INTERNATIONAL YEARBOOK BRANDS & COMMUNICATION DESIGN 2020/2021

[Edited by PETER ZEC]

VOL 2

The cover design is inspired by two projects that won awards in this year's competition: the "Human Rights Tattoo" project, whose website – designed by the Dutch agency Freshheads – was this year awarded a Red Dot: Grand Prix, and the Söhne Collection font family for which Klim Type Foundry in New Zealand received a Red Dot: Best of the Best from the jury. The resulting design is a fusion of both award-winning projects. While the shape of the letters is based on the Söhne Mono typeface, the colours of the letters reflect the different skin colours of the people who, as part of the "Human Rights Tattoo" project, had themselves tattooed with one of the 6,773 letters contained in the Universal Declaration of Human Rights. The text reproduced on the cover is part of this declaration, published by the United Nations General Assembly in 1948. You can read more about both projects on pages 94–95 and 174–175.

Contents

- 4 **Publishing & Print Media**
- 64 **Posters**
- 92 **Typography**
- 116 **Illustrations**
- 126 **Sound Design**
- 138 **Film & Animation**
- 172 **Online**
- 206 **Apps**
- 236 **Interface & User Experience Design**
- 336 **Spatial Communication**
- 426 **Red Dot: Junior Award Vol. 2**
- 564 **Designer Profiles Vol. 2**
- 642 **Jury Portraits**
- 668 **Index Vol. 2**
- 684 **Imprint**

Find more in Volume 1
Red Dot: Agency of the Year – Brands – Brand Design & Identity
Corporate Design & Identity – Annual Reports – Advertising
Packaging Design – Fair Stands – Retail Design
Red Dot: Junior Award Vol. 1 – Designer Profiles Vol. 1

Publishing & Print Media

Publishing & Print Media	Posters	Typography	Illustrations	Sound Design	Film & Animation	Online
4	64	92	116	126	138	172

Red Dot: Grand Prix

Anaptár, Intersection of Art and Science

[Special Publication]

The aim of "Anaptár" has been to, first, explore and implement in a visually easy-to-understand manner the scientific and artistic relationships concerning antecedents of radial calendars from a scientific and art-history perspective, and second, to examine whether the motion of the moon had been depicted in a similar way in the past. Starting off with extensive historical and scientific research, the information obtained was processed in an interdisciplinary approach and the plethora of data then presented following a specially developed presentation method. The abundance of enticing historical illustrations from physics, art and astronomy, as well as the creative visualisation of the immense amount of pure numbers, makes for an engaging, detailed and lovingly designed read. The hand-manufactured cover pays homage to women from the early days of astronomy, especially Cecilia Payne.

Statement by the jury
The quality of this publication, which extends across all areas of the design, is downright outstanding. From the first impression created by the threads, which are integrated radially into the cover, to the rhythm of the illustrations and the use of typography, this work is an excellent showcase in a truly literal sense of how good design can make even academic art-historical content stimulating to read.

Apps	Interface & User Experience Design	Spatial Communication	Red Dot: Junior Award	Designer Profiles	Jury Portraits	Index
206	236	336	426	564	642	668

reddot winner 2020
grand prix

Client
Hungarian University of Fine Arts
Doctoral School
Budapest, Hungary

Design
Anna Farkas
Anagraphic
Budapest, Hungary

Project Team
Prof. Dr. László Beke, CSc, dr. habil.
(Supervisor)

→ Designer profile on page 586

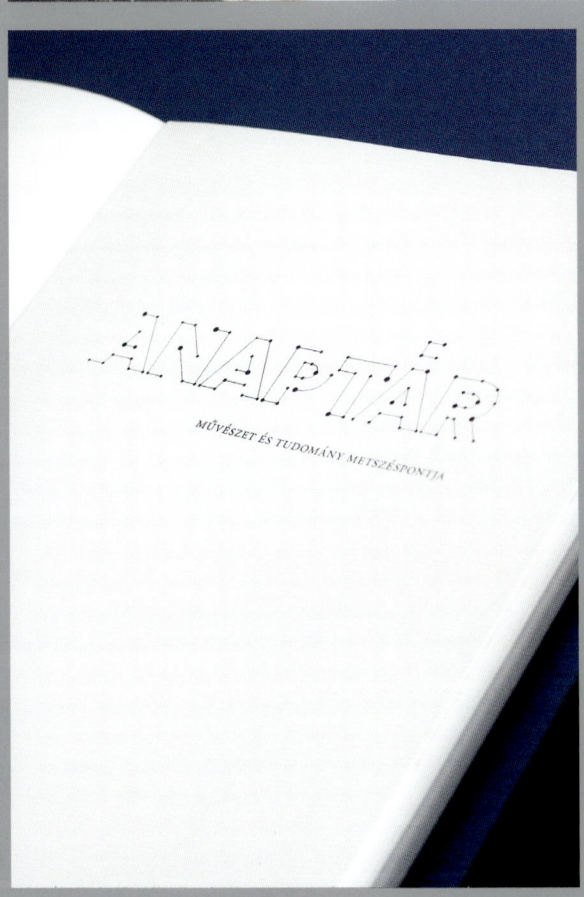

Red Dot: Best of the Best

Volkhonka. The Unhurried Walk
[Guidebook]

"Volkhonka. The Unhurried Walk", which is about the history and architecture of Volkhonka, one of the oldest streets in Moscow situated near the Kremlin, is far more than just an elaborately designed guidebook. Based on extensive historical and archival research, it reveals new thrilling aspects in the history of the district and is richly illustrated with both modern and historical materials, many of which are published for the first time. Three introductory articles telling about the role of the district in the urban planning of Moscow are followed by the main section, which presents 30 buildings chosen for their architectural, cultural and historical significance. Every article is structured into sections to cover modern photos, characteristics of the building, its development and evolution, as well as essays about famous persons whose life was connected to the buildings, turning this book into an unusual print product. In addition, the book cover is made in numerous expert steps that can only be carried out by hand.

Statement by the jury
The "Volkhonka. The Unhurried Walk" guidebook about one of the oldest streets in Moscow fascinates at first glance with its complexity and comprehensiveness. The illustrations and typography are used in a highly sensitive manner and in their sheer abundance have resulted in an impressive overall work. The cover with embossing was produced in a technically sophisticated manner to pique curiosity about the content.

Apps	Interface & User Experience Design	Spatial Communication	Red Dot: Junior Award	Designer Profiles	Jury Portraits	Index
206	236	336	426	564	642	668

Client
White City Project Foundation
Moscow, Russia

Design
White City Project Foundation
Moscow, Russia

Project Team
White City Project Foundation:
Ivan Aleksandrov (Art Direction)
Ekaterina Yumasheva (Graphic Design)
Elena Byalaya (Graphic Design)

Elena Olshanskaya (Publisher)
Federica Rossi (Idea/Author)
Tatiana Dudina (Author)
Dmitry Shvidkovsky (Author)

Printmanagement Plitt GmbH
(Production)
Tipografia Esperia (Printing)
FopmaWier boekbinderij (Bookbinding)

→ Designer profile on page 630

Red Dot: Best of the Best

English Journey

[Book]

In this book, renowned photographer John Angerson retraces the steps that English writer J. B. Priestley took in his 1934 classic "English Journey". Taken over three years, the photos in the book are a contemporary photographic record of England and carefully document today's cultural and economic landscape, including service stations and fast-food chains. With 20 different covers reminiscent of English road signs on high-quality coloured linen binding, the book has been designed as a collector's piece. The inside was printed on uncoated paper, while the photos on the uncoated glossy paper are "tipped" to make them look almost as if glued into a photo album in order to create an artistic contrast. On a foldable map in the style of the time accompanying the book, the route and places that John Angerson visited are precisely recorded and can thus easily be traced back. Gill Sans was used for the typeface within the book, including the inline cut.

Statement by the jury
The book, which reconstructs a journey through England undertaken by J. B. Priestley in 1934, impresses with its consistently high-quality processing showing in all details. Realistic photographs of the journey stations as they look today and the meticulous attention to materials and printing techniques reveal a deep passion for design that aims to bridge the past and the present by permeating every aspect of this jewel of a book.

Apps 206	Interface & User Experience Design 236	Spatial Communication 336	Red Dot: Junior Award 426	Designer Profiles 564	Jury Portraits 642	Index 668

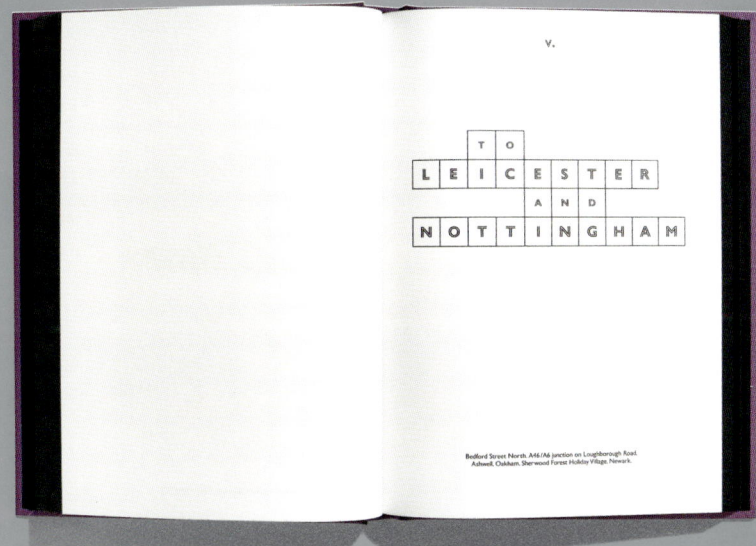

Client
John Angerson, Photographer
London, United Kingdom

Design
B&W Studio
Leeds, United Kingdom

Project Team
John Angerson (Photography)

B&W Studio:
Lee Bradley (Creative Director)
Jimmy Smith (Senior Designer)
Scott Cockerham (Senior Designer)

Lee Hanson (Writing)
Harry Mount (Writing)

Made by Team (Printing)
Diamond Print Services
(Foil Blocking & Binding)
Fedrigoni UK (Paper)
Ratchford Ltd. (Tissue Lined Cloth)

→ Designer profile on page 575

Red Dot: Best of the Best

Andreas Oster Weinkellerei
[Catalogue]

The Andreas Oster Weinkellerei – a 400-year old family-run business, wine merchant and professional bottling company – ranks among the leading major winemakers in Germany with an international portfolio. The standard range they offer is being showcased for the first time in a detailed catalogue, with each growing region being presented individually and the most distinctive grape varieties shown respectively as mock-ups. The individual wine families are also clearly presented in a kind of trip to the wine-growing regions around the world. Particular focus has been placed on the label series, which represents the affiliation of the individual wines to the winemaker's standard range and presents their individuality in detail using the respective grape variety. The design language of the labels is continued on the catalogue pages in the background as a design element, so that each double page reflects the winery's love for the quality of its products. Running titles provide information about the respective wine-growing region.

Statement by the jury
The catalogue for the Andreas Oster Weinkellerei convinces with an implementation that is unusual for a winery, as well as fine graphic details that are also reflected in the uniquely evocative visual language and the high sensitivity projected by the typography. A stringent graphic concept harmoniously integrates the design of the labels and fascinates with its overall independent and self-reliant appearance.

| Apps | Interface & User Experience Design | Spatial Communication | Red Dot: Junior Award | Designer Profiles | Jury Portraits | Index |
| 206 | 236 | 336 | 426 | 564 | 642 | 668 |

Client
Andreas Oster Weinkellerei
Cochem, Germany

Design
Jäger & Jäger
Überlingen, Germany

Project Team
Olaf Jäger (Creative Direction)
Tanja Weich (Art Direction)
Regina Jäger (Project Management)

→ Designer profile on page 599

Publishing & Print Media	Posters	Typography	Illustrations	Sound Design	Film & Animation	Online
4	64	92	116	126	138	172

Kloster Karree®
[Special Publication]

New residences are being created in the former Carmelite convent in the heart of Bamberg. A high-quality slipcase with folding maps and the Kloster Karree catalogue was produced to promote the refectory of the listed buildings. A visually simplified stucco ceiling rose embellishes the handcrafted case and is used as a recurring design element to guide users through the contents. Folded floor plans demonstrate different ways of using the premises. Hand-drawn maps of Bamberg's old town structure the catalogue into chapters. The high-quality finish and stylish design thus reflect the character of this historic property.

Client
terraplan Grundstücksentwicklungs-
gesellschaft mbH
Nuremberg, Germany

Design
grafikatelier Engelke & Neubauer
Nuremberg, Germany

Project Team
Tania Engelke (Graphic Design)
Kurt Neubauer (Graphic Design)
Nina Beckert (Graphic Design)

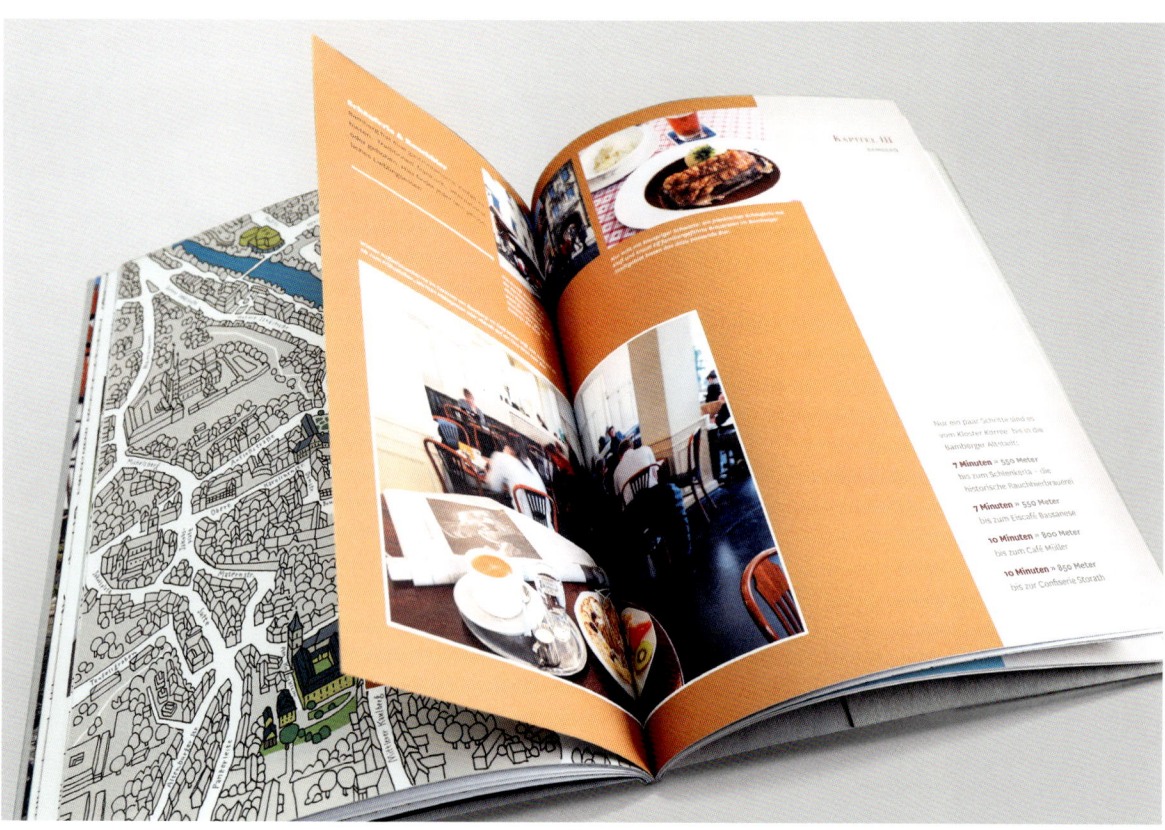
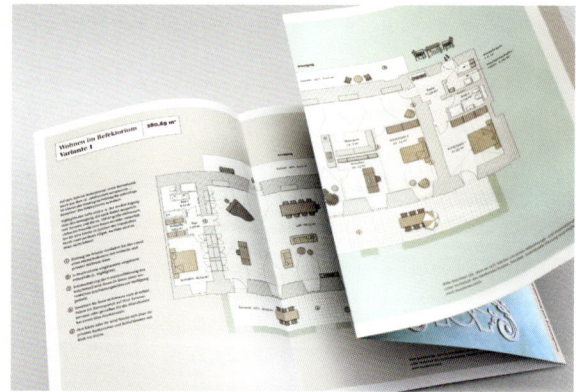
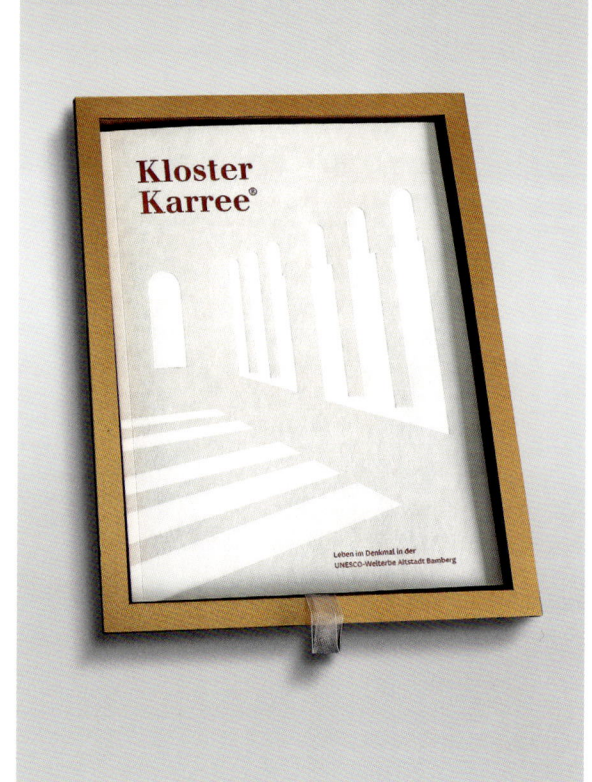

La Loupe

[Magazine]

La Loupe is a magazine with an integrated guide. Each issue is dedicated to an appealing destination like Salzburg, St. Anton, Kitzbühel, or Kampen & Lech Zürs. Brimming with personal stories and fascinating images, the bilingual pocket magazine (German/English) aims to inspire people all over the world who have an eye for detail. Its carefully chosen content introduces the urban readership to select, special local features, handpicked by the editor and the authors. The elegance of the design is matched by the high-quality feel of the paper and an elaborate cover that employs UV protective coating.

Client
La Loupe GmbH
Benjamin & Julia Skardarasy
Vienna, Austria

Design
La Loupe GmbH
Benjamin & Julia Skardarasy
Vienna, Austria

| Publishing & Print Media | Posters | Typography | Illustrations | Sound Design | Film & Animation | Online |
| 4 | 64 | 92 | 116 | 126 | 138 | 172 |

Bid Book
Hannover 2025

[Book]

Client
Landeshauptstadt Hannover
Bewerbungsteam ECoC 2025
Hannover, Germany

Design
peetz & le peetz design
Sebastian Peetz
Hannover, Germany

→ Designer profile on page 614
→ Clip online

Apps	Interface & User Experience Design	Spatial Communication	Red Dot: Junior Award	Designer Profiles	Jury Portraits	Index
206	236	336	426	564	642	668

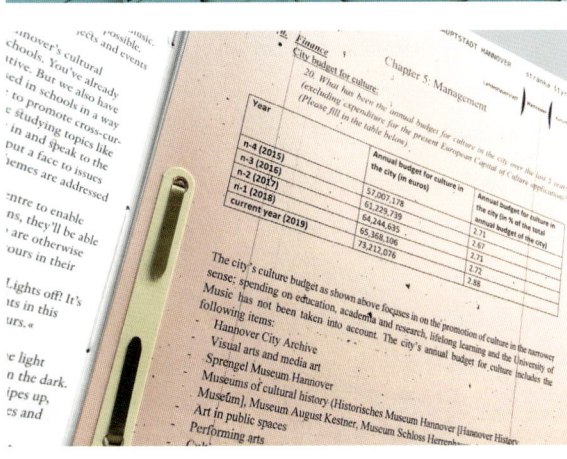

This book was created for Hannover's bid for European Capital of Culture 2025. Its eye-catching cover is a delicate laser-cut multilayer relief, which picks up on the formal language of "Merzbau" by Dada artist Kurt Schwitters and continues as a gap into the book. It also portrays the metaphor of the agora as a central marketplace where important European topics can be discussed and experienced. Inside the hand-bound book, meticulous design elements, microtypography and fantastic illustrations build tension and serve as a highly creative companion to the bid.

Shenzhen Case

[Special Publication]

The city of Shenzhen was the subject of an exhibition, including the regeneration process for the village of Dafen on the outskirts of the Chinese city. Within a few years, the village became a huge workshop for oil painting reproductions. The aim of the exhibition was also to express the unique nature of Shenzhen, a city aspiring to become a "global pioneering city", through contemporary architecture. The accompanying books were created after years of in-depth research. Carefully bound in a linen cover, they document the interventions into urban reality and the spirit behind them through a large number of photographs, maps and archive material.

Client
Urban Planning, Land & Resources
Commission of Shenzhen
Shenzhen, China

Design
SenseTeam
Shenzhen, China

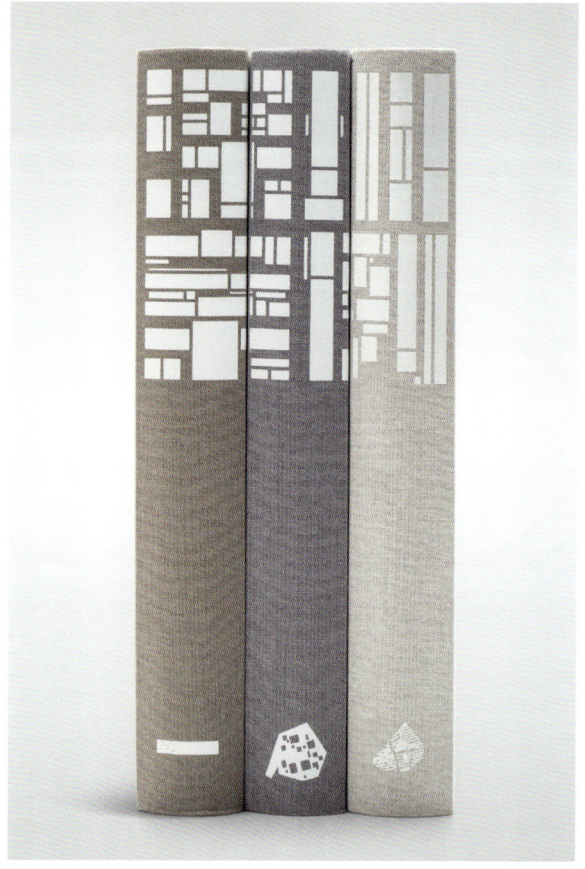

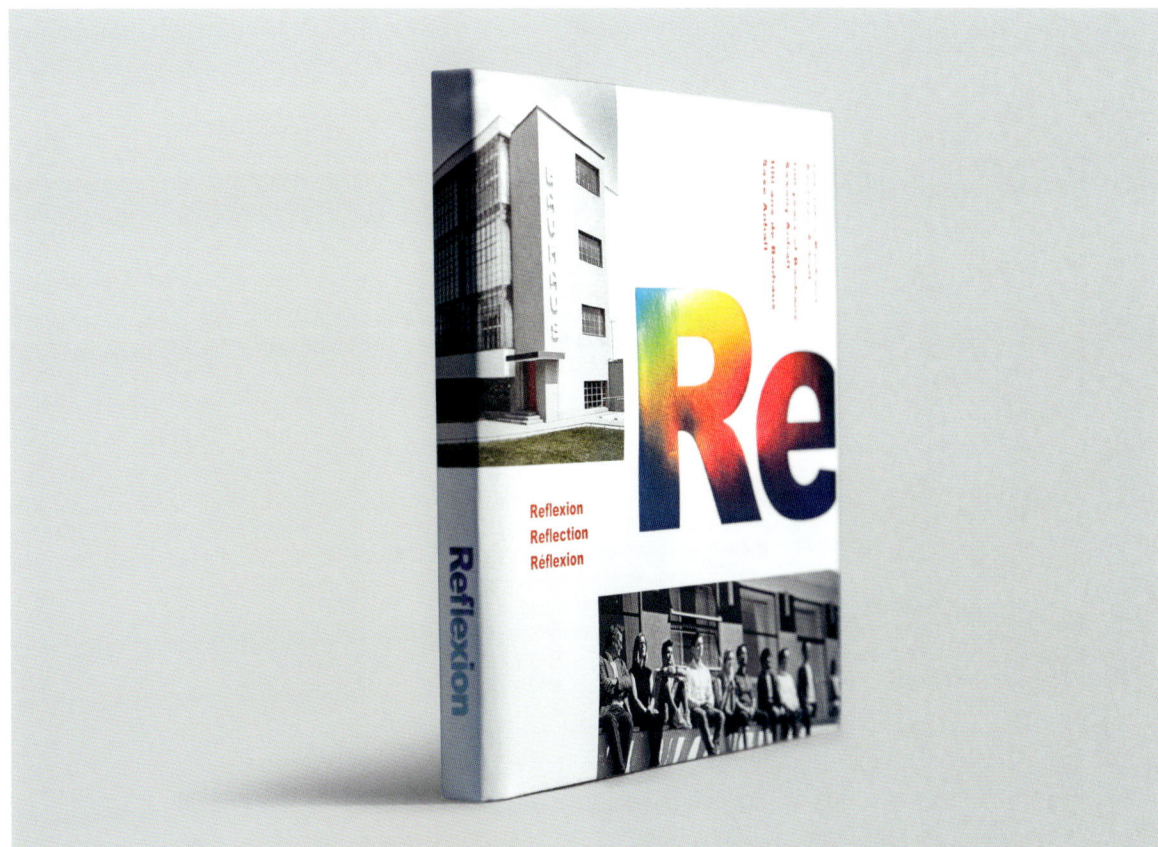

Reflexion
[Book]

In 2019, Saxony-Anhalt celebrated the 100th anniversary of the School of Design. Featuring all of the commemorative events, this yearbook invites the reader to browse and reminisce. It recounts stories of decision makers in art, culture and politics in three languages. The colour and format are a play on the Bauhaus style, which is characterised by rigidity and straight lines. The cover can be unfolded into a poster introducing the leitmotif. Shimmering hot-foil embossing, an exciting layout and foldable metre-wide double-page spreads lend opulence to the publication, which features a clear structure and nuanced images.

Client
Staatskanzlei und Ministerium für Kultur des Landes Sachsen-Anhalt
Magdeburg, Germany

Design
Genese Werbeagentur GmbH
Magdeburg, Germany

Project Team
Andreas Georgi (Concept)
Sebastian Kahl (Concept)
Hagen Nessler (Graphic Design)
Isabel König (Project Management)

Publishing & Print Media	Posters	Typography	Illustrations	Sound Design	Film & Animation	Online
4	64	92	116	126	138	172

BEETS, ROSES AND THE MEANING OF LIFE – RE['RU:]TING HILDESHEIM

[Special Publication]

The city of Hildesheim released this book as part of its application to become a European Capital of Culture 2025. Carefully selected and edited images guide readers from chapter to chapter. A special, experimental binding and neon Pantone colours underscore the city's cultural attributes and its aim to become a Capital of Culture. Starting from the laser-engraved Finnboard cover with a premium feel, a neon magenta thread runs through the book. Important facts are presented in a reader-friendly and appealing way and blurred images create a contextual reference to the future, which is never crystal clear.

Client
Stadt Hildesheim
Hildesheim, Germany

Design
HAWK University of Applied Sciences and Art, Faculty of Design
Hildesheim, Germany

Project Team
Prof. Dominika Hasse
Anna-Lena Schotge
Timo Strüber
Sophie Stillig
Tatjana Rabe

Duddjot

[Exhibition Catalogue]

This publication was developed to accompany the "Duddjot" exhibition in Paris, showcasing the indigenous culture of the Sámi people from northern Scandinavia. With works by artisans and artists, the exhibition focused on Sámi culture and handicraft, also known as "duodji". The catalogue reflects this strong focus on the fabrication process, which requires a deep knowledge of natural materials, through the hand-stitched binding and shows the quality of the raw materials through the natural papers used. Combined with special graphic patterns, this achieves a tactile and authentic identity.

Client
Institute finlandais
Paris, France

Design
Kuudes
Helsinki, Finland

Project Team
Kuudes:
Piëtke Visser (Design)
Kirsi Rauhala (Production)

Sofia Okonen (Portfolio Photography),
Duotone

Publishing & Print Media	Posters	Typography	Illustrations	Sound Design	Film & Animation	Online
4	64	92	116	126	138	172

Maximilian Schell

[Book]

The book accompanying the "Maximilian Schell" exhibition presents the career of the multi-talented actor over its more than 300 pages. It creatively highlights the contrasts between Hollywood glamour and the Schell estate in the Austrian Alps. Documents such as diaries, letters and drafts of screenplays are printed on small pages of uncoated paper, making them appear particularly vivid. Seventeen authors explore Schell's great acting talent, share behind-the-scenes insights and focus on the knowledgeable art collector, film director and lover of Shakespeare. The book has a printed linen cover with metallic embossing.

Client
DFF – Deutsches Filminstitut & Filmmuseum e.V.
Frankfurt/Main, Germany

Design
mind the gap! design
Karl-Heinz Best
Frankfurt/Main, Germany

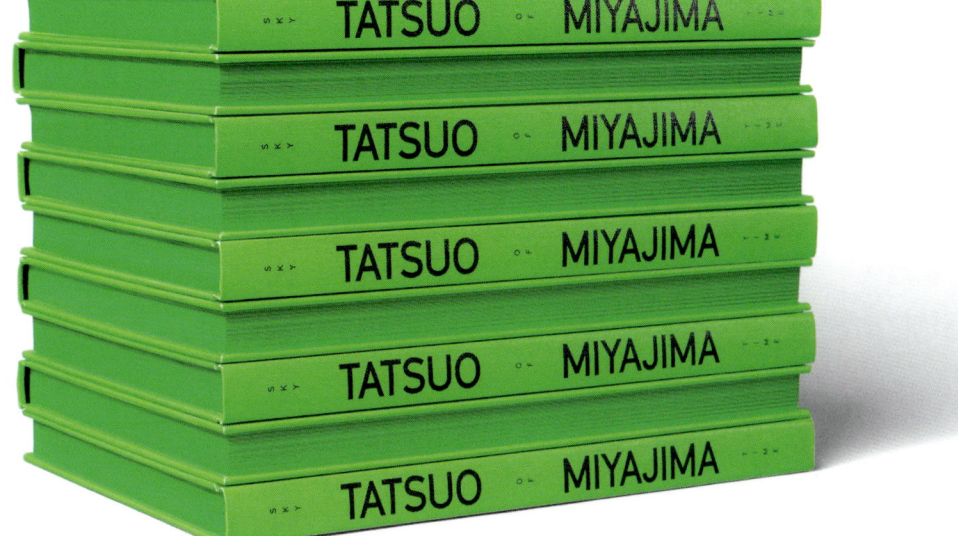

Tatsuo Miyajima – "Sky of Time"

[Exhibition Catalogue]

Sky of Time is the title of an exhibition by the famous Japanese artist Tatsuo Miyajima. It consists of a number of LED devices, twinkling in a dark room like stars to reflect concepts such as infinity and eternity. The choice of the neon green colour was inspired by the northern lights the artist witnessed on his visit to Rovaniemi. The same green was chosen as the main colour of the accompanying publication, which uses letters in a mechanical typeface to create a link to Miyajima's LED numbers. Images of the exhibition are printed with special colour profiles that allow the use of an additional spot colour – the characteristic neon green.

Client
EMMA Espoo Museum of Modern Art
Espoo, Finland

Design
Kuudes
Helsinki, Finland

Project Team
EMMA Espoo Museum of Modern Art:
Pilvi Kalhama (Author)
Päivi Karttunen (Author)
Mami Kataoka (Author)
Arja Miller (Author)
Inka Laine (Production Director)
Ari Karttunen (Photography)

Kuudes:
Jari Danielsson (CEO)
Tony Eräpuro (Art Direction)
Vesa Viljakainen (Production)
Sonja Söderholm (Project Management)

stories/spaces

[Exhibition Catalogue]

The 10th anniversary of architectural brand agency 1zu33 was celebrated with an experiential installation at the AIT-ArchitekturSalon in Munich. The "stories/spaces" exhibition unveiled the creative processes behind the agency's work. Enveloped by ever-changing light and sound, it uses four double-sided screens to show the duality of results and processes. The design of the accompanying catalogue is equally intricate, echoing this duality and combining two separately bound booklets. One covers the film level, while the other presents the exhibition's architecture.

Client
1zu33 Architectural Brand Identity
Munich, Germany

Design
1zu33 Architectural Brand Identity
Munich, Germany
OFF OFFICE
Munich, Germany

Project Team
OFF OFFICE:
Markus Lingemann (Art Direction)
Johannes von Gross (Art Direction)
Oliver Schwamkrug (Graphic Design)

Georgia Kareola (Text), Not A Pipe
Nicole Makowski (Printing), Druckerei Makowski

Jerritt Clark (Photography)
Verena Kathrein (Photography)
Bodo Mertoglu (Photography)
Manfred Jarisch (Photography),
Myrzik & Jarisch
Ludger Paffrath (Photography)
Robert Rieger for FvF Productions (Photography)
Robert Sprang (Photography)

Apps	Interface & User Experience Design	Spatial Communication	Red Dot: Junior Award	Designer Profiles	Jury Portraits	Index
206	236	336	426	564	642	668

2020 Arphic Font Library
[Catalogue]

Aiming for greater convenience, diversity and ecological stewardship, the Arphic Font Library has adopted a new design in order to reduce paper consumption and environmental pollution. The compendium includes more than a thousand fonts from the leading font foundry and is organised into four collections which are ingeniously bound using metal clips so that they can be taken out and assembled individually. The volumes are titled Decoration, Calligraphy, Collection of Design, and Classics, and offer a tremendous number of options to combine visual experiences with multiple functions.

Client
Arphic Technology Co., Ltd.
New Taipei City, Taiwan

Design
Hong Da Design Studio
New Taipei City, Taiwan

Project Team
Arphic Technology:
Ethan Chiou (Marketing Manager)
Rina Lin (Marketing Specialist)

Hong Da Design Studio:
Hong-Da Jiang (Graphic Design)

Si-Jia Sun (Photography),
Grandvity Visual Integration Co., Ltd.
Ta-Wei Yo (Printing), JIL Print Co., Ltd.

Publishing & Print Media	Posters	Typography	Illustrations	Sound Design	Film & Animation	Online
4	64	92	116	126	138	172

Die Weltköche zu Gast im Ikarus, Band 6

[Book]

Client
Benevento Publishing
Elsbethen, Austria

Design
wir sind artisten
Salzburg, Austria

→ Designer profile on page 632

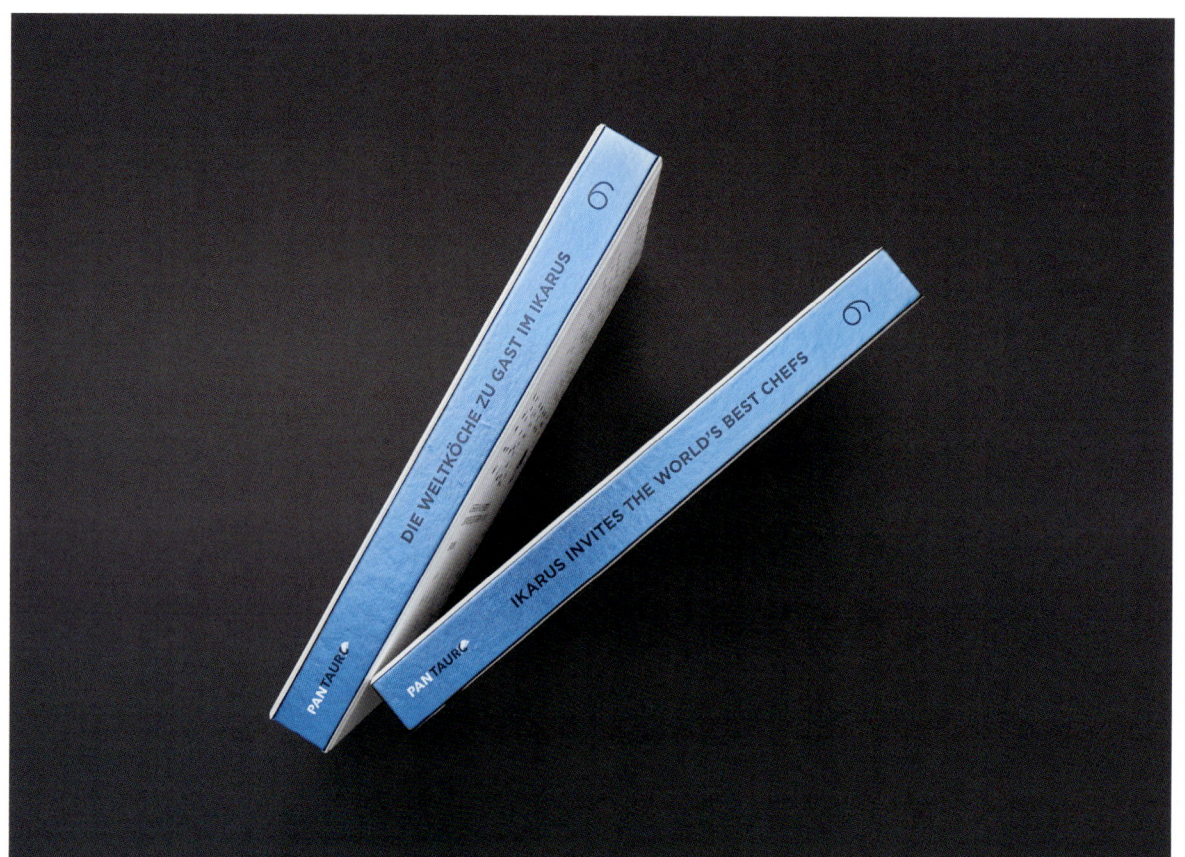

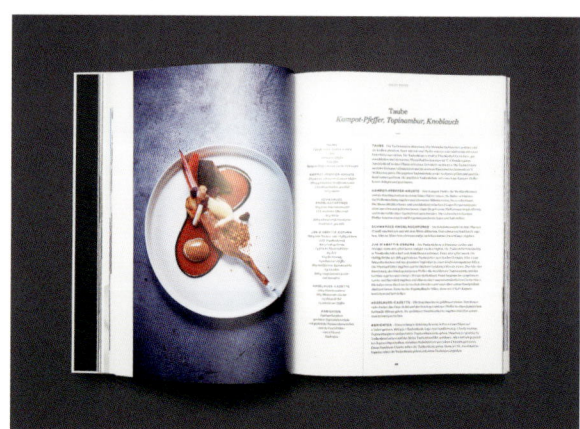

At Hangar-7 located at Salzburg Airport, the renowned Restaurant Ikarus serves up exciting concepts dreamt up by the world's best chefs, who take turns each month to be the restaurant's guest chef. The 6th volume of the series "Ikarus invites the world's best chefs" travels to restaurant kitchens around the globe. To highlight the personality of each guest chef, the book features expressive portraits and focuses on the tools of their trade: their hands. Hand-pasted tracing paper features background information on each guest chef and their signature. The premium appearance of the book is seasoned with hot-foil stamping and embossing.

PARADISE CITY
Brand Book

[Special Publication]

Client
PARADISE GROUP
Seoul, South Korea

Design
Killing Mario
Seoul, South Korea
PARADISE GROUP Brand & Design Dept.
Seoul, South Korea

→ Designer profile on page 600

Apps	Interface & User Experience Design	Spatial Communication	Red Dot: Junior Award	Designer Profiles	Jury Portraits	Index
206	236	336	426	564	642	668

The large PARADISE CITY "art-tainment" resort in Northeast Asia provides unique enjoyment with its more than 3,000 pieces of artwork and diverse entertainment facilities. This book introduces the PARADISE GROUP's brand philosophy and the resort's key facilities. The guiding design motif was Jogakbo, used in an artistic and metaphorical way to illustrate the company's patchwork philosophy of bringing different elements together to create a whole that is more beautiful and remarkable than each element would be on its own.

Publishing & Print Media	Posters	Typography	Illustrations	Sound Design	Film & Animation	Online
4	64	92	116	126	138	172

LOTTE DUTY FREE

[Corporate Publishing]

Client
LOTTE DUTY FREE
Seoul, South Korea

Design
Daehong Communications
Seoul, South Korea
Killing Mario
Seoul, South Korea

→ Designer profile on page 600
→ Clip online

This book explores the heritage of LOTTE DUTY FREE, the large duty-free retailer that celebrated its 40th anniversary in 2020. The first half of the book examines the value of the brand, initially established with 40 products, and discusses each decade's duty-free retail trends. The second half recounts the beginnings of the global duty-free industry and the company's efforts to introduce innovation and culture into the duty-free shopping experience. The red colour of this lavishly designed, modern book is symbolic of the company and reflects the festive mood of the 40th anniversary celebrations.

Publishing & Print Media	Posters	Typography	Illustrations	Sound Design	Film & Animation	Online
4	64	92	116	126	138	172

Samsung KX

[Book]

Samsung KX is a unique event space in the north of London where visitors can use Samsung technology to monitor the latest trends in culture and innovation. The space offers a breath-taking, dynamic brand experience with creative workshops and a vast range of presentations to let visitors discover, experience and learn new things. The KX vision book documents the company's approach to strategy and design and provides a visual narrative of the overall experience in Samsung KX. The aim is to inspire other cities to create their own tailored travel destination for digital culture.

Client
Samsung Electronics Co., Ltd.
Suwon, South Korea

Design
Cheil Worldwide
Seoul, South Korea
SPIN
London, United Kingdom

Project Team
Cheil Worldwide:
Simon Hong (Executive Creative Director)
Jaehun Heo (Creative Director)
Heeyoung Lee (Senior Designer)
Soyeon Yoo (Senior Designer)
Seungtae Kim (Designer)

SPIN:
Tony Brook (Creative Director)
Claudia Klat (Design Director)
Patricia Finegan (Project Director)
Jonathan Nielsen (Designer)

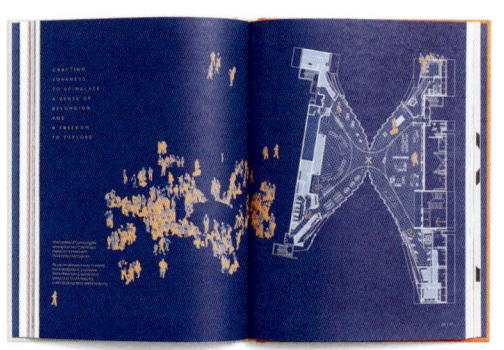

Polestar 2 – Into the Light

[Book]

The book about the electric car Polestar 2 shows how a collective vision, coupled with determination and attention to detail, enabled the car to turn from theory into reality, merging avant-garde design and innovative technology. The publication is intended as a physical extension of the car, capturing the spirit and ambitions of the brand before the first car deliveries in the form of a photographic journey all the way from the birth of the brand to the launch of its first all-electric car. The reader gets an in-depth insight into the entire craft and the level of sophistication involved.

Client
Polestar
Gothenburg, Sweden

Design
Stockholm Design Lab
Stockholm, Sweden
Polestar
Gothenburg, Sweden

Publishing & Print Media	Posters	Typography	Illustrations	Sound Design	Film & Animation	Online
4	64	92	116	126	138	172

Nextview

[Anniversary Publication]

Nextview uses Design Thinking to help clients create positive impact with technological solutions. The book focuses on people, especially on customers during the past ten years, and takes the reader through the company portfolio. In the middle of the pages, a cut-out has been made for a smaller booklet. On the cover of this booklet is a mirror. The reader looks to the future through the eyes of the teenagers portrayed here, who answer questions about how they see the future. In this way, the past and future are brought together in a visually striking manner in this anniversary book.

Client
Nextview Netherlands B.V.
Eindhoven, Netherlands

Design
52 graden noorderbreedte
Noordwijkerhout, Netherlands

Project Team
52 graden noorderbreedte:
Sandra Geerlings (Account Management)

Esther den Hertog (Text)
René Koster (Photography)
Stephan Wassenaar (Printing), Easyprint

Architekturkultur

[Corporate Publishing]

Euroboden is a leading developer of architecturally sophisticated real estate and urban planning projects in Munich, Berlin, Frankfurt and Hamburg. The company's love of architecture is evident in its projects. To mark its 20th anniversary, Euroboden published "Architekturkultur" (architecture culture), a book which addresses the topic of building culture in various – sometimes controversial – ways. With clean, reduced typography and high-quality black-and-white photographs, it also presents the company's position and the architects it collaborates with, thus making a valuable contribution to the discourse about architectural culture.

Client
Euroboden GmbH
Munich, Germany

Design
Herburg Weiland
Munich, Germany

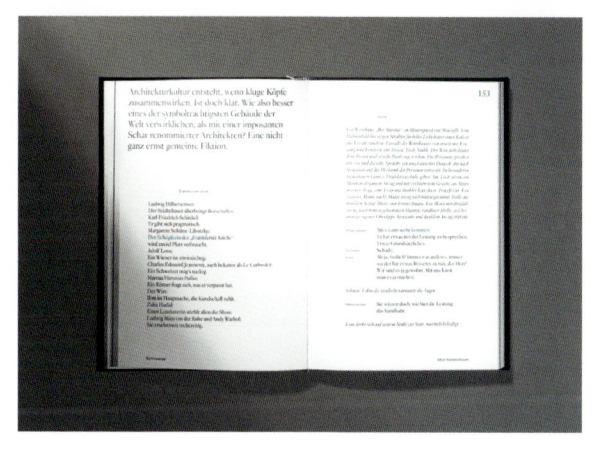

Publishing & Print Media	Posters	Typography	Illustrations	Sound Design	Film & Animation	Online
4	64	92	116	126	138	172

Unbroken

[Corporate Publishing]

Client
YCH Group Pte. Ltd.
Singapore

Design
Yellow Octopus Pte. Ltd.
Singapore

Project Team
Yellow Octopus:
Kevin Thio (Concept)
Kai Jun Tan (Art Direction)
Siow Yu-Ming (Copywriting)

Wai Kay Ho (Photography)

Apps	Interface & User Experience Design	Spatial Communication	Red Dot: Junior Award	Designer Profiles	Jury Portraits	Index
206	236	336	426	564	642	668

This book recounts the history of Singapore's large logistics firm YCH, which has remained true to its values for 60 years. The title "Unbroken" expresses its unfaltering spirit to connect Asia by road and create integrated ecosystems that serve the community. The carefully produced design of the cover stands out due to the embossed silver lines that form a wireframe model of the new company headquarters or lead to and away from the building, in order to portray the group's extensive network in Asia Pacific as a logistics hub.

Publishing & Print Media	Posters	Typography	Illustrations	Sound Design	Film & Animation	Online
4	64	92	116	126	138	172

Faust and The Divine Comedy

[Book]

This new series of richly illustrated classics from around the world has for the first time published both parts of "Faust" in Slovak collected in a single volume and has also issued The "Divine Comedy". The extensive text and large number of vivid illustrations called for a large-format presentation. The result is an artistic book whose subtle graphic and typographic design leaves room for illustrations, and yet still allows for natural interaction with the text. The books are printed on uncoated paper and bound in a beige linen hardcover with a dust jacket.

Client
Spolok svätého Vojtecha
Trnava, Slovakia

Design
Pergamen s.r.o.
Trnava, Slovakia

Project Team
Pergamen:
Juraj Demovič (Graphic Design)
Juraj Vontorčík (Graphic Design)
Ervín Gejdoš (Layout)

Miroslav Cipár (Illustration)
Ema Lančaričová (Photography)

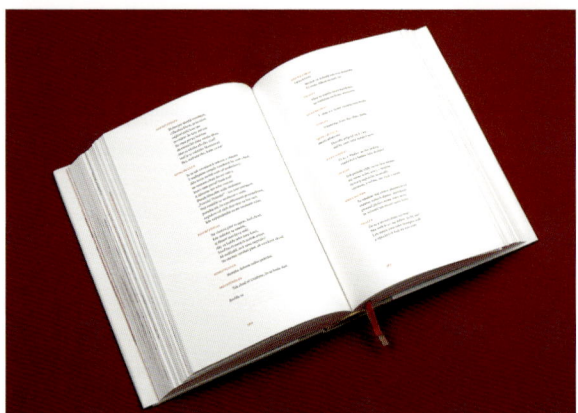

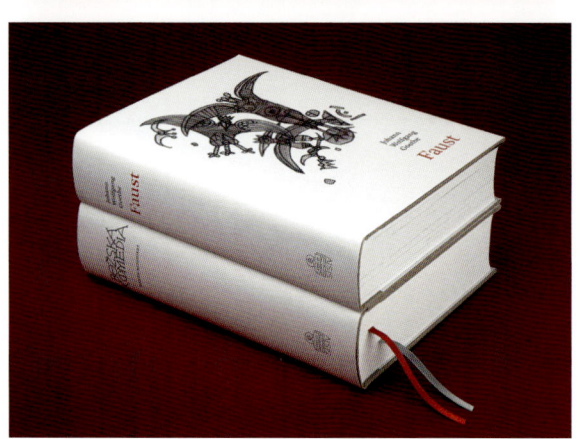

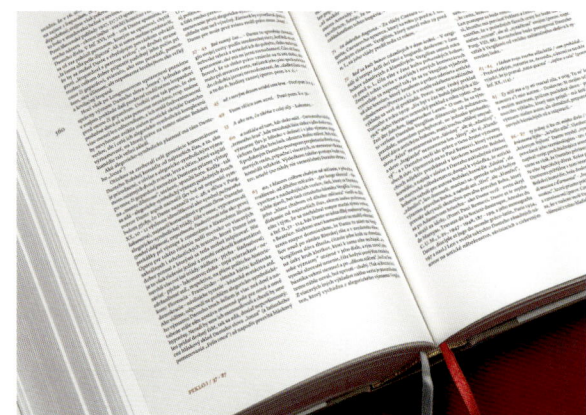

Authors' Boras

[Book]

As part of the Rijeka European Capital of Culture project, 16 writers spent a month in the Kvarner Gulf and on its islands. On the sea of the Kvarner Gulf, bora wind often breaks seawater into very tiny droplets and foam, creating a thin, misty layer referred to as the "smoking sea". The short stories in this project were written in this unique environment. The design of the book seeks to evoke the authors' emotional and physical experience of the bora. The text is printed on tracing paper in such a way that the letters overlap and resemble the watery dust caused by the bora at sea. The reader has to turn the page to be able to read the next.

Client
Rijeka 2020 d.o.o.
Rijeka, Croatia

Design
Studio Sonda
Vižinada, Croatia

Project Team
Rijeka 2020:
Iva Kelentric (Project Management)

Studio Sonda:
Jelena Fiskus (Creative Direction)
Sean Poropat (Creative Direction)
Matko Plovanic (Graphic Design)
Rajko Ban (Graphic Design)
Mladen Gvozden (Account Management)

FAQ YOU

[Special Publication]

The modern sex-education book "FAQ YOU" from the NGO Youth Against AIDS answers the most frequently asked questions as determined by a survey conducted among young people. Generally, sex-education textbooks tend to be quite unappealing to young people, but this book is colourful, loud and modern. The design takes its readers seriously. The photographic look is authentic, and the illustrations are as diverse and explicit as possible. The book, however, also borrows useful elements from reference books and textbooks, such as underscored text and highlighted information boxes, as well as the Tiempos typeface, modified to suit contemporary reading habits.

Client
Youth against AIDS
Hamburg, Germany

Design
loved GmbH
Hamburg, Germany

Project Team
Mieke Haase (Chief Creative Officer)
Alexander Müsgens (Creative Director)
Sabine Cole (Editor-in-Chief)
Valerie Bachert (Editor-in-Chief)
Jana Maria Herrmann (Art Direction)
Yannic Hefermann (Art Direction)
Susanne Sauer (Designer)
Isabella Bigler (Text)

Apps	Interface & User Experience Design	Spatial Communication	Red Dot: Junior Award	Designer Profiles	Jury Portraits	Index
206	236	336	426	564	642	668

ATLAS – Das Magazin von Gebrüder Weiss

ATLAS is the B2B customer magazine of the Gebrüder Weiss logistics firm and is inspired by an interest in processes that go beyond the obvious. Issue 13/2019 deals with the topic of "normal" and focuses on the everyday and the unremarkable. Both the semantic meanings of "normal" and the creative application of the term are explored in the 92-page bilingual edition. As a rule, people consider what they know to be normal. But what is considered normal varies from generation to generation, from culture to culture. The magazine is distributed in the 30 countries in which the company has subsidiaries.

Client
Gebrüder Weiss Gesellschaft m.b.H
Lauterach, Austria

Design
Groothuis. Gesellschaft der Ideen und Passionen mbH
Hamburg, Germany

Publishing & Print Media	Posters	Typography	Illustrations	Sound Design	Film & Animation	Online
4	64	92	116	126	138	172

The Unseasonal – Prelude Issue

[Magazine]

As an international magazine, The Unseasonal features timeless pictorials, in-depth stories, and unique collaborations with personalities from the fields of fashion, contemporary art, and celebrity culture. Each project, story and partnership are carefully selected. In contrast to a time of fast fashion and the madness of social media, the magazine offers great artistic quality and embodies a feeling of escapism, of getting away, slowing down, exoticism, passion and the lightness of being. Exciting photography and dramatic typography reinforce this avant-garde aspiration.

Client
The Unseasonal
Los Angeles, USA

Design
Ger Ger
Los Angeles, USA

Apps	Interface & User Experience Design	Spatial Communication	Red Dot: Junior Award	Designer Profiles	Jury Portraits	Index
206	236	336	426	564	642	668

OTON

[Magazine, Seasonal Preview]

OTON magazine is published annually together with a season preview. In addition to classical music, the magazine also covers themes affecting society. The current theme is "volume". Volume is, needless to say, present in music and is becoming increasingly relevant with the recent digital development of mass media communication. Alongside programme information, the magazine features photo series, essays and interviews that firmly establish Tonhalle Düsseldorf amongst the city's residents. The concept is rounded out with clear and intelligent language, creative formats and a design that marries high-quality content with modernity.

Client
Tonhalle Düsseldorf
Düsseldorf, Germany

Design
Grand Quest
Düsseldorf, Germany

Project Team
Tonhalle Düsseldorf:
Michael Becker (Publisher)
Torger Nelson (Publisher)
Udo Flaskamp (Head of Marketing)
Stephanie Fuchs (Marketing)
Uwe Sommer-Sorgente (Editorial Work)
Marita Ingenhoven (Editorial Work)

Grand Quest:
Till Paukstat (Creative Direction)
Tim Turiak (Creative Direction)
Daniel Bonrath (Graphic Design)
Vincent Mertens (Graphic Design Intern)

Luci

[Magazine]

Luxembourg is a cosmopolitan country in the heart of Europe, known for its European institutions, tourist sights, UNESCO World Heritage monuments and numerous museums. Luci is a new magazine aimed at an international audience looking for authentic local experiences that are off the beaten track and at those who are interested in the country, its people, their lives, culture, nature and customs. Presented in a timeless layout, inspiring travel stories bring together places and people as well as thoughts and emotions, while the magazine's classic typography leaves room for vibrant photography.

Client
Luxembourg For Tourism
Luxembourg-Kirchberg, Luxembourg

Design
ampersand.studio
Bascharage, Luxembourg

Apps	Interface & User Experience Design	Spatial Communication	Red Dot: Junior Award	Designer Profiles	Jury Portraits	Index
206	236	336	426	564	642	668

Rugged

[Magazine]

Rugged, a magazine about running, covered Luxembourg's 14th night marathon in June 2019. A team of three photographers were deployed to capture the atmosphere and emotions of the large street party on that exceptional evening when thousands of gasping, sweating runners were cheered on as they made their way through the streets. The magazine is full of inspiring stories and honest, unfiltered photographs that do not necessarily stand out for their beauty but for their authenticity. The clean, reduced design and the distinctive typeface underscore the passion behind this sport.

Client
ampersand.studio
Bascharage, Luxembourg

Design
ampersand.studio
Bascharage, Luxembourg

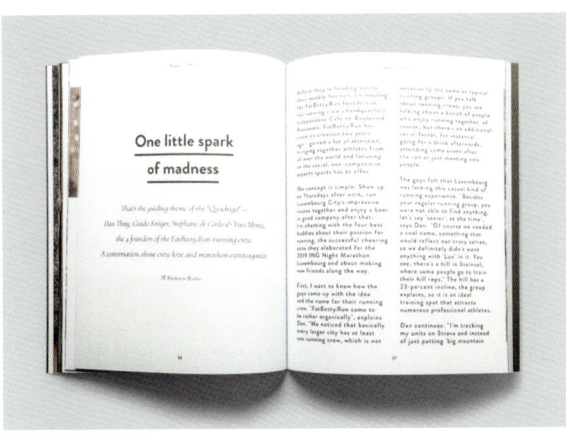

New York, New York

[Special Publication]

The work "New York, New York" was inspired by a journey and is itself a virtual voyage of discovery through the neighbourhoods of the global metropolis. Map-like graphic representations were created to provide a bird's-eye view of the well-known urban canyons in the city. They show abstract footprints of the buildings, and the scalable skyscrapers in various bright colours can be placed on these footprints. In this way, users can reinterpret the city and experience it using an interactive app that marries the analogue and the digital.

Client
AURORA School for ARtists/INKA Research Group, HTW Berlin – University of Applied Sciences
Berlin, Germany

Design
Sarah Müller
Berlin, Germany

Project Team
AURORA School for ARtists:
Maja Stark (Project Management)
Leonid Barsht (Programming)

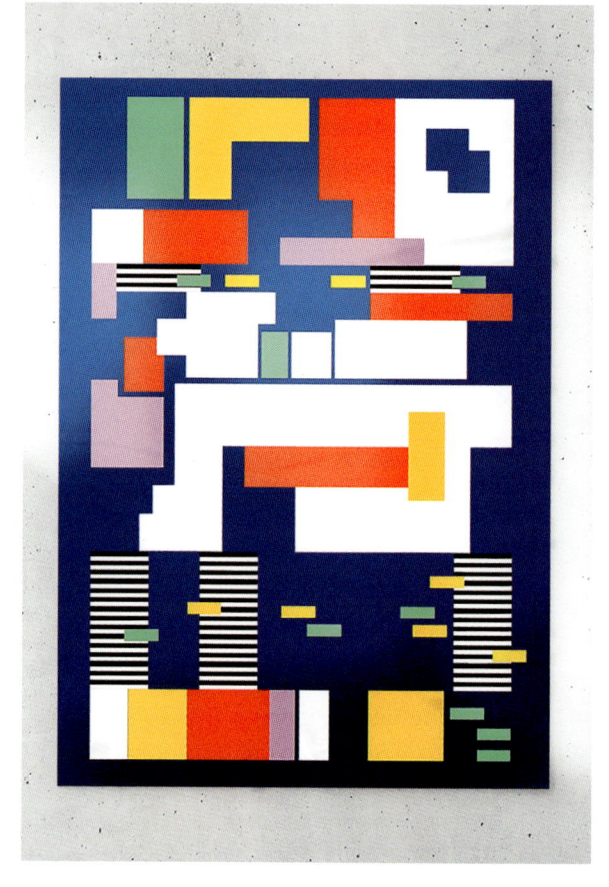

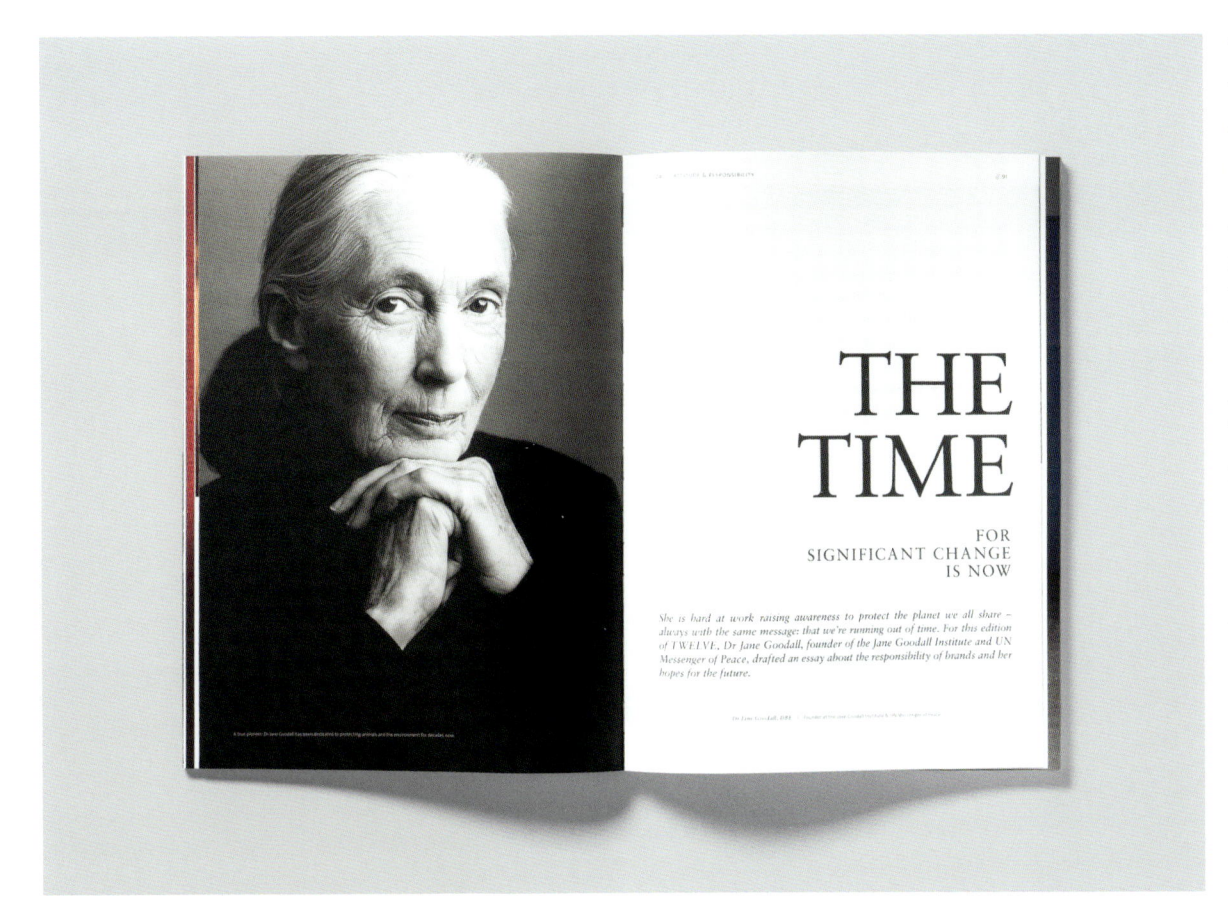

TWELVE – the magazine for brands, media and communication

[Corporate Publishing]

TWELVE was developed as an individual annual review by the Serviceplan Group for the media and communications industry. The magazine provides an insight into the personalities and topics that have accompanied the group in the past year and also showcases its portfolio. The articles in the magazine aim to inspire, move and surprise people and also to shift the spotlight onto niche topics. In the sixth edition, prominent guest authors and experts present astute analyses and thought-provoking inspiration on the overarching topic of "Purpose". The pieces are accompanied by a series of striking photos produced by internationally renowned photographers.

Client
Serviceplan Group
Munich, Germany

Design
Serviceplan Group
Munich, Germany

Project Team
Serviceplan:
Beate Gronemann
(Executive Creative Direction)
Julia Becker (Concept)
Franziska Siebald (Project Management)
Katy Pergelt (Production)

Alexandra Berger (Text)
Leica Photographers (Photography)

The Business Value of Design

[Special Publication]

The Business Value of Design is a research series by McKinsey Design aimed at elevating design's value for businesses and organisations. An analysis of the design actions and financial performance of thousands of organisations found that design has a significant impact on business. The series aimed at CEOs features a versatile design that at the same time reflects the brand identity of the management consulting firm. The concept is inspired by paper, the place where designers bring their ideas to life, and demonstrated, for example, through the paper cut illustration style.

Client
McKinsey Design
New York, USA

Design
Human After All
London, United Kingdom
McKinsey Design
New York, USA

The Audi Magazine

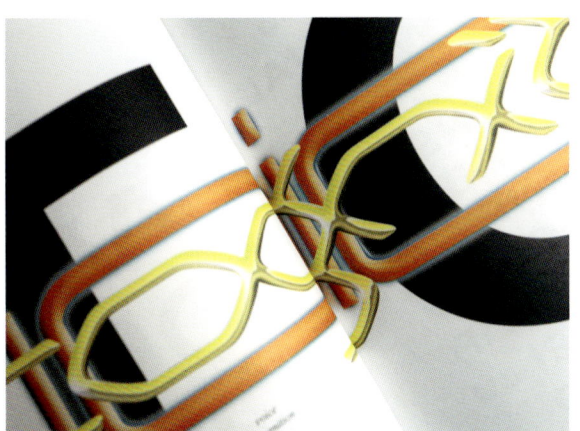

The Audi Magazine is a key part of the company's communication strategy as an expert in modern, sustainable mobility. Each issue is focused on a neutral topic, rolled out in a brand- and media-appropriate manner in terms of relevance and depth. In addition, each issue contains a journey "From A to" the mobility questions of the future, as well as a journey to real places and people. The magazine's visuals and imagery are generous, varied and opulent in design, an impression that is heightened by its high-quality look and feel. Headline questions printed in red set the tone and are answered in subsequent articles.

Client
AUDI AG
Ingolstadt, Germany

Design
loved GmbH
Hamburg, Germany

Project Team
loved:
Mieke Haase (Chief Creative Officer)
Julia Kerschbaum (Art Direction)
Stefan Kaetz (Designer)
Jana Maria Herrmann (Designer)
Birte Mußmann (Text)
Peggy Wellerdt (Head of Photography)

Mirko Borsche (Creative Director),
Bureau Borsche

ZUKUNFTSSTARK – SICHERHEIT

[Magazine, Corporate Publishing]

The magazine ZUKUNFTSSTARK is published as a supplement to the annual report of Bechtle AG, one of Europe's main IT service providers. Dedicated to one main topic each time, this year's magazine covers security in general and IT security in particular. For example, it explores topics such as how to counter online con artists and fake news, what it is that makes clouds watertight or where we should stand on the issues of security versus openness and risk avoidance versus innovative ability. The magazine presents these topics with a vibrant layout that underscores the content in a versatile and thought-provoking manner.

Client
Bechtle AG
Neckarsulm, Germany

Design
waf.berlin GmbH
Berlin, Germany

Kepler Tribune

[Special Publication]

Moving away from traditional campus newspapers, the Kepler Tribune aims to promote knowledge in society (Wissen in Gesellschaft) and to set a journalistic milestone in Austrian academia. The large size of the broadsheet format also reflects the magnitude of the content. High-profile editors from established newspapers as well as prominent guest authors and renowned scientists guarantee the high quality of the quarterly newspaper. It was designed and developed from scratch in terms of its size, name, layout, typography, structure and headings. It is published at the university and as an insert in major daily newspapers.

Client
JKU Johannes Kepler Universität Linz
Linz, Austria

Design
kest werbeagentur gmbh
Linz, Austria

Project Team
JKU Johannes Kepler Universität Linz:
Elke Strobl (Head of Marketing)
Meinhard Lukas (Concept)

kest werbeagentur:
Christoph Kerschner (Editorial Work)

Publishing & Print Media	Posters	Typography	Illustrations	Sound Design	Film & Animation	Online
4	64	92	116	126	138	172

Fakultät der Künste

[Catalogue]

Client
Hochschule Macromedia
Faculty of Creative Arts
Munich, Stuttgart, Freiburg, Cologne,
Hamburg, Leipzig, Berlin, Germany

Design
Prof. Dirk Wachowiak
Stuttgart, Germany

Project Team
Prof. Tanja Schmitt-Fumian
(Dean of the Faculty)
Prof. Dirk Wachowiak (Concept)
Prof. Karin Jobst (Concept)

→ Clip online

The catalogue for the newly founded Faculty of Arts at Macromedia University of Applied Sciences presents the artistic and design works of the different programmes. Printed in A3 format on high-gloss paper with three special metallic colours, it comprises folded-up DIN A1 posters printed on both sides that can also be hung on the walls of the university's different campuses in Germany. The design thus succeeded in satisfying the narrative and sequential requirements for a brochure while also accounting for the requirements for poster design.

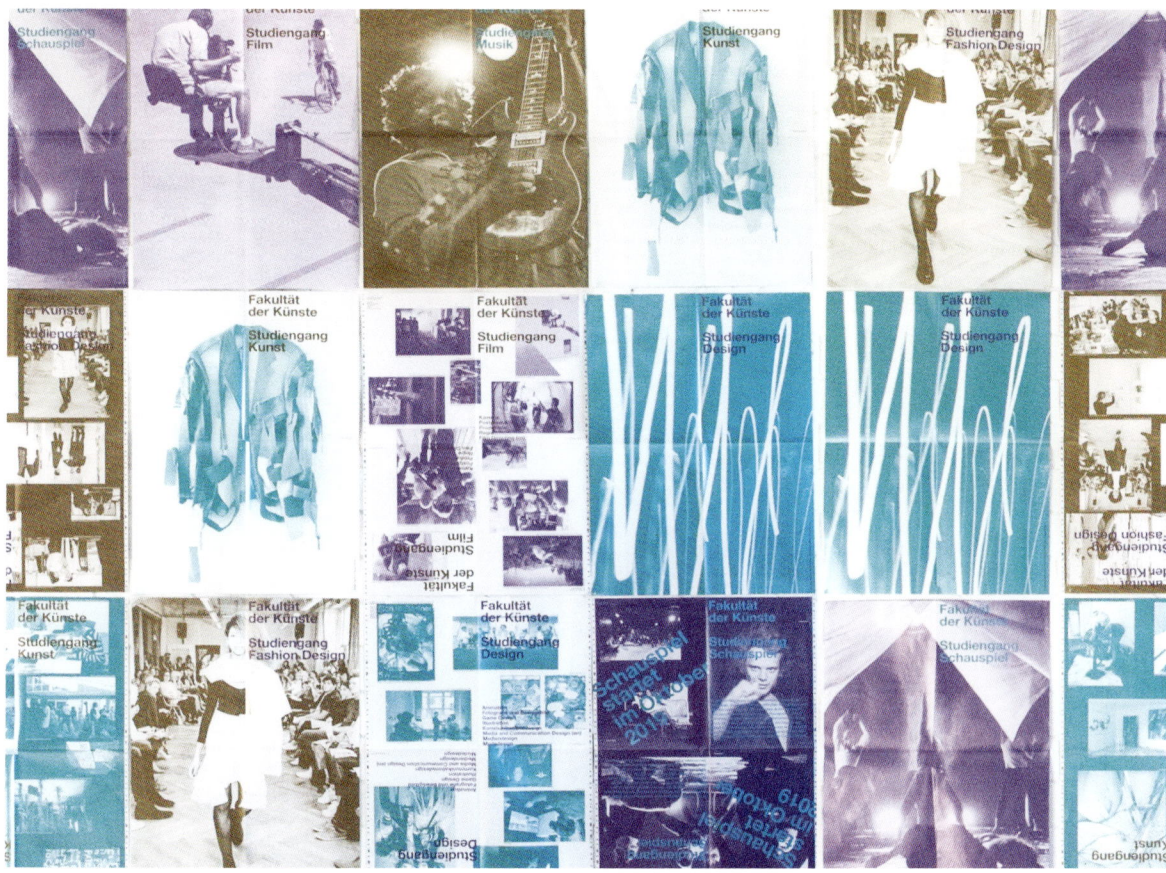

SieMatic

[Brand Brochure]

Client
SieMatic Möbelwerke GmbH & Co. KG
Löhne, Germany

Design
Bay Designagentur
Bastian Nemitz
Hamburg, Germany

Project Team
Christine Graf (Text)
Mario Düsterhöft (Photography),
Klemme.Photos

Apps	Interface & User Experience Design	Spatial Communication	Red Dot: Junior Award	Designer Profiles	Jury Portraits	Index
206	236	336	426	564	642	668

The SieMatic brand brochure is structured according to the brand's three main attributes: family, form and function. In addition to exploring the traditions of the family business, it also highlights the sophisticated design of its kitchen furniture and the highly functional, first-class components. The feel of the fine paper and the luxurious appearance of the gold colour form the creative link between the elegance of the kitchen design and SieMatic's 90th anniversary in 2019. Finely printed in duplex, a removable anniversary booklet emphasises the company history and leaves space in the main section for a modern layout with high-quality images.

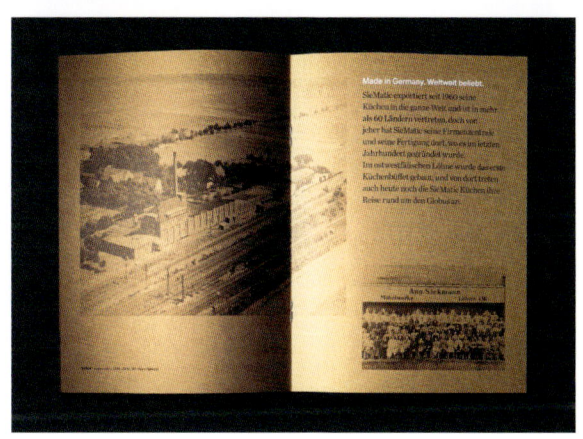

Publishing & Print Media	Posters	Typography	Illustrations	Sound Design	Film & Animation	Online
4	64	92	116	126	138	172

The Seeds of Faith
[Special Publication]

The design of the admission letter, notebook and enrolment guidelines for Beijing Forestry University is a nod to the image of a seed. Students at the university are likened to seeds, which release their power through cultivation and irrigation in order to make important contributions in the future. The shape of the letter on a dark-green background symbolises the round sky and the square Earth – an ancient metaphor in China. Millions of seeds in gold and silver are growing in its centre, with the four different admission letters representing the phases of cultivation, germination, growth and flourishing.

Client
Beijing Forestry University
Beijing, China

Design
Xianming Hu
Beijing, China

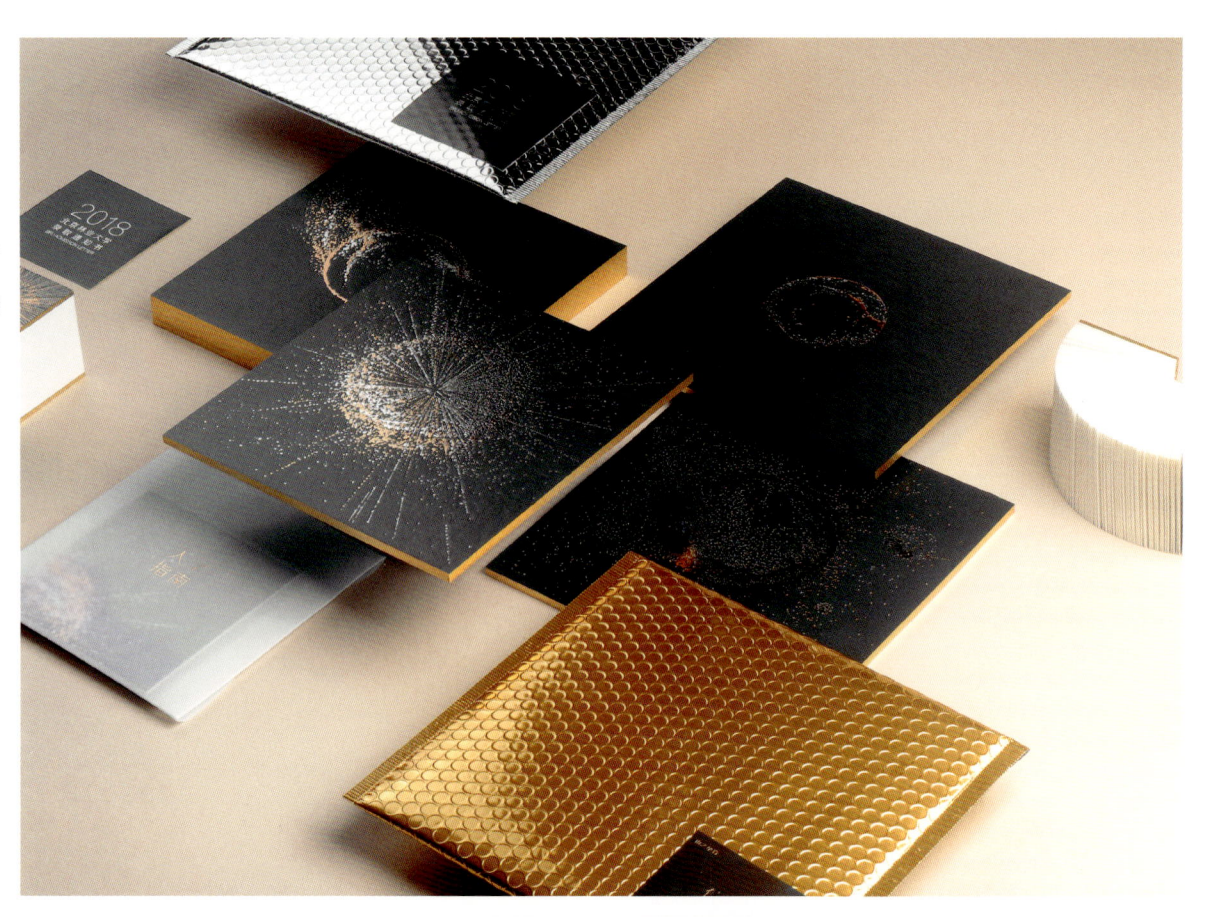

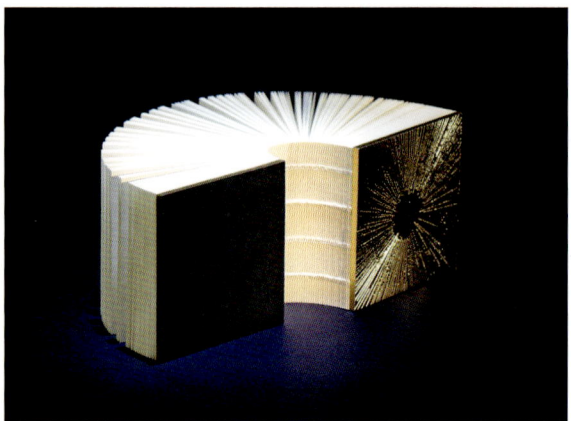

STARLUX Airlines – Menu

[Special Publication]

The Taiwanese STARLUX Airlines celebrated the launch of its inaugural flights in January 2020. Its aim was to offer its guests a relaxed and pleasant atmosphere while providing a surreal flying experience – against the scenery of boundless starlight beyond the horizon. The idea of flight as a gravity-defying process was incorporated as a core visual theme in the design of the in-flight menu and the packaging of the in-flight items. The results are images of fruit appearing to float weightlessly in the in-flight menu as well as fascinating photos of aesthetically presented splashing cocktails.

Client
STARLUX Airlines
Taipei City, Taiwan

Design
Transform Design
Taipei City, Taiwan

Publishing & Print Media	Posters	Typography	Illustrations	Sound Design	Film & Animation	Online
4	64	92	116	126	138	172

Dinbilidanbala

[Educational Board Game]

Dinbilidanbala is an onomatopoeic word derived from the action of rocking. It is the name of a board game that invites pupils to leave the classroom in order to investigate, learn about and shape the world as a team. The intangible heritage of the community of Navarre is used effectively as part of the game. Not confined by the aesthetic principles of familiar board games, the game features a free board with a colour code, primary symbols as well as a modular structure to build a child's individual "personality". Through knowledge, recognition and appreciation of heritage, the game works on the content of the curriculum in an entertaining, collaborative and fun way.

Client
Bitartean
Navarra, Spain
Gobierno de Navarra
Navarra, Spain

Design
Bronce Estudio
Pamplona, Spain

Project Team
Germán Úcar (Creative Direction)
Alicia Puebla (Project Management)
Miguel Ayesa (Design)

Apps	Interface & User Experience Design	Spatial Communication	Red Dot: Junior Award	Designer Profiles	Jury Portraits	Index
206	236	336	426	564	642	668

Infinity joy – Grenzenlose Freude

[Calendar]

This calendar, marking the 150th anniversary of the Epple Druckfarben firm, offers a coloured tour of a world with a wealth of multisensory enhancements. The aim is to make the breadth of the company's product range come to life. The calendar therefore includes a number of refinements that illustrate the diversity of the target audience and wide range of applications. From food printing to fully sustainable colour systems to the sophisticated effects achieved with UV printing, the calendar depicts all levels of printing complexity extremely effectively and conveys the power of colours.

Client
Epple Druckfarben AG
Neusäß, Germany

Design
monsun media GmbH
Osnabrück, Germany

→ Designer profile on page 610

The Legends

[Calendar]

This 2020 charity calendar with handwritten numbers was released to raise funds for the Polish branch of UNICEF, an organisation known for its commitment to helping children worldwide. The main concept was to present legends from countries such as Syria, Sudan, Niger and Yemen in an attractive and distinctive way. A leaflet featuring an entire story is attached to each page, while the back of the calendar can be folded into a box for storing the 12 legends. The front cover can be turned into a mask for use as wall decoration, allowing the calendar fulfil more than one function.

Client
UNICEF Poland
Warsaw, Poland

Design
TOFU Studio
Gdansk, Poland

Project Team
TOFU Studio:
Adam Chylinski (Creative Direction)
Daniel Naborowski (Creative Direction)
Paulina Kozicka (Art Direction)
Ola Kaługa-Mokwa (Copywriting)
Ksawery Kirklewski (Web Development)

Paweł Morawczyński (Printing), NORMEX

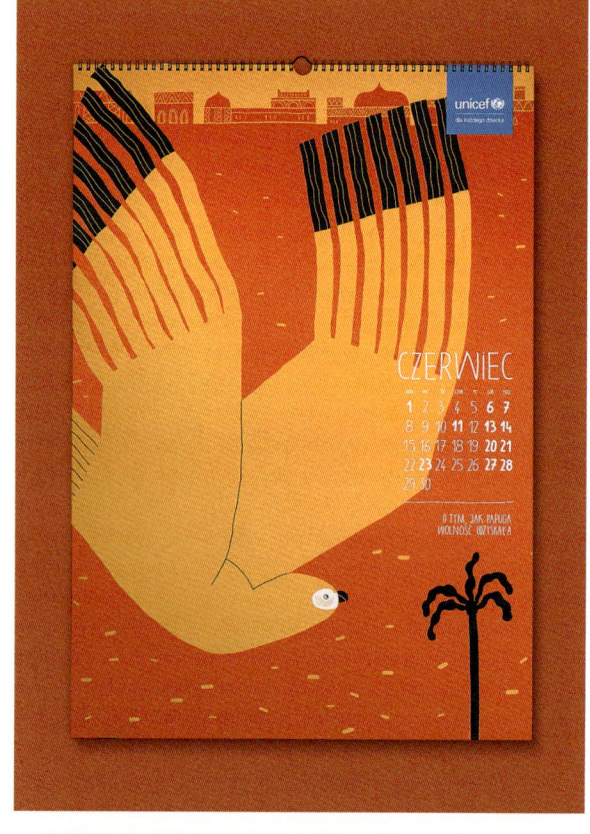

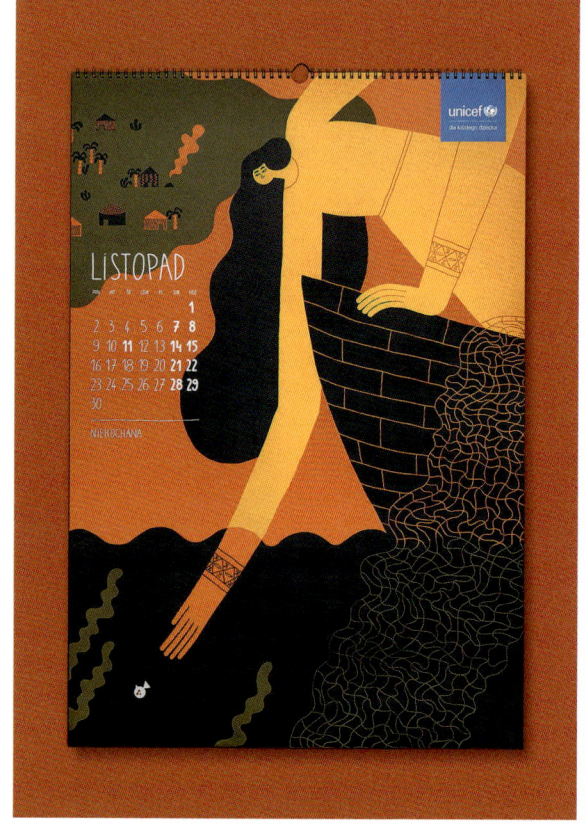

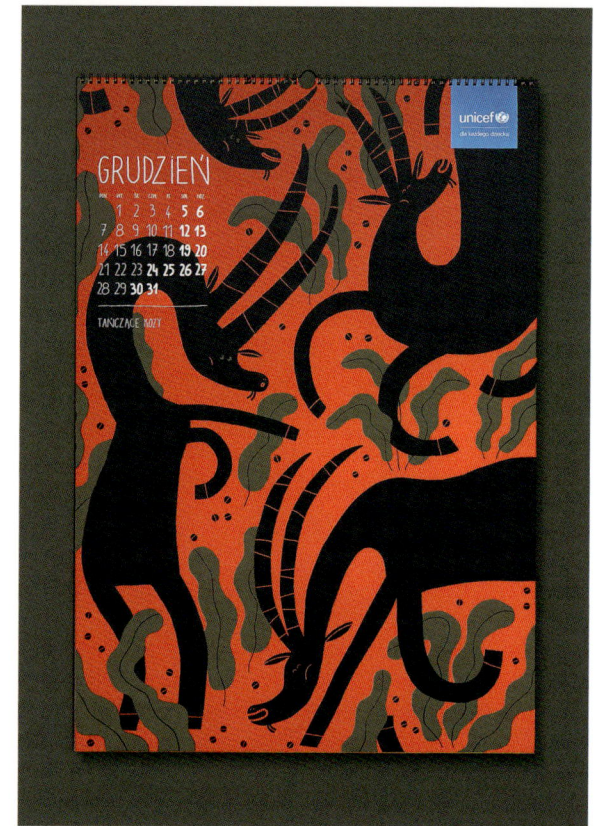

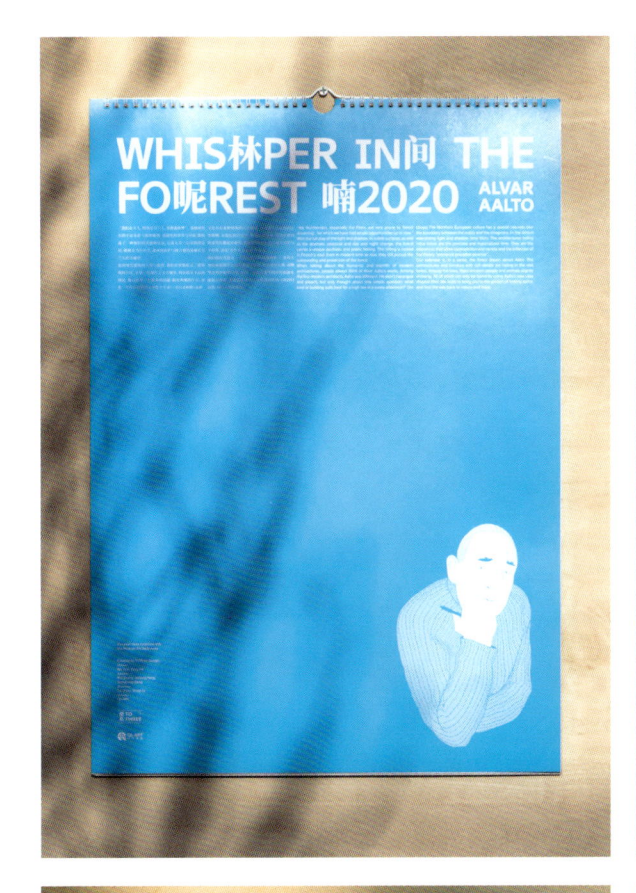

Whisper in the Forest
[Calendar]

"Forest dreaming" is well-known in Finland. This calendar links the dreams with the buildings of the renowned architect Alvar Aalto. Finns believe that the unique poetic feeling generated by the forest and its interplay of light and shadows, as well as the dramatic change of the seasons is rooted in the Finnish soul. As a trailblazer of modernity, Alvar Aalto aimed to established a close connection between buildings and countryside, as shown here as yellow silhouettes on the forest and landscape depicted in blue. The trick: the outline of his famous vase acts as a filter and makes the yellow areas appear black.

Client
ToThree Design
Beijing, China

Design
ToThree Design
Beijing, China

Publishing & Print Media	Posters	Typography	Illustrations	Sound Design	Film & Animation	Online
4	64	92	116	126	138	172

Daily Milk – 2019 Calendar

Much like tearing a page off a calendar, drinking milk is among the things many people do each morning. This calendar was conceptualised as a milk carton to reflect this connection. The daily content of the calendar can thus also be viewed as human nourishment. In addition to indicating the date, the desktop calendar contains illustrations, reminders of public holidays and the lunar date for each day. Printed in the primary colours blue and red, the calendar offers plenty of room for annotations and reminders on its appealing yet unobtrusive pages.

Client
where studio
Taitung, Taiwan

Design
where studio
Taitung, Taiwan

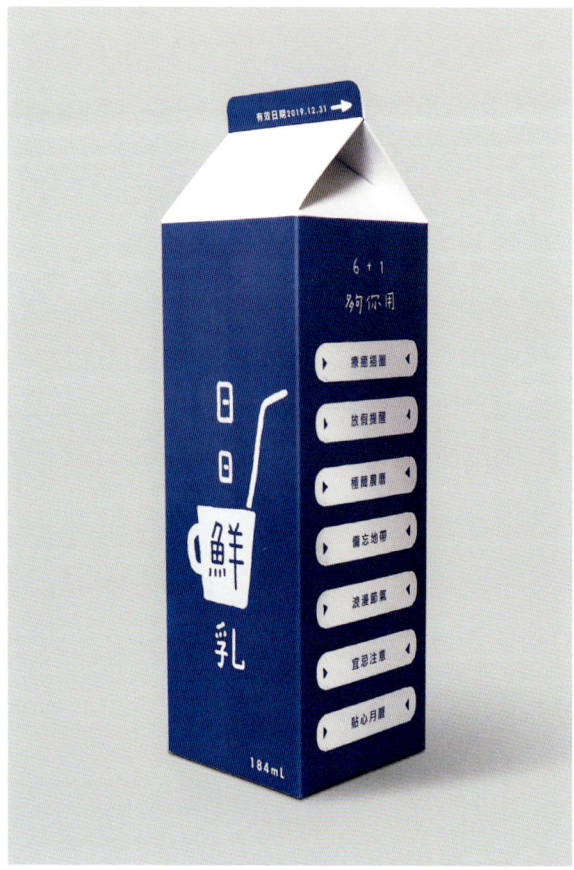

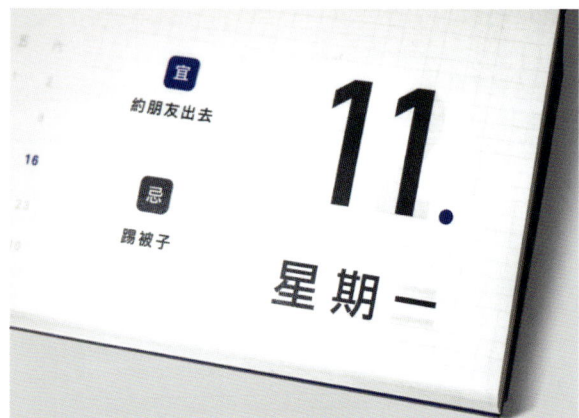

The color of memories – Die Farben der Erinnerung

[Calendar]

Floating Homes designs and builds floating houses for residential and commercial use. The mechanism of this annual calendar works by extracting specific colour stimuli from a key visual on or near the water and covering them with transparent interleaves to produce a filtered colour carpet. This highlights the fleeting nature of the moments one experiences when living on water and also expands one's view of life. The orderly graphic and striking layout are supplemented by barely visible, but tactile print finishes that round off the high-quality appearance of this print product.

Client
Floating Homes GmbH
Verden, Germany

Design
monsun media GmbH
Osnabrück, Germany

→ Designer profile on page 610

Posters

València World Design Capital 2022

[Poster]

The Spanish city of Valencia has been designated "World Design Capital 2022". This series of posters was part of the application and will also accompany the future event. The motifs are based on a natural, modular construction with great variability. The initials VWDC for Valencia World Design Capital are geometrically simplified and communicate news of the event in a universal, timeless and modern language. This first edition has been made in black serigraphy against a yellow and white background, the corporate colours of the Valencia World Design Capital.

Client
Associació València Capital del Disseny
Valencia, Spain

Design
Ibán Ramon – Design Studio
Valencia, Spain

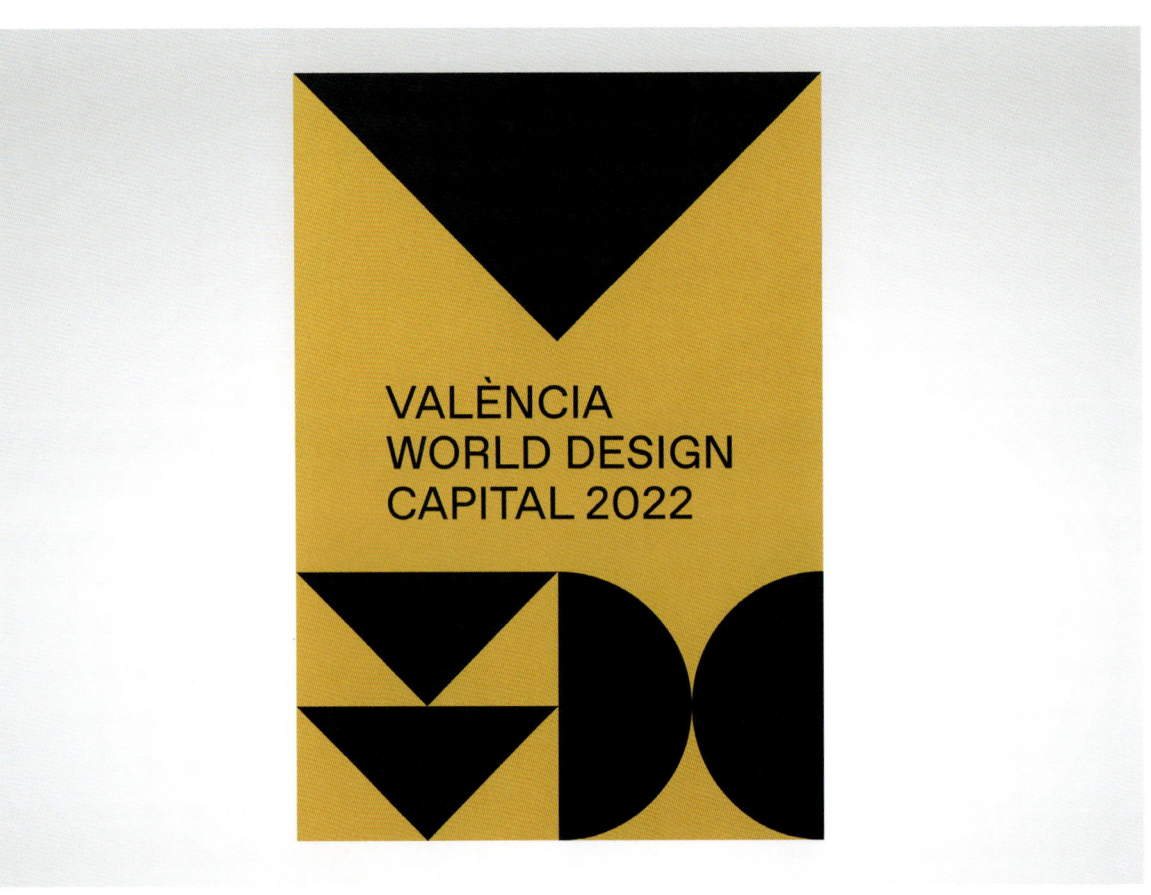

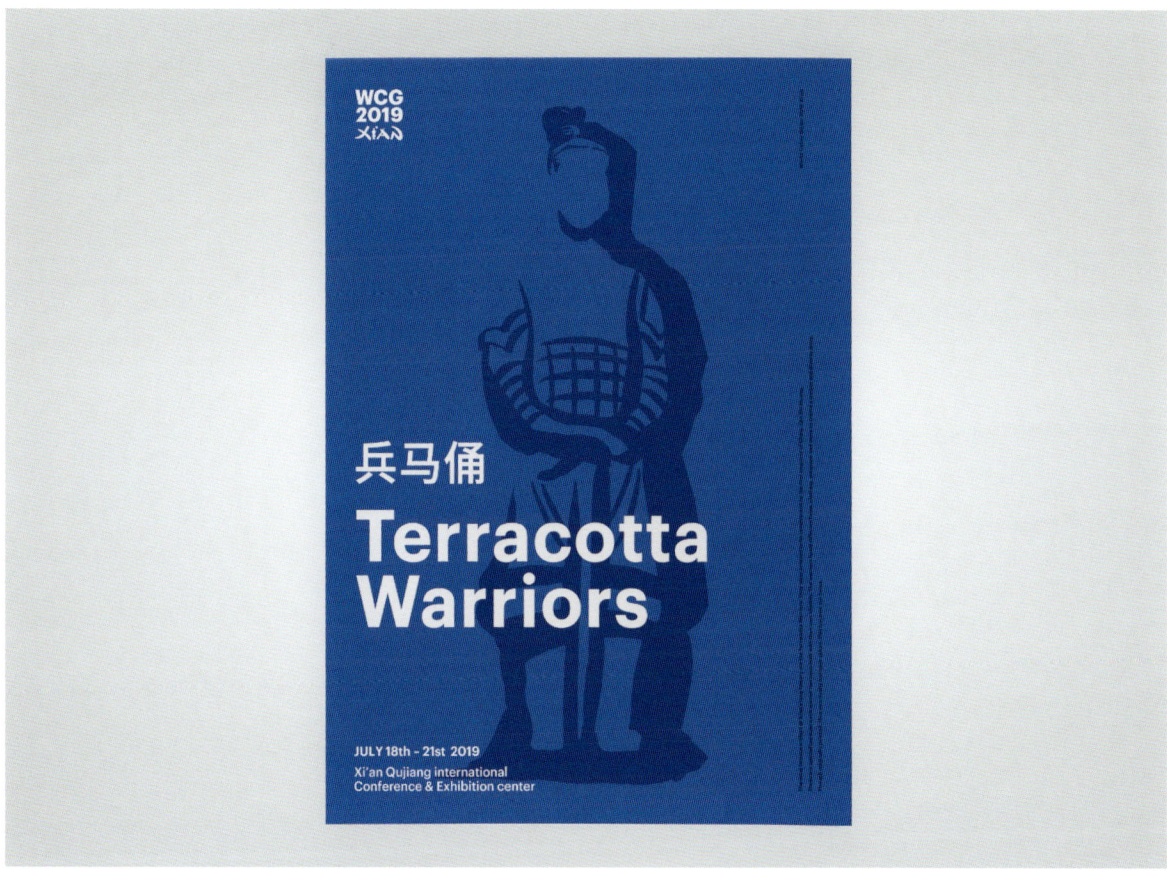

Apps	Interface & User Experience Design	Spatial Communication	Red Dot: Junior Award	Designer Profiles	Jury Portraits	Index
206	236	336	426	564	642	668

WCG 2019
[Event Poster]

The terracotta army is a symbol of the Chinese city of Xian, partner to the return of the World Cyber Games 2019. The famous clay warriors became the key visual for the campaign to advertise the international tournament. They also adorned the corresponding poster series in powerful, contrasting colours and equipped with modern, technical accessories like Segways and controllers. In this way, the partnership between the city and the event was communicated effectively, and a visual link was created between tradition and modernity.

Client
WCG, Smilegate
Seongnam, South Korea

Design
Eidetic Korea
Seoul, South Korea

Project Team
Yohan Choi (Executive Sponsor)
Justin Donghyuk Choi (Creative Director)
Kenneth Nienhuser (Verbal Strategist)
Ji Hye Shin (Senior Brand Designer)
Kimmi Miyeon Kim (Senior Event Designer)
Yun Jeong Seok (Graphic Designer)
Hak Jae Jung (Senior Graphic Designer)
Yeon Dan Choi (Senior Event Designer)
Min Hwan Jung (Account Management)

Publishing & Print Media	Posters	Typography	Illustrations	Sound Design	Film & Animation	Online
4	64	92	116	126	138	172

City Vision
[Exhibition Poster Series]

"City Vision" is the title of the Shanghai contemporary art exhibition, where 72 artists have developed and created a joint stance on contemporary art in the city. The motifs on the posters also play with the idea of "reconstruction". The individual letters look like small scaffoldings which combine to create the exhibition title and other buzzwords, like "city resonance", and thus visualise an art scene in transition; an art scene which, under the influence of major social upheaval, renews itself beyond the realm of conventional thought.

Client
Artsway Media (Shanghai) Co., Ltd.
Shanghai, China

Design
Bangqian Zheng
Shanghai, China

Project Team
Bangqian Zheng (Creative Director)
Binhao Zhang (Photography)
Hui Zhang (Image Editing)

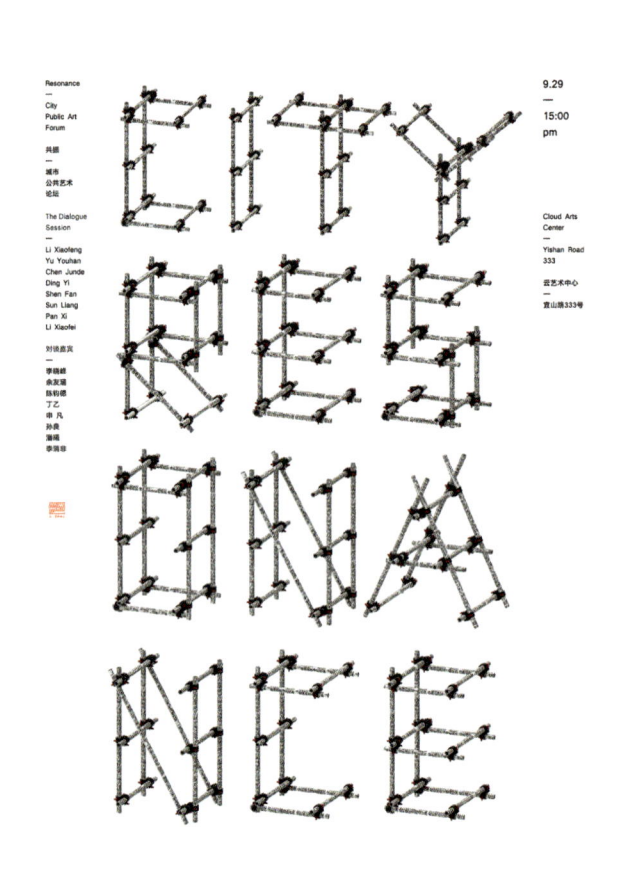

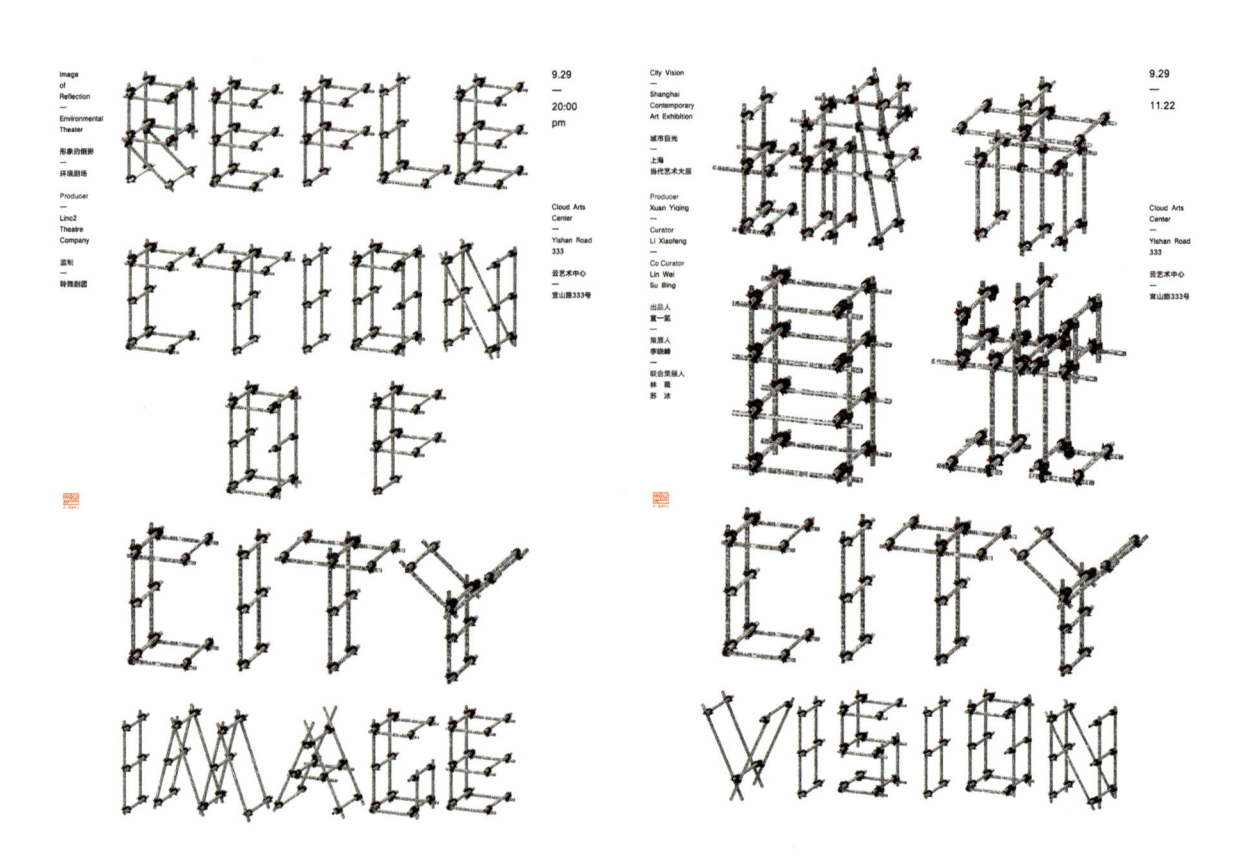

Apps	Interface & User Experience Design	Spatial Communication	Red Dot: Junior Award	Designer Profiles	Jury Portraits	Index
206	236	336	426	564	642	668

Pieces
[Exhibition Poster]

The posters for "Pieces", a photographic artwork and exhibition by Mingmei Meng, are an appealing and effective way of setting a scene for an art project which is related to the body, relationships, childhood memories, limitations and ideals. The title of the exhibition and the name of the artist are deliberately fragmented. Letters of small white squares dissolve gradually as they approach the middle of the posters until finally form a Chinese character for "piece" on the upper right corner. The subtle arrangements of these fragments ensure the idea recognisably for the visitor, who can easily grasp the crucial details.

Client
May Art Foundation
New York, USA

Design
T9 Brand
Shanghai, China

Project Team
Hui Pan (Art Director)
Dawang Sun (Designer)

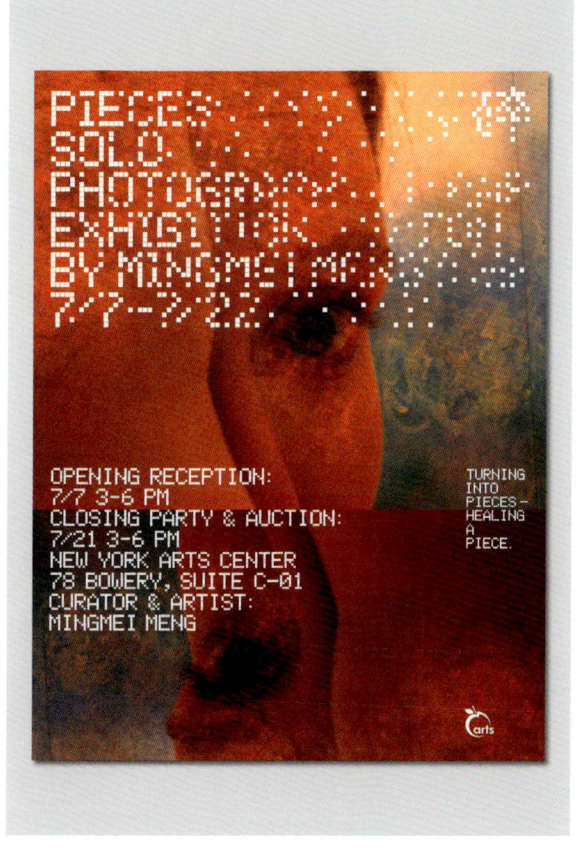

Publishing & Print Media	Posters	Typography	Illustrations	Sound Design	Film & Animation	Online
4	64	92	116	126	138	172

Ten Thousand Li of Rivers and Mountains

[Art Poster Series]

Experimental characters based on writings from traditional Chinese cultures provide the motifs for the poster series "Ten Thousand Li of Rivers and Mountains". They complement each other, criss-cross and overlap, forming diverse patterns and shapes which in turn produce abstract landscapes with trees, mountains, rivers and grasslands. In addition, deliberately used black-and-white contrasts and finely nuanced grey hues create an expressive play of light and shade, and give the motifs printed on the scrolls a special expressiveness.

Client
Shenzhen Luyao Culture Media Ltd.
Shenzhen, China

Design
Shenzhen Sandulixian Design Ltd.
Shenzhen, China

Project Team
Shenzhen Luyao Culture Media:
Xiaozhong Chen (Manager)

Shenzhen Sandulixian Design:
Lixian Xu (Creative Director)
Zhangchi Shi (Design Team Leader)
Tao Zhang (Art Director)
Liang Lin (Art Director)
Yuan Fang (Designer)
Lirong Xu (Project Manager)

Jiangnan Context
[Art Poster]

This series of posters pays homage to the beauty and diversity of the scenery in the Jiangnan region in China. The ink drawings show motifs from the Jiangnan gardens. Typical plants such as bamboo and the plum blossom as well as the formations of the well-known Taihu Lake stone make up the logo of the region, turning them into ambassadors for Jiangnan. The geometrically shaped frames around the motifs are a well-executed detail which act like a window through which the visitor can catch a glimpse of the gardens in Jiangnan.

Client
Suzhou SoFeng Culture Media Co., Ltd.
Suzhou, China

Design
Suzhou SoFeng Culture Media Co., Ltd.
Suzhou, China

Project Team
Sha Feng (Creative Direction)
Jiayi Lu (Art Direction)

Beethoven 2020

[Billboard]

Ludwig van Beethoven is generally considered to have been unconventional. His avant-garde hairstyle is the central design element of the billboard by the Bielefeld Philharmonic Orchestra advertising a nine-part concert series to be held to commemorate his 250th birthday. The background is made up of the composer's name, printed in capital letters in different colours and in narrow and wide formats. The outline of his hairstyle is suspended in front of the letters, directly at the centre of the billboard above the orchestra's logo. Even without recognisable facial features, there is a direct visual link to the composer.

Client
Bielefelder Philharmoniker, Bühnen und Orchester der Stadt Bielefeld
Bielefeld, Germany

Design
beierarbeit GmbH
Bielefeld, Germany

Project Team
Bühnen und Orchester der Stadt Bielefeld:
Michael Heicks (Intendant)
Alexander Kalajdzic (Musical Director)
Martin Beyer (Managing Director)
Jana Wörmann (Marketing Management)

beierarbeit:
Christoph Beier (Creative Direction)

Benjamin Wolf (Design)
Silke Nehring (Illustration)

Beethoven 2020

[Promotional Poster]

The typical Beethoven hairstyle is the key visual for this poster series by the Bielefeld Philharmonic Orchestra. The outline of his distinctive and unusual hairstyle forms the basis for an eye-catching motif reflecting the composer's unconventional personality, which gives him the cult status of a pop star even 250 years after his birth. The central Beethoven lettering in the background uses the trend of elision to omit the vowels and create an unmistakeable logo which establishes a direct link to the Beethoven anniversary year as well as it serves as a hashtag for social media.

Client
Bielefelder Philharmoniker, Bühnen und Orchester der Stadt Bielefeld
Bielefeld, Germany

Design
beierarbeit GmbH
Bielefeld, Germany

Project Team
Bühnen und Orchester der Stadt Bielefeld:
Michael Heicks (Intendant)
Alexander Kalajdzic (Musical Director)
Martin Beyer (Managing Director)
Jana Wörmann (Marketing Management)

beierarbeit:
Christoph Beier (Creative Direction)

Benjamin Wolf (Design)
Silke Nehring (Illustration)

Publishing & Print Media	Posters	Typography	Illustrations	Sound Design	Film & Animation	Online
4	64	92	116	126	138	172

Korea Infographic Poster Series

The posters of this series present Korean traditions and cultural assets in the form of infographics. Every month, a new motif appears in the magazine Street H. The topics covered are as diverse as the design of the individual motifs, ranging from traditional clothing to individual regions of the country or culinary specialities. Clearly structured infographics with many facts and images break down even complex topics in a way that makes them intuitive for readers, regardless of their cultural and linguistic background.

Client
Street H – Culture Magazine for Hongdae Area
Seoul, South Korea

Design
203 X Infographics Lab
Seoul, South Korea

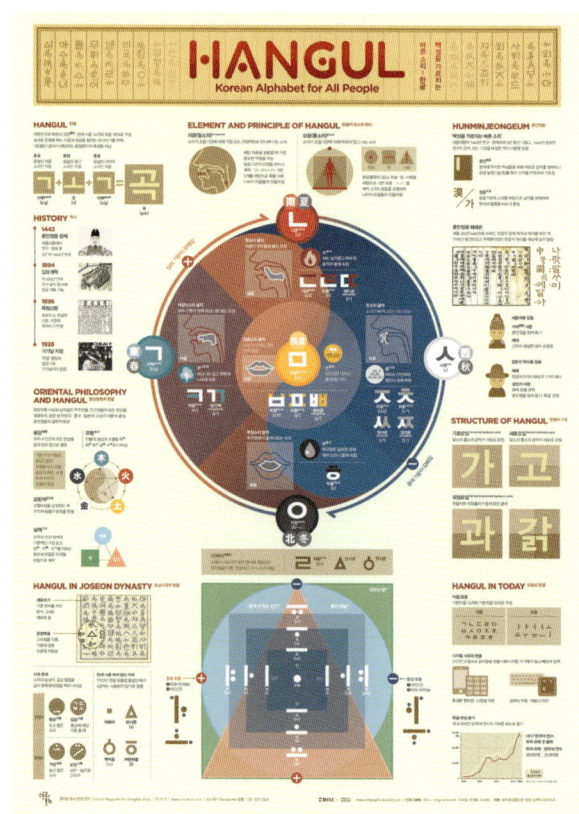

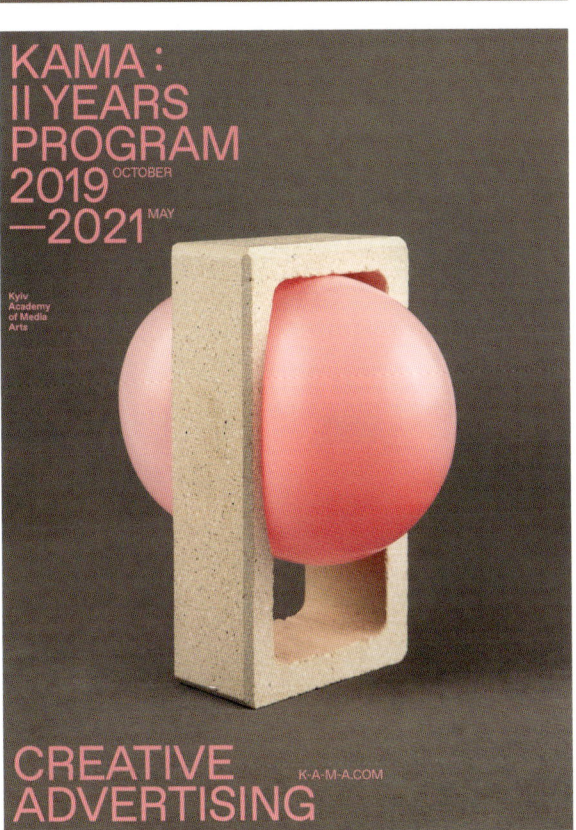

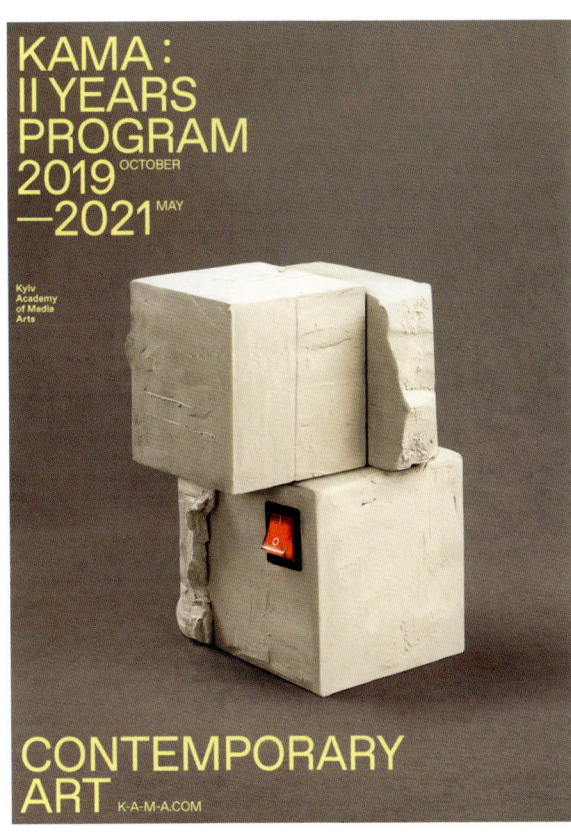

Apps	Interface & User Experience Design	Spatial Communication	Red Dot: Junior Award	Designer Profiles	Jury Portraits	Index
206	236	336	426	564	642	668

Kyiv Academy of Media Arts – II Years Program

[Promotional Poster Series]

The Kyiv Academy of Media Arts uses these poster motifs to advertise its two-year programmes in Contemporary Arts, Creative Advertising and Graphic Design. The combination of items with different characteristics in one object is what distinguishes the Academy's individual style, which is also reflected in this series. Natural materials, such as stone, concrete, clay and glass, are combined with elements which stand out in terms of their properties and colours. The resulting sculptural works are at the heart of the posters and create a metaphor which visualises the focus of the respective course.

Client
Kyiv Academy of Media Arts
Kyiv, Ukraine

Design
CREVV
Kyiv, Ukraine

Project Team
Natalia Ivanova (Design)
Anton Ivanov (Design)
Eugene Sulimenko (Photography)

Publishing & Print Media	Posters	Typography	Illustrations	Sound Design	Film & Animation	Online
4	64	92	116	126	138	172

Don't forget !)

[Poster Campaign]

The NGO Youth against AIDS wants to educate young people about the importance of safer sex. Six motifs were developed which link the serious topic of safer sex to a playful graphic design. The posters show phallic shapes with a knot tied in them in the same way people used to tie a knot in their handkerchief in order to remember something. This is a fun way to remind people to use a condom. All of the motifs, from rockets to sausages, share the same basic idea but with different visualisations. The style is aimed at young adults and shows a style mix of CI elements and illustration.

Client
Youth against AIDS
Hamburg, Germany

Design
loved GmbH
Hamburg, Germany

Project Team
Alexander Müsgens (Creative Director)
Lukas Weber (Copywriting)
Marc Huth (Art Buying)
Lilli Oldag (Account Management)

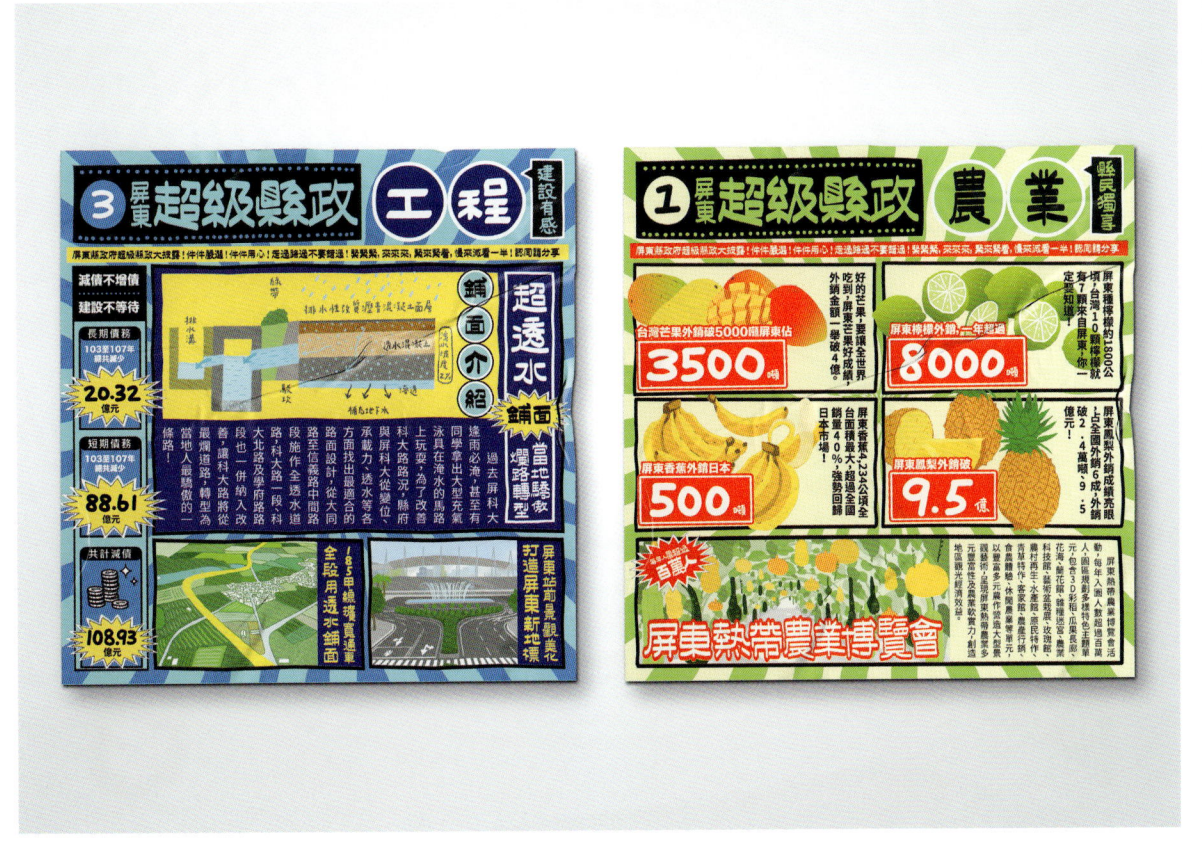

Apps	Interface & User Experience Design	Spatial Communication	Red Dot: Junior Award	Designer Profiles	Jury Portraits	Index
206	236	336	426	564	642	668

Super Policy
[Poster Series]

These posters aim to present official government documents in an attractive design. Nine motifs communicate the political objectives of Pingtung County Government and were exhibited as part of the Taiwan Design Expo. The brightly coloured posters, designed to look like supermarket flyers, pique the interest of, and are, at the same time, familiar to a lot of people who know the design from their everyday lives. It is common practice in Taiwan to fold flyers into origami figures. And this also happened to these posters during the exhibition: they were folded into nine gemstones.

Client
Pingtung County Government
Pingtung, Taiwan

Design
Mengdom Design Lab
Taipei City, Taiwan

Project Team
Mengdom Design Lab:
Meng Chih Chiang (Creative Direction)
Chi Chun Chang (Graphic Design)
Sunday Huang (Graphic Design)
Pei Rong Lu (Project Management)

James Lin (Photography)
Daya Chang (Illustration)

Publishing & Print Media	Posters	Typography	Illustrations	Sound Design	Film & Animation	Online
4	64	92	116	126	138	172

Alles könnte anders sein
[Promotional Poster]

"Alles könnte anders sein" (Everything could be different), the 2020/2021 season motto of Theater Bielefeld is ambiguous. It can inspire us to reflect on the extraordinary nature of our present age, to imagine our future in both dark and light colours, or to look back at the past. On the poster for the new season, the motto is shown on a spiral with sweeping handwriting on both sides. The focus shifts from one word or part of a sentence to another, opening up new perspectives and allowing for different interpretations. The shimmering colourful background creates an atmospheric contrast to the black-and-white inscription.

Client
Theater Bielefeld, Bühnen und Orchester der Stadt Bielefeld
Bielefeld, Germany

Design
beierarbeit GmbH
Bielefeld, Germany

Project Team
Bühnen und Orchester der Stadt Bielefeld:
Michael Heicks (Intendant)
Charlotte Höpker (Head of Marketing)
Jennifer Nüßing (Design)

beierarbeit:
Christoph Beier (Creative Direction)
Sina Stuke (Graphic Design)

Apps	Interface & User Experience Design	Spatial Communication	Red Dot: Junior Award	Designer Profiles	Jury Portraits	Index
206	236	336	426	564	642	668

Existence
[Poster Series]

The poster series "Existence" tackles the issue of depression and coping with depression. All of the motifs are designed in black and white, and each of them depicts different aspects of the illness as well as related existential questions in a very individual way. As sketches or in reduced form, together the posters visualise and interpret the impact of depression and how to overcome it. The central symbol in the series is the semicolon, symbolising the development from melancholy essence to a new and free existence.

Client
Island-image Art Club de Taipei
Taipei City, Taiwan

Design
Ming-Chi Ken Hsieh,
Ming-Chi Hsieh Art Studio
Taipei City, Taiwan

Chih-Chun Lai, The Graduate Institute of
Design Science, Tatung University
Taipei City, Taiwan

→ Designer profile on page 593

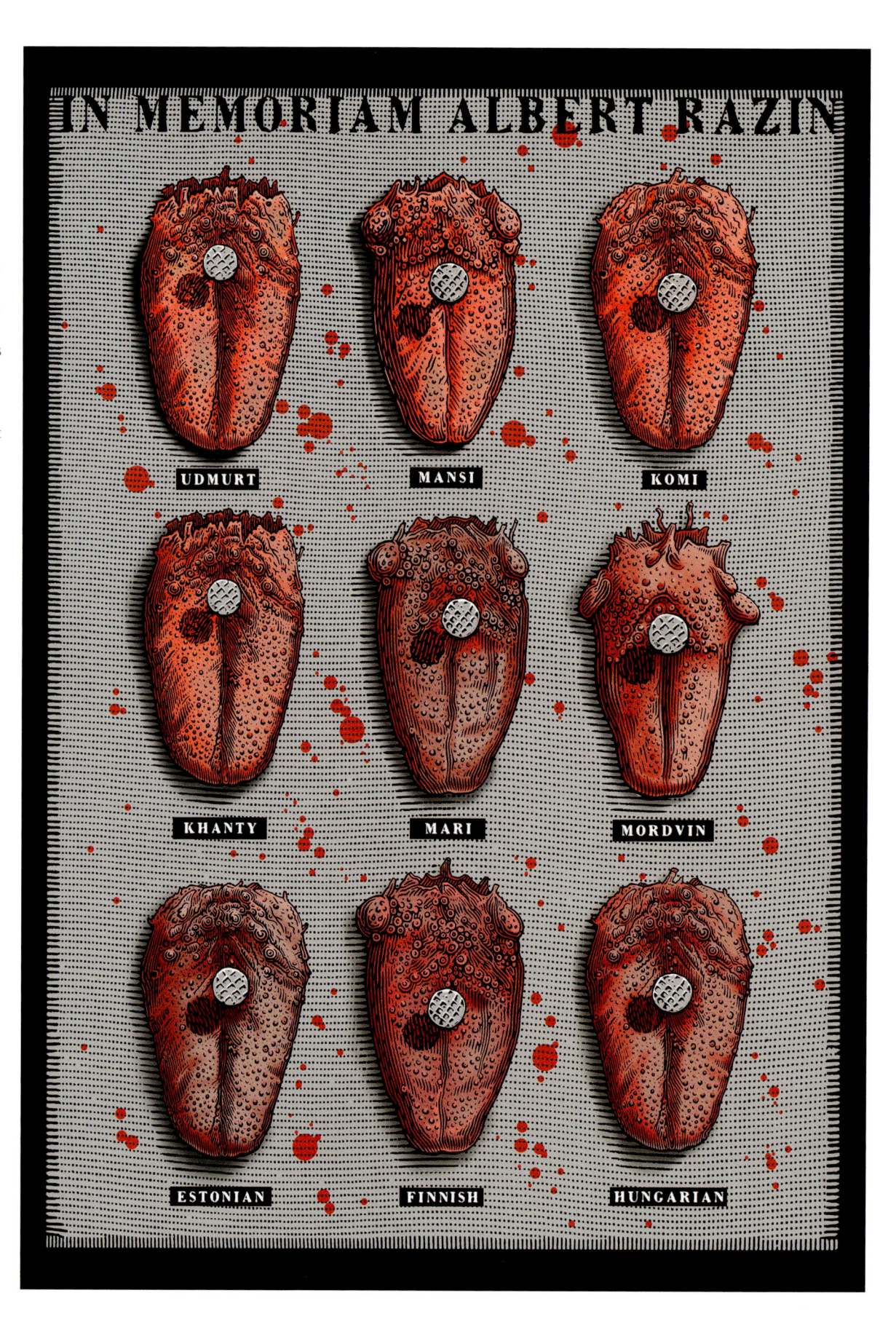

In Memoriam Albert Razin

[Political Poster]

In 2019, philosopher Albert Razin set himself on fire in protest against the language policy of the Russian government and the oppression of Uralic languages such as Udmurt. The poster "In memoriam Albert Razin" commemorates this act and makes an unequivocal statement with its stark motif: illustrated tongues, torn out and nailed to a grey background, hanging above signs bearing the names of Uralic languages, blood splattered across the entire surface of the poster. This representation creates a powerful image of the conflict and calls uncompromisingly for this issue to be addressed.

Client
István Orosz
Budakeszi, Hungary

Design
István Orosz
Budakeszi, Hungary

Apps	Interface & User Experience Design	Spatial Communication	Red Dot: Junior Award	Designer Profiles	Jury Portraits	Index
206	236	336	426	564	642	668

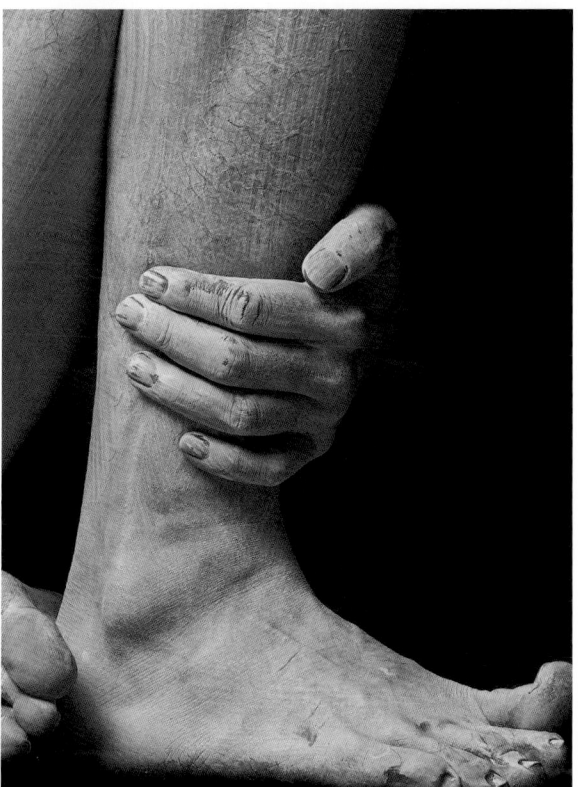

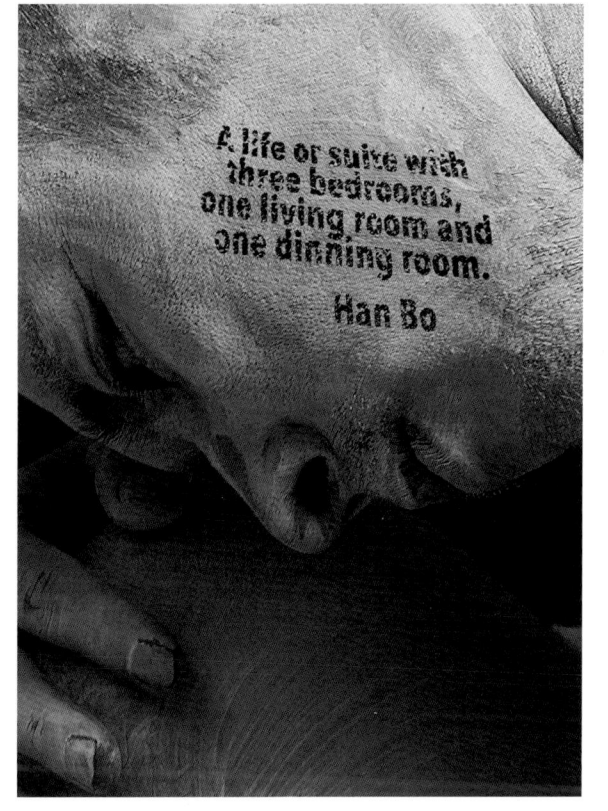

Three Rooms and Two Halls

[Poster Series]

These posters provide the images for the book "Three Rooms and Two Halls" by Chinese poet Han Bo. The title describes the idea of the ideal living environment many contemporaries in China have, but also the boundaries of their view of the world. These boundaries are reflected in the motif: a man squats all alone at the centre of the image. He is naked and covered only in white paint. His gaze is directed downward into empty space. The writing on his cheek creates a direct link to the book, showing the title and the author's name in black letters.

Client
Zhejiang Literature &
Art Publishing House
Shanghai, China

Design
Shanghai Dongxiang Culture
Communication Co., Ltd.
Shanghai, China

Project Team
Bangqian Zheng (Creative Director)
Fei Wei (Photography)
Xuezhou Zhang (Film Production)
Bin An (Project Management)
Hui Zhang (Image Editing)

Publishing & Print Media	Posters	Typography	Illustrations	Sound Design	Film & Animation	Online
4	64	92	116	126	138	172

War No More – Poster Poem by Peter Bankov

[Poster Series]

"War No More" is a series of posters to commemorate the 75th anniversary of the end of the Second World War. These posters are a graphic tribute to those who suffered during the war and, at the same time, a memorial for younger generations. Fragments of war-time poems are combined with modern illustrations to create poster art. The illustrations are fresco-style portraits drawn with gouache and show faces inspired by war-time poems and the artist's childhood memories of veterans. The inscriptions were painted with a hand-crafted typeface.

Client
RT
Moscow, Russia

Design
Peter Bankov
Prague, Czech Republic

Project Team
Peter Bankov (Graphic Designer)
Kirill Karnovich-Valua (Creative Director)
Margo Tskhovrebova (Project Manager)
Lilly Kazakova (Project Manager)
Revaz Todua (Lead Designer)
Gleb Burashov (Producer)
Eldar Salamov (Producer)
Ania Fedorova (Producer)
Katya Motyakina (Editor)
Ivan Fursov (Editor)
Lena Medvedeva (Producer)
Ivor Crotty (Producer)

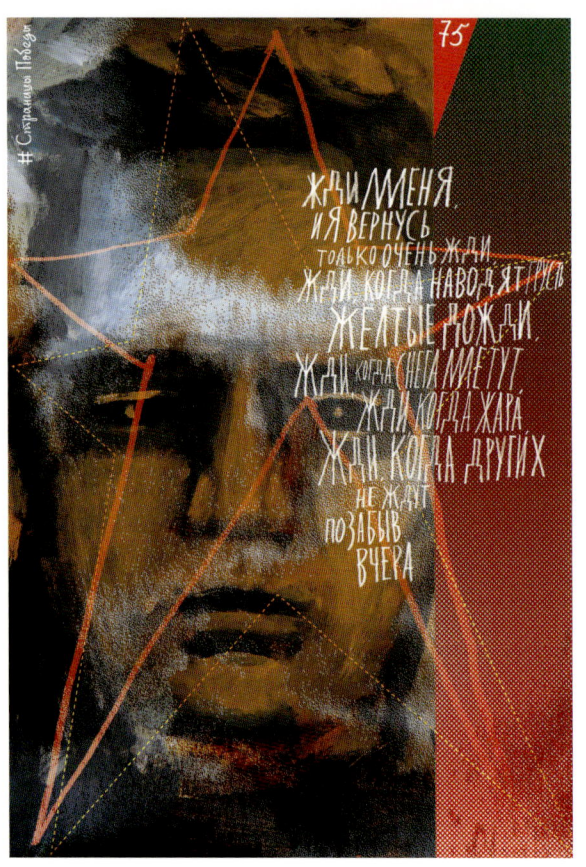

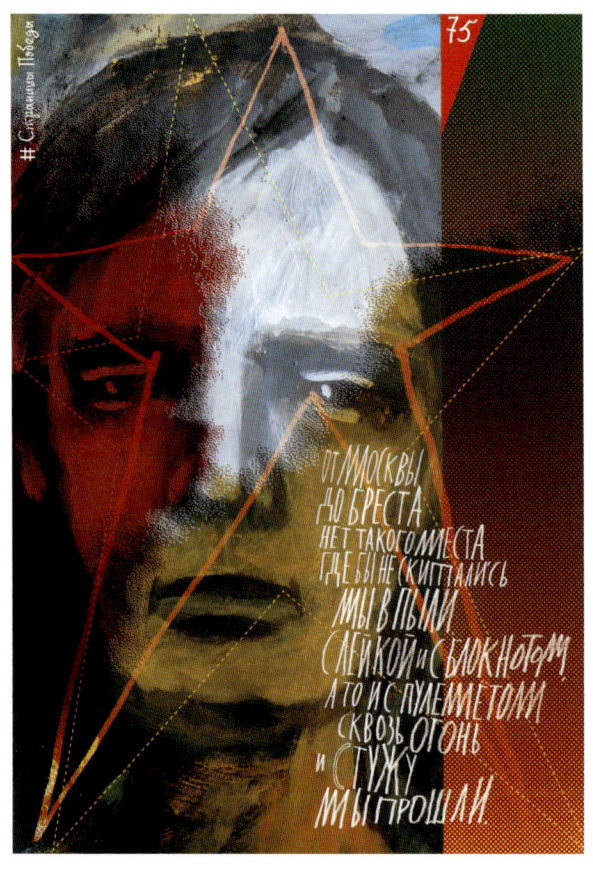

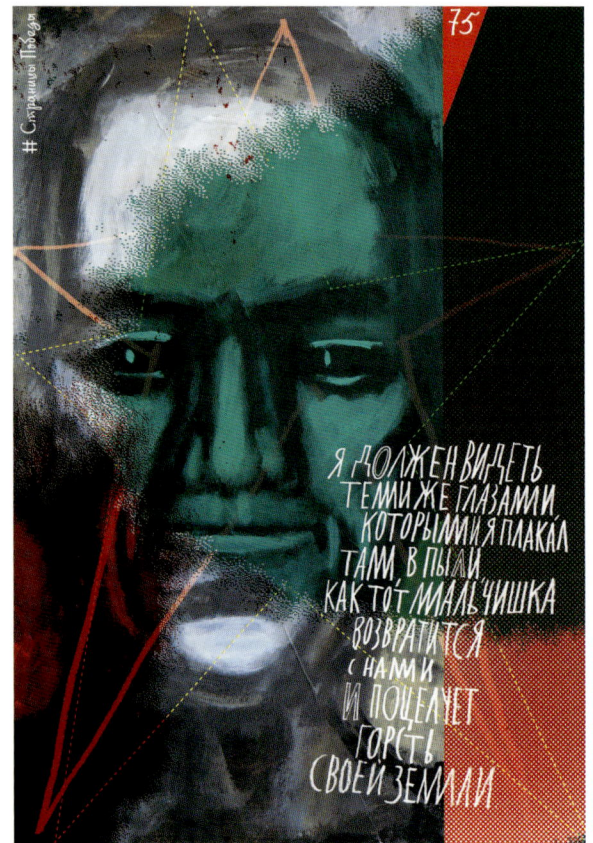

Autumn Sound & Spring View

[Poster Series]

Chinese poetry and characters provided the inspiration for the design of the poster series "Autumn Sound & Spring View". Creative fonts and graphic elements were used to develop large-scale motifs depicting a visual interpretation of poems. The fine lines and clear geometric shapes are put together differently in every motif and give each representation its very own character and personality. This effect is emphasised by the colours used, with one motif showing a contrasting and rather cool black-and-white pattern, while another is dominated by warm gold and brown tones.

Client
Shenzhen Yiqi Culture Development Ltd.
Shenzhen, China

Design
Shenzhen Sandulixian Design Ltd.
Shenzhen, China

Project Team
Shenzhen Yiqi Culture Development:
Shenglei Rui (Manager)

Shenzhen Sandulixian Design:
Lixian Xu (Creative Director)
Zhangchi Shi (Design Team Leader)
Tao Zhang (Art Director)
Liang Lin (Art Director)
Yuan Fang (Designer)
Lirong Xu (Project Manager)

Publishing & Print Media	Posters	Typography	Illustrations	Sound Design	Film & Animation	Online
4	64	92	116	126	138	172

Give a Hand to Wildlife
[Poster Series]

Client
UNITE DESIGN
Taipei City, Taiwan

Design
UNITE Design
Taipei City, Taiwan

Project Team
Jen-Jiun Wang (Graphic Design)

Apps	Interface & User Experience Design	Spatial Communication	Red Dot: Junior Award	Designer Profiles	Jury Portraits	Index
206	236	336	426	564	642	668

Lending a hand to animal rights: that is the message depicted on the three motifs of the poster series "Give a Hand to Wildlife". The subtle relationship between humans and animals is conveyed in a simple, reduced yet moving way. Two seemingly abstract sketches in black and white combine to create the picture. Fine lines depict the face and hand of a human and, together with the black shapes, show a human giving a protective hug to the outlines of different animals, a rhino, an elephant and an elk.

Publishing & Print Media	Posters	Typography	Illustrations	Sound Design	Film & Animation	Online
4	64	92	116	126	138	172

VIA – Wink the World

[Social Campaign Poster]

This poster series uses subtle irony to comment on environmental exploitation and pollution. The three motifs, depicting a fish, a bird and a bat, look like watercolour paintings. The most striking thing about the motifs is the face mask worn by all three creatures. Painted in simple brush strokes, this small aid, which people are currently using in the fight against COVID-19, is enough to convey the serious message in a clear yet humorous manner. Since the human race is not learning from its mistakes in its dealings with nature and the environment, the creatures' only choice is to protect themselves.

Client
Island-image Art Club de Taipei
Taipei City, Taiwan

Design
Ming-Chi Ken Hsieh, Ya-Wen Paulina Lee,
Ming-Chi Hsieh Art Studio
Taipei City, Taiwan

Chih-Chun Lai, The Graduate Institute of Design Science, Tatung University
Taipei City, Taiwan

→ Designer profile on page 593

Return of the Turtle
[Social Campaign Poster]

This poster aims to raise awareness of the plight of the green turtle. The motif design works with strong contrasts and colours which appear counterintuitive at first, with a bright-red turtle set against a dark-green background. The poster takes advantage of the complementary afterimage, which is a special effect occuring when looking at the poster for a long time. Anyone who focuses on the image for a few seconds and then closes their eyes will see the image in reverse colours before their mind's eye. The green turtle is swimming in a blood-red sea.

Client
Kaohsiung City Art Promotion Association, KAPAarts
Kaohsiung, Taiwan

Design
AMI DESIGN
Kaohsiung, Taiwan

Project Team
Pency Tsai (Editorial Work), Voiceoyster

→ Designer profile on page 570
→ Clip online

Publishing & Print Media	Posters	Typography	Illustrations	Sound Design	Film & Animation	Online
4	64	92	116	126	138	172

Restaurant Videgård

[Poster Series]

These posters were developed for the Swedish restaurant Videgård, which focuses on Japanese-Peruvian Nikkei cuisine. The designs are integrated in the interior as well as digitally on social media and celebrate the least common denominator in the Nikkei kitchen: the chopstick. The clear-cut figures display different silhouettes. For example, the graphic chopsticks take the shape of a grid or the random pile of Mikado pick-up sticks. The precise and playful motifs on the posters can be understood at a glance and are easily recognisable.

Client
Erik Videgård, Stureplansgruppen
Stockholm, Sweden

Design
Gabor Palotai Design AB
Stockholm, Sweden

Project Team
Gabor Palotai (Art Direction)
Clara Axtelius (Graphic Design)

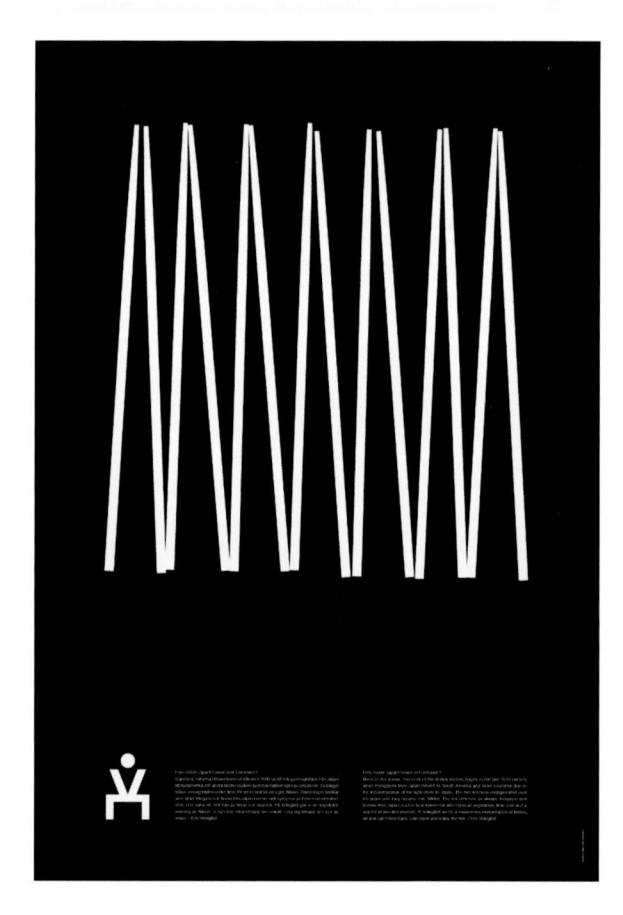

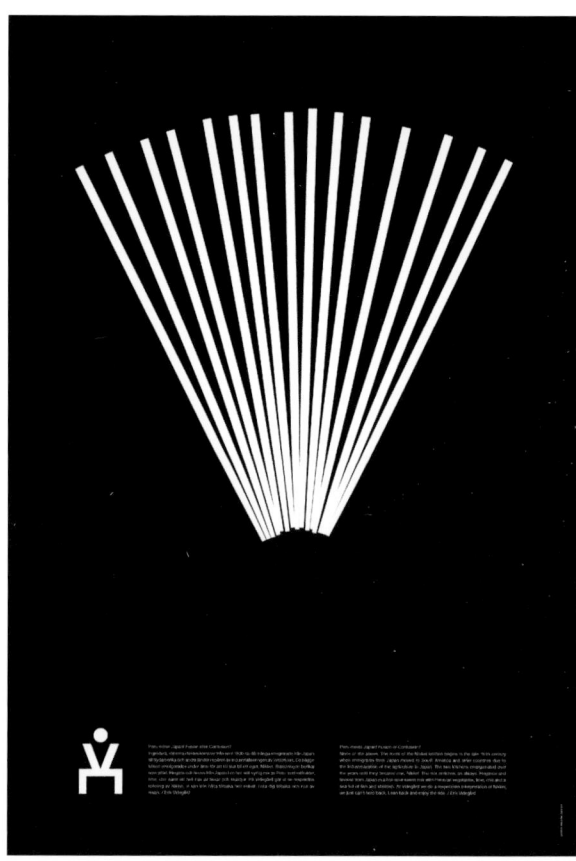

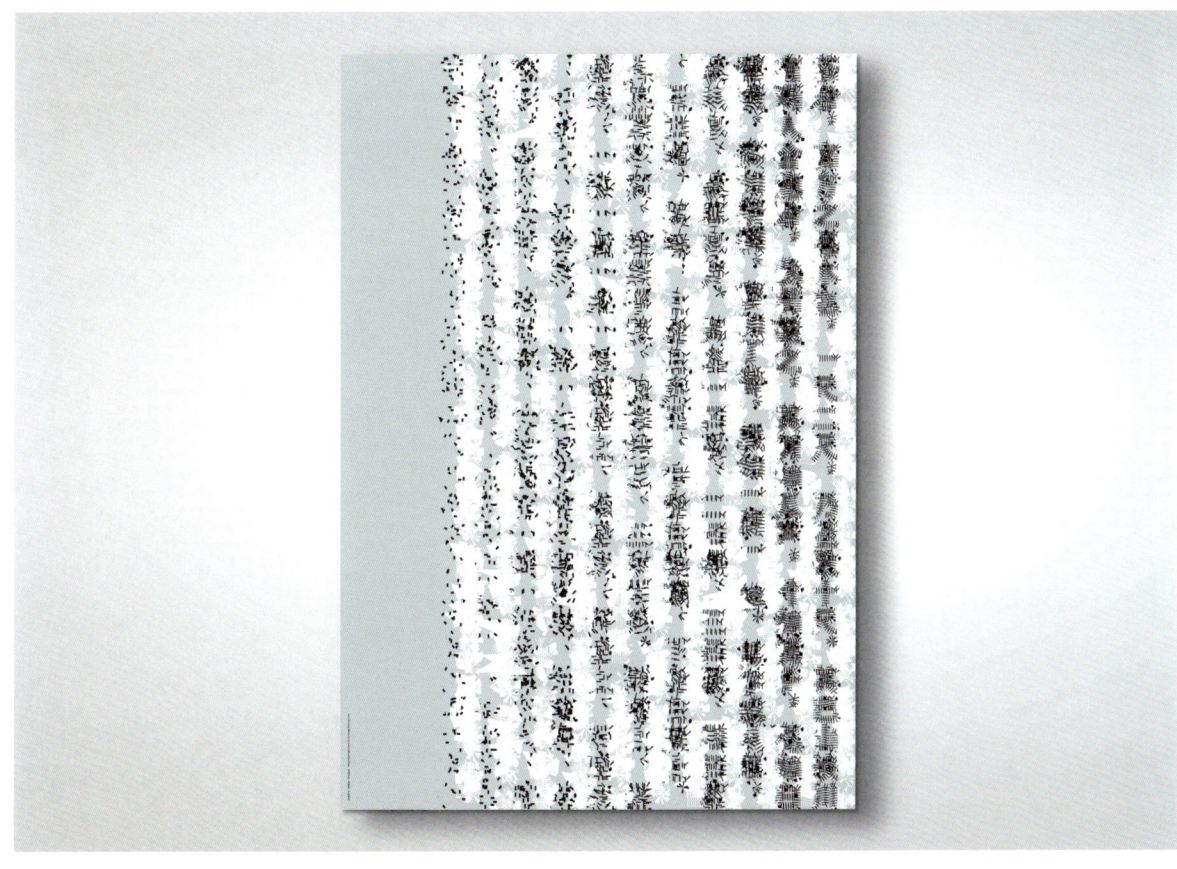

The Classic of Herbal of Shennong
[Poster Series]

Classic Chinese texts inspired this series of posters. Excerpts from the historical books "The Classic of Tea" on tea-making and tea culture, and "The Classic of Herbal" on herbalism and medicine were used as central elements. The design experiments with these well-known texts. The characters appear to flow into natural shapes reminiscent of blossoms and leaves. In this way they create their own new imagery. The words blend with the portrayals of nature to create a visually harmonious whole.

Client
Shenzhen Yiqi Culture Development Ltd.
Shenzhen, China

Design
Shenzhen Sandulixian Design Ltd.
Shenzhen, China

Project Team
Shenzhen Yiqi Culture Development:
Shenglei Rui (Manager)

Shenzhen Sandulixian Design:
Lixian Xu (Creative Director)
Zhangchi Shi (Design Team Leader)
Liang Lin (Art Director)
Jieyong Wu (Designer)
Yuan Fang (Designer)
Lirong Xu (Project Manager)

The Huge Wall – IFSC Climbing World Championships 2019

[Event Poster]

Client
International Federation of Sport Climbing
Turin, Italy

Design
PEN.Inc.
Tokyo, Japan
Japan Mountaineering & Sport Climbing Association
Tokyo, Japan

Project Team
Japan Mountaineering & Sport Climbing Association:
Ryusuke Fujieda (Creative Direction)

PEN.Inc.:
Taiji Kimura (Art Direction)

Dentsu On Demand Graphic Inc.:
Shinya Tamura (Printing)

Apps	Interface & User Experience Design	Spatial Communication	Red Dot: Junior Award	Designer Profiles	Jury Portraits	Index
206	236	336	426	564	642	668

The objective of developing the branding and design for the IFSC Climbing World Championships 2019 was to raise the profile of sport climbing in Japan. The letter "H" became the visual symbol, representing the venue where the games were held, Hachioji in Tokyo. The posters advertising the event feature a steep, gold or silver-coloured climbing wall. Part of the coloured surfaces overlap the event information, time and place, creating an interesting visual effect. When light falls on the posters, the text fades and the walls become more prominent.

Typography

Red Dot: Best of the Best

Söhne Collection
[Typeface]

The Söhne collection is a sans-serif font family that was developed in memory of Akzidenz-Grotesk that appeared in 1898 – back then a milestone in font design and a model for numerous later designs such as Helvetica. It was inspired by Unimark's legendary wayfinding system for the New York City Subway, which was traditionally set in Standard Medium, an American release of Akzidenz-Grotesk, and since then in Helvetica. "Framed through the reality of Helvetica", the style of the Söhne collection captures the analogue materiality of Standard Medium and retains the charm of its original style. Noticeably revised, the collection is clearly suitable for our digital age, comprising four families with a total of 64 fonts. Starting with the regular styles, the collection travels through the famous history of its role model in that it draws inspiration from all its disparate styles over a century of development and presents itself as a complete, contemporary typeface family for modern designers.

Statement by the jury
Söhne is an outstanding contemporary typeface that is the outcome of a meticulous and exciting development. It is quite a challenge to choose as a starting point the New York City Subway wayfinding system, which has been guiding millions of people safely every day. This new font family goes a step further and cleverly sets itself apart in that it achieves an appearance that is ideal for today's digital era.

Client
Klim Type Foundry
Wellington, New Zealand

Design
Klim Type Foundry
Wellington, New Zealand

Project Team
Dave Foster (Production)
Noe Blanco (Technical Direction)

→ Designer profile on page 601

Supersuperabundant
Autoabstract
Counterdogmatism
Semiplastic
Radiotelephonic
Equisignal
Angiospermae
Vitruvius

The matrices for this Neuste Titel-Versalien, Zehnte Sorte were imported from *Caslon & Livermore* in London.

Like other early British sans serifs, this *approximately* 36-pt face was an all-caps design.

It came from the German-language term for everyday commercial printing, *Akzidenzen*.

Halbfette Bücher-Grotesk, Accidenz-Grotesk specimen, Bauer & Co. and Berthold (*circa 1911*).

The typeface was *different* from the other Breite Grotesques sold by e.g., Ludwig & Mayer and Schelter & Giesecke.

Unfortunately we do not know the Bauer & Co. or Berthold employee who had this idea.

Akzidenz-Grotesk, on the other hand, is *not* as harmonious a family.

Lange was *Berthold's* longtime artistic director & the designer of several later versions of Akzidenz-Grotesk.

Red Dot: Best of the Best

Klim Type Foundry
[Typeface, Website]

Klim Type Foundry is a New Zealand-based independent design agency for typeface design and sales. The website has been relaunched in order to adequately address the target group of designers, inviting them to easily browse the different typefaces and their styles, as well as their uses and prices. An integral part of the entirely redesigned website is Söhne, a collection of new typefaces. It was created by company founder and designer Kris Sowersby, who describes the type as "the memory of Akzidenz-Grotesk framed through the reality of Helvetica" and designed it as a profound appreciation of the role model. The passion for fonts, playing with them and illustrating their appropriate use depending on the content, is conveyed on the website in sophisticated and unusual animations that not only alternate quickly but implicitly also visualise the functionality of the fonts. Structured around responsive and variable layouts, the website is based on Swiss design principles embedded in CSS grids.

Statement by the jury
The new website of Klim Type Foundry is agile, responsive and powerful. The visitor immediately gains the feeling of being engaged in a real narrative. Based on typography, the website projects a staging that is unusual and extremely exciting. The company's services and products, and their uses in particular, are expressed in an emotional and authentic manner.

| Apps | Interface & User Experience Design | Spatial Communication | Red Dot: Junior Award | Designer Profiles | Jury Portraits | Index |
| 206 | 236 | 336 | 426 | 564 | 642 | 668 |

Client
Klim Type Foundry
Wellington, New Zealand

Design
Klim Type Foundry
Wellington, New Zealand
Springload
Wellington, New Zealand

Project Team
Klim Type Foundry:
Kris Sowersby (Creative Direction)
Jess Sowersby (Head of Marketing)

Springload:
Dan Newman (Creative Direction)
Zak Brown (Web Design)
Mitch Ryan (Programming)
Peter Dekkers (Programming)

→ Designer profiles on pages 601, 624

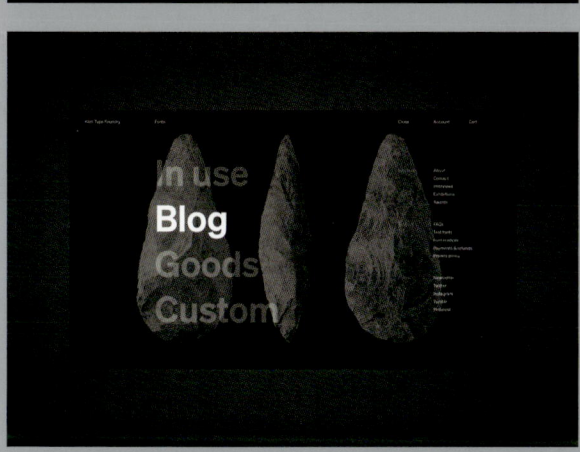

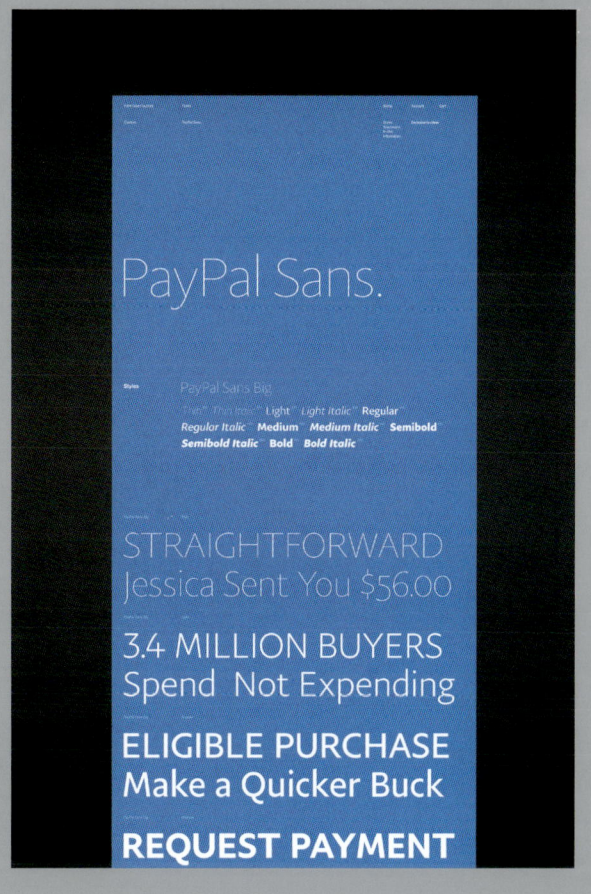

Red Dot: Best of the Best

Macklin
[Typeface]

The Macklin typeface superfamily, published in April 2020, is inspired by the work of the British typographer Vincent Figgins and represents a gently irreverent take on the 19th-century display type. Its innovation lies in that it takes the letterforms, which became famous by the rise of early-1900s attention-grabbing advertisements and posters, and gives them an elegant twist that updates them with sharp yet graceful forms for modern use. With roots in this pivotal period of type history, where fonts transitioned alongside the boom of the industrial era, Macklin today reflects modern publishers' next evolution to new media interfaces. Comprising four subfamilies designed with the same underlying skeleton, 54 fonts, nine weights and a variable font, Macklin offers a broad palette for expression in everything from packaging, luxury products and editorial content. In addition, it delivers a bold twist on what modernity is now.

Statement by the jury
The Macklin typeface has been very carefully crafted and combines two essential aspects that are relevant for contemporary typeface design. First, it is extremely flexible and adaptable because, thanks to the various font styles, it can perfectly be adapted to user needs. Second, it is a font family in response to digital touchpoints and thus creates a high-quality typeface in any application.

One family. Many styles. A voice for every moment.
Macklin™ Superfamily by *Malou Verlomme* of the Monotype Studio.

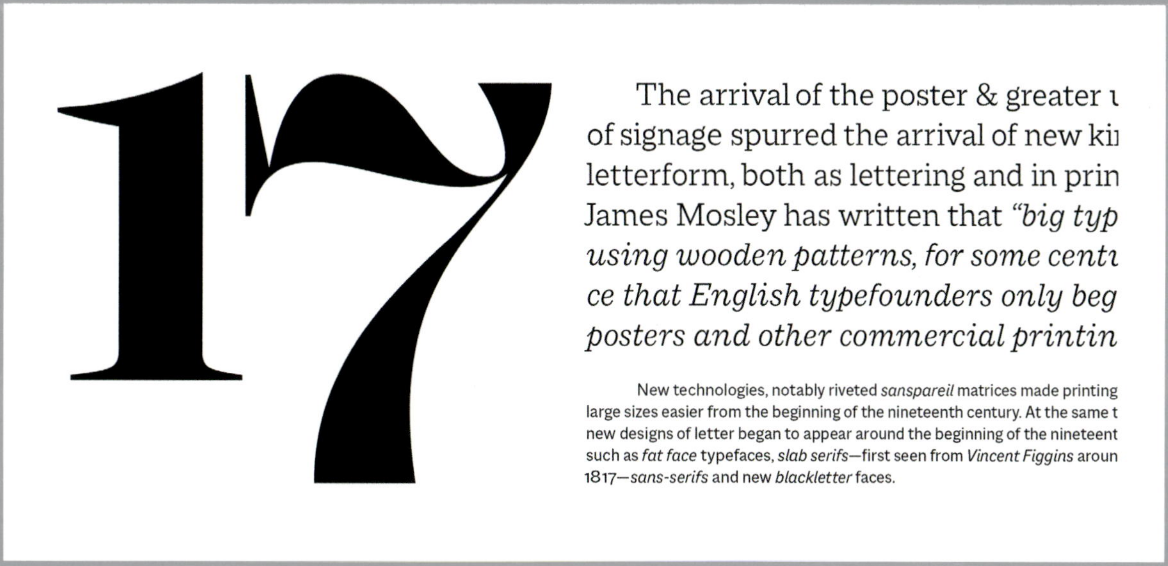

Apps	Interface & User Experience Design	Spatial Communication	Red Dot: Junior Award	Designer Profiles	Jury Portraits	Index
206	236	336	426	564	642	668

Client
Monotype
Woburn, USA

Design
Monotype
Woburn, USA

Project Team
Malou Verlomme/Monotype Studio
(Typeface Design)

→ Designer profile on page 609

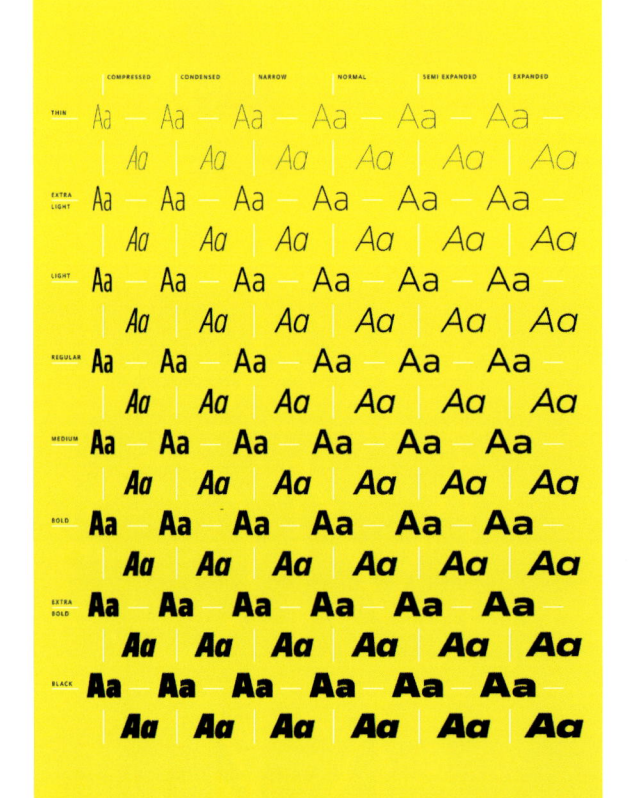

Fact

[Typeface]

Inspired by the Frutiger typeface created in 1975, Fact was conceived as an open sans serif type system. While the Regular style is slightly modernised, yet still quite close to Frutiger, changing the weight or width makes the differences in the design more pronounced. Fact's range of styles is particularly wide, including weights from Fact Thin to Fact Black and widths from Fact Compressed to Fact Expanded. The Fact type system contains 48 upright styles and 48 italic styles with variations in width and weight, giving it the versatility to be used even for applications such as information boards in public spaces.

Client
Paratype Ltd.
Moscow, Russia

Design
Paratype Ltd.
Moscow, Russia

Project Team
Manvel Shmavonyan (Designer)
Alexandra Korolkova (Designer)

Circe Slab

[Typeface]

Circe Slab was created as a slab serif typeface family. It contains variations in weight and contrast, including three regular styles that range from non-contrasting geometric (Circe Slab A) to an almost typical book serif contrast style (Circe Slab C). In addition, each of the styles also comes in a narrow version. The font's character set includes small caps, old-style figures and a wide variety of alternative capitals and small caps. The regular styles of Circe Slab are suitable for long texts, while the light and bold versions of the typeface lend themselves to headlines.

Client
Paratype Ltd.
Moscow, Russia

Design
Paratype Ltd.
Moscow, Russia

Project Team
Alexandra Korolkova (Designer)
Oleksa Volochay (Assistant)

Monotype Helvetica Now & DIN

[Poster Series]

In April 2019, as part of the Alibaba Group's UCAN Design Conference, a new generation of Helvetica fonts was launched, called Helvetica Now and Helvetica DIN. A series of posters was created for the two of them, to draw attention to the contemporary update to this well-known font family. A total of 17 poster motifs, printed in different sizes, were designed to showcase the various new features of the two fonts in terms of different font levels, typefaces and layout effects. All of the posters were created in shades of blue and grey to strengthen their recognition value.

Client
ALIBABA GROUP
Hangzhou, China

Design
Zhejiang Gongshang University
Hangzhou, China

Project Team
Kan Zhao (Designer)
Chun-Lei He (Designer)
Yi-Fan Zhang (Designer)

→ Designer profile on page 641

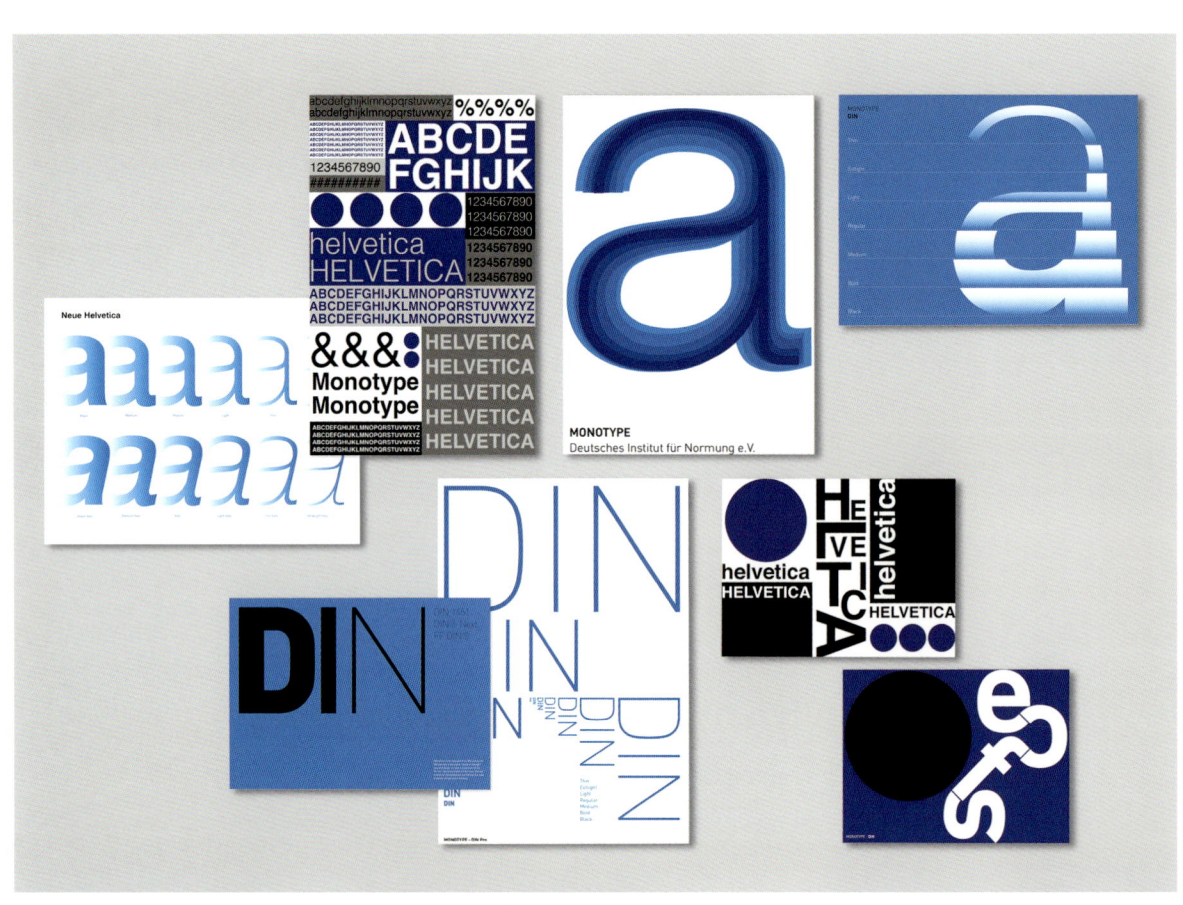

LG Smart UI Typeface Family

[Corporate Typeface]

The LG Smart UI typeface is applied to user interfaces and the physical surfaces of electronic products, providing a consistent visual identity by integrating the fonts used in all customer product and service contacts in the course of the company's marketing activities. The corporate typeface expresses LG Electronics' philosophy of "Respect for human dignity" and "Customer-oriented innovation" in its smooth curves and open forms. This is a flexible font family optimised for the characteristics of both display and print, as well as being implemented in products. It supports 49 languages and ensures a unified brand experience.

Client
LG Electronics Inc.
Seoul, South Korea

Design
LG Electronics Inc.
Seoul, South Korea

Project Team
Kunsik Lee (Creative Direction)
Sooyoung Yang (Creative Direction)
Jeongin Park (Typography)
Eunji Roh (Typography)

Publishing & Print Media	Posters	**Typography**	Illustrations	Sound Design	Film & Animation	Online
4	64	92	116	126	138	172

Alles könnte anders sein

[Billboard]

"Alles könnte anders sein" (Everything could be different) – the motto for Theater Bielefeld's 2020/2021 season is ambiguous. It aims to inspire readers to reflect on the extraordinary nature of the present or to imagine the future. And finally, it is also a motivating call to take the future into one's own hands. The typographic design underlines the passage of time by stringing together the season's motto in a kind of endless spiral. In this way, the visible words can be combined to form a complete sentence. The semi-transparent spiral also allows the words at the back to dimly shine through.

Client
Theater Bielefeld, Bühnen und Orchester der Stadt Bielefeld
Bielefeld, Germany

Design
beierarbeit GmbH
Bielefeld, Germany

Project Team
Bühnen und Orchester der Stadt Bielefeld:
Michael Heicks (Intendant)
Charlotte Höpker (Head of Marketing)
Jennifer Nüßing (Design)

beierarbeit:
Christoph Beier (Creative Direction)
Sina Stuke (Graphic Design)

Good is like Water

[Poster]

The 2019 Gwangju Design Biennale addresses social issues through the value and role of design within the theme of humanity. The exhibition highlights design for a sustainable society and human community. The typographically focused poster presents a quote by Chinese philosopher Lao Tzu: "Good is like water." The typeface of the quote in English is covered with drops of water, which act like a prism and distort the typeface. Thus, the quote can only be read clearly by taking a closer look. The three-dimensional contours of the drops form the Chinese character for "good".

Client
Gwangju Design Biennale
Gwangju, South Korea

Design
Ying Gao, Chaosheng Li
Zhejiang Gongshang University
Hangzhou, China

Refuse to kill

[Poster Series]

Environmental pollution, the indiscriminate killing of animals and the destruction of their habitats by humans have all contributed to numerous animal species being wiped out. These posters draw attention to this issue by using the oldest Chinese hieroglyphs, which depict images of nature from ancestral observations. The characters feature individual design elements made of charcoal burned at a high temperature. In addition, animals can be seen in the contours of the key visuals. The slogan "Refuse to kill" calls upon people to rethink and cherish animals instead of killing them.

Client
Appedu Design Institute
Taipei City, Taiwan

Design
Appedu Design Institute
Taipei City, Taiwan

Project Team
Ming-Lung Yu (Art Direction)

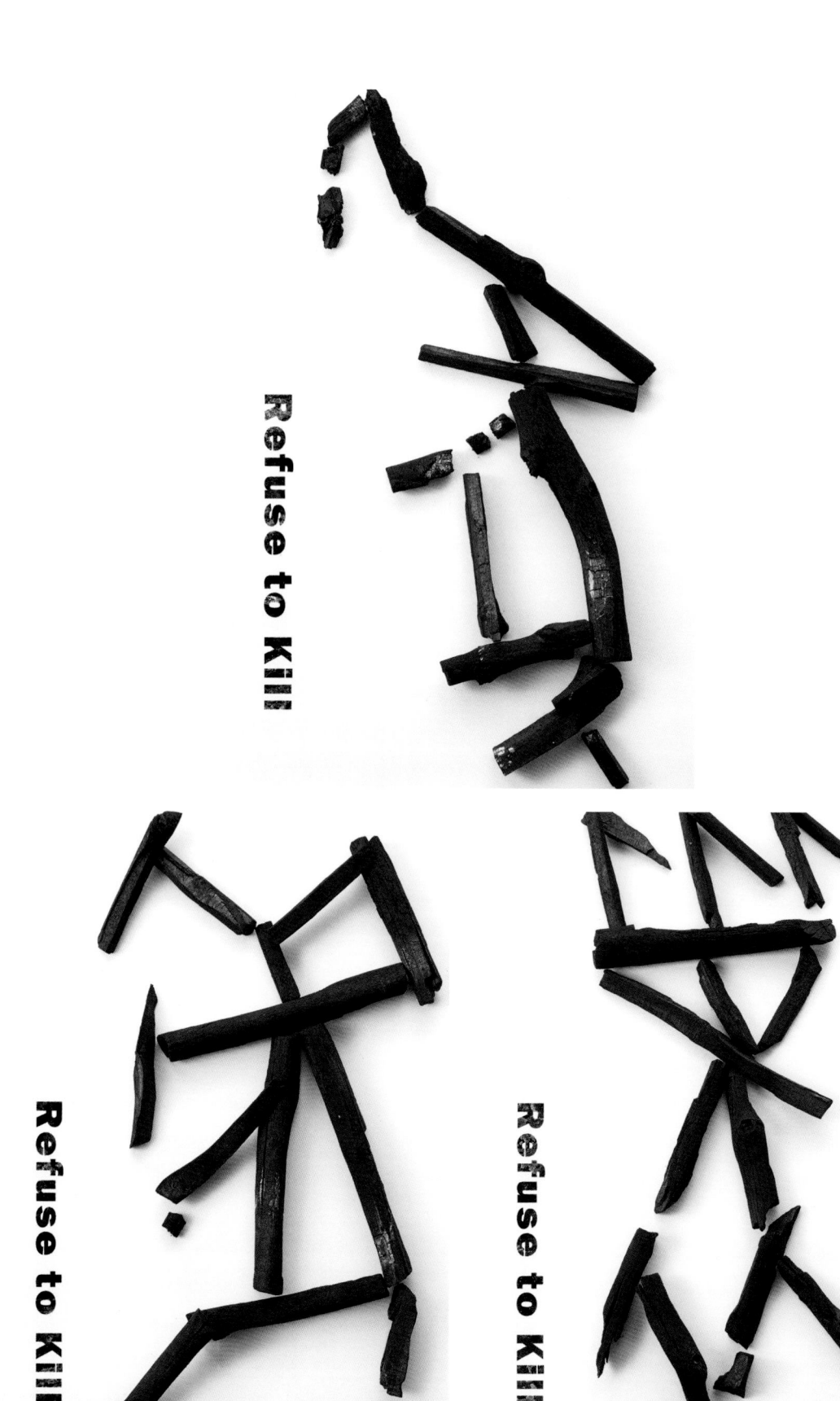

Apps	Interface & User Experience Design	Spatial Communication	Red Dot: Junior Award	Designer Profiles	Jury Portraits	Index
206	236	336	426	564	642	668

It is not a beautiful hill/mountain/island

[Poster Series]

This poster series was created with the aim of motivating people in China to reduce household waste. The three motifs show the Chinese characters for hill, mountain and island, each featuring a subtle reference to the topic of waste. For example, the traditional character for "island" in Chinese is much like a pictograph, which shows a bird standing on the top of a mountain. In this typography, the element that depicts the mountain has been replaced by rubbish bags. The vertical lettering "This is not a beautiful island" refers to the hidden criticism concerning those mountains of rubbish.

Client
Appedu Design Institute
Taipei City, Taiwan

Design
Appedu Design Institute
Taipei City, Taiwan

Project Team
Ming-Lung Yu (Art Direction)

War No More – Poster Poem by Peter Bankov

[Poster Series]

Millions of Russians died during World War 2. "War No More" is an artistic tribute to the 75th anniversary of Victory Day, which marks the capitulation of Nazi Germany. The poster series features illustrated excerpts inscribed by the artist and separately painted with a hand-crafted typeface, giving the poems a strong individual character. Although the typeface varies, the typography is easy to read. The illustrations are fresco-style portraits painted with gouache mixed with egg yolk and are inspired by both wartime poems and the artist's childhood memories of veterans who lived in his neighbourhood.

Client
RT
Moscow, Russia

Design
Peter Bankov
Prague, Czech Republic

Project Team
Peter Bankov (Graphic Designer)
Kirill Karnovich-Valua (Creative Director)
Margo Tskhovrebova (Project Manager)
Lilly Kazakova (Project Manager)
Revaz Todua (Lead Designer)
Gleb Burashov (Producer)
Eldar Salamov (Producer)
Ania Fedorova (Producer)
Katya Motyakina (Editor)
Ivan Fursov (Editor)
Lena Medvedeva (Producer)

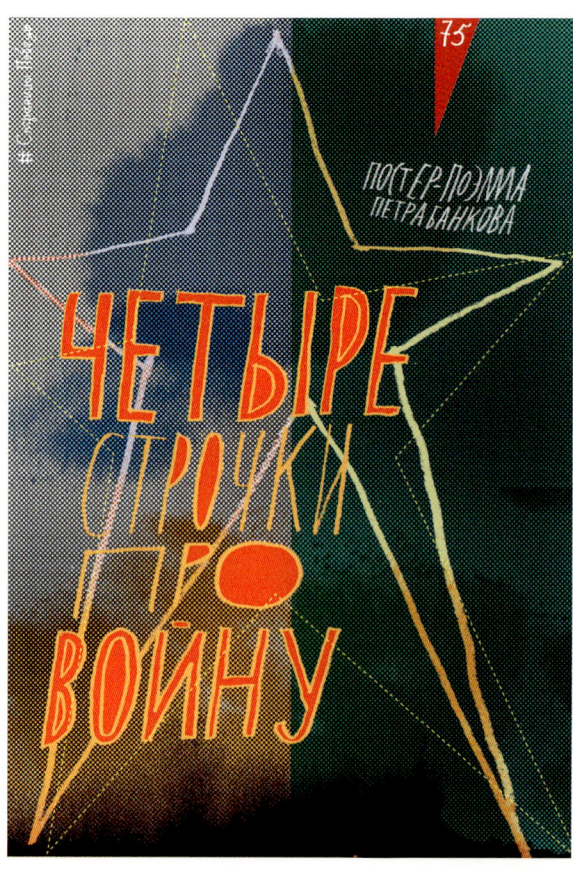

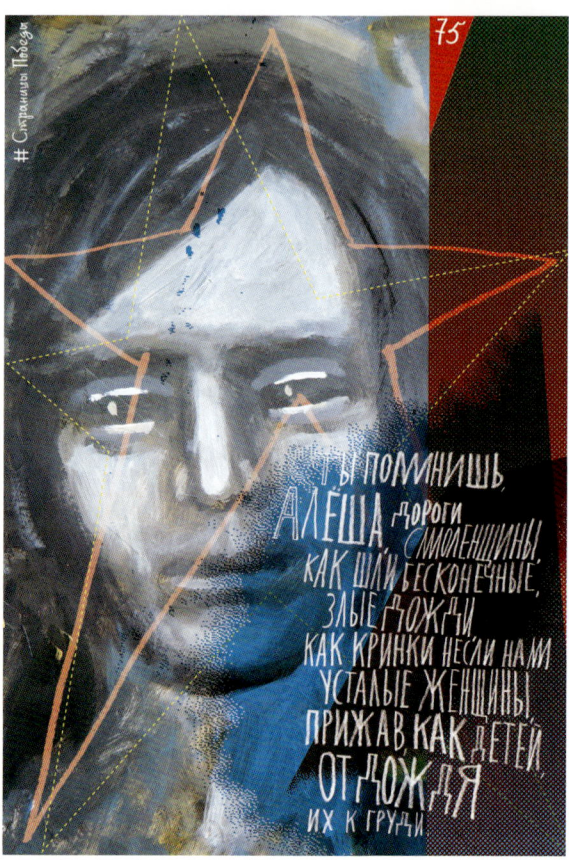

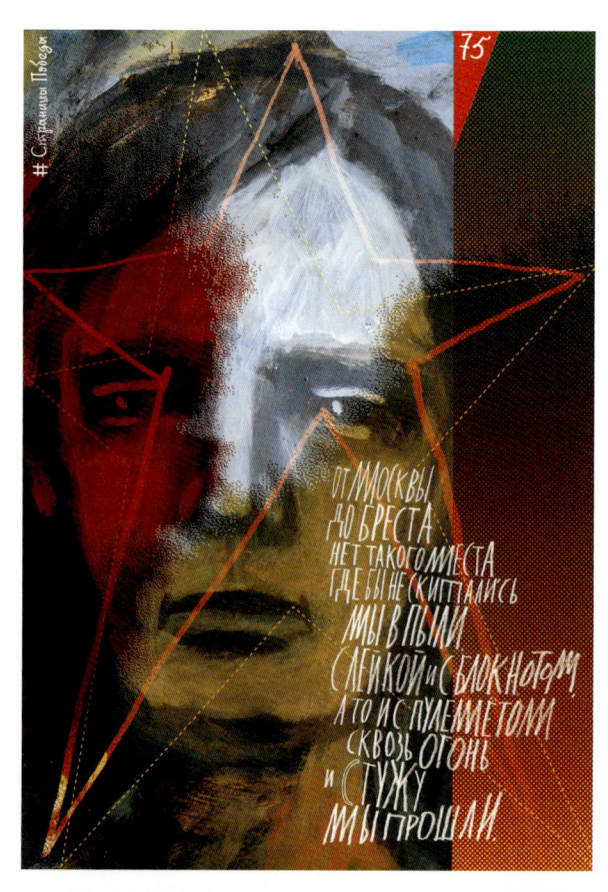

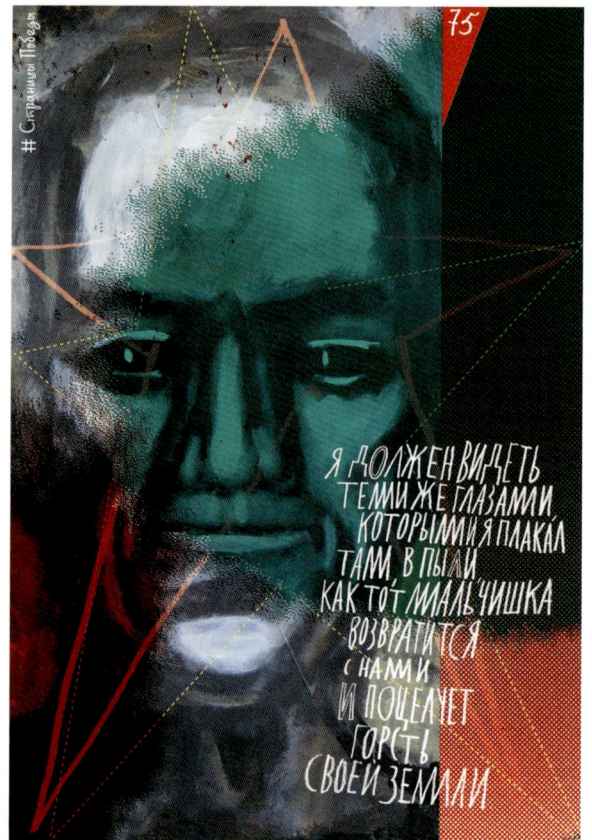

Apps	Interface & User Experience Design	Spatial Communication	Red Dot: Junior Award	Designer Profiles	Jury Portraits	Index
206	236	336	426	564	642	668

#VictoryFont May: A Typeface to Remember

As Nazi Germany capitulated in May 1945, thousands of soldiers left inscriptions on the walls of the Reichstag in Berlin. Today, most of these inscriptions can only be seen in photo archives and museums. To mark the 75th anniversary, the #VictoryFont May was created as the core element of the #VictoryPages project, which is a versatile social media documentary. The font is based on hundreds of original historical inscriptions studied during months of research. It is a tool designed to commemorate the veterans and convey a message of peace. Through its characters and symbols, the font aims to create a link between the past and the present.

Client
RT
Moscow, Russia

Design
Contrast Foundry
Moscow, Russia

Project Team
Kirill Karnovich-Valua (Creative Director)
Revaz Todua (Original Idea)
Maria Doreuli (Typeface Designer)
Liza Rasskazova (Typeface Designer)
Nikita Sapozhkov (Typeface Designer)
Ania Fedorova (Producer)
Gleb Burashov (Producer)
Eldar Salamov (Producer)
Katya Motyakina (Editor)
Ivan Fursov (Editor)
Lena Medvedeva (Producer)
Ivor Crotty (Producer)
Lilly Kazakova (Producer)
Margo Tskhovrebova
(Administrative Manager)

Publishing & Print Media	Posters	Typography	Illustrations	Sound Design	Film & Animation	Online
4	64	92	116	126	138	172

Extraordinary Time, Ordinary Lives: Flying Over Wuhan

[Book]

In 2020, the coronavirus pandemic has had a serious impact on people worldwide. This publication responds to this by inviting authors to write about what their lives were like in February 2020. The authors used a variety of forms, such as text, photography and painting, to record their situation. Proceeds from the book's sales will be donated to the Taiwan CDC to support medical staff. The cover design employs geometric forms and lines, to show the passage of time in a static manner. The butterfly embodies people's hope. The typography picks up the colours of the cover, effectively underlining the aesthetics of the characters.

Client
Ding Ding Co., Ltd.
Taipei City, Taiwan

Design
Hufax Arts
Taipei City, Taiwan
Fu Jen Catholic University
New Taipei City, Taiwan

Project Team
Fa-Hsiang Hu (Creative Direction)
Yun Liu (Concept)
Alain Hu (Concept)
Jin-Yan Zhong (Typography)
Di Hu (Typography)
Fei Hu (Typography)
Natasha Liao (Editor)
Gayle Wang (Editor)

→ Designer profile on page 597
→ Clip online

PF Marlet

[Typeface]

Marlet is a new typeface based on a minimalist approach in order to express elegance. It takes cues from the 1920s and 1930s, decades that embraced women's independence. The font aims to bring femininity and all its complexities into the limelight, with lean lines concluding in subtle curves that reference simplicity and emphasise the font's distinctive character. Its thick-thin, sans serif strokes also underline the modernity of the fashion industry. The type system incorporates contrasts progressing from low through medium to high, and offers differentiated letter widths for titling, as well as 64 eclectic patterns.

Client
Parachute Typefoundry
Athens, Greece

Design
Panos Vassiliou
Athens, Greece

CHENGJIAN-Xin kai

[Typeface]

Client
FounderType,
Beijing Founder Electronics Co., Ltd.
Beijing, China

Design
Fojun Li,
Guangzhou City Construction College
Guangzhou, China

→ Designer profile on page 591

代各建勝塔標示自斯東北二千餘里入大雪山至
尼波羅國純信於佛僧有二千大小兼學城東有池
中有天金光浮水上古老傳云彌勒下生用為首飾
或有利其寶者夜往盜之但見火聚騰燄都不可近
今則流深巨窺其底水又極熱難得措足唐國使者
試火投之燄便涌起因用煮米便得成飯其境北界
卽東女國與吐蕃接境比來國命往還率由此地約
指為語唐梵相去一萬餘里自古廻邅致途遠阻又
從梵吠舍南濟硤河達摩揭陀國卽摩竭提之正號
也其國所居是為中印度矣今王祖胤繼接無憂無

Apps	Interface & User Experience Design	Spatial Communication	Red Dot: Junior Award	Designer Profiles	Jury Portraits	Index
206	236	336	426	564	642	668

Based on expertise drawn from more than 20 years of calligraphy, as well as the inspiration of traditional calligraphy, this font design is a round-up of various periods in the history of representative calligraphers' instructions in essence. Reflecting the requirements of current printing technology and graphic design, the typeface merges a traditional style with contemporary design standards. By combining the essence of the work of each generation of calligraphers and removing the individual aspects of their writing styles, the emerging characters yield an evenly aesthetic, elegant overall appearance.

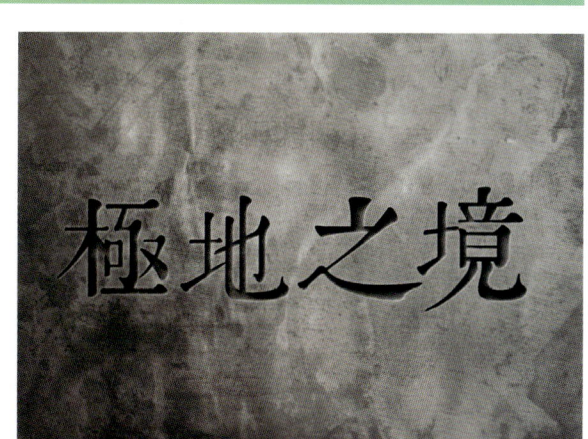

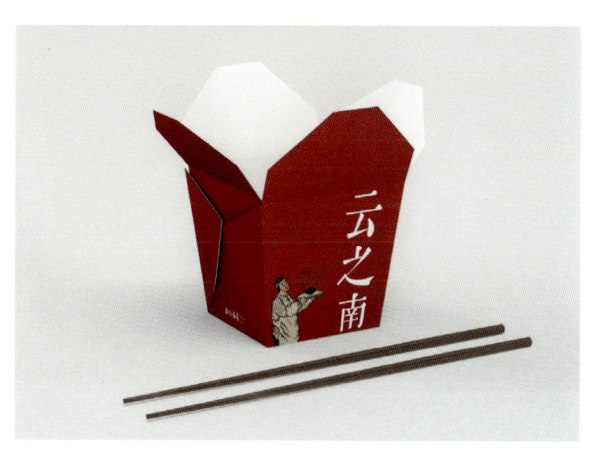

Founder Yuzhi Font

[Typeface]

Client
FounderType,
Beijing Founder Electronics Co., Ltd.
Beijing, China

Design
Xiangguo Kong
Zhongshan, China

This Chinese typeface benefits from a particularly aesthetic structure. It has both thick and thin strokes, each one being curved on the right and straight on the left, combining hardness with softness. The typography design was inspired by a classic painting from the Tang Dynasty called "Ladies with Head-pinned Flowers", as well as the script style of Yan Zhenqing, a traditional calligrapher. The sharp contours of each character create a dynamic and powerful impression. Nevertheless, the characters convey lightness even in large font sizes, which makes them also well suited for headlines.

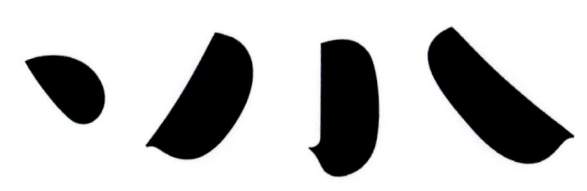

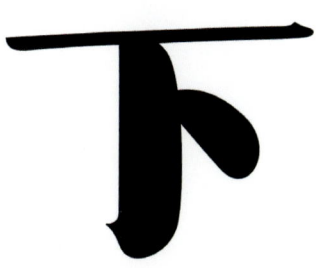

XIANG GUO KONG

Illustrations

Controlling & Management Review

[Cover Illustration]

Client
Springer Fachmedien Wiesbaden GmbH
Wiesbaden, Germany

Design
Jörg Block
Hamburg, Germany

These cover illustrations from the Controlling & Management Review journal series from 2018, 2019 and 2020 pick up key words from the headline and subheading of the current issue. Several elements, which refer to these key words or to further relevant topics, are combined in an unexpected way in a more or less surreal scene. In this way, the illustrations visually break down the rather abstract and not immediately intuitively accessible key topics from the area of controlling and management, and provide a lively and humorous introduction to the respective subject.

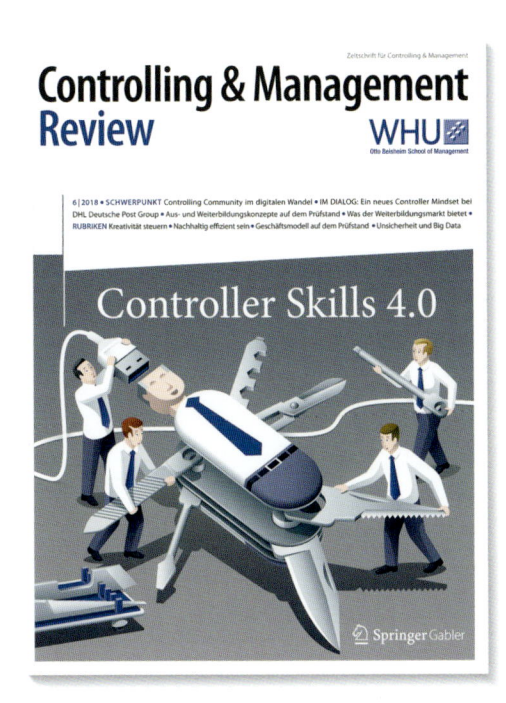

Traveling and Me

[Caricatures]

The "Traveling and Me" campaign is intended to inspire a desire to travel. A flamingo was chosen as the brand character. It can be found in the centre of all the billboards, posters and other marketing material. This comic-style Mr Flamingo, with his pink feathers, blue bill and red sports shoes, has a high recognition factor and is complemented by eye-catching, brightly coloured illustrations. Appearing in different outfits and equipped for different holiday activities, such as diving or a safari, the flamingo is a jolly travel companion and, at the same time, an ambassador for the diversity of travel.

Client
China International Travel Service
Head Office
Beijing, China

Design
Zhengbang Creative Beijing
Branding & Technology Co., Ltd.
Beijing, China

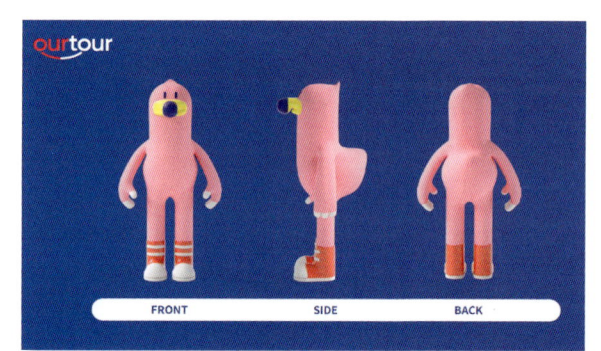

FAQ YOU

[Editorial Illustration]

The sex education book "FAQ YOU" from Youth against AIDS answers the 50 most frequently asked questions about sex and love. The explanations are accompanied by illustrations which depict, interpret and complement the information provided. These illustrations all derive from the respective content and create visually striking companion pieces to the texts. They reflect a variety of styles and techniques, from pen sketches to 3D renderings. Yet these highly individual illustrations still form a harmonious whole and complement the existing vector illustrations of the corporate identity of Youth against AIDS without eclipsing these.

Client
Youth against AIDS
Hamburg, Germany

Design
loved GmbH
Hamburg, Germany

Project Team
Mieke Haase (Chief Creative Officer)
Alexander Müsgens (Creative Director)
Sabine Cole (Editor-in-Chief)
Valerie Bachert (Editor-in-Chief)
Jana Maria Herrmann (Art Direction)
Yannic Hefermann (Art Direction)
Susanne Sauer (Designer)
Isabella Bigler (Text)

Lessons of Auschwitz

[3D Computer Graphics]

"Lessons of Auschwitz" is a social experiment to mark the 75th anniversary of the liberation of the Auschwitz concentration camp which is intended to encourage, above all, young people to learn about the Holocaust. The innovative project mixes virtual reality images of young artists and their virtual avatars with moving and touching video sequences. History, the personal emotions of teenagers, the lament of a theremin, an electronic instrument played without physical contact, and innovative immersive technology combine to create a haunting work which keeps commemoration and remembrance alive in today's digital world.

Client
RT
Moscow, Russia

Design
RT
Moscow, Russia
Phygitalism Studio
Moscow, Russia

Project Team
Kirill Karnovich-Valua (Creative Director)
Denis Semionov (Director)
Peter Theremin (Composer)
Eldar Salamov (Sound Design)
Elena Medvedeva (Producer)
Ania Fedorova (Producer)
Ekaterina Sidorova (3D Artist)
Valeria Fimina (Project Manager)
Vlad Krutenyuk (3D Artist)
Aleksandr Kryuchkov (Developer)
Pavel Postnikov (3D Artist)
Vanya Yunitskiy (Project Manager)
Aleksey Lushnikov (Developer)
Nikita Semionov (VR Artist)
Sasha Volkov (VR Artist)
Misha Borisov (VR Artist)
Dima Kaderkaev (VR Artist)
Zhenya Timoshenkova (VR Artist)
Vlad Sarychev (VR Artist)
Nata Makashvili (VR Artist)
Dima Sobaev (VR Artist)
Lera Agescheva (VR Artist)

→ Designer profiles on pages 611, 616

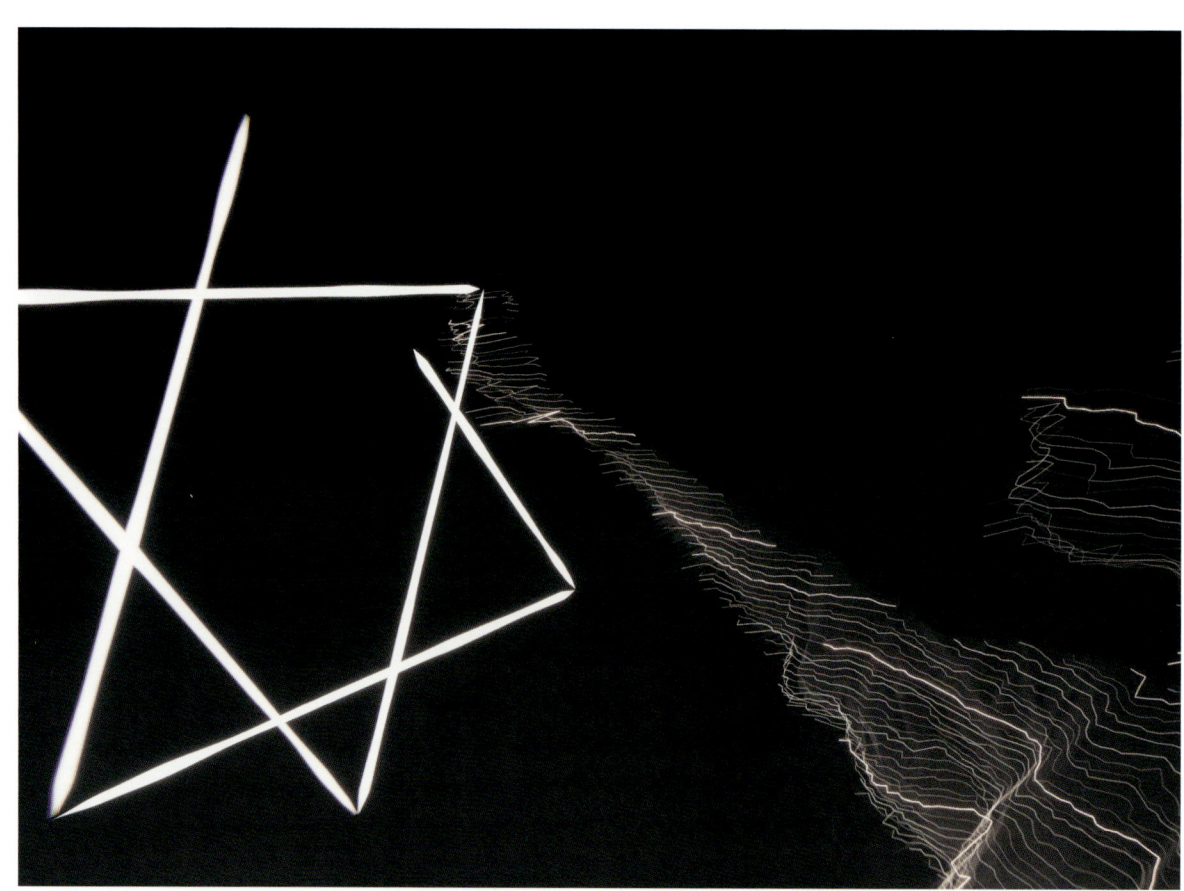

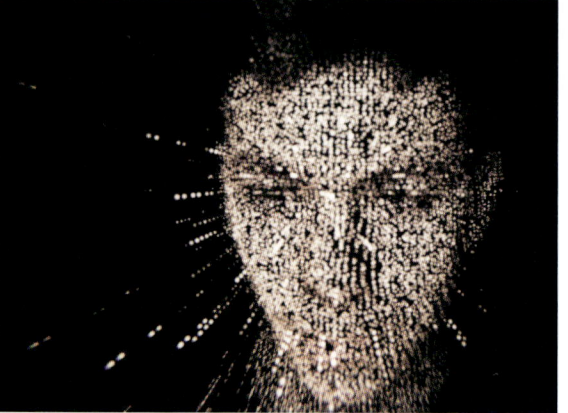

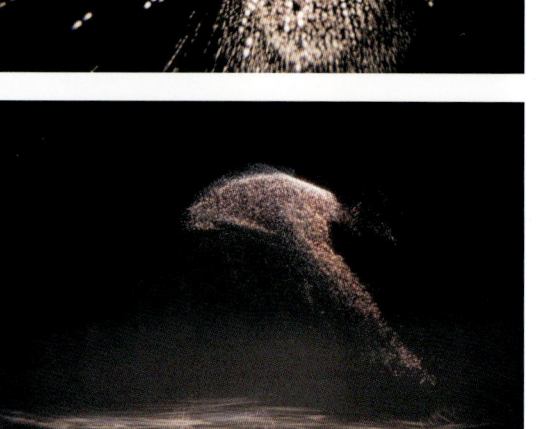

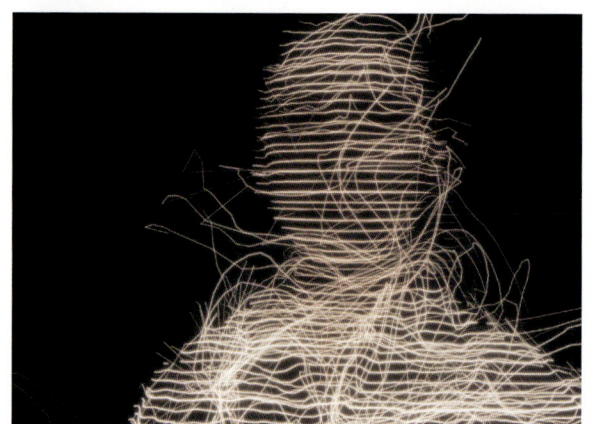

The Bestiary. Russia's Ten Epic Monsters

[Educational Illustration]

The Bestiary website impressively brings to life ten mythological beasts from various regions of Russia, together with their stories. The black, richly detailed illustrations of these creatures from Slavic, Caucasian, Finno-Ugric, Turkish and Manchu-Tungus folklore stand out thanks to their bold lines. The monsters are clearly categorised with individual profiles, while matt background colours help the viewer to visually distinguish between the creatures' respective habitats. Their portrayal within the environment of present-day Russia creates an effective contrast between myth and modernity.

Client
TASS Russian News Agency
Moscow, Russia

Design
TASS Russian News Agency
Moscow, Russia

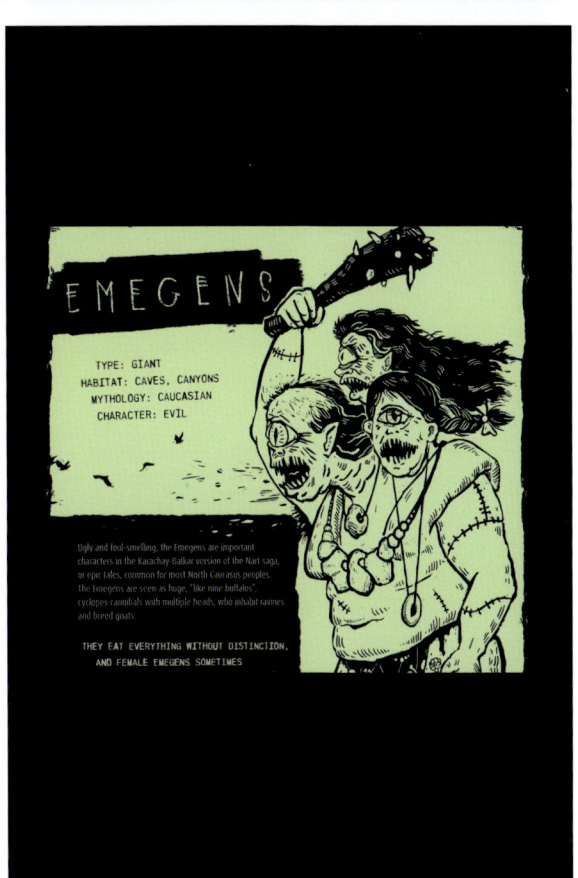

Publishing & Print Media	Posters	Typography	**Illustrations**	Sound Design	Film & Animation	Online
4	64	92	116	126	138	172

Hanbrand Image

[Poster Illustration]

This series of the finely illustrated and subtly coloured Hanbrand images focuses on the art of the Han dynasty. Preserved fragments of stone paintings and totem decorations from that era were combined with new design elements to develop scenarios which reflect the way of life, the craftsmanship and the aesthetic of stone-painting of the period. Thus, the cultural heritage of the Han dynasty becomes closely associated with the modern brand, which seeks to use the illustrations to create a new awareness of ancient traditions.

Client
Huagang Building Decoration Materials Co., Ltd., Hanbrand Company
Changsha, China

Design
Biwei Zhu, Wilbur Design Studio
Changsha, China

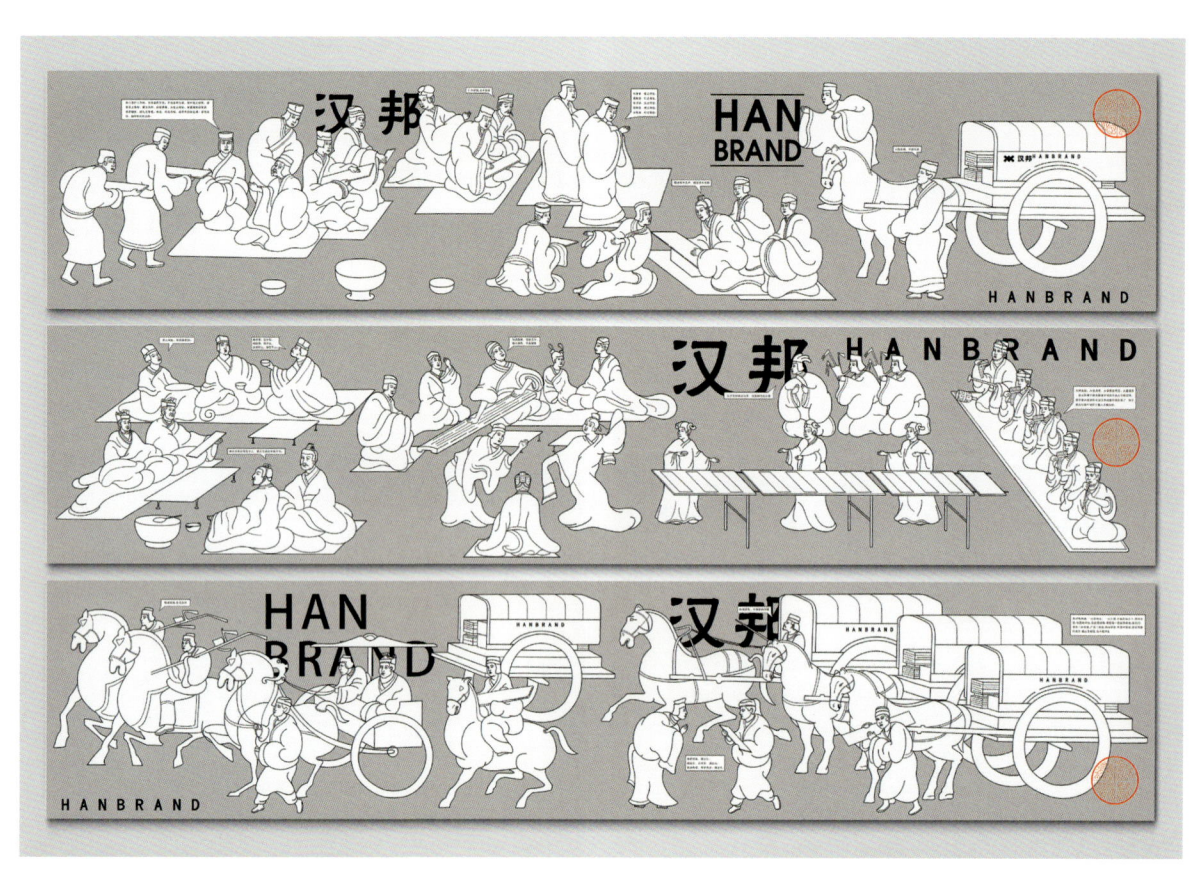

Apps	Interface & User Experience Design	Spatial Communication	Red Dot: Junior Award	Designer Profiles	Jury Portraits	Index
206	236	336	426	564	642	668

THE SILENT KILLER
MARINE POLLUTION

THE SILENT KILLER
LAND POLLUTION

THE SILENT KILLER
AIR POLLUTION

The Silent Killer

[Poster Illustration]

The consequences of land, air and sea pollution are visible in the illustrations of The Silent Killer. They show animals suffocated by exhaust fumes or dying of contaminated soil and oil-polluted water – a creeping process communicated by the deliberately chosen pointillist technique. Dot by dot, the black-and-white illustrations converge to create a whole – just like the smallest amount of pollution caused by humans can lead to environmental damage of catastrophic proportions.

Client
Appedu Design Institute
Taipei City, Taiwan

Design
Wei-Ching Lin
Taipei City, Taiwan

→ Designer profile on page 573

Sound Design

Red Dot: Grand Prix

Siemens Healthineers Brand Sound
[Corporate Sound Concept]

In order to differentiate its position on the increasingly complex global market and to further strengthen it in medical technology, Siemens Healthineers sharpened its brand strategy in 2018. The aim was to provide an experience of the brand for all the senses and to thus create an emotional link to the public. For the sound logo, the word mark was pictured on a piano by playing each letter in "Healthineers" on a correspondingly assigned piano key. The letters that have no corresponding piano keys were turned into the sound of a digital heartbeat. The new sound was inspired by both the brand values and the nine-part "Dot Pulse" of the logo, which is derived from the Fibonacci sequence. These dots were then adapted horizontally for the rhythm and vertically for the pitch. In addition to developing a soundscape that covers all main brand touchpoints, a piece of health-oriented music was composed to improve the user experience in computer tomography as the music supports relaxation, mindfulness and stress relief.

Statement by the jury
The corporate sound concept for Siemens Healthineers impresses with its unique and holistic acoustic appeal in that it pushes the boundaries to set new standards in the field of corporate sound design. It integrates excellently into the brand architecture and has been implemented to creative, professional and emotionally convincing effect. Particularly noteworthy is the sound element inspired by the dot matrix of the logo with its forward dribbling beat.

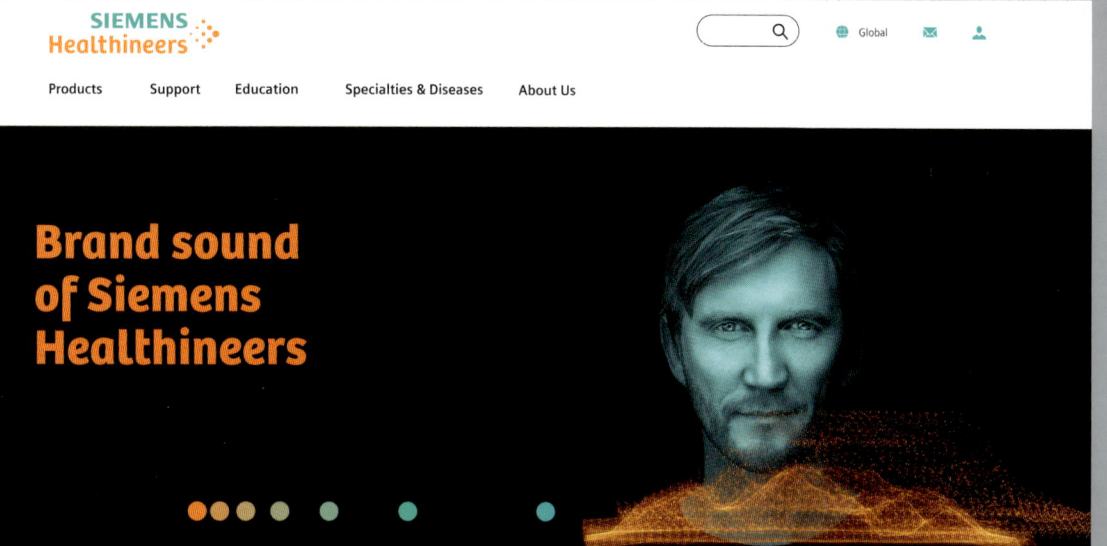

Apps	Interface & User Experience Design	Spatial Communication	Red Dot: Junior Award	Designer Profiles	Jury Portraits	Index
206	236	336	426	564	642	668

reddot winner 2020
grand prix

Client
Siemens Healthineers,
Siemens Healthcare GmbH
Erlangen, Germany

Design
why do birds
Berlin, Germany

Project Team
Siemens Healthineers:
Michael Schmidt (Senior Design Director Brand Engagement)
Silke Schumann (Head of Brand Management)

why do birds:
Alexander Wodrich (Managing Director)
Leopold Hoepner (Creative Director)
Johannes Lehniger (Sound Design)

→ Designer profile on page 631
→ Clip online

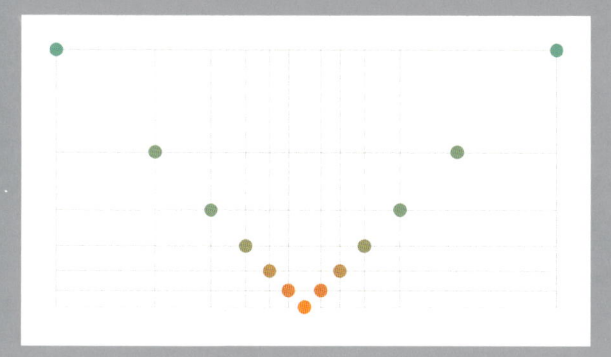

Telekom – New Sound Identity

[Audio Logo]

Client
Deutsche Telekom AG
Bonn, Germany

Design
Klangerfinder
Stuttgart, Germany
S12
Munich, Germany

Project Team
Deutsche Telekom:
Alexander Engelhardt
(Creative Management)
Christian Hammerschmidt
(Creative Direction)

→ Clip online

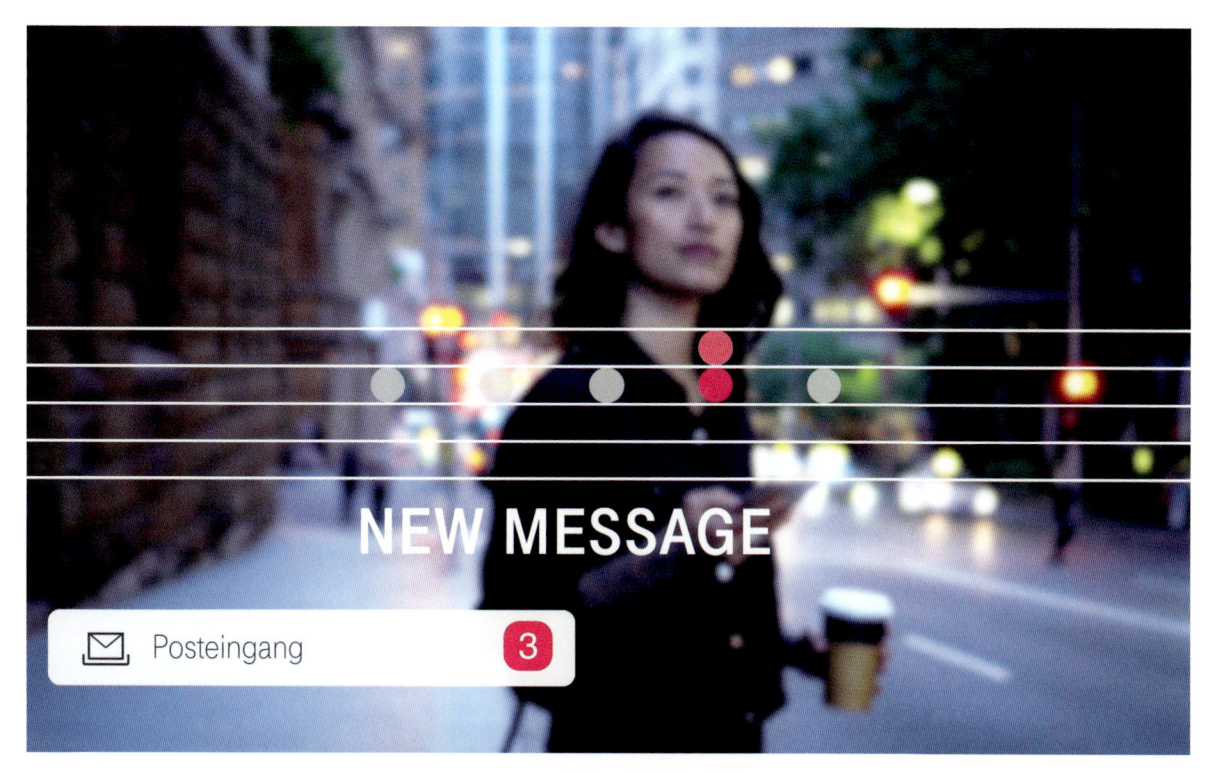

Deutsche Telekom introduced its sound logo in 1999. Today, the sound sequence of five tones is well-known across Europe and associated with the brand and its products. For its 20th anniversary, the sound logo has now been modernised. The tone sequence remains unchanged, yet the new logo has more nuances and a wider audible frequency range. It creates the basis for a growing number of functional sounds that can be developed to expand the acoustic brand. Use is allowed in 12 different keys (from C major to B). The result is a new and expanded sound identity, yet one based on the familiar.

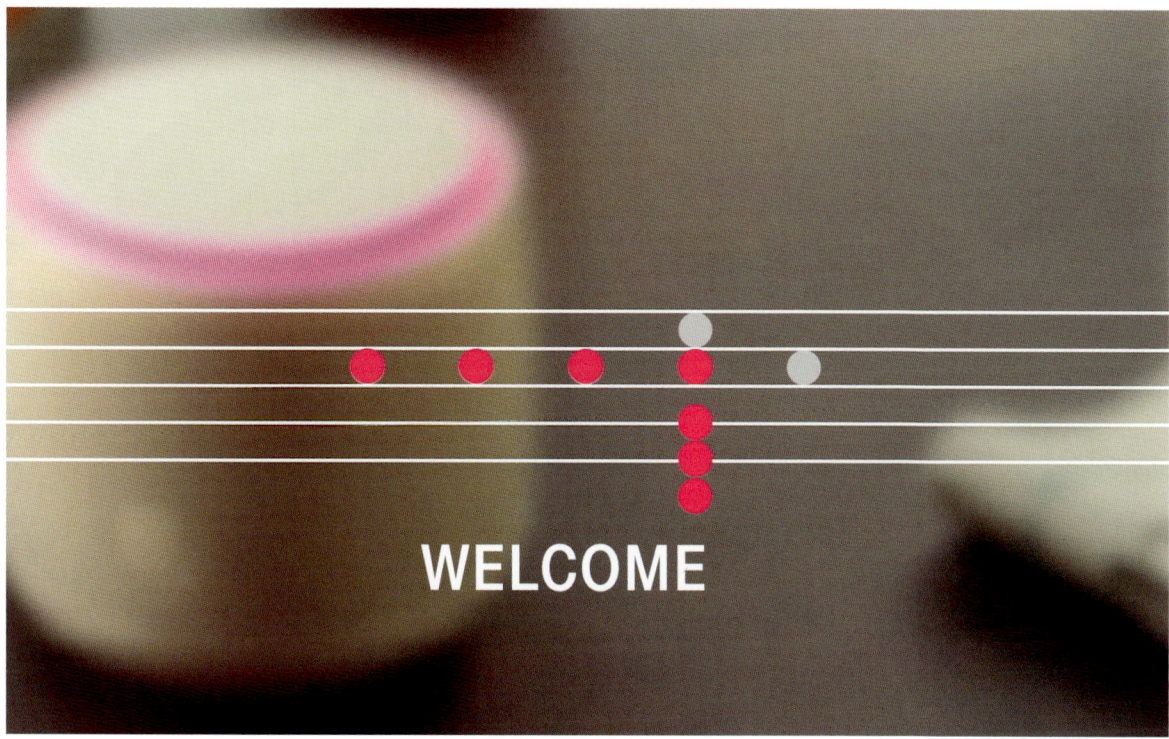

Ready for the Future Today

[Ambient Sound]

This experience room was designed to embody the company's leading idea at trade fairs and shows, expressed through the slogan "Ready for the Future Today". A special audiovisual presentation was created to highlight the innovative ideas and key advantages of the products, as well as their aesthetic value. The sounds were taken from digitalised recordings and then reconstructed into musical landscapes, melodies and rhythms, merging the recognisable exhaust system sounds with musical composition. These fundamental elements were then enhanced with digital animations to create the "Sound of Akrapovič" experience.

Client
Akrapovič d.d.
Ivančna Gorica, Slovenia

Design
Slavojka Akrapovič
Ljubljana, Slovenia
Gregor Zemljič
Ljubljana, Slovenia

Project Team
Akrapovič Kreativa d.o.o.:
Andrej Perčič (Animation)
Robert Cankar (Animation)
Jan Mohorič (Animation)

Benjamin Česen (Film Production)

→ Clip online

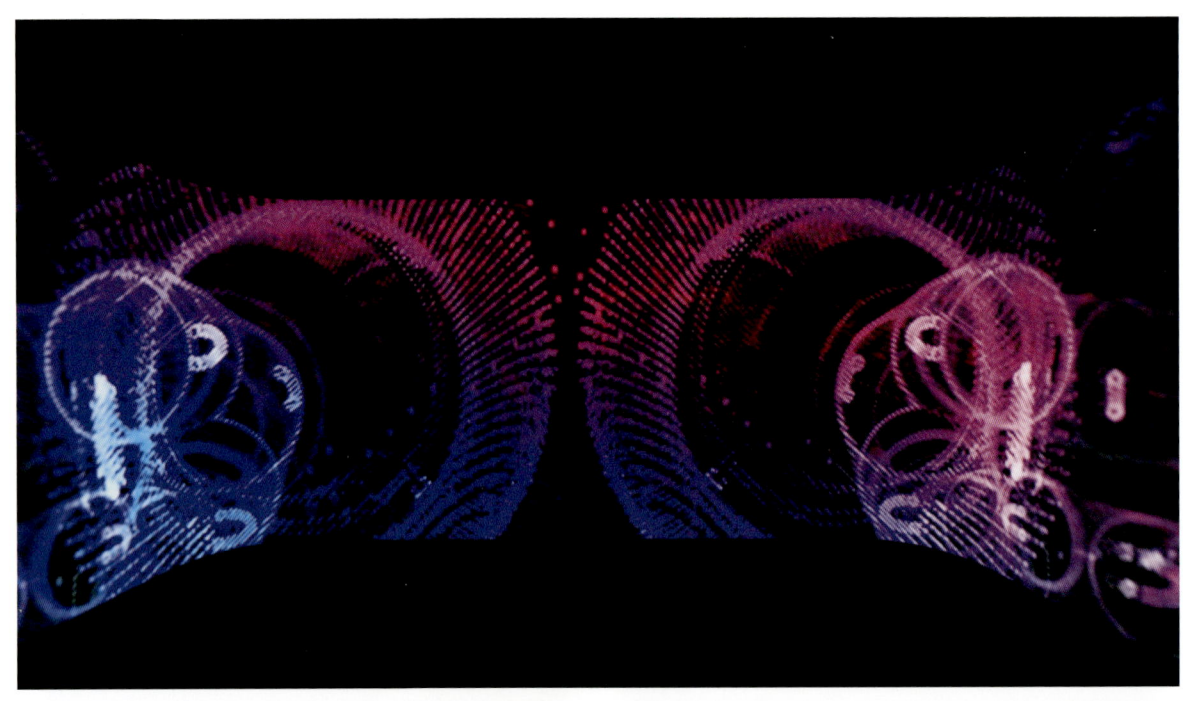

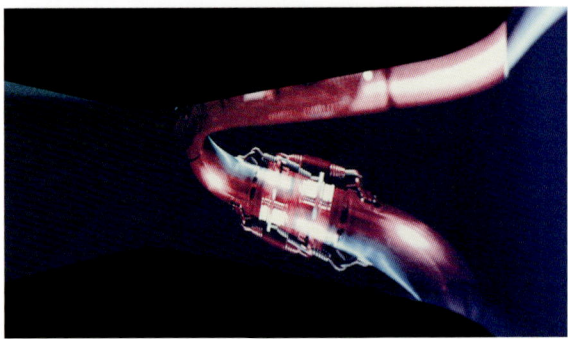

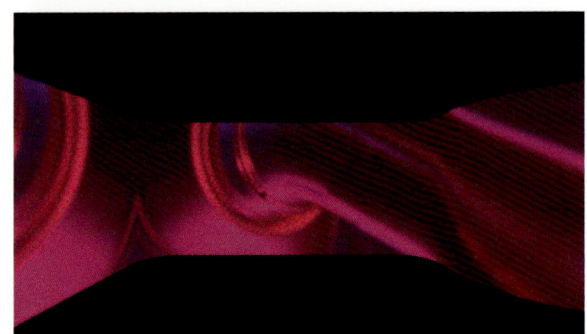

T-Roc Bob
[Commercial Sound]

In this film, the subcompact crossover SUV model T-Roc R visually delivers a race with a four-seater bobsleigh. "It's all about power, speed and control." This comment by the Austrian bobsleigh pilot Benny Maier accompanies the action like a resonant mantra. As the four-seater bobsleigh picks up speed, so does the film. The breath of athletes training their speed strength in the gym picks up the beat and quickens the pace into a pumping rhythm. It is the sound design and the unobtrusive composition that give the film the dynamics that so effectively underline the analogies between bobsleigh and vehicle, athlete and sports equipment.

Client
Volkswagen AG
Wolfsburg, Germany

Design
loved GmbH
Hamburg, Germany

Project Team
loved:
Mieke Haase (Chief Creative Officer)
Sabine Cole (Editor-in-Chief)
Alexander Müsgens (Creative Director)
Nadine Kaminski (Text)

Marc Schölermann (Director/DOP)
Simon Roloff (Camera)
Matthias Morick (Camera)
Sören Görth (Film Editing)
Boris Salchow (Music/Sound Design)

→ Clip online

Publishing & Print Media	Posters	Typography	Illustrations	**Sound Design**	Film & Animation	Online
4	64	92	116	126	138	172

Axel Springer Audio Branding

[Corporate Sound Concept]

Client
Axel Springer SE
Berlin, Germany

Design
why do birds
Berlin, Germany
Superunion
Berlin, Germany

Project Team
why do birds:
Alexander Wodrich (Strategic Planning)
Leopold Hoepner (Creative Direction)
Holger Schuhmann (Sound Production)

Superunion:
Martin Steinacker (Creative Direction)
Anna Jüttner (Account Management)

Tobias Belker (Drums)

→ Designer profile on page 631
→ Clip online

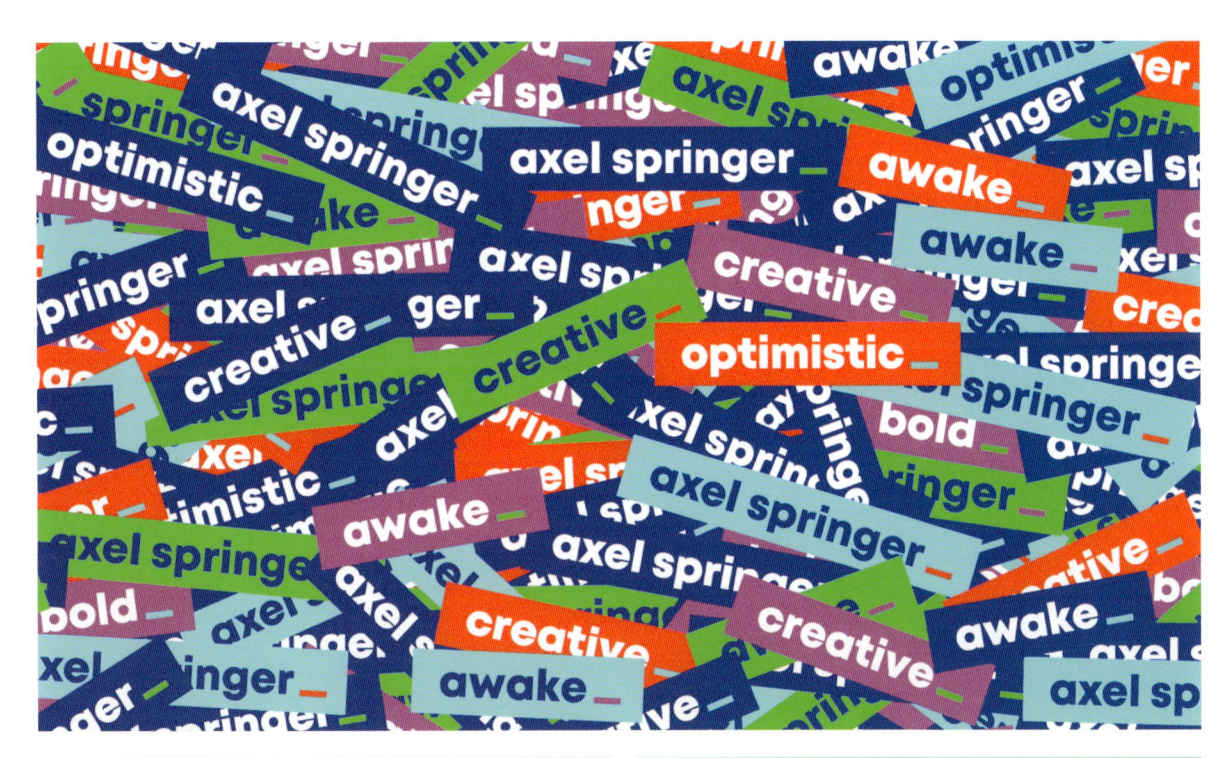

Apps	Interface & User Experience Design	Spatial Communication	Red Dot: Junior Award	Designer Profiles	Jury Portraits	Index
206	236	336	426	564	642	668

In 2019, Axel Springer sharpened its brand positioning to reflect its forward-thinking, transformative attitude and business strategy. The new brand vision: "We Empower Free Decisions." The inspiration was derived from the company founder's belief in the vital role that freedom plays for democracy and the rule of law. Excerpts from his voice were reinterpreted with drums that mimic the phonetic sounds of words, while consonants and vowels received different rhythmic elements. The sound language thus has the effect of a bold punchline and embodies a radical form of freedom in the sense of free expression, as the resulting rhythm is ever-changing in measure and structure.

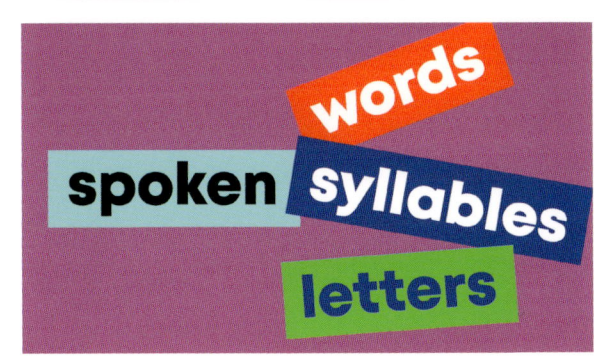

Publishing & Print Media	Posters	Typography	Illustrations	Sound Design	Film & Animation	Online
4	64	92	116	126	138	172

Discovery Dock – Mixed Reality 3D Sound Experience

[Soundscape]

At the Discovery Dock, visitors can explore the Port of Hamburg interactively along with state-of-the-art VR technology, projections and live simulations. Using specially developed software and audio concepts, this world has been brought to life through music and sound design. Typical harbour sounds like the air horns of ships, cranes, wind or water were captured using a 3D microphone array in an eight-capsule design. Interactive soundscapes and algorithmic compositions change constantly in depth and complexity. Based on a specially designed 3D network of 50 speakers that allows music and sounds to be heard from all directions, a new level of immersion has been achieved.

Client
Morgenpost Verlag GmbH
Hamburg, Germany

Design
WESOUND GmbH
Hamburg, Germany

Project Team
WESOUND:
Lars Ohlendorf (Creative Direction)
Janek Newjoto (Media Engineer)
Dr. Cornelius Ringe (CEO)

Florian Gläser (Creative Direction),
Demodern GmbH
Tobias Soffner (Executive Producer),
Demodern GmbH

Susan Molzow (former CEO),
Morgenpost Verlag GmbH
Antje Dittrich (Consulting),
fischerAppelt, advisors

→ Clip online

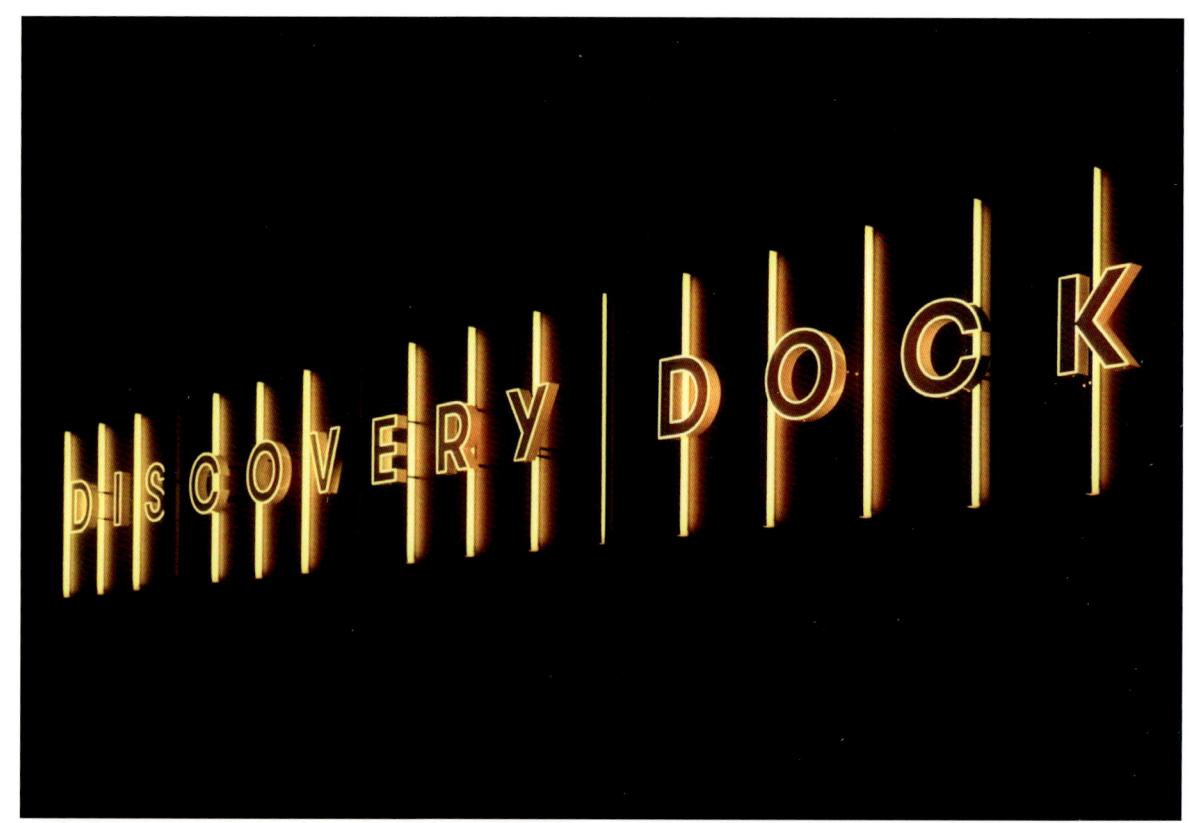

Underwater

[Ambient Sound]

This ambient sound design project for the exhibition "Taiwan New Wave" in Paris featured one track filled with the sounds of water and breathing underwater. It echoed the exhibition's main art film, which was shot underwater, and thus provided the overall atmosphere that filled the entire venue. The intention was to bring the climate experience of Taiwan, as an island surrounded by the sea with humid and rainy weather conditions, to the audience in Paris. The underwater sounds were mixed with samples from daily life in Taiwan, taken from the surrounding environment, such as streets or temples, and then combined with melody lines.

Client
alamak!project
Taipei City, Taiwan

Design
Yu Te Chou (ODd)
Taipei City, Taiwan

Project Team
Yoichi Nakamuta (Curator)
Henry Hsiao (Curator)
Pon Ding (Co-Curator)
Clear Gallery (Co-Curator)
Yeelon Lin (Assistant Curator)
nbt.STUDIO (Organiser)
Joy Cheng (Co-Organiser)
Jasmine Lu (Co-Organiser)
Manabu Koga (Underwater Film)

→ Clip online

Film & Animation

Publishing & Print Media	Posters	Typography	Illustrations	Sound Design	Film & Animation	Online
4	64	92	116	126	138	172

Was ist Deine Geschichte?
[Christmas ID]

Client
ARD Design und Präsentation
Munich, Germany

Design
Luxlotusliner
Munich, Germany

Project Team
ARD Design und Präsentation:
Henriette Edle von Hoessle
(Head of ARD Design and Presentation)
Werner Mayer (Art Director)

Luxlotusliner:
Gabi Trojan-Madračević
(Creative Director)
Tatjana Živanović-Wegele
(Executive Producer)
Nadja Doth (Post-Production Supervisor)

Keno Langbein (Songwriter)
Dominik Giesriegl (Music Composer)

Moland Film:
Asger Leth (Film Director)
Christian Bévort (Film Producer)

→ Clip online

Apps	Interface & User Experience Design	Spatial Communication	Red Dot: Junior Award	Designer Profiles	Jury Portraits	Index
206	236	336	426	564	642	668

In its 2019 Christmas campaign, ARD made a plea for solidarity, raising the question "Was ist Deine Geschichte?" (What's your story?) and focusing on what is especially important at Christmas: the community. For the main clip, 300 people from all over Germany were invited to sing a song especially written for this event while standing on stages arranged as a map of the country. The video premiered on the first of December 2019, just before the evening news, and was aired on all other ARD channels and social media afterwards. It was accompanied by portrait stories featuring individual singers, all linked by the song. The invitation to sing along and participate gave rise to a variety of contributions.

MDR

[Station ID, Brand Design]

A confident and timeless visual identity was designed for MDR in its capacity as a seasoned market leader among the regional broadcasters which make up the German broadcasting consortium ARD. The brand design consists of a modular system of elegant, functional, classy but discrete guiding elements which inform viewers about the programme and which, at the same time, are pleasing to the eye. In addition, the design works for all channels of communication and has a strong connection to the MDR umbrella brand, so as to ensure a high level of recognition among the general public.

Client
Mitteldeutscher Rundfunk
Leipzig, Germany

Design
UNFOLD Design & Motion Studio
Hamburg, Germany

Project Team
MDR:
Doreen Zörkler (Art Direction)
Klaus Schuntermann (Art Direction)
Ulrike Zoller (Project Management)

Florian Lakenmacher (Music/
Sound Design), Supreme Music

→ Clip online

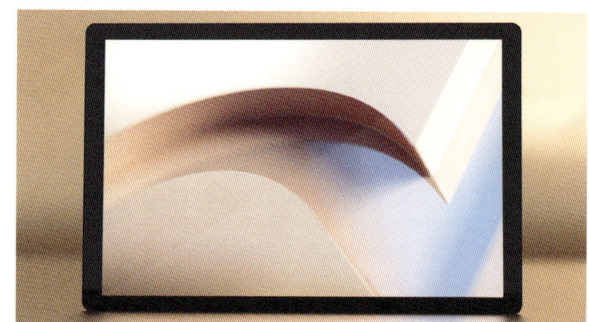

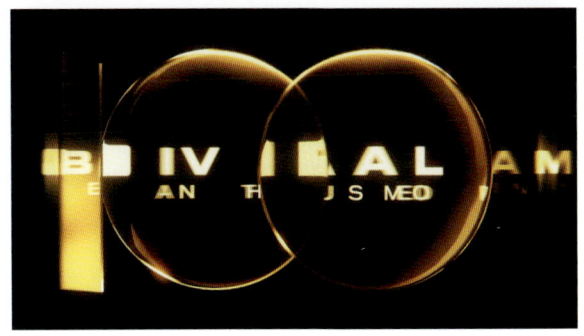

Bavaria Film – One Hundred Years in Motion

[Corporate Clip, Logo Design]

The "One Hundred Years in Motion" anniversary campaign by Bavaria Film inspired the creation of a golden "100 years" logo. This animation design is characterised by imagery which is immediately emotionally accessible. The clip begins with the image of a typewriter to allude to the historical background of the campaign and the fact that, to this day, every film begins with a script. The full stops on the paper inserted into the typewriter change into the perforations of a reel of film. They form a line down which two film cans roll and, ultimately, become the circular zeroes of the golden "100 years" logo.

Client
Bavaria Film GmbH
Geiselgasteig, Germany

Design
mattweis
Munich, Germany

Project Team
mattweis:
Matthias Meier-Stuckenberger (Creative Direction)
Gunther Weis (Creative Direction)
Sandra Thoms (Senior Design)

Jochen Hirschfeld (Creative Direction), Living Room Pictures
Jesse James Jones jr. (Motion Design), Living Room Pictures

→ Clip online

Publishing & Print Media	Posters	Typography	Illustrations	Sound Design	Film & Animation	Online
4	64	92	116	126	138	172

Münchner Runde – Political Talk Show

[Graphic Design, Set Design]

Münchner Runde is the foremost political talk show on the Bavarian TV channel BR Fernsehen. Since 1996, the format has stood for critical journalism and explores topical issues from a Bavarian point of view. The design concept takes the title of the show literally: Münchner Runde translates as the Munich Circle. Each individual element centres on the focal point of attention, originates from the circle and finally returns there. The set design aims for maximum reduction to allow viewers to concentrate on the panel lists and the discussion.

Client
Bayerischer Rundfunk, BR Fernsehen
Munich, Germany

Design
Feedmee
Cologne, Germany

Project Team
BR Fernsehen:
Uwe Kassner (Lead Design and Promotion)
Thorsten Timm
(Project Management Design)
Silvia Renauer
(Project Management TV Editing)

Feedmee:
Susanne Frericks (Creative Director)
Monika Jagla (Designer)
Julia David (Designer)
Tina Haffke (Producer)
Tom Gugel (Set Designer)

Frank Cremers (Set Planning)

→ Clip online

Second First Steps
[Online Film]

"Second First Steps" shares the story of Korean para-athlete and archer Jun-Beom Park who had lost the ability to walk in a car accident. The online film for Hyundai Motors Robotics shows how the young man takes his second first steps towards his parents, aided by the wearable robotics technology. For dramatic effect, this moment is linked to home-made videos of small children also taking their first steps. The emotionally touching visual language aims to underline the brand's philosophy that future technologies must be human-centric.

Client
Hyundai Motor Company
Seoul, South Korea

Design
Innocean Worldwide
Seoul, South Korea

Project Team
Kiyoung Kim (Executive Creative Director)
Hyunsuk Lee (Manager)
Saemi Shin (Senior Manager)
Hyunchul Lim (Art Director)
Jisoo Kim (Art Director)
Daehyun Kim (Art Director)
Jisoo Kim (Art Director)
Daeyoung Eum (Copywriter)
Moonhwi Lee (Copywriter)
Daeun Lee (Copywriter)
Gye Eun Chang (Account Management)
Bo Kyung Kim (Account Management)

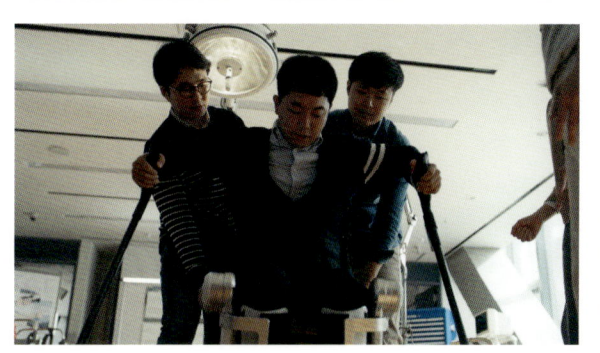

→ Clip online

PRO X Gaming Headset – Play to Win

[Corporate Film]

The Pro X Gaming Headset by Logitech allows users to hear exactly what their voice sounds like before they begin competing. Developed by and for professionals, this corporate film shows e-sport athletes from around the world on a black background, putting on the headset in preparation for their next match. Contrary to expectations, one does not hear their voices. The film breaks off at the moment when well-known gaming professional Myth lowers his microphone in order to start. The tension created is released by a product animation in which the headset moves in time to the driving beat of the music.

Client
Logitech
Lausanne, Switzerland

Design
Logitech
Newark, CA, USA
Chapeau Studios
Los Angeles, USA

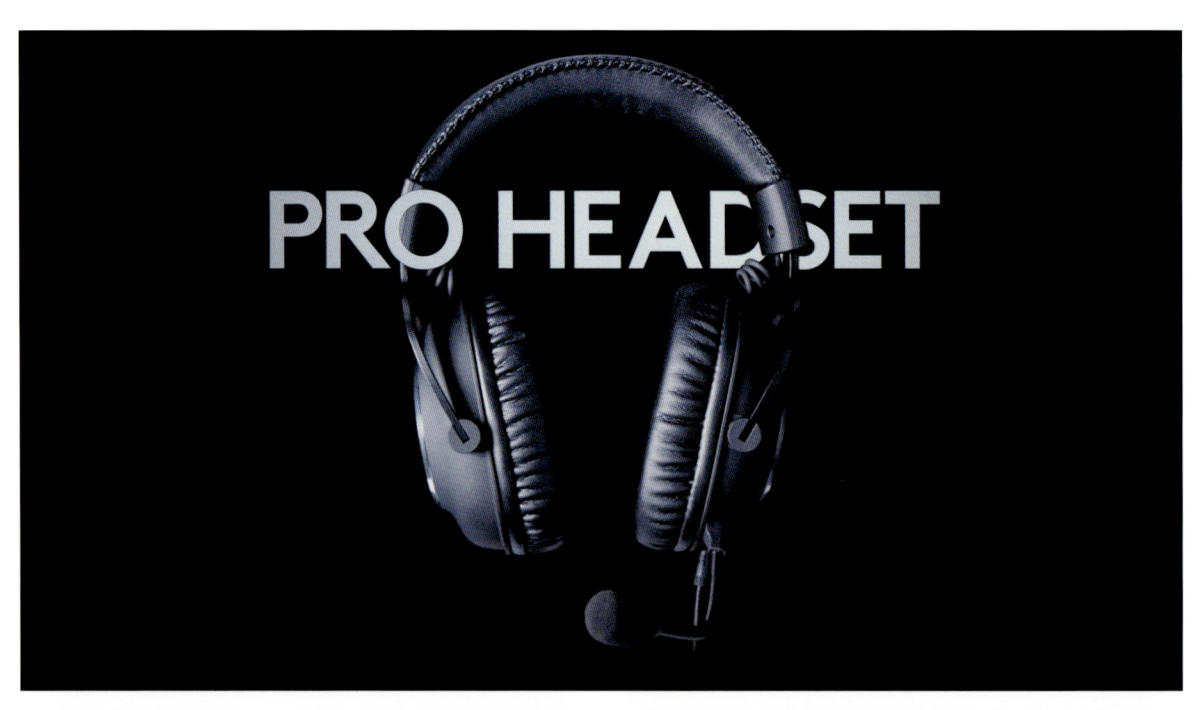

→ Clip online

Logitech G915 Wireless Gaming Keyboard

[Corporate Film]

In this video, the Logitech G915 wireless gaming keyboard becomes a portal to a hypercomplex world of infinitely reflected geometries which represent new dimensions of playing. Gradually, the complexity of the shapes is scaled back and a growing number of keyboard details become visible. In a split-screen montage, macro-shots of the keyboard are contrasted with the abstract patterns so that the link between the two becomes increasingly apparent. Finally, an impossible shape magically unfolds to become a real version of the keyboard, signifying that the G915 encompasses all dimensions.

Client
Logitech
Lausanne, Switzerland

Design
Logitech
Newark, CA, USA
ManvsMachine
London, United Kingdom

→ Clip online

ROG III – The Age of Gamers

[Brand Video]

With the ROG Saga, Republic of Gamers, a manufacturer of gaming hardware, has created a unique fantasy world which effectively relates to the brand. This brand video offers fans a detailed preview of the characters, environments, and the developing plot of the story. The film depicts traditional and futuristic styles, mechanical and biological life forms, analogue and digital blending, all of which are contradictions and normally do not co-exist in the same world. From the dark streets and glowing neon signs of Tokyo to the long bridges of Kaohsiung, almost all elements of this Cyberpunk world are derived from real world environments.

Client
ASUS
Taipei City, Taiwan

Design
ASUS
Taipei City, Taiwan

Project Team
MoonShine Animation

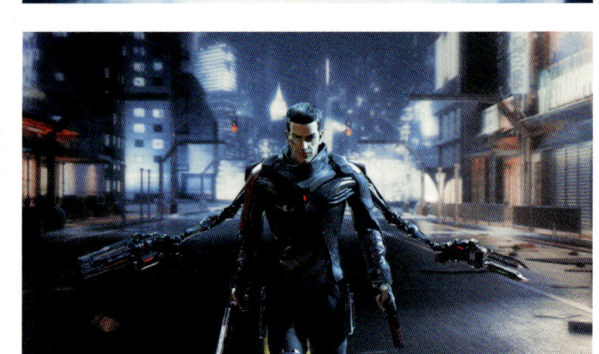

→ Clip online

ROG Zephyrus S17

[Online Clip]

This online clip for the ROG Zephyrus S17 uses modern storytelling techniques to highlight the specifications of the gaming laptop. The S17 is personified by Se7en, a character from the ROG fantasy world, developed specifically for marketing purposes. The individual scenes symbolise the design features of the product, e.g. Se7en's narrow escape from enemies illustrates how slim and strong the laptop is. The highly cinematic CGI imagery allows the brand to connect more closely with its audience of passionate gamers who commonly see this type of footage in video game cutscenes.

Client
ASUS
Taipei City, Taiwan

Design
ASUS
Taipei City, Taiwan

→ Clip online

ASUS VivoBook – #WowTheWorld

[Brand Video]

The #WowTheWorld brand video promotes the 2020 ASUS VivoBook laptop series, which has been designed for Generation Z. The video was shot with a street-style-feel and focuses on the spirit and lifestyle of young people. It features creative personalities from the fields of music, augmented reality, athletics and fashion design, shows the impact their ideas and talent have on the world, and the role the brand's laptops play in their lives. Since music has a big influence on the target group, the company collaborated with female artist Godi J, who wrote the theme song for the video.

Client
ASUS
Taipei City, Taiwan

Design
ASUS
Taipei City, Taiwan

Project Team
Bollywood Productions:
Dominique Esmenard (Production)
Dorothée Hernandez (Production)

C41.eu:
Leone Balduzzi (Film Direction)
Giuseppe Favale (Film Production)

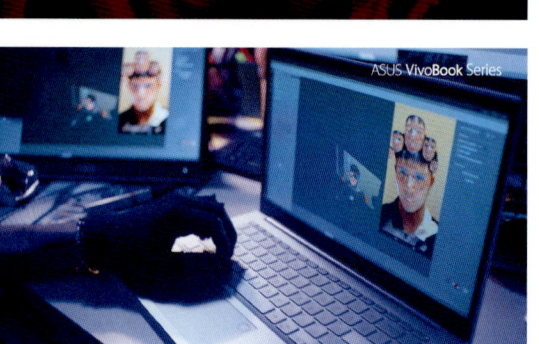

→ Clip online

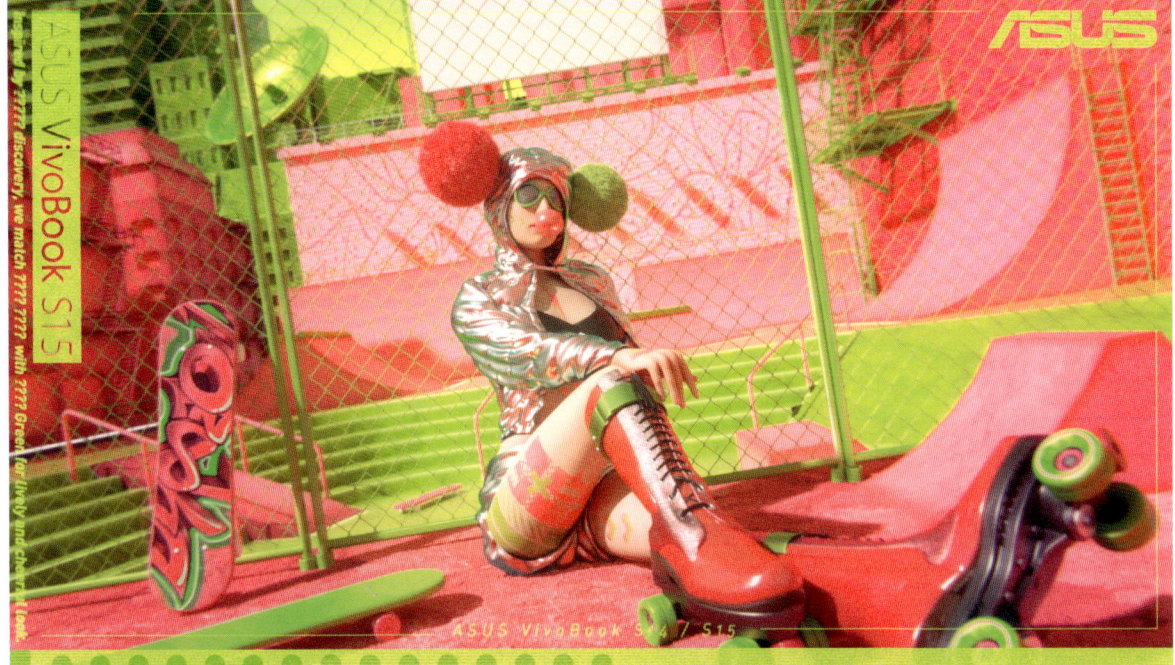

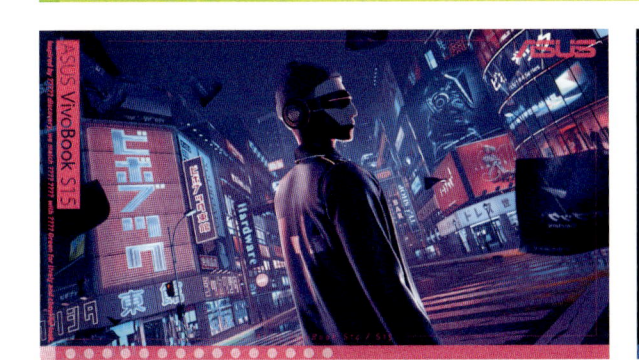

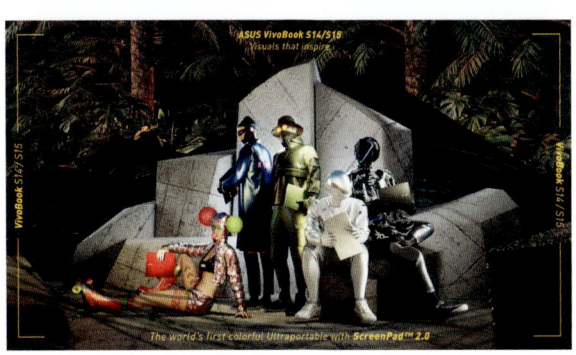

ASUS VivoBook S14/S15 – Visuals that inspire
[Promotional Clip, Computer Animation]

In order to promote the various colours of the ASUS VivoBook S14/S15, five animated characters were created to represent different types and styles of users. Based on various colour schemes, which have names such as Punk Pink and Moss Green, each character has been given not only a unique look but also a virtual setting which perfectly showcases the product's characteristics. The design of the promotional clips lies somewhere between reality and imagination, thereby reflecting the product slogan "Visuals that inspire".

Client
ASUS
Taipei City, Taiwan

Design
Timothy Motion
Taipei City, Taiwan

Project Team
Timothy Motion (Production)
Timothy Chang (Director)
Ying Ren Liu (Project Manager)
Ling Chih Hung (Character Design)
Ruo-Jia Liang (Character Design)
Huang Ching Chieh (Product Modelling)
Sean Wen (3D Artist)
Troy Lin (Music/Sound Design)

→ Clip online

EasyWallet

[Commercial]

EasyWallet is a mobile payment service by EasyCard Corporation. Designed to give the impression of being filmed in one single shot, this commercial aims to show how this service makes life more convenient. The actor moves through different scenes and uses his smartphone to pay and seamlessly change locations, e.g. a bookshelf opens when he swipes across his phone. An underground train appears behind it and he boards. The usage scenarios are enhanced with fantastical elements such as a bicycle ride past the moon in order to convey the message that the opportunities for cashless payments are almost limitless.

Client
EasyCard Corporation
Taipei City, Taiwan

Design
Merry Go Round Inc.
Taipei City, Taiwan

Project Team
Tien-Hau Hua (Creative Direction)
Yung-Chiao Chang
(Account Management)
Gui-Rong Chen (Account Management)
Hsin-Yi Tung (Strategic Planning)
Nai-Fang Zheng (Film Direction)
Ha-Ying Pak (Art Direction)
Yu-Hsuan Chien (Film Editing)

→ Designer profile on page 606
→ Clip online

Welcome to a Wireless World – Logitech POWERED

[Corporate Film]

Designed as a cinematic counterpart to the product slogan "No matter what your world looks like, we can help transform it into a wireless one", this corporate film shows the wireless charging devices of the Logitech Powered product range in a variety of flamboyant interiors. The field of view is always the same with the product as the focal point. Only the room and the hand which places the smartphone on the charging station and picks it up again change. The eccentricity of the interior reveals the variety of people who use the product and, at the same time, gives the film a touch of humour.

Client
Logitech
Lausanne, Switzerland

Design
Logitech Creative Team America
Newark, CA, USA

→ Clip online

Publishing & Print Media	Posters	Typography	Illustrations	Sound Design	**Film & Animation**	Online
4	64	92	116	126	138	172

ANSSil
[TV Commercial]

Client
ANSSil
Seoul, South Korea

Design
APOLLO Content Company
Seoul, South Korea
Loocreative
Seoul, South Korea

Project Team
APOLLO Content Company:
Dongkyu Nam (Executive Producer)
Soyoung Kim (Creative Director)

Loocreative:
Tackzun Lee (Director)
Chase Kwon (Motion)
Sumin Kwon (Animation)

→ Designer profile on page 572
→ Clip online

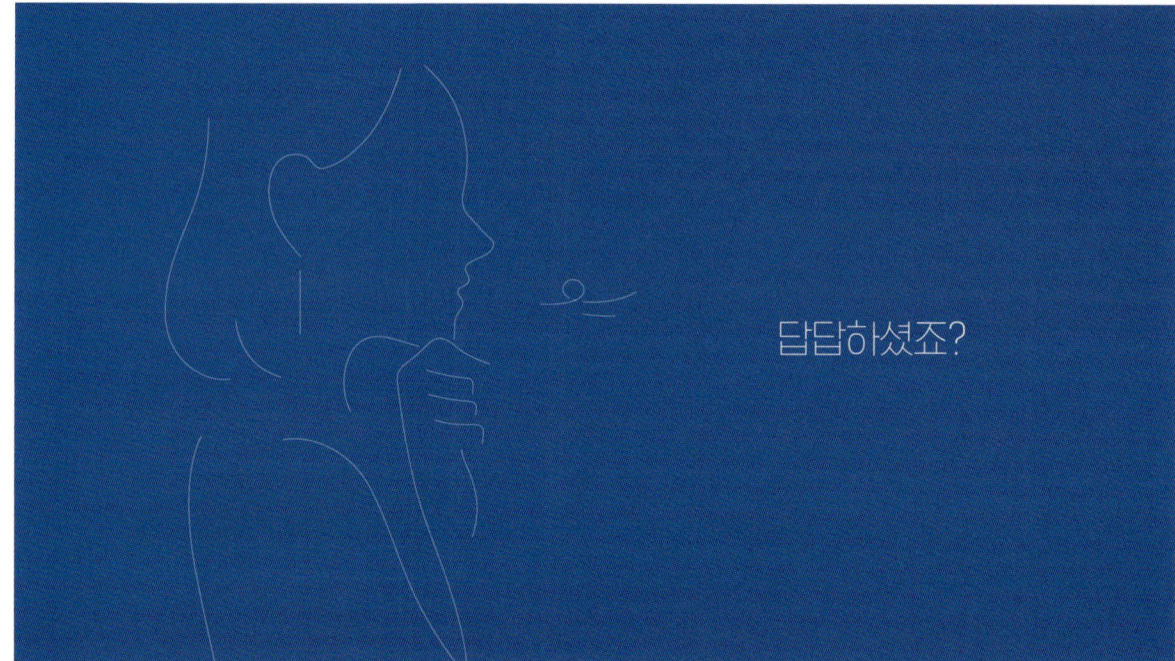

Apps	Interface & User Experience Design	Spatial Communication	Red Dot: Junior Award	Designer Profiles	Jury Portraits	Index
206	236	336	426	564	642	668

왜 평생 쓰지는

왜 평생 쓰지는 못하는 걸까?

The mattress manufacturer ANSSil was founded to provide answers to fundamental questions such as: why do mattresses not last a lifetime? What would happen if you could individually adjust the firmness of a mattress to suit your needs? The company has developed highly flexible mattresses made of strings and produced using 3D technology. For the brand launch, five television commercials were developed, each focusing on one of the key questions which had occupied the company since its foundation. The videos reference the motif of strings, with the animations primarily consisting of minimalist contour lines.

Publishing & Print Media	Posters	Typography	Illustrations	Sound Design	Film & Animation	Online
4	64	92	116	126	138	172

Leader iCase Refrigerator

[Motion Graphics Design, Commercial]

The Chinese brand Leader manufactures domestic appliances for a young, style-conscious target group. The visual appeal of the colourful motion graphic video for the iCase refrigerator range is lively. It employs various dynamic 3D animation effects in order to convey the special features of the products. Inspired by the brand logo and the product design, the round shape of a ball is a recurring graphic element. Different living situations, which change in front of the audience's eyes, communicate the adaptability of the refrigerator to the lifestyle of the respective customer.

Client
Haier Group
Qingdao, China

Design
Haier Innovation Design Center
Qingdao, China
Qingdao Hairigaoke Model Co. Ltd.
Qingdao, China

Project Team
Haier Innovation Design Center:
Yu Yiping
Huang Zeping
Wan Lulu
Xu Ningyang
Huang Yi
Zhou Heng

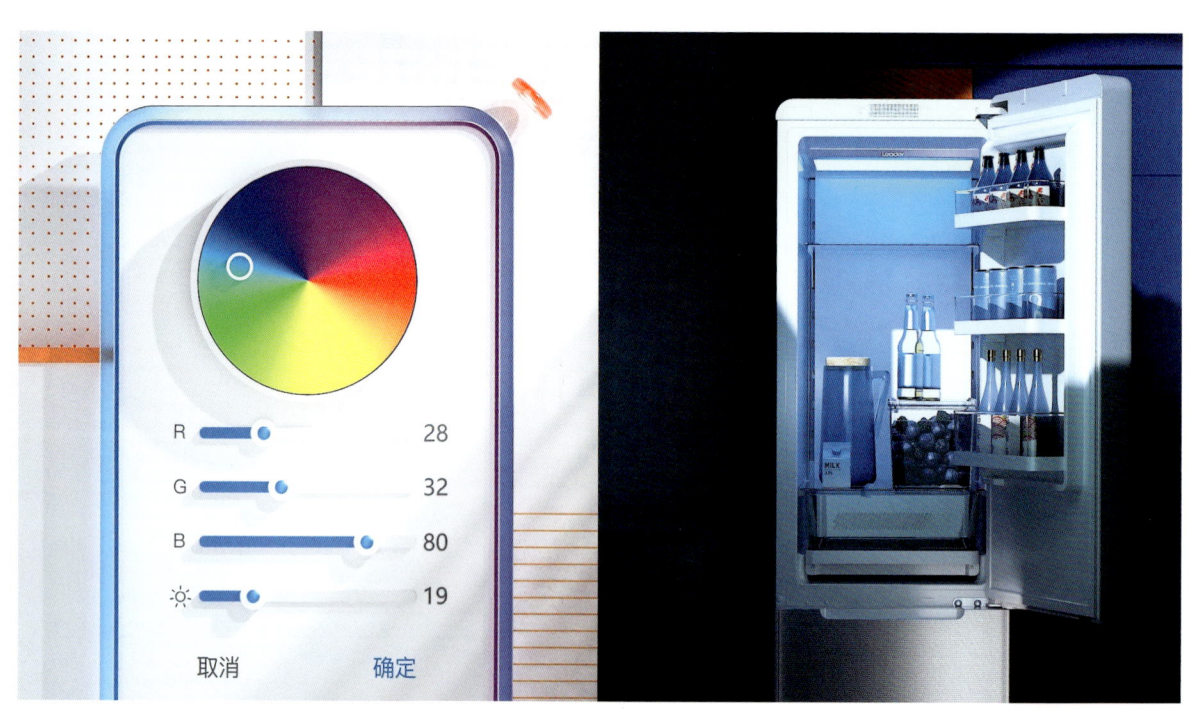

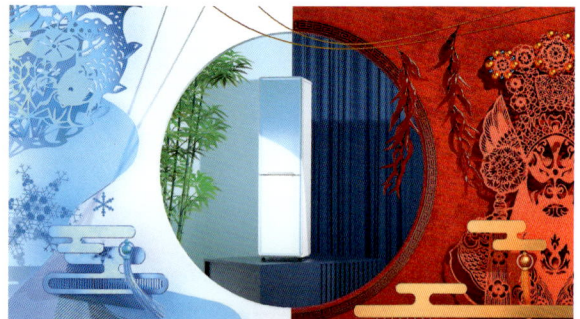

→ Clip online

Casarte Stone Series Refrigerator

[Motion Graphics Design, Commercial]

The motion graphic design for this commercial featuring the Casarte Raw Gemstone refrigerator range gets across the principles of the premium brand: smart technology and Italian elegance. Starting with the rough stone surface of the exterior casing, the fridge materialises from pieces of rock in a bizarre landscape at the beginning of the clip. Various image effects, such as slow motion, close-ups and a camera flight through the interior of the fridge, are used to accentuate the technical highlights. At the end, the video shows the refrigerator in a high-end room to emphasise its aesthetic quality.

Client
Haier Group
Qingdao, China

Design
Haier Innovation Design Center
Qingdao, China
Qingdao Hairigaoke Model Co. Ltd.
Qingdao, China

Project Team
Haier Innovation Design Center:
Yu Yiping
Wu Jian
Huang Zeping
Wang Yisen
Bao Changliang
Liu Haibo

→ Clip online

Akrapovič Tribute to Superbikes

[Promotional Video]

Akrapovič is a manufacturer of premium exhaust systems for motorcycles and performance cars. Released on various social media channels, this promotional video portrays the feeling of riding a superbike equipped with one of those systems. The viewer experiences the power of the bike as they start and their breathtaking speed when the riders open up the throttle on the racing circuit. The diffuse light of dusk creates a dramatic atmosphere. The visual impact is heightened by a stunning soundtrack, giving the viewer the opportunity to experience the unique sound of the exhausts.

Client
Akrapovič d.d.
Ivančna Gorica, Slovenia

Design
Akrapovič Kreativa d.o.o.
Ivančna Gorica, Slovenia
Sixtyseven Pictures GmbH
Mainz-Kostheim, Germany

Project Team
Akrapovič Kreativa d.o.o.:
Aljoša Gomilšek (Video Concept)
Andrej Ravnikar (Video Concept)

→ Clip online

T-Roc Bob
[Online Promotional Clip]

This promotional clip demonstrates the power and agility of the VW T-Roc by contrasting it with the raw energy of a bobsleigh run. The clip switches between the footage of a bobsleigh team in an ice tunnel and a T-Roc driven in the snow – when the team accelerate or turn a corner, so does the car. Tension is created through the sound of the ever-faster breathing of one of the bobsledders, which is mirrored by the increasing speed of the cuts. Finally, the sleigh crosses the finishing line and the mood eases. The idea of rapid breathing conveys the story and underscores the essence of bobsledding: speed, power and control.

Client
Volkswagen AG
Wolfsburg, Germany

Design
loved GmbH
Hamburg, Germany

Project Team
loved:
Mieke Haase (Chief Creative Officer)
Sabine Cole (Editor-in-Chief)
Alexander Müsgens (Creative Director)
Nadine Kaminski (Text)

Marc Schölermann (Director/DOP)
Simon Roloff (Camera)
Sören Görth (Film Editing)
Boris Salchow (Music/Sound Design)

→ Clip online

BMW Press Conference Toolkit 19–22

[Computer Animation]

A modular design system for press conferences at international motor shows has been developed as part of BMW's new trade-fair strategy. The physical stand is digitally expanded and the umbrella brand and the sub-brands are translated into 11 individual brand rooms. The architecture of the rooms intentionally establishes connections and differences between the brands. The materials used and the interplay of light and shadow convey the specific character of the brand. The theatrical assembly and dismantling of the rooms create excitement and offer a virtual stage for vehicle-specific content.

Client
BMW Group
Munich, Germany

Design
Elastique. GmbH
Cologne, Germany

Project Team
Andreas Schimmelpfennig (Creative Direction)
Philipp Alfes (Art Direction)
André Britz (Art Direction)
Christoph Große Hovest (Art Direction)
Hadrien Ledieu (Motion Design)
Mariusz Becker (Motion Design)
Peter Pannes (Motion Design)
Felix Kapfer (Motion Design)
Maximiliane Wadler (Motion Design)
Christin Flosbach (Project Lead)

Susanne Gocht (Strategy),
Blue Scope GmbH

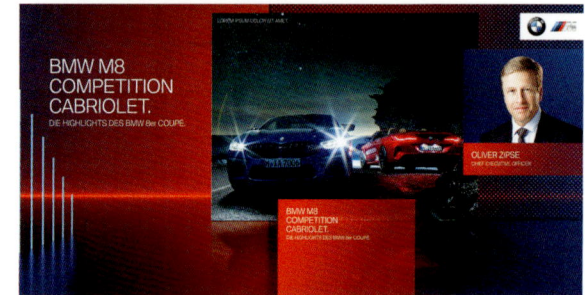

→ Clip online

BMW Trade Fair Media 19–22

[Computer Animation]

The redesign of the visual appearance for BMW in trade fair and press conference media follows an unusual approach as it focuses on the feel of the brand instead of promoting new products by providing facts and figures. This is achieved by transforming selected materials from the cars' exteriors and interiors into hyper-real animations. The 15-minute-long motion design, music and sound design drama contains relaxing and dynamic sections as well as a large-scale augmented reality installation in which a real car is, amongst other things, virtually doused in paint and dragged underwater by a giant octopus.

Client
BMW Group
Munich, Germany

Design
Elastique. GmbH
Cologne, Germany

Project Team
Sarah Böckenhüser (Creative Direction)
Andreas Schimmelpfennig
(Creative Direction)

Annika Meyer (Motion Design)
Felix Kapfer (Motion Design)
Peter Pannes (Motion Design)
Justus Jäger (Motion Design)
Christopher Wöltjen (Motion Design)
Misha Shyukin (Motion Design)
Dmitry Zakharov (Motion Design)

Philipp Schneider (Edit)
Ioannis Mihailidis (Technical Director AR)
Kerstin Kohle (Account Management)
Ole Reinsberger (Project Manager)

Marvin Keil (Sound Design)
TRO (Music)

→ Clip online

Publishing & Print Media	Posters	Typography	Illustrations	Sound Design	Film & Animation	Online
4	64	92	116	126	138	172

Gapwaves 5G Antenna

[Promotional Video, Computer Animation]

This promotional video for Gapwaves, a Swedish technology company, uses storytelling and graphical illustrations to explain the value and story behind the brand's complicated 5G antenna, built with waveguide technology. The visual style and tone of voice are tailored to suit even non-technical audiences. The film addresses three key topics: the problem statement, the company's solution and the future vision. All three sections share the same likeable, simplified design style and are closely interconnected. That creates a direct link between the world's macro problems and the micro-solution offered by the 5G product.

Client
Gapwaves AB
Gothenburg, Sweden

Design
The Techno Creatives
Gothenburg, Sweden

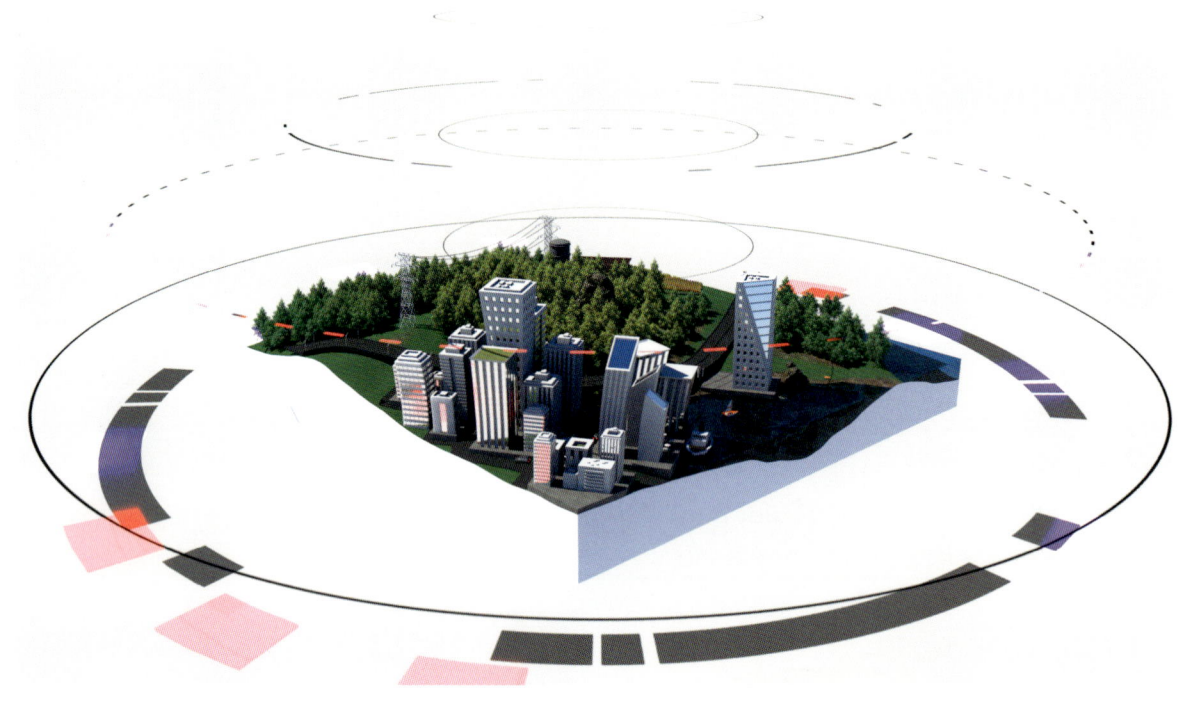

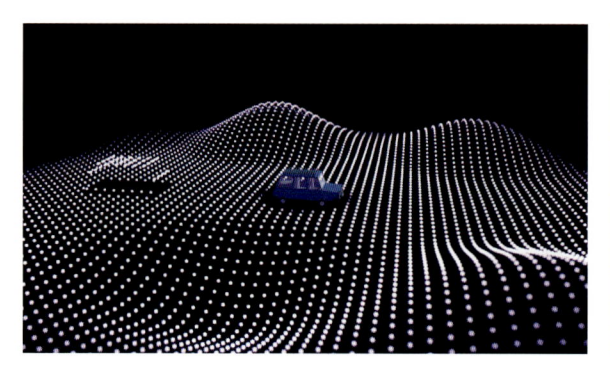

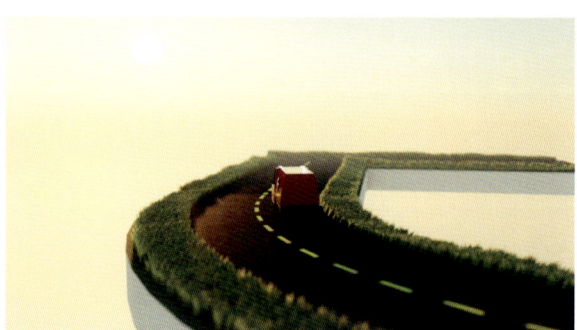

→ Clip online

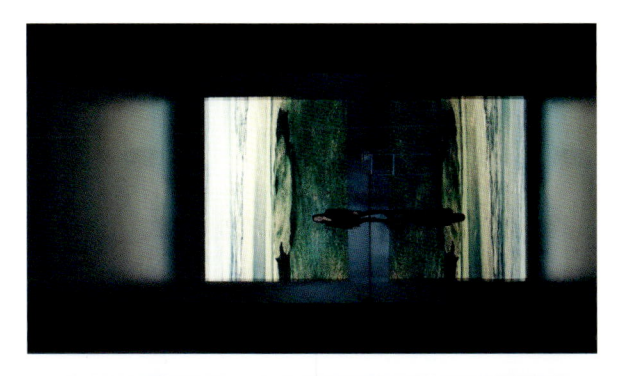

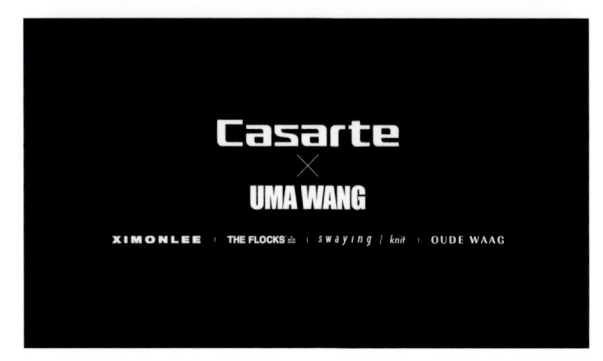

Casarte "Black Label"
[Promotional Video Series]

This promotional video for Casarte is intended to point out that incorrect washing of clothing can have a serious environmental impact. The brand's Black Label range of washing machines helps to protect the environment by extending the life of clothes. The video combines an information section filmed in a studio and presented by various fashion designers with images of nature which translate the facts presented into memorable visual images. The composition of light, sound and editing creates a strong atmosphere which underscores the urgency of the message.

Client
Haier Group
Qingdao, China

Design
Haier Innovation Design Center
Qingdao, China
Qingdao Hairigaoke Model Co. Ltd.
Qingdao, China

Project Team
Haier Innovation Design Center:
Cheng Chuanling
Li Jinyuan
Jin Hua
Wang Wei
Yu Yiping
Huang Zeping

→ Clip online

Publishing & Print Media	Posters	Typography	Illustrations	Sound Design	Film & Animation	Online
4	64	92	116	126	138	172

Röben Kaleidoscope
[Online Clip]

Creativity is the important starting point of every project. However, the journey from idea to implementation is a long one. Inspired by the motto "You've got the idea. We've got the brick", an online campaign for the German ceramics company Röben was created to encourage architects to adhere to their creative ideas. The clips show complex, kaleidoscopic architectural images which keep forming into new geometric patterns. Amidst all this activity we see the products of the brand, providing inspiration and bringing the abstract world of creativity to life.

Client
Röben Tonbaustoffe GmbH
Zetel, Germany

Design
Kopfkunst, Agentur für Kommunikation GmbH
Münster, Germany

Project Team
Simon Hattrup (Creative Direction)
Florian Zimmermann
(Senior Art Direction)
Jens Kallfelz (Strategic Planning)
Dirk Knepper (Production)
Christoph Lojak (Web Design)
Dennis Harwardt (Animation Design)
Marc Fielers (Text)

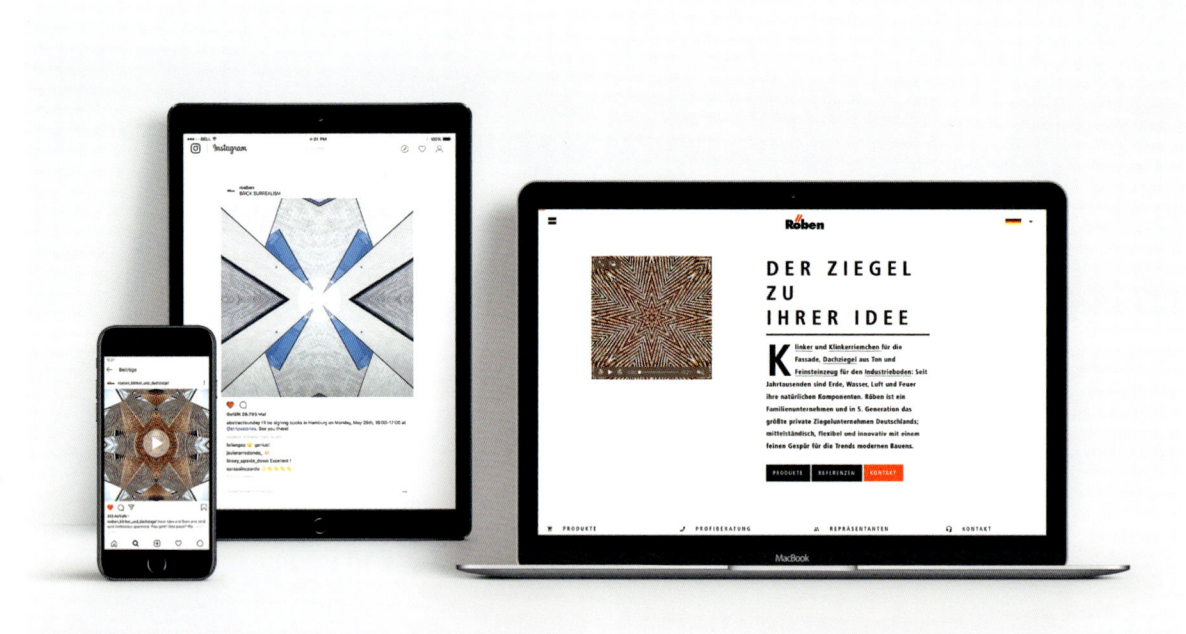

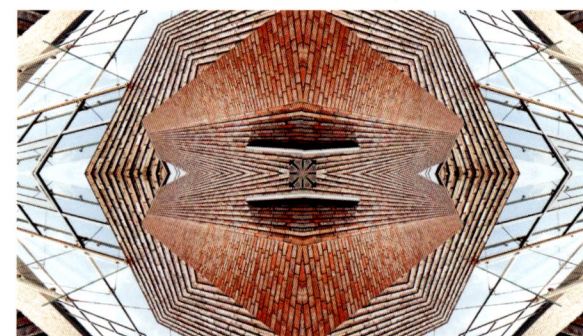

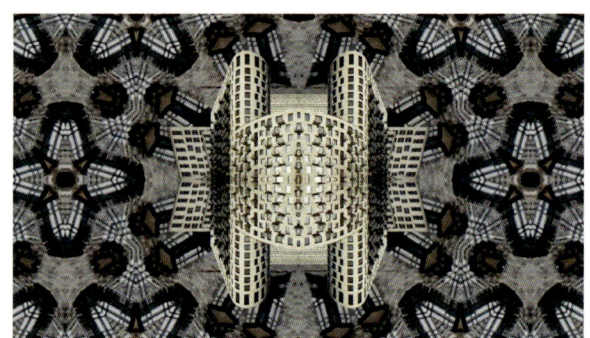

→ Clip online

Reveal Your Thaidentity – Experience the Thai way in Thailand

[Cel Animation]

The "Reveal Your Thaidentity" campaign aims to make Thailand attractive again as a holiday destination for tourists from Singapore. The design strategy centres around presenting Thailand and its culture, which is familiar to most Singaporeans, through cartoons in an unfamiliar way. The three animated clips each show a tourist experiencing the prime attractions Singaporeans associate with a holiday in Thailand: shopping, food and entertainment. Once they have overcome their initial culture shock, the characters start to go wild and become a part of the colourful scenery, embracing their hidden "Thaidentity".

Client
Tourism Authority of Thailand – Singapore Office, Royal Thai Embassy Singapore

Design
Aught Pte. Ltd.
Singapore
Fuum Studio
Bangkok, Thailand

Project Team
Aught:
Tomaz Goh (Creative Direction)
Mark Lawrence Ong (Creative Direction)
Jessica Gan (Art Direction)
Marie Chong (Graphic Design)

Fuum Studio:
Panop Koonwat (Animation)

Sathapat (Tum) Teeranitayapap (Music/Sound Design), No Sound in Space

→ Designer profile on page 574
→ Clip online

Lessons of Auschwitz

[Short Film]

The short film "Lessons of Auschwitz" aims to show how history can be retold and reimagined by younger generations through digital art. Marking the 75th anniversary of its liberation, nine students from a Moscow high school, between 13 and 16 years old, were taken to the memorial in Poland. After the trip, they were asked to express their reactions and emotions in VR. Using innovative XR film technology, a new kind of commemorative tribute emerged aiming to engage and touch younger viewers and inspire them to learn more about the Holocaust.

Client
RT
Moscow, Russia

Design
RT
Moscow, Russia
Phygitalism Studio
Moscow, Russia

Project Team
Kirill Karnovich-Valua (Creative Director)
Denis Semionov (Director)
Peter Theremin (Composer)
Eldar Salamov (Sound Design)
Elena Medvedeva (Producer)
Ania Fedorova (Producer)
Ekaterina Sidorova (3D Artist)
Valeria Fimina (Project Manager)
Vlad Krutenyuk (3D Artist)
Aleksandr Kryuchkov (Developer)
Pavel Postnikov (3D Artist)
Vanya Yunitskiy (Project Manager)
Aleksey Lushnikov (Developer)
Nikita Semionov (VR Artist)
Sasha Volkov (VR Artist)
Misha Borisov (VR Artist)
Dima Kaderkaev (VR Artist)
Zhenya Timoshenkova (VR Artist)
Vlad Sarychev (VR Artist)
Nata Makashvili (VR Artist)
Dima Sobaev (VR Artist)
Lera Agescheva (VR Artist)

→ Designer profiles on pages 611, 616
→ Clip online

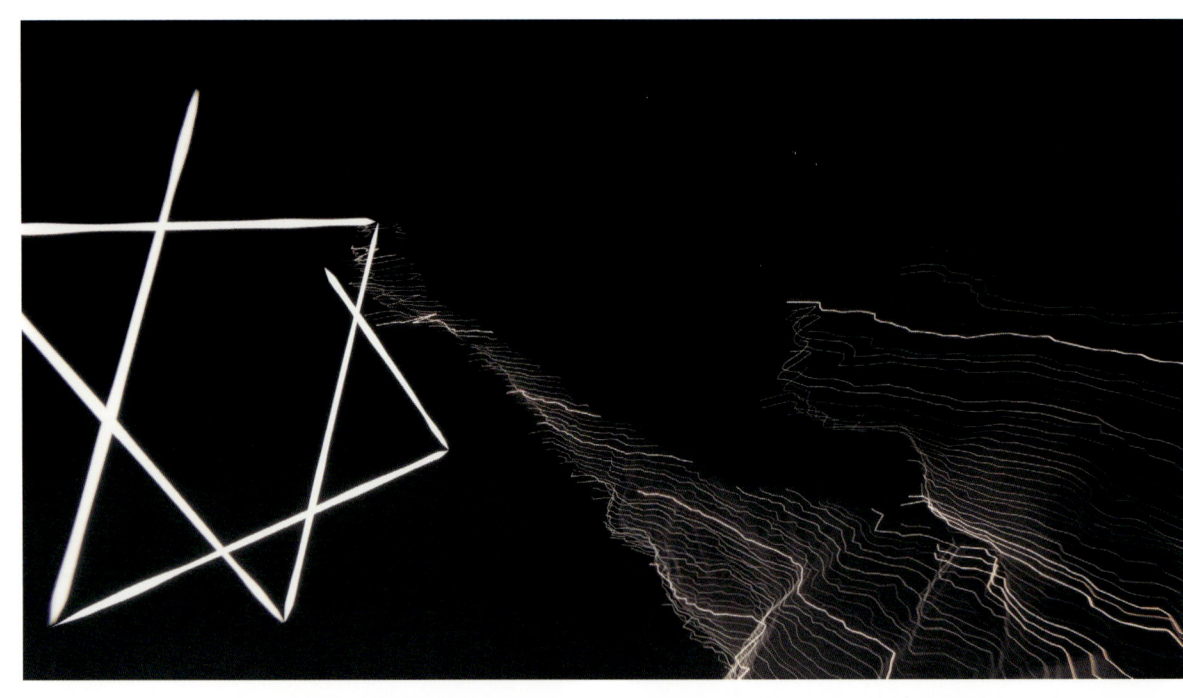

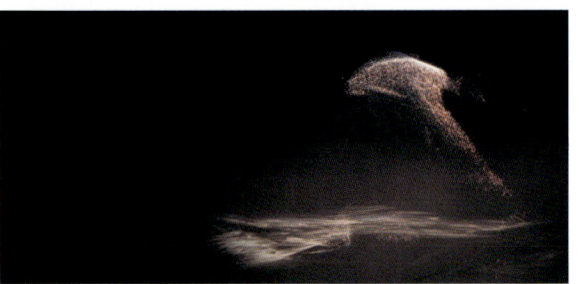

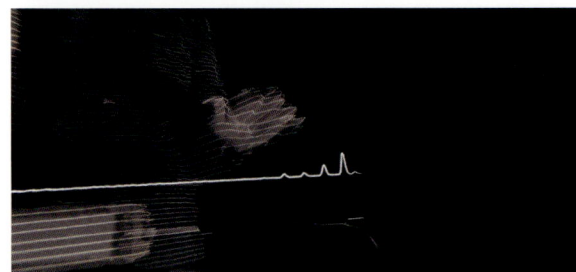

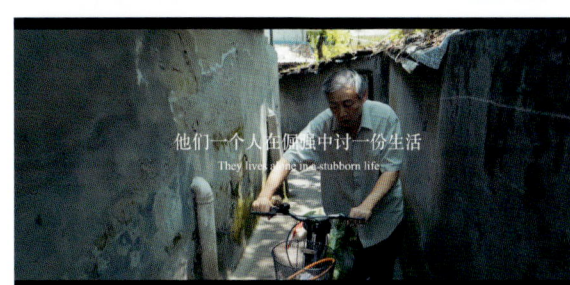

Leave Me Alone
[Short Film]

The number of elderly singles in China is rising. This short film is a reminder that people should look more after their senior citizens, even if they say that they want to be left alone. The film documents the everyday life of an elderly man. The calm flow of images indicates how slowly his days pass. The camera angle focuses the viewers' attention on details such as a dripping tap or the man's worn out shoes. The message of the film is to pay more attention to these details and that even small gestures, such as the new pair of shoes, which the old man is given by his daughter at the end of the film, can have an effect.

Client
Hangzhou Yizhijia Network
Technology Co., Ltd.
Hangzhou, China

Design
Hangzhou Yizhijia Network
Technology Co., Ltd.
Hangzhou, China

Project Team
Qi Han (Project Management)
Shangtan Li (Project Management)
Jing Shu (Producer)
Fang Meng (Director)
Bingshuai Wang (Photography)
Chenyan Jin (Graphic Design)
Shucheng Liao (Graphic Design)

→ Clip online

Feel Better, Do Better

[Computer Animation]

How can ergonomics be translated into a graphic language which is simple, vibrant and youthful? That was the challenge this project sought to address for the launch of a range of ergonomic devices by Logitech. The solution consists of various static and animated 3D characters to present different key topics. The focal point of the design was to make these characters easy to distinguish. Morphological aspects played just as important a role as the styling of the figures. In a direct reference to the brand logo, in which the letter "g" is partially invisible, the characters have no midsection.

Client
Logitech
Lausanne, Switzerland

Design
Logitech Creative Team Europe
Lausanne, Switzerland
Clim Studio
Barcelona, Spain

→ Clip online

Apps	Interface & User Experience Design	Spatial Communication	Red Dot: Junior Award	Designer Profiles	Jury Portraits	Index
206	236	336	426	564	642	668

Mazu Pilgrimage
[Computer Animation]

The goddess of seafarers and fisherman, Mazu, is one of the best-known deities in Taiwan and China. Every year, hundreds of thousands of people take part in a pilgrimage to honour the goddess. This animation expresses belief in prayer and in Mazu's blessing. The motif of the Mazu pilgrimage is combined with a music box depicting the temple from which the procession sets out, with the goddess being carried on a palanquin. Instead of the usual, lurid colours of religious processions, the colours used in the animation are restricted to the natural hue of the wood to emphasise the sincerity of the film's message.

Client
Knock-Knock Animation
Taipei City, Taiwan

Design
Knock-Knock Animation
Taipei City, Taiwan

→ Clip online

Taipei Music Center

[Brand Video]

The turbulent rise of a band from their early beginnings in a small backstreet garage to their break-through concert in a big venue, the Taipei Music Center, is shown in this video. The visual presentation of the gradual development of the band, represented by the members of the Taiwanese pop group EggPlantEgg, shows the transformation of the protagonists from real people to animated cartoon characters on changing concert posters. The different drawing styles of the posters symbolise the increasing professionalism of the band and, at the same time, allude to the diversity of music in general.

Client
Taipei City Government,
Department of Cultural Affairs
Taipei Music Center
Taipei City, Taiwan

Design
Grass Jelly Studio
Taipei City, Taiwan

Project Team
Muh Chen (Film Direction)
Nigel Huang (Post-Production)
Grass Jelly Studio Team

→ Clip online

Qing Feng Wu – Spaceman

[Music Video]

The touching music video for "Spaceman" by Qing Feng Wu is set in two different worlds: a fantasy world, which exists only in the imagination of a young illustrator, and the real world, in which the illustrator falls in love with his flatmate. In the fantasy world, the illustrator is a prince living on a distant planet. The post-apocalyptic landscape reflects his loneliness until he, one day, meets an astronaut, an embodiment of his flatmate, who puts an end to his unhappiness. Both worlds are characterised by their own visual aesthetics and differ markedly.

Client
The Harlequin's Carnival Ltd.
Universal Music Ltd., Taiwan
Taipei City, Taiwan

Design
Grass Jelly Studio
Taipei City, Taiwan

Project Team
Muh Chen (Film Direction)
Greg Miao (Post-Production)
Grass Jelly Studio Team

→ Clip online

Online

Red Dot: Grand Prix

Human Rights Tattoo
[Website]

The Universal Declaration of Human Rights is a legally non-binding resolution consisting of 30 articles promulgated by the United Nations General Assembly in 1948. As these rights are important for everyone, but they are far from being respected all over the world, the Human Rights Tattoo project was launched. Since 2012, Human Rights Tattoo is tattooing the 6,773 letters of this declaration one by one on 6,773 people worldwide. People of different cultures and various groups are to be inspired to stand up for human rights in their own way, for example, by taking a tattoo, simply donating or simply making their voices heard otherwise. Together, all participants in their commitment to the campaign form a movement and a living artwork of individual letters. The website thus connects people across all borders. It shares their exciting stories as well as their individual motivation to get the tattoo in order to feel part of a larger community with the common goal of together forming a front for equal rights worldwide.

Statement by the jury
This extraordinary project sees itself as a committed defender of human rights and, in so doing, literally gets under the skin. Through their individual letter tattoo, the participants are all part of a work of art and together are a personification of human rights. This radical idea is as great as it is pertinent because, beyond compromise, it gets straight to the heart of the issue and the reality of the message. The stories on the website complement the relevance of the work and its quality outstandingly.

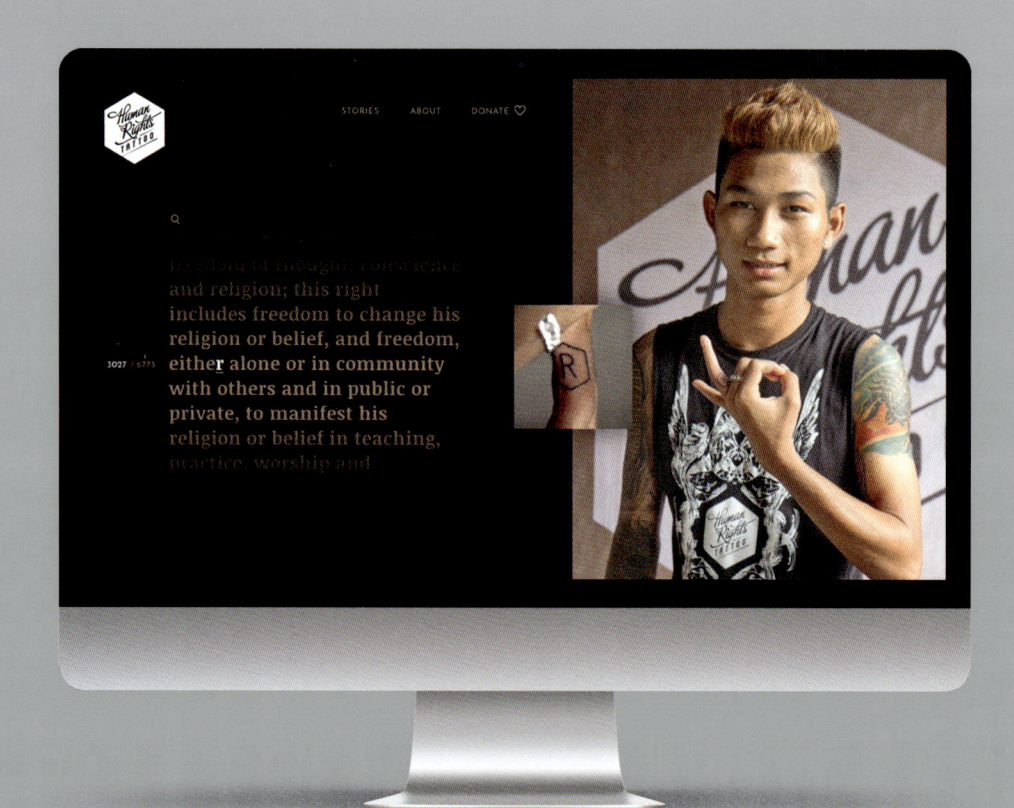

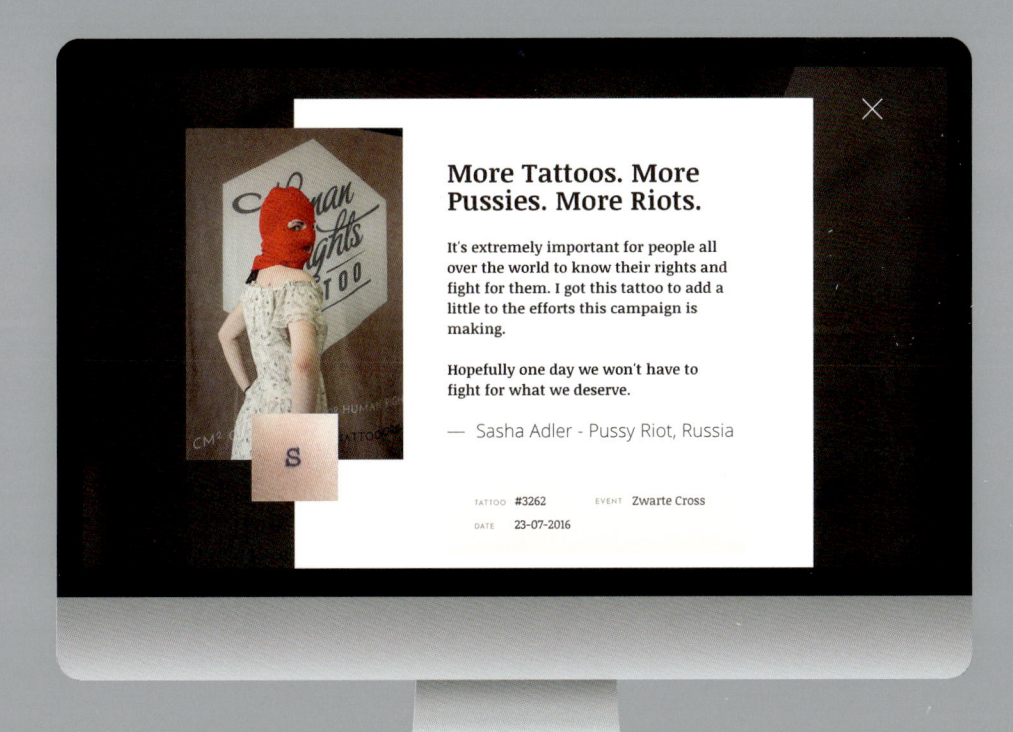

Apps	Interface & User Experience Design	Spatial Communication	Red Dot: Junior Award	Designer Profiles	Jury Portraits	Index
206	236	336	426	564	642	668

reddot winner 2020
grand prix

Client
Human Rights Tattoo
Tilburg, Netherlands

Design
Freshheads
Tilburg, Netherlands

→ Designer profile on page 587

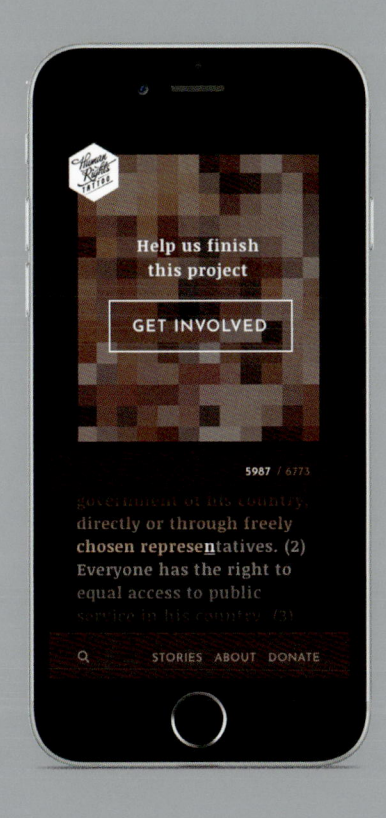

Publishing & Print Media	Posters	Typography	Illustrations	Sound Design	Film & Animation	Online
4	64	92	116	126	138	172

Red Dot: Best of the Best

Lessons of Auschwitz
[Web Special]

"Lessons of Auschwitz" is a social experiment that aimed to show how history is experienced by younger generations and how it is then retold and reimagined by them through digital art. To mark the 75th anniversary of the liberation of Auschwitz, nine students from a Moscow high school visited the Memorial in Poland to personally undergo this experience. After the trip, they learned under the creative guidance of Russian XR artist Denis Semionov how to express their experiences and reactions using XR film technology. The students amalgamated their impressions into individual, immersive productions and thus created a new kind of commemorative tribute and dealing with the past, which is intended to engage and touch younger viewers and inspire them to learn more about the Holocaust. History, personal emotions and latest technology thus united in a multifaceted manner and emerged as a powerful, engaging website that incorporates the idea of touching the senses in order to sustain historical memory in a digital world.

Statement by the jury
"Lessons of Auschwitz" is a significant project in that it invited young people to use VR to express their impressions of and reactions to the Holocaust. The website with its outstandingly impressive design documents the reactions as commemorative tribute and as a record of the technological explorations, presenting itself in artistic versatility that can be experienced at all sensual levels. Overall, it is a successful digital commemoration for the 21st century.

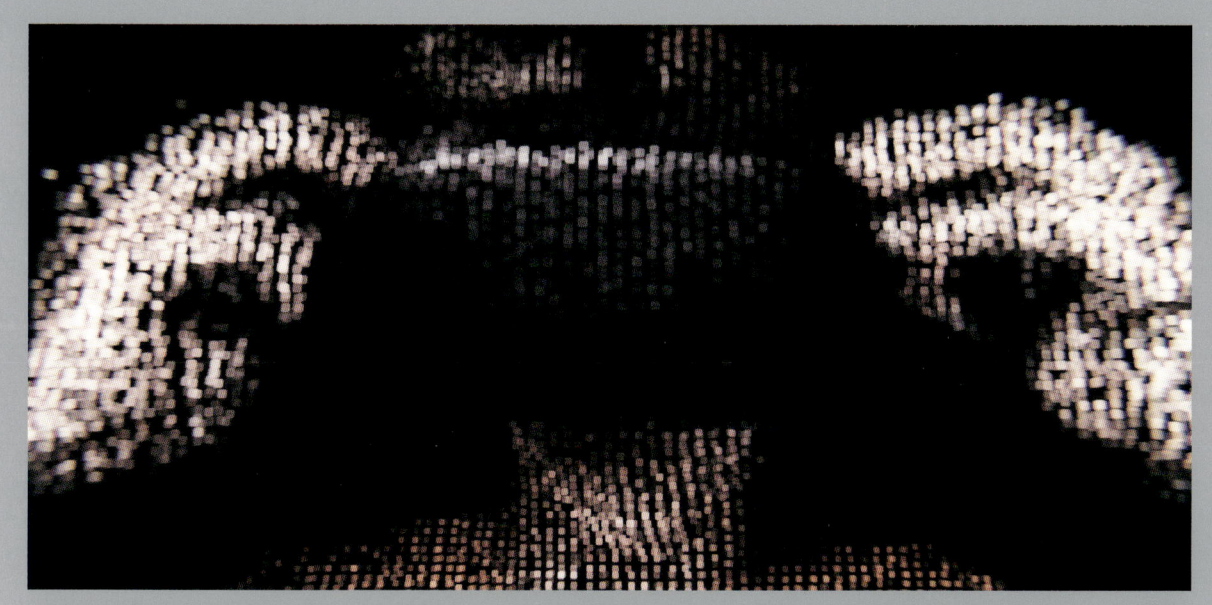

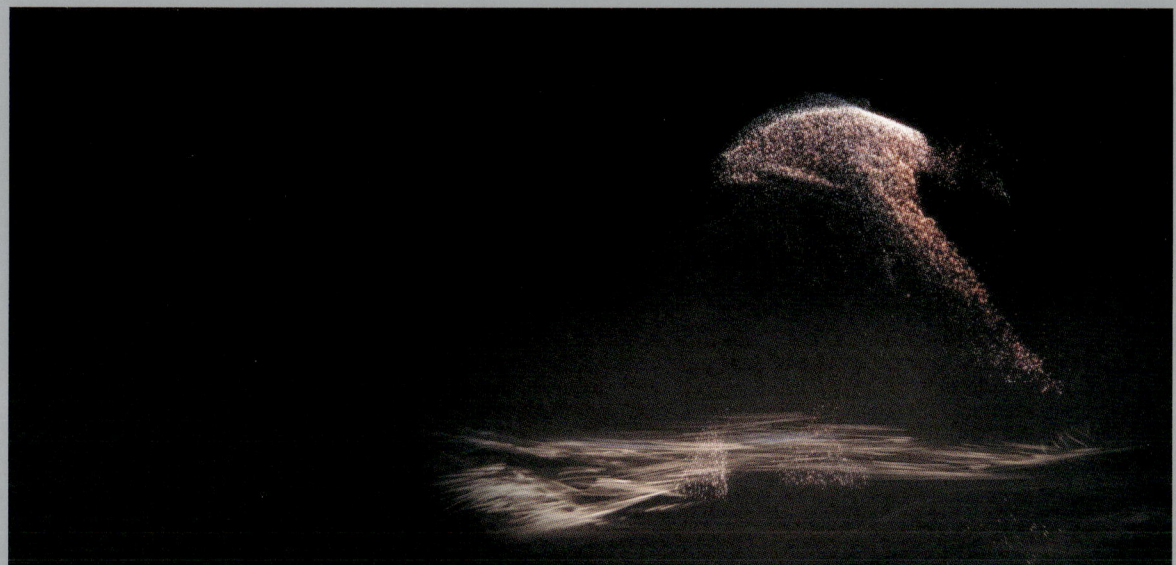

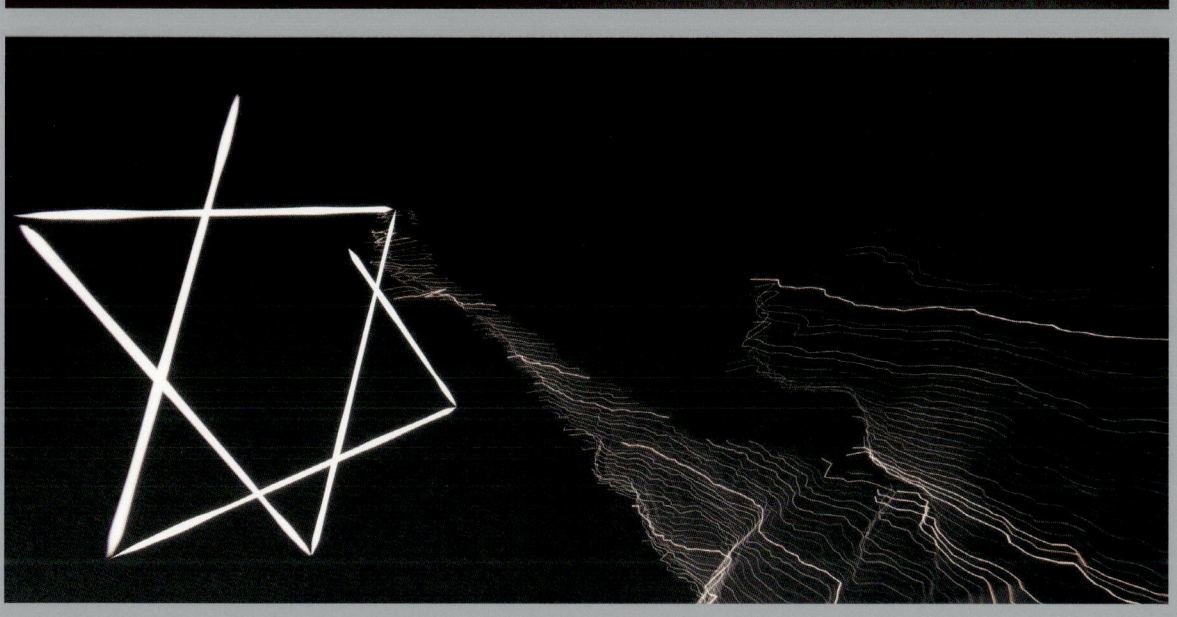

Client
RT
Moscow, Russia

Design
RT
Moscow, Russia
Phygitalism Studio
Moscow, Russia

Project Team
Kirill Karnovich-Valua (Creative Director)
Denis Semionov (Director)
Peter Theremin (Composer)
Eldar Salamov (Sound Designer)
Elena Medvedeva (Producer)
Ania Fedorova (Producer)
Ekaterina Sidorova (3D Artist)
Valeria Fimina (Project Manager)
Vlad Krutenyuk (3D Artist)
Aleksandr Kryuchkov (Developer)
Pavel Postnikov (3D Artist)
Vanya Yunitskiy (Project Manager)
Aleksey Lushnikov (Developer)
Nikita Semionov (VR Artist)
Sasha Volkov (VR Artist)
Misha Borisov (VR Artist)
Dima Kaderkaev (VR Artist)
Zhenya Timoshenkova (VR Artist)
Vlad Sarychev (VR Artist)
Nata Makashvili (VR Artist)
Dima Sobaev (VR Artist)
Lera Agescheva (VR Artist)

→ Designer profiles on pages 611, 616
→ Clip online

Red Dot: Best of the Best

SMK Open
[Public Online Art Collection]

The art must be set free. This is one of the visions of SMK, the National Gallery of Denmark, which holds the entire country's joint art collection of more than 260,000 works. Anyone visiting the gallery to see all the exhibited works will only have seen 0.7 per cent of the collection, as a total of 99.3 per cent of the collection is in archives in the basement. In order to make this huge inventory accessible in a public online art collection, a website has been developed featuring a design that is clearly shaped by the envisioned function. A purist black-and-white background makes each work stand out concisely, and, with the reduced-scale view, creates a minimalist expression that provides clarity and focus on the many functions through which users can navigate. The advanced search feature makes it possible to search intuitively without having to decide in advance what to look for – be it a motif, artist, colour, period or material. The layout is flexible while the navigation is fluid, so that visitors can at all time clearly see the result of their choices.

Statement by the jury
By making its enormous art collection accessible to the public online, the SMK website has successfully emerged as an opportunity to present all of the collected works of art. The works stand out to particularly expressive effect against the unobtrusive, elegant background. The many different search functions, including a customisable search, allow easy intuitive navigation and inspiring interaction with the works.

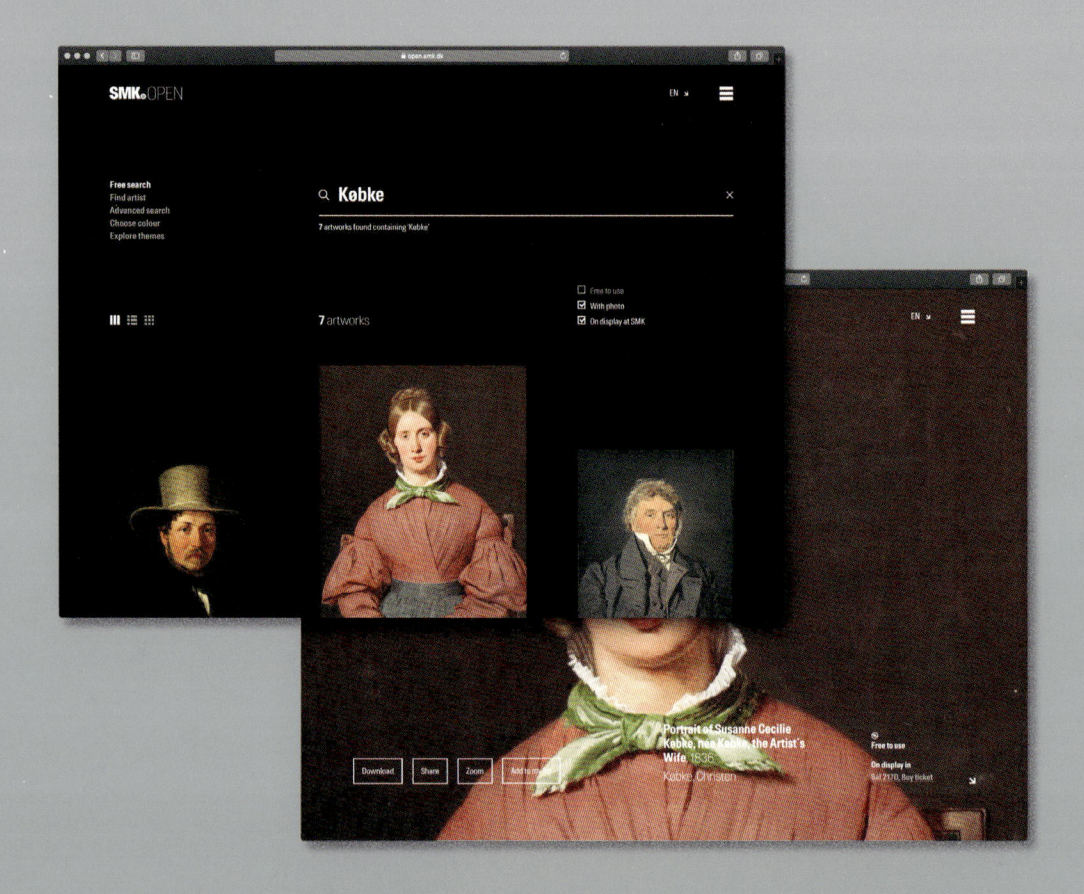

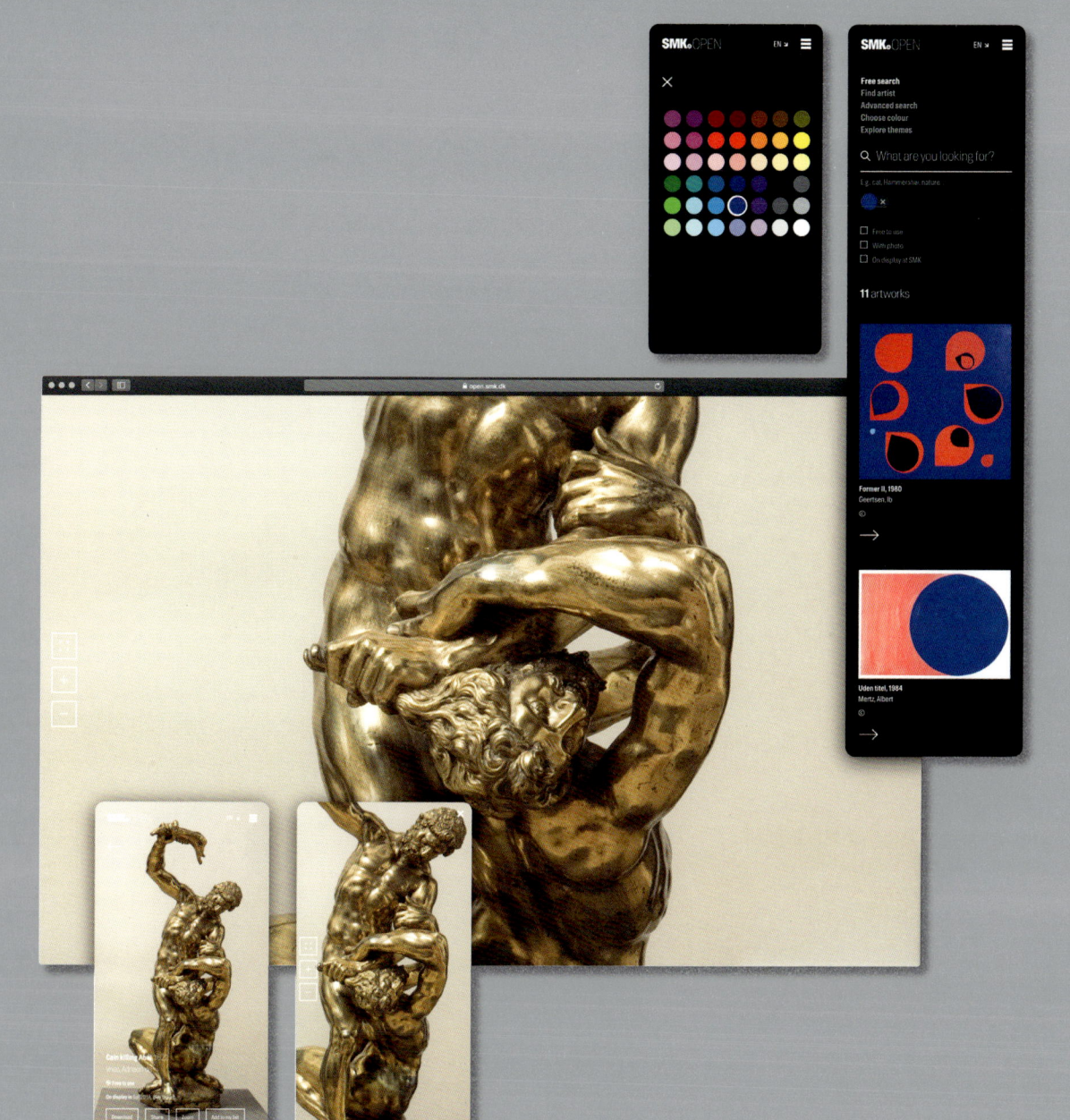

Apps	Interface & User Experience Design	Spatial Communication	Red Dot: Junior Award	Designer Profiles	Jury Portraits	Index
206	236	336	426	564	642	668

Client
SMK Statens Museum for Kunst
Copenhagen, Denmark

Design
1508
Copenhagen, Denmark
Strömlin
Copenhagen, Denmark

Project Team
1508:
Christoffer Kildahl (Designer)
Tore Rosbo (Designer)
Per C. Jackson (Front-End Developer)

Strömlin:
Anton Stonor (Back-End Developer)
Thomas Clement Mogensen
(Back-End Developer)
Pernille Charlotte Mardell (Client Lead)

→ Designer profile on page 566

Red Dot: Best of the Best

SZ Plus. The perfect fit.
[Digital Campaign]

"SZ Plus. The perfect fit." is the title of an online campaign with which the Süddeutsche Zeitung daily newspaper, published in Munich, Germany, is promoting its contemporary digital subscription model. The aim was to appeal to the new target group of millennials, by attracting their attention and putting them under the paper's spell. Under the motto "digital, flexible, affordable", six animations were created for use across various social media channels to communicate what makes the new digital subscription model stand out. The message is that it does not slightly fit the target group's requirements – rather it fits perfectly. In collaboration with Swedish motion designer Andreas Wannerstedt, the central idea of "the perfect fit" was translated into a visually captivating effect. Viewers can hardly escape the visual pull created by the various geometric elements that move towards and away from each other following a precise rhythm and, in so doing, naturally encapsulate the message.

Statement by the jury
The online campaign for the new Süddeutsche Zeitung daily newspaper subscription model impresses with the high quality with which it makes form and content coalesce to create a metaphor that is as impressive as it is captivating. Using new 3D technologies, the message of the slogan is coherently conveyed, while also communicating the high standards of the newspaper company in a smart manner and with a wink.

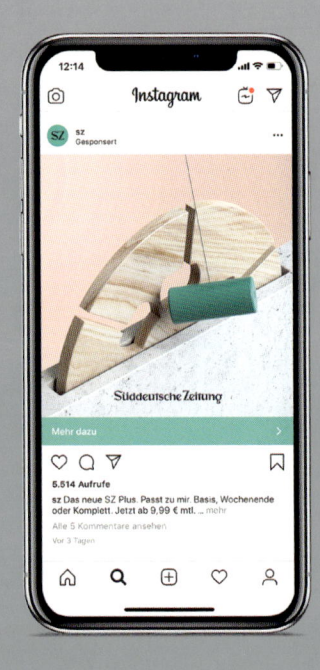

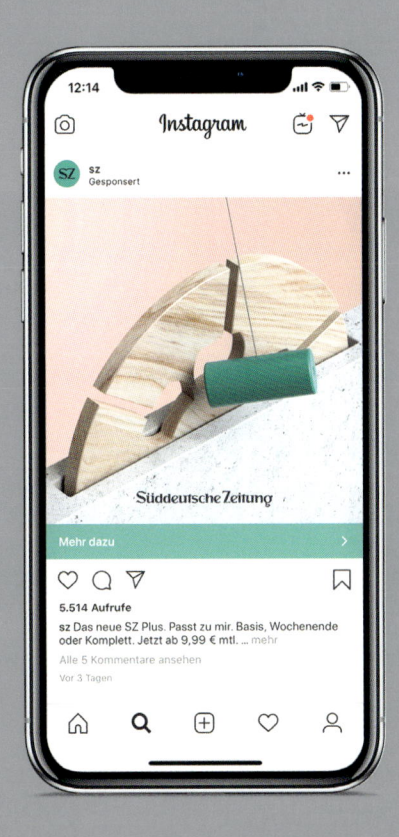

Apps	Interface & User Experience Design	Spatial Communication	Red Dot: Junior Award	Designer Profiles	Jury Portraits	Index
206	236	336	426	564	642	668

Client
Süddeutsche Zeitung Digitale
Medien GmbH
Munich, Germany

Design
Zeichen & Wunder
Munich, Germany

Project Team
Zeichen & Wunder:
Irmgard Hesse (Managing Partner)
Marcus von Hausen (Managing Partner)
Annika Kaltenthaler (Brand Design)
Nicole Hector (Brand Strategy)
Alexander Fackler (Design Director)
Caroline Gouy (Project Management)
Claudia Less (Design)

Andreas Wannerstedt (Motion Design),
Kloon Production AB

→ Designer profile on page 639
→ Clip online

Red Dot: Best of the Best

Bro&Tips

[Website]

Bro&Tips is a Korean skincare range developed exclusively for men. The range caters to male consumers, who in general are not much concerned about skincare, with easy-to-use all-in-one products. The message featuring on the website reads "live a half-hearted life", which conveys a sense of carefree coolness in a credible manner. The brand name Bro&Tips is made up of "bro" for brothers – and refers to the close, almost intimate relationship between them – and "tips" in the sense of practical advice that friends and brothers give each other. The individual products have names such as "Never Oily", "Never Dry" or "Super Natural" for the individual skin types and are packaged in simply designed tubes featuring humorous illustrations. The website appeals to the target group of casual, trendy young men, who want to have fun, with a combination of easy-to-like cartoons, bold typography and animated illustrations, conveying information such as on ingredients and ways of application in a clear and immediately-to-find manner.

Statement by the jury
This website for men-only skincare products impresses with its quirky approach with which it addresses the target group of the young male generation. The entire conception of how copy, imagery and – in the animations – even rhythm work together has been implemented in an unusual yet highly consistent, loud and gaudy manner. The distinctive design is simple, easy-to-recognise and highly functional.

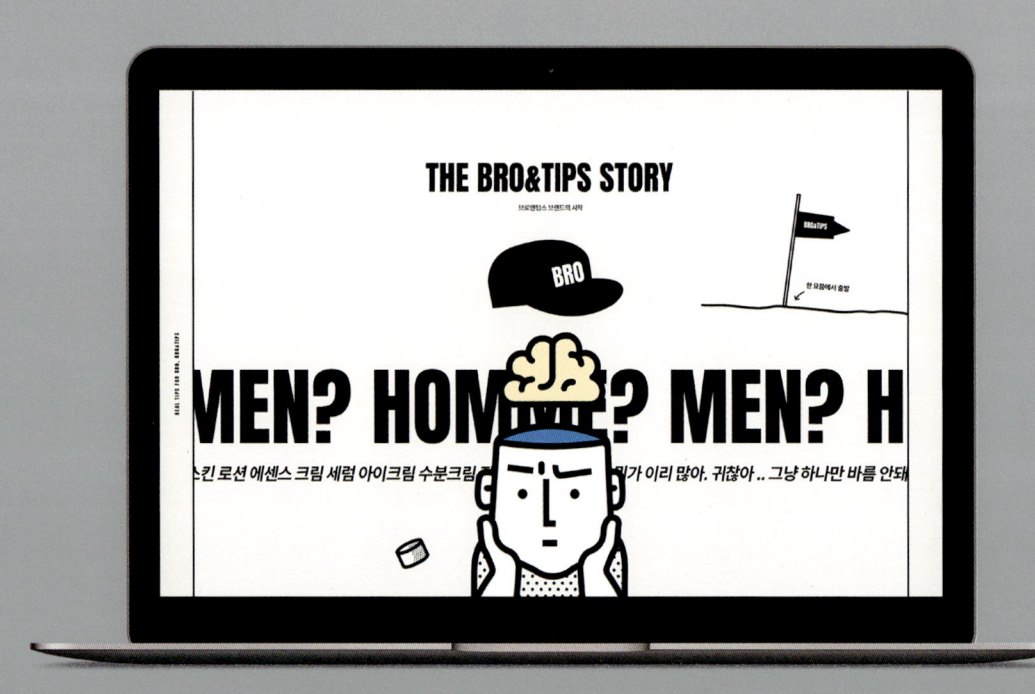

Client
Amorepacific
Seoul, South Korea

Design
Amorepacific
Seoul, South Korea

Project Team
Amorepacific:
Seokhoon Choi
Kanghwan Jeon (Web Design)
Dooyeon Kim (Art Direction)
Sangwoo Shin (Photography)

Studio-JT:
Seungoh Yang (Project Management)
Dawon Jung (Web Design)
Jisoo Lee (Web Design)
Nicolas Chauvet (Programming)

→ Designer profile on page 571

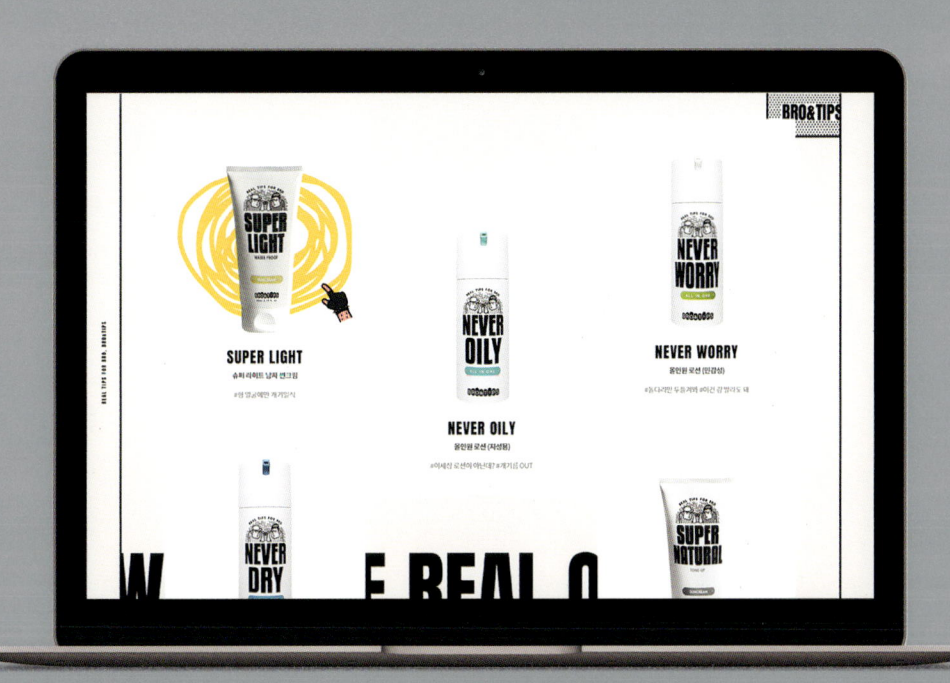

Red Dot: Best of the Best

Klim Type Foundry
[Website]

The website of Klim Type Foundry, a type foundry and design office in New Zealand, underwent a complete redesign with the aim of placing the customers and designers centre stage. They are invited to browse the huge variety of different typefaces for use across physical and digital applications and to choose the ones that are right for them. An integral part of the new website is Söhne, a collection of new typefaces described as "the memory of Akzidenz-Grotesk framed through the reality of Helvetica". The relaunched site is an ambitious combination of speed, functionality and elegance, which is expressed, for example, in extraordinary animations of individual letters. Structured around responsive and variable layouts, the site is based on classic Swiss design principles embedded in CSS grids. The type specimen generation is randomised and based on a set of defined rules for how type should be displayed.

Statement by the jury
The concept of this new website impresses with a powerful and self-reliant design including animations that are innovative in this context. Despite all the sophistication, the site offers a practical user interface with a clear and self-explanatory navigation. The aim of placing the designer as customer at the centre of the browsing and buying experience has thus been implemented and fulfilled to outstanding effect.

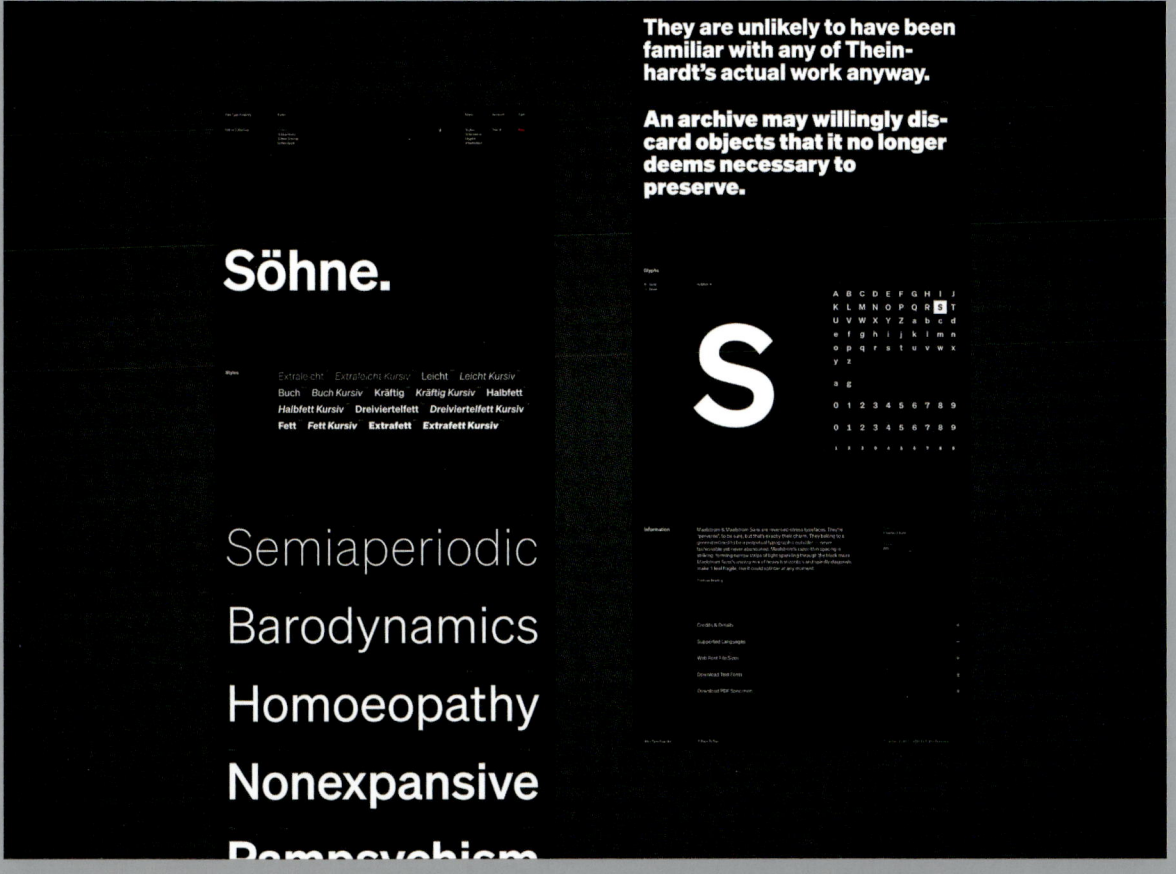

Apps	Interface & User Experience Design	Spatial Communication	Red Dot: Junior Award	Designer Profiles	Jury Portraits	Index
206	236	336	426	564	642	668

Client
Klim Type Foundry
Wellington, New Zealand

Design
Klim Type Foundry
Wellington, New Zealand
Springload
Wellington, New Zealand

Project Team
Klim Type Foundry:
Kris Sowersby (Creative Direction)
Jess Sowersby (Head of Marketing)

Springload:
Dan Newman (Creative Direction)
Zak Brown (Web Design)
Mitch Ryan (Programming)
Peter Dekkers (Programming)

→ Designer profiles on pages 601, 624

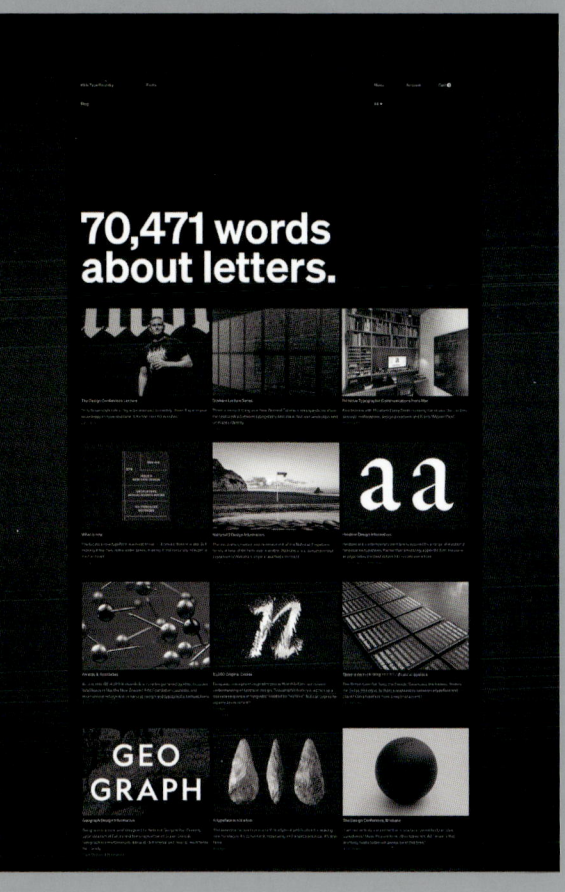

Publishing & Print Media	Posters	Typography	Illustrations	Sound Design	Film & Animation	Online
4	64	92	116	126	138	172

Samsung Clinician Dashboard

[Digital Innovation]

Client
Samsung Research America
Mountain View, CA, USA

Design
Samsung Research America
Mountain View, CA, USA

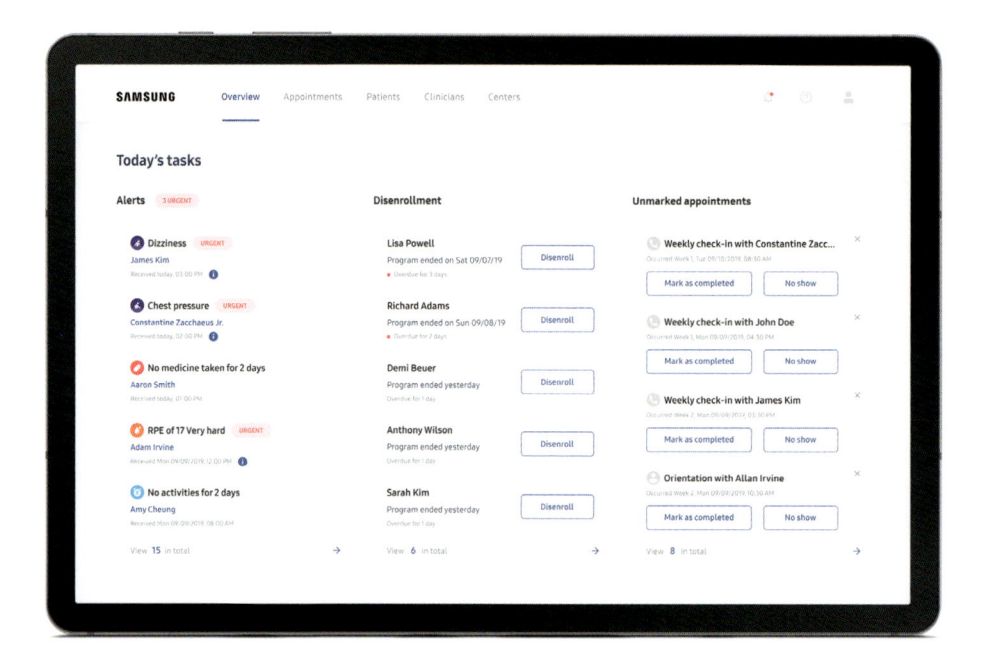

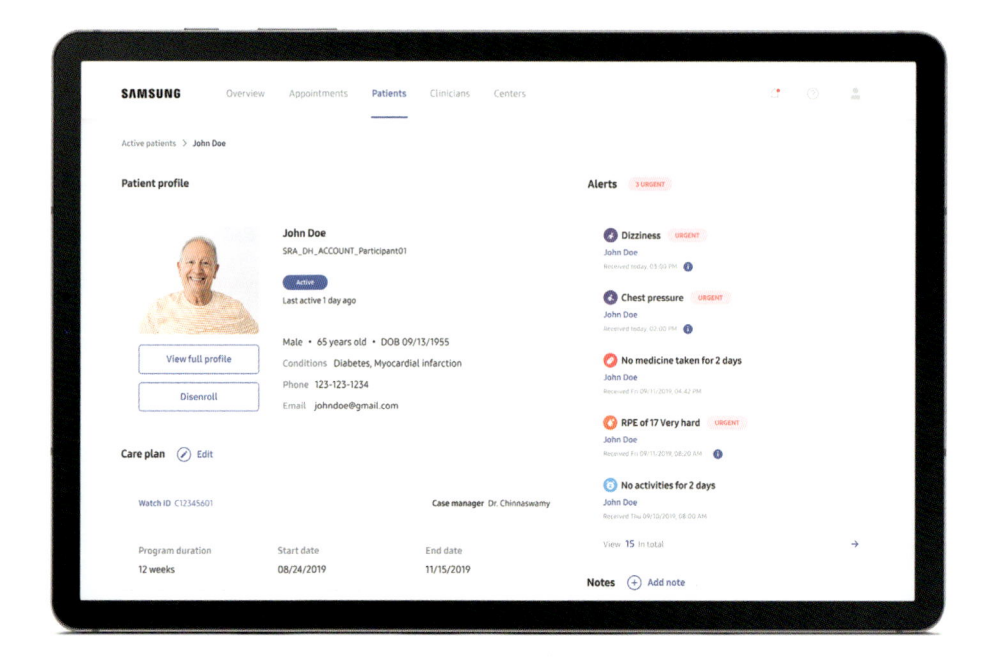

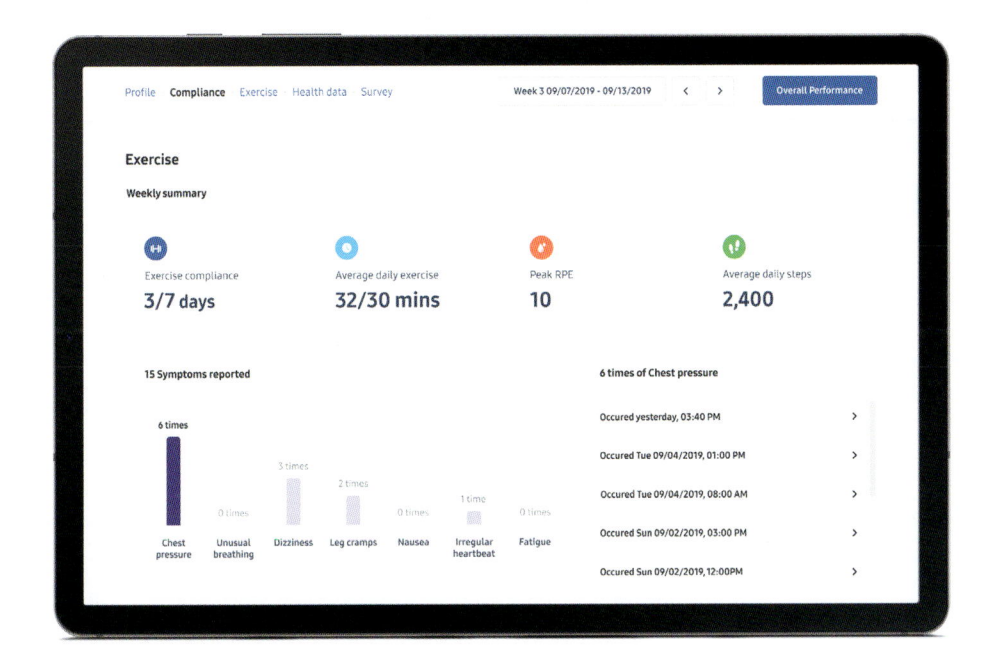

The Samsung Clinician Dashboard is an all-in-one portal for remote patient monitoring. It collects real-time data from patients' mobile and wearable devices and displays it through an intuitive interface that can be implemented in different hospital outpatient and rehabilitation programmes. Its integrated tools and analytics help clinicians easily tackle their administrative tasks and keep up with the progress of their outpatients. They can remotely monitor their recovery, assign new exercise goals and thus more easily organise and prioritise their day. It enables a stronger focus on patient care.

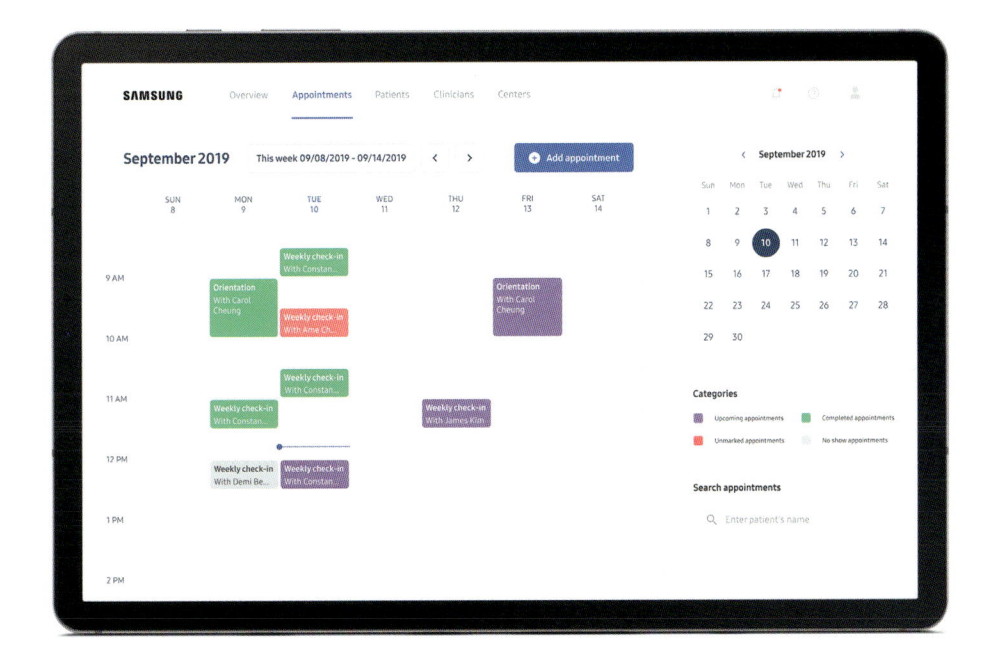

Publishing & Print Media	Posters	Typography	Illustrations	Sound Design	Film & Animation	Online
4	64	92	116	126	138	172

Steam Birdseye
[Web-Based Interactive Visualisation Tool]

In Abu Dhabi, the Department of Municipalities and Transport operates and maintains the transport sector. It plans and develops new infrastructure projects by using advanced modelling tools in order to understand the current and projected future state of the transport sector. However, the enormous volume and complexity of data from different sources have made it difficult to combine, analyse or share it with stakeholders and decision makers. Steam Birdseye has been developed as an interactive tool that allows one to easily explore and visualise complex data sets and predictive models in a consistent, visually appealing form.

Client
Department of Municipalities and Transport
Abu Dhabi, United Arab Emirates

Design
Pixonal
Dubai, United Arab Emirates
CLEVER°FRANKE
Utrecht, Netherlands

Project Team
Transpo Group (Technical Consultant)

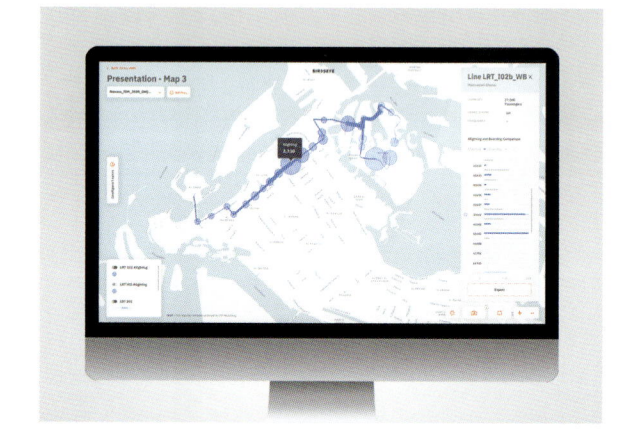

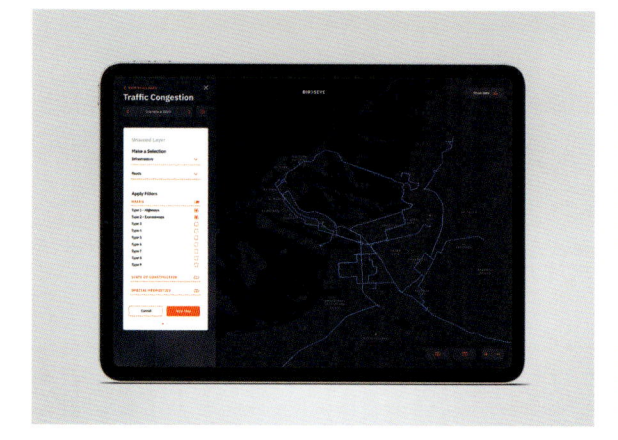

188

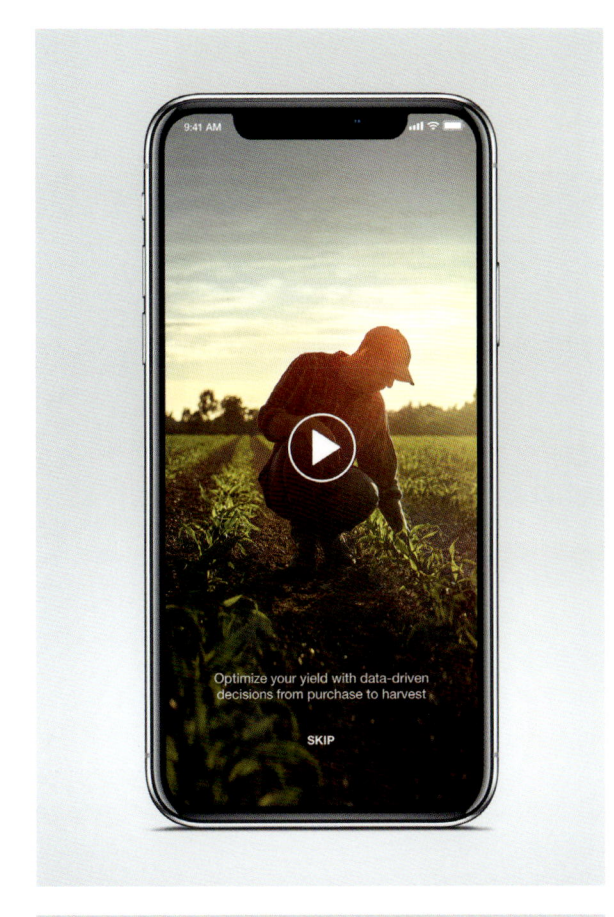

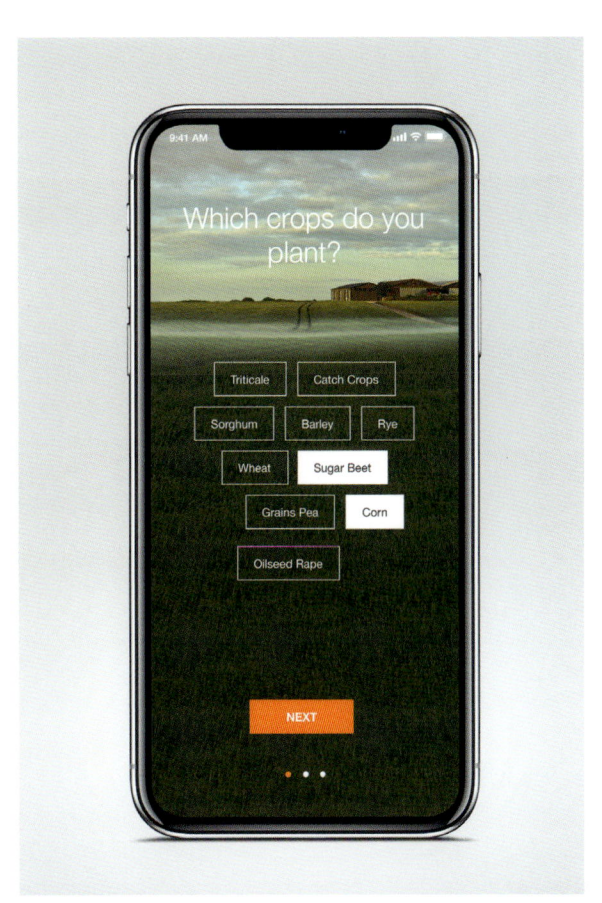

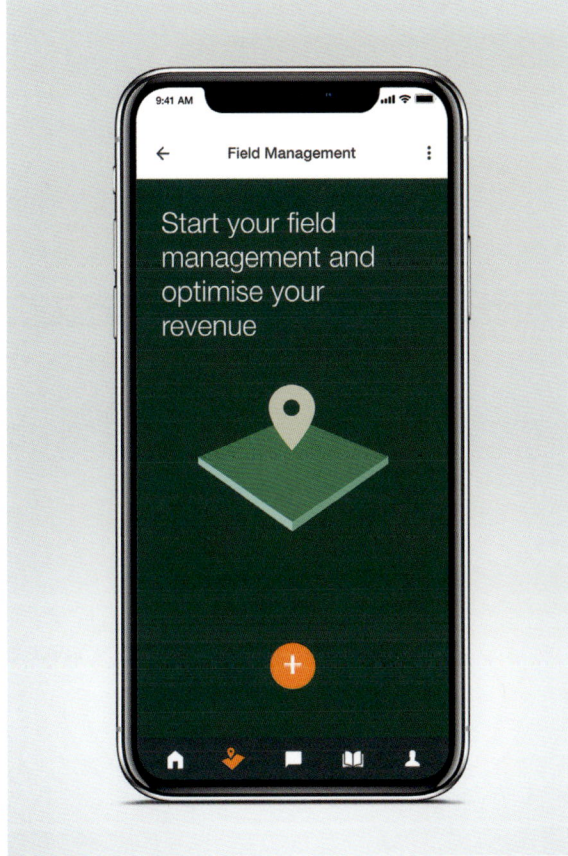

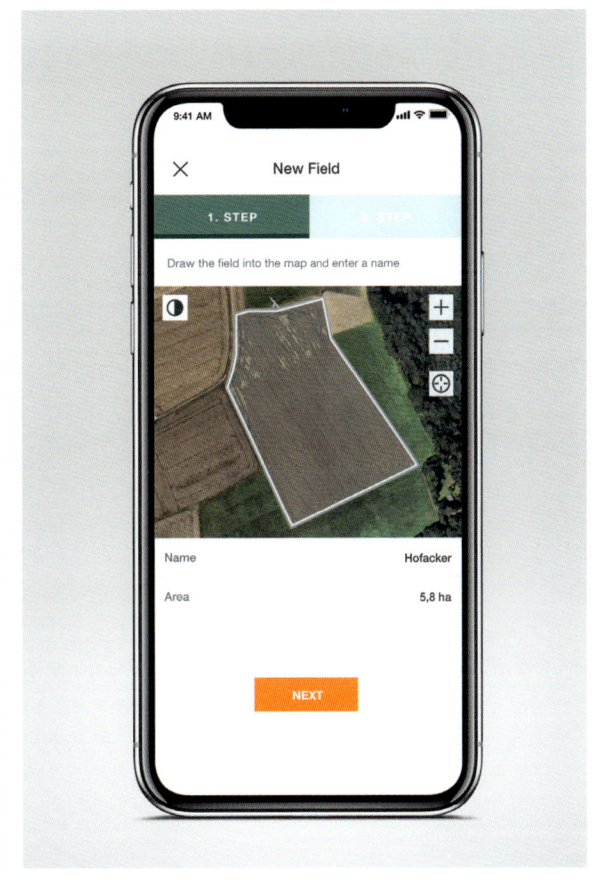

Apps	Interface & User Experience Design	Spatial Communication	Red Dot: Junior Award	Designer Profiles	Jury Portraits	Index
206	236	336	426	564	642	668

myKWS

[Customer Service Platform]

Since feeding the world in a sustainable manner has become a major challenge, this one-stop service platform addresses farmers across the globe. It is free to use and provides expert advice as well as more than 20 tools for data-driven decision-making. The map-based field dashboard enables farmers to easily optimise their acreage, from seed selection to harvest and beyond. High-tech apps use satellite imagery to monitor fields from space, to determine the best harvest time and to provide essential data across the season. Thus, farmers are assisted in increasing their harvest yield without using chemicals.

Client
KWS SAAT SE & Co. KGaA
Einbeck, Germany

Design
chilli mind Design Team
Kassel, Germany

Project Team
SUTSCHE (Digital Consulting)
comspace GmbH & Co. KG (Programming)
newcubator GmbH (Programming)
hmmh multimediahaus AG
(Programming)

Publishing & Print Media	Posters	Typography	Illustrations	Sound Design	Film & Animation	Online
4	64	92	116	126	138	172

Siemens Predictive Analytics

[Digital Innovation]

SiePA is a predictive analytics system that helps customers to turn collected plant data into valuable insights. Based on the in-depth analysis of historical data via integrated AI, it helps predict potential failures of equipment and processes, identify root causes, search for valuable maintenance experience and suggest preventive measures before the real failures happen. The system integrates plant data monitoring, condition prediction and smart diagnosis, as well as a series of visual analysis tools, in order to simplify the professional data analysis procedure in the form of intuitive and user-friendly tasks.

Client
Siemens
Shanghai, China

Design
Siemens AG/Siemens Ltd.
Digital Enterprise Lab (DE-L),
Process Automation,
Digital Industry
Shanghai, China

Project Team
Dr. Wu Wenchao (Product Owner)
Que Yilin (UX Designer)
Li Tian (Developer)
Wang Yin (Developer)
Tang Qi (Technical Support)
Tian Pengwei (Technical Support)
Monica Florentina Hildinger
(Business Owner)
Yue Sheng (Business Owner)
Dr. Yao Jun (Supervising Management)
Steffen Wagner
(Supervising Management)

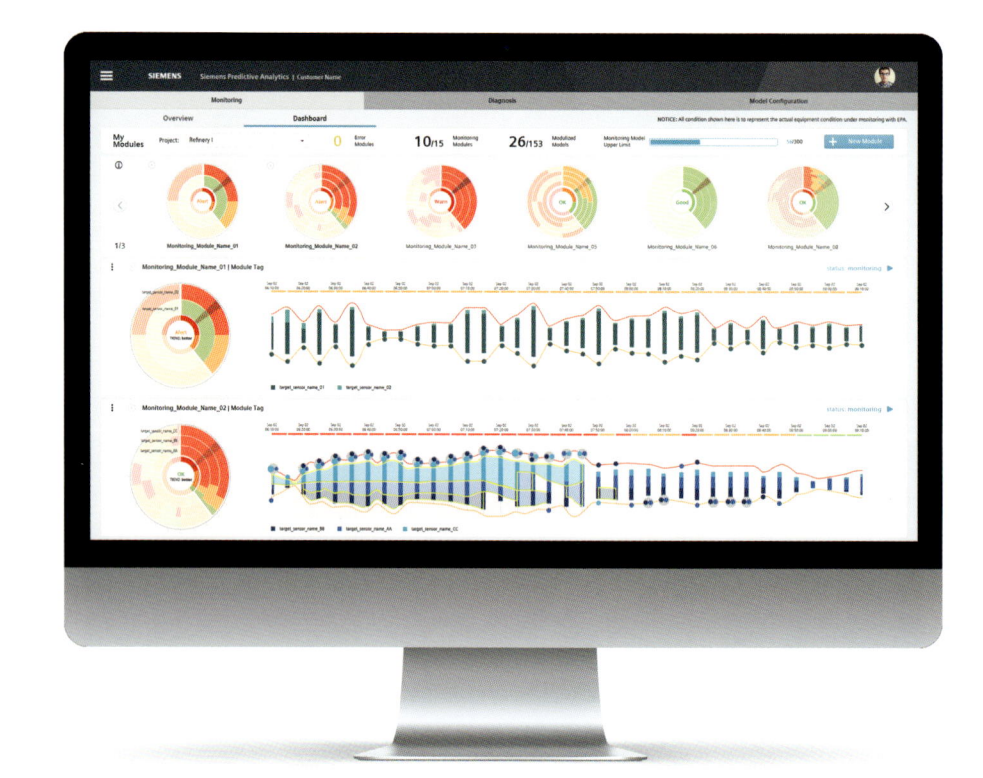

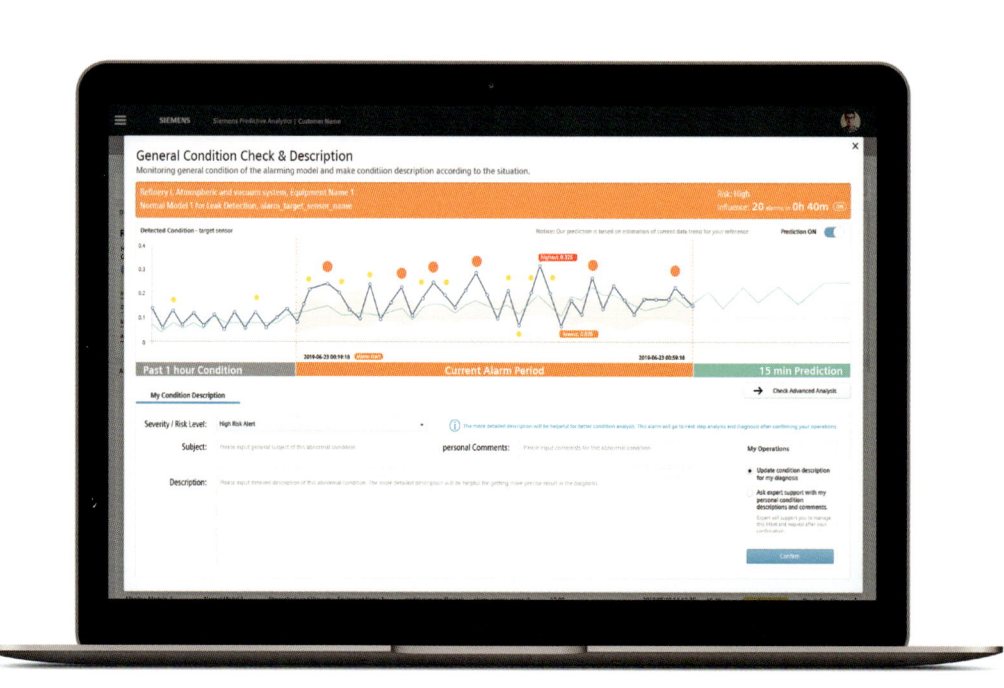

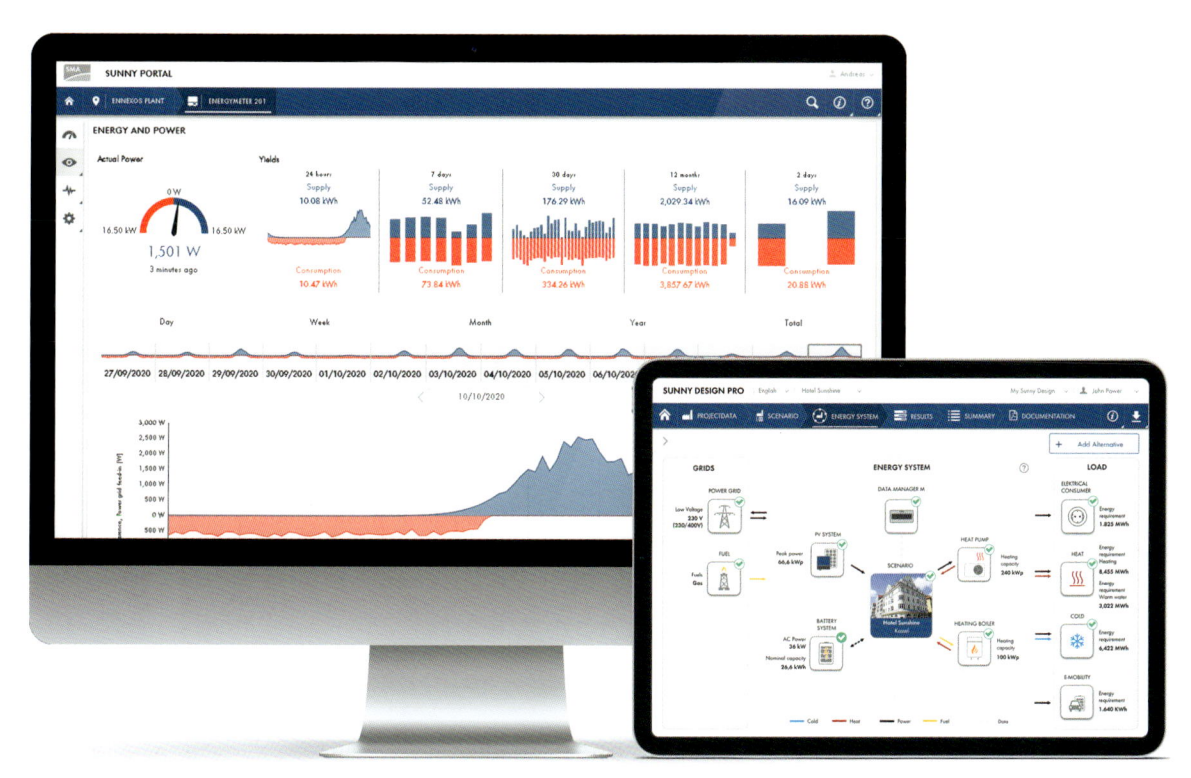

ennexOS

[Online Platform]

This cross-sector portal platform supports the planning, set-up and operation of energy systems with complex asset hierarchies. As software for commercial and private energy consumers, it optimises the energy management of photovoltaics, battery storage, heat pumps, boilers and combined heat and power plants. Offering clear and fast user flows through all system hierarchies, such as portfolios, plant groups, plants, units and devices, as well as efficient analysis dashboards, UX-monitoring functions and customised modules, it makes for a new dimension of intelligent energy management.

Client
SMA Solar Technology AG
Niestetal, Germany

Design
chilli mind Design Team
Kassel, Germany

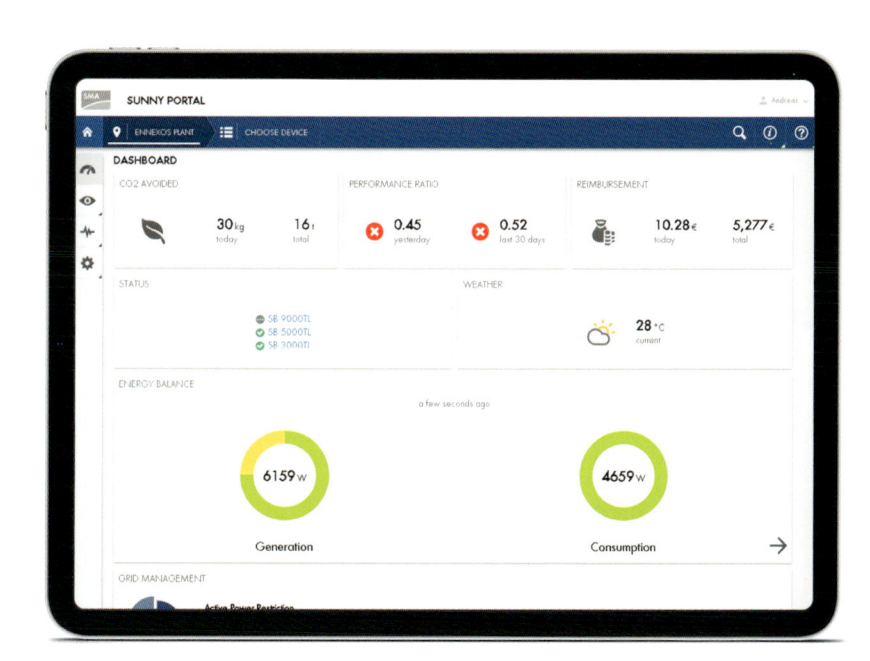

Publishing & Print Media	Posters	Typography	Illustrations	Sound Design	Film & Animation	Online
4	64	92	116	126	138	172

Mercedes-Benz Buses Online

[Website]

The aim of this website is to guide potential customers through the purchase initiation process. Serving as a central source for prospective buyers to gain rapid access to relevant information, it offers the possibility of downloading product and technology brochures in PDF format to make the search for information fast and easy. Combining nationally and internationally relevant content and updates from the Mercedes-Benz Bus World with appealing visuals, a clear structure and interactive components, the website is specially tailored to the needs of the target group and facilitates a comprehensive user experience.

Client
EvoBus GmbH
Stuttgart, Germany

Design
mensemedia Gesellschaft für
Neue Medien mbH
Düsseldorf, Germany

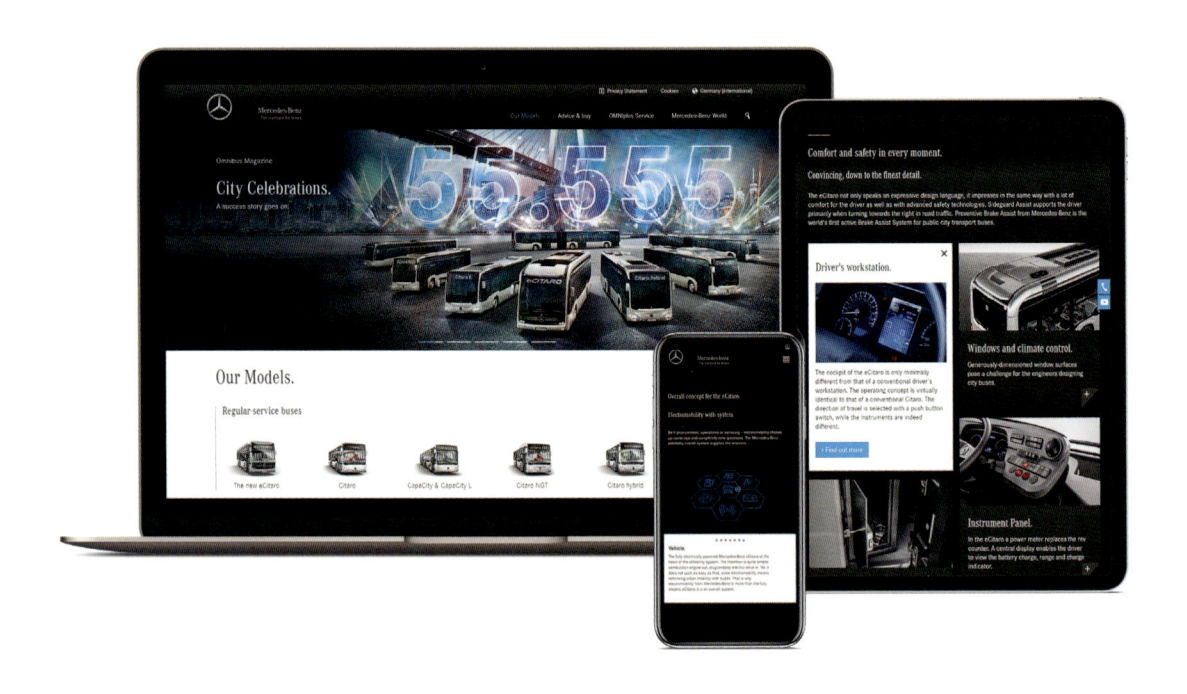

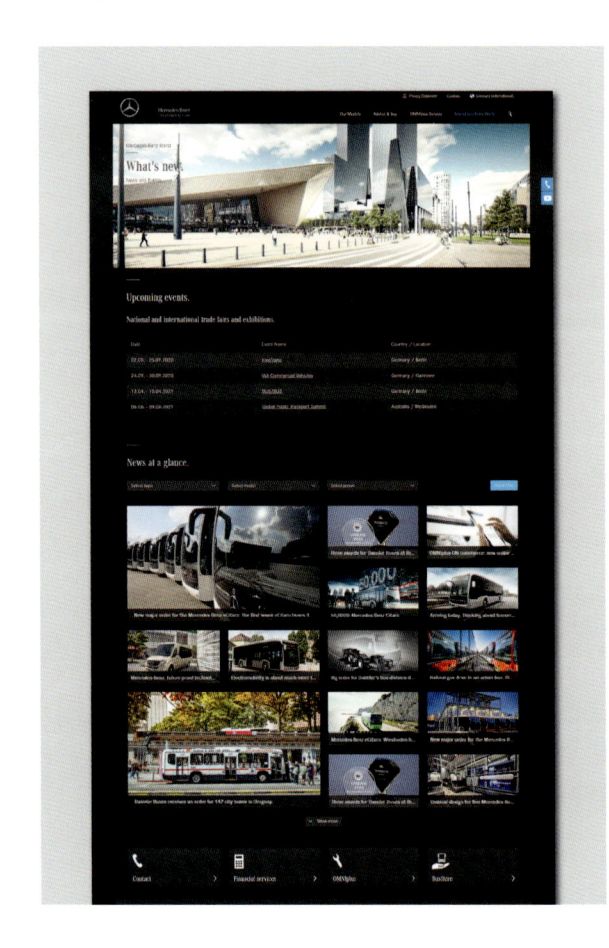

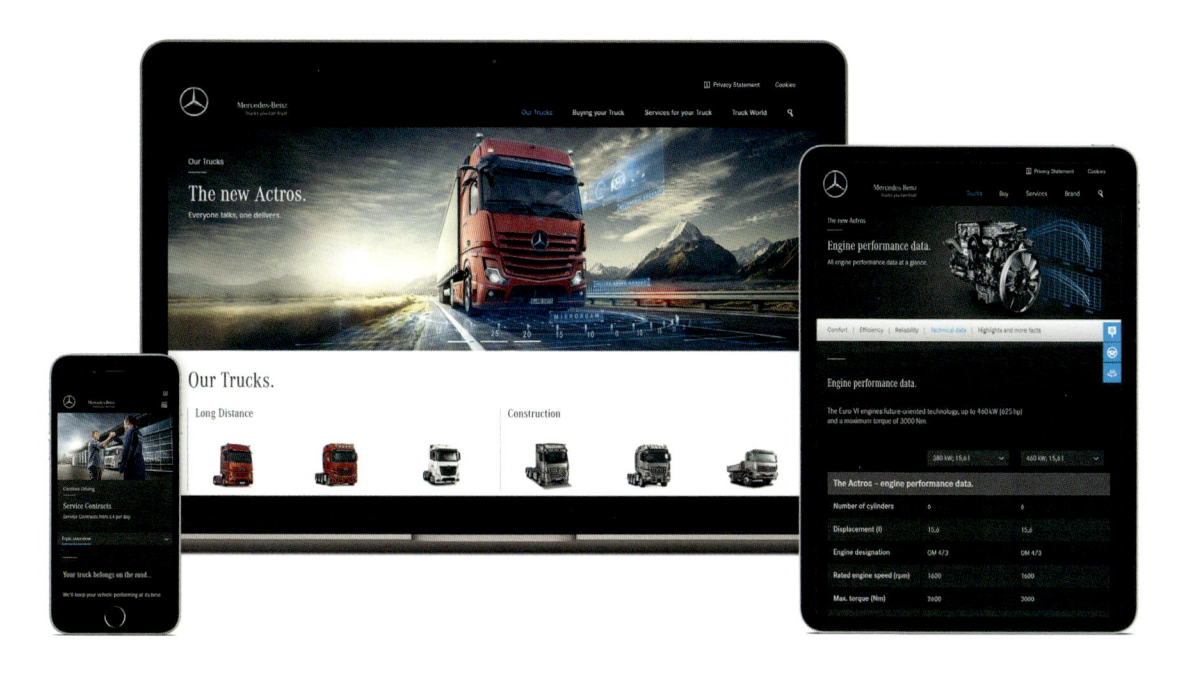

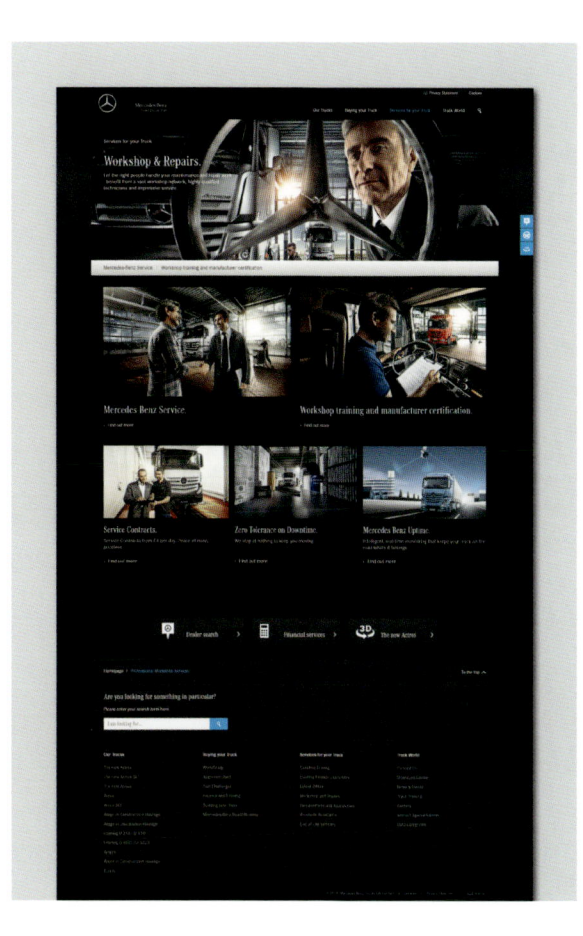

Apps	Interface & User Experience Design	Spatial Communication	Red Dot: Junior Award	Designer Profiles	Jury Portraits	Index
206	236	336	426	564	642	668

Mercedes-Benz Trucks Online

[Website]

The new corporate website of Mercedes-Benz Trucks constitutes a direct communication channel to the target and interest group. Its content primarily aimed at purchasing decision-makers. Following the core mission to fully accompany prospective customers through the entire purchasing process, clear navigation and well-structured content make it possible to intuitively find all relevant information. Together with insight into the multifaceted brand world with its various offers and extras, the website presents a comprehensive picture of the truck division and a sustainable online experience.

Client
Daimler Truck AG
Stuttgart, Germany

Design
mensemedia Gesellschaft für Neue Medien mbH
Düsseldorf, Germany

Publishing & Print Media	Posters	Typography	Illustrations	Sound Design	Film & Animation	Online
4	64	92	116	126	138	172

iONE360

[Online Configurator]

iONE360 is a visual product configurator suited to various industries, such as the furniture industry. It can handle elaborate, customisable products including complex business rules and pricing. Users can generate configurations themselves and add 2D and 3D visuals, which are then translated to an easy, guided selling process that can be embedded in other applications. Companies are able to offer their customisable products on all channels consistently, thus providing 3D product configuration for web shops, AR, VR and even a room planner. Consumers can customise complex products and view them before making expensive purchases.

Client
Colijn IT
Goes, Netherlands

Design
Colijn IT
Goes, Netherlands

Project Team
Colijn IT:
Patrick van Keulen (Programming)
Jan Kruijt (Programming)
Matthijs Oomkens (Programming)
Nico Zwanenburg (Programming)
Ralf Eversen (Programming)
Dev Team (Programming)

Karel Klima (Programming), Salsita

→ Clip online

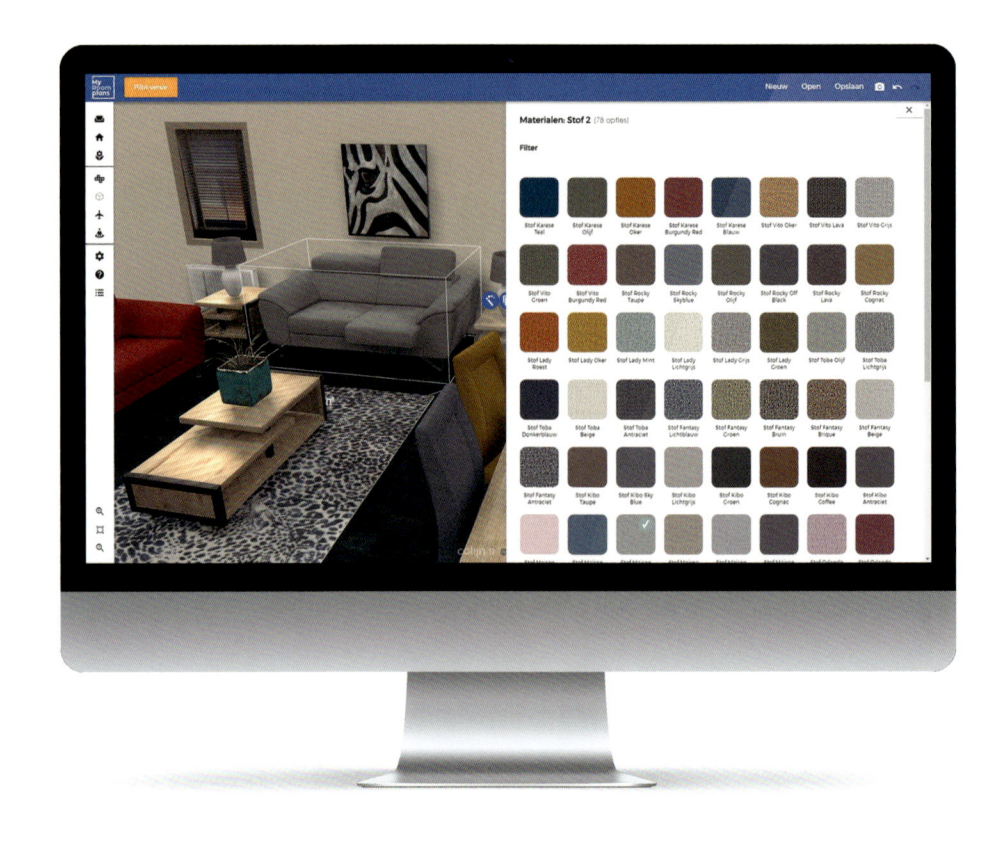

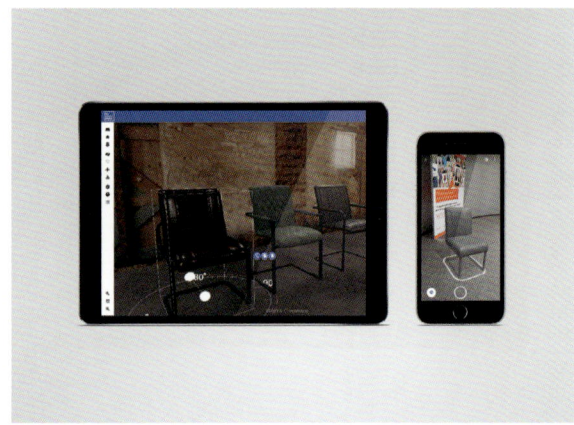

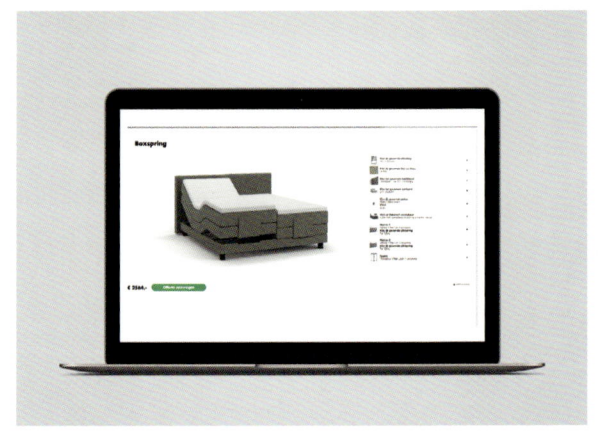

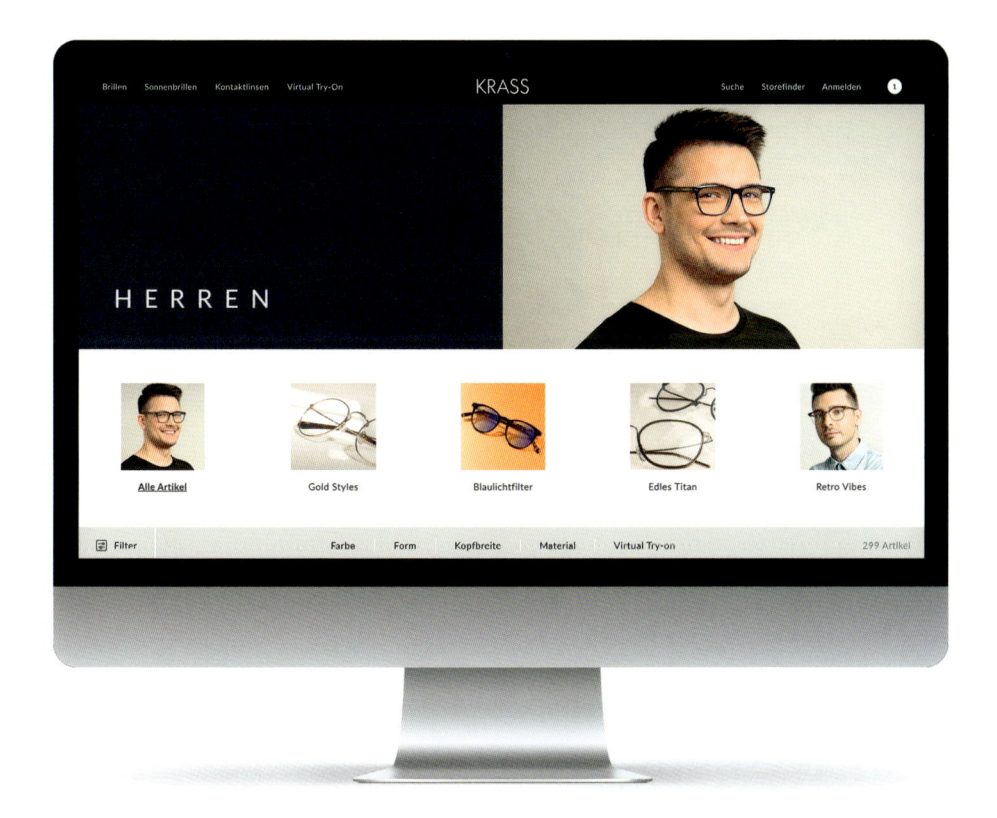

Krass Optik

[Online Shop]

Considering that selling spectacles online faces different challenges than customer service offline does, the relaunch of the e-commerce site of the German eyewear brand focused on a resharpening of the online brand appearance, an intuitive customer journey, an exciting user experience and a clear communication of medical details. The web shop represents the product range on a large scale and digitalises the consulting competence of the company. Each customer can try on, customise and order his or her individual glasses via "virtual try-on" and the "glasses configurator" on the website.

Client
Krass Optik
Dornach-Aschheim, Germany

Design
Y1 Digital AG
Munich, Germany

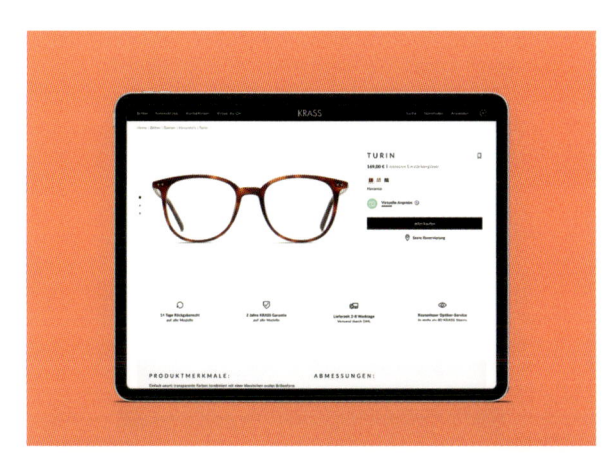

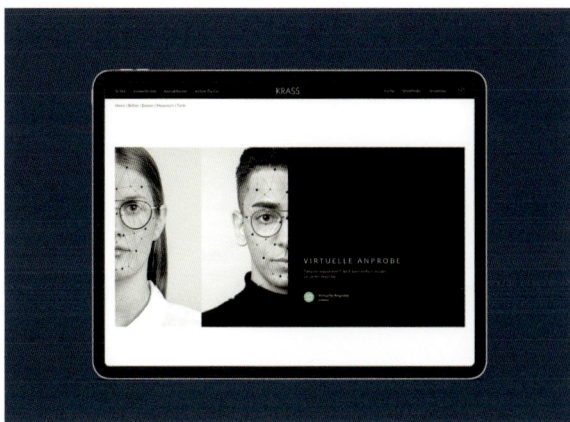

Publishing & Print Media	Posters	Typography	Illustrations	Sound Design	Film & Animation	Online
4	64	92	116	126	138	172

Fillvoid
[Website]

The name of this body-care brand is made up of the compound words "fill" and "void", representing a moment focused entirely on its own identity and a sensitive stimulus embracing the whole body. To effectively represent this moment, and the brand's message, the website uses enveloping music and large photos, as well as different types of videos and blur transition effects. Based on a design language inspired by Henri Cartier-Bresson's photobook "The Decisive Moment", it aims to help visitors enjoy and explore the different concepts of each product line in an emotionally appealing manner.

Client
Amorepacific
Seoul, South Korea

Design
Amorepacific
Seoul, South Korea

Project Team
Amorepacific:
Sangkyung Ryu
Kanghwan Jeon (Web Design)
Dooyeon Kim (Photography)

Studio-JT:
Mijin Lee (Project Management)
Dawon Jung (Web Design)
Yujin Song (Web Design)
Minseo Kim (Programming)
Youngil Lee (Programming)

→ Designer profile on page 571

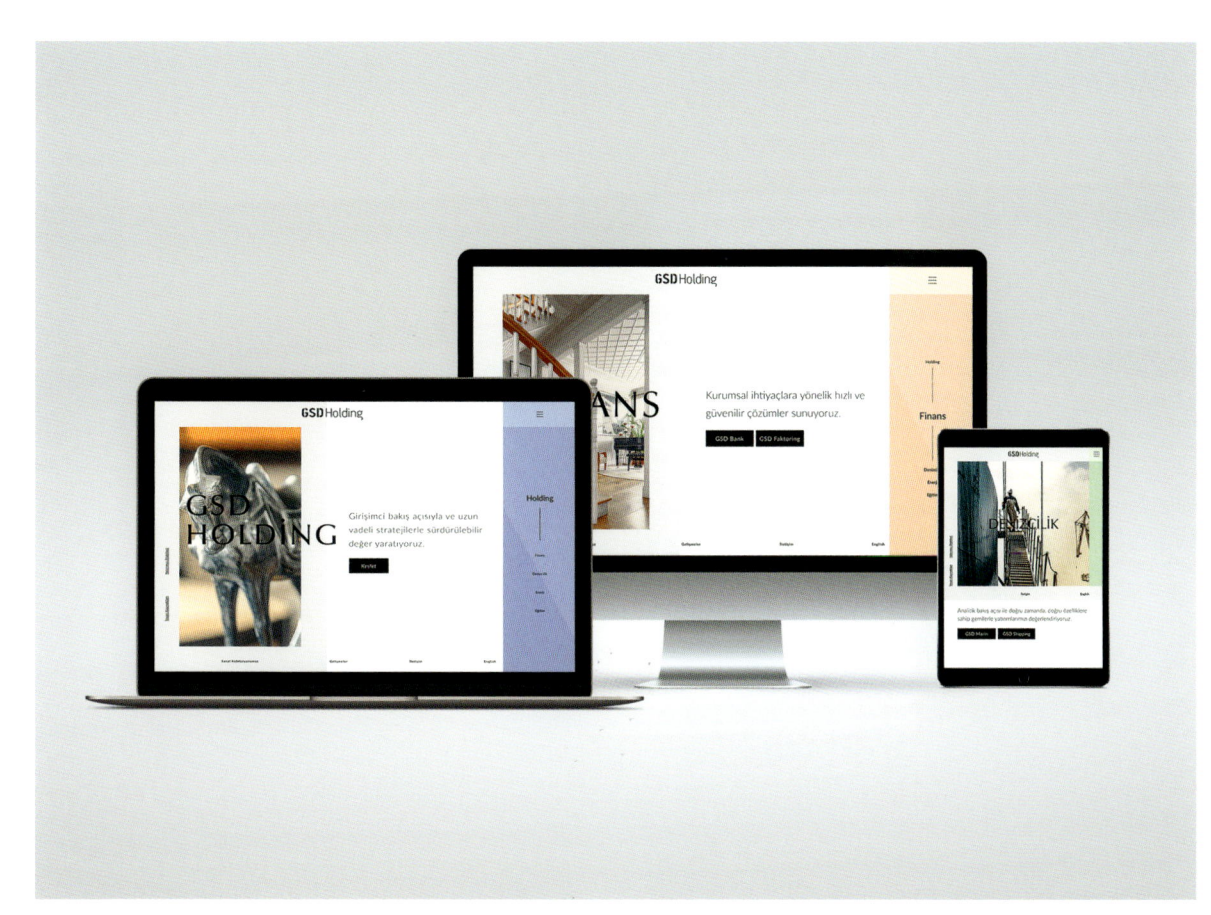

GSD Holding

[Website Redesign]

GSD Holding is a Turkey-based, publicly traded holding company engaged in financial services, maritime shipping, and the energy and education sectors. By reflecting on the story of the long-standing company culture, its website has been redesigned to present the various sectors of the company, as well as their activities and philosophy, with visual integrity. A clear and minimal design approach has resulted in a sorted overview, which makes all brief information easily accessible. Photography is used as an essential element to reflect the visual culture of the company as a means of brand communication.

Client
GSD Holding
Istanbul, Turkey

Design
Design In Situ
Istanbul, Turkey

Project Team
Design In Situ:
Nagehan Kurali Alan (Creative Direction)
Selin Oezcelik Mörth (Creative Direction)
Murat Durusoy (Photography)

InsideOut (Editorial)
Martian Digital (Programming)

→ Designer profile on page 584

Publishing & Print Media	Posters	Typography	Illustrations	Sound Design	Film & Animation	Online
4	64	92	116	126	138	172

PlusX
[Website]

Witty details such as dynamic and rhythmic motions, kinetic shuffles and a dark/light mode characterise this website and aim to catch the users' attention and add to their fun. It serves as a platform for presenting the agency's design projects and experimenting with development at the same time. Users can feel the website flowing as they scroll, due to the smooth transition between the pages. The pages of individual companies are shown in a different colour each, yet at the same time the feeling of consistency within the overall website is maintained by using similar shapes for the figures presented.

Client
PlusX
Seoul, South Korea

Design
PlusX
Seoul, South Korea

Project Team
Sabum Byun (Creative Direction)
Ki Hyun Kim (Programming)
Seung Hyun Ma (Programming)
Faris Kassim (Programming)
Minji Kwon (Programming)

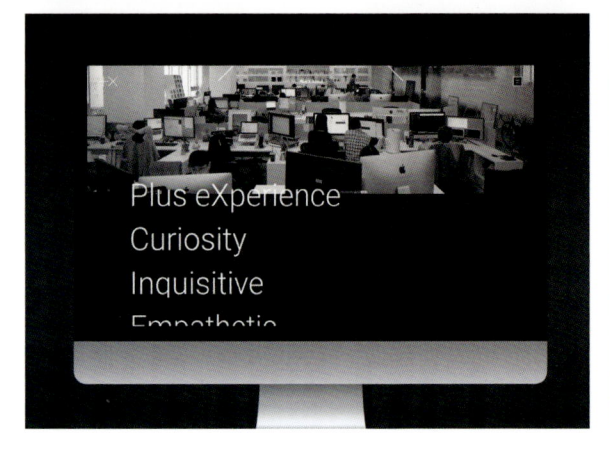

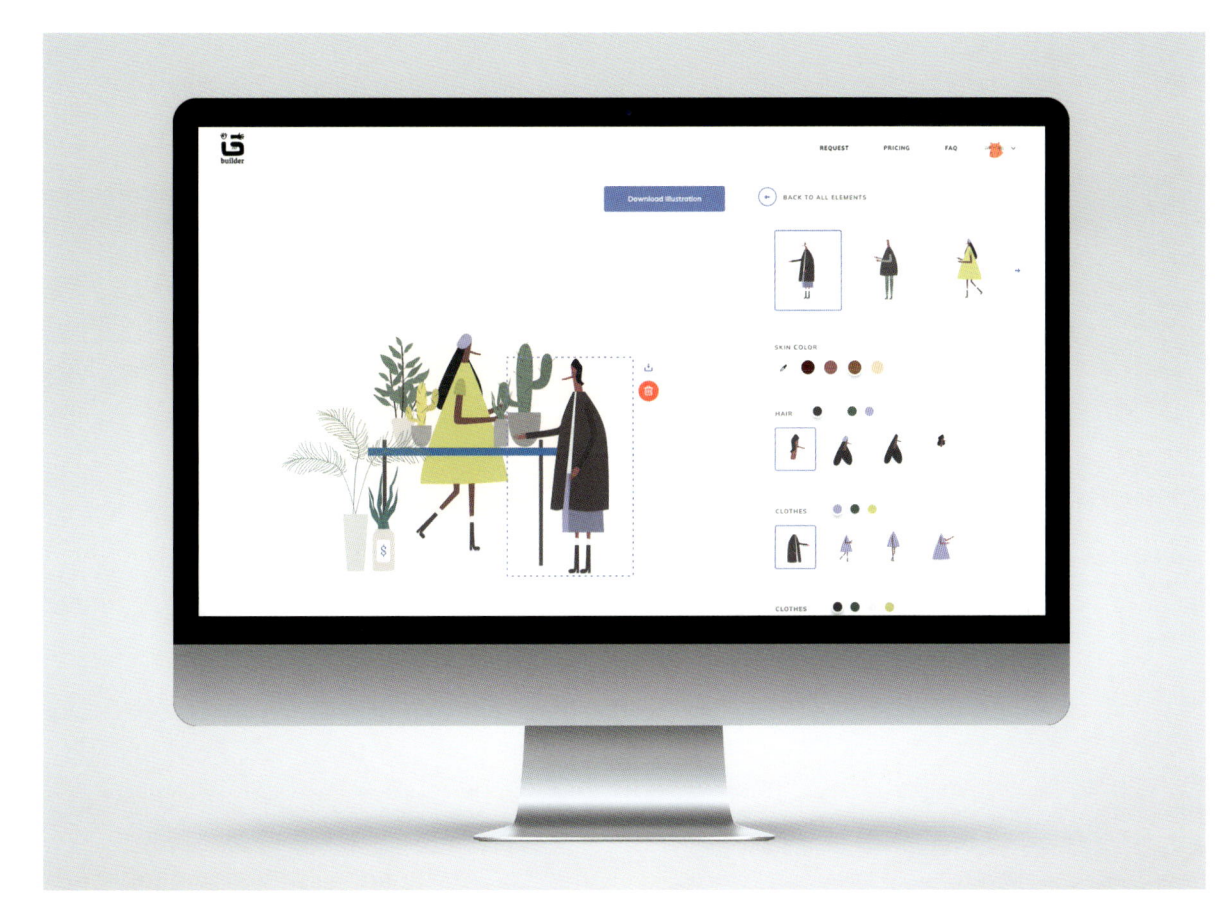

ITG.digital

[Online Platform]

ITG.digital is an online builder of illustrations, as used for websites, apps, social media posts or presentations to communicate ideas visually. It was developed with the objective of providing people with a tool to easily find and customise illustrations according to individual needs, without any special software or knowledge. ITG.digital serves as a platform that allows one to automatically create custom illustrations from predefined elements, which are available in high resolution and vector graphics (JPG, PNG, SVG). Users can edit the elements and apply specific brand colours as required.

Client
ITG.digital
Kharkiv, Ukraine

Design
Netrix Digital
Kharkiv, Ukraine

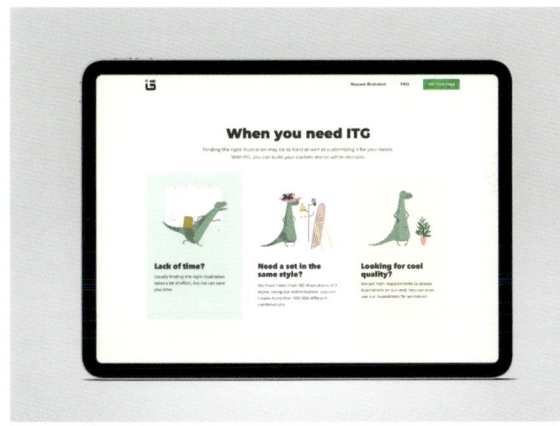

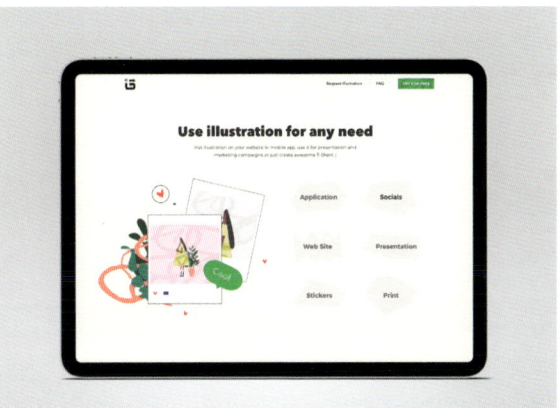

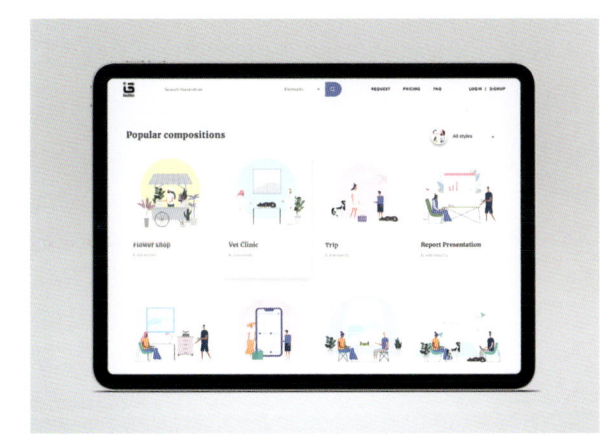

Publishing & Print Media	Posters	Typography	Illustrations	Sound Design	Film & Animation	Online
4	64	92	116	126	138	172

Human

[Corporate Website]

Human is an interaction company focused on making interactions between humans and computers a joy. The company's goal is to bring to the digital world an understanding of human-computer interactions – by making them easy, fun and innovative. The new website, as part of the company's rebranding, aims to reflect the brand values, so it needs to be engaging, bingeworthy, informative, smart and funny, all at the same time. The content was built around small stories written by the employees, with photos that have not been photoshopped, and the website was turned into a fun and engaging user experience.

Client
Human, Burza d.o.o.
Zagreb, Croatia

Design
Human, Burza d.o.o.
Zagreb, Croatia

Project Team
Vanja Bertalan (Strategic Planning)

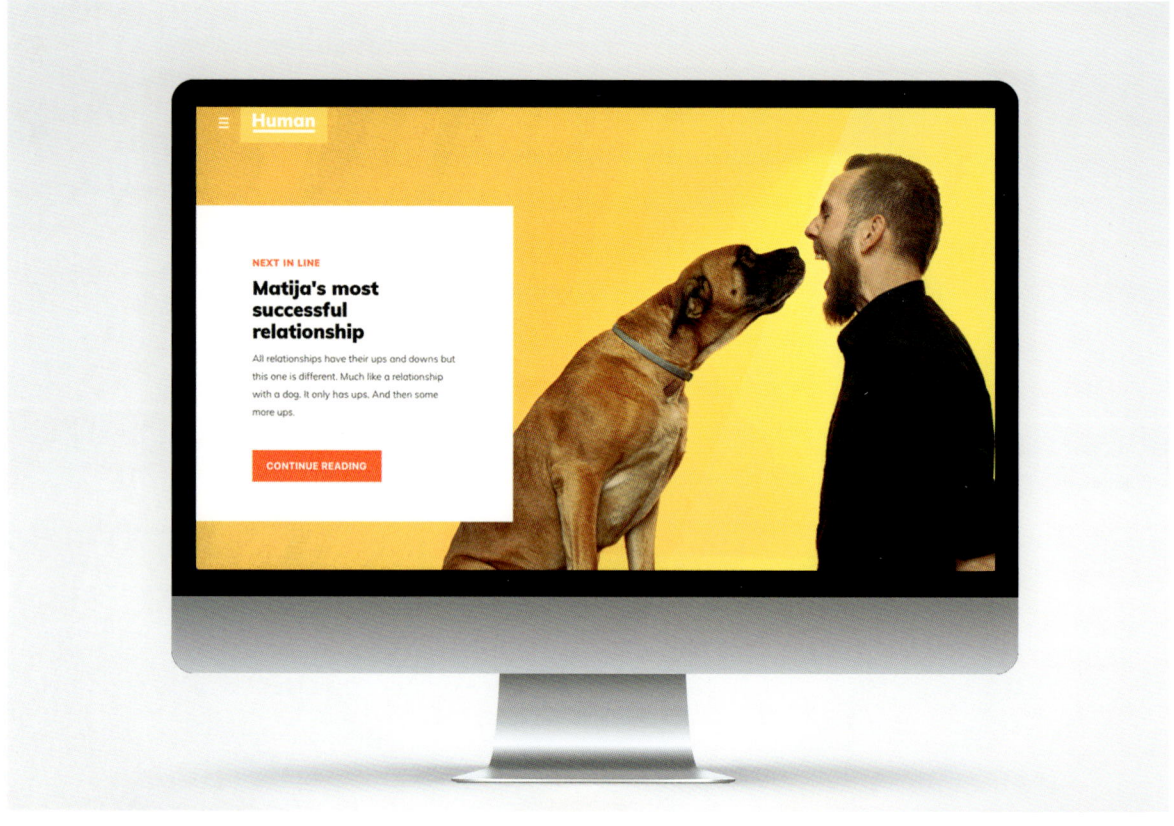

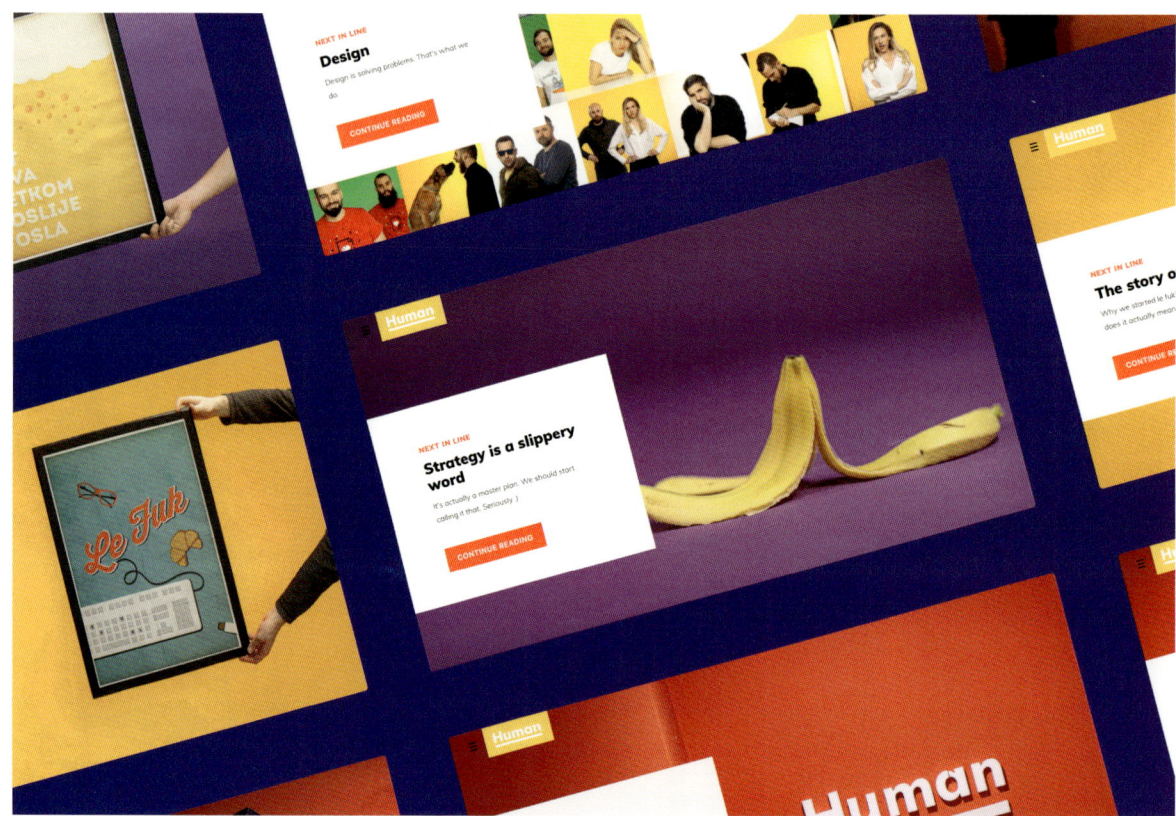

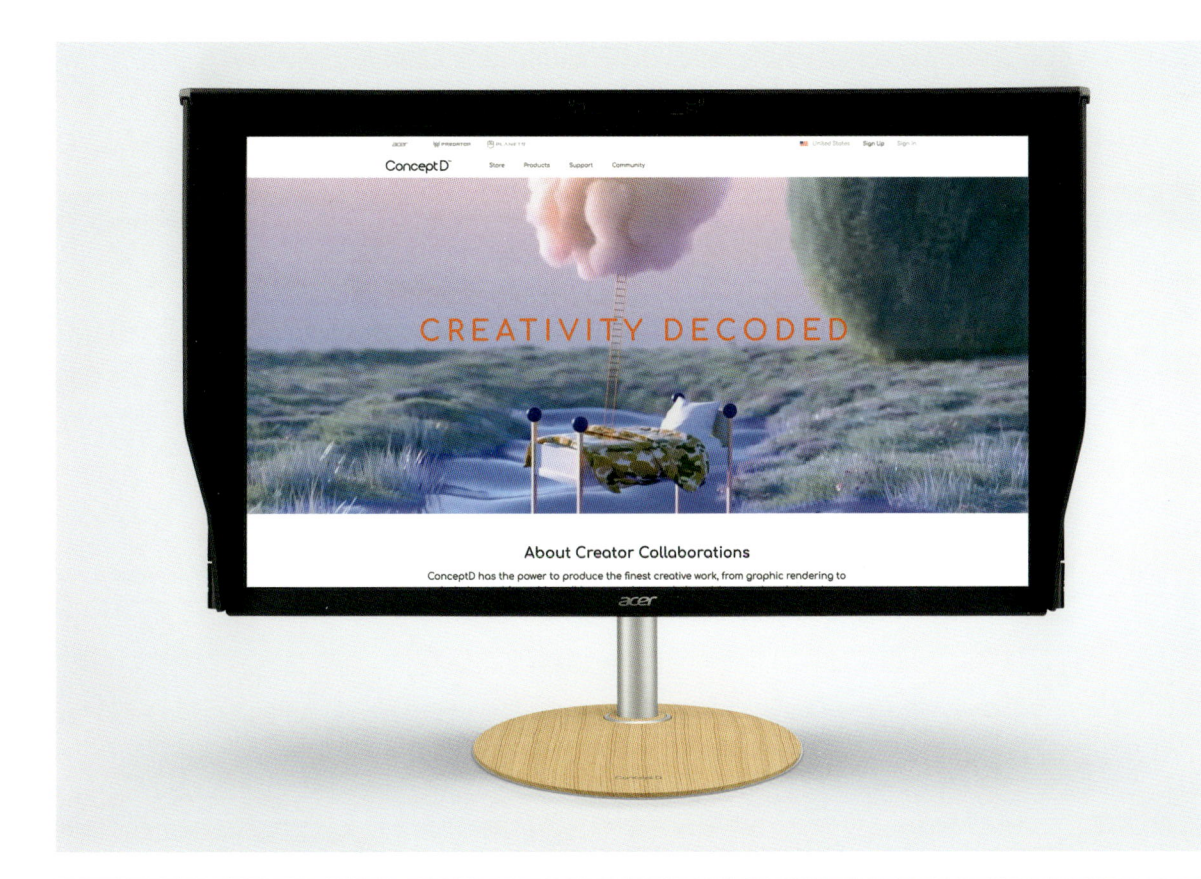

ConceptD
Creativity Decoded

[Digital Campaign]

This global campaign comprises a series of mixed-media films and strives to highlight the innate versatility and performance capability of the company's computers, showcasing them as ideal working companions for creatives and design professionals. Each episode of the series presents a finished piece by an artist or studio and has three parts: one in which the brand slogan "Let Creators Be Creators" was put into action, one presenting the production steps and the functionality of the devices involved, and one featuring a series of interviews with the creators about the creative process and hardware needs.

Client
Acer Inc.
New Taipei City, Taiwan

Design
Acer Inc.
New Taipei City, Taiwan
We Are Social
Shanghai, China

Project Team
We Are Social:
Jason Breen (Creative Director)
Nathan Baker (Group Account Director)
Kristina Knut (Associate Account Manager)

→ Designer profile on page 628
→ Clip online

Publishing & Print Media	Posters	Typography	Illustrations	Sound Design	Film & Animation	Online
4	64	92	116	126	138	172

Google x BASIC®

[E-Commerce]

Client
Google
Mountain View, CA, USA

Design
BASIC® x Google
Mountain View, CA, USA

Project Team
Strahan McMullen (Creative Direction)

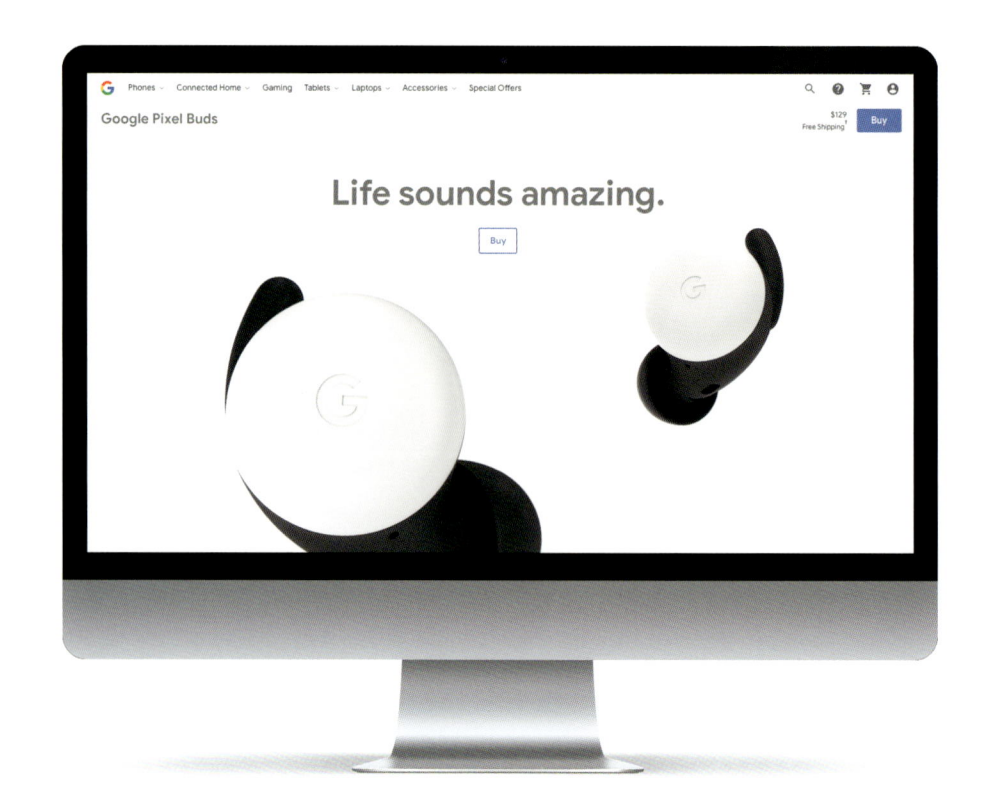

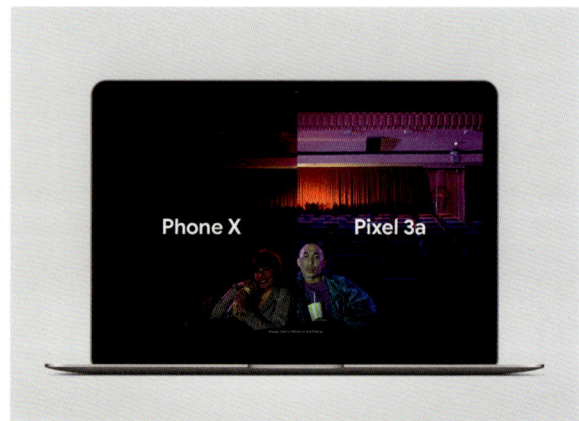

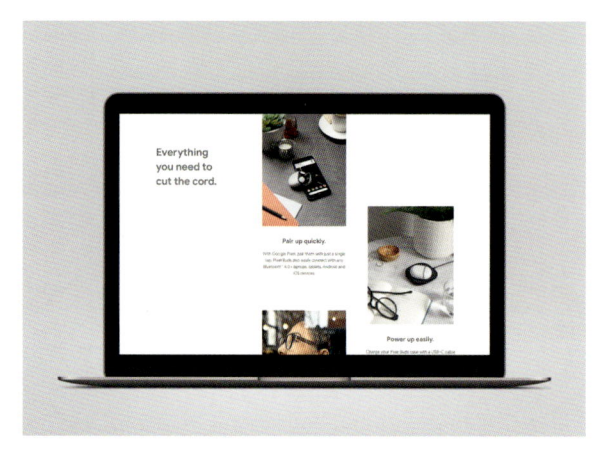

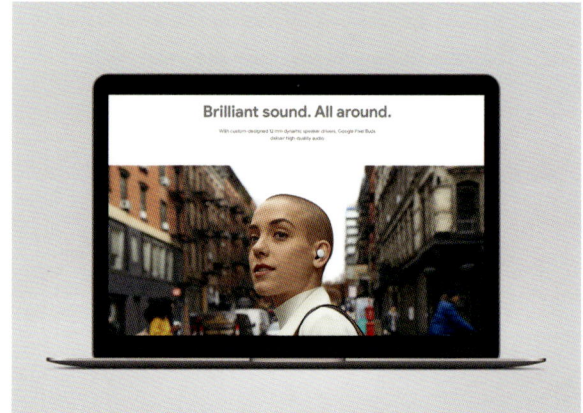

202

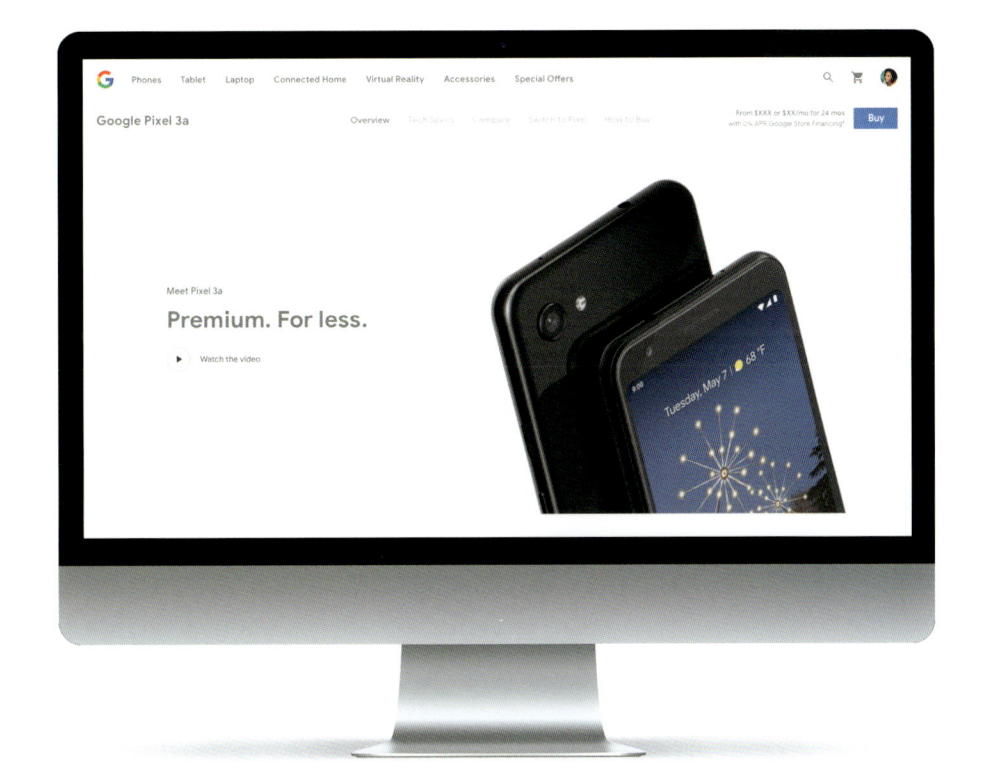

Apps	Interface & User Experience Design	Spatial Communication	Red Dot: Junior Award	Designer Profiles	Jury Portraits	Index
206	236	336	426	564	642	668

The idea behind this website was to replicate the physical shopping experience online. It enables e-commerce customers to "touch and try" products before buying them and creates more ways to interact with new devices. Users can get to know products and features through immersive, scroll-based storytelling and contextual utilities that highlight how hard- and software work together. Rich content activates product features, while motion drives engagement. Moreover, newly added functionality, including product comparisons, bundling and streamlined navigation, have enhanced shopability and increased the conversion rate.

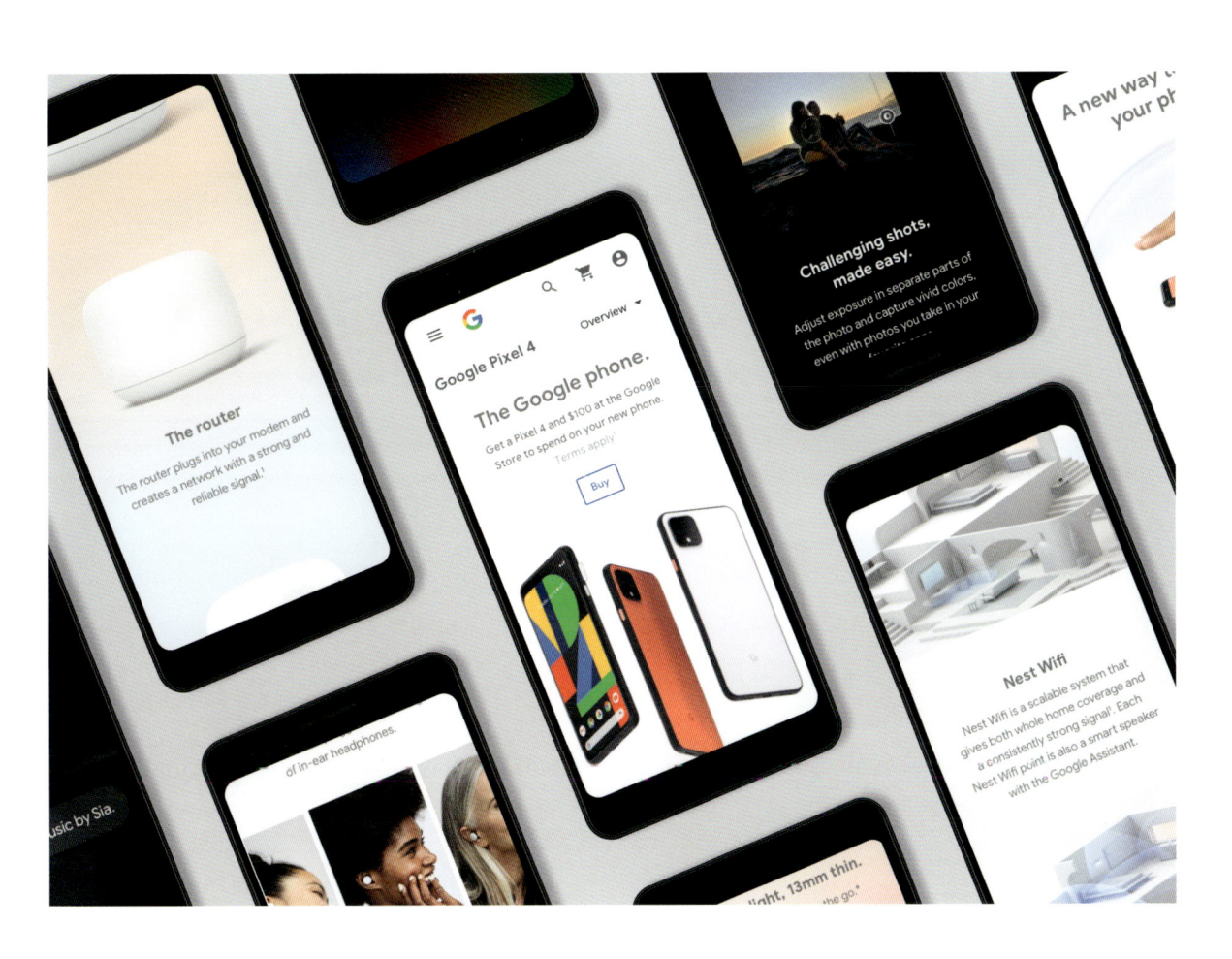

Publishing & Print Media	Posters	Typography	Illustrations	Sound Design	Film & Animation	Online
4	64	92	116	126	138	172

fromAtoB.
Travel Your Way.

[Website]

To facilitate travelling and to help people make smart travel decisions, this online travel agency, already established in Germany, Austria and Switzerland, aims to provide all available options in a transparent way, in order to give travellers freedom of choice. Whether the fastest, cheapest or most eco-friendly mode of transport is preferred, the options are shown according to individual needs and comprise everything that is essential for a safe and easy journey, door to door, including tickets for public transport and information about places and times of connection, as well as possible accommodation.

Client
Pinion Digital GmbH
Berlin, Germany

Design
Pinion Digital GmbH
Berlin, Germany

Project Team
Saltanat Tashibayeva (Design)

→ Designer profile on page 614

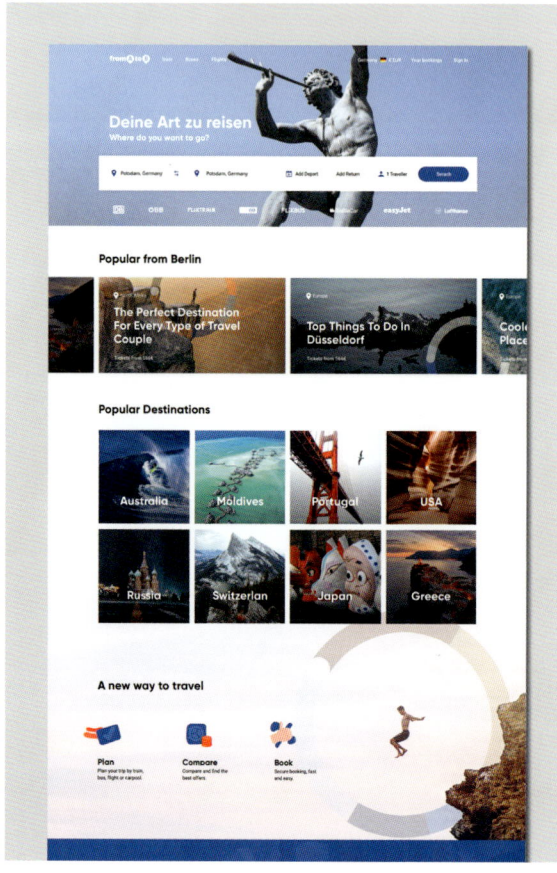

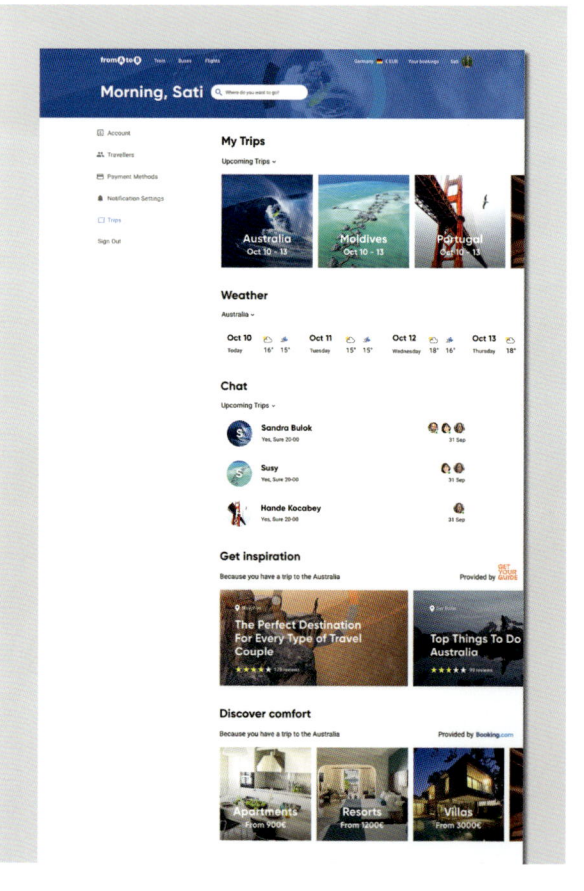

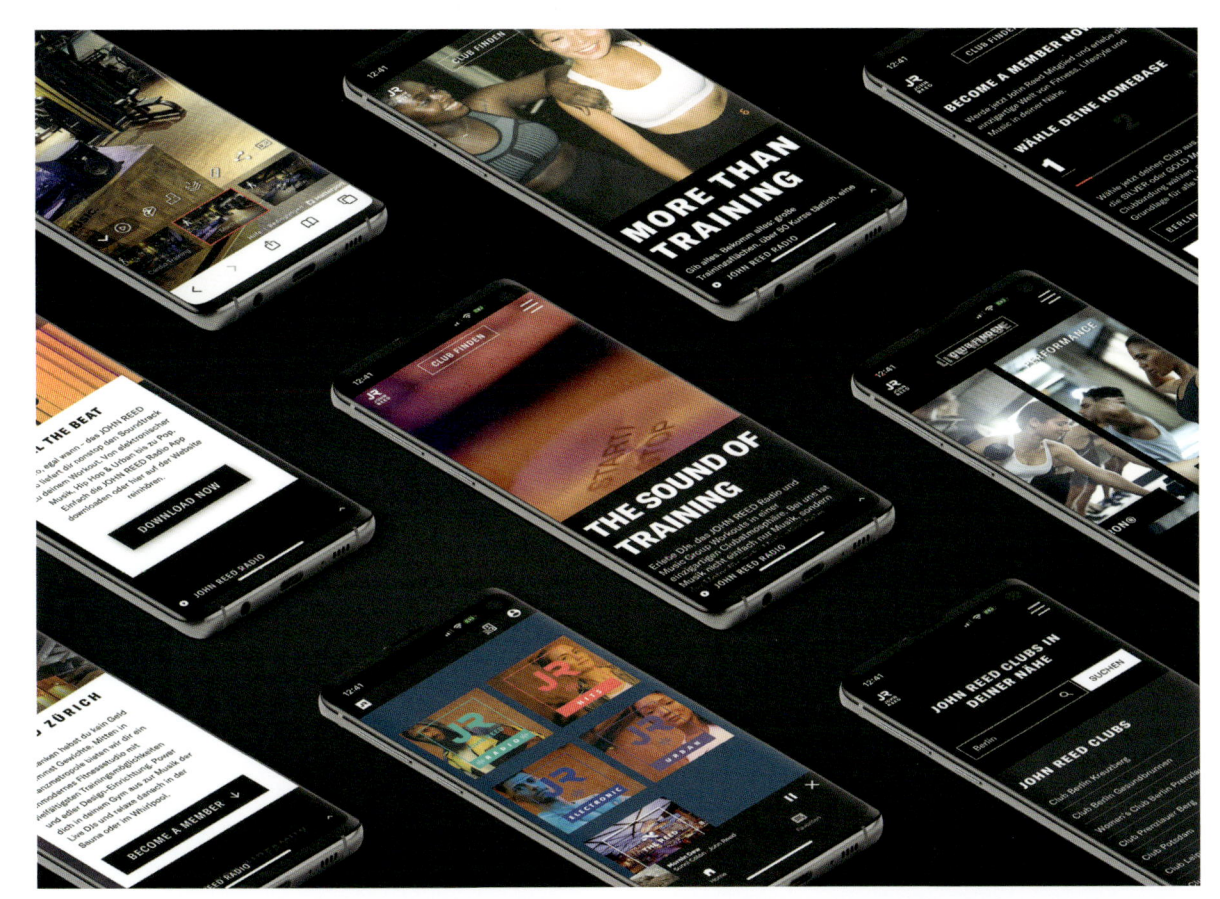

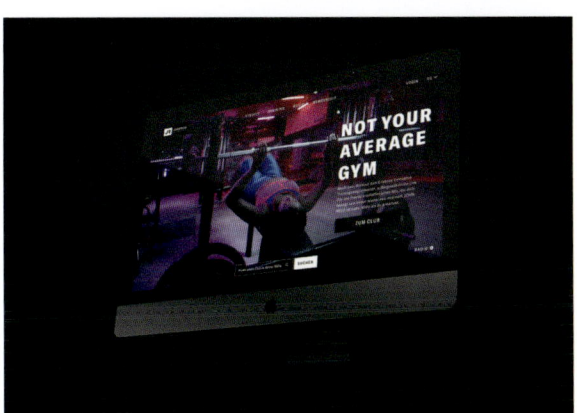

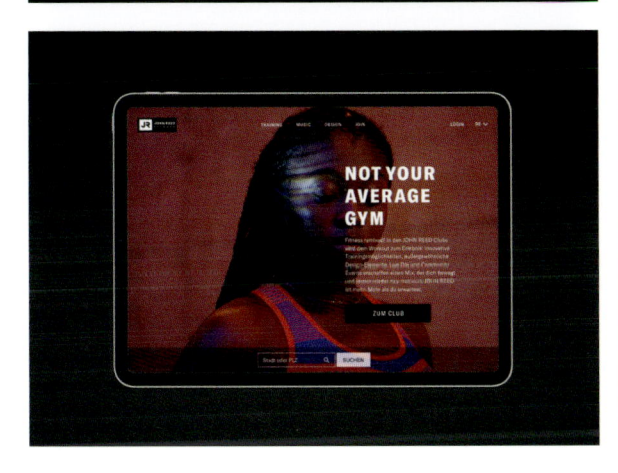

JOHN REED Fitness

[Website Relaunch]

The aim of the website relaunch was to transport and clearly reflect the brand's USP digitally with a high focus on mobile usability. The site features a vivid brand experience and an interface design that offers an engaging UX. With animated video stages and images, micro animations and a music player, users are immersed directly in the brand's flair by taking part in live courses or events in which the DJs become directly tangible. As the development is API-driven, services provided by third parties, such as a radio player, studio finder, membership agreement or lead management, can be easily integrated.

Client
RSG Group GmbH
Schlüsselfeld, Germany

Design
brandung GmbH & Co. KG
Berlin, Germany

Project Team
RSG Group/JOHN REED Fitness:
Marcus Adam (Head of Marketing & Music)
Martin Meyer (Team Lead Marketing)

brandung:
Thomas Mrasek (UX/UI Designer)
Stella Raab (UI Designer)
Johannes Rackles (Front-End Lead)
Tim Woldt (Front-End Developer)
André Wenk (Back-End Lead)
Steffen Rütten (Key Account Manager)
Johannes Manz (Project Manager)

→ Clip online

Apps

Red Dot: Grand Prix

FYEO

[Entertainment App]

FYEO (For Your Ears Only) has set itself the goal of becoming number one in terms of diverse and unusual listening experiences. On the platform developed by audio experts, stories from the neighbourhood meet great entertainment and newcomers meet scene sizes – with content that aims at being inspiring. Classic podcasts (over one million of them are free, including radio plays) are hosted there, complemented by the FYEO Originals of high-quality stories, talks, documentaries and audio blockbusters. The design presents the formats with a visual appearance that is as simple as it is concise, unmistakably conveying the high standards in bold typography against a black background. The overall simple user interface shows what FYEO is all about: enabling and facilitating access to the content with a new visual experience. Real podcast lovers regularly compile recommendations making it easy to discover new content.

Statement by the jury

The design of the FYEO app succeeds in clearly and loudly expressing the focus on the audio experience in times of visual overstimulation. The self-confident, trendy appearance with its simple font on a black background perfectly suits the service, which advertises itself with high quality and very differently prepared formats. Overall, the app projects an innovative appearance for an intuitive-to-operate service.

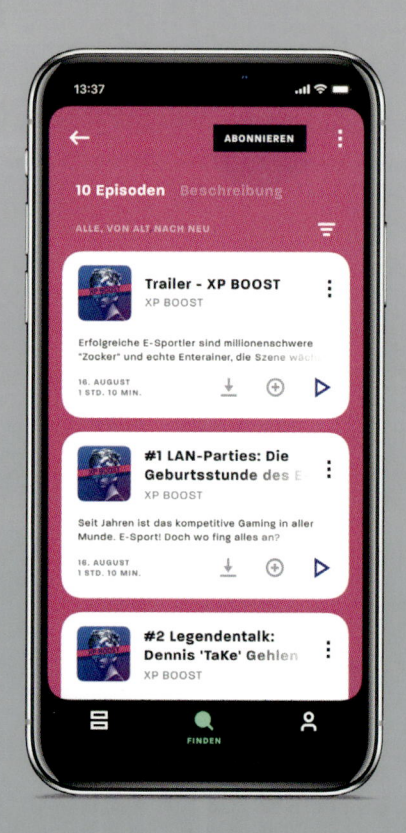

Apps	Interface & User Experience Design	Spatial Communication	Red Dot: Junior Award	Designer Profiles	Jury Portraits	Index
206	236	336	426	564	642	668

reddot winner 2020
grand prix

Client
ProSiebenSat.1 Digital GmbH
Unterföhring, Germany

Design
COBE GmbH
Munich, Germany
P7S1 Experience Design
Unterföhring, Germany

Project Team
ProSiebenSat.1 Experience Design Team:
Benjamin Risom
Tristan Lehmann
Luca Hirschfeld

COBE:
Daniel Wagner (Managing Director)
Felix Menzel (Direction)
Melchior Schramm (UX/UI Design)
Roland Lehle (UX/UI Design)
Pauline Våge (UX/UI Design)
Andreas Kuhnen (UX/UI Design)
Adrian Spiegelt (UX/UI Design)
Tim Kawohl (UX/UI Design)
Julia Roming (Research/Strategy)
Pamela Zotz (Research/Strategy)
Sherilyn Austen (Project Management)

→ Designer profile on page 581

Publishing & Print Media	Posters	Typography	Illustrations	Sound Design	Film & Animation	Online
4	64	92	116	126	138	172

EF Hello
[Educational App]

EF Hello is a conversation-driven language learning app that is free of charge and can be used on any mobile device. It features a chat-based interface and teaching through conversation, encompassing all skills needed to learn English, including vocabulary, speaking, reading, writing, listening, grammar and expressions. Thus, the app provides an English-learning environment that reflects real life, while also building upon well-understood chat design patterns that every user is familiar with. Complex learning tasks become as easy as sending a chat message, recording a voice message or attaching a file.

Client
EF Education First
London, United Kingdom

Design
EF Hello
London, United Kingdom

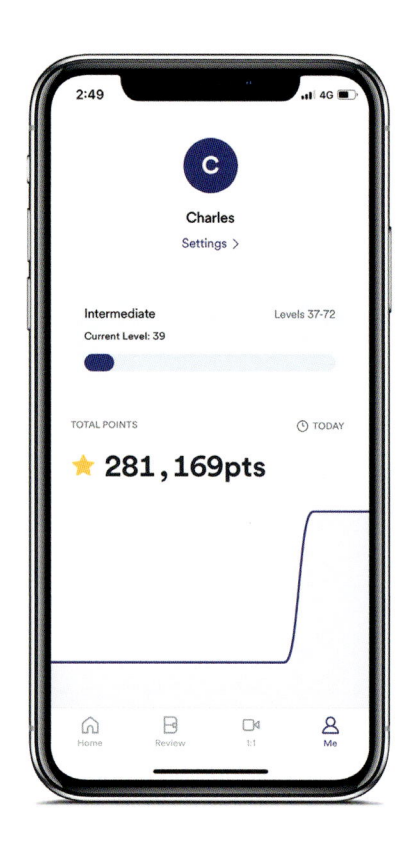

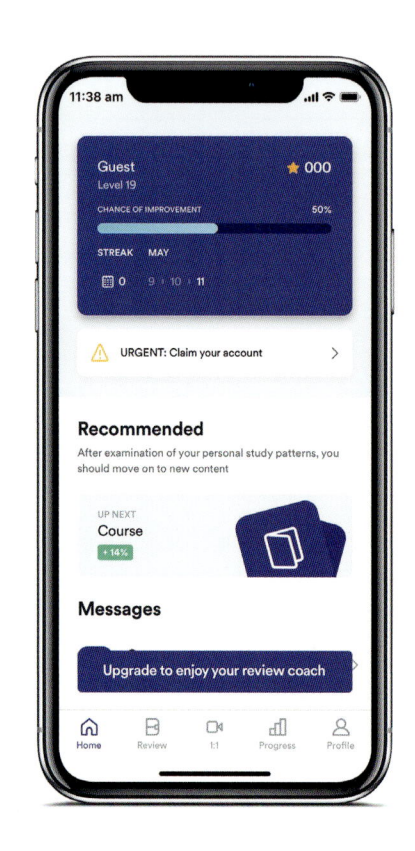

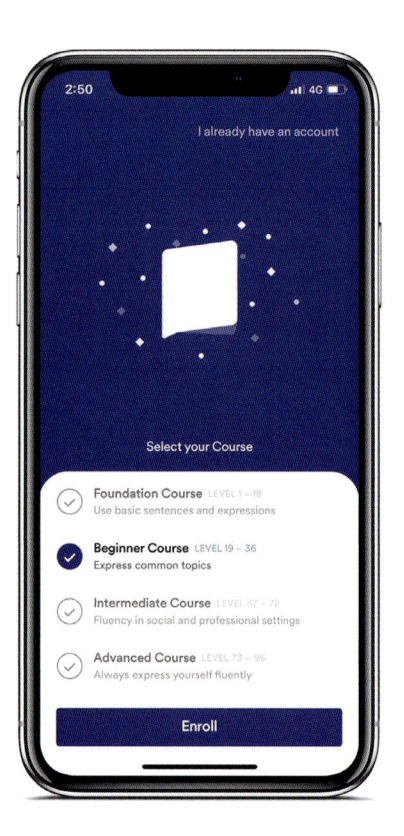

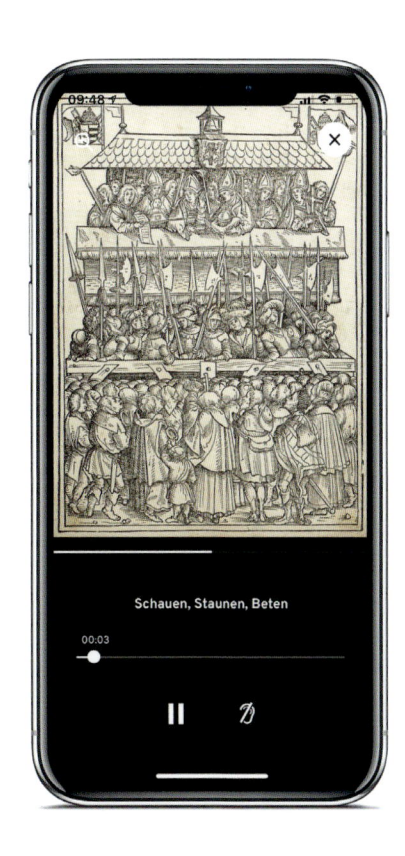

Apps	Interface & User Experience Design	Spatial Communication	Red Dot: Junior Award	Designer Profiles	Jury Portraits	Index
206	236	336	426	564	642	668

1519

[History Experience App]

Emperor Maximilian I transformed Tyrol during his reign and left it changed after his death in 1519. This project spans a historical web across the region of the Alps and illustrates social life at the turn of the modern age in ten different locations. The app 1519 provides users with a historical on-site experience, audible and visible, and guides them to bygone yet still intact monumental structures. A narrative audio guide tells stories about the everyday lives of the residents at the time and draws a line from past to present: street art, animation and dance performances make historical traces contemporarily available.

Client
Land Tirol
Innsbruck, Austria

Design
florianmatthias
Innsbruck, Austria
Rath & Winkler
Innsbruck, Austria

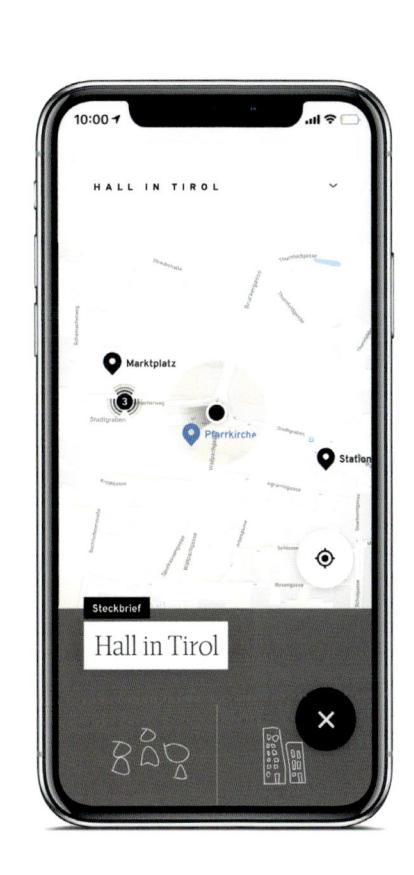

Publishing & Print Media	Posters	Typography	Illustrations	Sound Design	Film & Animation	Online
4	64	92	116	126	138	172

Halyk Travel

[Travel App]

Laid-back travel was the initial inspiration for the development of the Halyk Travel app. The main idea was to unite all needed services in one place. Thus, the app offers a linear flow for purchases of plane and train tickets. It gives users the opportunity to select what they need and to go anywhere in the world. By using the budget calculator, it is possible to estimate costs in advance and avoid miscalculations. Moreover, apartments and cars can also be rented. A light and rounded design, with different kinds of cute loading animations that speak to the audience in a joyful tone, makes using the app a pleasant experience.

Client
Halyk Bank
Almaty, Kazakhstan

Design
Alty
Kyiv, Ukraine

→ Designer profile on page 569
→ Clip online

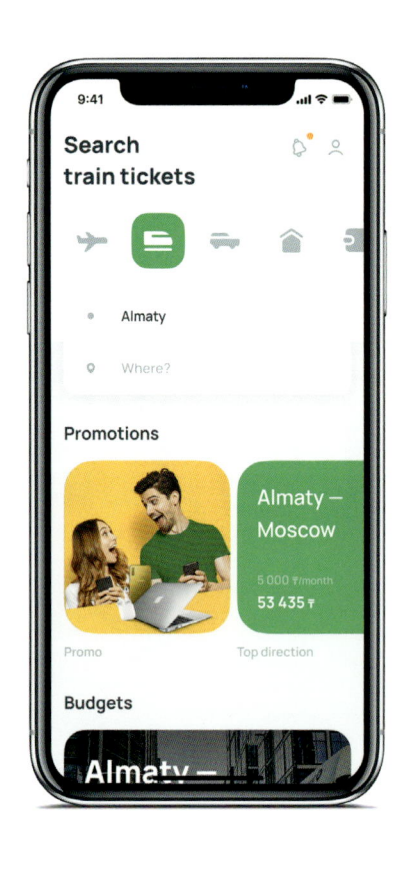

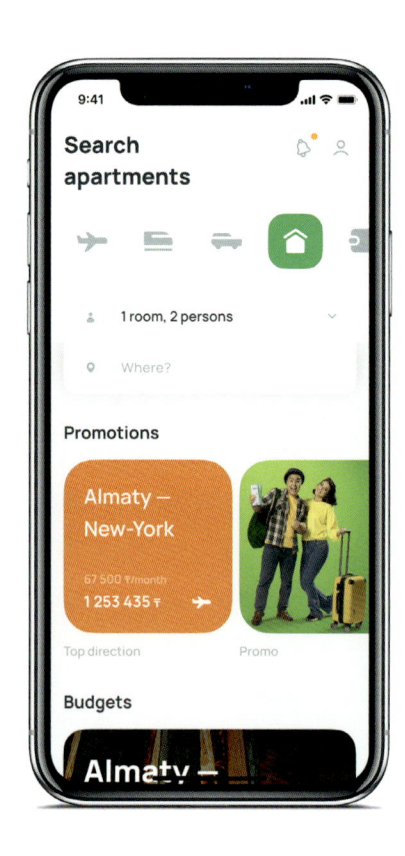

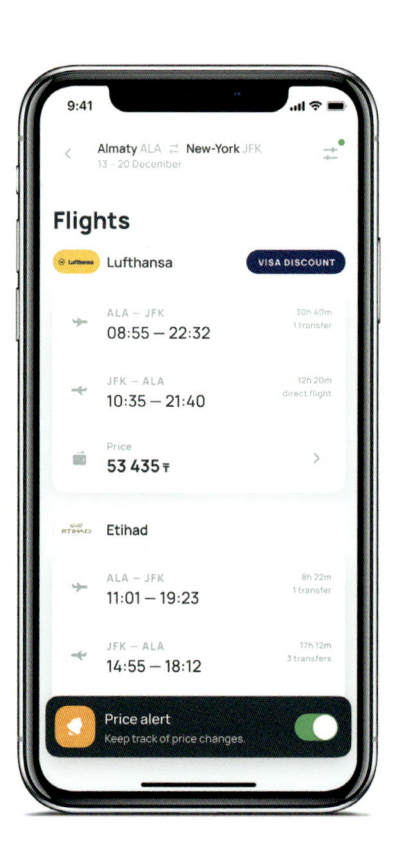

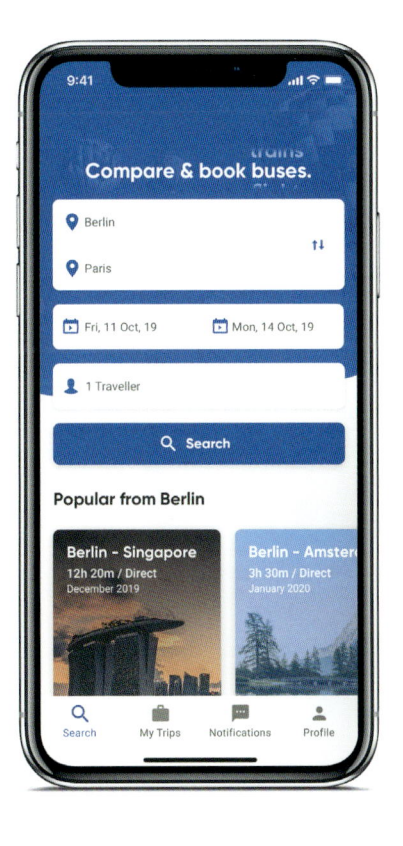

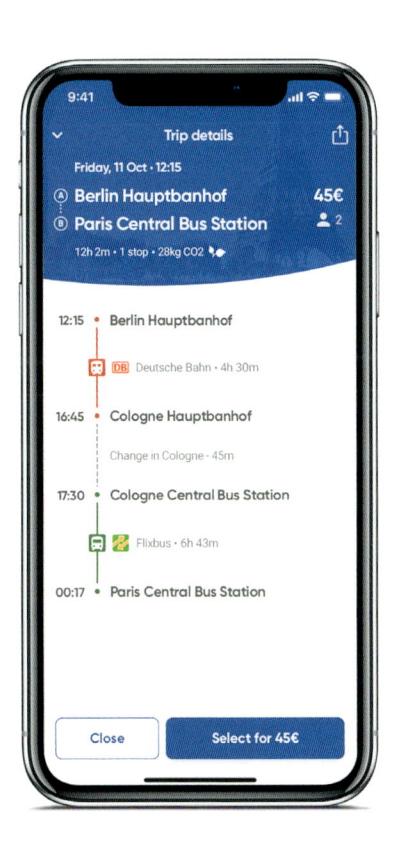

fromAtoB.
Travel Your Way.

[Travel App]

Since every individual is different, with needs that vary for each unique journey, this travel agency app aims to help travellers easily find the fastest, cheapest or most eco-friendly option, whichever one is preferred. Determined to not stop exploring and moving towards innovation, the developers designed the app to give travellers a full freedom of choice by providing all available options in a transparent way. In order to facilitate travel bookings, it creates everything that is needed in one click, including public transport tickets on the way to and from the airport and possible connecting flights.

Client
Pinion Digital GmbH
Berlin, Germany

Design
Pinion Digital GmbH
Berlin, Germany

Project Team
Saltanat Tashibayeva (Design)

→ Designer profile on page 614

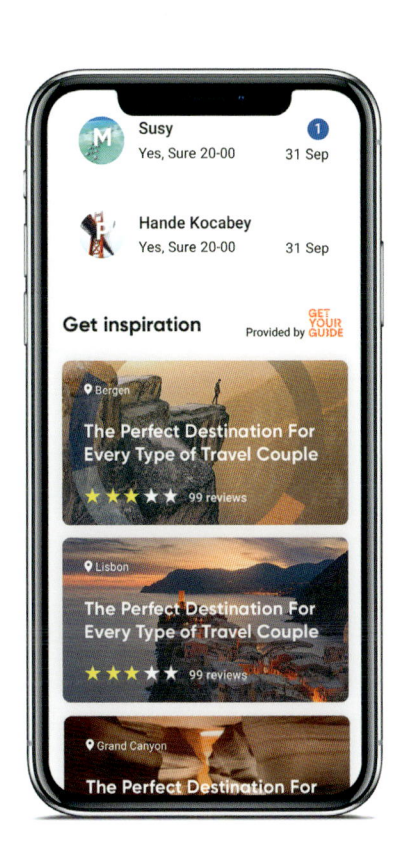

MIUI Weather App

Client
Beijing Xiaomi Mobile Software Co., Ltd.
Beijing, China

Design
MIUI Design Team
Beijing Xiaomi Mobile Software Co., Ltd.
Beijing, China

Project Team
Shao Chen (Art Direction)
Zhuoqun Sun (UI Design)
Anqi Wen (UI Design)
Jiayan Li (Animation)
Jiawei Liu (Animation)
Tianyu Zhou (Animation)

→ Designer profile on page 634
→ Clip online

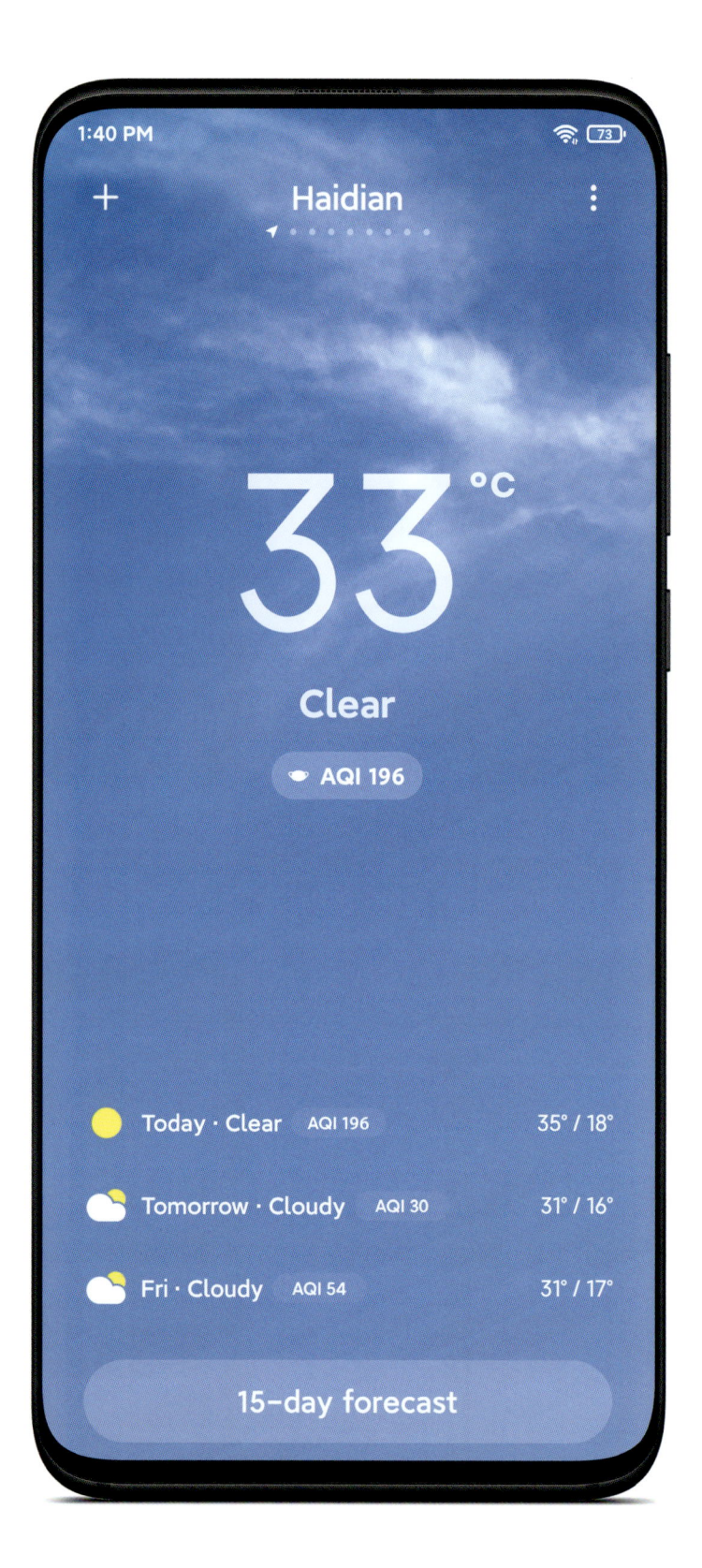

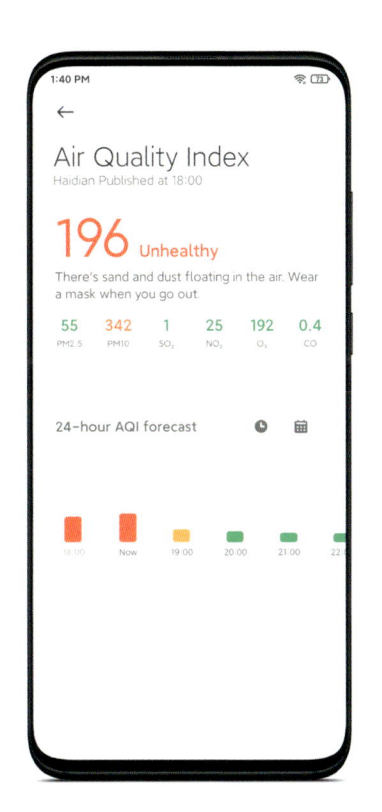

Based on user satisfaction research, the MIUI Weather App was updated and optimised in all dimensions. It is designed to provide users with new visual effects and an immersive interactive experience. The menu shows, for instance, the current temperature, air quality and wind speed. All of this information is displayed by the hour and now offers more accurate weather distinctions, thus giving users the chance to reliably plan their day. The information is presented for the entire week – for a particular city or anywhere else in the world. Some dramatic features are integrated into specific weather scenes. The MIUI Weather App is fun to use and offers users a realistic overview, allowing them to check weather information in a more natural way.

FUJIFILM PhotoBank

[Service App]

This photographic cloud service converts and preserves photos taken with smartphones and digital cameras, as well as filmed scenes and print photos, as digital data. Under the design concept of "Encounter", the aim of this app is to enable people to re-experience life moments. As a service that prevents precious photos from being forgotten, it incorporates pictures of great moments and relationships in living spaces. An environment which integrates AI, automatic tags shown in text for easy editing, user-generated tags and tag-filtered searches makes it easy for users to find whatever they are looking for at any time.

Client
FUJIFILM Corporation
Tokyo, Japan

Design
FUJIFILM Corporation Design Center
Tokyo, Japan

Apps	Interface & User Experience Design	Spatial Communication	Red Dot: Junior Award	Designer Profiles	Jury Portraits	Index
206	236	336	426	564	642	668

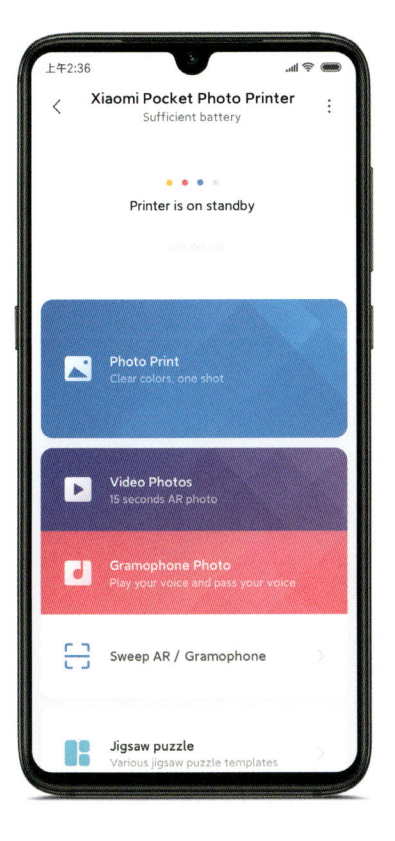

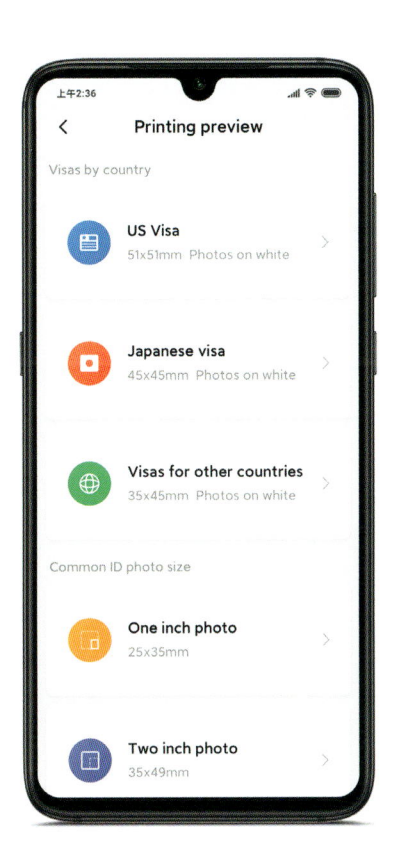

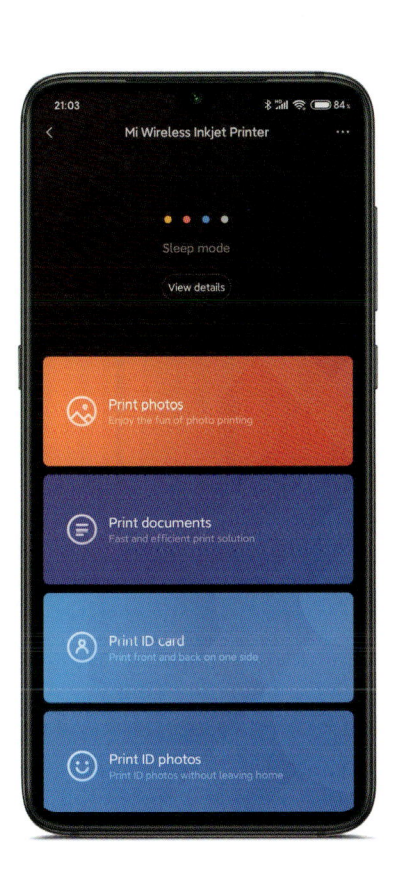

Xiaomi Printer Series

[Printing App]

Following the concept of making printing a simple matter, the Mijia app has been developed to offer smart printing in just one step. Accompanying the Xiaomi printer series, it provides simple and intelligent installation and ensures high-level printing quality. This results in a personalised, convenient, reliable and efficient printing experience, so that every user's idea can be set to paper. With a variety of built-in, certified photo templates and filters, no other Photoshop app is needed; users can simply edit their photos or graphics directly within the app and print them out.

Client
Beijing Xiaomi Mobile Software Co., Ltd.
Beijing, China

Design
Beijing Xiaomi Mobile Software Co., Ltd.
Beijing, China

Project Team
Yan Xie (Supervision)

→ Designer profile on page 635

Publishing & Print Media	Posters	Typography	Illustrations	Sound Design	Film & Animation	Online
4	64	92	116	126	138	172

PRISM Live Studio

[Entertainment App]

PRISM Live Studio is a live-streaming app which allows users to create engaging live streams, videos and photos through various effects. With a UX design that is centred around the concept of facilitating premium live-streaming experiences, it strives to offer broadcasting that is enjoyable and accessible. Multiple features, such as the option to share the screens of mobile devices or AR interactive filters, make it easy to produce professional-level content. The broadcasting interface design enables content creators to effortlessly manage their live-stream feeds and interact with viewers.

Client
NAVER Corp.
Seongnam, South Korea

Design
NAVER Corp.
Seongnam, South Korea

Project Team
Sung Yul Yang (Creative Direction)
Jiyoung Park (UI Design)
Youngok Choi (UI Design)
Yukyung Chun (UI Design)
Sun Lee (UI Design)
Ara Lee (Graphic/Motion Design)
Gyuwon Kim (Graphic/Motion Design)
Juhyeon Jang (Graphic/Motion Design)
Junseok Jang (Graphic/Motion Design)
Minhyung Chun (Graphic/Motion Design)

→ Clip online

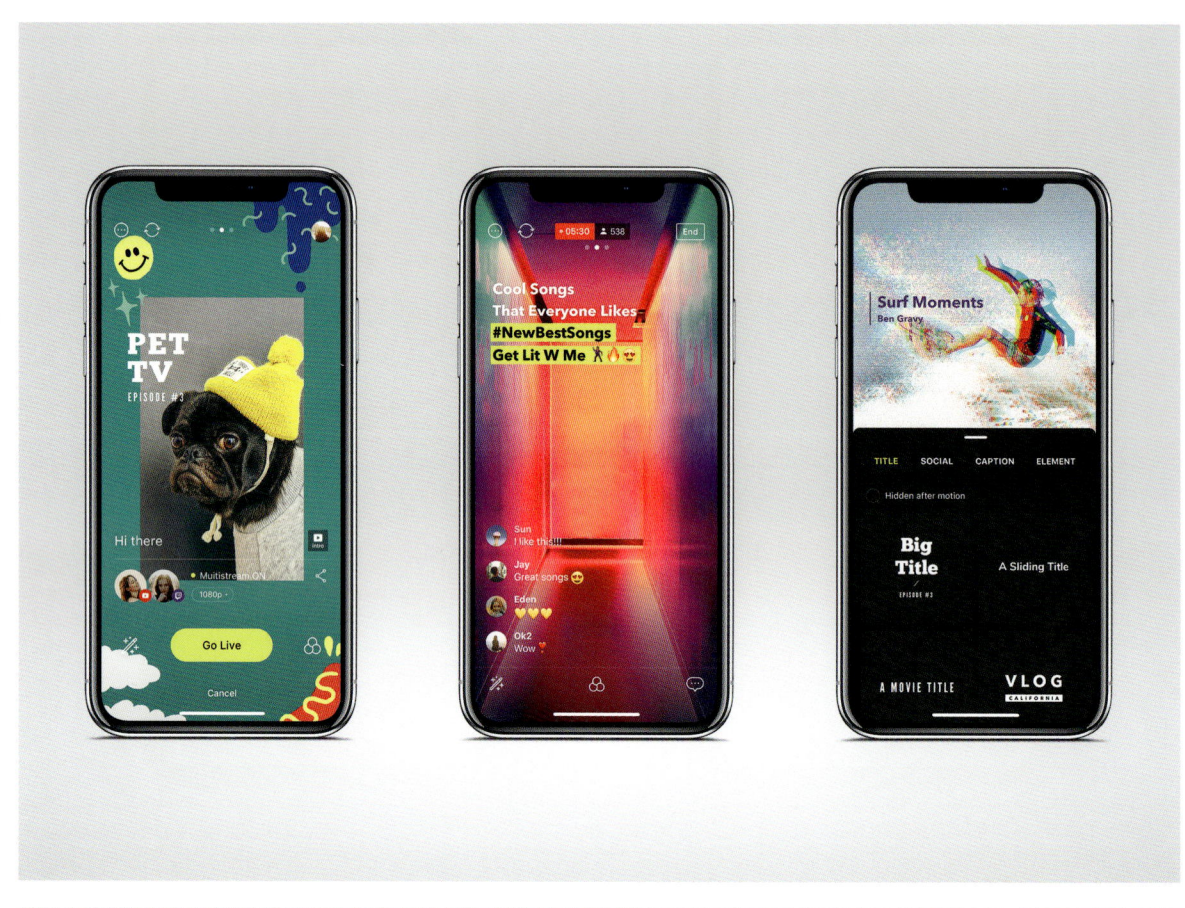

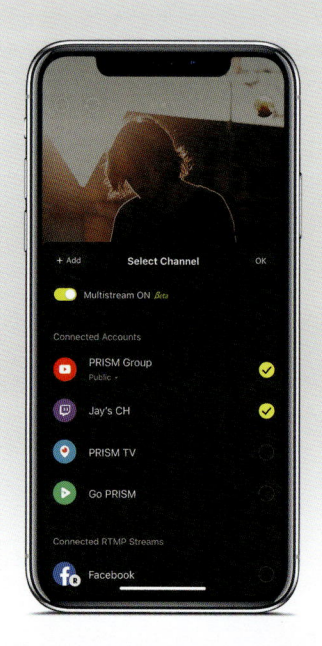

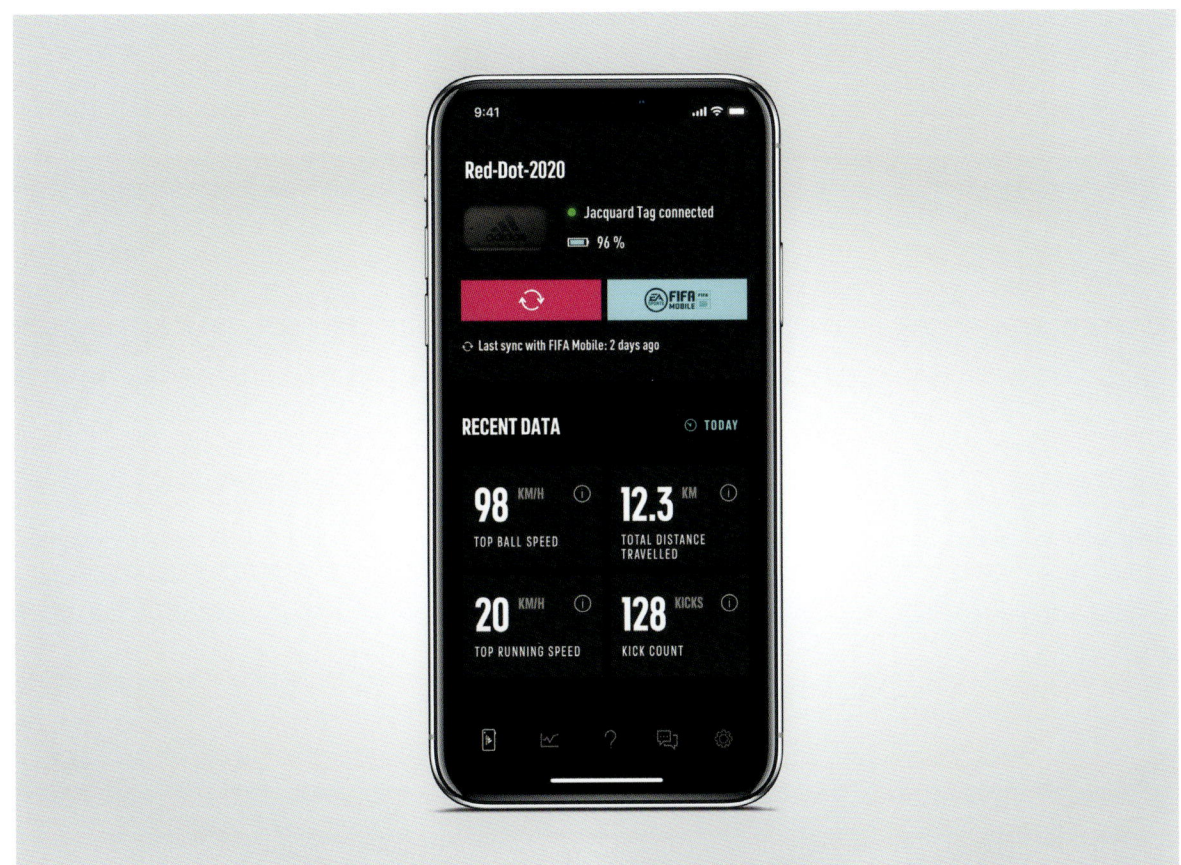

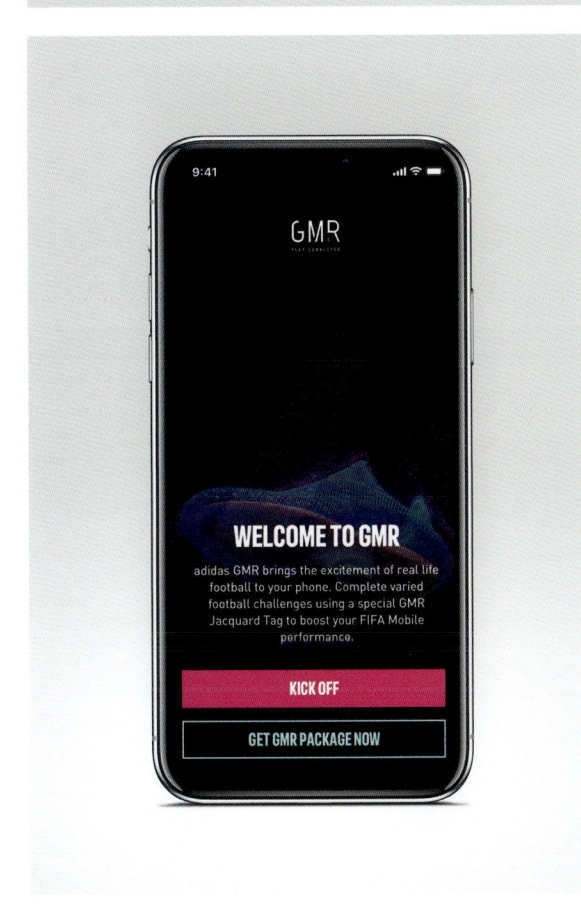

adidas GMR

[Sports App]

The GMR app is an experience that connects the analogue with the digital world. It features an insole with a smart tag which is capable of detecting football-specific movement. The app guides users through the journey, from collecting and syncing data on real playfields to the virtual stadiums of EA SPORTS FIFA Mobile in order to improve the skills of the team. The app offers a user journey with easy and fast onboarding and a dashboard where the recurring syncing of the tag is managed and where recent statistics are displayed. It is also used to set up and manage the tag and includes support chat in real time.

Client
adidas AG
Herzogenaurach, Germany

Design
intive GmbH
Munich, Germany

Project Team
Michael Ehrnböck (UX Design)
Johannes Dornisch (UX Design)
Alexander Kalinowski (UX Design)

U+Game Live

[Entertainment App]

Client
LG Uplus
Seoul, South Korea

Design
LG Uplus
Seoul, South Korea
Amoeba
Seoul, South Korea

Project Team
LG Uplus:
Minhyung Cho (Creative Direction)
Seowoo Lee (Creative Direction)
Juhyun Park (Publisher)

Amoeba:
Sangmin Yoo (Designer)

→ Designer profile on page 603

Apps	Interface & User Experience Design	Spatial Communication	Red Dot: Junior Award	Designer Profiles	Jury Portraits	Index
206	236	336	426	564	642	668

The U+Game Live app is a service for LGU+ 5G customers that offers vivid and accurate game streaming combined with the information about specific players that a viewer wants to see. Through this game-streaming platform, which is free of buffering, up to three live videos and matches of favourite players can be selected. The game information can also be checked in real time, and users enjoy analysing the game like experts. The app provides multiple features, such as the ability to replay scenes or watch them in slow motion or to have the champion characteristics shown that were used by a certain player during the game.

Publishing & Print Media	Posters	Typography	Illustrations	Sound Design	Film & Animation	Online
4	64	92	116	126	138	172

hOn
[Smart Home App]

Client
Haier Europe
Brugherio, Italy

Design
Enhancers S.p.A.
Turin, Italy

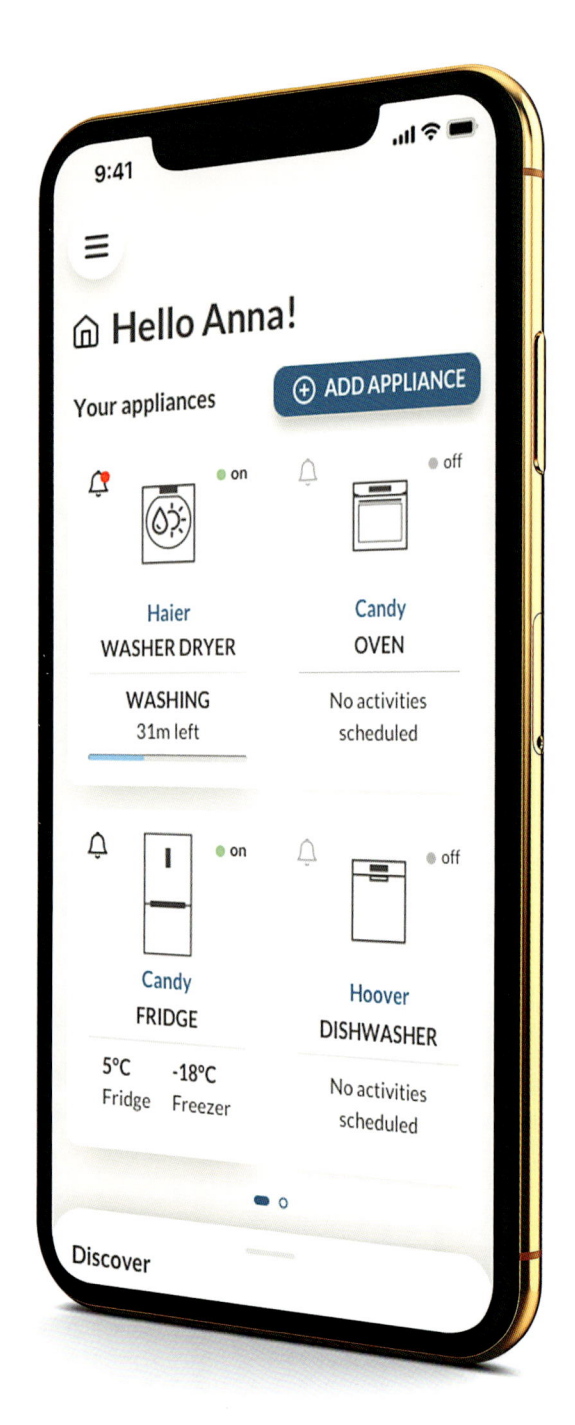

→ Clip online

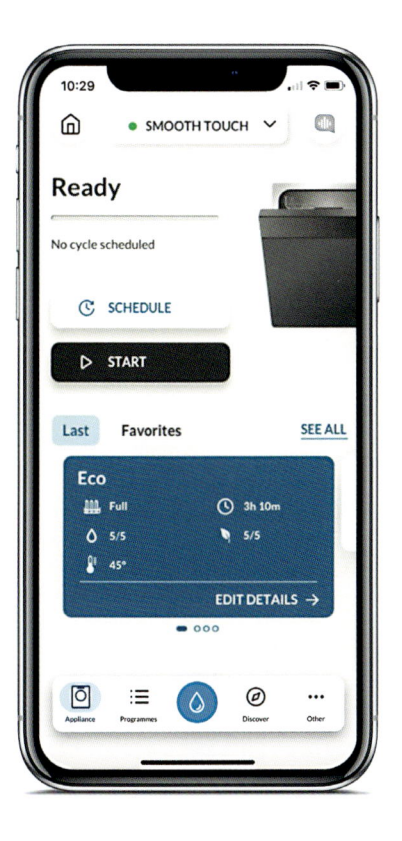

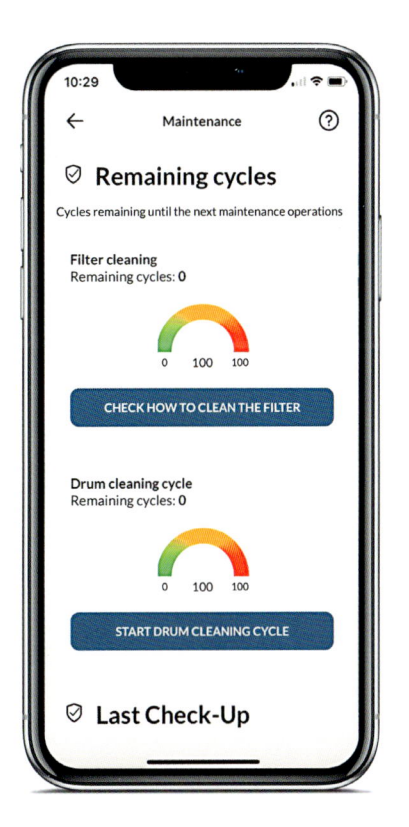

The hOn app is a digital environment which enables users to conveniently manage and control connected appliances in their home. Alongside useful functions such as a remote control, access to tips and guided tutorials, efficiency statistics, maintenance management and setting reminders, it combines innovative features enabled by artificial intelligence, image recognition and special algorithms. Labels can be scanned and products managed using voice via the chatbot within the app. Moreover, it suggests suitable programmes for a dishwasher or washing machine and can track air quality and activate conditioning treatments.

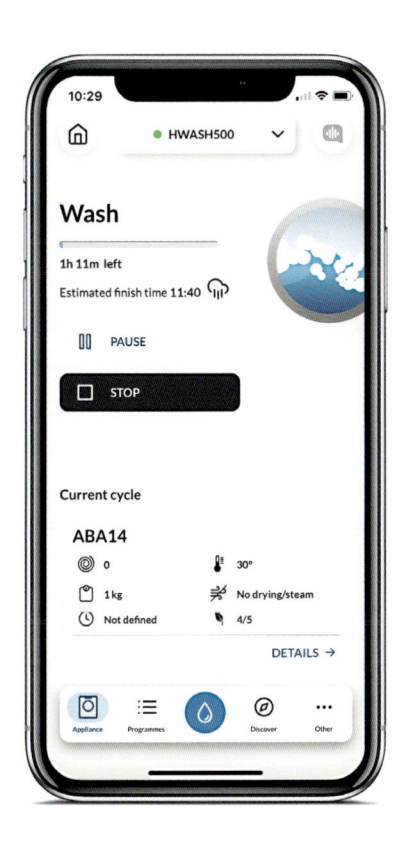

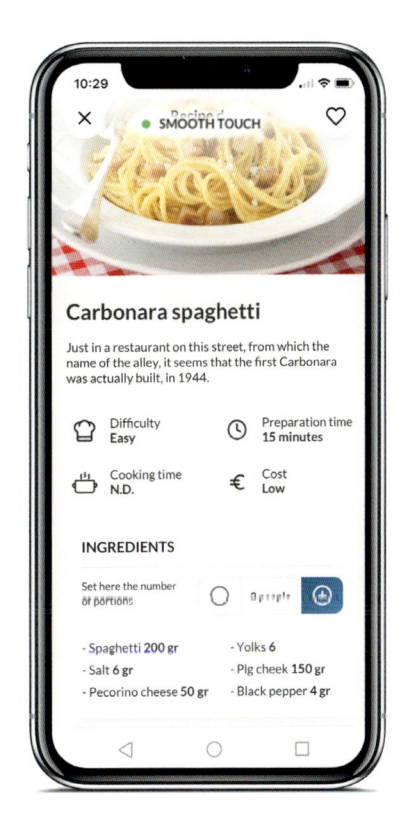

Publishing & Print Media	Posters	Typography	Illustrations	Sound Design	Film & Animation	Online
4	64	92	116	126	138	172

EGGER Decorative Collection App

[Service App]

EGGER produces wood-based materials in various decor variants. This app has been developed to complement the company's physical catalogues and decor samples as a smart marketing tool. Aimed to facilitate activities for customers when picking suitable decor for their projects or finding information about the availability of the selected materials, the app offers intuitive digital navigation through the entire product range. This includes 3D visuals, real-time information and project folders for customer presentations. The scanning of order numbers in the catalogue opens up direct access to all information, and samples are ordered with just one tap.

Client
FRITZ EGGER GmbH & Co. OG
St. Johann in Tirol, Austria

Design
Netural GmbH
Linz, Austria

Project Team
Evelyn Rendl (UX Design)
Elisabeth Hofmanninger (UX Design)
Dominik Brandlberger
(Software Engineering)
Florian Eckerstorfer
(Software Engineering)
Peter Gollowitsch (Concept)
Katharina Liedl (Concept)

→ Clip online

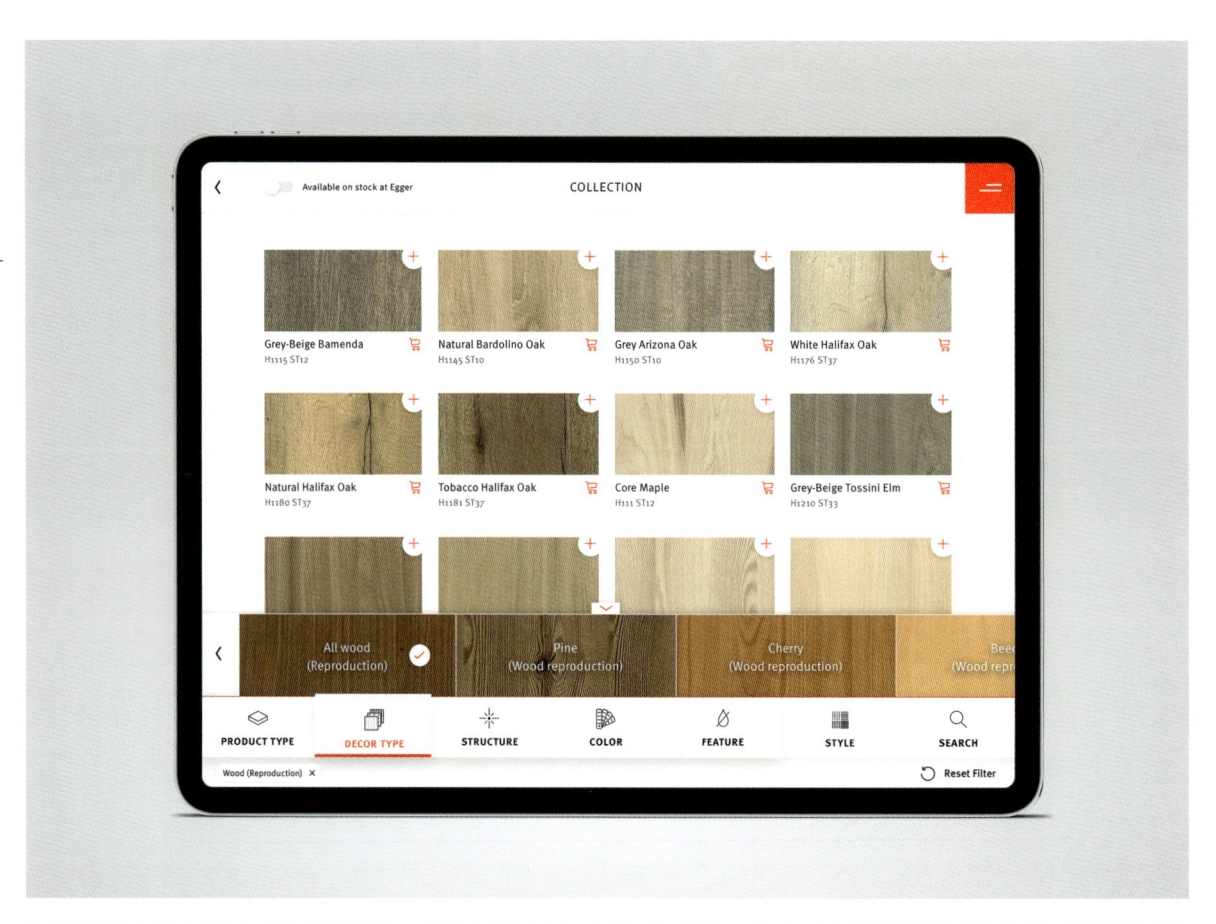

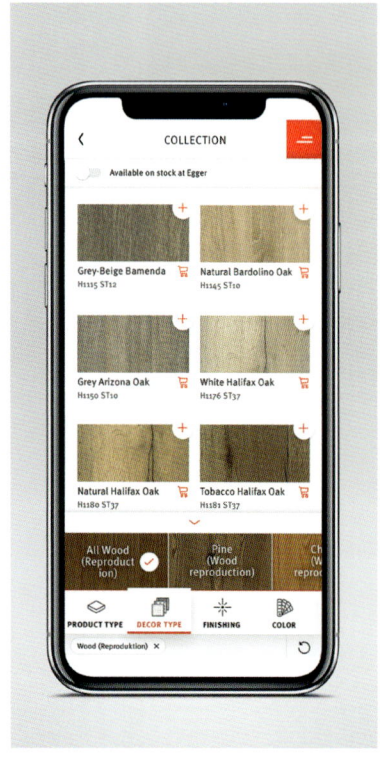

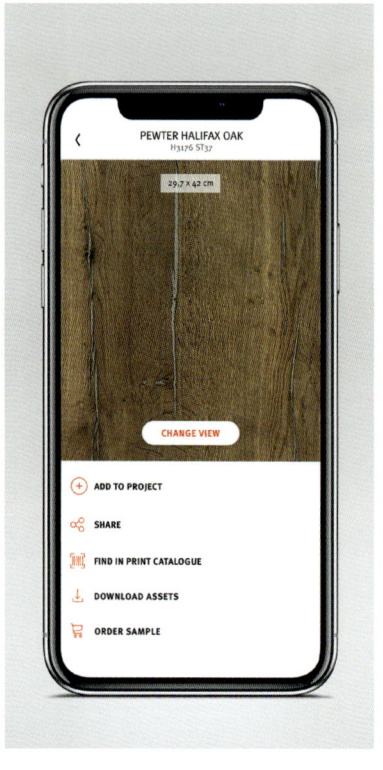

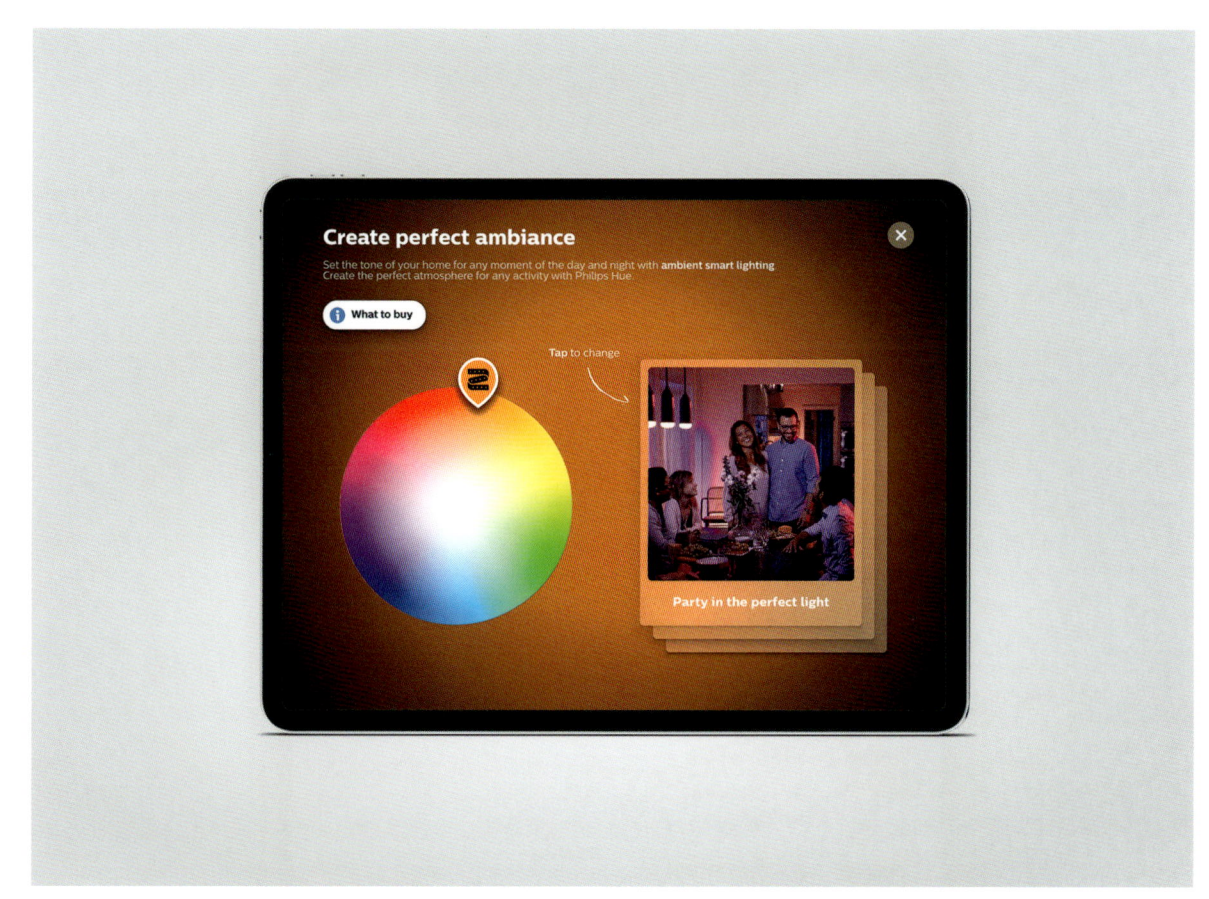

Philips Hue In-Store App gen2

[Interactive Demo App]

The Philips Hue In-Store App gen2 is a premium point of sale tablet app offering shops a way to demonstrate the potential of the smart, controlled, atmospheric, lighting system. It guides users interactively through the various products and ways of use. In a 360-degree immersive experience, they can explore all of the possibilities. It is a one-stop information point for potential customers to find beneficial information on the Hue smart lighting platform. With its easy-to-use and visually attractive interface, the app makes all important information conveniently accessible in a single place.

Client
Signify
Eindhoven, Netherlands

Design
Signify Design team
Eindhoven, Netherlands

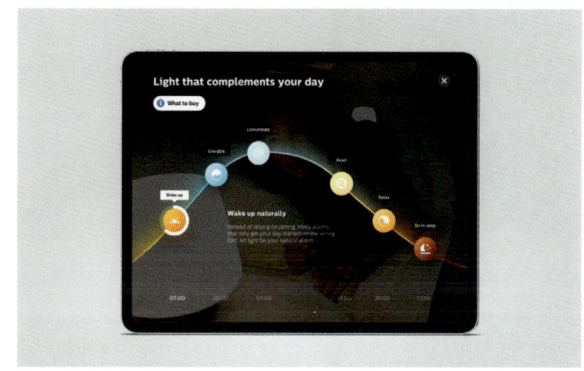

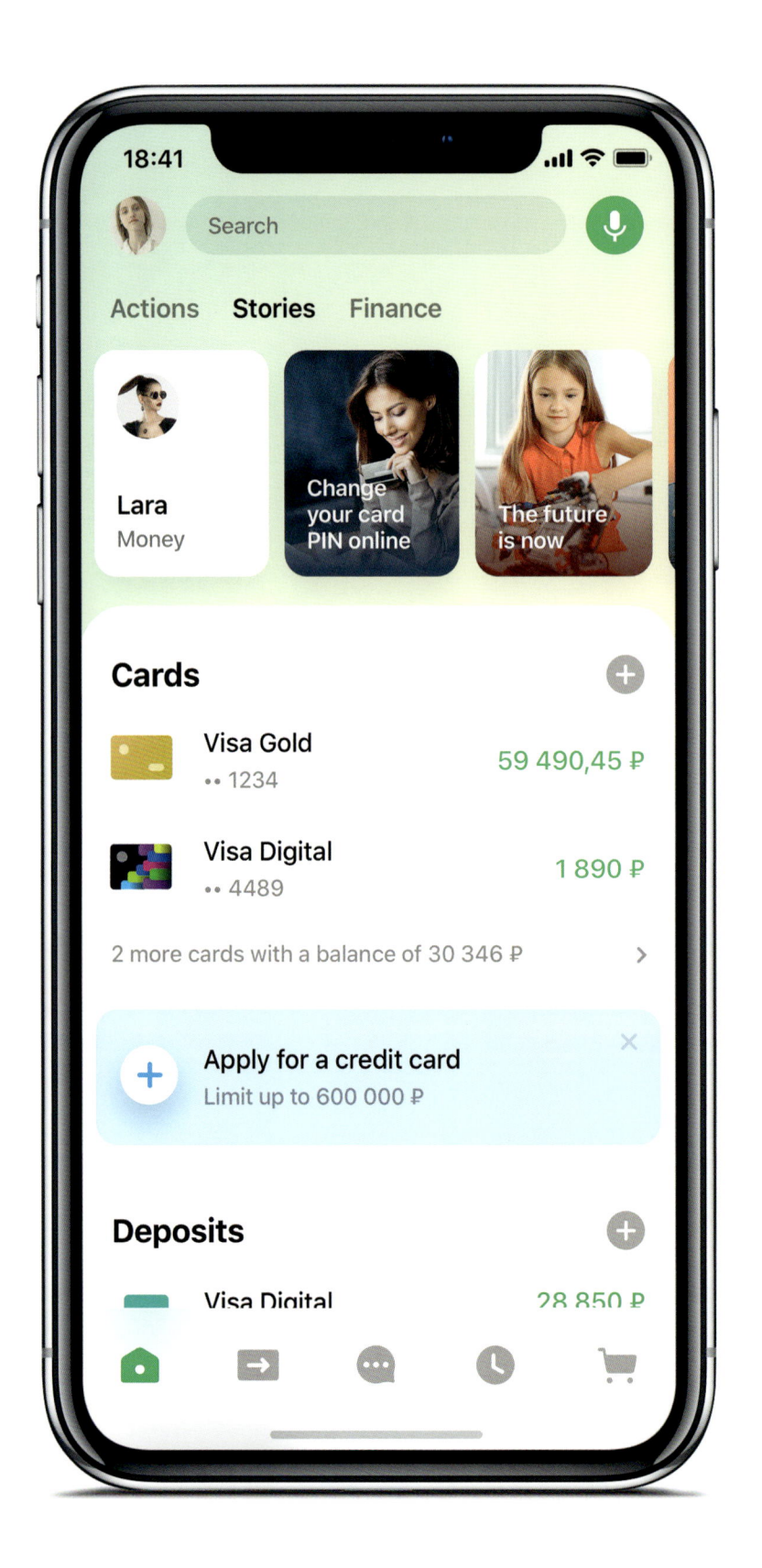

Publishing & Print Media	Posters	Typography	Illustrations	Sound Design	Film & Animation	Online
4	64	92	116	126	138	172

Sberbank Online

[Finance App, Edutainment App]

Client
Sberbank
Moscow, Russia

Design
Sberbank
Moscow, Russia

→ Clip online

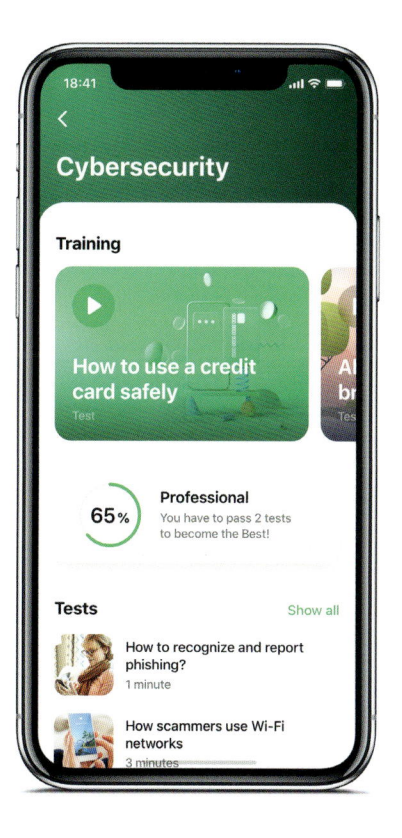

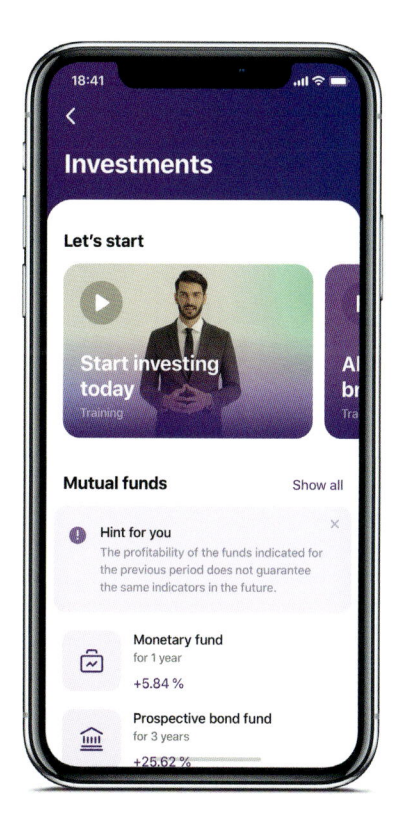

Apps	Interface & User Experience Design	Spatial Communication	Red Dot: Junior Award	Designer Profiles	Jury Portraits	Index
206	236	336	426	564	642	668

The Sberbank Online app gives access to almost all of the financial products and services of this Russian bank. It comprises an integrated edutainment platform that aims to explain financial themes and products. How-to videos in the product sections help customers to choose a product or service which best suits an individual life scenario. Thematic channels are implemented for those who are more into texts and details, thus allowing further research. The cybersecurity centre offers articles, videos and tests which teach customers to safely use banking cards, smartphones and computers and to recognise fraudsters.

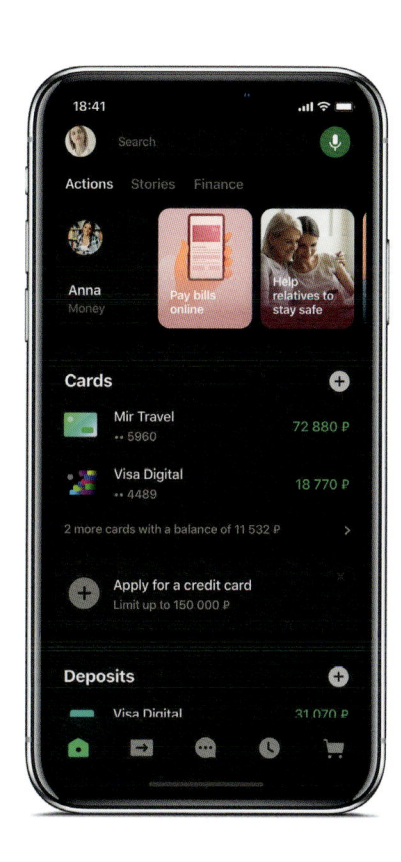

Publishing & Print Media	Posters	Typography	Illustrations	Sound Design	Film & Animation	Online
4	64	92	116	126	138	172

Akbank Mobile
[Finance App]

Akbank Mobile is a finance app that provides a new perspective in terms of a social, smart, future-proof and rewarding experience in traditional banking. It sets out to speak the users' language by featuring contact thumbnails, simplified actions, and phrases and concepts that are familiar to them, rather than being based on system-oriented terms. In a human-first approach, with a personalised area on the main page, the app offers users a convenient overview to ease their financial tasks and reduce stress. The AI engine thereby gives smart insights, and users can also share their feedback and needs directly with the bank.

Client
Akbank T.A.S
Istanbul, Turkey

Design
Akbank T.A.S
Istanbul, Turkey

Project Team
Akbank Design Studio
Akbank Design and Development Team

R/GA London Team

→ Clip online

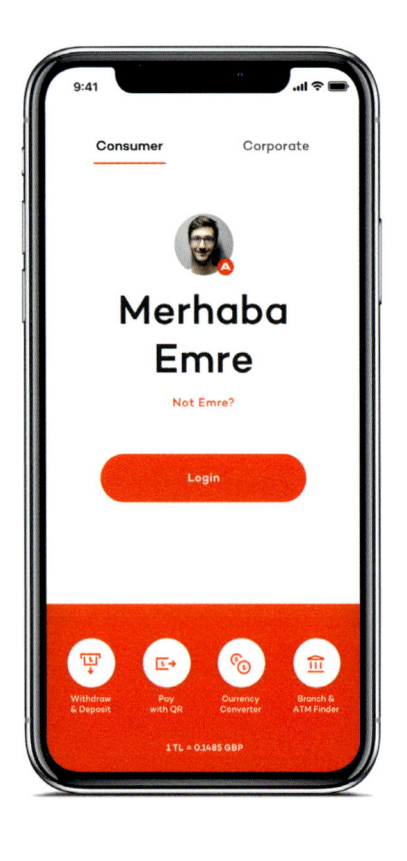

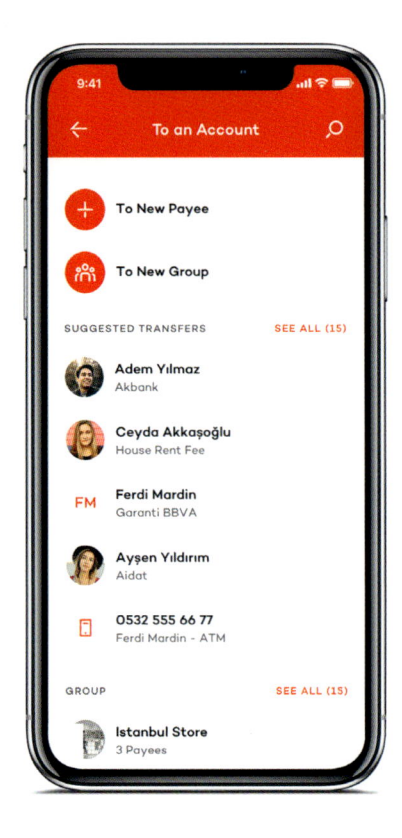

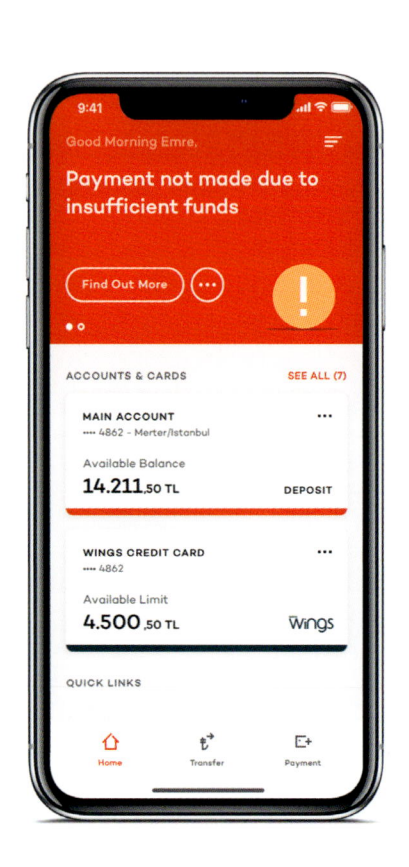

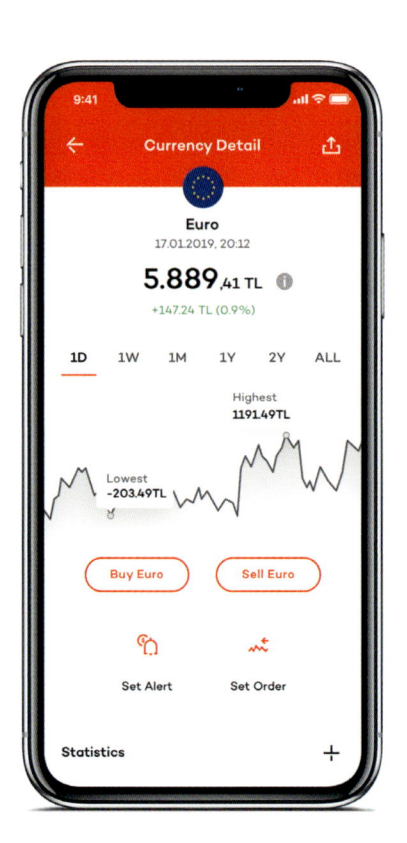

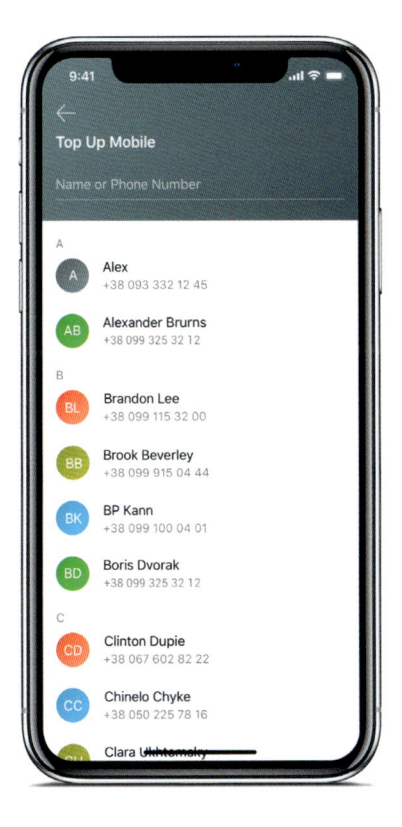

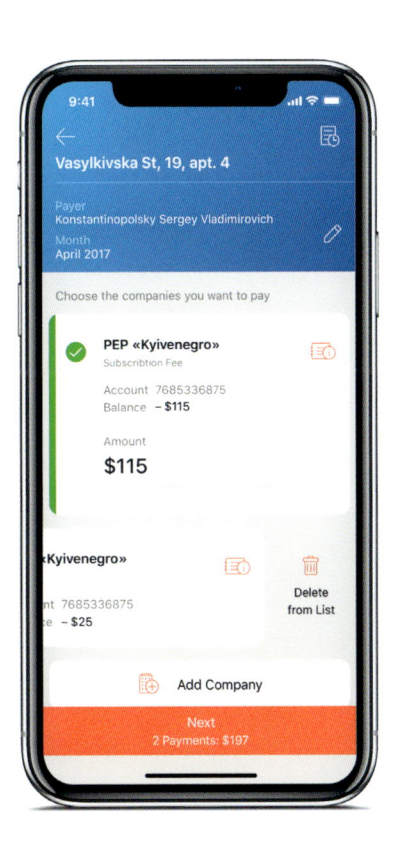

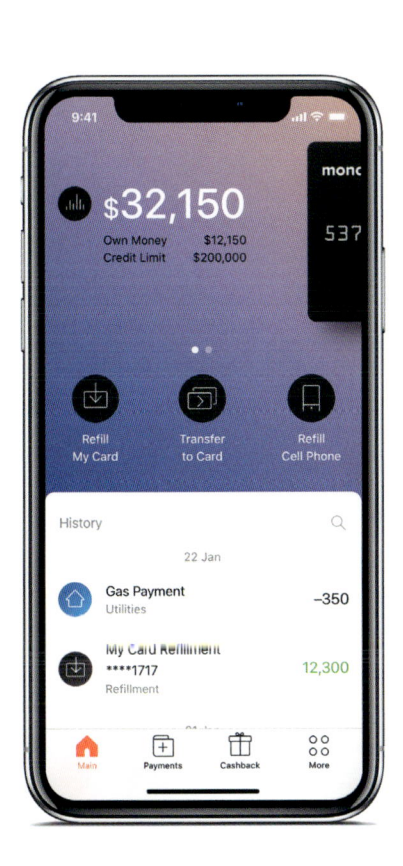

Apps	Interface & User Experience Design	Spatial Communication	Red Dot: Junior Award	Designer Profiles	Jury Portraits	Index
206	236	336	426	564	642	668

Monobank

[Finance App]

Monobank is the first Ukrainian mobile-only bank. Since this financial institution has no branches, the service is provided solely through a mobile app which allows users to open a bank account and make full use of all offered products. The account-opening process has been simplified by dividing it into three easy steps. Potential customers only need a phone, and it takes just five minutes to become a client. The app offers a variety of banking services: from free money transfer and the paying of utility bills with no commission to loans and cashback. Customer support is provided through the most popular messenger services and by telephone.

Client
Fintech Band
Kyiv, Ukraine

Design
Alty
Kyiv, Ukraine

→ Designer profile on page 569
→ Clip online

Publishing & Print Media	Posters	Typography	Illustrations	Sound Design	Film & Animation	Online
4	64	92	116	126	138	172

bob
[Service App]

bob is a brand of A1 Telekom Austria in the field of mobile communications services. In line with the development of a completely new brand appearance, the user concept for the bob app has also been revised after integrating collected user feedback. The aim was to create an intuitive, uniform and user-centred brand. The app enables users to quickly check their mobile phone costs and consumption, to adjust settings and to browse through current offers. Featuring a clear overview, it provides them with complete, transparent control over expenses, to avoid any nasty surprises at the end of the month.

Client
A1 Telekom Austria
Vienna, Austria

Design
Nicole Zimmermann
Vienna, Austria

→ Clip online

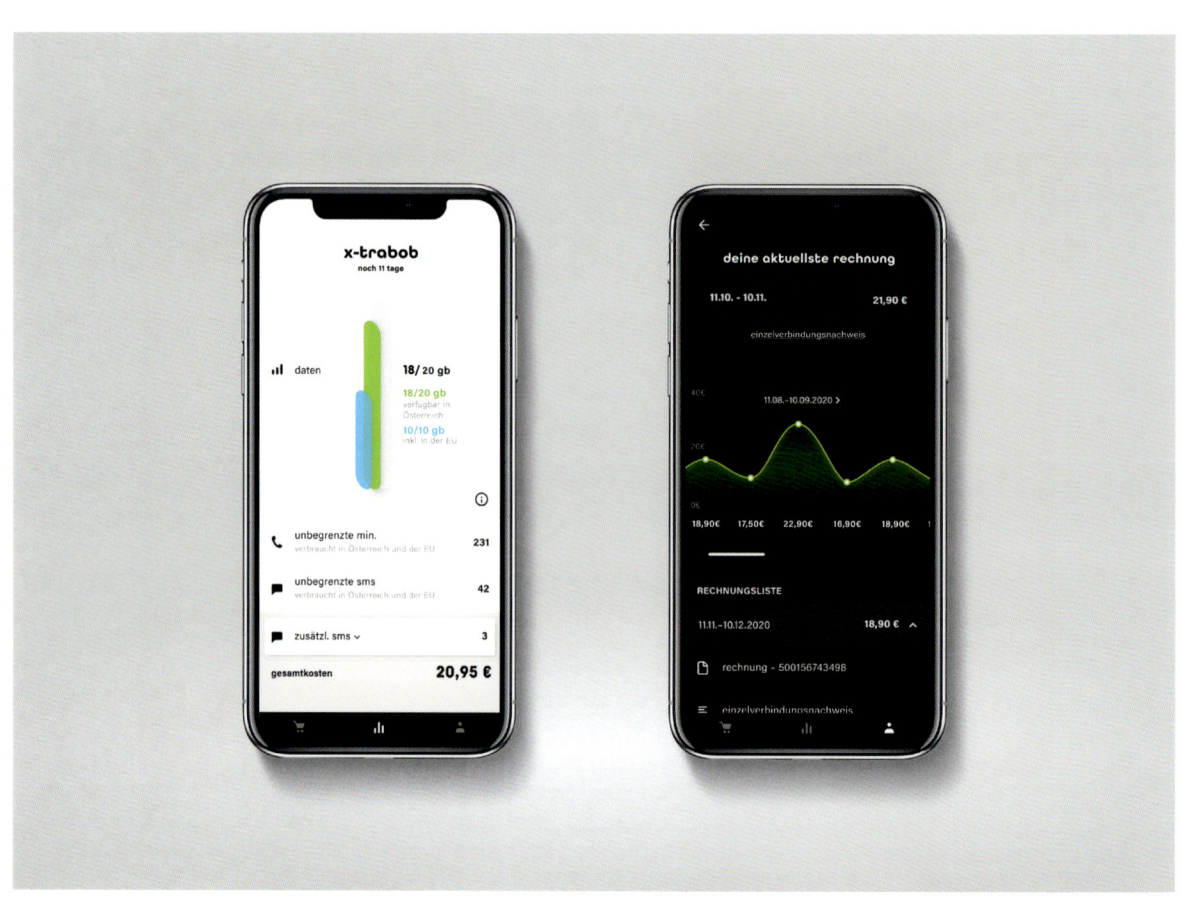

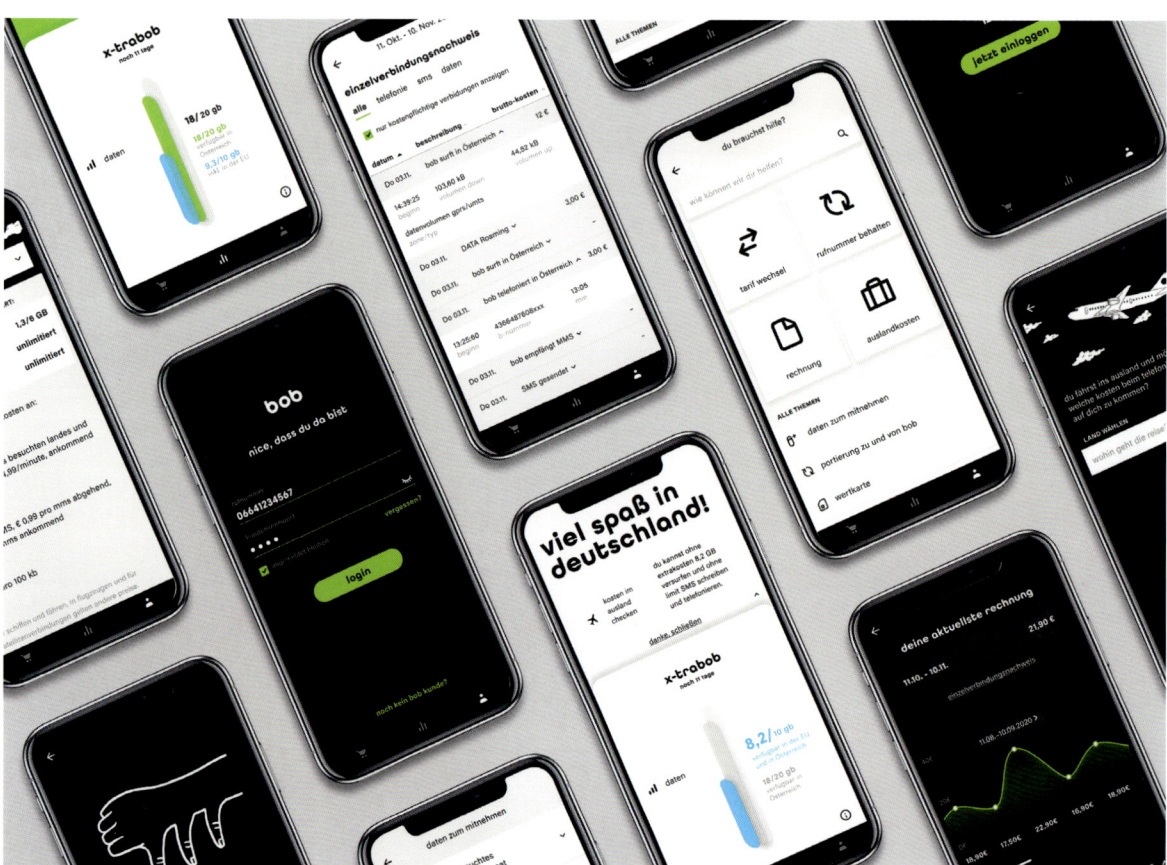

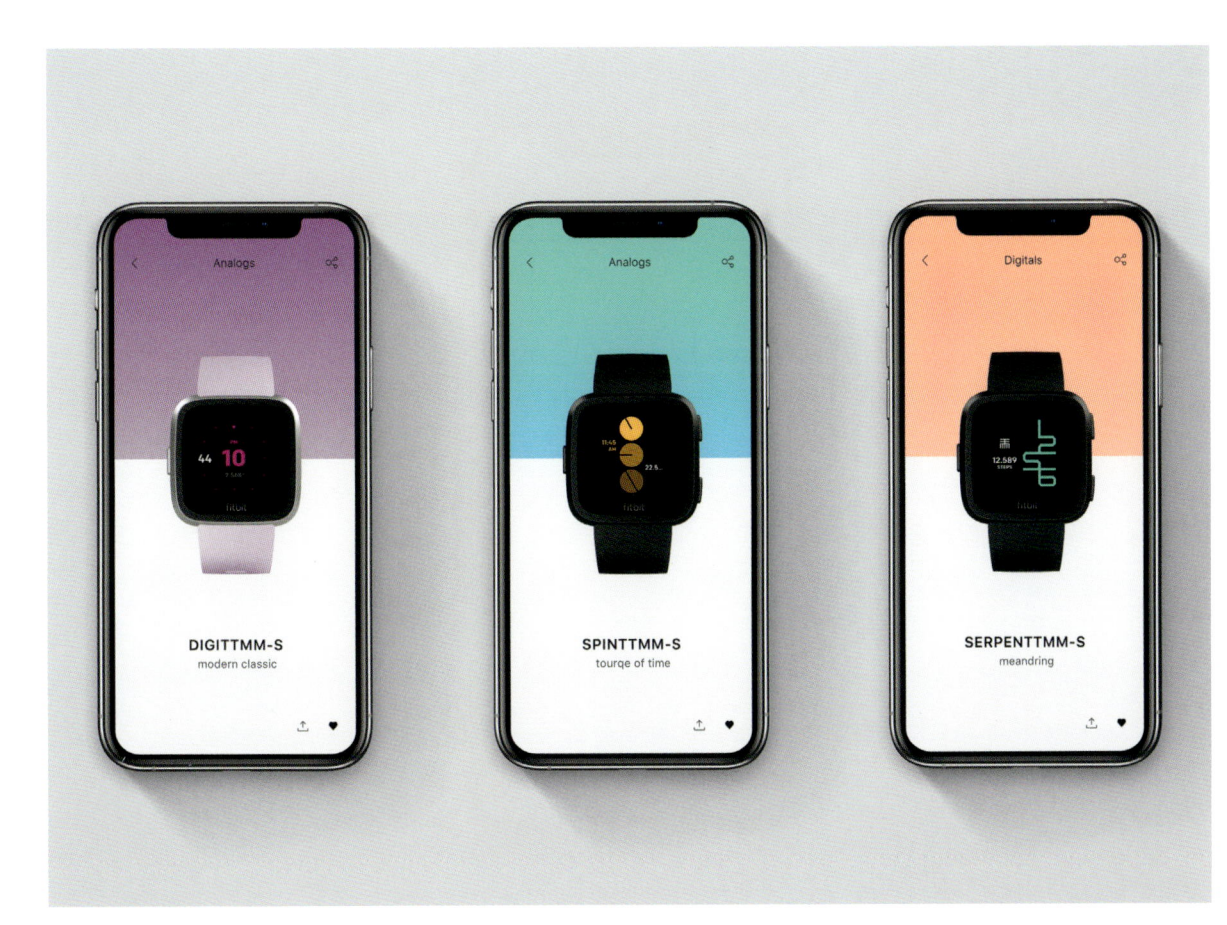

TTMM-S for Fitbit Versa

[Service App]

The TTMM-S app offers a collection of clock faces for Fitbit Versa smartwatches. It is equipped with a feature displaying weather conditions and air quality and is offered in a monthly subscription plan. The clock face designs range from highly functional, through minimalist and elegant, to abstract and futuristic, presented in four categories. Some are additionally equipped with a stopwatch, a timer, an alarm or a torch. The app offers a view of the watch body settings and provides search features. The clock faces are equipped with three types of alerts: dangerous weather conditions, high UV radiation and unhealthy air quality.

Client
TTMM Sp. z o.o.
Warsaw, Poland

Design
TTMM Sp. z o.o.
Warsaw, Poland

Project Team
TTMM:
Albert Salamon (Brand Design)
Rafał Gorczyński (iOS Programming)
Arkadiusz Banaś (iOS Programming)
Piotr Kamiński (Fitbit Programming)
Wiktor Hołubowicz (Fitbit Programming)
Gregoire Sage (Fitbit Programming)

Leszek Juraszczyk (UX Design),
Parabolic Playground
Marcin Berendt (Marketing Consultant),
Maxmall

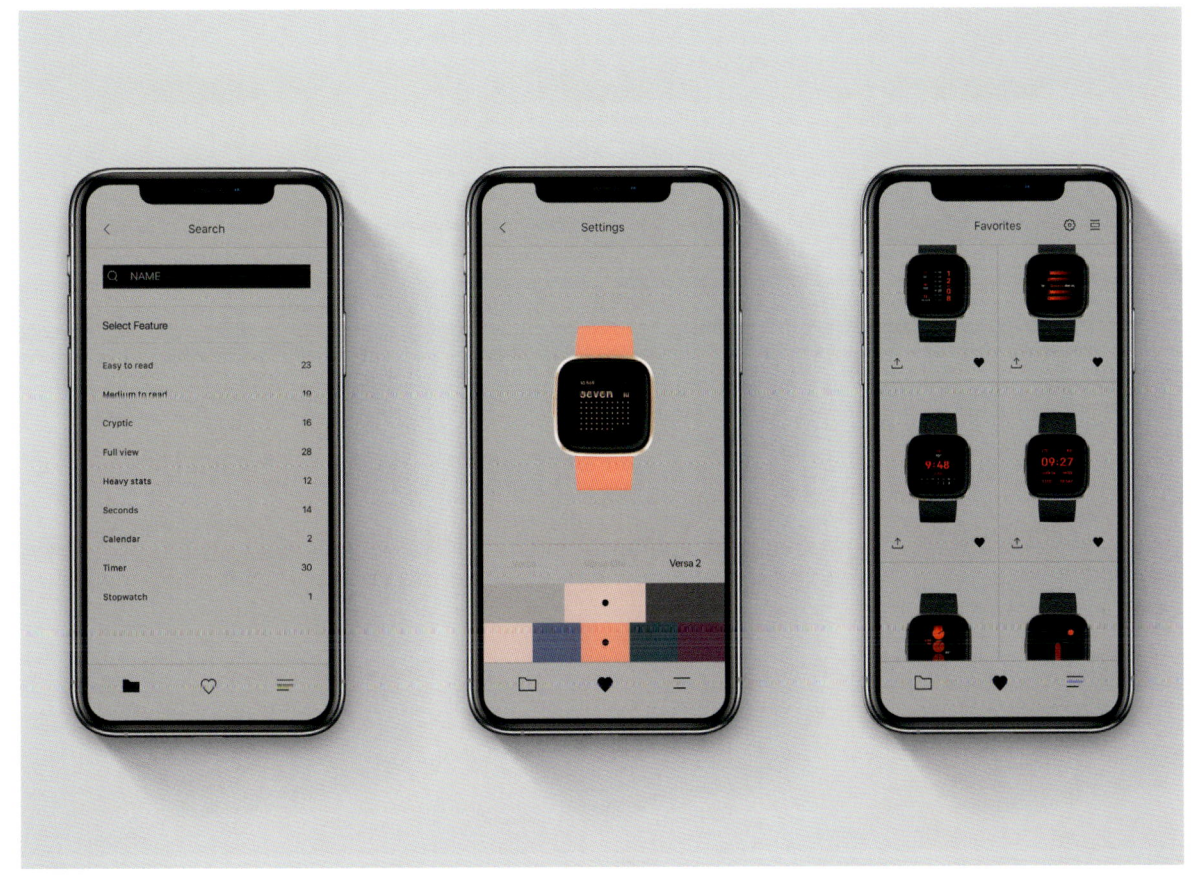

CREON Mobile

[Finance App]

CREON Mobile is the stock-trading app of Daishin Securities, a Korea-based company specialised in financial investment. Moving away from the standardised layout of stock-trading apps that simply list information, the focus has been placed on the users' purpose and pattern. Readability and information delivery were enhanced by adjusting the screen layout. Complex processes were reduced and functions simplified, thus enabling users to manage their tasks easily and to customise the menus they frequently use. The app provides research information, a search service to explore stocks that are worth investing in and an AI chatbot function.

Client
Daishin Securities,
Daishin Financial Group
Seoul, South Korea

Design
Daishin Securities,
Daishin Financial Group
Seoul, South Korea

Project Team
Bongchan Kim (Creative Direction)
Ilsik Chae (Project Management)
Seeun Park (Strategic Planning)
Jihoon Kang (Graphic Design)
Jiyoon Chae (Graphic Design)
Gayoung Kim (Graphic Design)
Youngmi Park (Graphic Design)

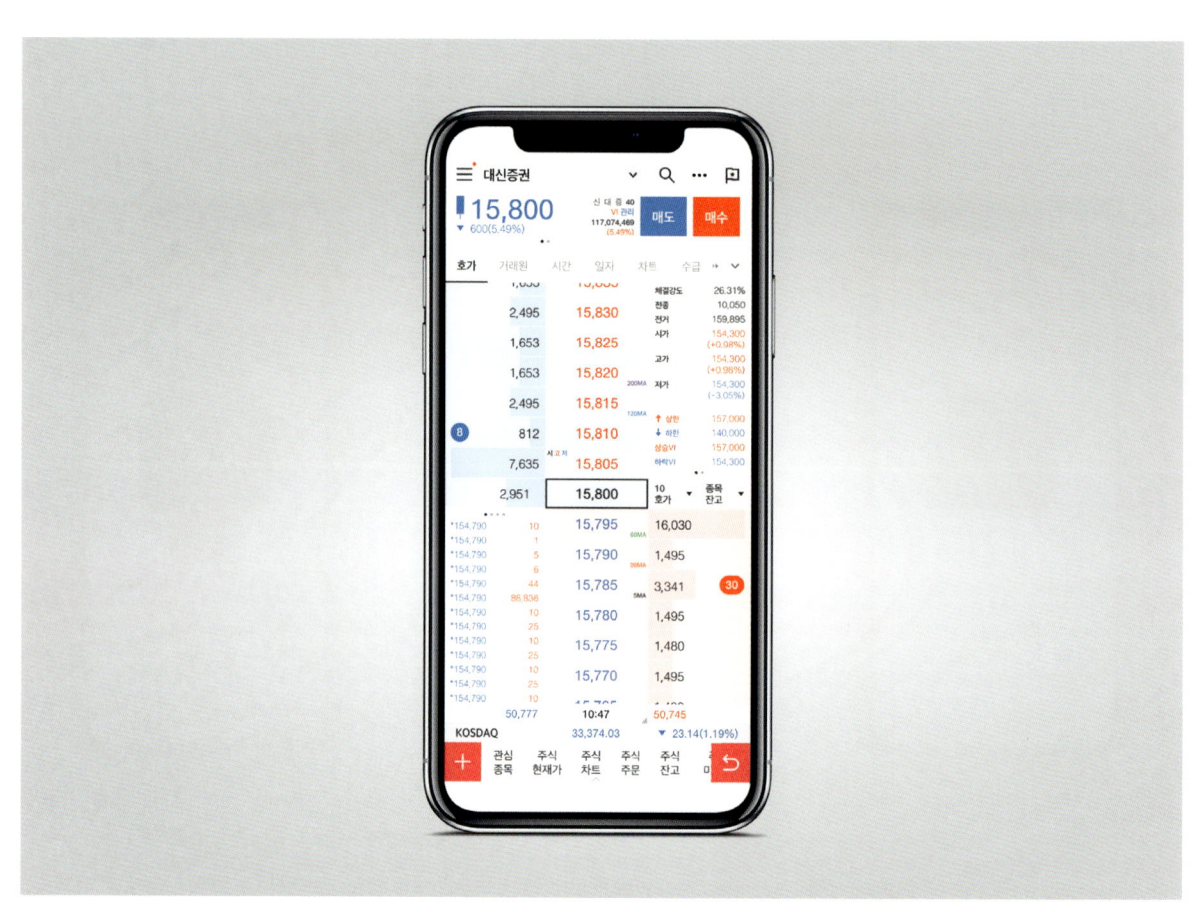

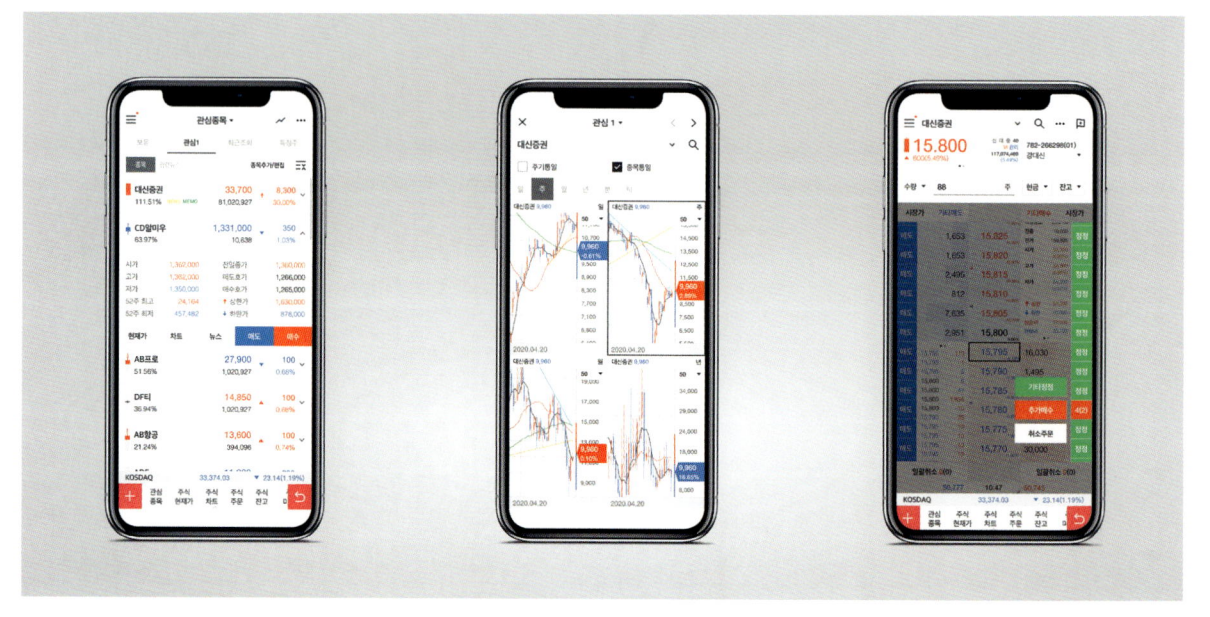

SIOS – The World of Industry Service

[Service App]

Operating or repairing industrial machinery can be a time-consuming challenge. SIOS is a one-stop service app with all of the information on Siemens machinery, providing access to more than 300,000 documents about the products. This includes FAQs, application examples, manuals, certificates and product notes. Access and usage are facilitated by various options: barcode scanning, fast forum Q&A, comprehensive library, optimised search and quick links. The app supports problem-solving during the implementation of a project, as well as troubleshooting and the expanding or restructuring of the system. It is available in six languages.

Client
Siemens AG
Nuremberg, Germany

Design
chilli mind Design Team
Kassel, Germany

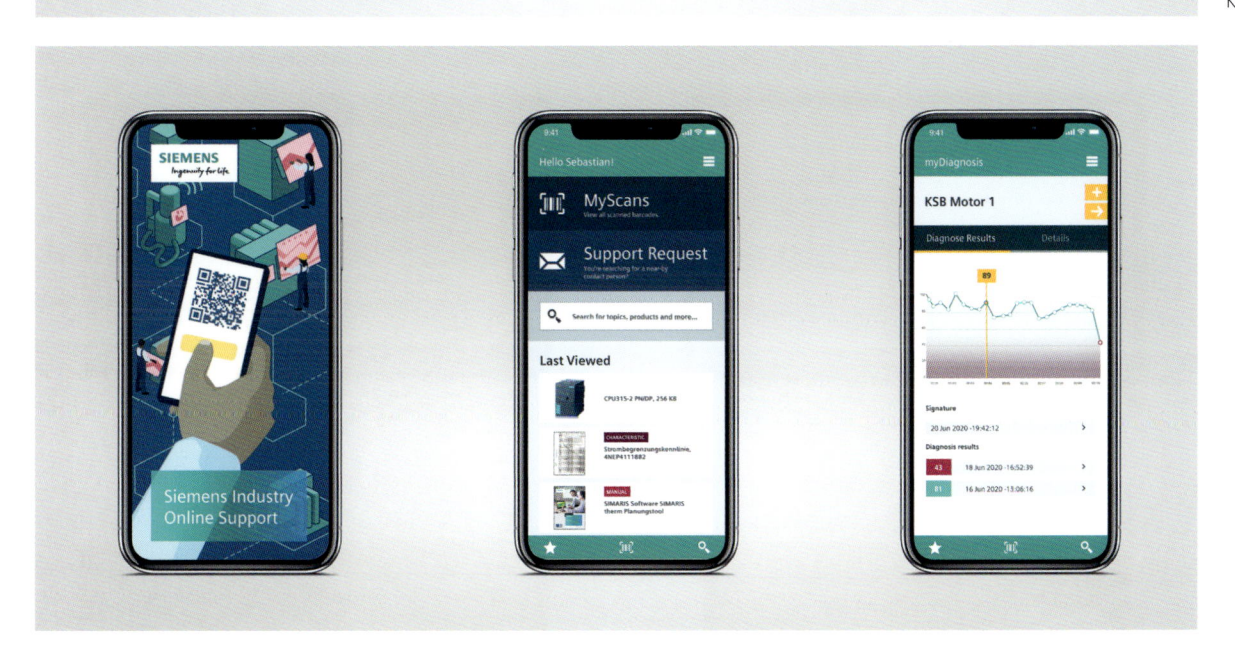

Steam Birdseye

[Web-Based Interactive Visualisation Tool]

Steam Birdseye has been designed as an interactive tool that allows the Department of Municipalities and Transport (DMT) in Abu Dhabi to easily explore and visualise complex data sets and predictive models in a consistent, visually attractive way. The app is designed to help non-technical stakeholders and decision-makers interact and compare proposed scenarios for the given infrastructure. It allows them to understand the current and forecasted future state of the transport sector by giving direct access to all data sources. It also offers features for the easy designing and sharing of maps based on project stories.

Client
Department of Municipalities and Transport
Abu Dhabi, United Arab Emirates

Design
Pixonal
Dubai, United Arab Emirates
CLEVER°FRANKE
Utrecht, Netherlands

Project Team
Transpo Group (Technical Consultant)

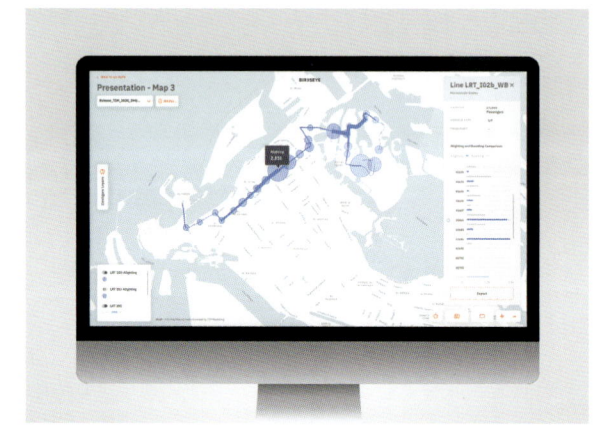

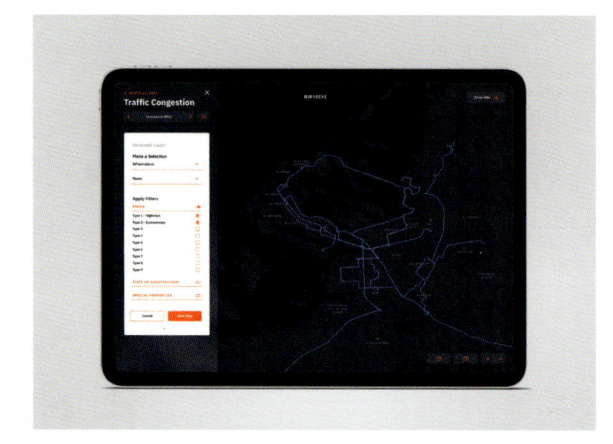

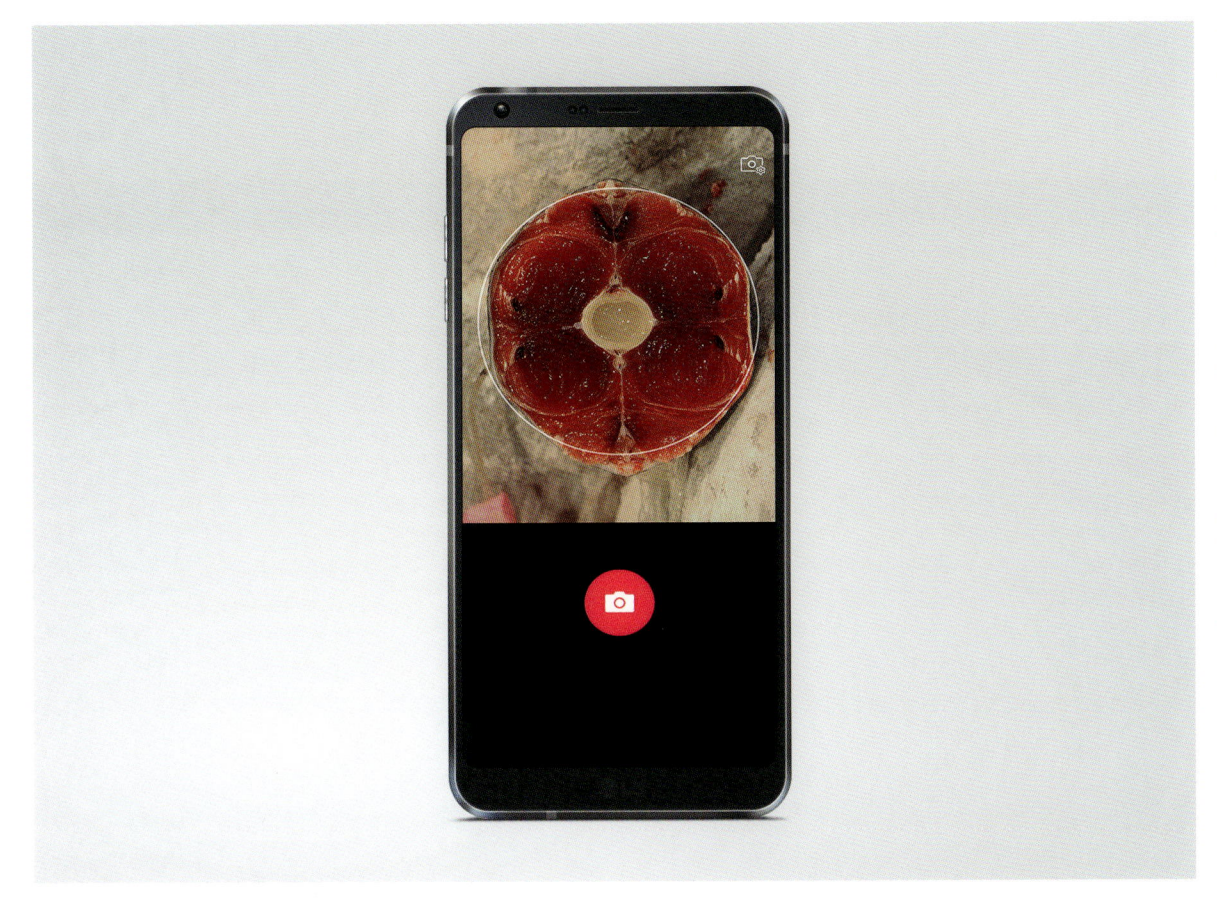

Apps	Interface & User Experience Design	Spatial Communication	Red Dot: Junior Award	Designer Profiles	Jury Portraits	Index
206	236	336	426	564	642	668

TUNA SCOPE

[Service App, AI Development]

Tuna quality examination is a tacit skill that is cultivated by years of training and gained experience, but the number of master artisans specialised in this area has fallen significantly in recent years. TUNA SCOPE is an AI-based system that instantaneously determines the quality of the tuna based on vital data to be found in the cross-section of its tail. Through deep learning analysis of recorded cross-sectional data, a sophisticated traditional Japanese skill was turned into an AI system. The app makes it possible to assess the quality of tuna anywhere in the world with remarkable accuracy.

Client
Dentsu Inc.
Tokyo, Japan

Design
Dentsu Inc.
Tokyo, Japan

Project Team
Kazuhiro Shimura (Creative Director)
Akimichi Hibi (Business Producer)
Ryo Sasaki (Communication Planner)
Daisuke Matsunaga (Art Director)

→ Designer profile on page 583

Interface & User Experience Design

Red Dot: Best of the Best

Lessons of Auschwitz
[VR Project]

"Lessons of Auschwitz" is both a social and artistic experiment dealing with the history of the Holocaust. After visiting the Memorial in Poland, Russian schoolchildren between the ages of 13 and 16 were invited to use XR film technology as a basis to express the personal experiences they had together with their knowledge and their emotional reactions to the Holocaust. In powerful, moving and creative images, they translated their individual experiences and recollections into rich collages that animate historical photo material and transform it into gloomy, blurred film sequences or that show the hand-drawn silhouettes of people dissolve. The background of this social experiment is to show how younger generations perceive history; how they can retell and reimagine it through digital art. Using innovative film technology, the students created a new form of commemorative tribute that appeals in particular to younger viewers at various sensual levels, touches them and inspires them to learn more about the Holocaust.

Statement by the jury
"Lessons of Auschwitz" was conceived as a social experiment that shows in a highly impressive manner how young people not only perceive history, but also how they translate and express it artistically. With the help of innovative XR technology, the students manage to stage their experiences and emotions in a highly creative and individual manner, creating an outstanding experience that touches viewers through all the senses.

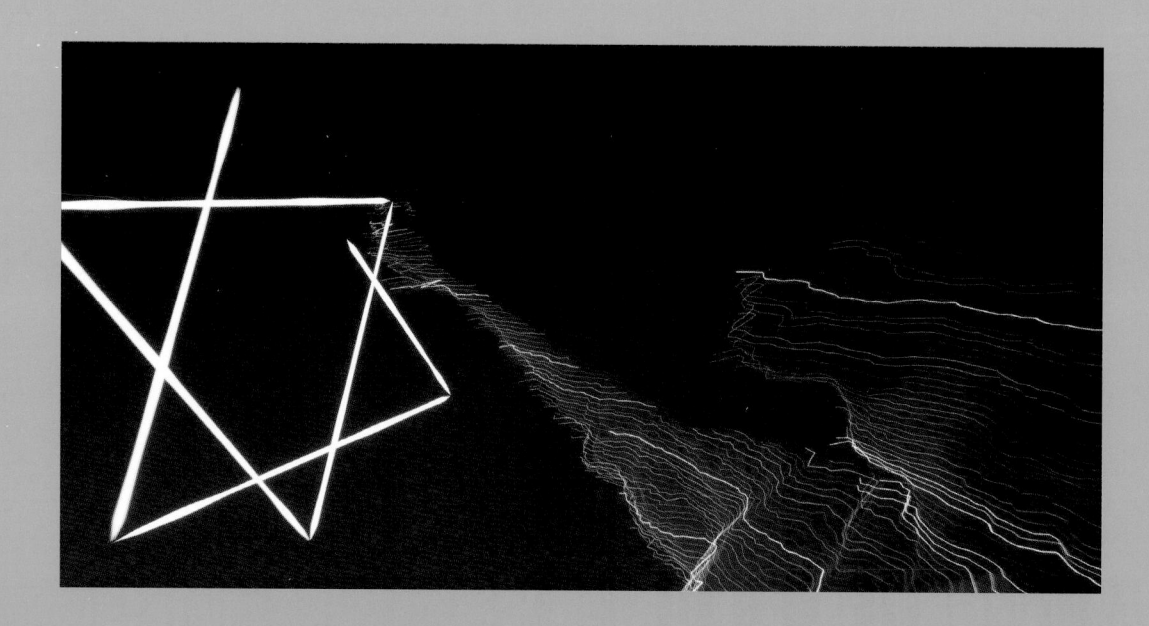

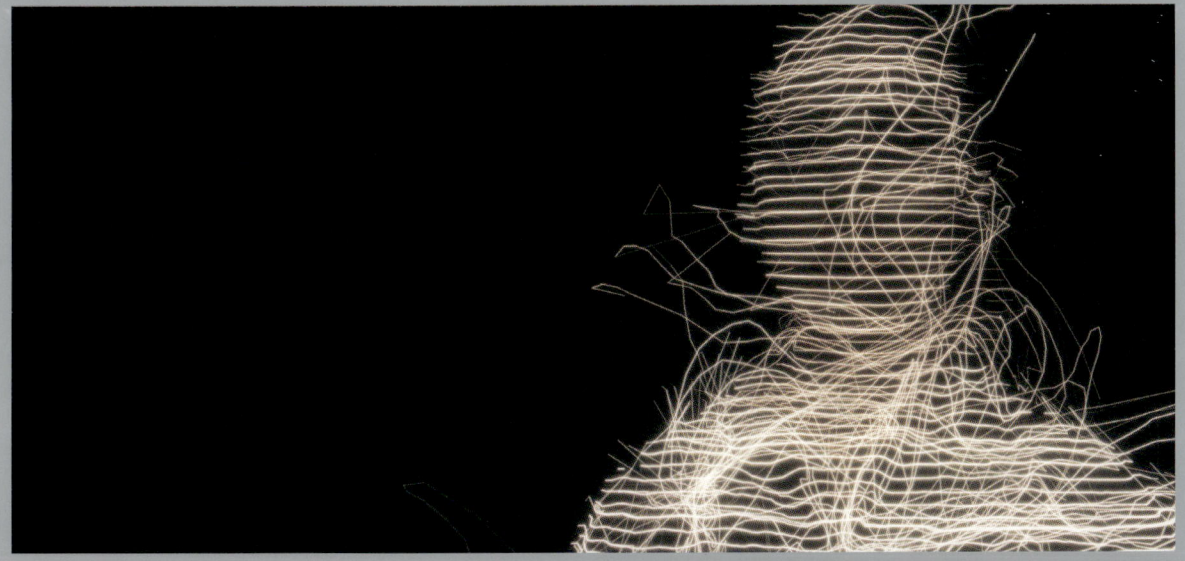

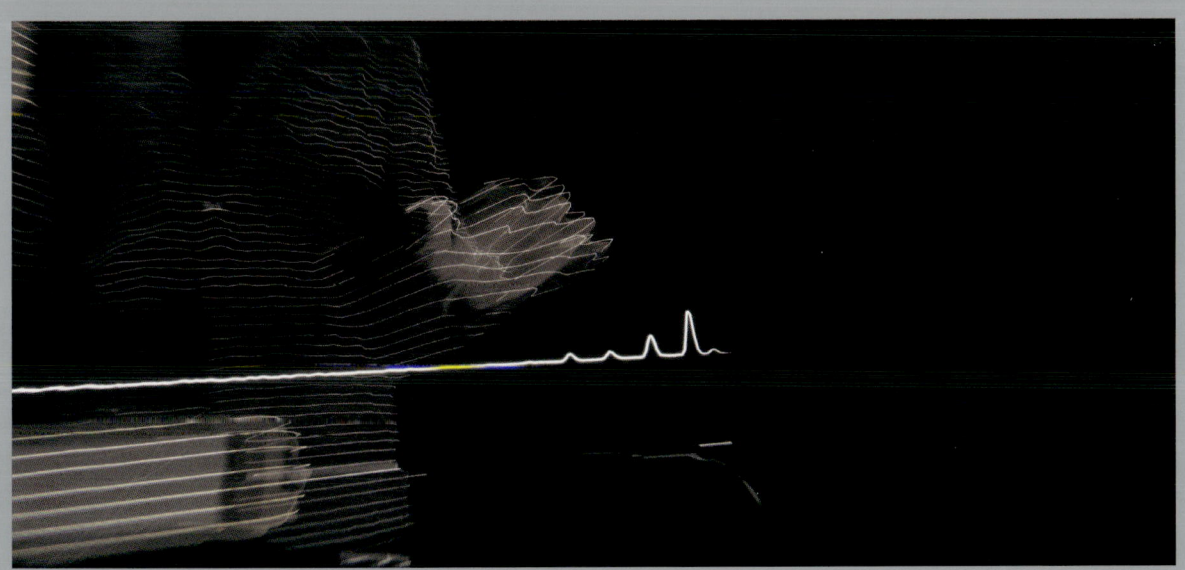

Client
RT
Moscow, Russia

Design
RT
Moscow, Russia
Phygitalism Studio
Moscow, Russia

Project Team
Kirill Karnovich-Valua (Creative Director)
Denis Semionov (Director)
Peter Theremin (Composer)
Eldar Salamov (Sound Design)
Elena Medvedeva (Producer)
Ania Fedorova (Producer)
Ekaterina Sidorova (3D Artist)
Valeria Fimina (Project Manager)
Vlad Krutenyuk (3D Artist)
Aleksandr Kryuchkov (Developer)
Pavel Postnikov (3D Artist)
Vanya Yunitskiy (Project Manager)
Aleksey Lushnikov (Developer)
Nikita Semionov (VR Artist)
Sasha Volkov (VR Artist)
Misha Borisov (VR Artist)
Dima Kaderkaev (VR Artist)
Zhenya Timoshenkova (VR Artist)
Vlad Sarychev (VR Artist)
Nata Makashvili (VR Artist)
Dima Sobaev (VR Artist)
Lera Agescheva (VR Artist)

→ Designer profiles on pages 611, 616

Red Dot: Best of the Best

discovering hands 3D diagnostic app
[Health Solution]

"discovering hands" closes a crucial gap in the field of breast cancer prevention with its tactile diagnosis and thus is a response to the 70,000 women who are diagnosed with breast cancer every year. Specially trained blind women examine patients according to a scientifically based method. To further support the tactile diagnosis, a software-based medical application was developed that allows the results of the tactile examination to be accurately documented and processed appropriately for the patient and further diagnosis. Thus, blind medical tactile examiners (MTEs) can digitally record the findings and visualise them in a 3D thoracic model and a 2D frontal view. The intuitive user interface also allows them to conveniently enter their tactile results in Braille. These are then recorded in a 3D grid and show the exact location of tissue changes. Similar to an X-ray image, the application provides precise information about the location of findings, providing ideal support for specialists in their diagnostic consultation with the patient.

Statement by the jury
The "discovering hands" project impresses with its clever approach of combining the special tactile sensitivity of visually impaired women in detecting breast cancer with an AI-based user interface into which these women can directly enter their findings. This not only facilitates faster, easier and, in particular, more precise diagnostics – and thus saving human lives – the design also impresses with an aesthetic appeal that is both elegant and clear.

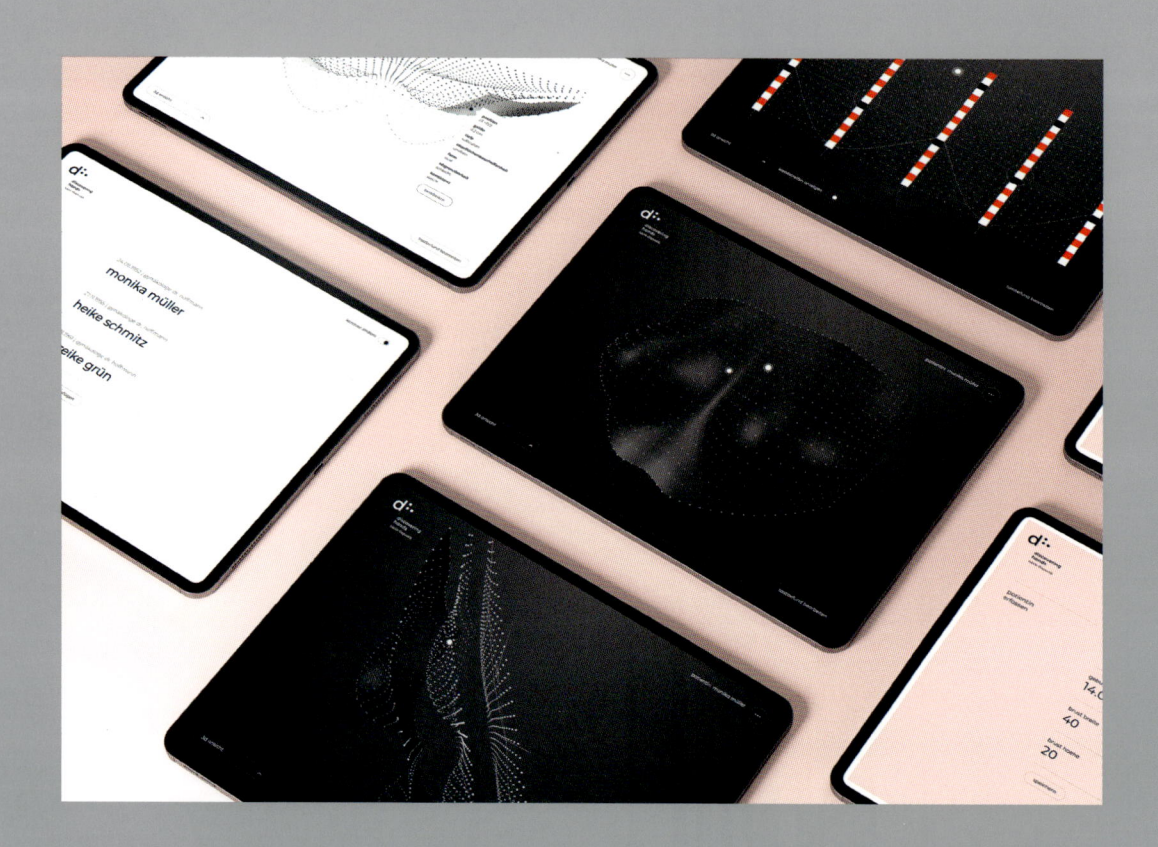

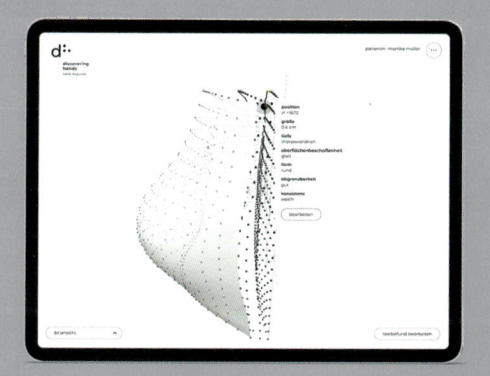

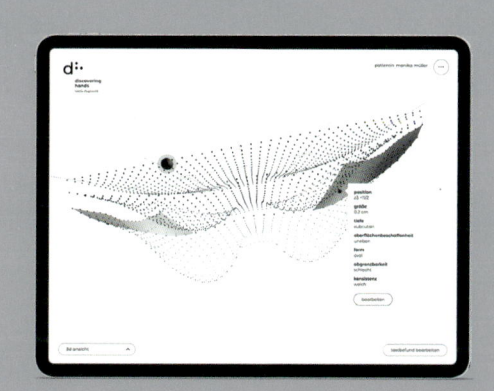

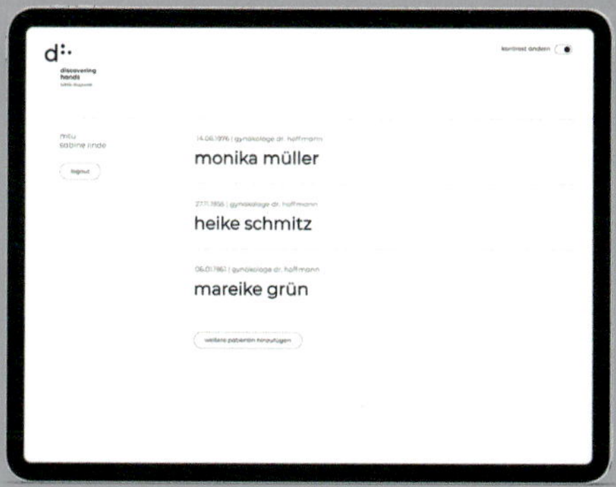

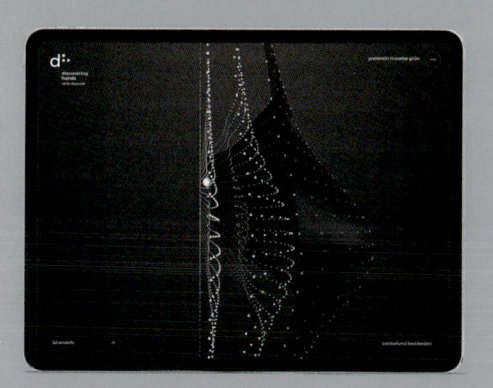

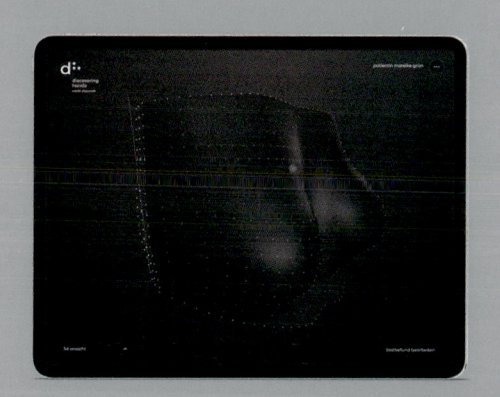

Apps	Interface & User Experience Design	Spatial Communication	Red Dot: Junior Award	Designer Profiles	Jury Portraits	Index
206	236	336	426	564	642	668

Client
discovering hands Service GmbH
Mülheim/Ruhr, Germany

Design
Grey Germany/KW43 BRANDDESIGN
Düsseldorf, Germany

Project Team
Prof. Rüdiger Goetz
(Managing Director Creation)
Tim Liedtke (Creative Director)
Miriam Hugo (Senior Art Director)
Marc Schaede (Senior Art Director)
Tim Wimmer (Junior Art Director)
Lucie Benavides (Junior Art Director)
Michael Draheim (Senior Copywriter)
Emma Foerster (Account Director Digital)
Marc Dittmann (Frontend Developer)

→ Designer profile on page 602

Red Dot: Best of the Best

Huawei EIHealth
[User Interface Design]

EIHealth is an artificial intelligence R&D platform, which provides professional services in the areas of genomic analysis, drug discovery, medical imaging and others. With hyperscale computer-aided drug screening abilities, the platform can perform homology modelling of the protein structure for all target proteins of a virus, molecular dynamics simulation and computer-aided molecular docking of billions of small-molecule compounds. Thanks to this technology and the simulations, a large number of measurements and scenarios can be carried out in less time in the event of a pandemic such as COVID-19, which effectively provides information and helps researchers, for example, in narrowing the scope of drug screening in the development of anti-epidemic drugs. The design of this effective platform is based on human centric design and uses a variety of graphic visualisations in 2D and 3D in order to clearly arrange the enormous amounts of data. The platform thus delivers an intuitive user experience that makes navigating this complex and powerful tool more transparent.

Statement by the jury
The AI-based user interface for Huawei EIHealth impresses with the enormous variety of approaches with which it can process huge amounts of complex data and, in this process, always remains clear and plausible. The design has successfully emerged with an appearance that intuitively guides the user and which organises the processed data into easy-to-understand 3D images or tables and diagrams.

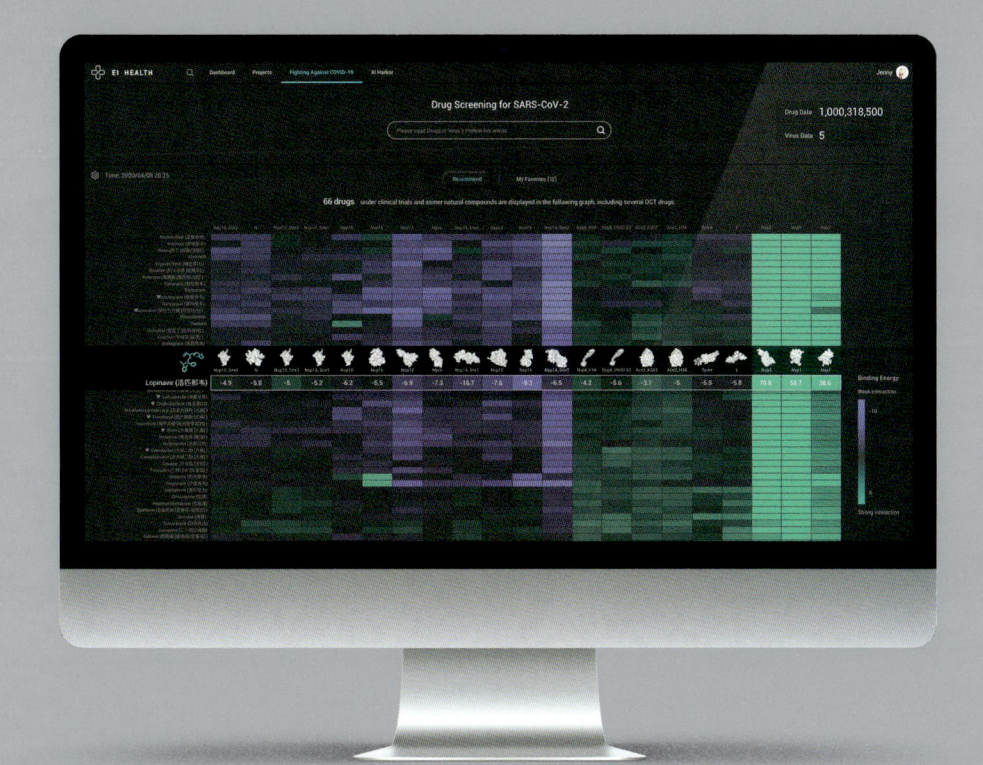

Apps	Interface & User Experience Design	Spatial Communication	Red Dot: Junior Award	Designer Profiles	Jury Portraits	Index
206	236	336	426	564	642	668

Client
Huawei Technologies Co., Ltd.
Shenzhen, China

Design
Huawei Technologies Co., Ltd.
UCD Center
Beijing, China

Project Team
Binghua Xu (Design)
Zhenzhen Li (Design)
Yilin Wang (Design)
Xue Yang (Animation Design)
Huimei Wei (Animation Design)
Nan Qiao (R&D)
Xin Meng (R&D)
Chi Xu (R&D)

→ Designer profile on page 595

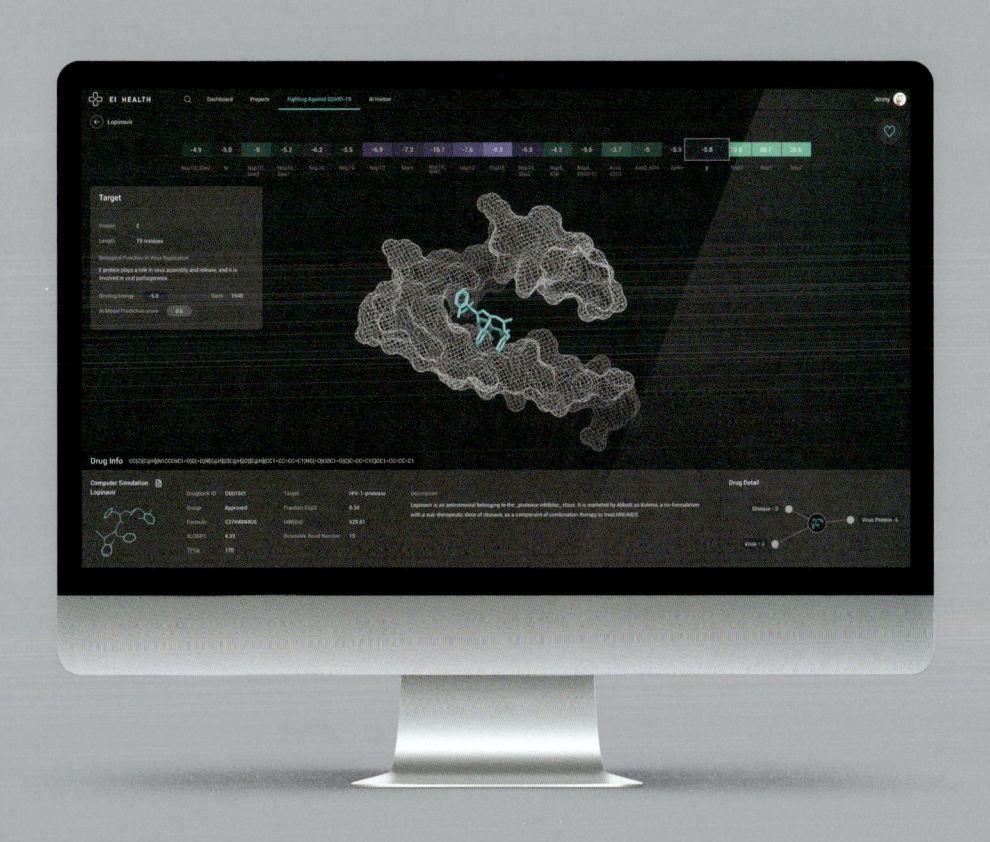

Red Dot: Best of the Best

KIEFEL – HMI for packaging machines
[User Interface Design]

KIEFEL is an international manufacturer of machines and tools for processing plastics. The new human-machine interface (HMI) for its packaging machines is based on self-explanatory illustrations and animations. For example, clear messages and status displays not only help monitoring the production process, they also assist in adding material in time and keeping the machine running continuously. Intelligent diagrams, clear animations and vivid illustrations reduce the complexity and a sophisticated colour and form guide system ensures correct assignment of parameters, components and their movement curves – even for people with poor colour vision. An ergonomically designed sidebar provides for short operating paths and maximum space at screen height. The modular machine visualisation facilitates easy navigation and clear status display, and like the modular expander controls, it ensures the efficient and economical adaptation of the HMI to any equipment variant.

Statement by the jury
The new user interface design for the automated KIEFEL packaging machines is an excellent example of how design and technology can be combined intelligently for the purpose of achieving not only higher performance and effectiveness but also higher ease of use for the operator. The well-thought-out design ensures an almost intuitive control of the system and a quick understanding of its functions.

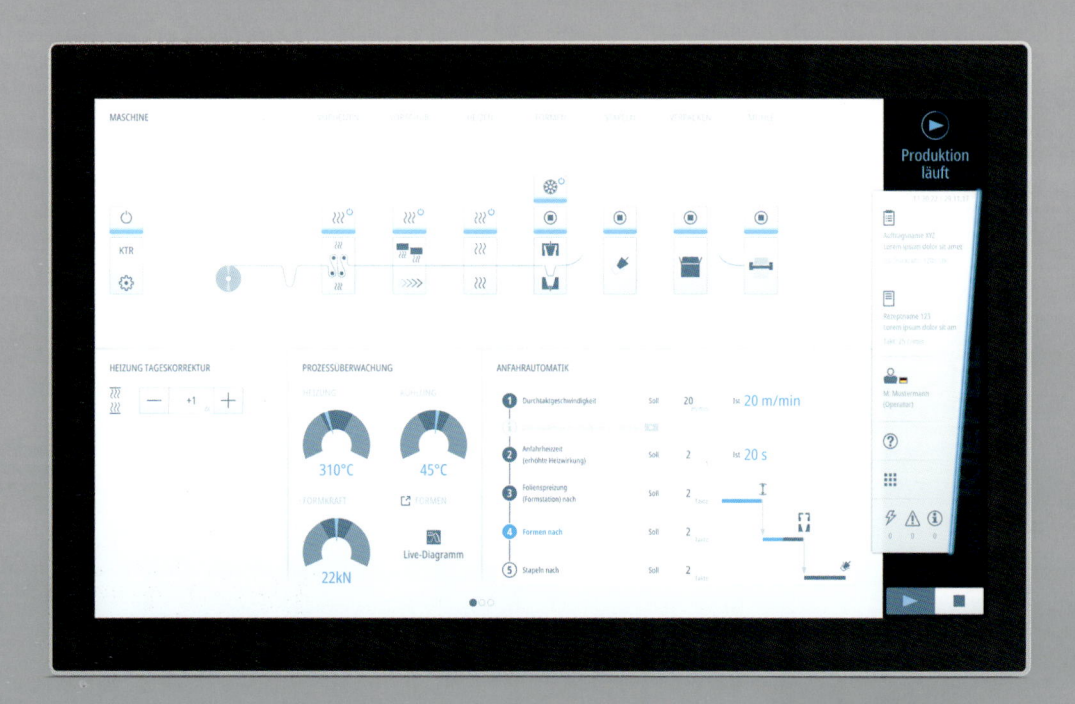

Apps	Interface & User Experience Design	Spatial Communication	Red Dot: Junior Award	Designer Profiles	Jury Portraits	Index
206	236	336	426	564	642	668

Client
KIEFEL GmbH
Freilassing, Germany

Design
CaderaDesign GmbH
Würzburg, Germany

Project Team
Tom Cadera (Creative Direction)
Amelie Reich (Creative Direction)
Henning Muschko (Graphic Design)
Anna Radlbeck (Graphic Design)
René Fleischer (Concept)
Eva Wolz (Concept)

→ Designer profile on page 578
→ Clip online

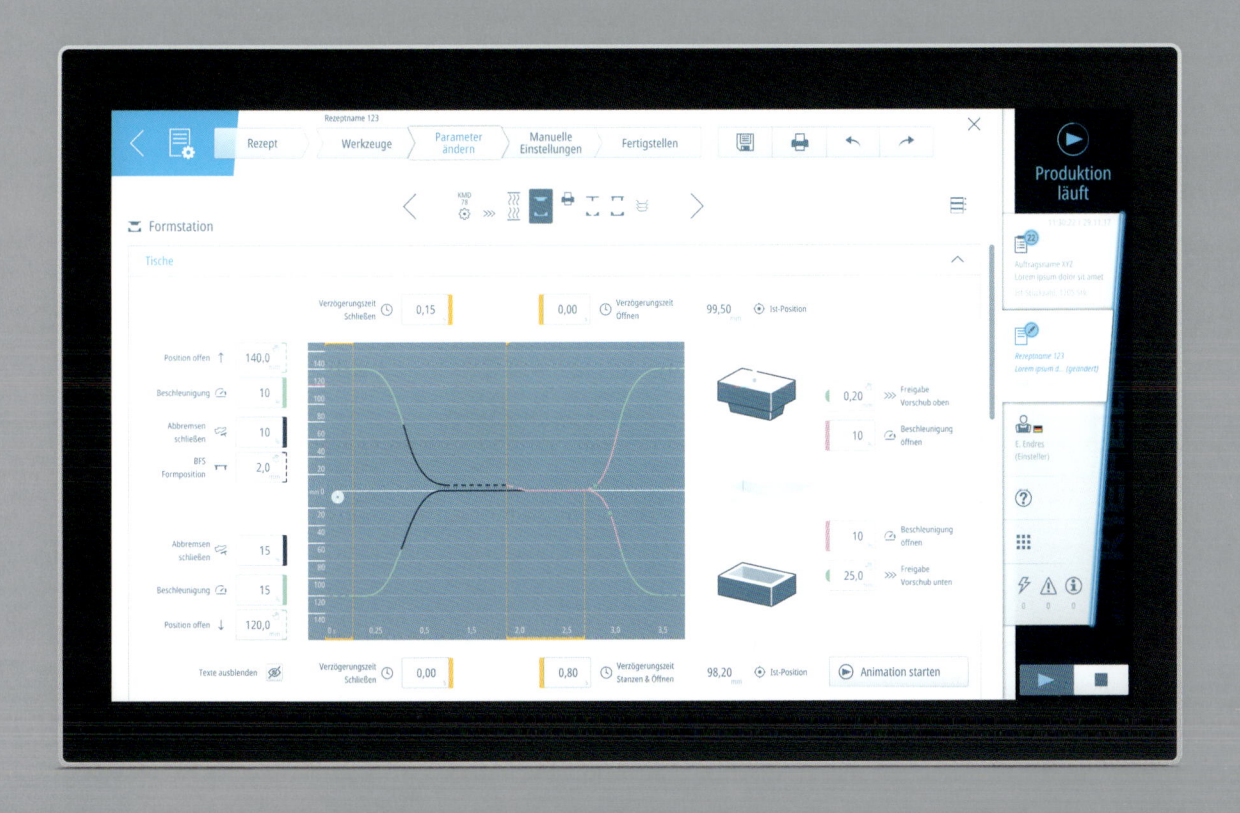

Publishing & Print Media	Posters	Typography	Illustrations	Sound Design	Film & Animation	Online
4	64	92	116	126	138	172

Edison Design System
[Health Solution]

Edison Design System is defined as a platform of user-validated design, code and standards for creating consistent, modern and intuitive health software. Launched in 2020, the system aims to evolve the industry and unify UX across the company GE Healthcare with improved usability and consistency. As craftsmanship is a core tenet, every component features detailed designs, codes and redlines. The system is tailored for healthcare with components such as patient banners, medical specialty icons and guidelines, as well as custom colours for use in dark and light rooms.

Client
GE Healthcare
Seattle, USA

Design
GE Healthcare
Seattle, USA

Project Team
Beverly May (Executive Creative Director)
Kevin Yuda (Creative Director)
Jay Christensen (UX Director)
Prasad Aluru (Director UI Engineering)
Adelina Green (Visual Design)
Lucia Choi (Visual Design)
Ambar de Kok-Mercado (Visual Design)
Deanna Liceaga (Graphic Design)

→ Clip online

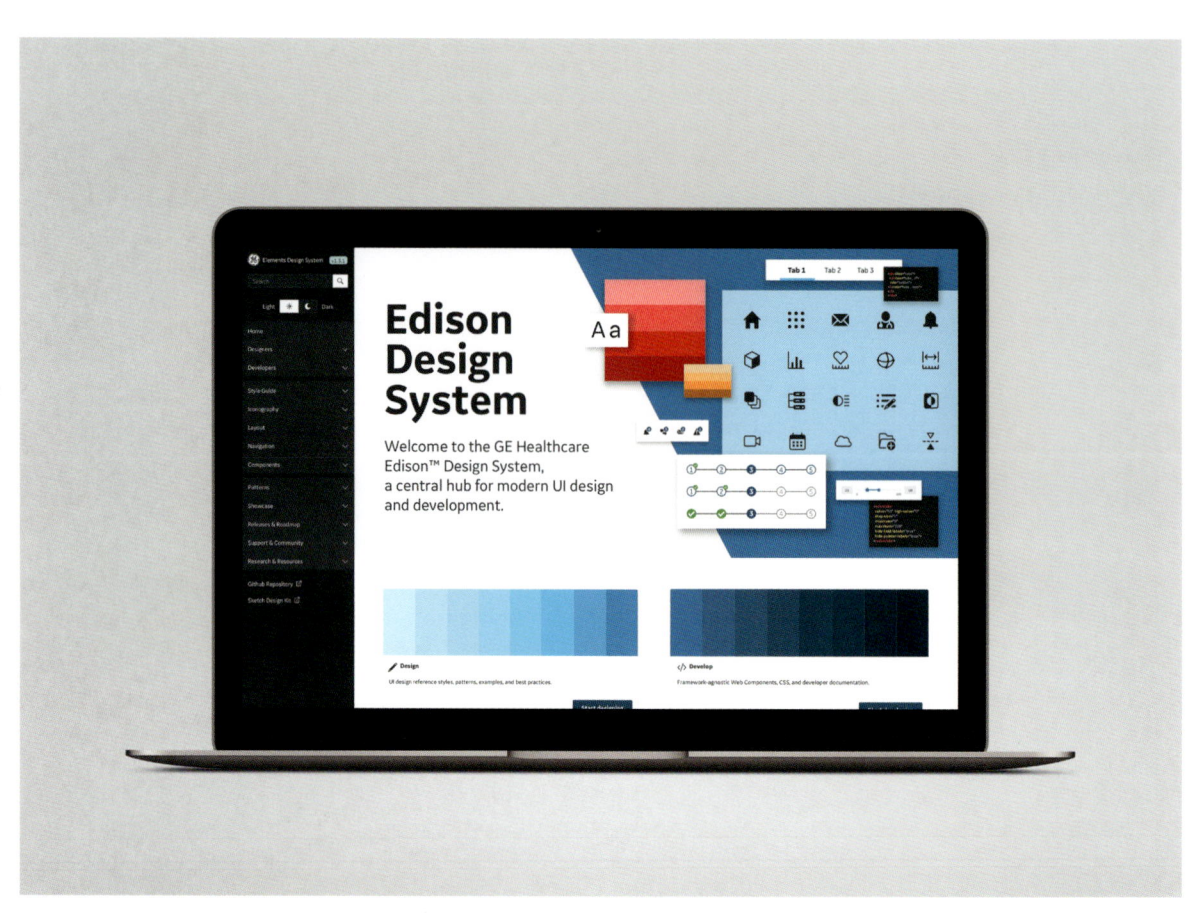

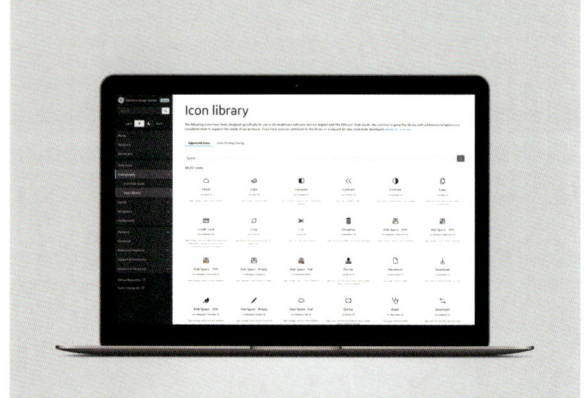

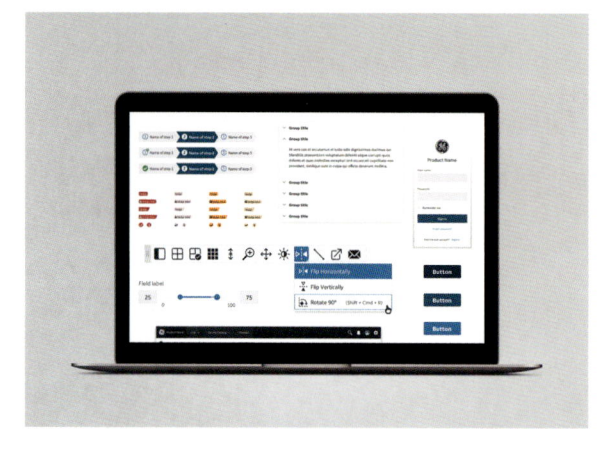

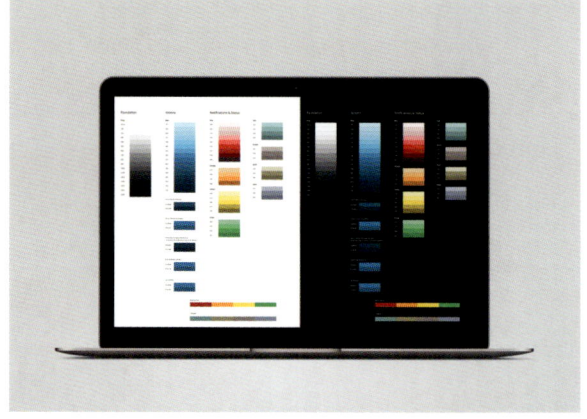

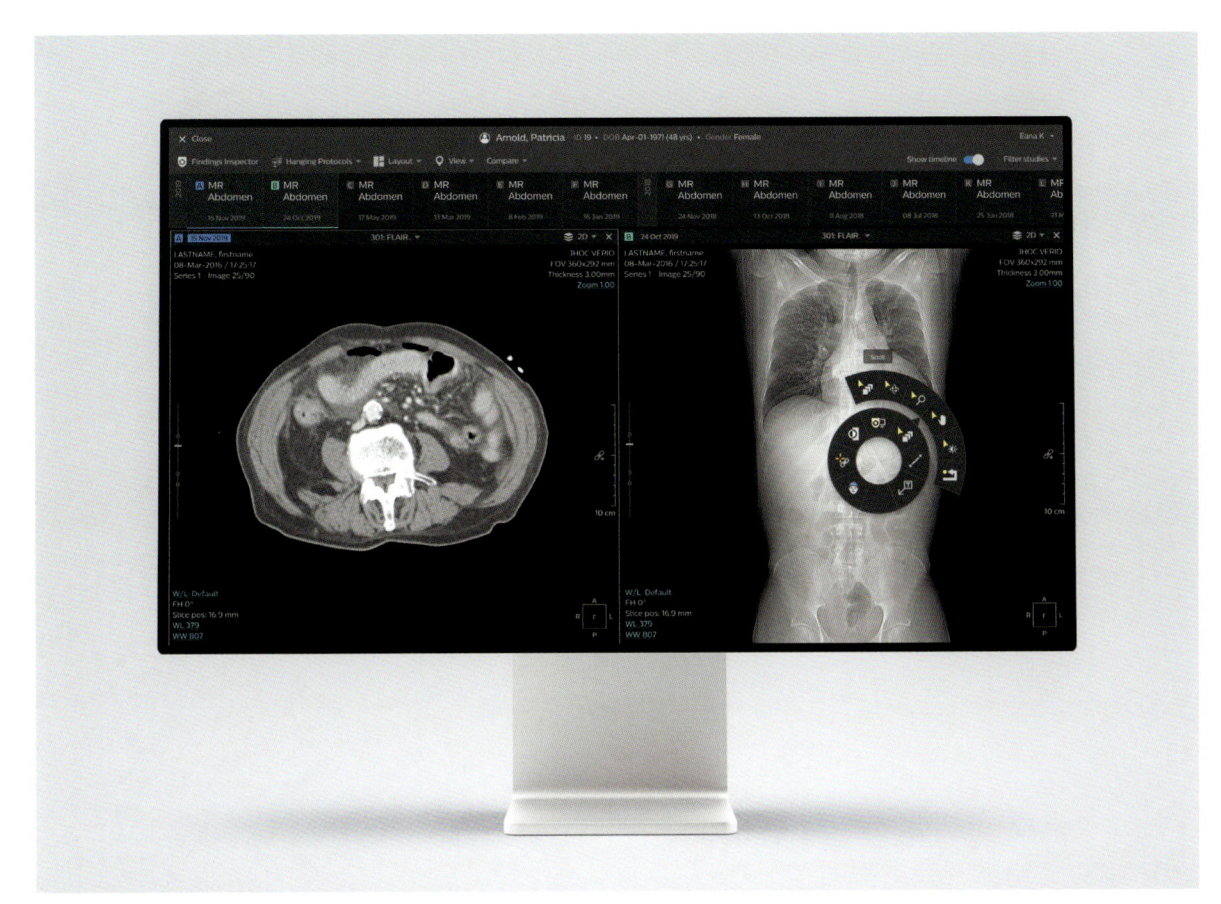

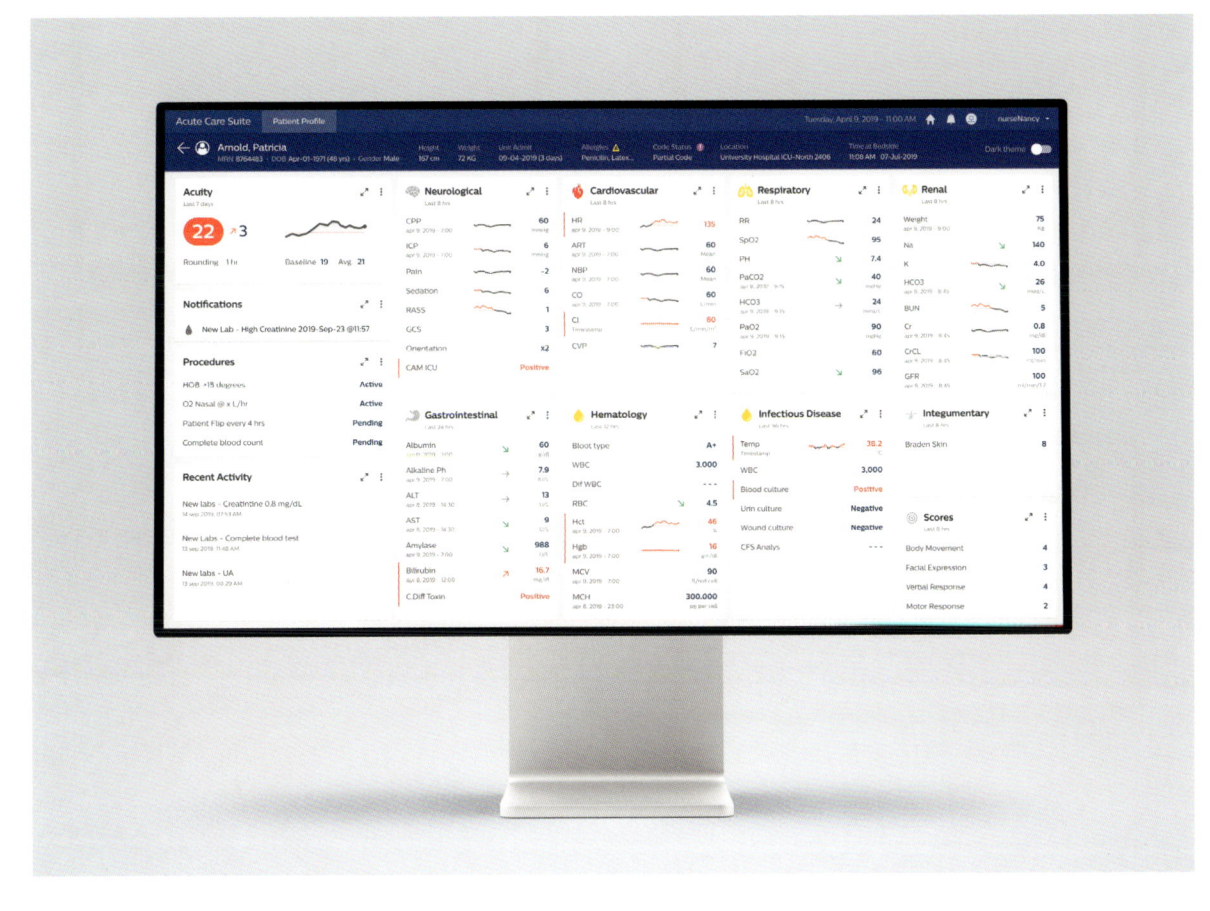

Modular Healthcare Informatics User Interface System

[Health Solution]

This modular healthcare informatics user interface system is a new type of tool for medical professionals in making diagnostic and treatment decisions. It addresses the specific workflow needs of multiple users across a complex and evolving ecosystem. The user experience design first identified shared user needs and engineering requirements across the portfolio and then developed a modular approach. The concept of these user-friendly, interacting modules has emerged as a simplified and consistent system of informatics apps that reduce the cognitive load for users.

Client
Philips
Eindhoven, Netherlands

Design
Philips Experience Design team
Blumenau, Brazil
Cambridge, USA
Haifa, Israel
Eindhoven, Netherlands
Pleasanton, USA
Bangalore, India

Publishing & Print Media	Posters	Typography	Illustrations	Sound Design	Film & Animation	Online
4	64	92	116	126	138	172

IPS Gate® 2.0
[Health Solution]

IPS Gate® 2.0 is used to facilitate the easy management of medical cases concerning patients in need of an implant. The entire process from the first contact to the implementation of patient-specific implants is realised and mapped on a single platform. Surgeons, healthcare professionals and implant designers can work together on cases securely and efficiently and track them throughout the entire workflow. Thanks to the chat function, all persons involved in a case are in contact with each other during the entire process.

Client
KLS Martin Group
Tuttlingen, Germany

Design
CADS GmbH
Perg, Austria

Project Team
Mario Moser (Project Management)
Michael Schultz (Designer)
Melanie Marksteiner (Designer)
Bárbara Gonzáles Iglesias (Artwork)

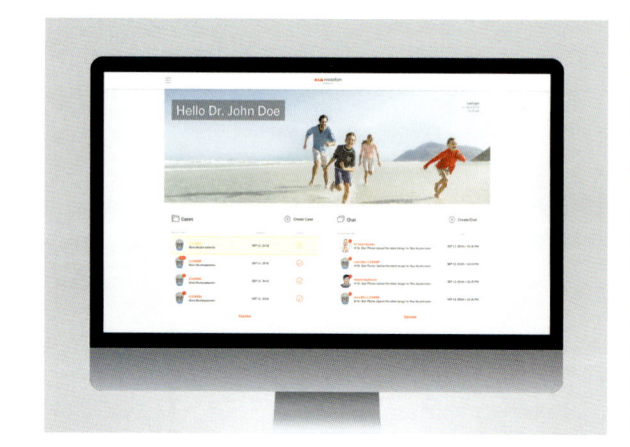

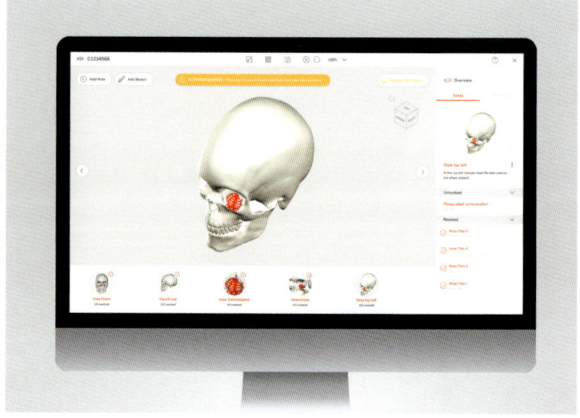

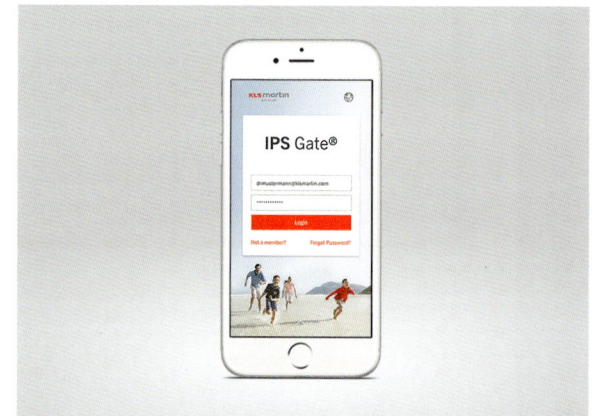

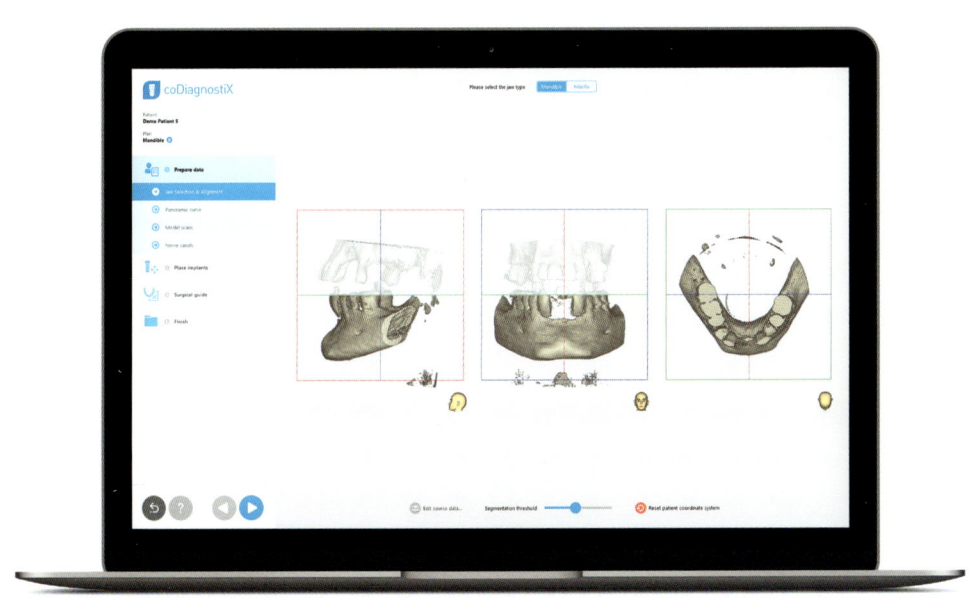

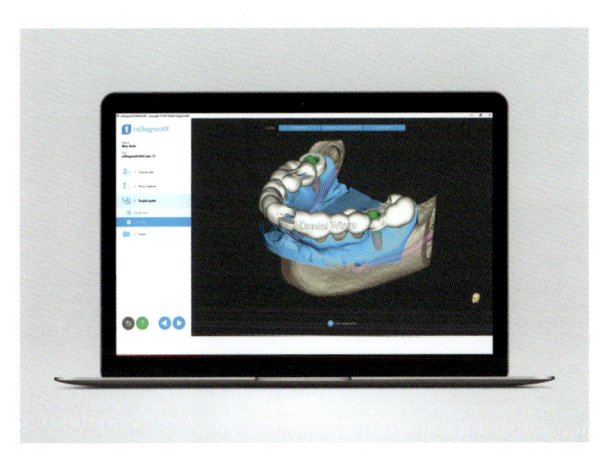

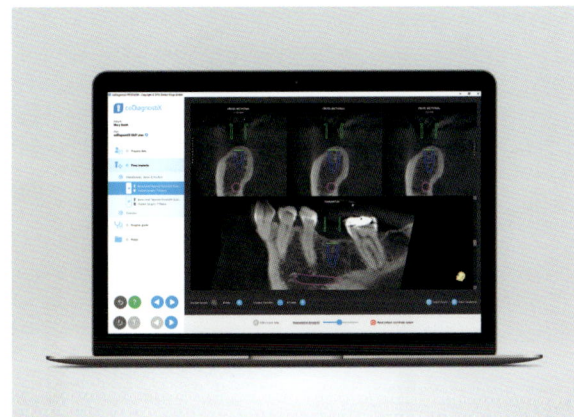

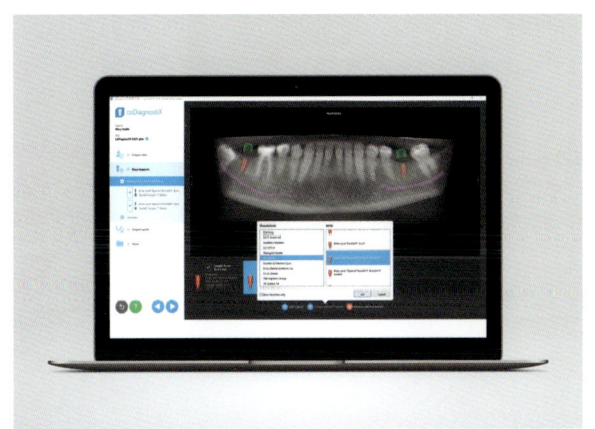

coDiagnostiX EASY Mode

[Health Solution]

The software coDiagnostiX for implant planning enables dental professionals to plan and design surgical guides that ensure an exact and aesthetically pleasing fit of their patient's tooth restoration. EASY mode is a new and intuitive UI specially tailored to new users. The design has been streamlined to make it self-explanatory, reduce learning time and speed up the planning process. It offers a fully guided workflow that contains only the essential planning steps, easily identifiable controls and integrated quick-help and pre-aligned views instead of the entire coDiagnostiX toolkit.

Client
Dental Wings GmbH
Chemnitz, Germany

Design
Dental Wings GmbH
Chemnitz, Germany

IntelliSpace Cognition

[Health Solution]

The design of IntelliSpace Cognition combines well-established neurocognitive assessments with automation and adaptive intelligence. It thus helps neurologists to make more precise diagnoses and develop more targeted treatment plans. A primary goal of this solution is to facilitate robust and reliable cognitive assessment with far greater efficiency and scale than is possible using only traditional methods. As a digital, cloud-based assessment tool, it takes established neuropsychological tests and enables their administration by a medical assistant using a tablet in an office setting.

Client
Philips
Eindhoven, Netherlands

Design
Philips Experience Design team
Eindhoven, Netherlands

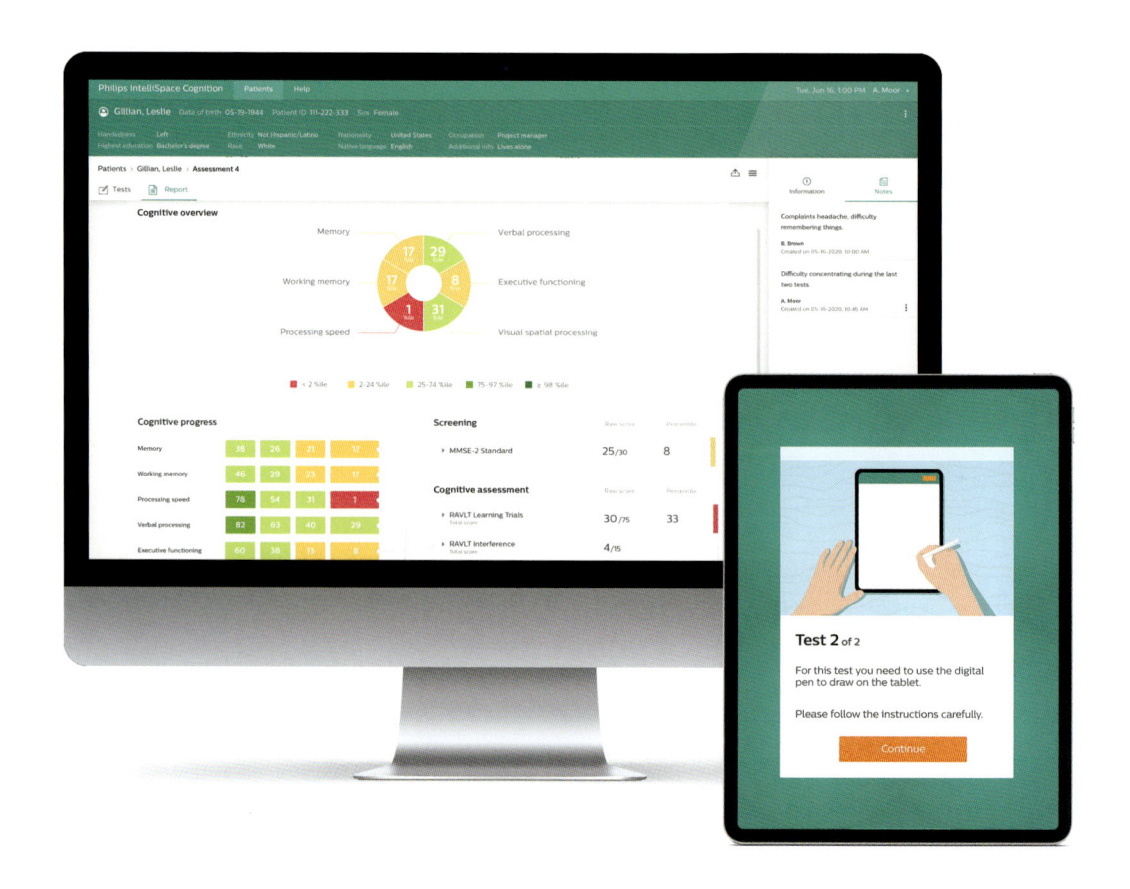

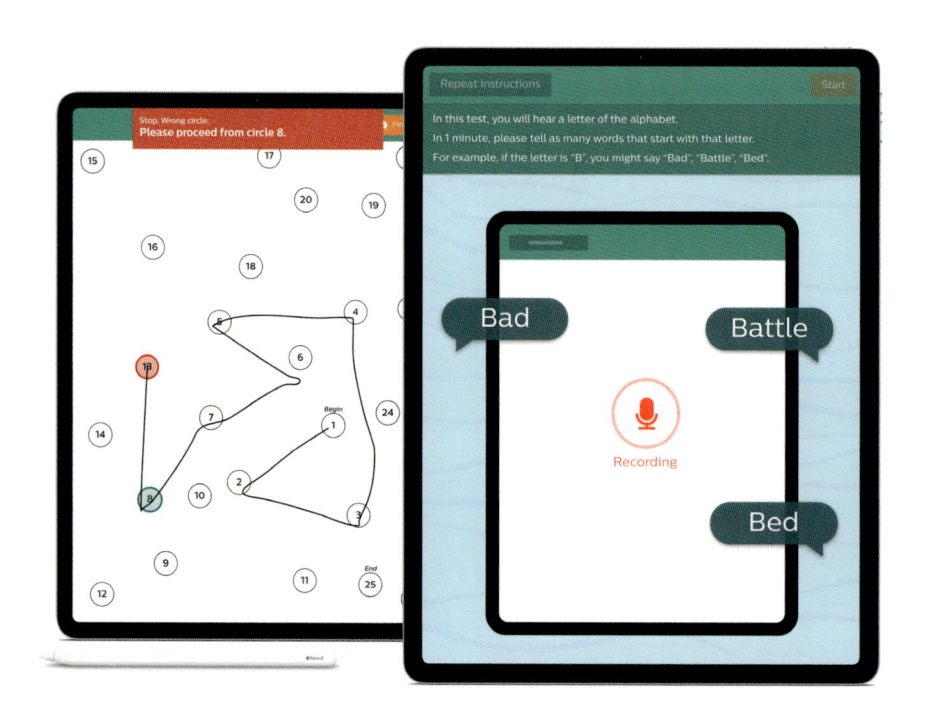

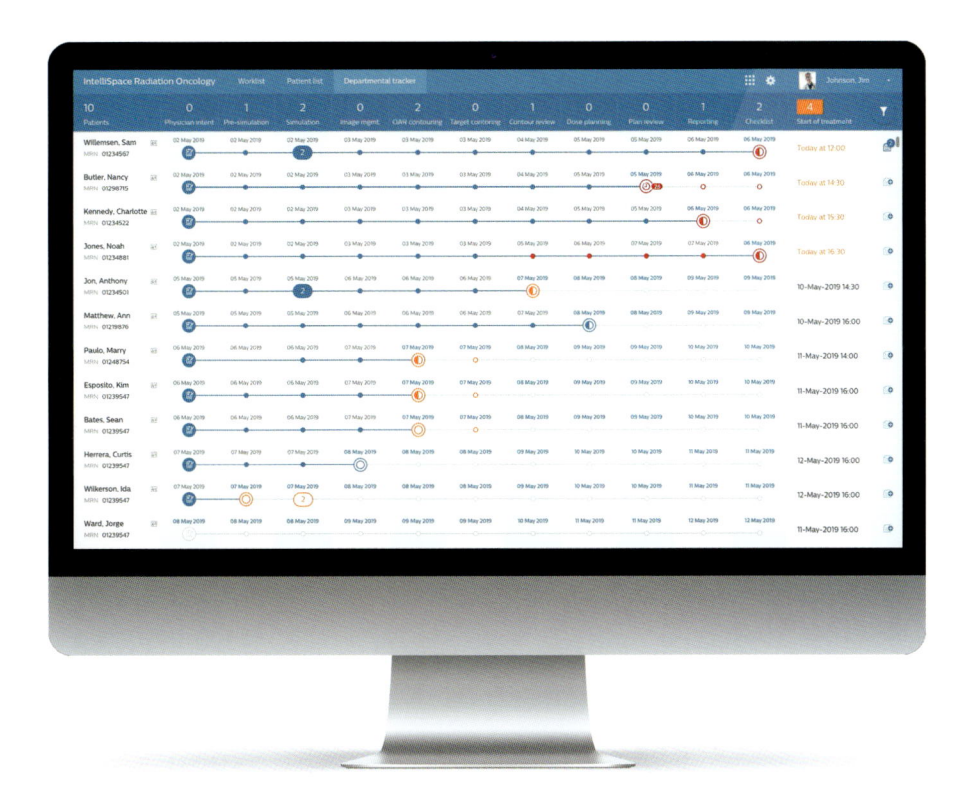

Apps	Interface & User Experience Design	Spatial Communication	Red Dot: Junior Award	Designer Profiles	Jury Portraits	Index
206	236	336	426	564	642	668

IntelliSpace Radiation Oncology

[Health Solution]

As radiation oncology processes are often fragmented and inefficient, IntelliSpace Radiation Oncology (IS-RO) aims to build bridges between these workflow tasks and information technology. It offers a simplified, consistent system of informatics apps that reduce cognitive load for users. Intuitive dashboards deliver relevant information to one's fingertips with direct access to external applications and a deep integration with hospital IT. As an intelligent patient management solution, IS-RO is designed to accelerate the time from patient referral to the start of treatment by helping to manage complexity, improve efficiency and enable operational excellence.

Client
Philips
Eindhoven, Netherlands

Design
Philips Experience Design team
Bangalore, India
Eindhoven, Netherlands

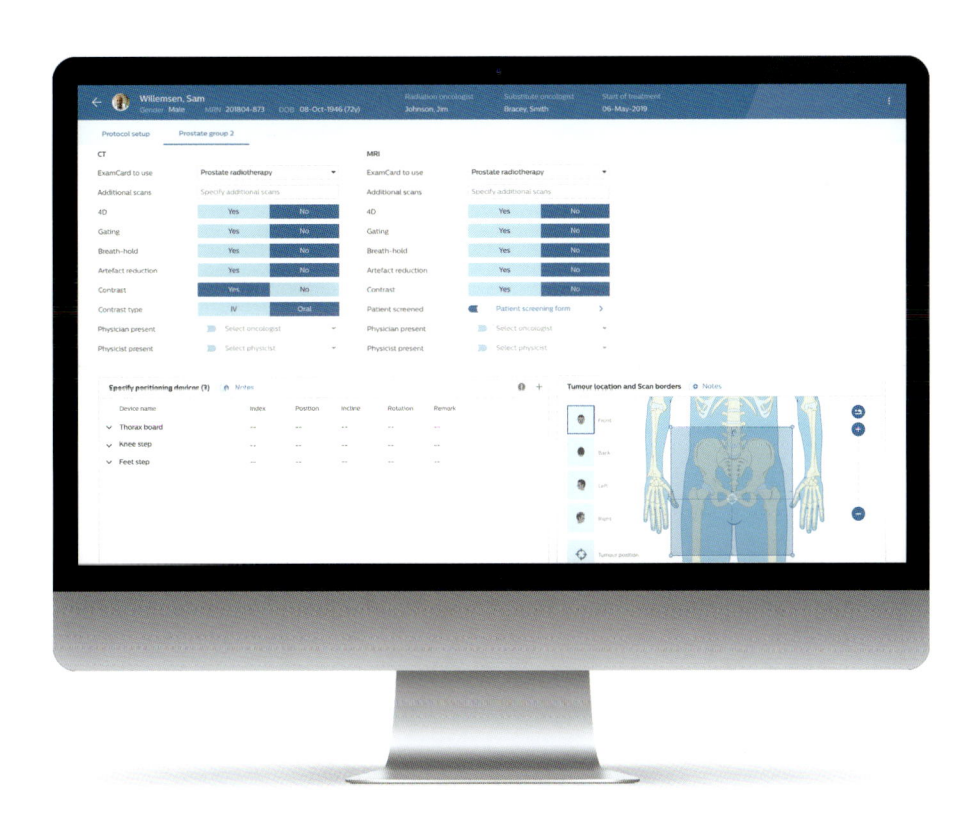

Publishing & Print Media	Posters	Typography	Illustrations	Sound Design	Film & Animation	Online
4	64	92	116	126	138	172

Huawei Medical Imaging – AI

[Health Solution]

As a user-friendly AI system, Huawei Medical Imaging offers the possibility of fast analysis of CT images, as well as a new way of experiencing the cooperation between AI and the doctor. Based on AI algorithms and an immersive user interface, the system can help to pre-identify Covid-19 infections and automatically generate diagnosis reports. In addition, the AI supports highly skilled doctors in the analysis of lesions and follow-up analyses. Analysing a CT image, which previously took around 15 minutes, is thus reduced to a range from two seconds to around two minutes.

Client
Huawei Technologies Co., Ltd.
Shenzhen, China

Design
Huawei Technologies Co., Ltd.
Shenzhen, China

Project Team
Shaolei Wang (UX Designer)
Ren Li (UX Designer)
Yuanfeng Chu (UX Designer)
Bijun Zhang (UX Designer)
Kai Kuang (UX Designer)
Yujing Wang (UX Designer)

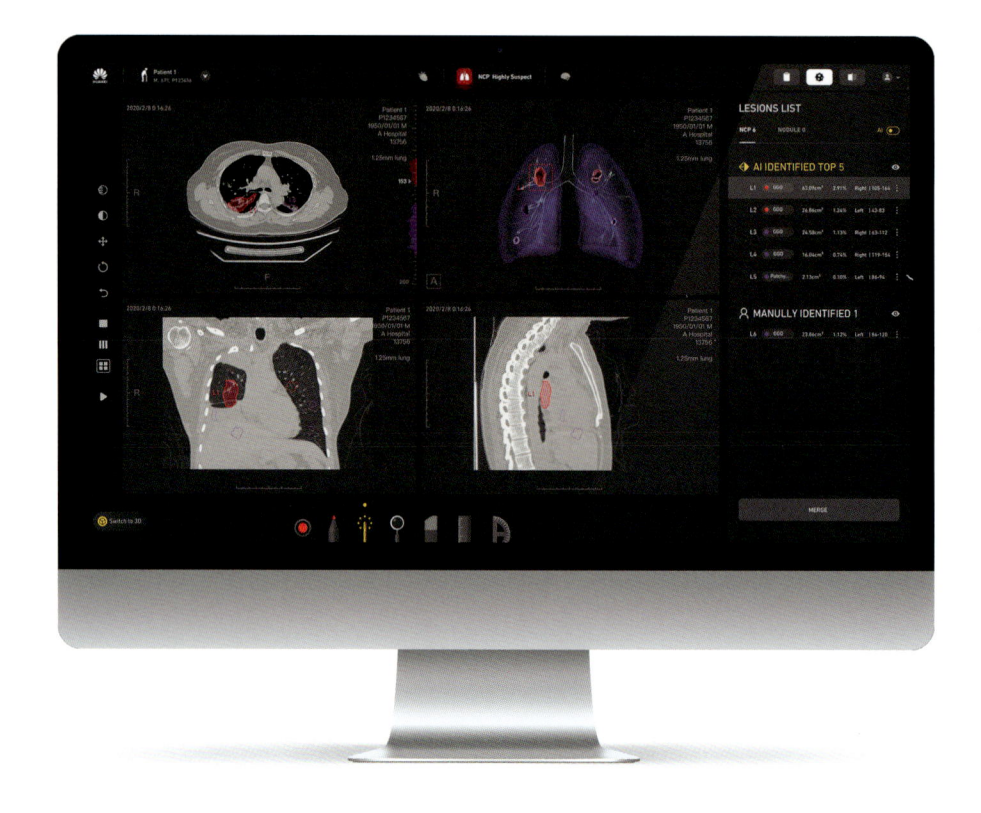

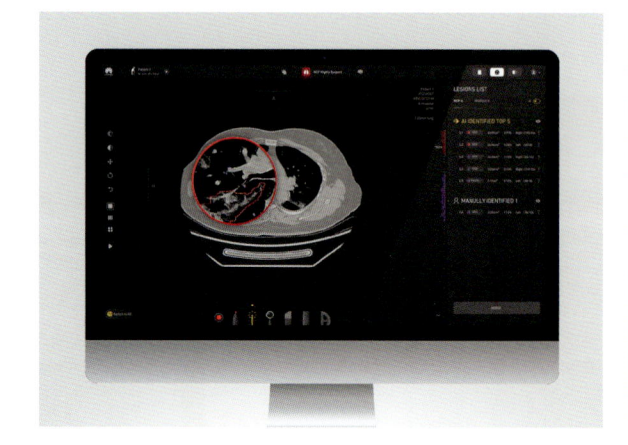

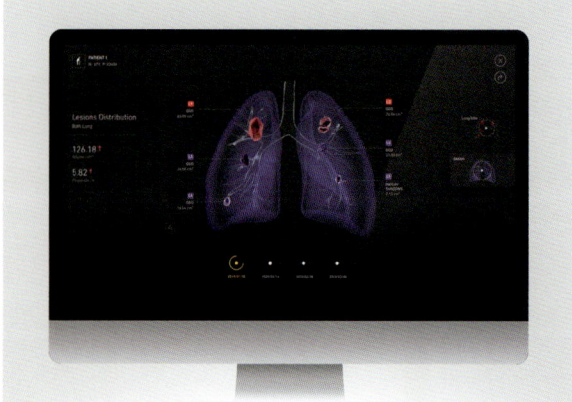

Apps	Interface & User Experience Design	Spatial Communication	Red Dot: Junior Award	Designer Profiles	Jury Portraits	Index
206	236	336	426	564	642	668

Lunit INSIGHT

[Health Solution]

Lunit INSIGHT is a medical AI software for analysing chest X-rays and mammography images with the aim of detecting major lung diseases or breast cancer. It can assist doctors as a "second reader" for a faster and more accurate diagnosis. Developed with a well-thought-out and user-friendly interface, it features a sleek dark mode and intuitive infographics. This AI solution indicates the location of the detected lesions in the form of heat maps and provides abnormality scores reflecting the probability of the existence of the detected lesion.

Client
Lunit Inc.
Seoul, South Korea

Design
Lunit Inc.
Seoul, South Korea

Project Team
Hyemin Shim (Creative Direction)
Taeyoung Yun (UX Design)

Publishing & Print Media	Posters	Typography	Illustrations	Sound Design	Film & Animation	Online
4	64	92	116	126	138	172

Vitrolife G-Series Interactive Hologram

[Interactive Exhibition, User Experience Design]

Vitrolife G-Series Holographic Demo is an installation that visualises and promotes the benefits of IVF-specific embryo mediums in this series. It aims to ensure, in a clear and eye-catching manner, how the G-Series media surrounds the embryos and gametes with optimised conditions in each stage of IVF (in vitro fertilisation). It visualises how each product in the G-Series is developed to resemble conditions in the female reproductive tract and to fulfil embryo growth. The interactive installation lets users select what medium to learn about by pressing the respective physical bottle.

Client
Vitrolife AB
Gothenburg, Sweden

Design
The Techno Creatives
Gothenburg, Sweden

Project Team
Jonas Lindberg (Designer)
Leticia Rezende (Designer)

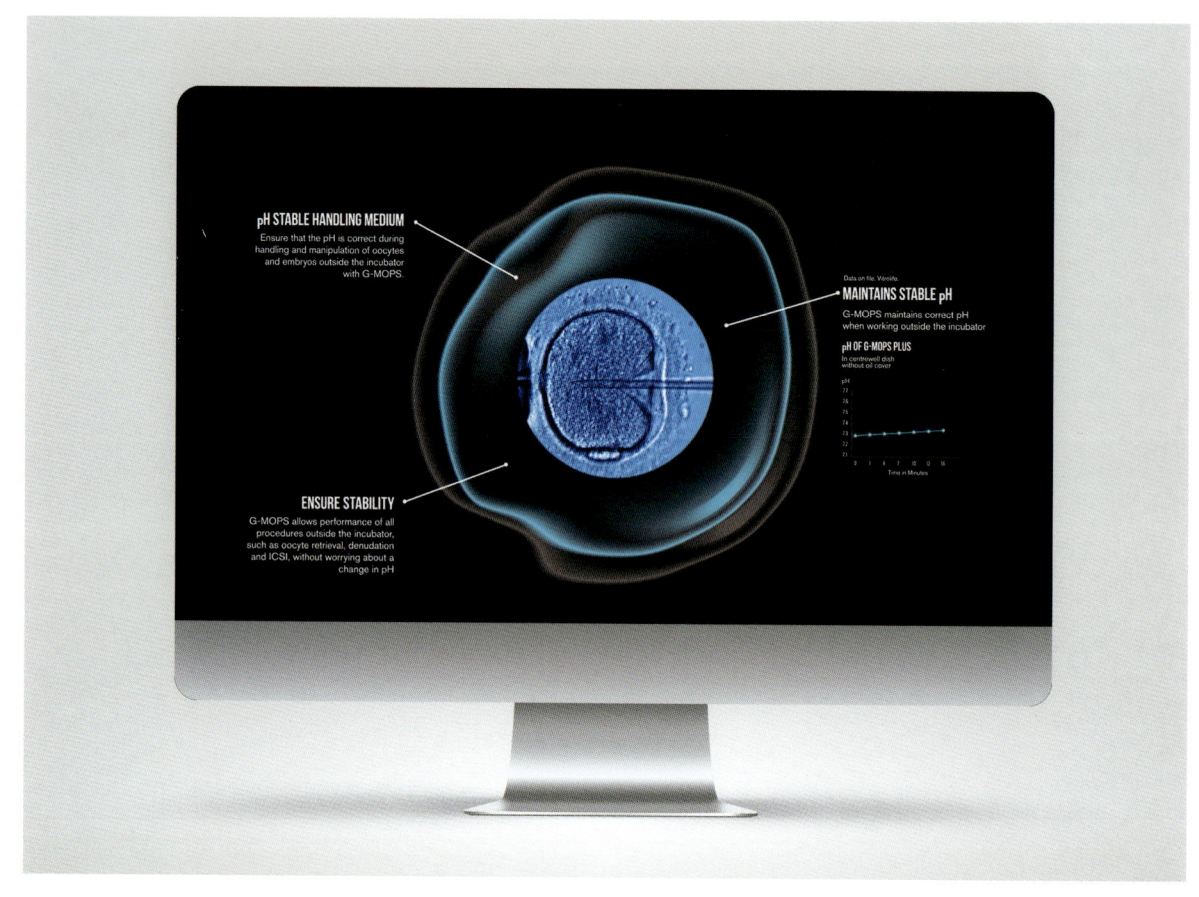

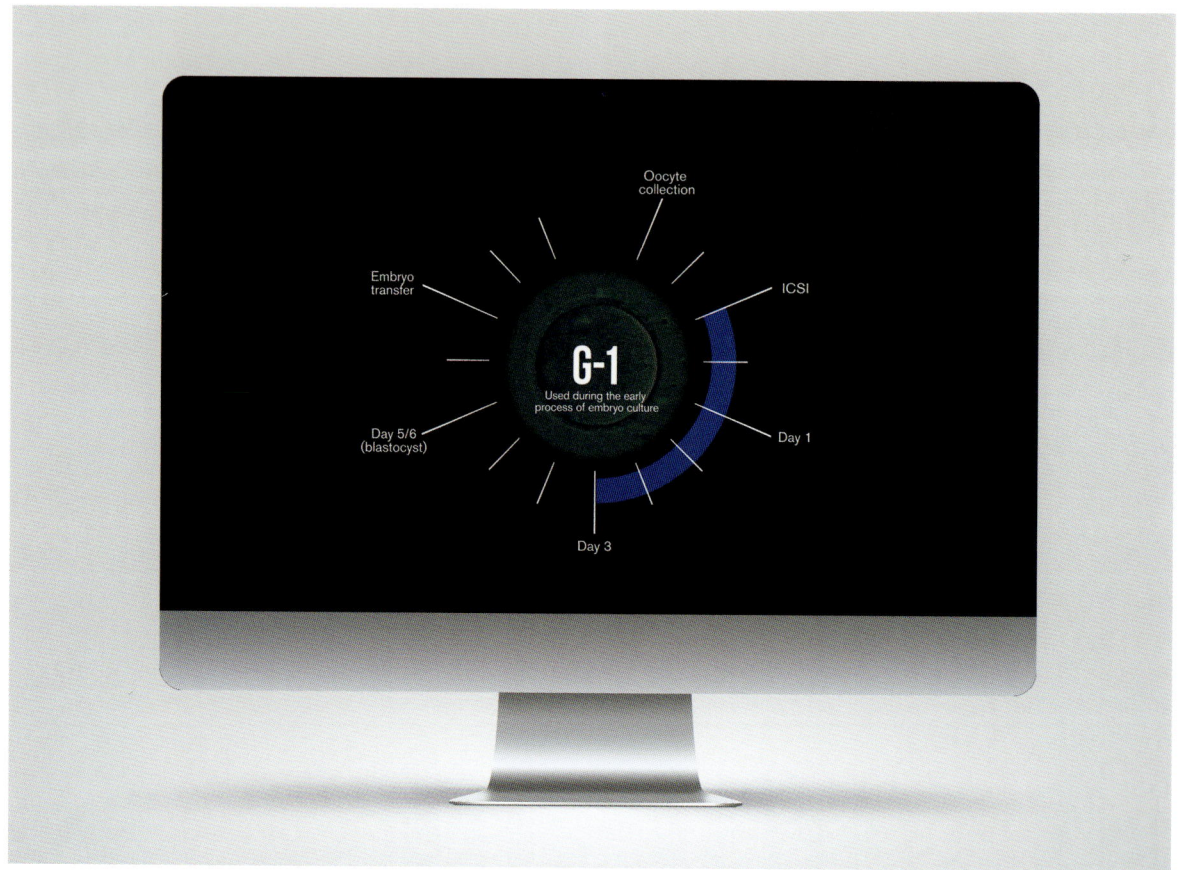

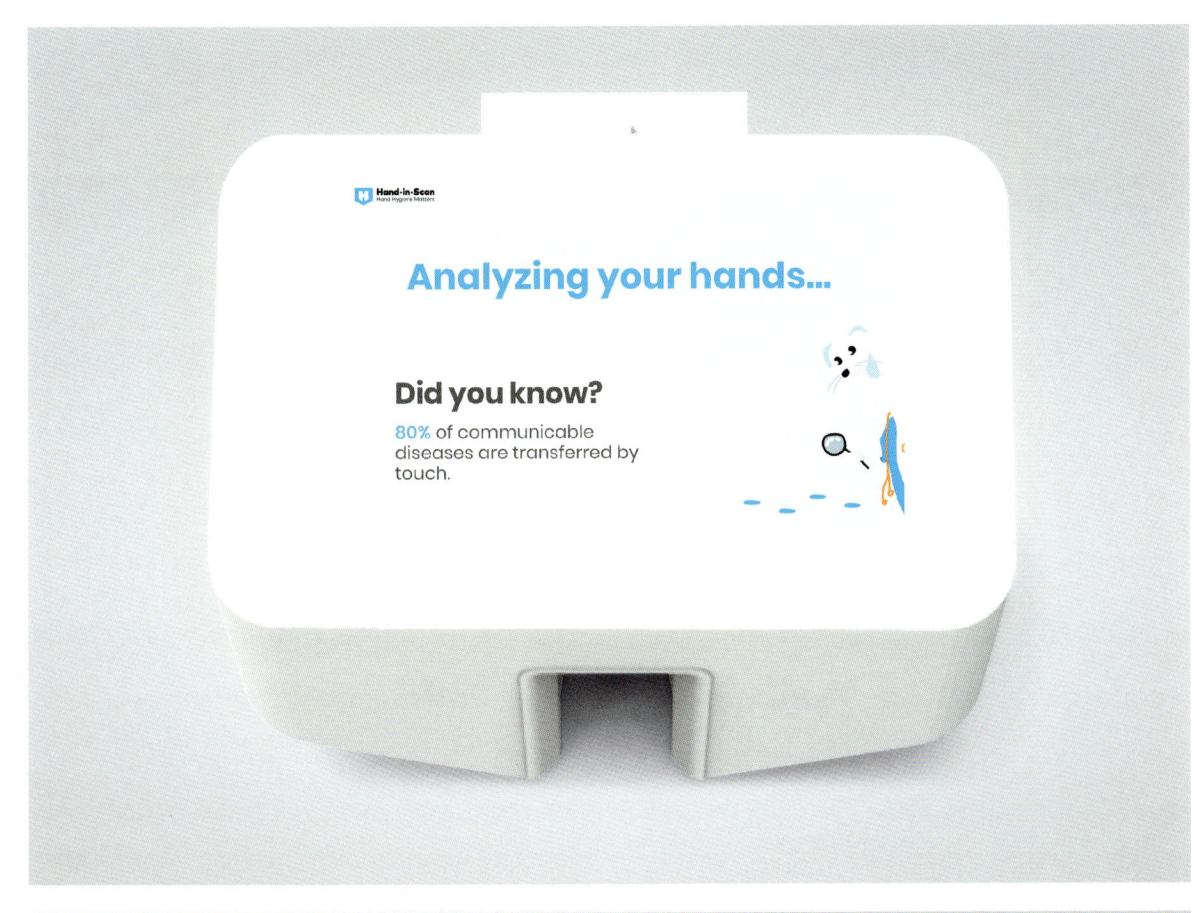

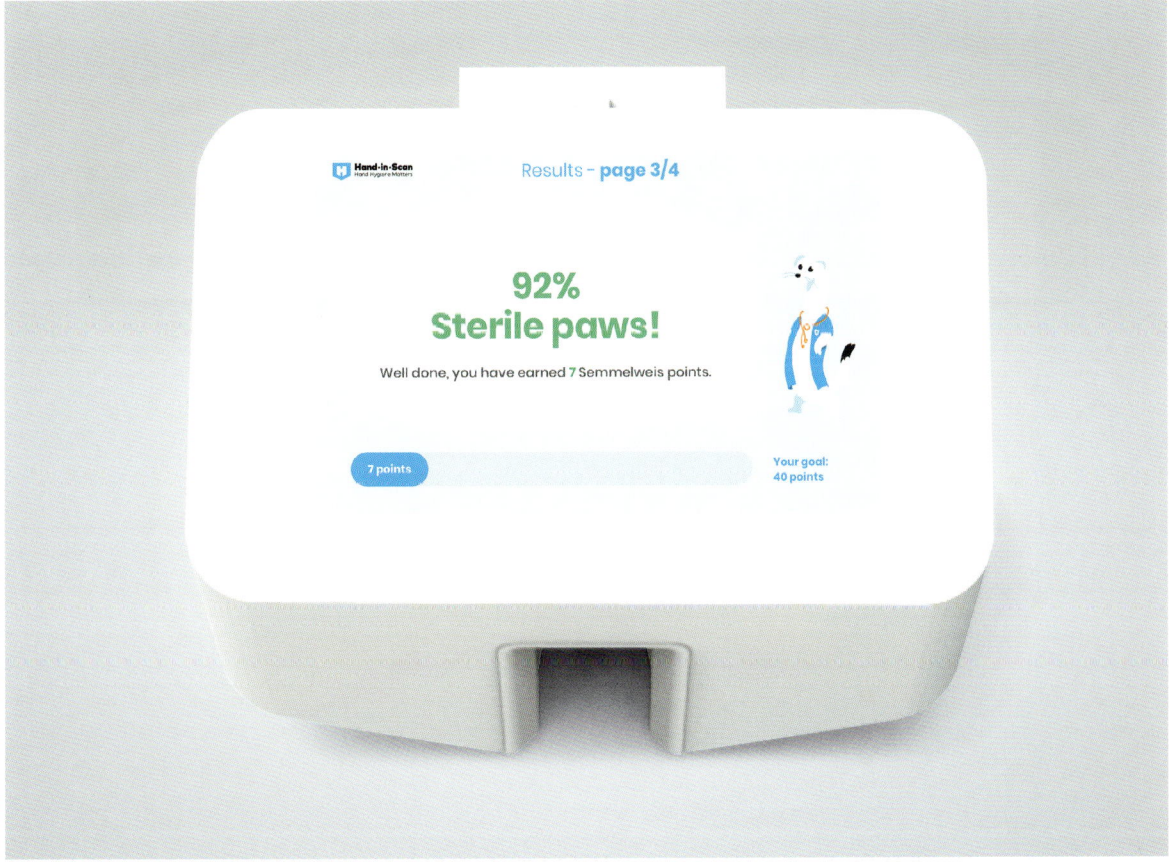

HandInScan

[Medical User Experience Redesign, Health Solution]

HandInScan aims to objectively measure and improve the hand hygiene practices of hospital staff. The goal was to teach users a proper technique for disinfection and thus decrease the number of hospital-acquired infections. In order to motivate staff members to use the device regularly, the entire product appearance has been redesigned to lend it an emotional appeal and to eliminate any need to touch the hardware. The new user experience innovatively connects the digital and physical worlds and strongly improves human behaviour.

Client
HandInScan Zrt.
Budapest, Hungary

Design
Supercharge
Budapest, Hungary

Project Team
Erika Somogyi (Visual Design)
Bence Lukács (UX Design)
Sára T. Kocsis (UX Design)
Judit Sándor (Project Lead)
Ádám Sándor (Art Direction)
Balázs Fónagy (Digital Concept)

→ Designer profile on page 626
→ Clip online

Publishing & Print Media	Posters	Typography	Illustrations	Sound Design	Film & Animation	Online
4	64	92	116	126	138	172

Ellie's MRI Journey
[Health Solution]

Client
Philips
Eindhoven, Netherlands

Design
Philips Experience Design team
Eindhoven, Netherlands

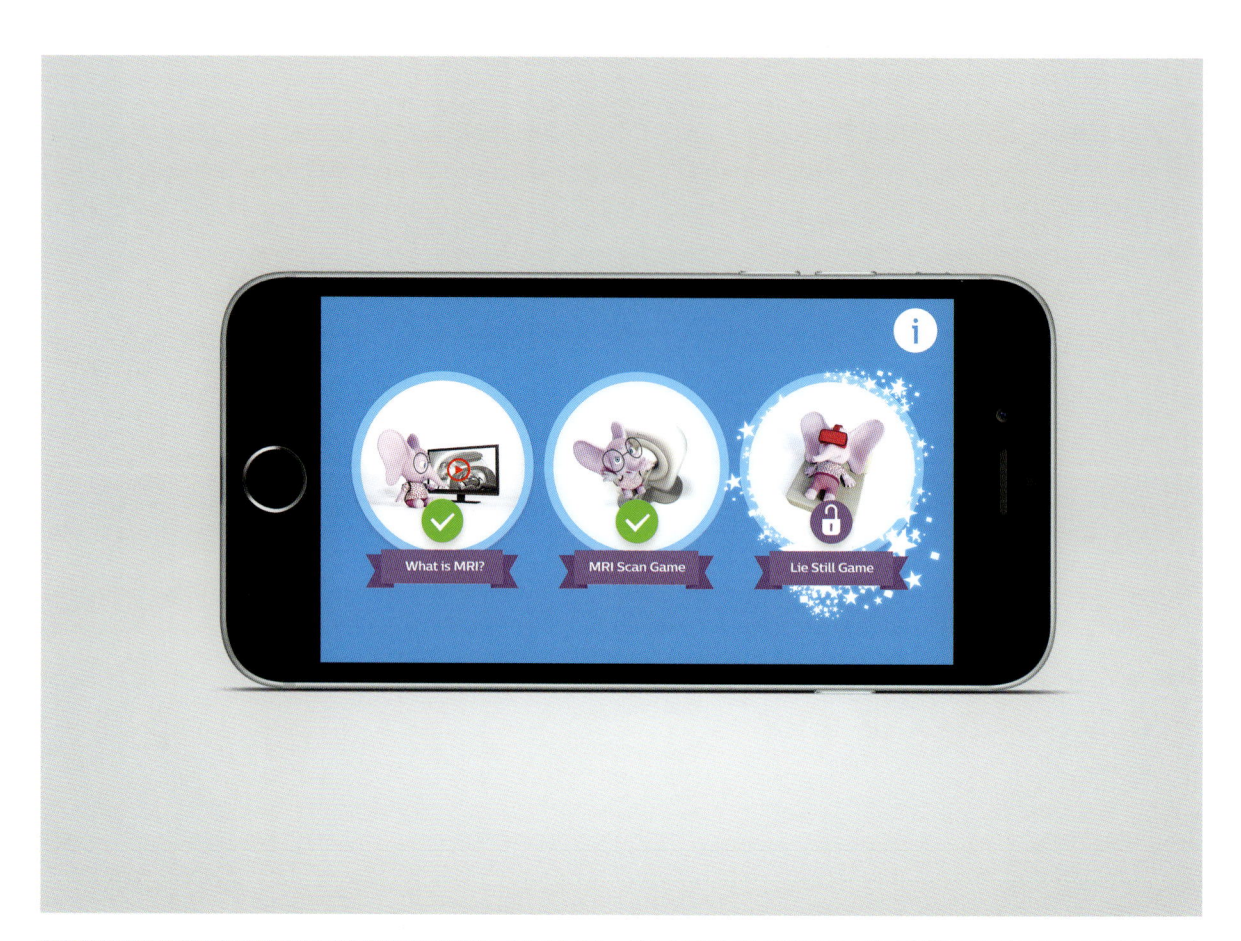

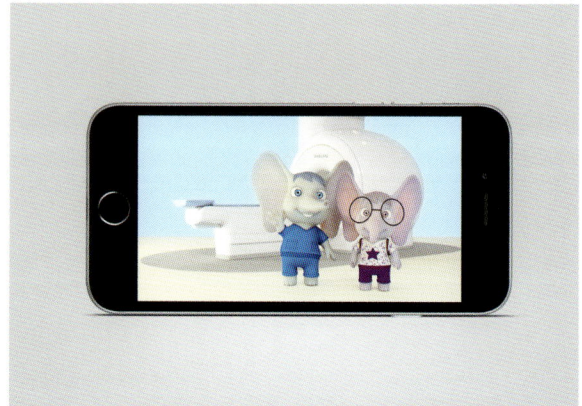

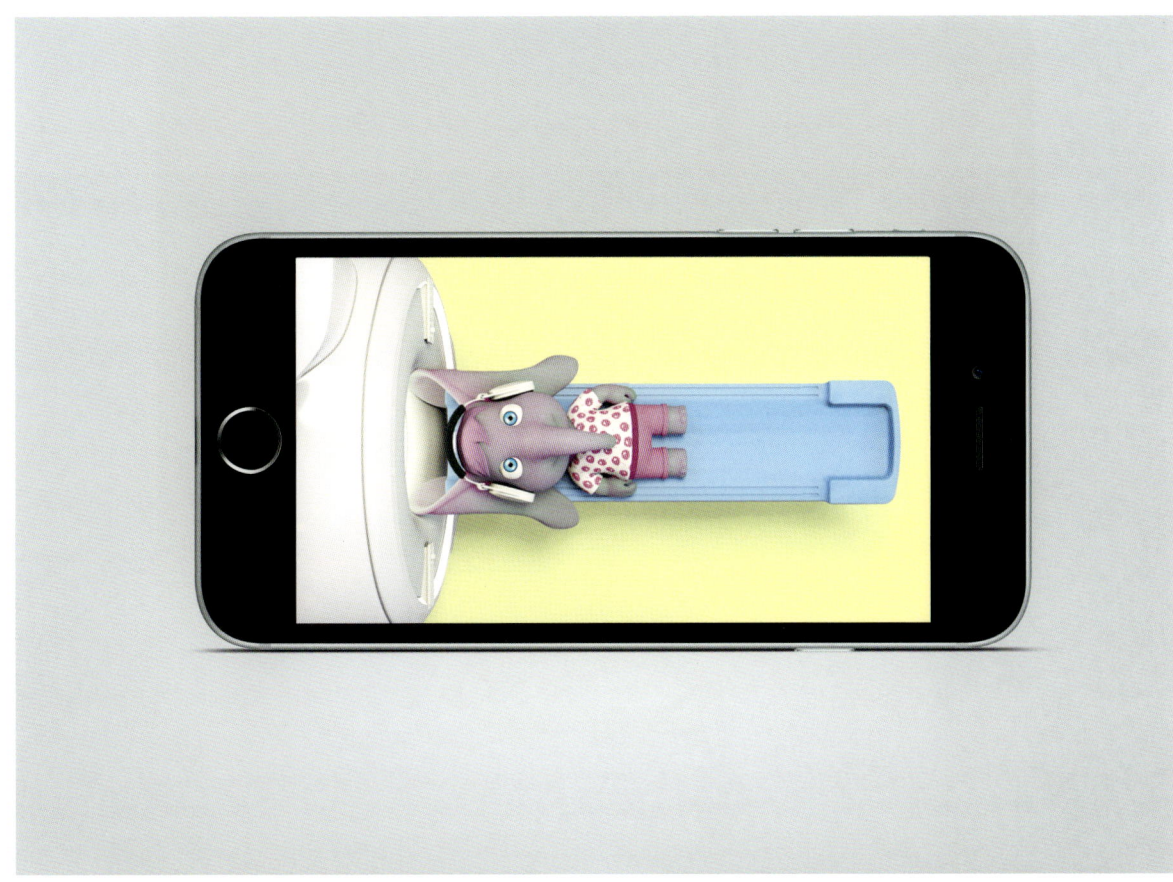

As an MRI scan can be a daunting experience for adults, let alone for children, this coaching service aims to help paediatric patients (aged 4 to 8) prepare for a smooth procedure with less anxiety. Using human-centric design and gamification, the tool employs a mobile app including an informative movie customised to the hospital, an interactive game where the patient takes a character through the procedure, and a VR experience to train the child to lie still. The experience can be expanded with educational colouring books and certificates.

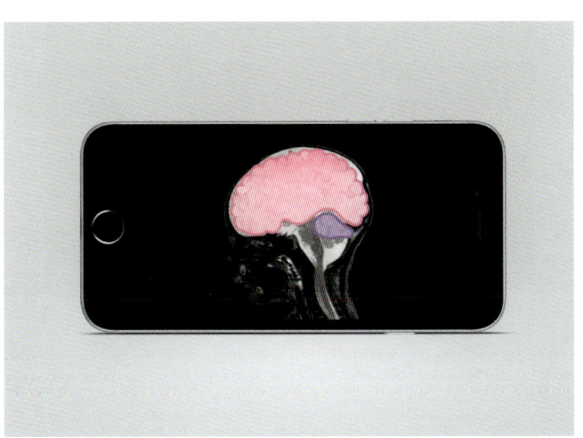

LMS Life – Line Monitoring System

[User Interface Design]

In this user interface design for use in the field of industrial IoT (Internet of Things), great importance was attached to intuitive navigation between the information levels. The system can be integrated into existing production environments where it monitors the performance and efficiency of the systems. The collected data is processed and presented in the form of easy-to-understand infographics. The target group is plant and shop floor managers, who need to quickly recognise the potential for error reduction and production optimisation.

Client
Schneider Electric Automation GmbH
Marktheidenfeld, Germany

Design
HMI Project GmbH
Würzburg, Germany

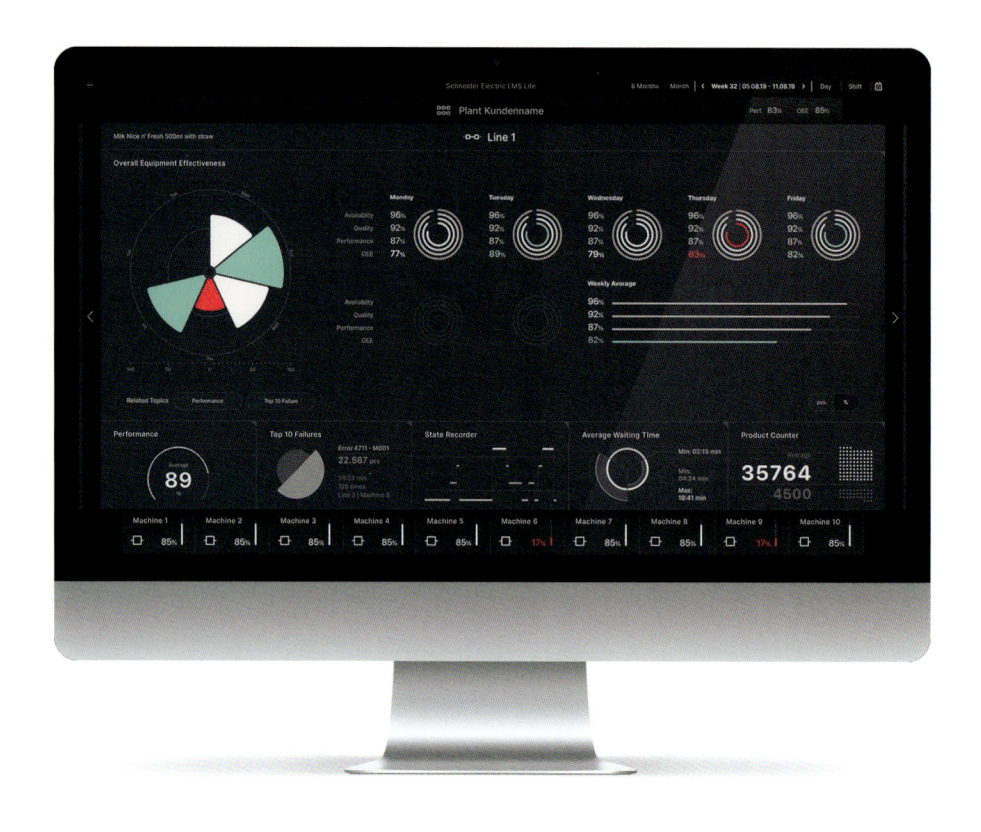

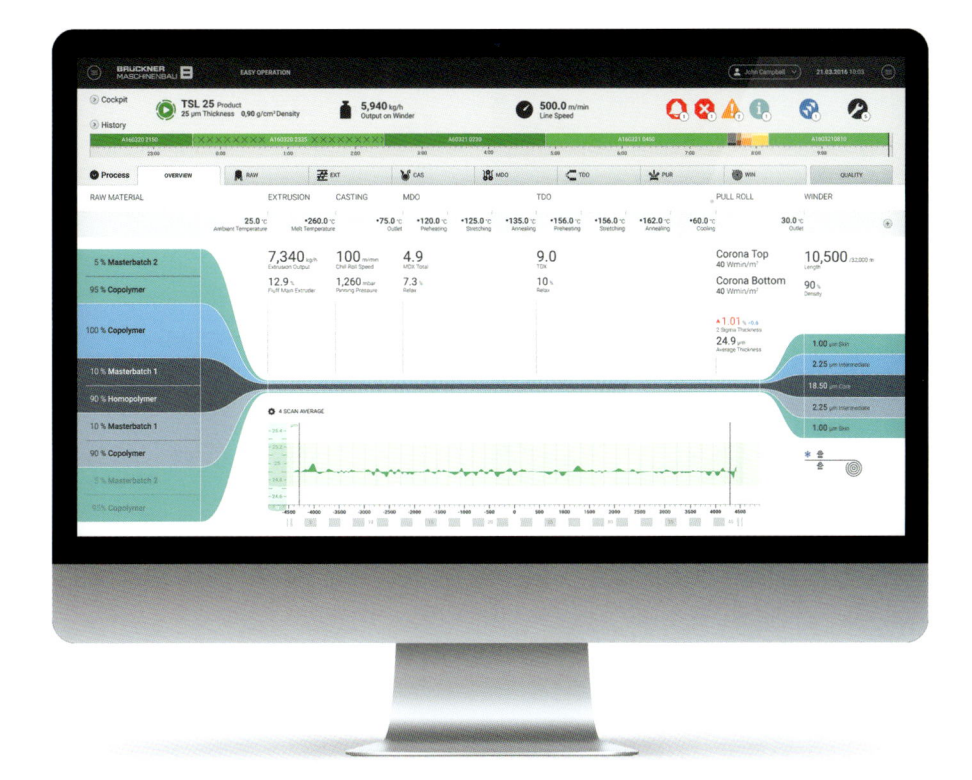

Apps	Interface & User Experience Design	Spatial Communication	Red Dot: Junior Award	Designer Profiles	Jury Portraits	Index
206	236	336	426	564	642	668

Easy Operation – Intelligent Line Management

[User Interface Design]

Developed for use in modern film-stretching systems, Easy Operation is a patented, newly integrated operating concept. By focusing on the process view, it allows intuitive operation using just a few parameters via a central cockpit. Based on a drill-down principle, the design of the responsive interface enables navigation up to the sensor level. Assistance systems provide comprehensive support in operating plants and guide the operator in an easy-to-understand manner using predefined, customisable steps.

Client
Brückner Maschinenbau GmbH & Co. KG
Siegsdorf, Germany

Design
HMI Project GmbH
Würzburg, Germany

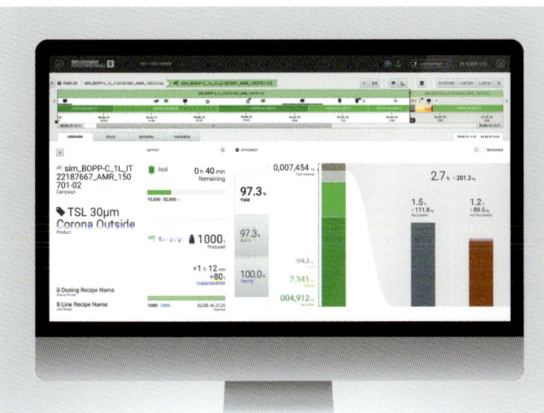

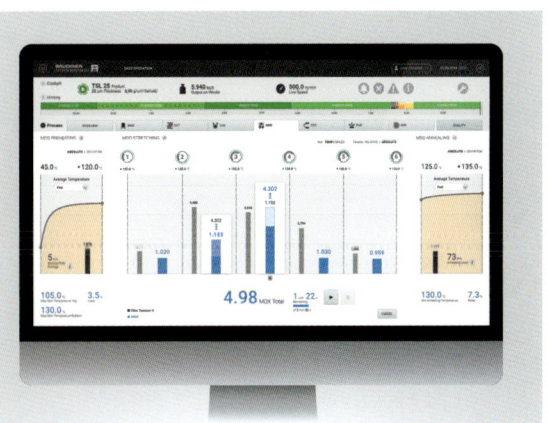

Huawei Industrial Internet – Spinning

[Smart Factory Solution]

Huawei Industrial Internet (Spinning) is an artificial intelligence system enabling the processes of a Smart Spinning Factory by assisting in its production and operation. Using IoT and AI in spinning manufacturing, the machines, data and humans are interconnected, allowing the factory to rapidly respond to changing needs. Featuring a clearly structured layout, the system realises the visualisation for individual machines, the production line, workspaces and the whole factory. Based on IoT, AI and immersive user interfaces, the system can monitor various equipment and process parameters in real time.

Client
Huawei Technologies Co., Ltd.
Shenzhen, China

Design
Huawei Technologies Co., Ltd.
Shenzhen, China

Project Team
Shaolei Wang (UX Designer)
Yuanfeng Chu (UX Designer)
Ren Li (UX Designer)
Yujing Wang (UX Designer)
Kai Kuang (UX Designer)

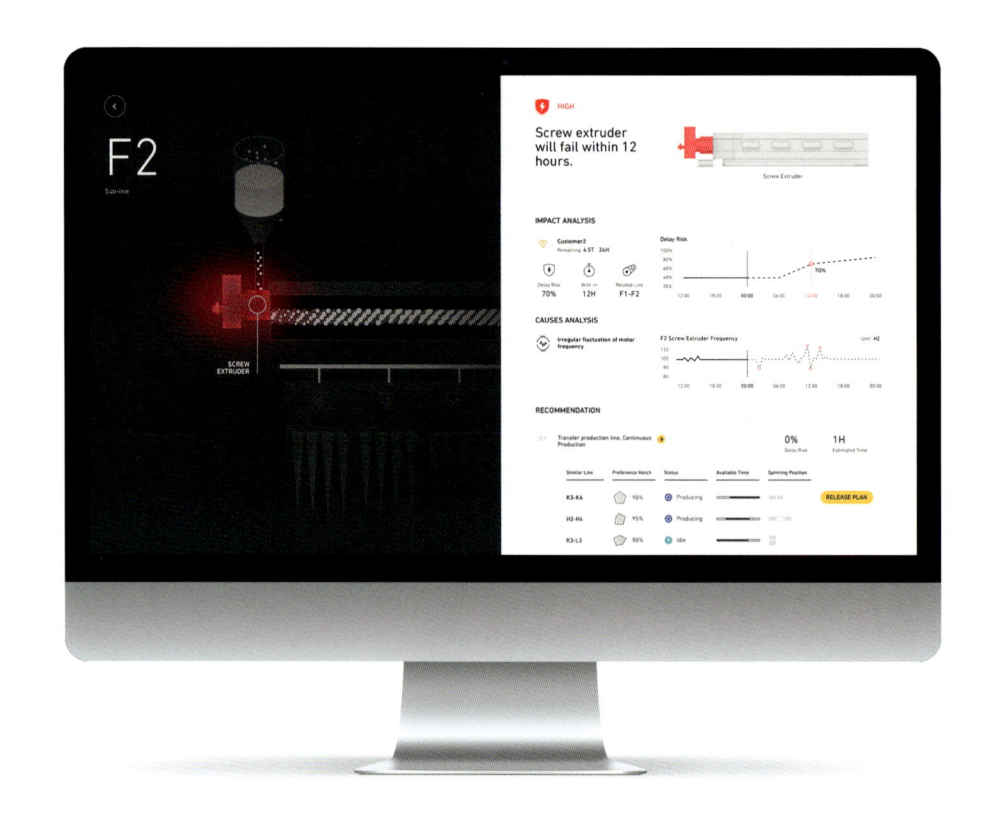

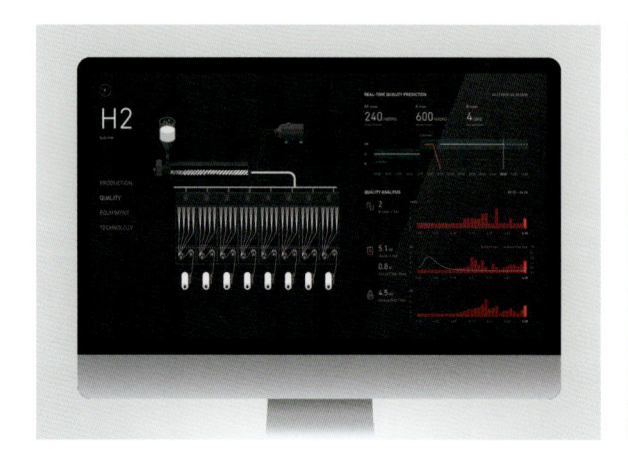

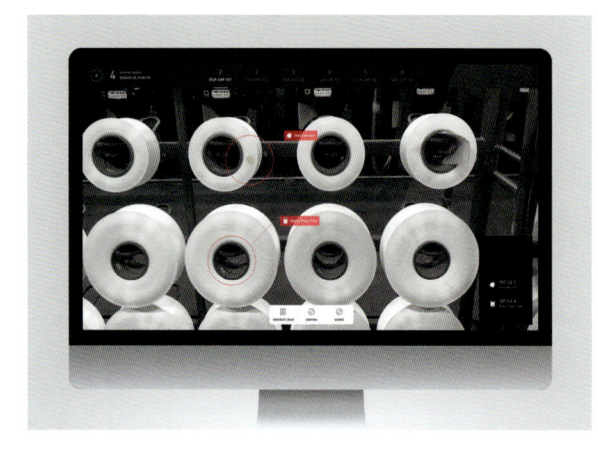

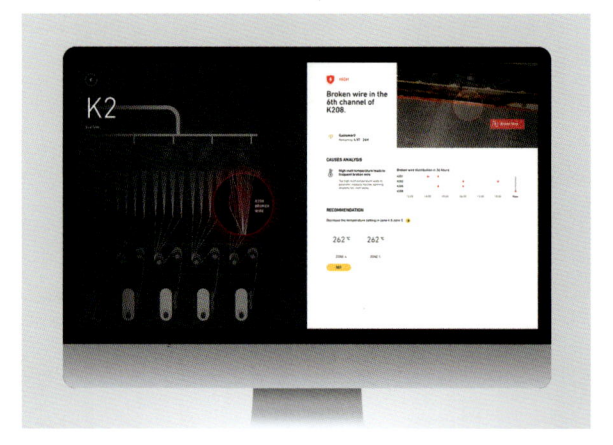

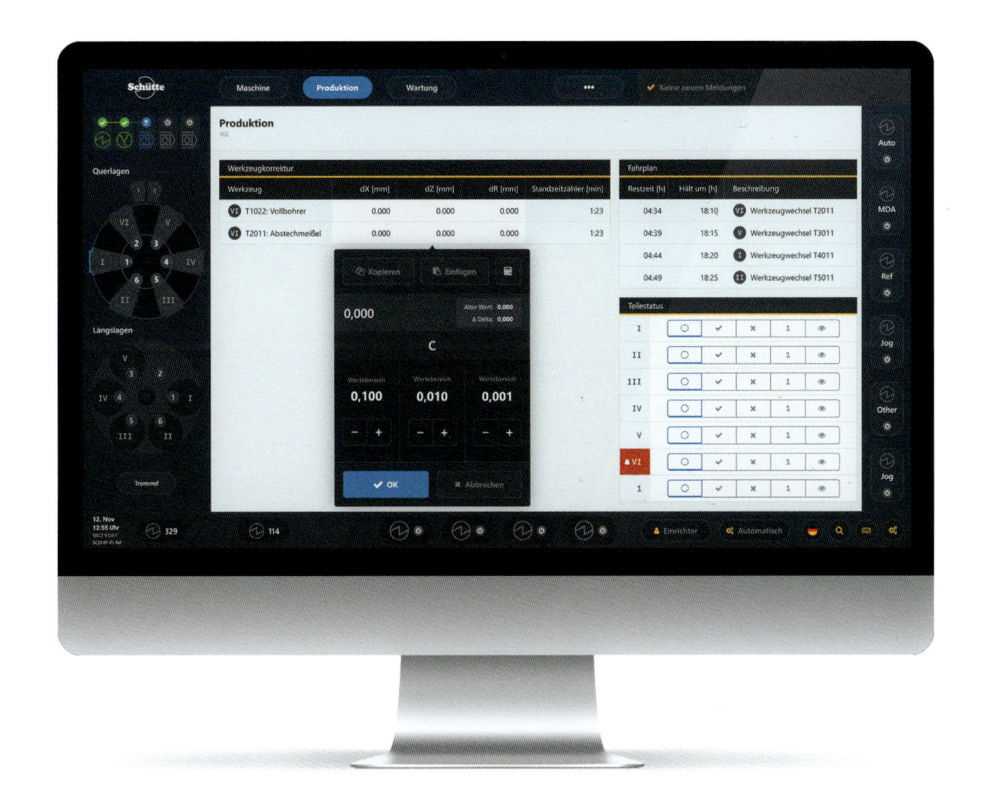

Apps	Interface & User Experience Design	Spatial Communication	Red Dot: Junior Award	Designer Profiles	Jury Portraits	Index
206	236	336	426	564	642	668

Modular Design System for a Multi-Spindle Automatic Lathe

[User Interface Design]

Considering the rapid change in technology, this user interface was designed with the requirement of individual configurability. Implemented with a systemic approach, it is based on a modular structure which aims to ensure that it can react flexibly to changes in the market. This human-machine interface was developed for the latest generation of multi-spindle automatic lathes from the company Schütte. Addressing the demand of being highly productive, precise, future-proof and flexible, it is custom-tailored to their machines.

Client
Alfred H. Schütte GmbH & Co. KG
Cologne, Germany

Design
Ergosign GmbH
Saarbrücken, Germany

Publishing & Print Media	Posters	Typography	Illustrations	Sound Design	Film & Animation	Online
4	64	92	116	126	138	172

Cognite Infield

[Service Solution, User Interface Design]

Cognite Infield is a responsive web application that provides field technicians with continuously updated information such as sensor data, 3D models, documents and work orders. By putting the information at their fingertips, there is no need to print out documents or search for and mentally integrate information from multiple complex interfaces before heading out. Infield allows users to plan and execute their daily tasks in one application, thereby facilitating better decision-making, avoiding hazardous situations and increasing efficiency and safety.

Client
Cognite AS
Oslo, Norway

Design
Cognite AS
Oslo, Norway

Project Team
Cemal Caglar Bektas (Designer)
Christoffer Lange (Designer)
Kristoffer Husøy (Designer)

→ Clip online

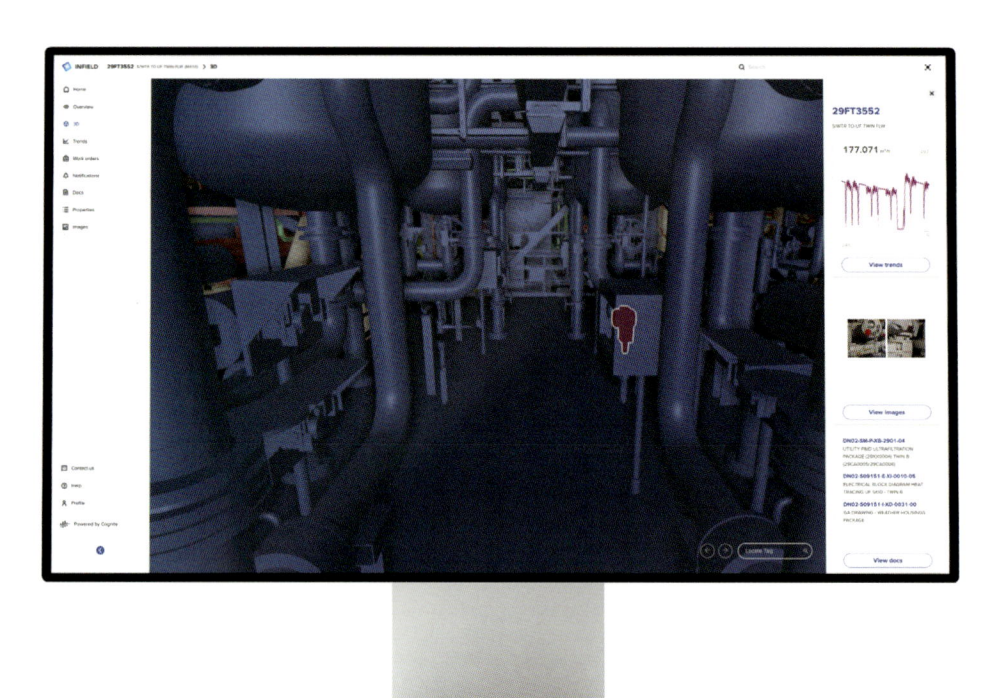

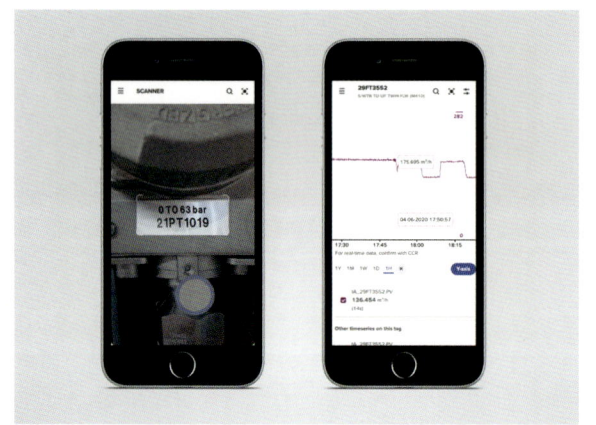

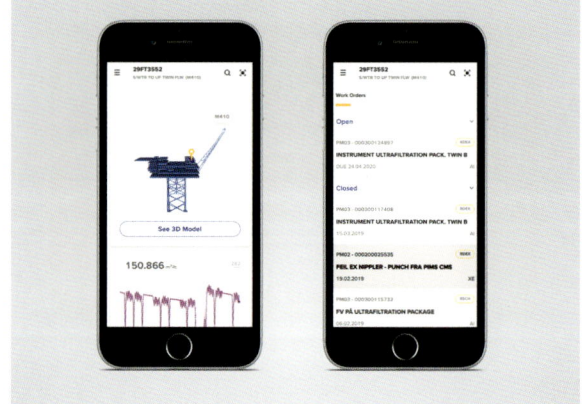

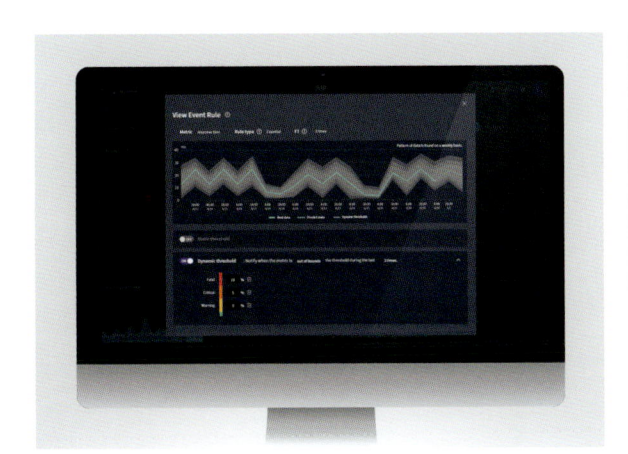

Monitoring Risk Tracker

[Integrated IT Monitoring Platform, User Interface Design]

The Monitoring Risk Tracker is an integrated monitoring platform designed to support IT system monitoring operators who are in charge of managing complex back-end systems such as servers, networks or databases. Although invisible to end users, a stable back-end system is highly essential, as it is the basis for providing a sustainable e-business. In order to solve system issues quickly and to maintain stability, the design solutions include troubleshooting flow, full-stack view and tactic knowledge visualisation.

Client
Samsung SDS
Seoul, South Korea

Design
Samsung SDS
Seoul, South Korea

Project Team
Jungwon Kim (Creative Direction)
Jaehwa Lee (Art Direction)
Dooyeon Kim (Digital Concept)

→ Designer profile on page 617

IBM Db2

[User Interface Design]

IBM Db2 Warehouse on Cloud is a software solution which helps businesses to better manage their data. It includes capabilities that allow users to quickly get a comprehensive view of their data so they can easily troubleshoot issues and keep their operations running. The software app provides an intuitive interface with a dashboard showing data visualisations, key data points and highlights, as well as a summary of data trends. The Db2 Warehouse on Cloud design is powered by machine learning und enables users to auto-scale their data and auto-allocate their resources.

Client
IBM
San Jose, USA

Design
IBM
San Jose, USA

Project Team
Kristyn Greenwood (Creative Direction)
Jessie Pahng (Creative Direction)
Rachel Miles (Creative Direction)
Huy Hua (Creative Direction)
Jingwei Wang (Creative Direction)
Natasha Yeh (Creative Direction)
Minsun Sang (Creative Direction)
Kelvin Esparza (Creative Direction)
Cory Marko (Creative Direction)
Jeff Levitt (Creative Direction)
Rimas Kalesnykas (Creative Direction)

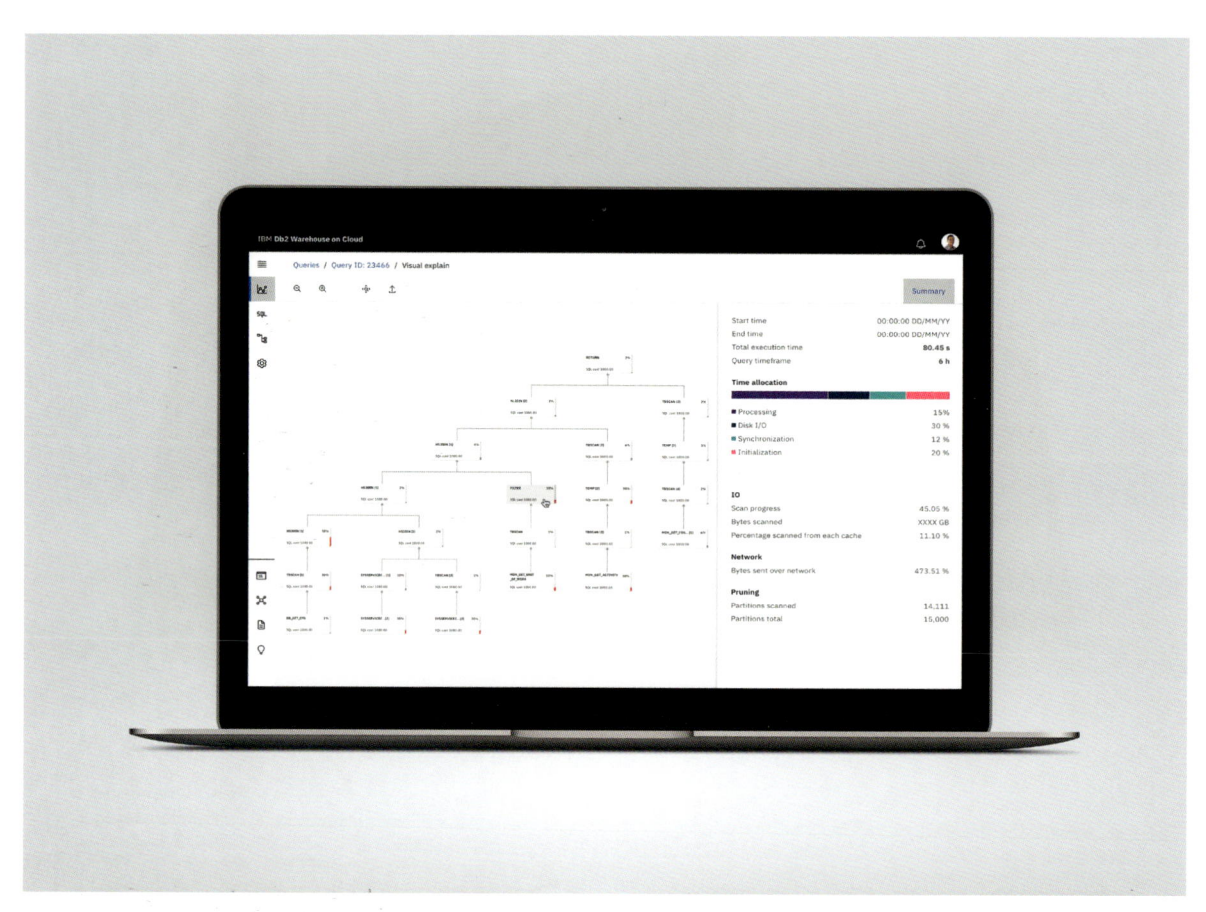

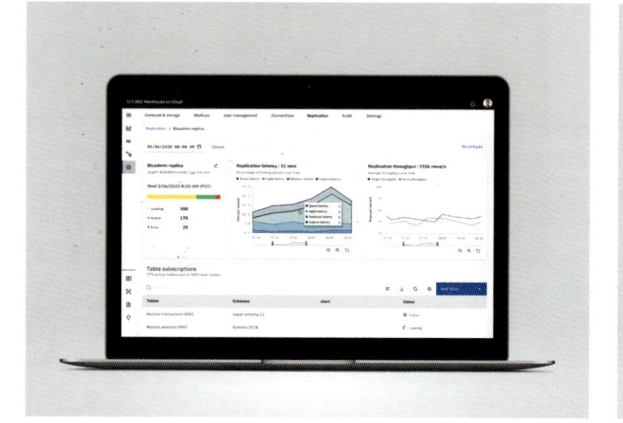

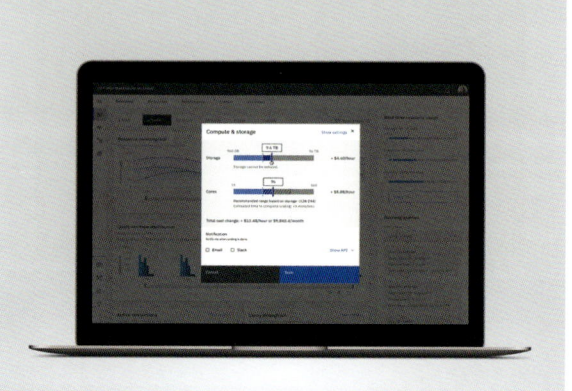

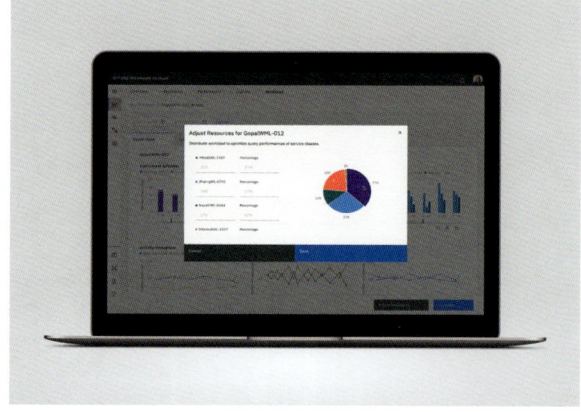

IBM Watson AutoAI

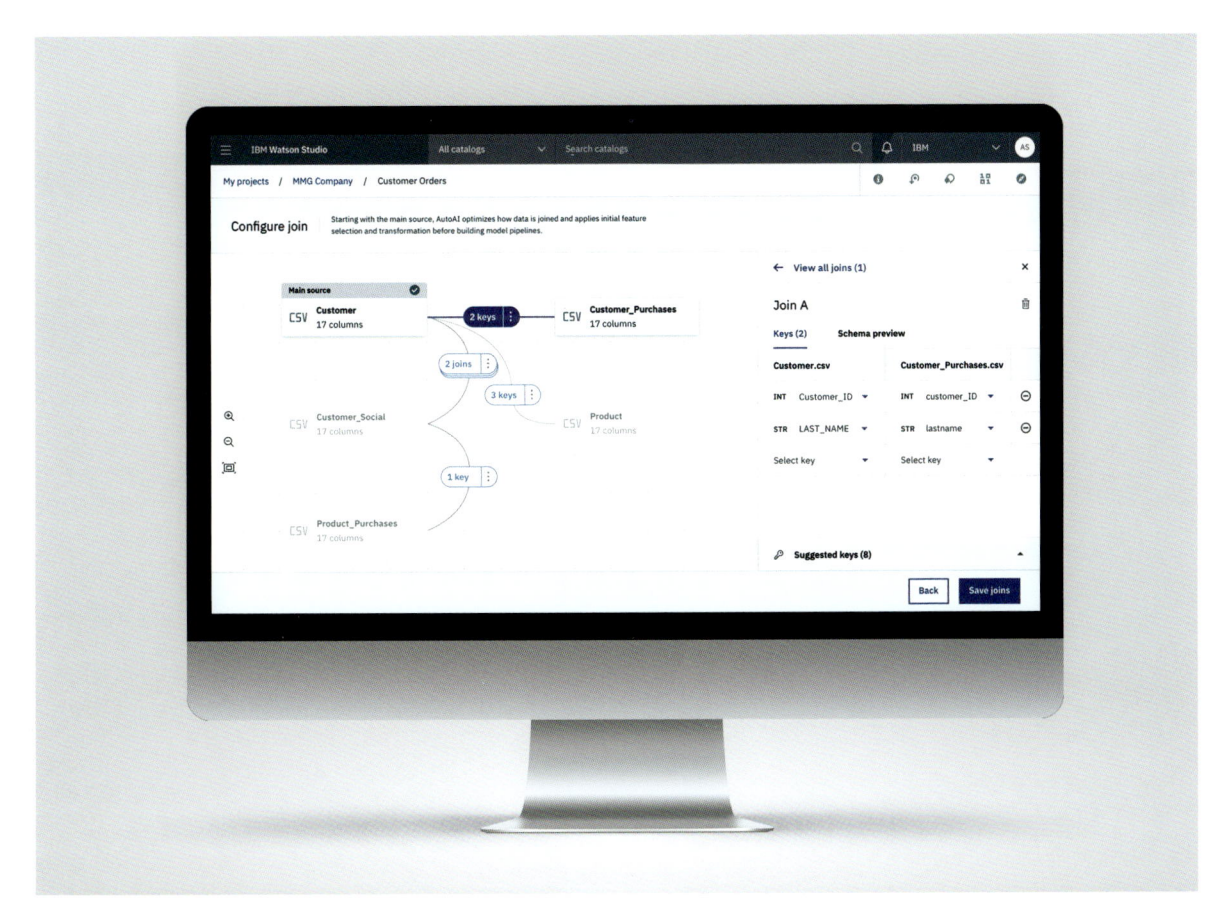

[User Interface Design]

IBM Watson AutoAI is a software feature that helps users simplify and automate how they use AI technology for business purposes. This tool helps users apply powerful AI tools to the process of data preparation, analysis, and model creation and training. Typical organisations that are looking to apply AI to their business and data operations are dealing with a gap in skills, as well as deployment and governance of their application. IBM Watson Auto AI helps users to automate AI to assist with the complex business and data operations of their organisations.

Client
IBM
Austin, USA

Design
IBM
Austin, USA

Project Team
Alex Swain (Design Director)
Dillon Eversman (Creative Director)
Voranouth Supadulya (Creative Director)

Publishing & Print Media	Posters	Typography	Illustrations	Sound Design	Film & Animation	Online
4	64	92	116	126	138	172

NetEco pro

[Data Centre Management System, User Interface Design]

This data centre management system was designed against the backdrop of environmental friendliness, saving energy and maximising the safety and efficiency of large data centres in particular. The user-friendly concept is based on "digital twins" that connect a building and everything inside, including cabinets, air conditioners and fire-fighting devices. Thus, it becomes a fully connected intelligent system. It automatically optimises the energy efficiency of the data centre through artificial intelligence.

Client
Huawei Technologies Co., Ltd.
Dongguan, China

Design
Huawei Technologies Co., Ltd.
Shenzhen, China

Project Team
Hai Huang (Main Designer)
Tao Qing Yang (Web Designer)
Weipan Guo (Web Designer)
Yucheng Zhong (Web Designer)
Zeqi Xu (Web Designer)

Huawei HoloSens Store

[User Interface Design]

The Huawei HoloSens store is an algorithm store based on the possibilities of machine vision. The innovative platform connects intelligent algorithms and camera users in the industry. On the one hand, the store uses algorithm videos as the key element for transferring algorithm advantages to the users; on the other hand, it features a convenient one-click-all-done function to help camera users quickly use the algorithm. By improving the user experience, the aim of the Huawei HoloSens store is to make AI more accessible to society.

Client
Huawei Technologies Co., Ltd.
Hangzhou, China

Design
Huawei Technologies Co., Ltd.
Hangzhou, China

Project Team
Feng Ye (UX Designer)
Rouchen Fu (UX Designer)
Wei Huang (Concept)
Kun Tan (Concept)
Shaofeng Fu (Concept)
Zhicheng Cao (Film Editing)

Plus10 – Die vernetzte Fabrik

[User Experience Design, Service Design]

Client
Plus10 GmbH
Augsburg, Germany

Design
F209 GmbH
Heidelberg, Germany

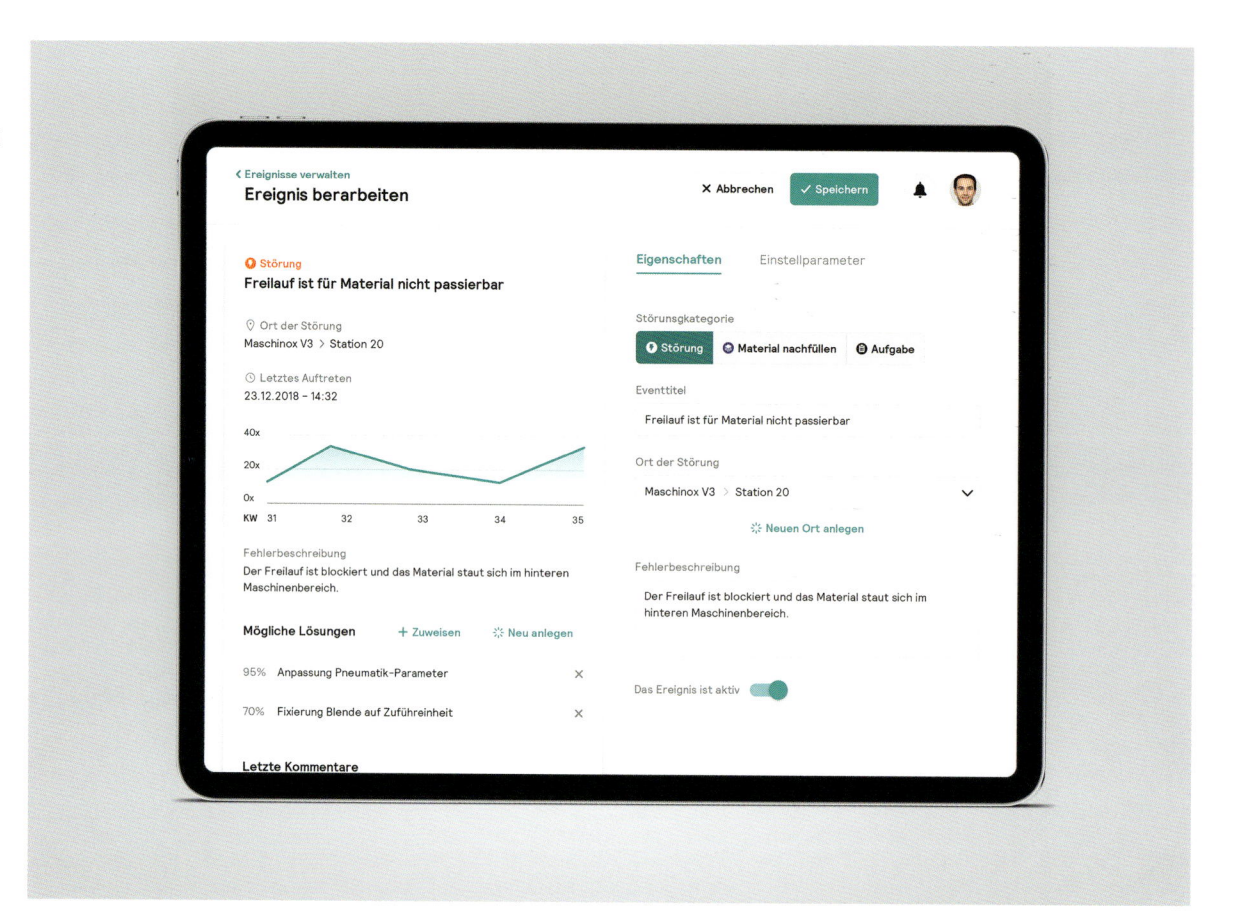

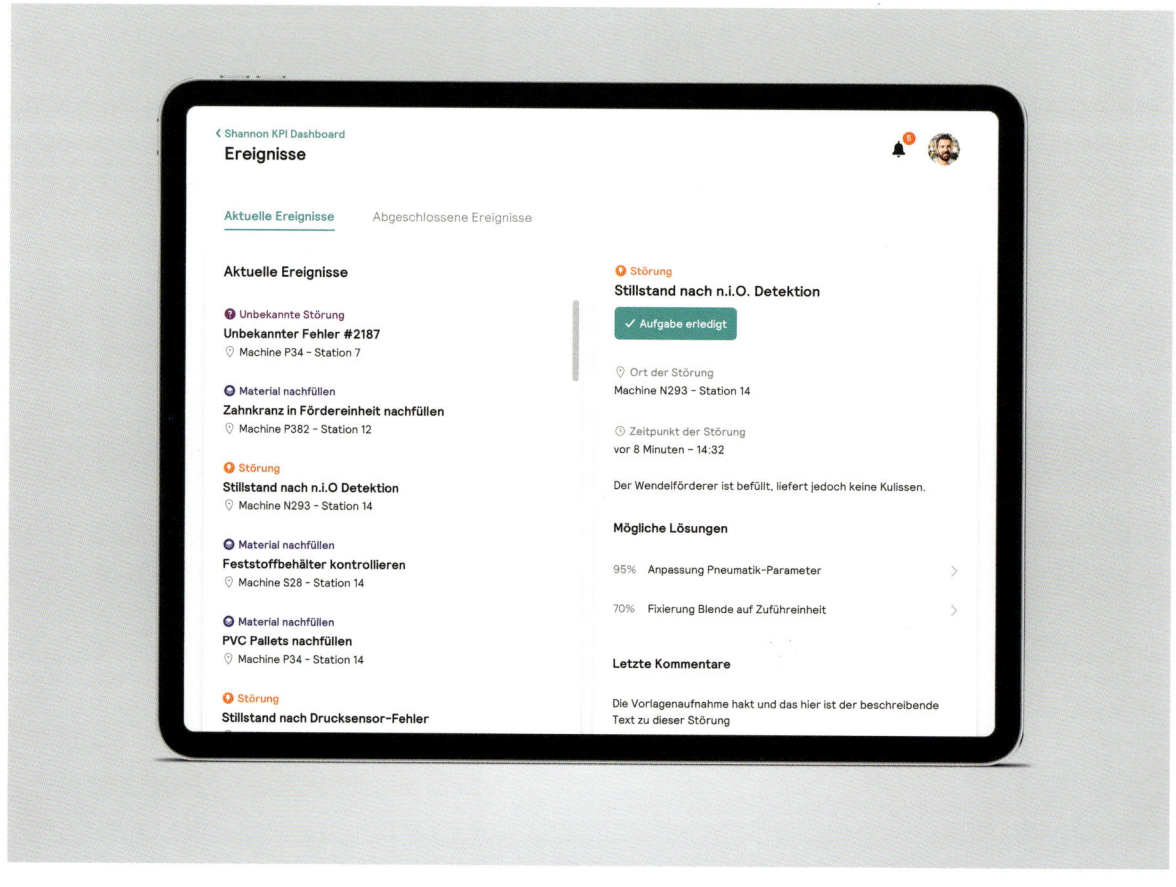

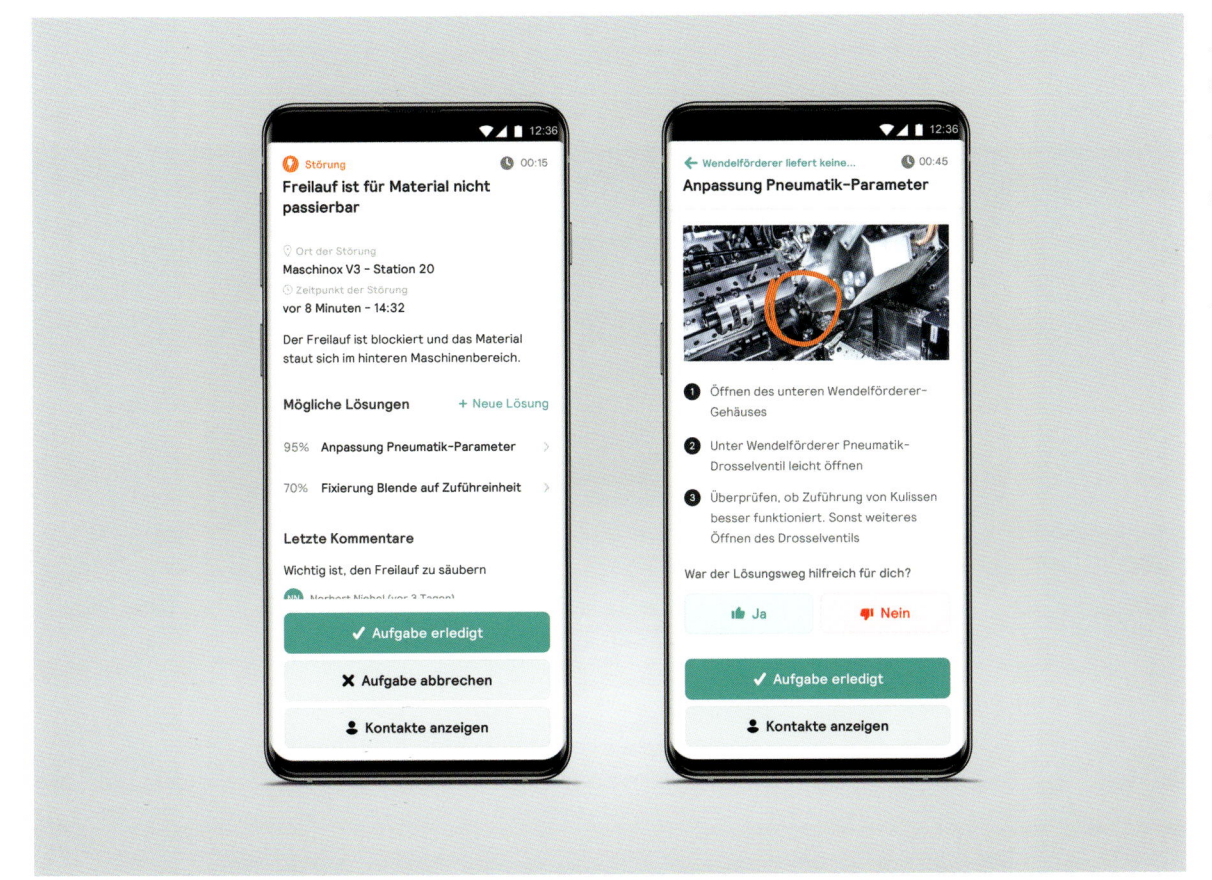

Apps	Interface & User Experience Design	Spatial Communication	Red Dot: Junior Award	Designer Profiles	Jury Portraits	Index
206	236	336	426	564	642	668

In order to enable workers in a factory to make autonomous and proactive decisions, thus facilitating more efficient production, this multi-device user interface has been structured for optimal problem solutions. By analysing all data streams, real-time data about the production process is collected and analysed, categorised and prioritised, using machine learning. The use of mobile devices and stationary terminals enables the workers to detect malfunctions and problems, to communicate them or to act directly based on suggested solutions.

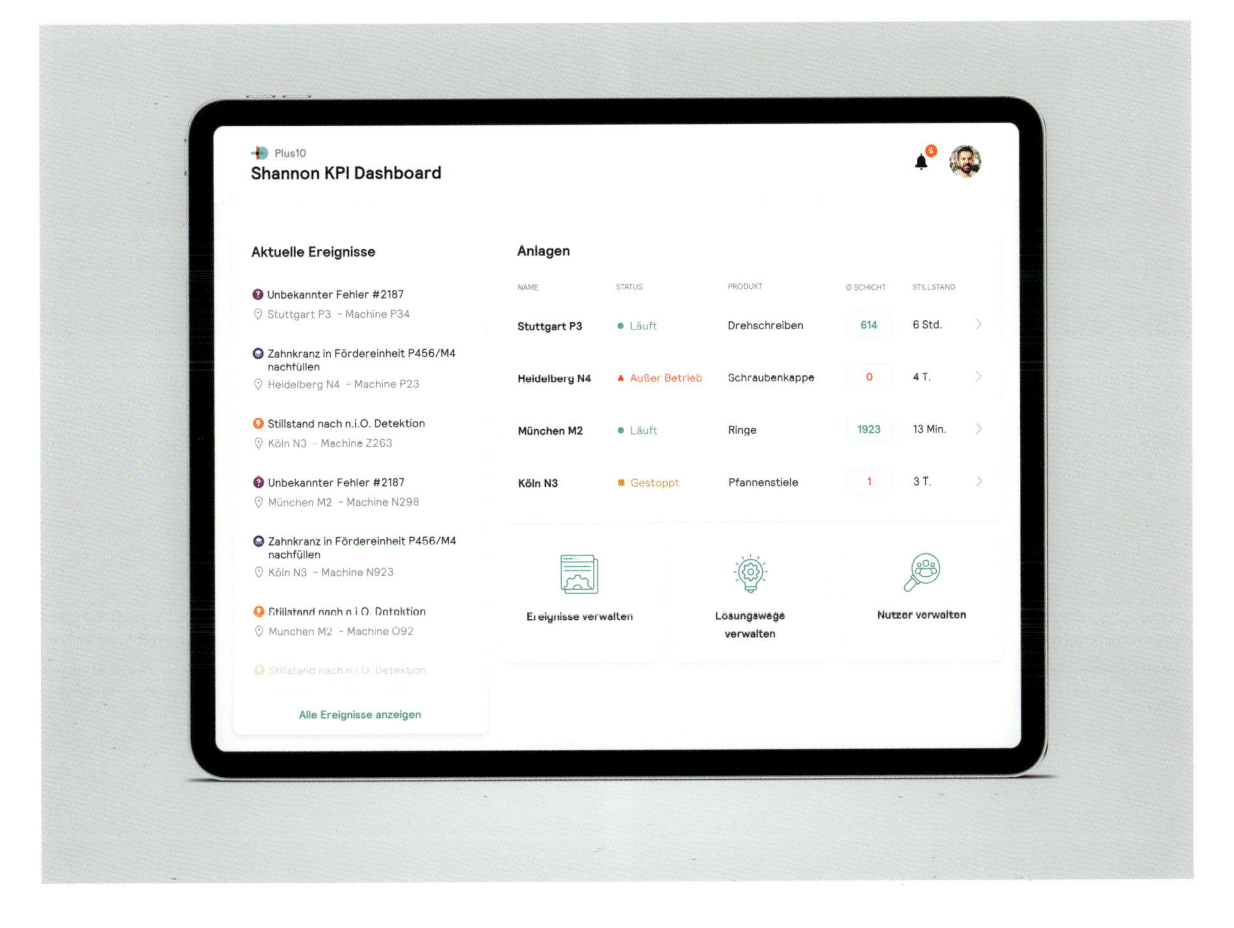

Rotary Evaporator Series Hei-VAP

[User Interface Design]

Following the product design language, the interface of the Hei-VAP rotary evaporator series showcases the devices' features. Integrating a multitude of parameters and information in an easy-to-read manner despite the small display was challenging. Thus, glow effects are used to emphasise the active areas on the device's screen. Additionally, coloured icons and design elements visualise the current status. Indicators in the user interface design show the respective tasks of the hardware control knobs.

Client
Heidolph Instruments GmbH & Co. KG
Schwabach, Germany

Design
User Interface Design GmbH
Ludwigsburg, Germany

Project Team
Heidolph Instruments:
Uwe Külz (Requirements Engineer)
Jürgen Heyder (Product Manager)
Patrick Bark (Project Manager)

User Interface Design:
Verena Reuter (Project Management)
Steffen Neumann (Art Direction)
Manfred Dorn (Creative Direction)
Tobias Stricker (UX Design)

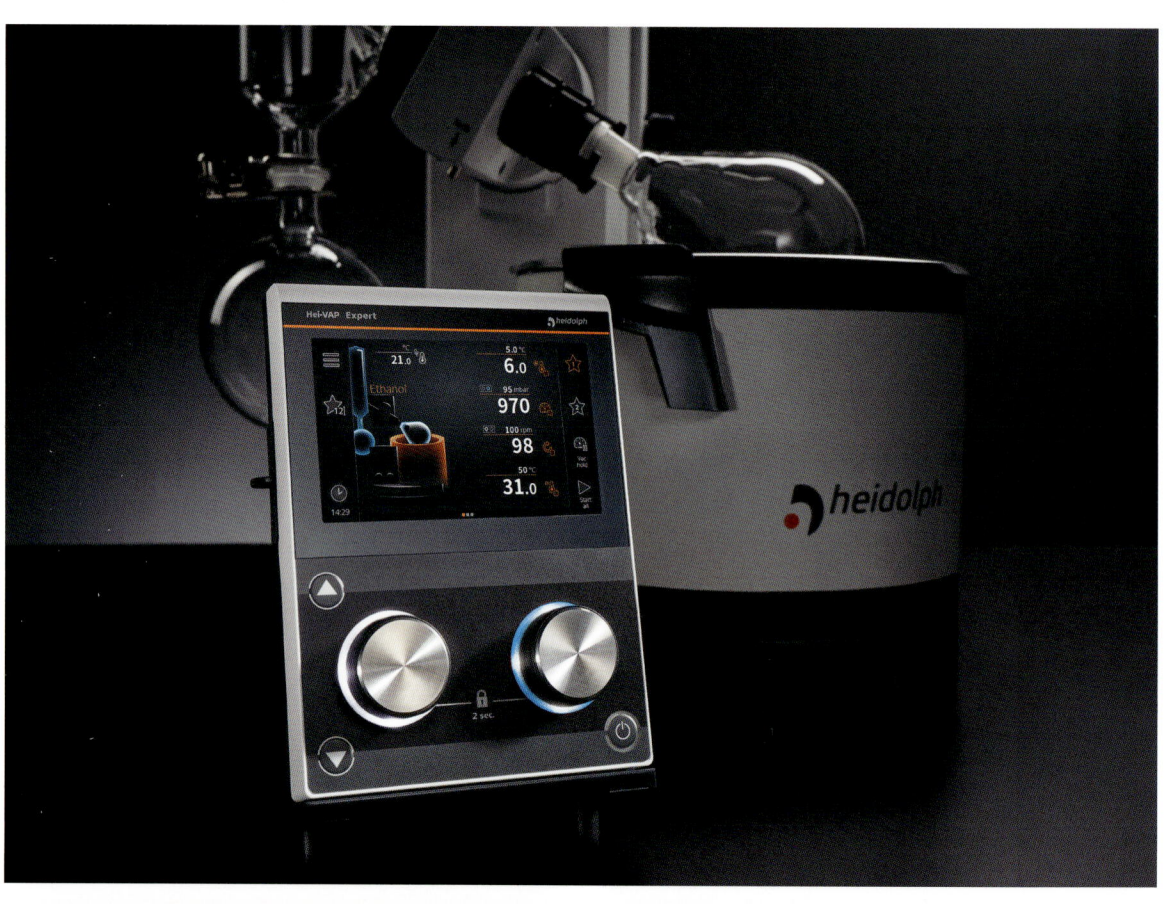

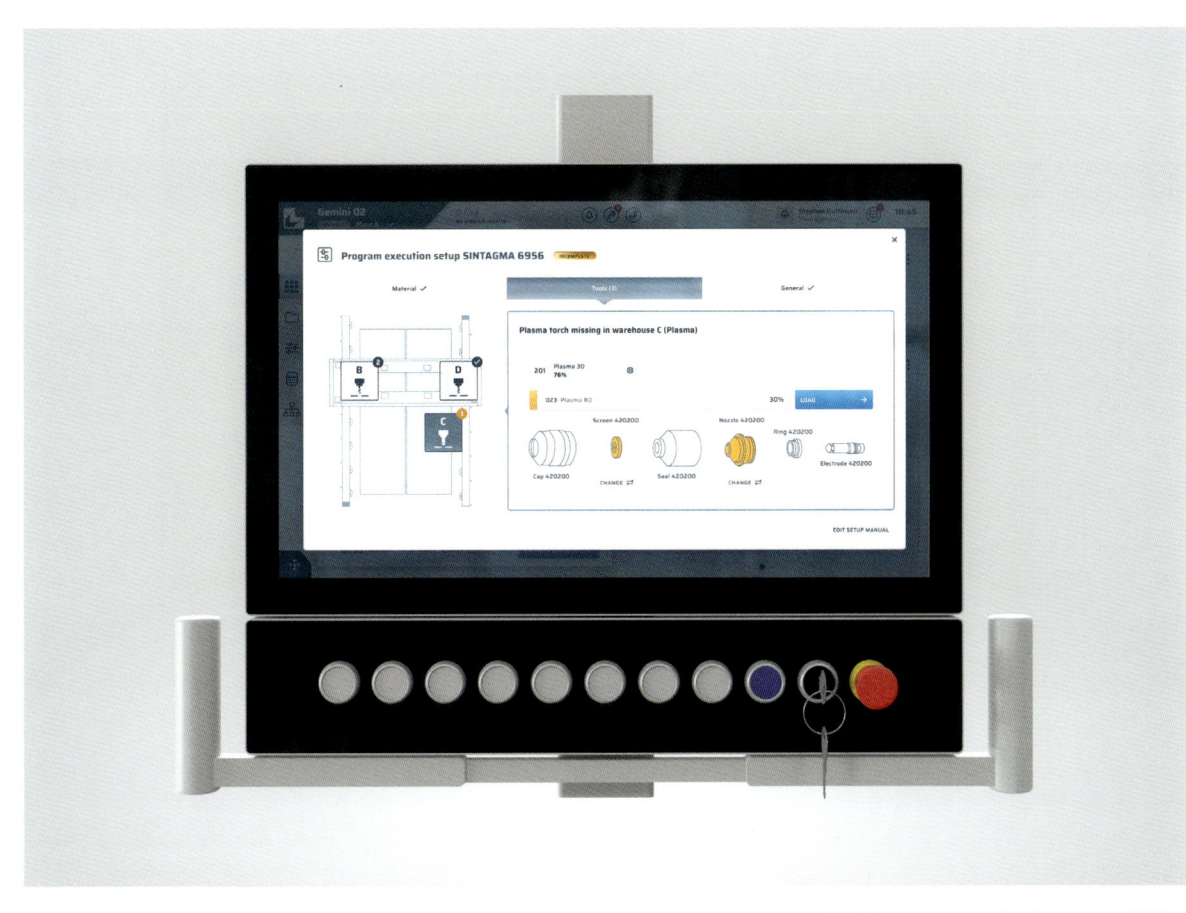

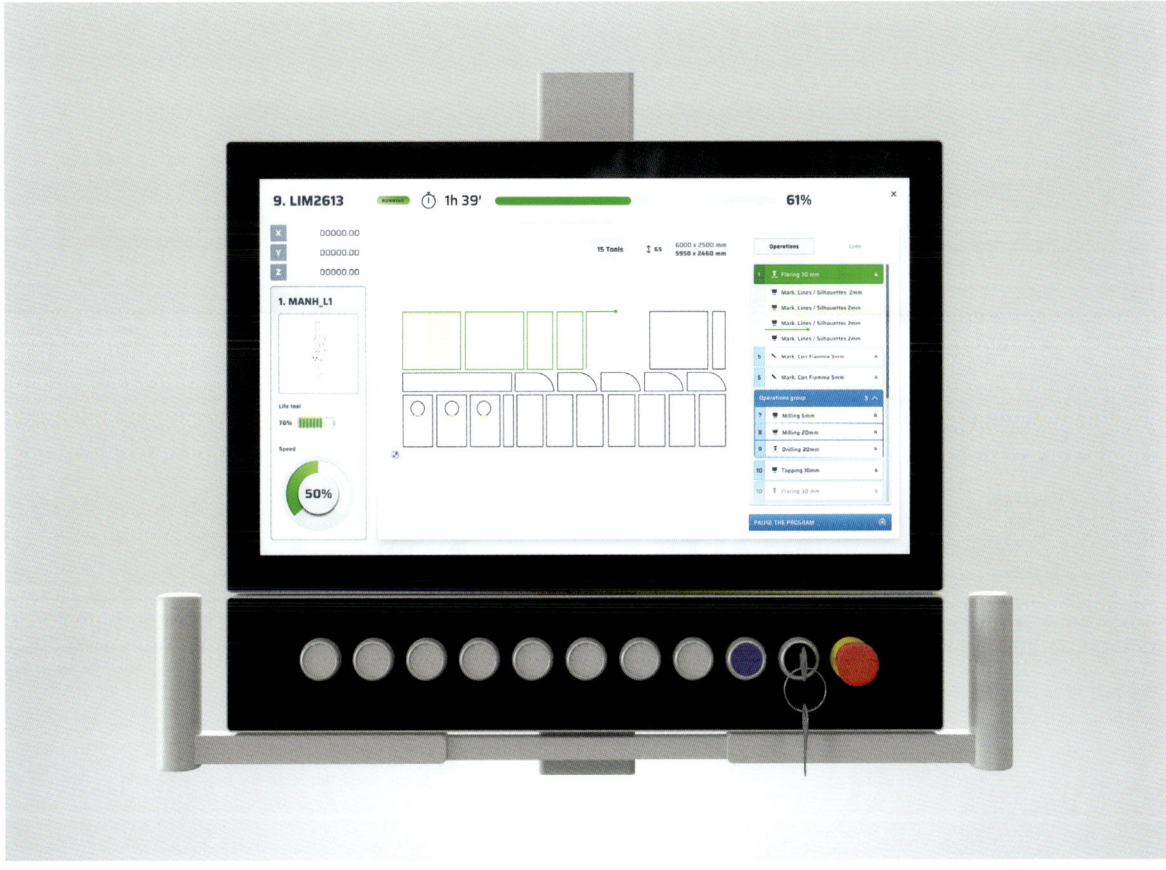

FICEP – Polaris

[Human Machine Interface Design]

This corporate operating system offers user interfaces for different types of machines. Polaris streamlines the whole process from planning and production to performance monitoring and analysis. As the cornerstone of the whole end-to-end process, it focuses on productivity improvement so as to guarantee full performance operativity even to inexperienced users across multiple shifts, a critical scenario in the steel construction industry. Polaris thus aims to provide a user experience involving seamless, consistent interaction that resonates with the roles of all users.

Client
FICEP S.p.A.
Varese, Italy

Design
NiEW Design
Modena, Italy

Project Team
Andrea Violante (Design Strategist)
Giancarlo Gamberini (Creative Director)
Andrea Cattani (UX Designer)
Vincenzo Melita (UX Designer)
Clara Reali (UI Designer)
Beatrice Cascio (UI Designer)
Daniele De Cia (Project Manager)

Publishing & Print Media	Posters	Typography	Illustrations	Sound Design	Film & Animation	Online
4	64	92	116	126	138	172

Huawei Intelligent Perception Platform for Yanchong Expressway

[Screen Design]

The Huawei Intelligent Perception Platform for Yanchong Expressway is a vehicle-road collaboration tool created for roadway managers. Since the Yanchong Expressway is going to be the main contact channel for the Beijing Olympic Winter Games in 2022, this platform intends to prevent accidents and emissions. Relying on digital visualisation interfaces and Huawei IoT services, managers can obtain timely road information and warnings of dangers in order to coordinate traffic lights and dispatch vehicles. The aim of the design is the integration of vehicles and roads.

Client
Huawei Technologies Co., Ltd.
Shenzhen, China

Design
Huawei Technologies Co., Ltd.
Shenzhen, China

Project Team
Lyuqian Bian (Creative Director)
Kun Tan (Animation)
Xiaofeng Zheng (Animation)
Xiaolan Zhou (Interaction Design)
Wei Huang (Interaction Design)
Yugang Wang (Graphic Design)
Qing Wang (Graphic Design)

Public Transportation Integrated Intelligent Monitoring System

[Mobility Solution]

This user interface design integrates data related to urban passenger flows, such as conventional buses, railways, taxis or online ride hailing. It builds a big data monitoring system for traffic operation through multidimensional, spatio-temporal data fusion and analysis. It analyses the situation and the rules of comprehensive traffic operation in order to grasp passenger behaviour, the allocation of transport capacities, traffic conditions and so forth, all in real time. The aim is to provide scientific support for the decision-making processes of comprehensive traffic supervision departments.

Client
Shenzhen Transportation Operation Command Center
Shenzhen, China

Design
Shenzhen Institute of Beidou Applied Technology Co., Ltd.
Shenzhen, China

Project Team
Tengfei Wu (Graphic Design)
Xiaohuan Xie (Graphic Design)
Shihao Li (Graphic Design)
Qian Yan (Concept)
Kai Huang (Project Management)
Danying Chen (Graphic Design)
Chuangye Liu (Graphic Design)
Xueying Zhu (Project Management)

Publishing & Print Media	Posters	Typography	Illustrations	Sound Design	Film & Animation	Online
4	64	92	116	126	138	172

Steam Birdseye
[Web-Based Interactive Visualisation Tool]

The goal of designing Steam Birdseye for the Department of Municipalities and Transport in Abu Dhabi was to develop an interactive tool for the transport sector. It is designed to easily explore and visualise complex data sets and predictive models in a consistent and visually attractive manner. The tool helps non-technical stakeholders and decision-makers to interact and compare between 1,000 proposed scenarios for the infrastructure every year. It gives direct access to all data sources, offering features such as the simple design of maps based on project stories, which can then be shared with stakeholders and leadership.

Client
Department of Municipalities and Transport
Abu Dhabi, United Arab Emirates

Design
Pixonal
Dubai, United Arab Emirates
CLEVER°FRANKE
Utrecht, Netherlands

Project Team
Transpo Group (Technical Consultant)

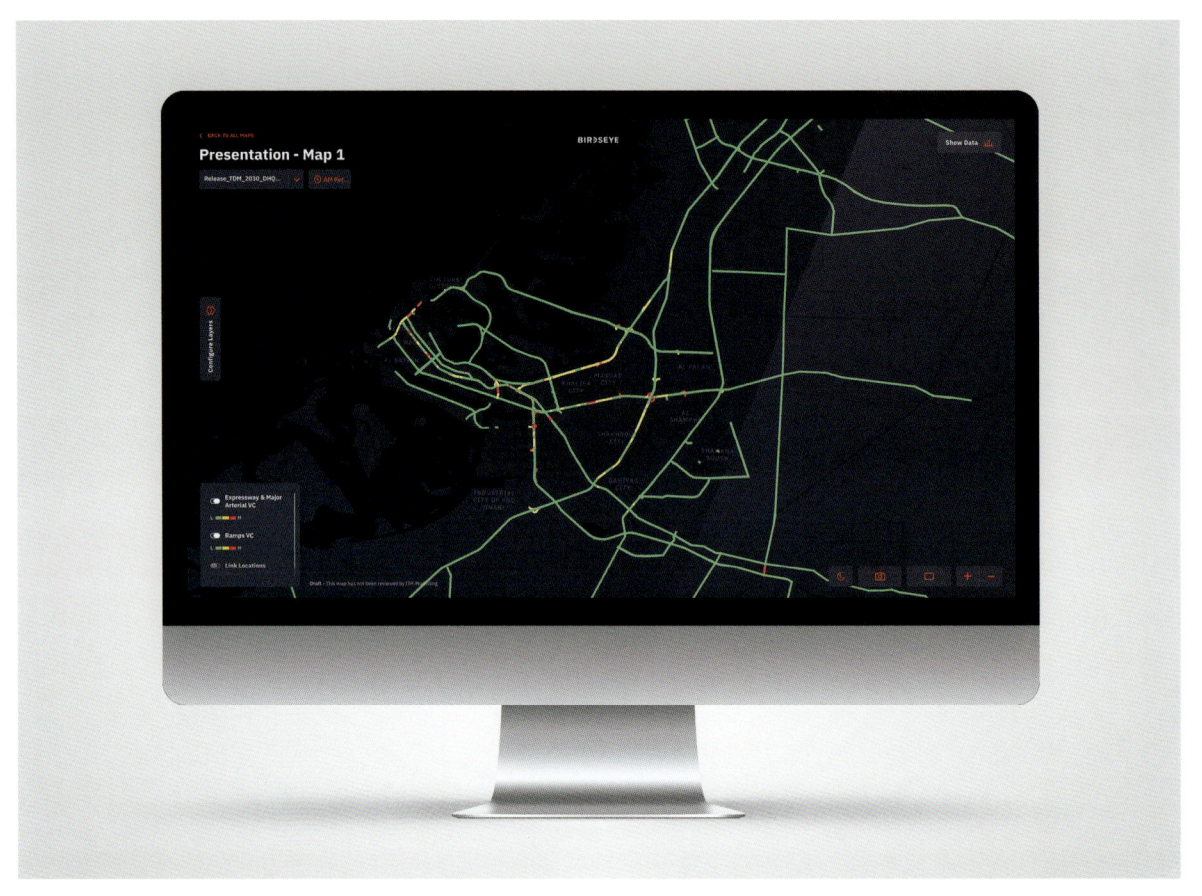

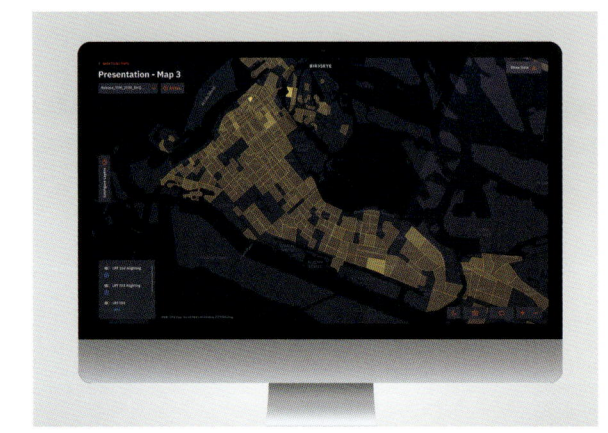

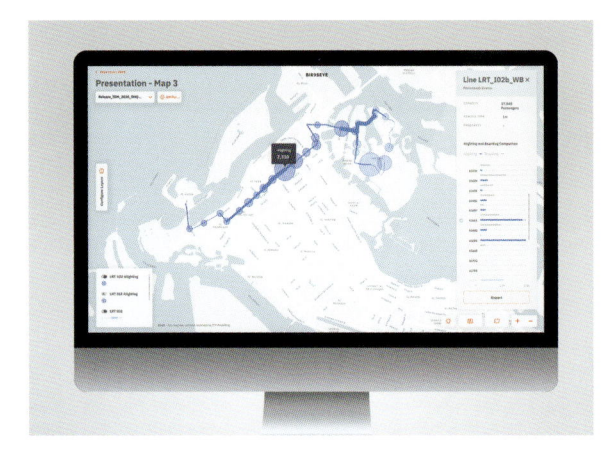

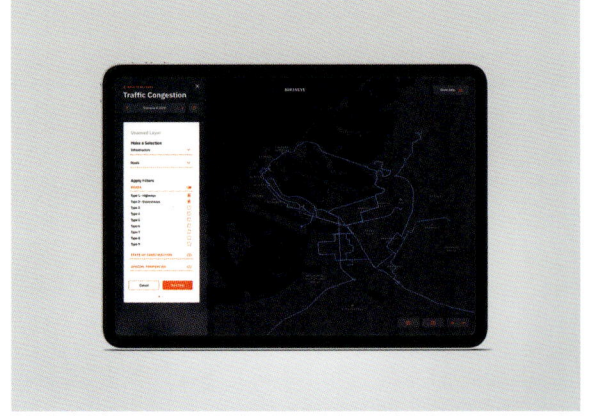

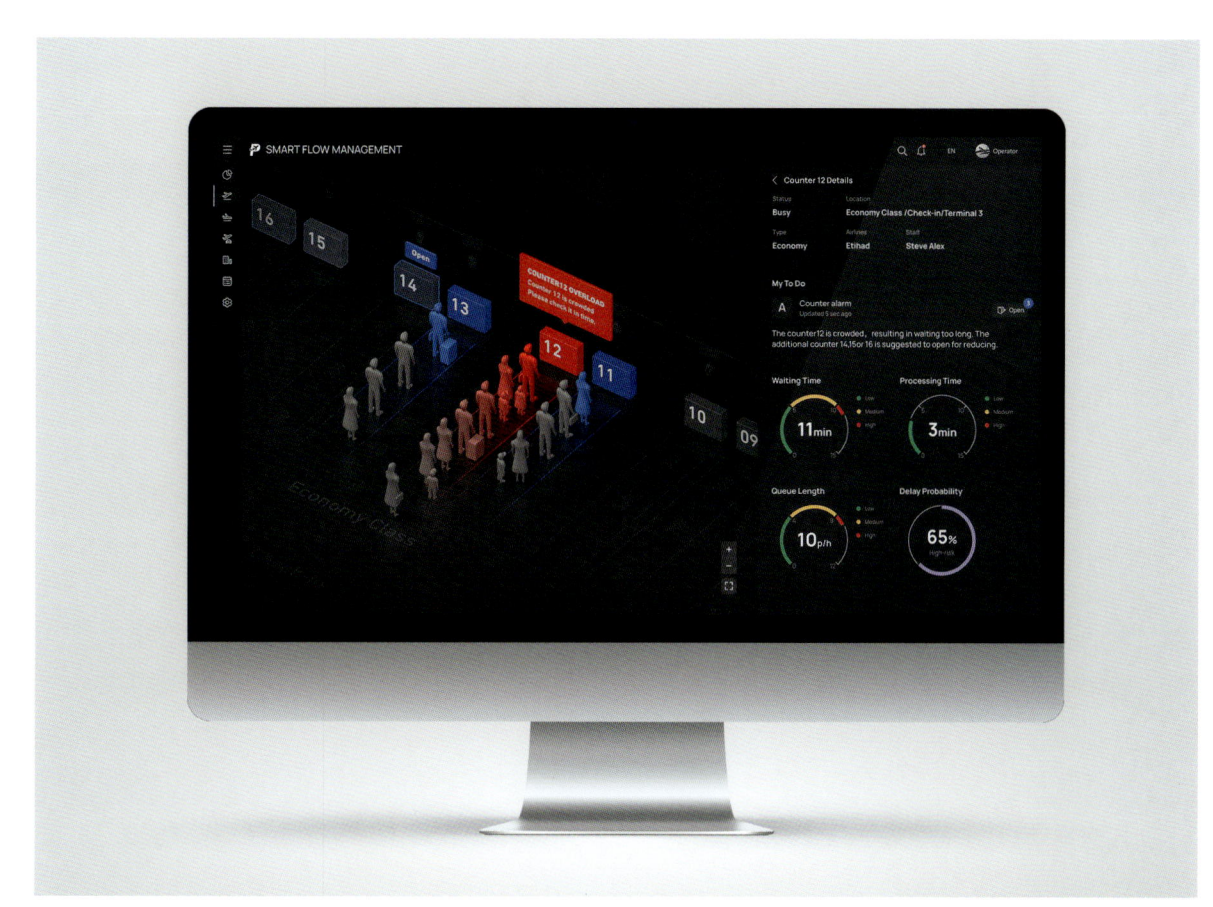

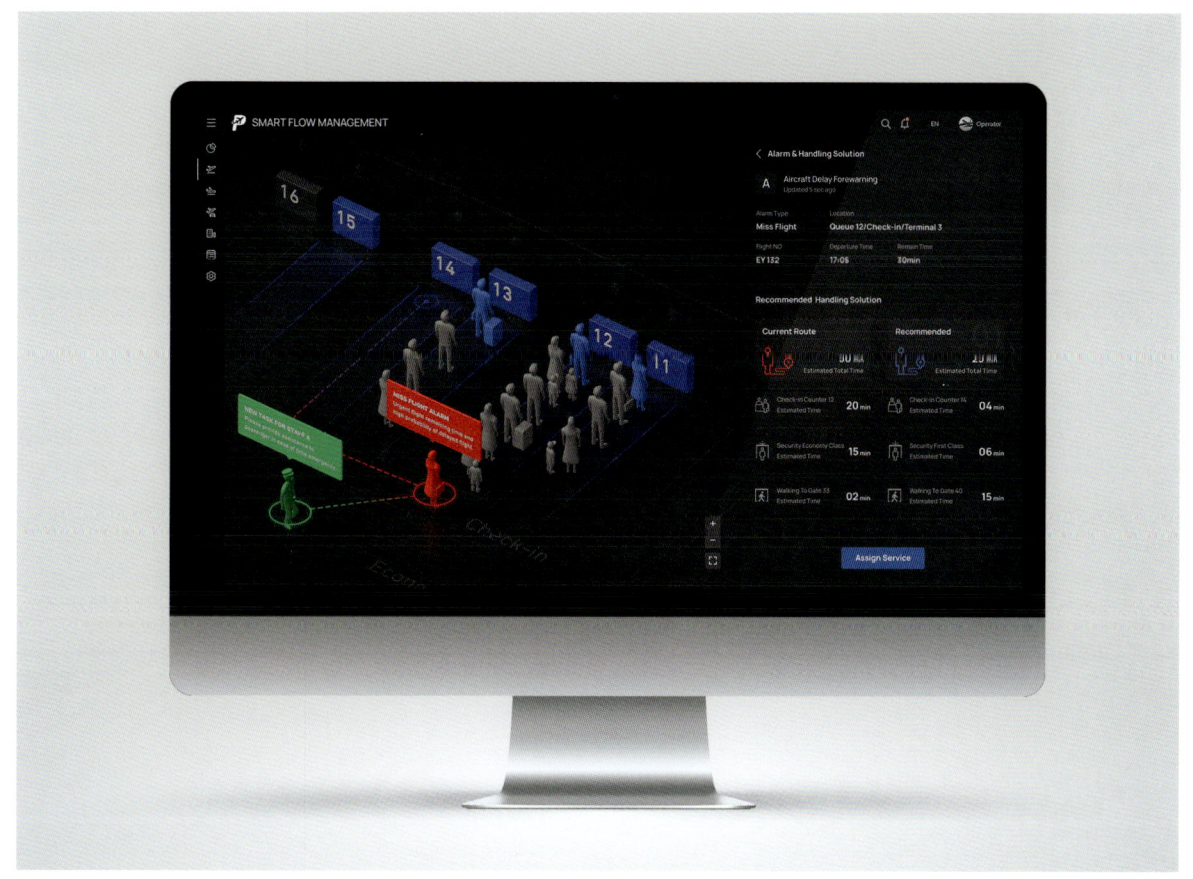

Huawei Smart Flow Management

[User Interface Design]

Huawei Smart Flow Management is dedicated to the phenomenon of stress during air travel. The user interface design addresses the fact that such stress is based on a lack of control and that people do not know what is going to happen in the case of congestion or delay. As an AI passenger-tracking system, Smart Flow Management provides anonymous real-time passenger counts as well as waiting time and service handling status monitoring for the airport. It allows the measuring of various queuing times (check-in, security, boarding) and helps to foresee bottlenecks before they can happen.

Client
Huawei Technologies Co., Ltd.
Nanjing, China

Design
Huawei Technologies Co., Ltd.
Nanjing, China

Project Team
Liangbing Lu (Project Manager)
Minmin Yang (Interaction Designer)
Wei Liu (Interaction Designer)
Shunji Jiang (Graphic Designer)
Yuan Wei (Interaction Designer)
Tingbin Xing (Web Designer)
Hongmei Li (Web Designer)

HI-SCAN 6040 CTiX

[User Experience Design,
User Interface Design]

Client
Smiths Detection Inc.
Wiesbaden, Germany

Design
Custom Interactions GmbH
Darmstadt, Germany

Project Team
Smiths Detection:
Robert Binias (Head of User Interface)
Christof Klopp
(Application Development Engineer)
Ingrid Oebekke (Project Management)
Parnian Tavakol (Software Programmer)

Custom Interactions:
Benjamin Franz (Project Management)
Sascha Hiller (Interaction Design)
Michaela Kauer-Franz
(Interaction Concept/User Research)
Philipp Kohl (Graphic Design)
Marta Piqué (Graphic Design)

→ Designer profile on page 582

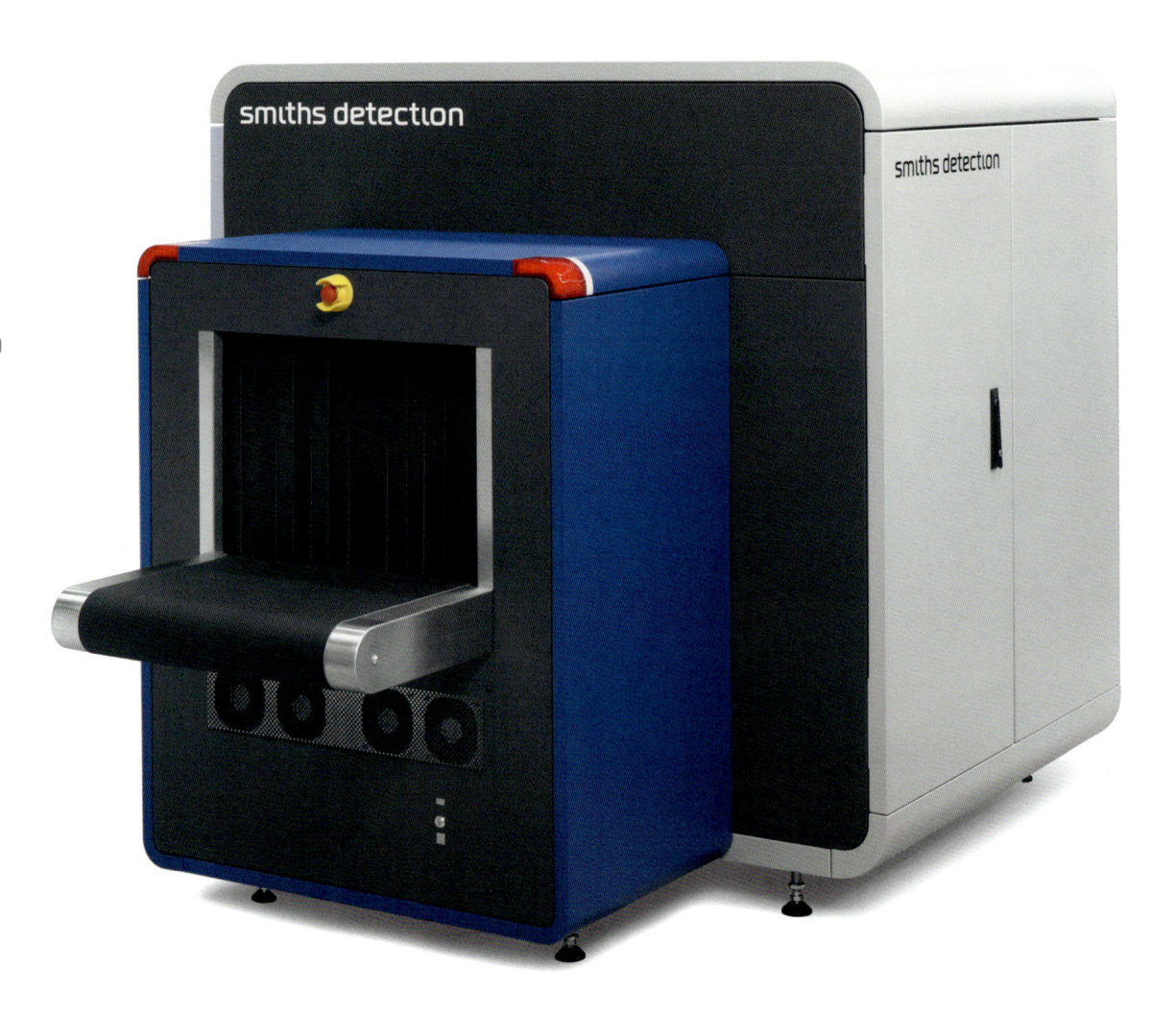

Apps	Interface & User Experience Design	Spatial Communication	Red Dot: Junior Award	Designer Profiles	Jury Portraits	Index
206	236	336	426	564	642	668

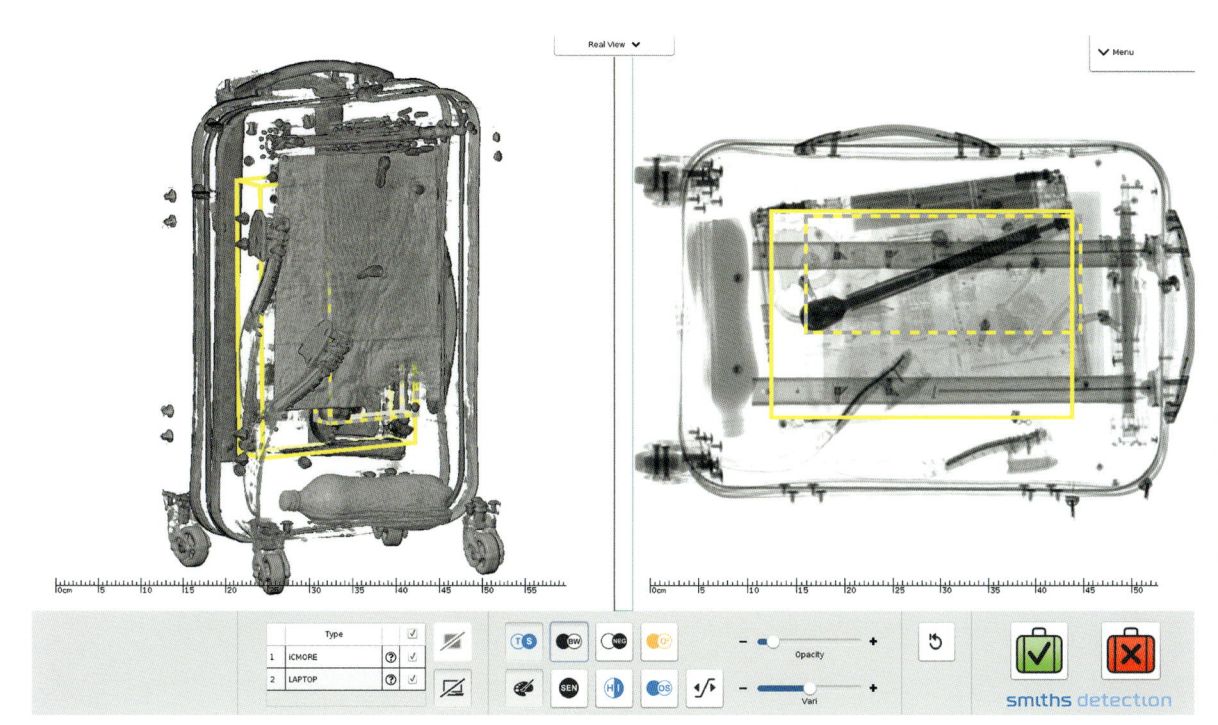

The HI-SCAN 6040 CTiX offers fully accessible, freely rotatable and zoomable 3D radiographic images of hand luggage for personnel working with luggage scanners at airports, as well as the automated detection and marking of potentially forbidden goods. Furthermore, it automatically disregards laptops without them needing to be unpacked from the luggage. This enables a quick and safe assessment of dangerous goods, prohibited items or safe luggage, and it gives the staff the certitude to make the right decision even under time pressure. This prevents long waiting queues and improves the working atmosphere. In addition, passengers no longer need to unpack electronic devices and liquids from their hand luggage.

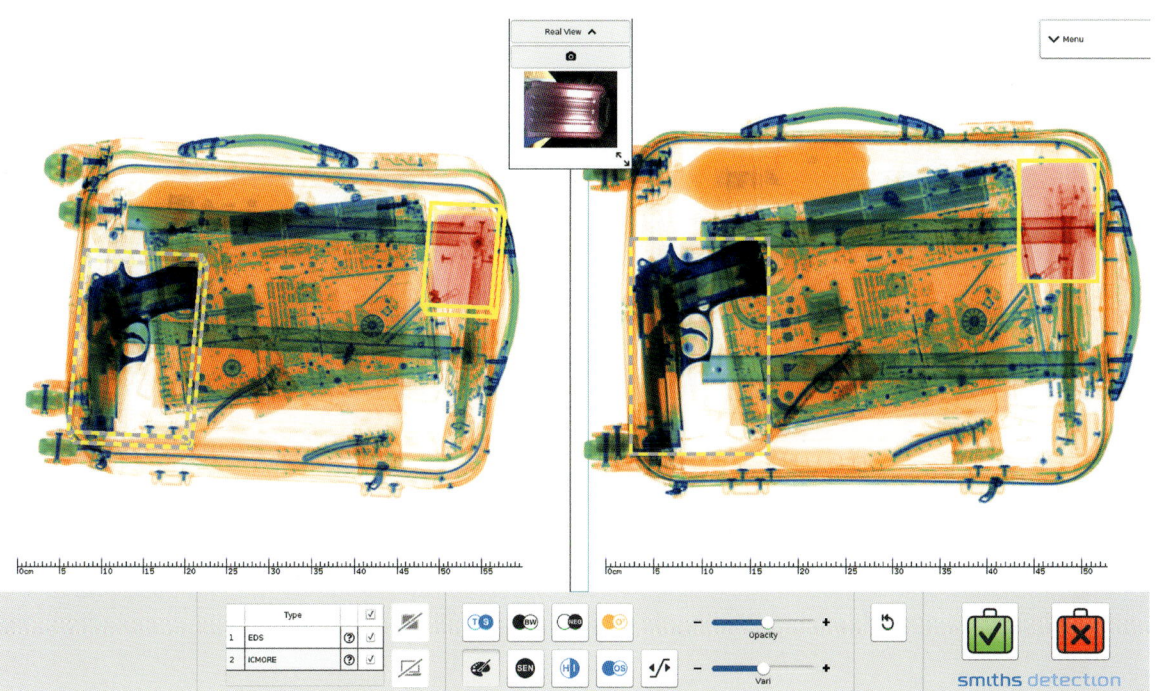

Publishing & Print Media	Posters	Typography	Illustrations	Sound Design	Film & Animation	Online
4	64	92	116	126	138	172

Veoneer Data Visualiser

[Exhibition User Experience Design, User Interface Design]

The Veoneer Data Visualiser showcased the demo "Collaborative Driving" at CES 2020, pointing out the significance of the two-way communication between user and vehicle for tomorrow's mobility. Interactive scenarios allowed visitors to approach a large TV screen and navigate through various scenes, each demonstrating different ways of how data insights can contribute to a safer and better driver experience. Additional key elements included accumulated data visualisation, a live data display and in-car demo apps, showcasing both existing and futuristic car features.

Client
Veoneer
Stockholm, Sweden

Design
The Techno Creatives
Gothenburg, Sweden

Project Team
Anderson Schimuneck (Art Direction)
Filip Svalander (Designer)
Jonas Lindberg (Designer)
Seungjun Jeong (Designer)
Leticia Rezende (Designer)

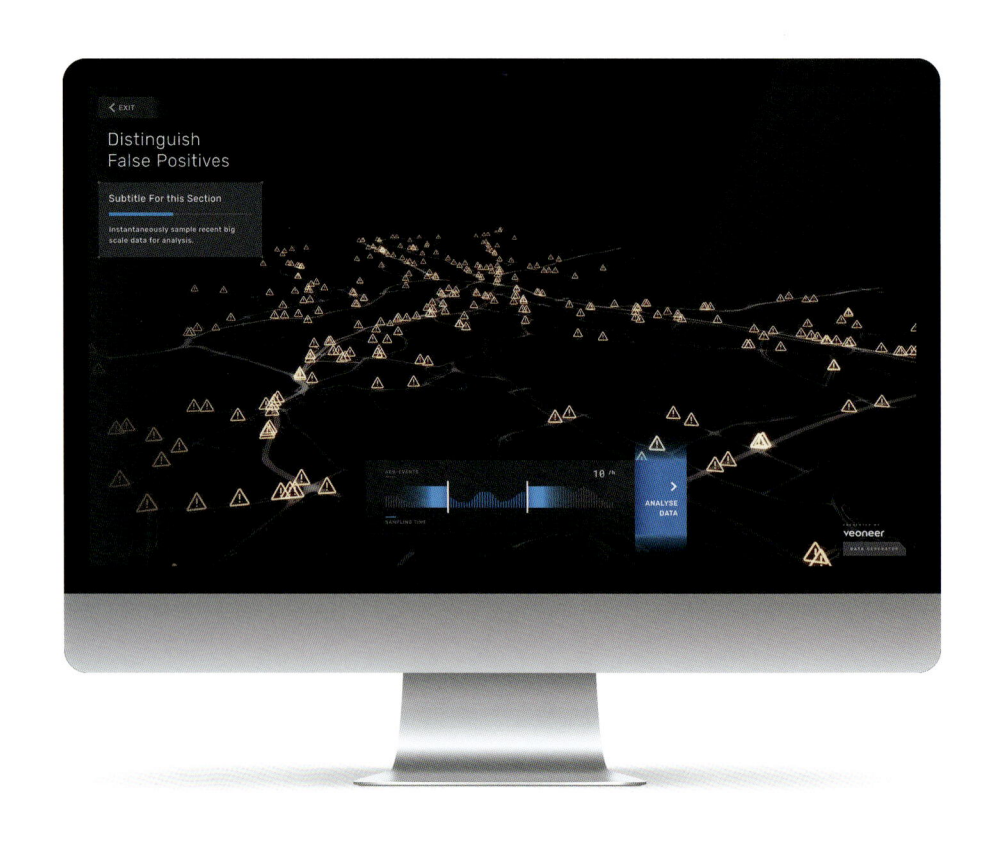

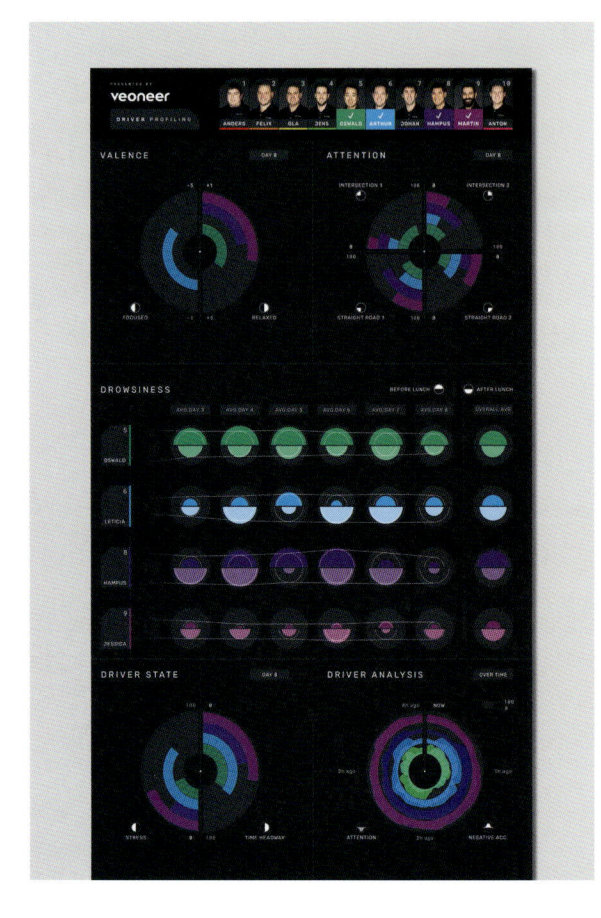

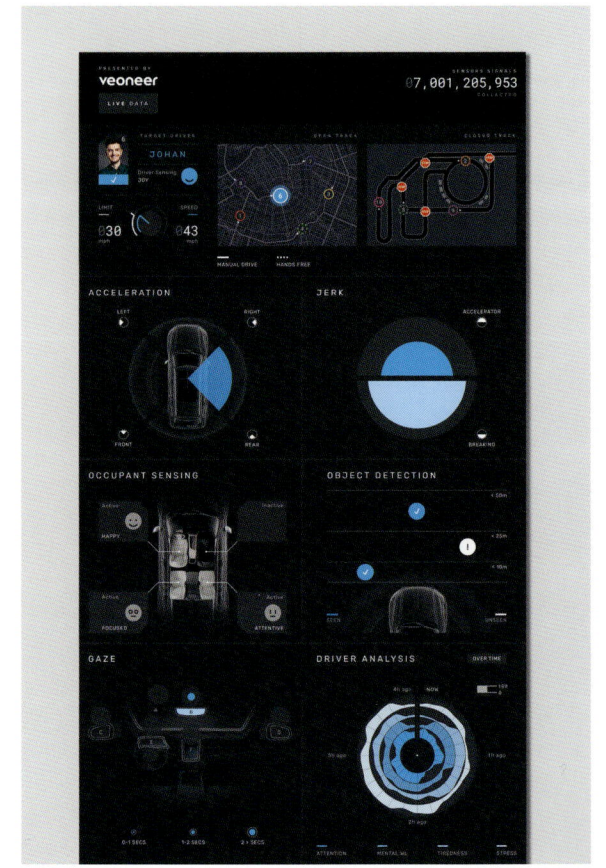

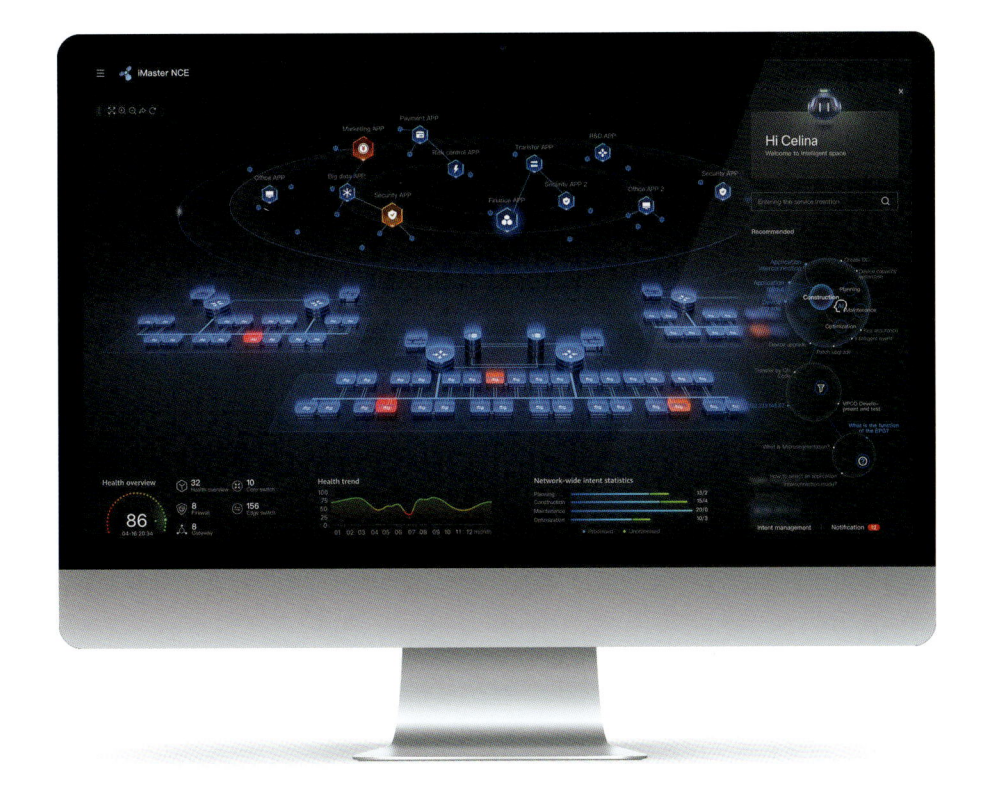

Apps	Interface & User Experience Design	Spatial Communication	Red Dot: Junior Award	Designer Profiles	Jury Portraits	Index
206	236	336	426	564	642	668

Huawei Data Center Autonomous Driving Network Solution

[Network Communication, User Interface Design]

The Huawei Data Center Autonomous Driving Network Solution addresses the trend of the extensive use of cloud computing, big data and mobile internet accelerating the launch of new services and thus creating even more data centre traffic. It therefore offers an intelligent network management and control system based on artificial intelligence and digital twin technology. O&M personnel can work on a visible and controllable virtual network carrier with digital twins. In addition, the system provides suggestions based on scenarios to assist with manual decision-making and close issues.

Client
Huawei Technologies Co., Ltd.
Shenzhen, China

Design
Huawei Technologies Co., Ltd.
Shenzhen, China

Project Team
Weipan Guo (Artwork)
Jian Gao (Artwork)
Junqiang Yin (Artwork)
Siwei Zhu (Artwork)
Wenfang Tang (Artwork)
Yanfang Tan (Artwork)
Yongzhen Zhao (Concept)
ToB Studio AUI (Concept)

Publishing & Print Media	Posters	Typography	Illustrations	Sound Design	Film & Animation	Online
4	64	92	116	126	138	172

Back-End System for Urban Water Quality Monitoring

[Web Design, User Interface Design]

The Yimu Back-End System is an integrated water-quality monitoring system that provides a text-based and graphical analysis, allowing users and management teams to grasp the water quality effectively. It allows one to forecast major or basin-water pollution accidents and to supervise the implementation of the total control system through continuous real-time and remote monitoring of the water quality. It can automatically monitor the water quality with regard to the parameters of turbidity, pH, residual chlorine, conductivity and temperature.

Client
Shenzhen Yimu Technology Co., Ltd.
Shenzhen, China

Design
Shenzhen Yimu Technology Co., Ltd.
Shenzhen, China

Project Team
Tianyi Chen (Lead Designer)
Zhiqiang Li (Lead Designer)
Tingran Li (Text)
Xiaozhu Yu (Designer)
Fei Zhou (Designer)
Nan Feng (Designer)
Zhengzheng Si (Designer)
Di Wu (Designer)

→ Designer profile on page 637

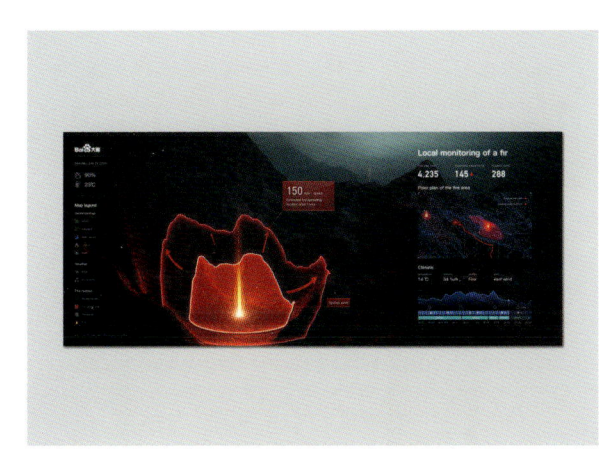

Intelligent Forest Fire Monitoring

[User Interface Design]

This user interface design uses AI technology to provide a full-process system for intelligent forest-fire monitoring. It can accurately detect forest fires globally while automatically triggering a warning system. Covering a wide range of detection scenarios, it meets the needs of institutions in different countries and regions. It detects overall fire parameters such as the fire status and the geographical environment. For instance, the system can intelligently deduce fire spread trends and automatically plan rescue routes.

Client
Baidu Online Network
Technology (Beijing) Co., Ltd.
Beijing, China

Design
Baidu Online Network
Technology (Beijing) Co., Ltd.
Beijing, China

Project Team
Zhao Huibin (Creative Direction)
Huang Xiaolin (Art Direction)
Ren Xiaohua (UX Design)
Liao Jiawei (UX Design)
Dong Zhaozhan (UI Design)
Zhong Pengfei (UI Design)
Che Weichun (UI Design)

Publishing & Print Media	Posters	Typography	Illustrations	Sound Design	Film & Animation	Online
4	64	92	116	126	138	172

MQ
[Mobile User Interface Design]

MQ is a design system for a product line of GIS-based software tools on mobile devices. It facilitates the inspection and condition management of trees, playground equipment and roads. The tasks can be performed directly through highly interactive list controls and modal dialogues without having to open any detail views. Overview and orientation are provided by a dynamic map view that connects with the list controls. Linked input fields with autocomplete suggestions accelerate the data entry and minimise errors.

Client
IP SYSCON GmbH
Hannover, Germany

Design
University of Applied Sciences Osnabrück
Osnabrück, Germany

Project Team
IP SYSCON:
Dr. Florian Hillen (Project Management)
Roland Hachmann (Managing Director)
Isabelle Poppe-Gierse (Marketing)

University of Applied Sciences Osnabrück:
Prof. Henrik Arndt (Creative Direction)
Niklas Garnholz (User Interface Design)
Ann-Christin Teigelkamp
(User Interface Design)

→ Clip online

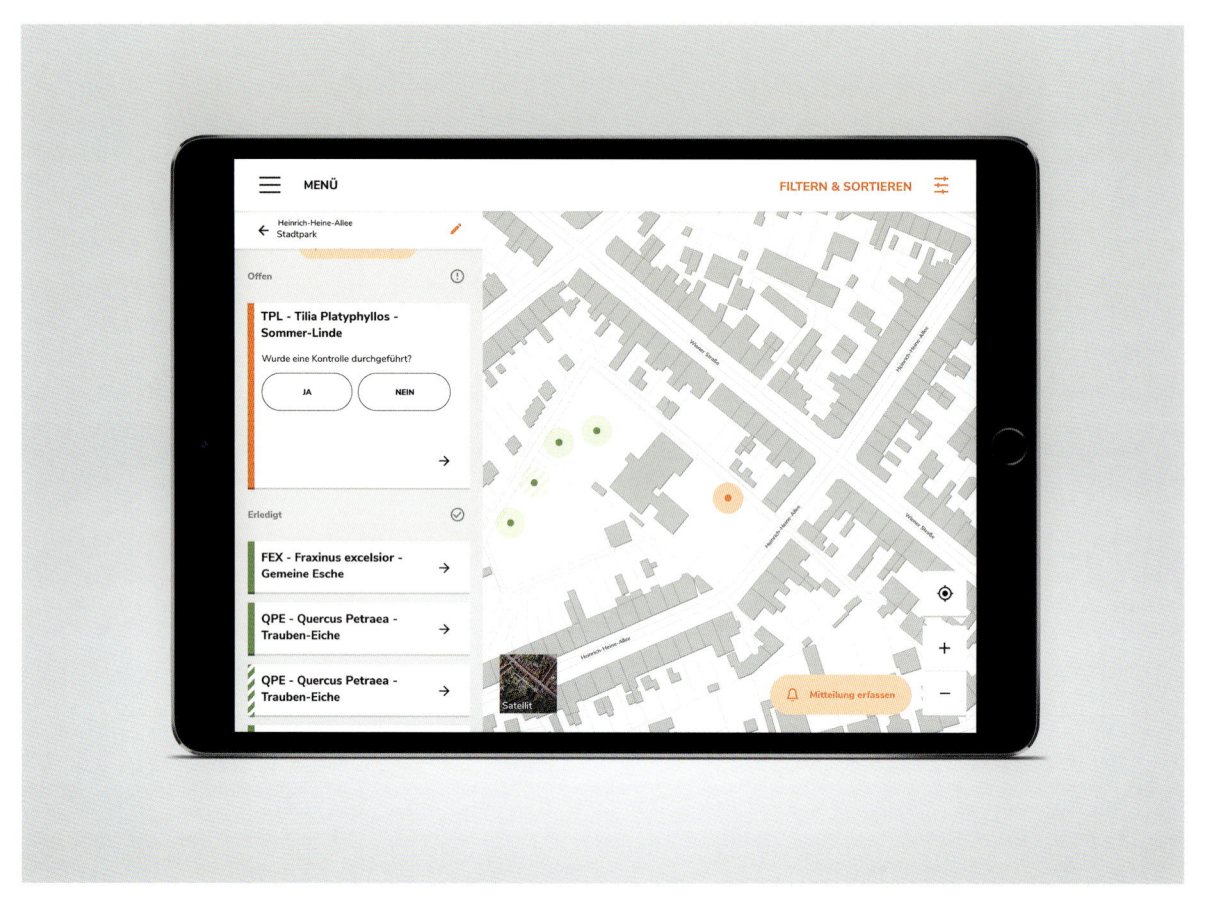

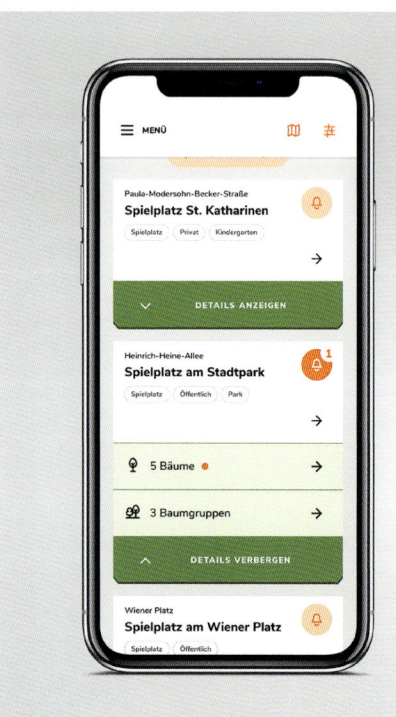

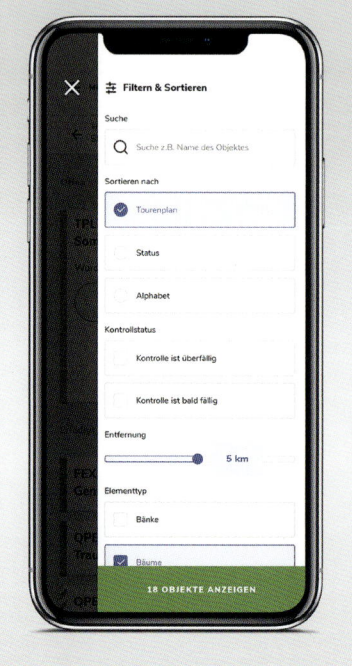

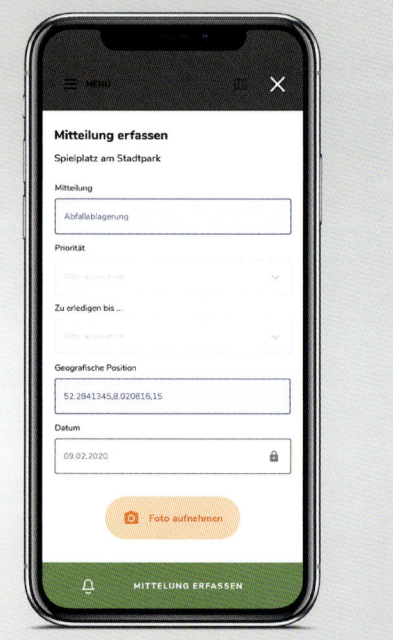

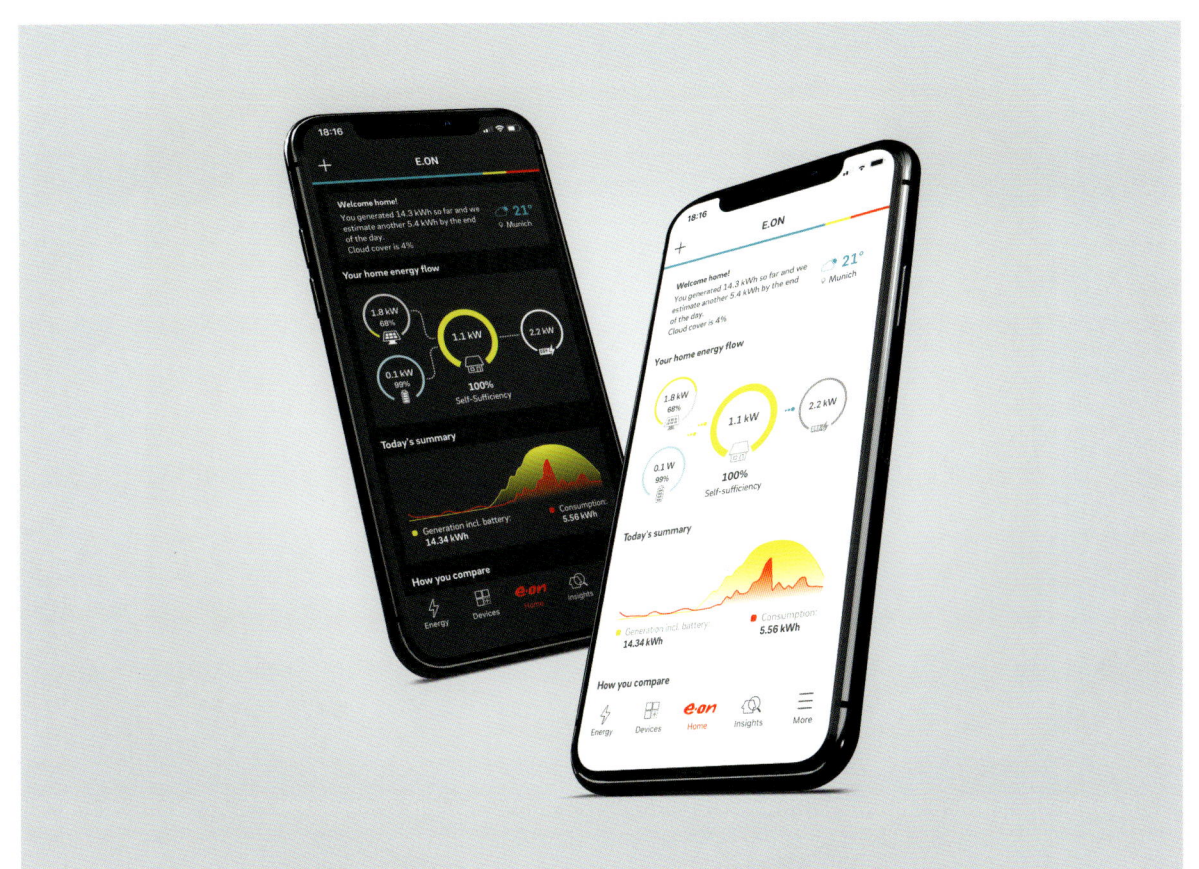

Apps	Interface & User Experience Design	Spatial Communication	Red Dot: Junior Award	Designer Profiles	Jury Portraits	Index
206	236	336	426	564	642	668

E.ON Home

[Smart Home Solution, Service Design]

Designed as a sector coupling solution, the application E.ON Home combines energy management and smart home functionality. The aim is to improve transparency and control. Adjusting automatically to individual configurations of solar panels and to home-battery, heating or cooling systems as well as electric car charging, the app focuses on relevant insights in order to optimise overall energy consumption and improve sustainability. The app is available in several languages and presents the energy components in a straightforward manner.

Client
E.ON Solutions GmbH
Essen, Germany

Design
E.ON Solutions GmbH
Essen, Germany

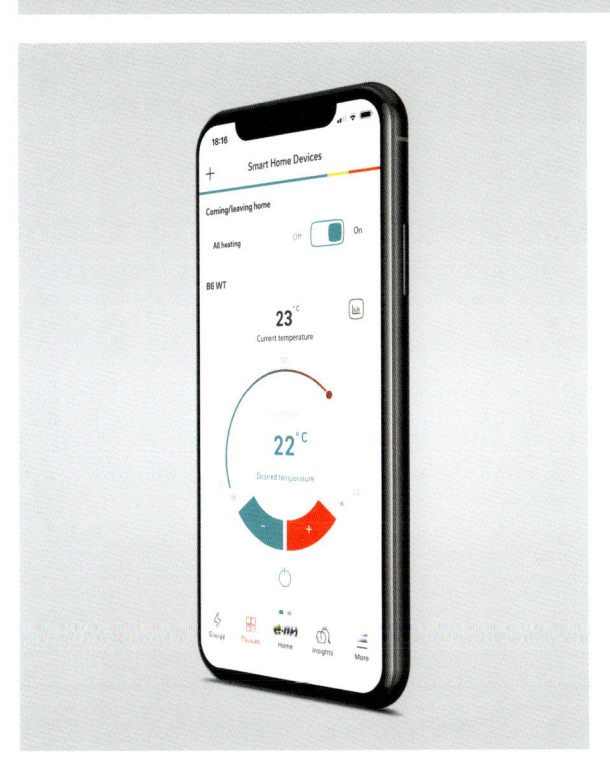

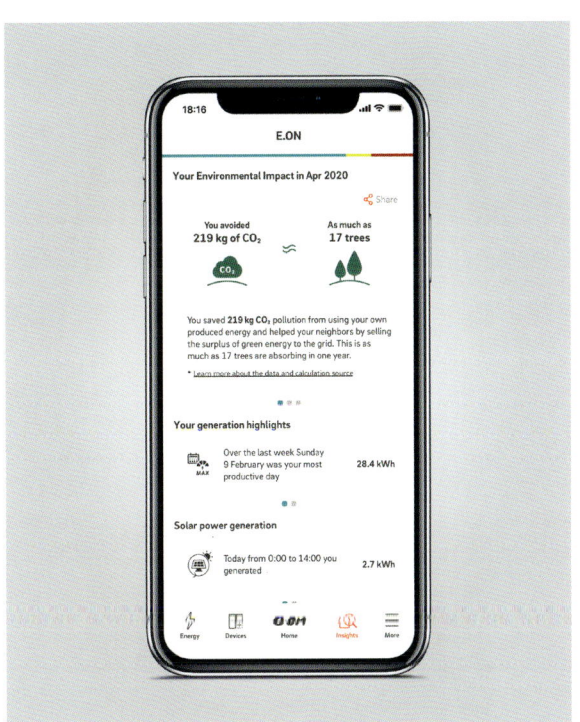

Publishing & Print Media	Posters	Typography	Illustrations	Sound Design	Film & Animation	Online
4	64	92	116	126	138	172

F-Box

[User Experience Design]

The F-Box platform allows the use of recyclable packaging boxes to be monitored in real time. Users receive information from their regions, including the times of recycling or the utilisation rate of the packaging. The home page is designed with a full-screen mode, which is convenient for real-time monitoring. The combination of various charts enriches the diversity of data visualisation. The colour matching of the interface aims to highlight the product characteristics of a shared express box.

Client
S.F. Express (Hong Kong) Limited
Shenzhen, China

Design
S.F. Express (Hong Kong) Limited
Shenzhen, China

Project Team
Qian Xu (Project Management)
Peiqi Li (UI Design)

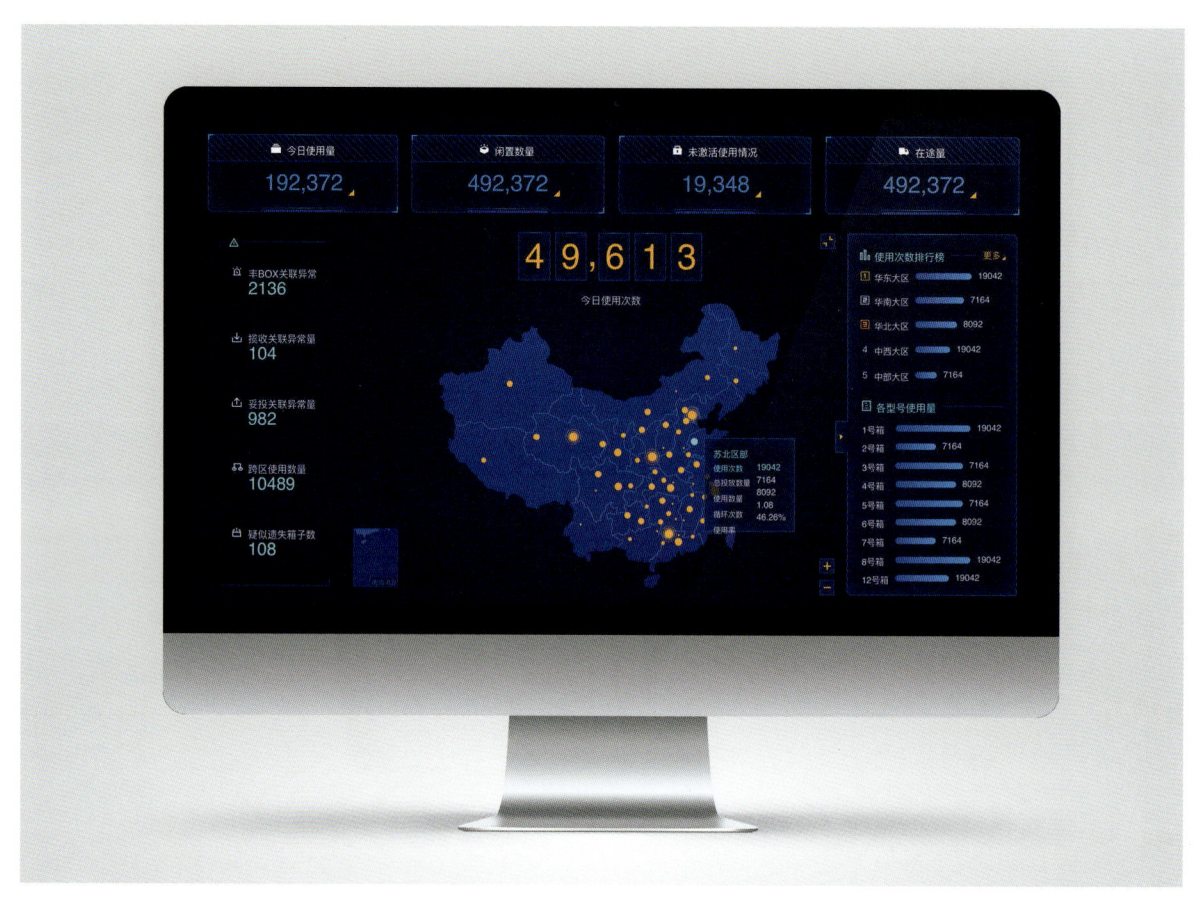

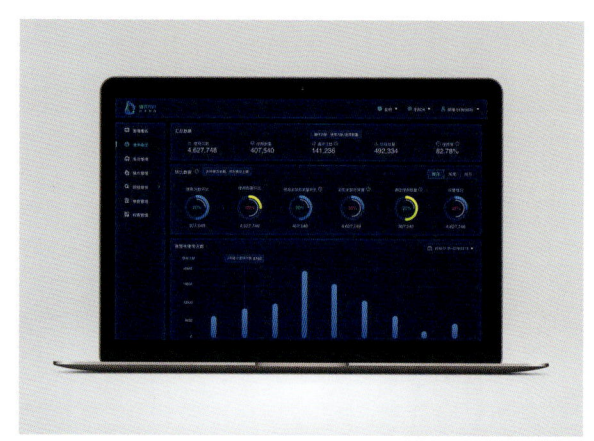

Bikespector

[User Interface Design]

This prediction website for bike sharing offers new possibilities against the backdrop of planning difficulty when it comes to sharing options. A prototype was developed for the app, along with a high-performance forecast model with an interface for the Bikespector front end. As result, it offers a user-friendly service, predicting bike sharing for days in advance by using a specifically developed AI trained on open source data. Thus, the sharing of bikes becomes a valid, plannable and eco-friendly alternative to driving cars.

Client
denkwerk
Cologne, Germany

Design
denkwerk
Cologne, Germany

Hivebox Smart Locker

[User Experience Design, Service Design]

The Hivebox smart locker enables the easy sending and temporary storage of goods, complemented by an essential pickup function service. The design provides a high degree of flexibility and convenience as compared to the traditional sending mode. It allows users to place orders online easily and quickly and to check the location and distance of the nearby Hivebox locker. This device – just like the WeChat official account, mini-program, app and official mobile website – also supports the use of multiple channels to place orders.

Client
Shenzhen Fengchao Technology Co., Ltd.
Shenzhen, China

Design
S.F. Express (Hong Kong) Limited
Shenzhen, China

Project Team
Jingwei Xiong (Project Management)
Peiqi Li (UI Design)
Yirong Tan (Illustration Design)

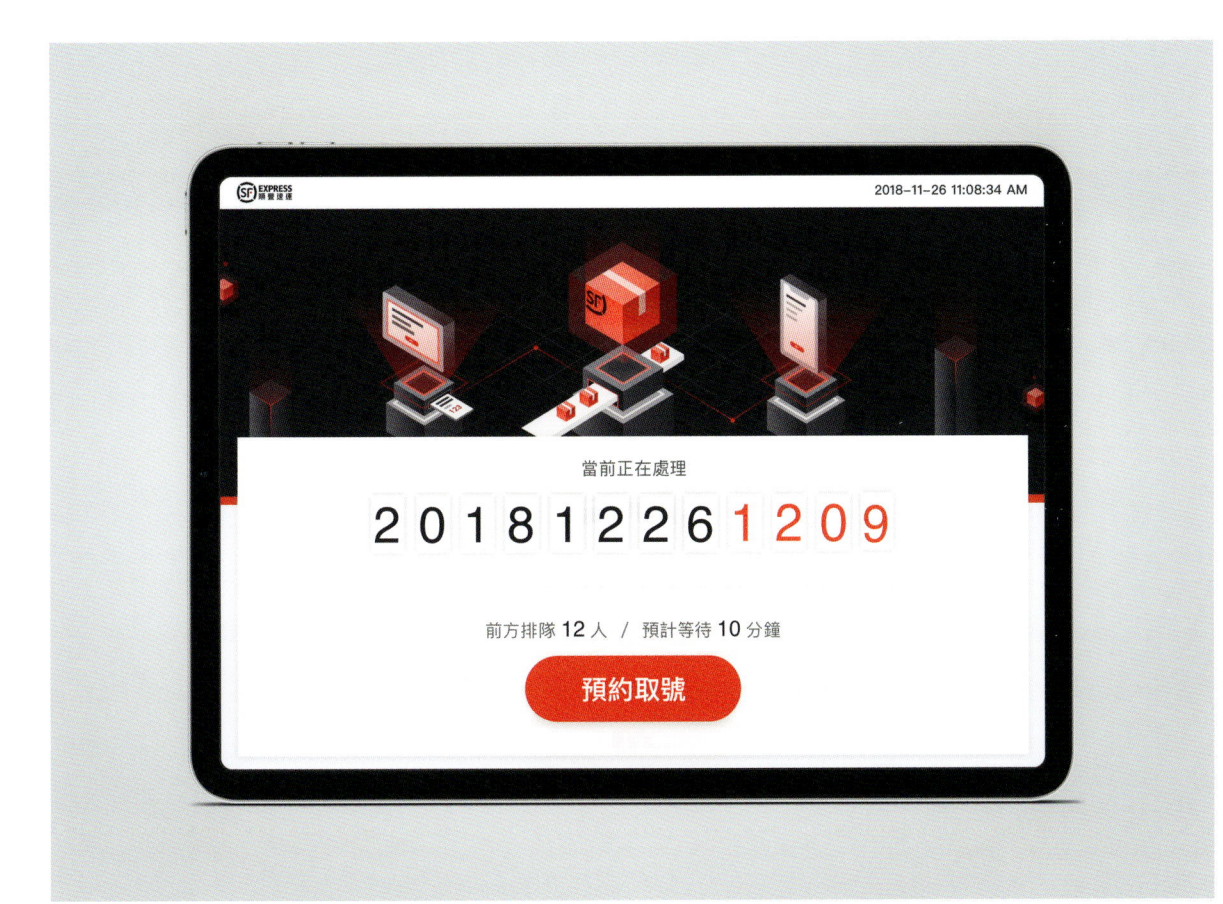

EF-Locker

[User Experience Design, Service Design]

The user experience design of the EF-Locker terminal, a product for a subsidiary of the company S.F. Express in Hong Kong, China, focused on optimising the "picking up", "checking" and "sending" functions. The goal of this intelligently designed interface was to offer end users the experience of a simple pickup service, available 24 hours a day. Another goal was to increase user trust in the brand and enhance its recognition value. The main colours of the interface design are red and black, originating from the S.F. logo.

Client
S.F. Express (Hong Kong) Limited
Shenzhen, China

Design
S.F. Express (Hong Kong) Limited
Shenzhen, China

Project Team
Peiqi Li (UI Design)
Peiwei Tang (UI Design)

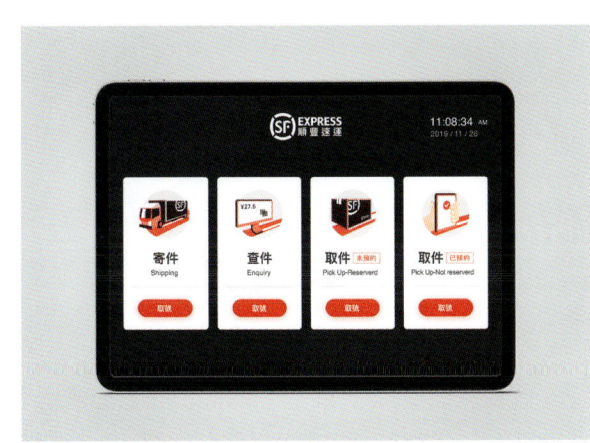

Publishing & Print Media	Posters	Typography	Illustrations	Sound Design	Film & Animation	Online
4	64	92	116	126	138	172

Digital Portal Diia

[User Experience Design,
User Interface Design]

With the objective of transparency, the concept of the digital portal Diia involved the development of the UX/UI and the creation of a design system for Ukraine government websites. It contains all federal services and gives users the possibility to order them directly from an electronic device. The services have been considerably simplified. Thus, thanks to a redesign of the private entrepreneur registration, for example, the number of fields a citizen needs to fill in has been decreased from 58 to 7. Every step of ordering a service is accompanied by tips and assistance.

Client
Ministry of Digital Transformation
of Ukraine
Kyiv, Ukraine

Design
Spiilka Design Büro
Kyiv, Ukraine

Project Team
Ministry of Digital Transformation
of Ukraine:
Mykhailo Fedorov (Manufacturer)
Mstyslav Banik (Project Management)

Spiilka Design Büro:
Vladimir Smirnov (Art Direction)
Nastya Zherebetska (Digital Concept)
Roman Sapielkin (Web Design)
Anna Sosnovska (Web Design)
Ani Kazarian (Project Management)

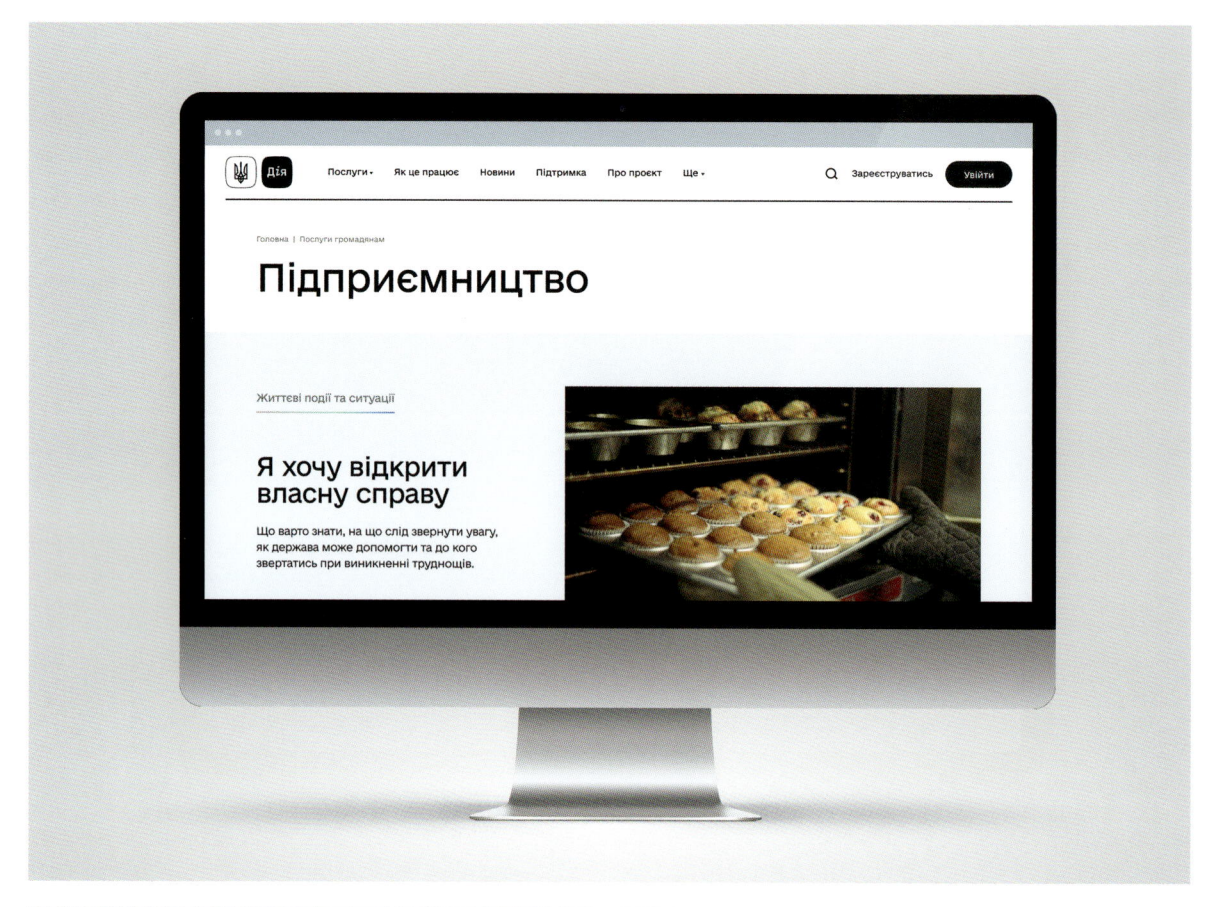

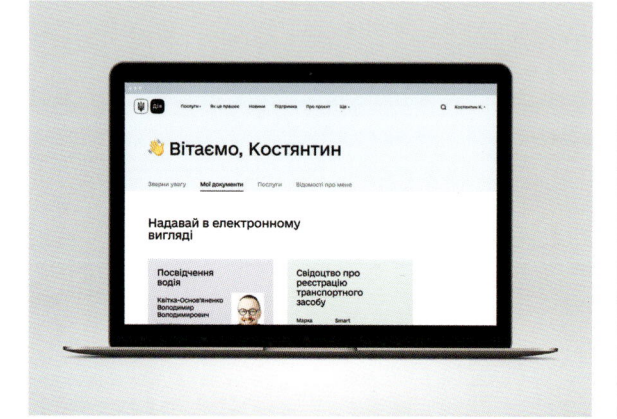

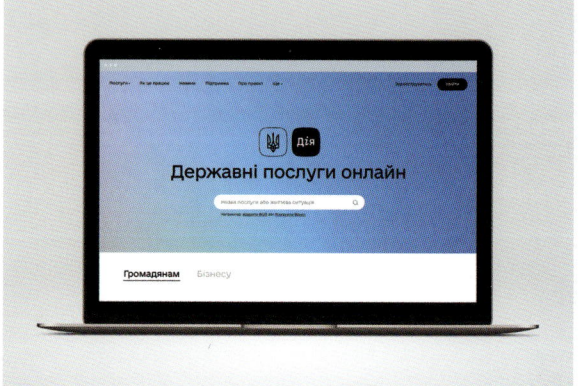

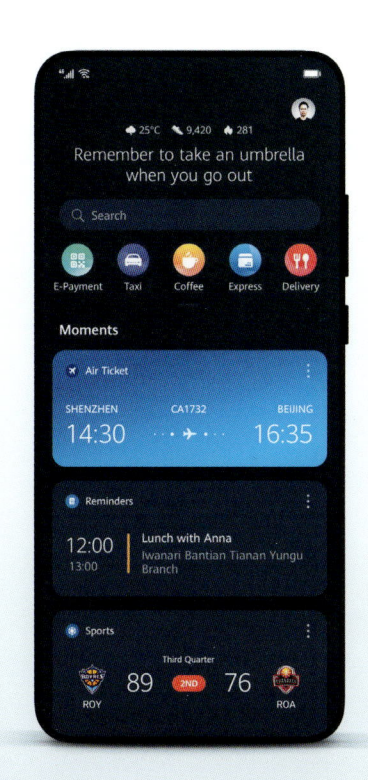

Huawei Assistant – Today

[User Experience Design, User Interface Design]

The design of the personal assistant "Huawei Assistant – Today" is focused on providing quick access to various services. The user can simply choose the preferred services without downloading the applications. Providing an open and sustainable ecosystem, all services and the entire information architecture have been aligned across different devices. In addition, SmartCards offer users an intelligent and dynamic way to search for the right application, while services are recommended when needed, based on artificial intelligence in all scenarios.

Client
Huawei Technologies Co., Ltd.
Shenzhen, China

Design
Huawei Technologies Co., Ltd.
Shenzhen, China

Project Team
Zhongli Dong (Project Management)
Zhaojie Xia (Project Management)
Hengguang Liao (Art Direction)
Shuangyan Xia (Production)
Zhuoxin Xu (Production)

SAP Road Map Explorer

[Service Design, Screen Design]

Client
SAP SE
Walldorf, Germany

Design
SAP SE – The Tools Team
Walldorf, Germany

Project Team
Astrid Kadel (Designer)
Sarina Claudia Walter (Designer)
Nikola Freudensprung (Designer)
Jonathan Edward Lee (Designer)

→ Designer profile on page 618
→ Clip online

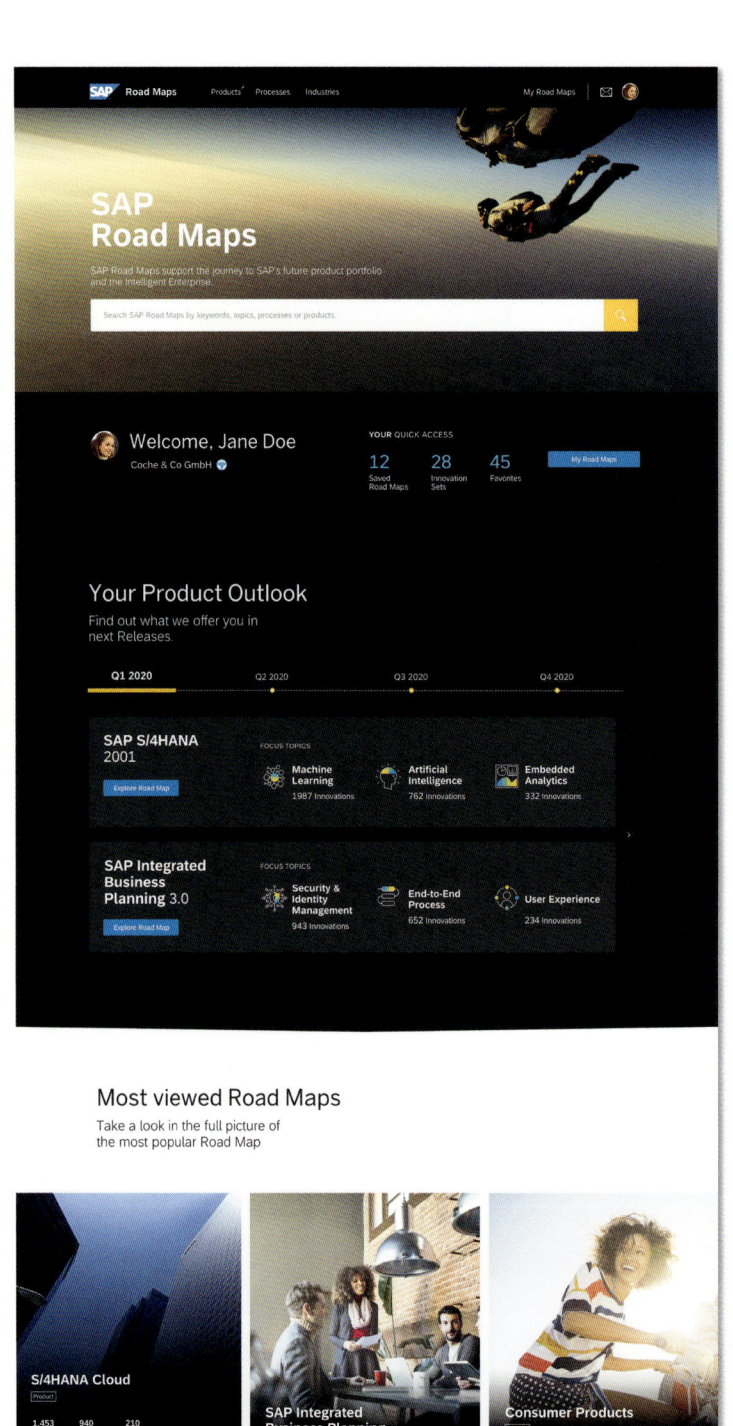

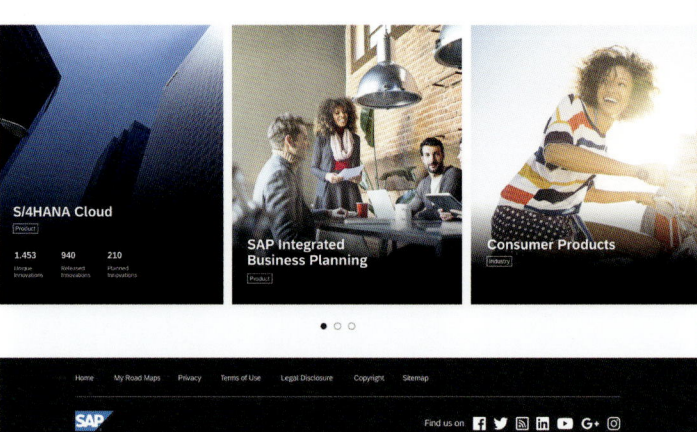

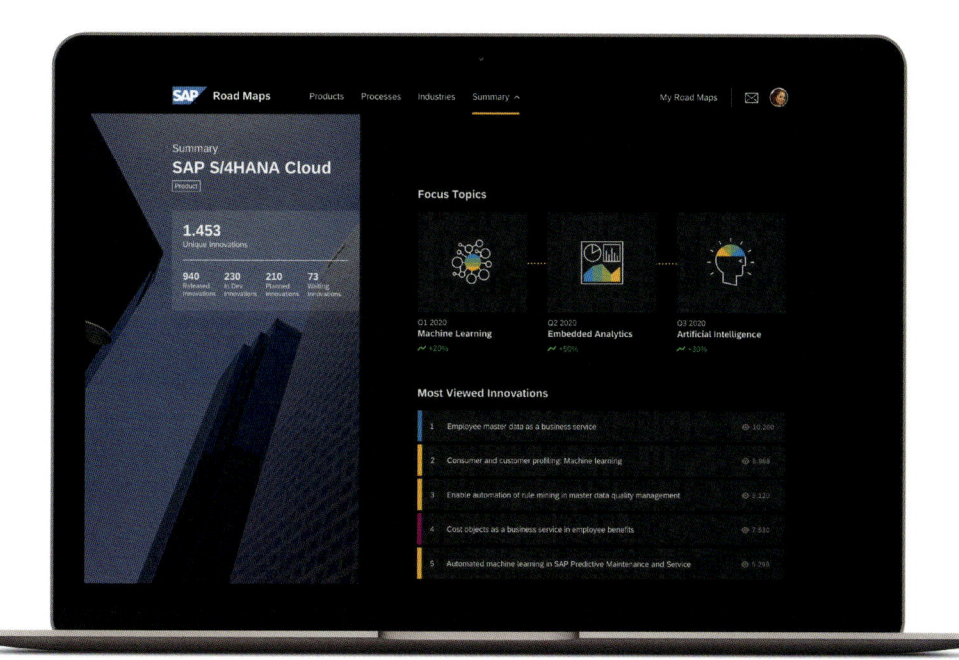

The concept of the SAP Road Map Explorer centres on the task of conveying a transparent, consistent and reliable experience of the company's current and future product direction. With searching and filtering road maps tailored to individual customer needs, this web application delivers an intuitive and efficient user interface, which makes it easy for a wide variety of customers to focus on the relevant information. The road maps, which are essential for the design, allow users to experience future releases and the adoption of the latest product and business process innovations.

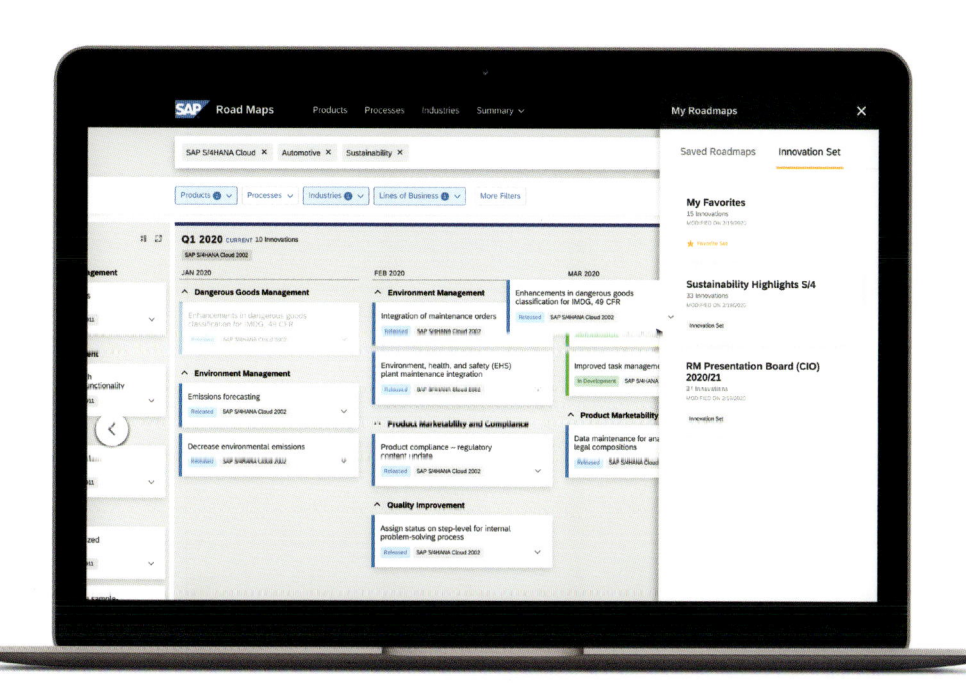

Publishing & Print Media	Posters	Typography	Illustrations	Sound Design	Film & Animation	Online
4	64	92	116	126	138	172

MuchSkills
[User Interface Design]

MuchSkills.com was launched in late April 2020 with the aim of giving individuals and organisations a better way to express and visualise their strengths and skills beyond the traditional CV. In addition to communicating an individual's history, the app also focuses on taking a look at the future and the goals of an individual or team. The patent-pending user experience on both desktop and mobile devices makes it easy for users to create and track their skill profiles over time, thus showcasing what is important to them in their work.

Client
Up Strategy Lab
Gothenburg, Sweden

Design
Up Strategy Lab
Gothenburg, Sweden

Project Team
Noel Braganza (Product Design)
Daniel Nilsson (Strategic Planning)

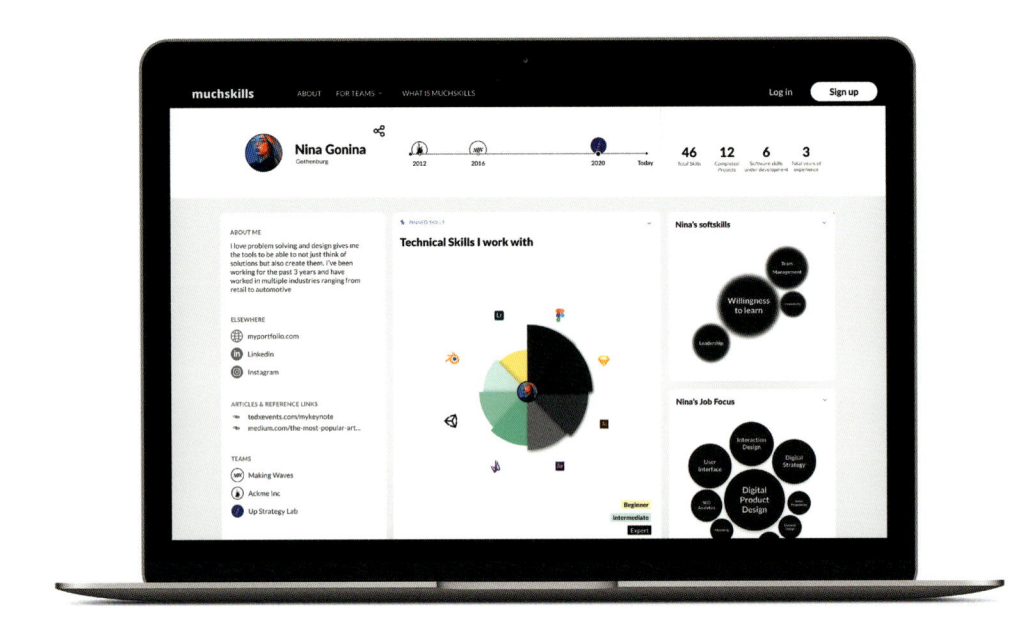

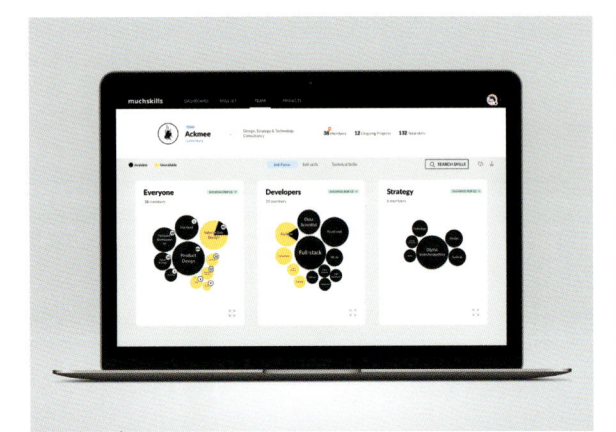

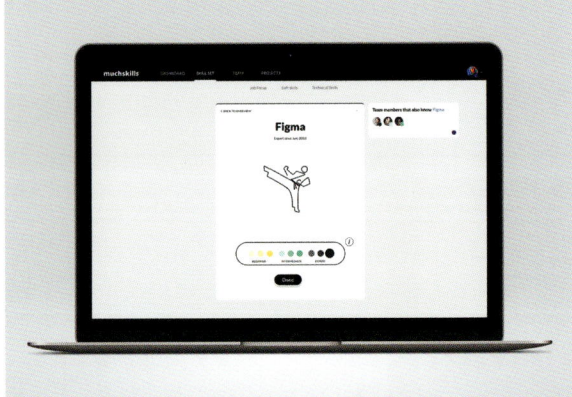

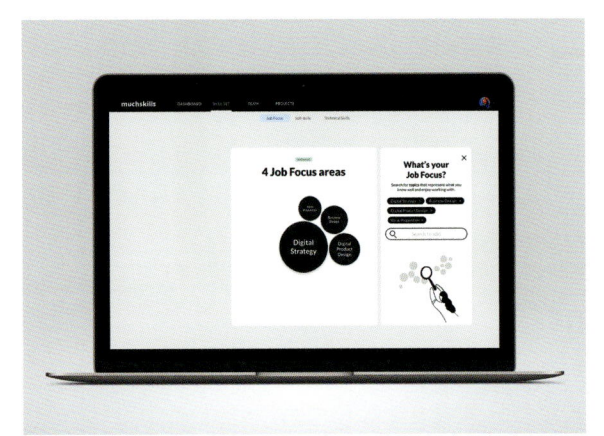

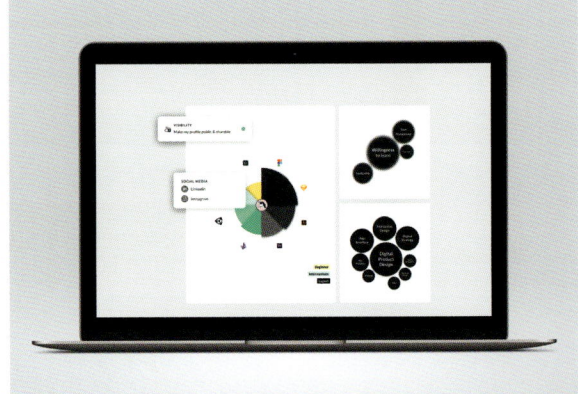

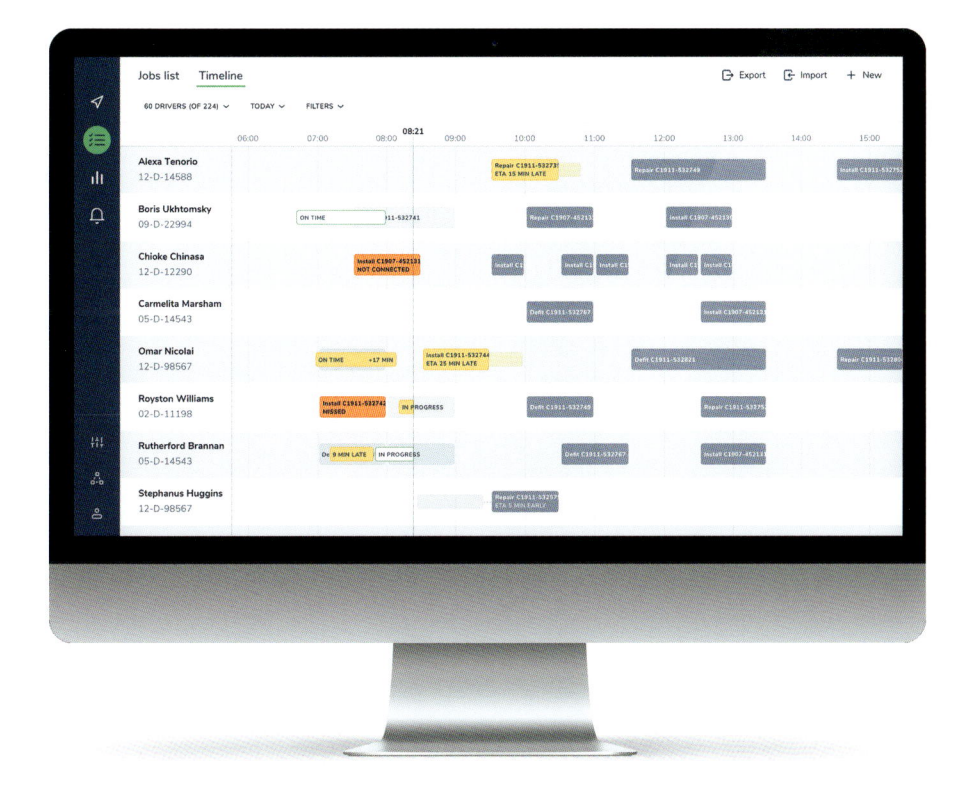

Masternaut On Time

[User Interface Design]

On Time is a module within the Masternaut Connect service platform, which provides fleet managers and operators with insight and tools to track and optimise vehicle utilisation. It allows the monitoring of job schedules as they are being planned and carried out in order to respond to live developments and optimise scheduling workflows. The user experience design is based on comprehensive customer feedback such as through interviews and user testing. It has been validated and refined through prototypes and various UI designs.

Client
Masternaut
London, United Kingdom

Design
Littlevoice
London, United Kingdom

→ Designer profile on page 605

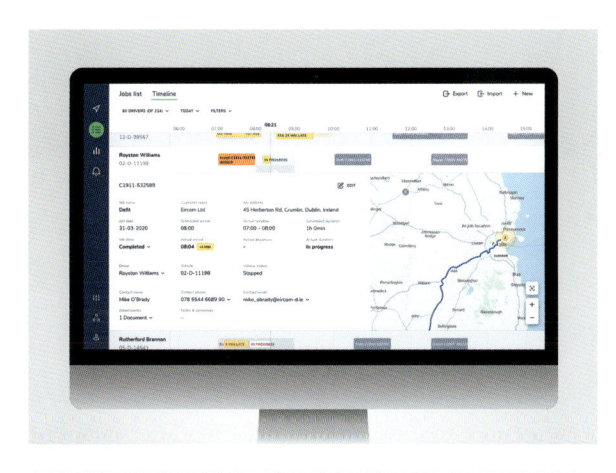

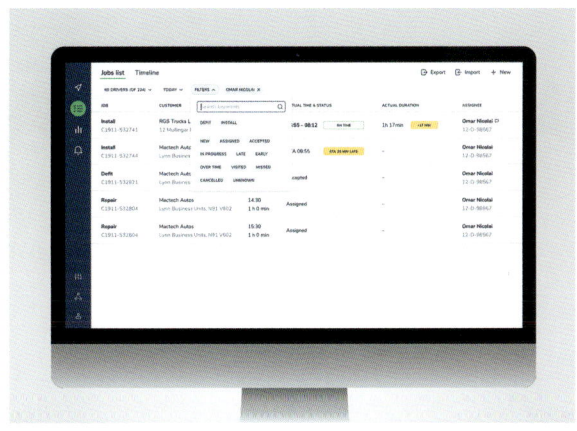

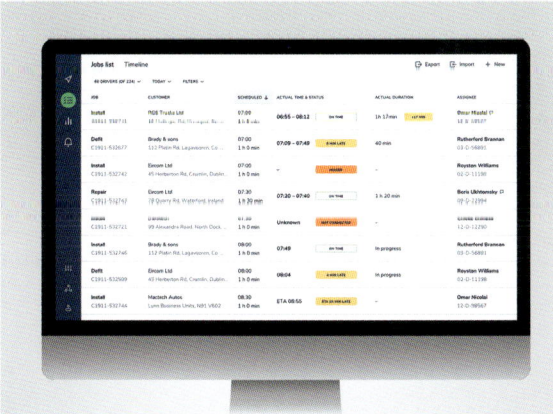

Publishing & Print Media	Posters	Typography	Illustrations	Sound Design	Film & Animation	Online
4	64	92	116	126	138	172

Huawei IdeaHub
[User Interface Design]

Huawei IdeaHub is a software system for digital whiteboards that promotes creativity as well as efficient and versatile team collaboration. Inspired by the current separation of office space, living space and entertainment space in the physical world, the design proposes a user experience architecture of "smart life", "creative collaboration" and "open ecosystems". The home page supports a standard mode with frequently used apps and a bulletin board mode for enterprise information. To switch between apps quickly, users can access a task centre to manage multitasking. The intuitive user experience architecture provides easy-to-learn interaction methods.

Client
Huawei Technologies Co., Ltd.
Shenzhen, China

Design
Huawei Technologies Co., Ltd.
Shenzhen, China

Project Team
Wei Huang (Experience Design)
Ruochen Fu (Visual Design)
Qin Xu (Experience Design)
Hui Yu (Experience Design)
Jinglong Zhang (Experience Design)

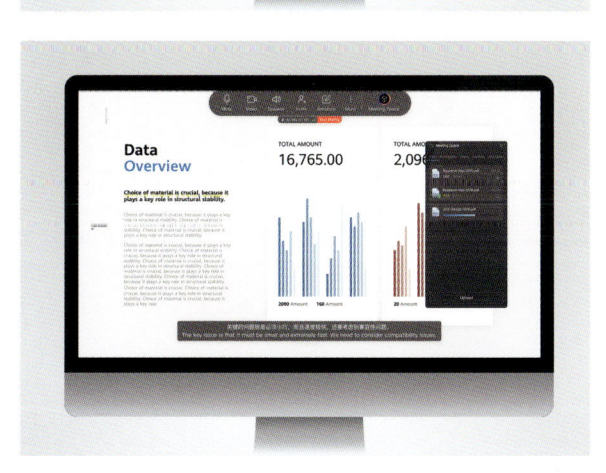

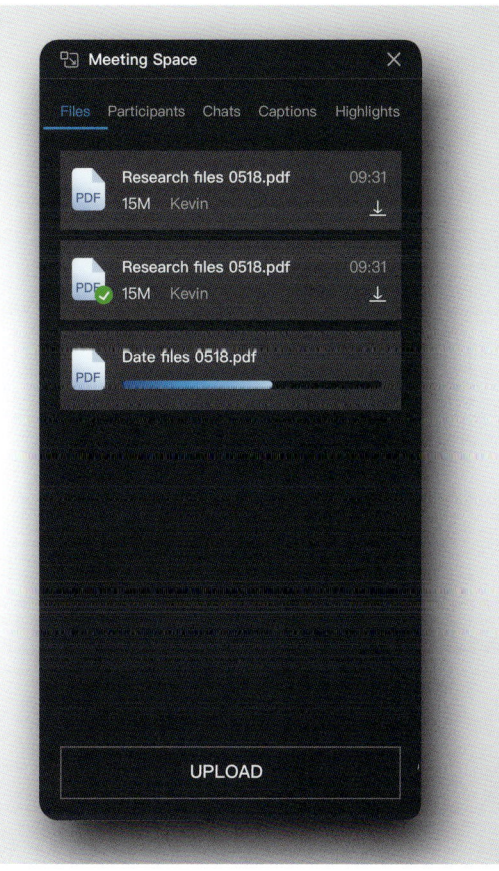

HUAWEI CLOUD Meeting

[User Interface Design]

The HUAWEI CLOUD Meeting system incorporates intelligent and professional software that provides cross-region and cross-enterprise communication as well as collaboration services. The idea is to help users facilitate conventional and unconventional meeting scenarios anytime with a meeting assistant that enables smoother communication and more efficient collaboration. In the generous meeting space, users have direct access to all features with just one click. This makes communicating very clear, as the person who is speaking is shown at the centre of the screen and in front of a sound wave background.

Client
Huawei Technologies Co., Ltd.
Shenzhen, China

Design
Huawei Technologies Co., Ltd.
Shenzhen, China

Project Team
Wei Huang (Design)
Rui Guan (Design)
Qing Wang (Artwork)
Yiting Zhao (Graphic Design)
Zhaotong Zhang (Motion Design)
Zixun Tu (Creative Design)
Mengdi Tang (Creative Design)
Xiang Kuang (Creative Design)

Publishing & Print Media	Posters	Typography	Illustrations	Sound Design	Film & Animation	Online
4	64	92	116	126	138	172

Huawei MeeTime

[Mobile User Experience Design]

Huawei MeeTime is an all-scenario video calling app supporting up to 1080p full HD video calls between the company's devices. It delivers a high-quality video call experience and allows users to share their screen during a call with the other party. Simultaneously, they can mark up the screen to collaborate with each other. Thus, people are able to connect with their family and friends anytime and anywhere through high-quality video calls, even in low-light or poor network conditions. This user experience design also comes with a range of features that make remote work highly productive.

Client
Huawei Device (Shenzhen) Co., Ltd.
Shenzhen, China

Design
Huawei Device (Shenzhen) Co., Ltd.
Shenzhen, China

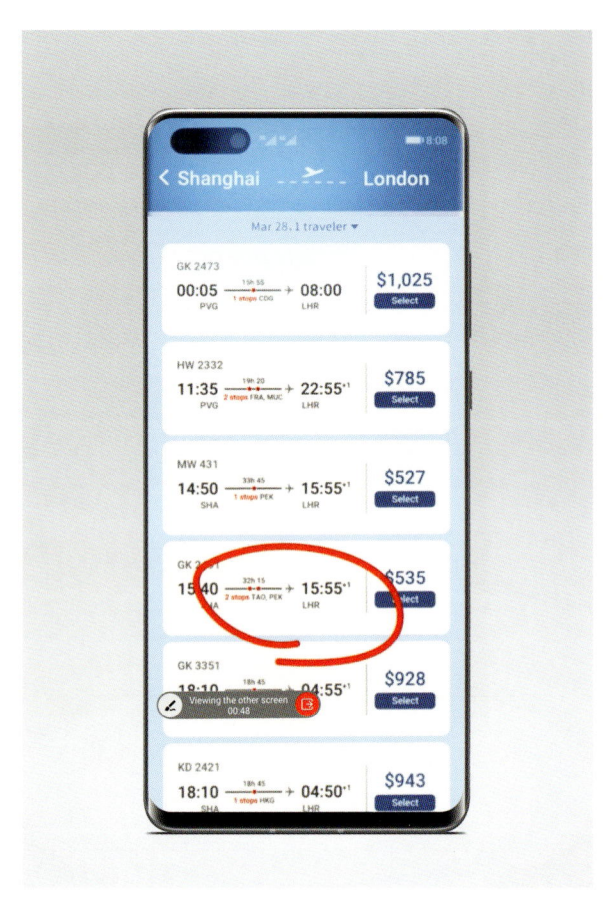

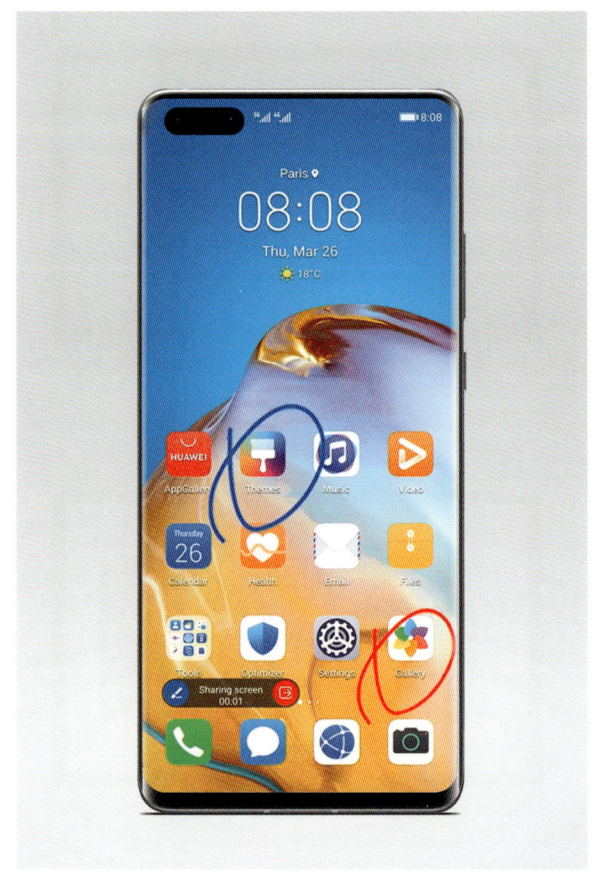

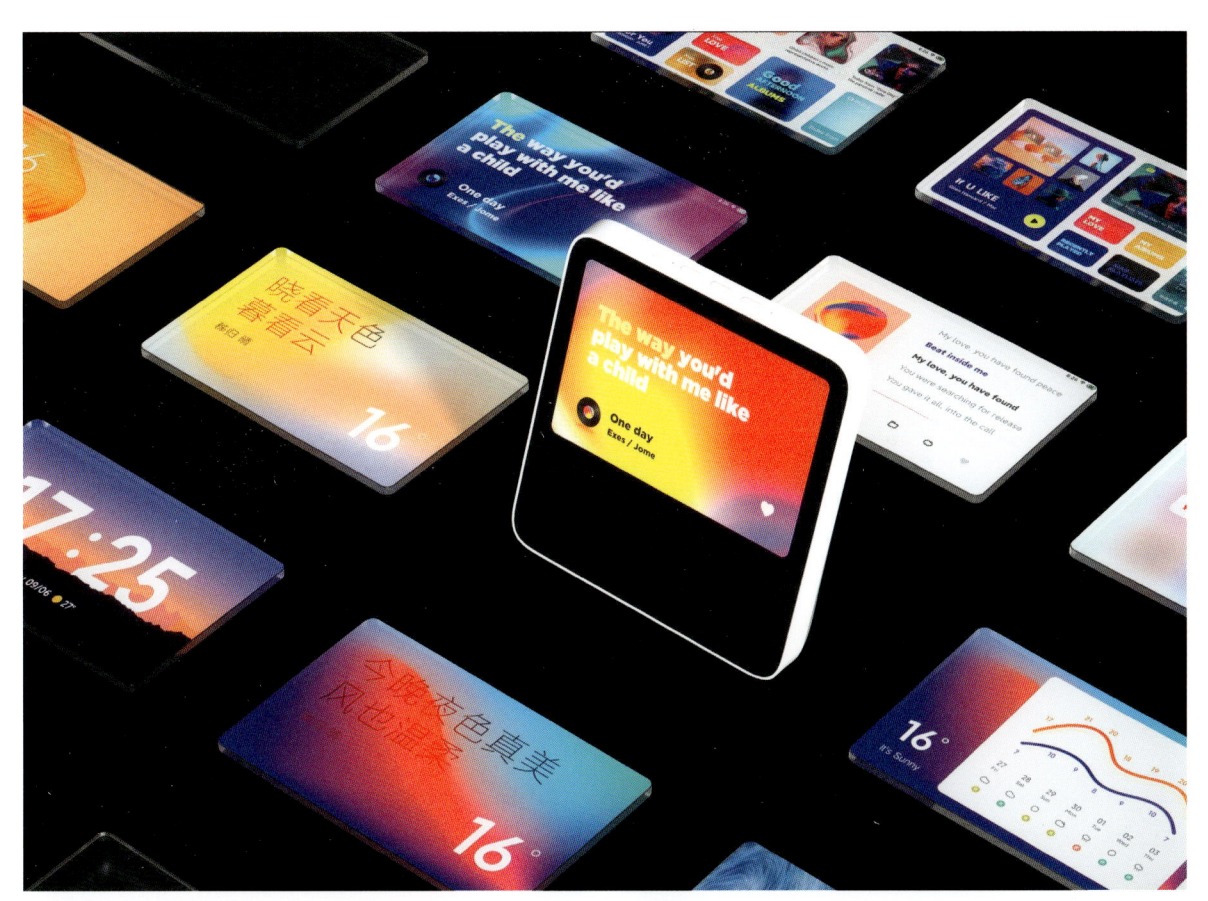

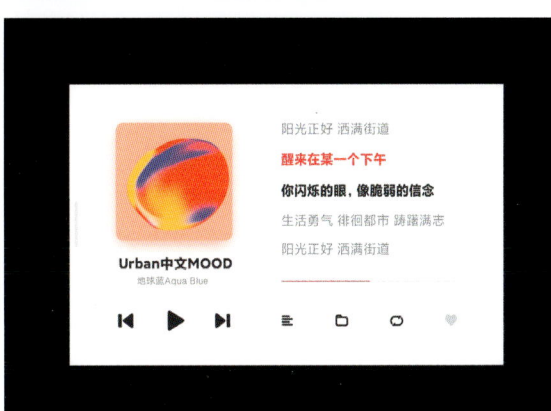

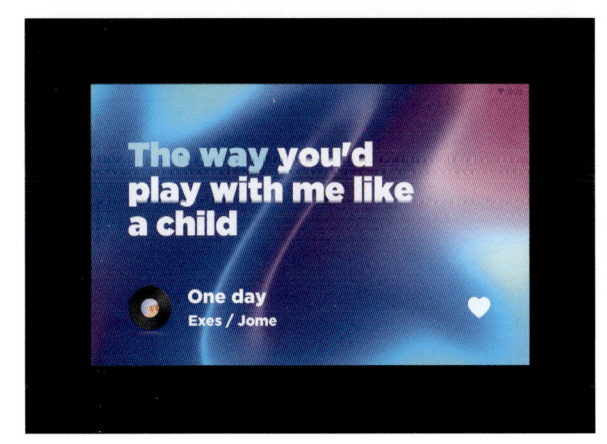

AIS'UI – Smart Speaker

[Interactive Operating System, Smart Home Solution]

AIS'UI is a multimode interactive operating system for an artificial intelligence touchscreen speaker with an 8" display. The user experience design focuses on improving efficiency in long-distance interaction. Aiming at a visual experience when using the music player, the system creates motion graphics with code generated by analysing the colour of the album's cover and the rhythm of the song to achieve a wide variety of different looks. Taking inspiration from Chinese ink painting, the design does without any specific graphics.

Client
Xiaomi Inc.
Beijing, China

Design
Xiaomi Inc.
Beijing, China

Project Team
Nandier
Xiaoxiao Shi
Wei Yu
Beiyi Zhang
Lipeng Ge
Liang Tan

→ Designer profile on page 633

HOME AI 2.0

[Smart Home Solution]

HOME AI 2.0 is a smart home operating system with a new aesthetic. It features an AI voice assistant that allows for a highly user-friendly smart home experience. As the third generation of a smart home system for the entire house, it integrates the four major interactive methods of buttons, touch, voice and app, integrating the whole life scene and nine functional systems. The concept was implemented by adopting a "One Step smart scene mechanism", thus supporting a continuous iterative upgrading of hardware, software and internet services.

Client
Shenzhen ORVIBO Technology Co., Ltd.
Shenzhen, China

Design
Shenzhen ORVIBO Technology Co., Ltd.
Shenzhen, China

Project Team
Shaobin Wu (Art Direction)
Xijiao Li (Designer)
Junbin Huang (Designer)
Lan Xiao (Designer)
Weina Li (Product Manager)
Qingquan Fu (Animation)

→ Designer profile on page 612

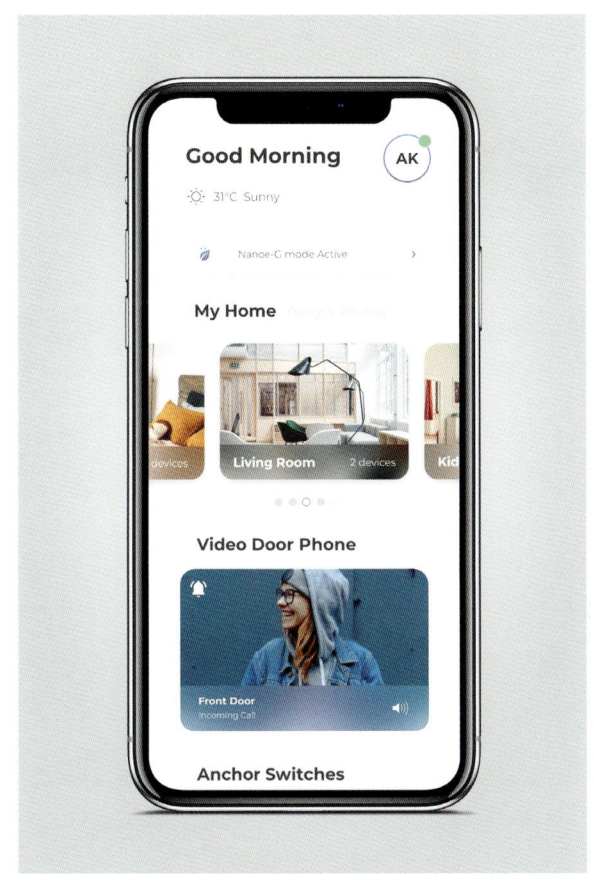

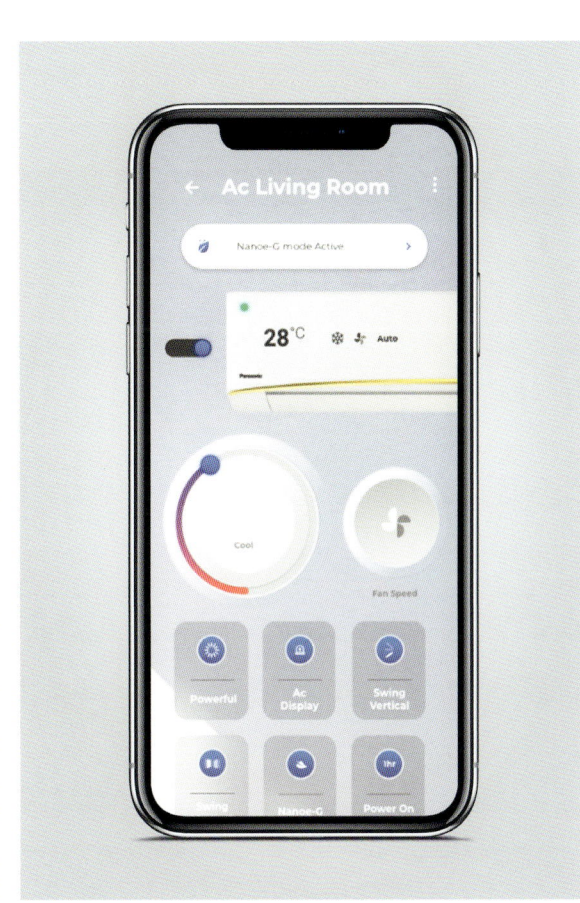

Apps	Interface & User Experience Design	Spatial Communication	Red Dot: Junior Award	Designer Profiles	Jury Portraits	Index
206	236	336	426	564	642	668

Panasonic MirAle
[Smart Home Solution]

The Panasonic MirAle smart home solutions aim to motivate even passive users by empowering them through an intuitive, gradual interface. The challenge is to offer a connected experience with a focus on engaging visual elements. Users are introduced to basic functionality and then slowly graduate to more complex functions like automation, sleep cycle, troubleshooting or data analytics. The concept is a seamless transition from object-based to digital experiences, while avoiding a steep learning curve.

Client
Panasonic India
Bangalore, India

Design
Analogy
Bengaluru, India

Project Team
Analogy:
Vyasateja Rao (Creative Direction)
Joel D'Silva (Digital Concept)
Arun Kumar (Digital Concept)

Panasonic:
Manish Mishra
Anurag Shrivastava

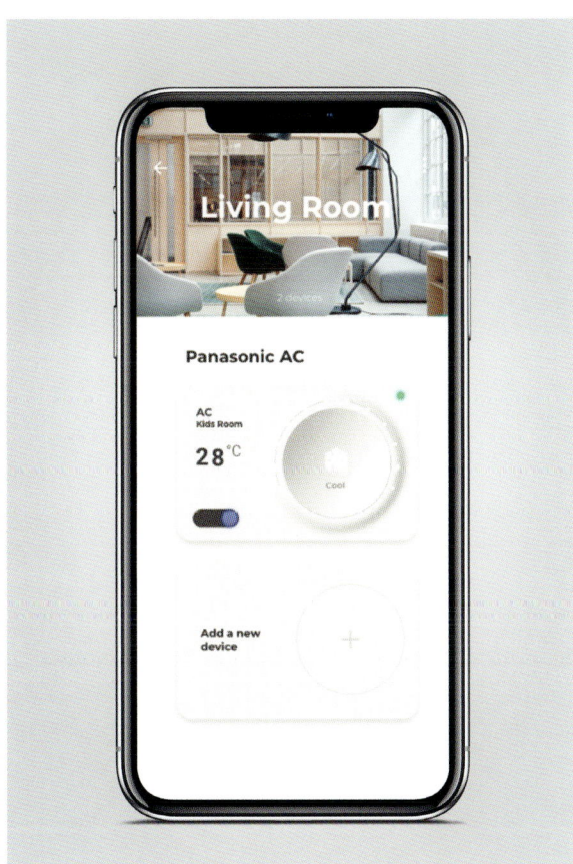

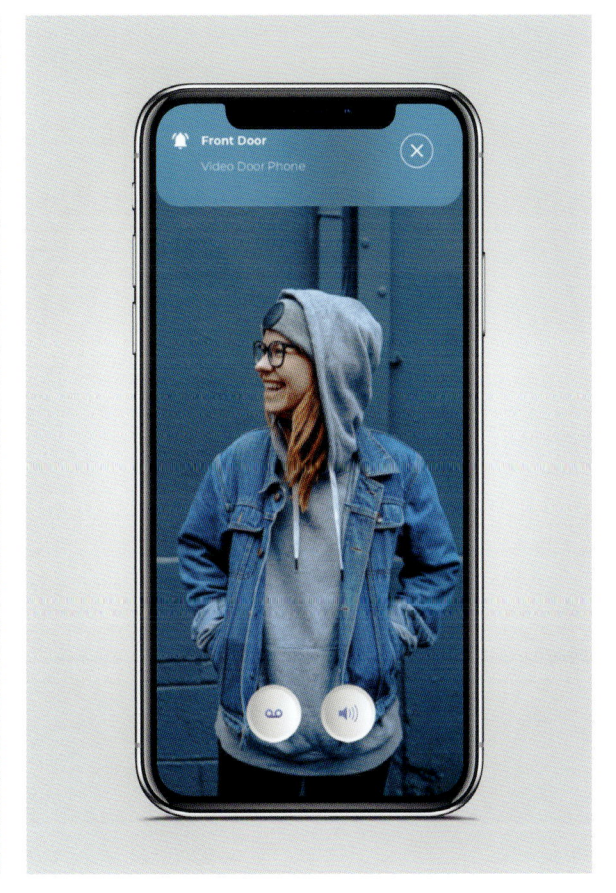

Publishing & Print Media	Posters	Typography	Illustrations	Sound Design	Film & Animation	Online
4	64	92	116	126	138	172

Busch-free@home® Next

[Smart Home Solution]

The completely redesigned "Busch-free@home Next" smart home solution enables easy and convenient control of the smart Busch-free@home control system. The basic principle of the design is focused on the more user-oriented, simplified and accelerated operation of individual devices or the entire system. Clearly arranged, the various functions can be used individually or combined with other application scenarios. Users determine the type and number of functions they want to control intelligently.

Client
Busch-Jaeger Elektro GmbH,
Mitglied der ABB-Gruppe
Lüdenscheid, Germany

Design
Busch-Jaeger Elektro GmbH,
Mitglied der ABB-Gruppe
Lüdenscheid, Germany

Project Team
Busch-Jaeger Elektro:
Till Martensmeier (Designer)

ABB:
Abdul Wahid (Designer)
Christian Aminoff (Designer)

HID Human Interface Design:
Prof. Frank Jacob (Designer)
Moritz Albert (Designer)
Johanna Döring (Designer)

→ Clip online

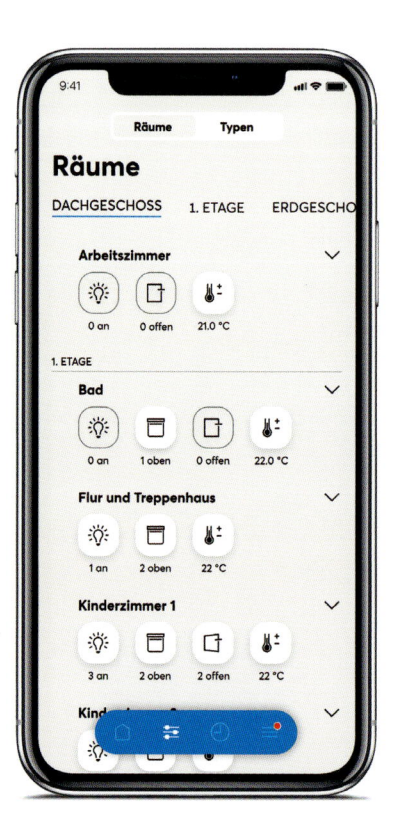

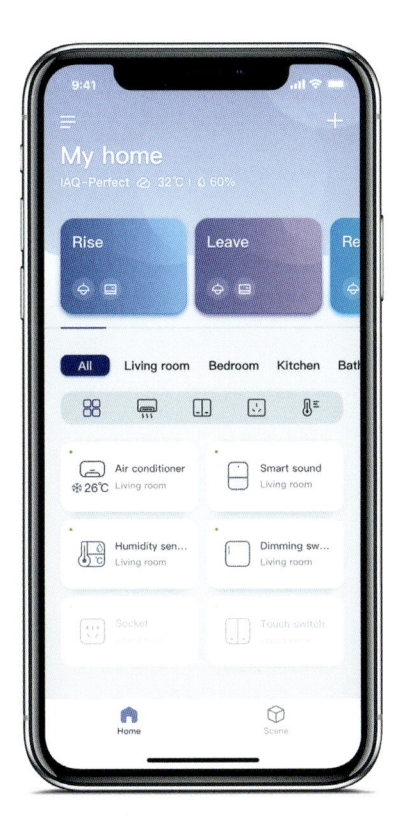

Apps	Interface & User Experience Design	Spatial Communication	Red Dot: Junior Award	Designer Profiles	Jury Portraits	Index
206	236	336	426	564	642	668

Simon Smart

[Smart Home Solution]

Simon Smart is an intuitive and user-friendly smart home application that has been developed to facilitate relaxed and enjoyable home automation experiences. The design consistency between its digital interfaces and the traditional physical way of operation aims to significantly shorten the users' learning curve. Preconfigured and also customisable scenes based on the daily routine of users are presented in animated illustrations. A simple layout and well-thought-out interactive components further boost a sense of intimacy and joyfulness.

Client
Simon Electric (China) Co., Ltd.
Shanghai, China

Design
Simon Electric (China) Co., Ltd.
Shanghai, China

→ Clip online

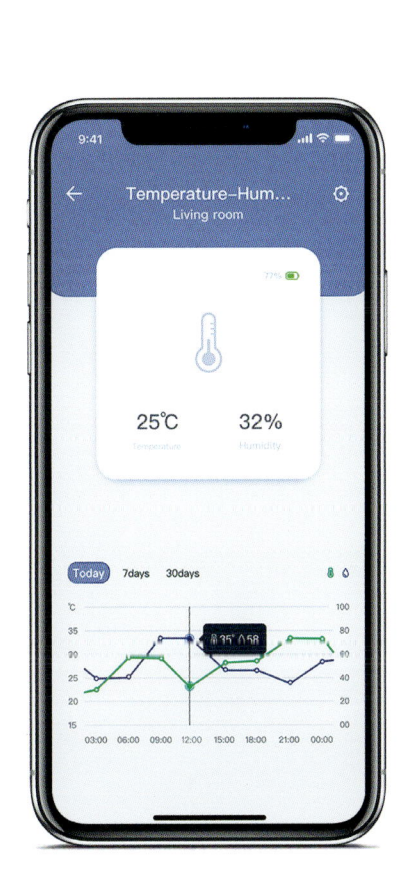

Casarte IOT Refrigerator

[User Interface Design]

The Casarte large-screen IOT refrigerator acts as an intelligent housekeeper to provide active services. Focusing on the care of users' eating health and health data visualisation, it creates a new experience of intelligent life. Based on the user's exercise, body index and eating habits, it can create a reasonable meal plan that is connected to a body fat scale. In addition, the fridge features a food material management clip and other surrounding intelligent hardware to better provide users with a diet service based on health science.

Client
Haier Group
Qingdao, China

Design
Haier Innovation Design Center
Qingdao, China
Qingdao Hairigaoke Model Co. Ltd.
Qingdao, China

Project Team
Haier Innovation Design Center:
Wen Yanbo
Yan Wen
Hang Cong
Ma Lulu
Wang Qiaoqiao

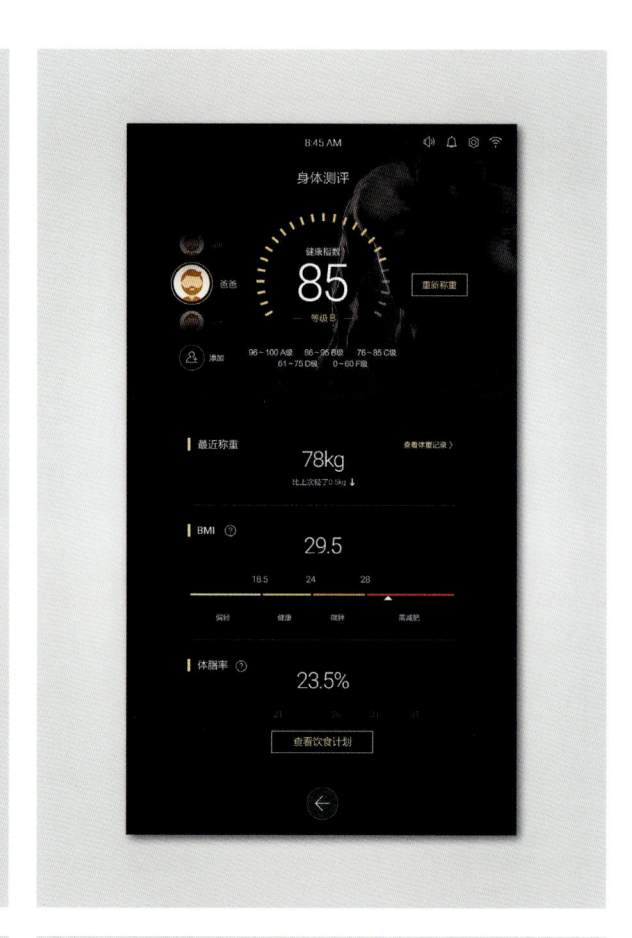

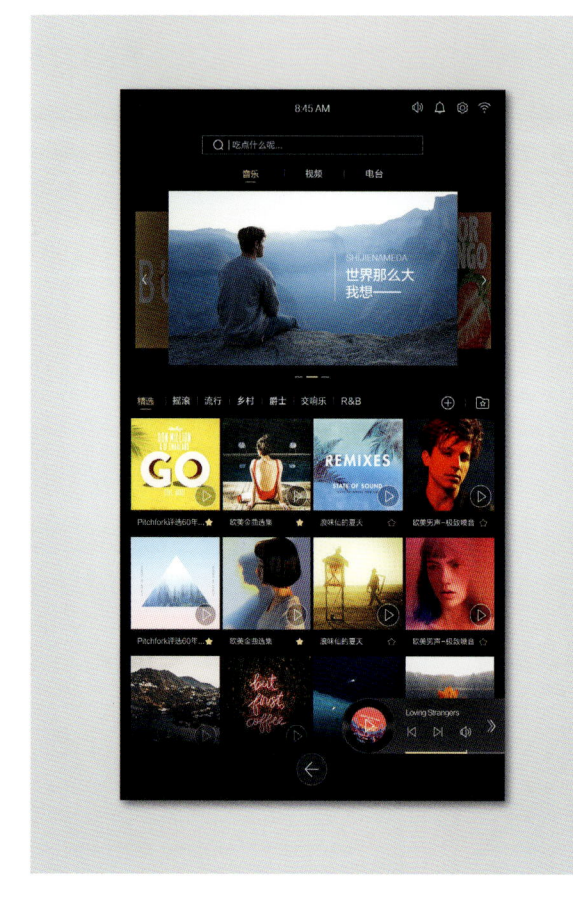

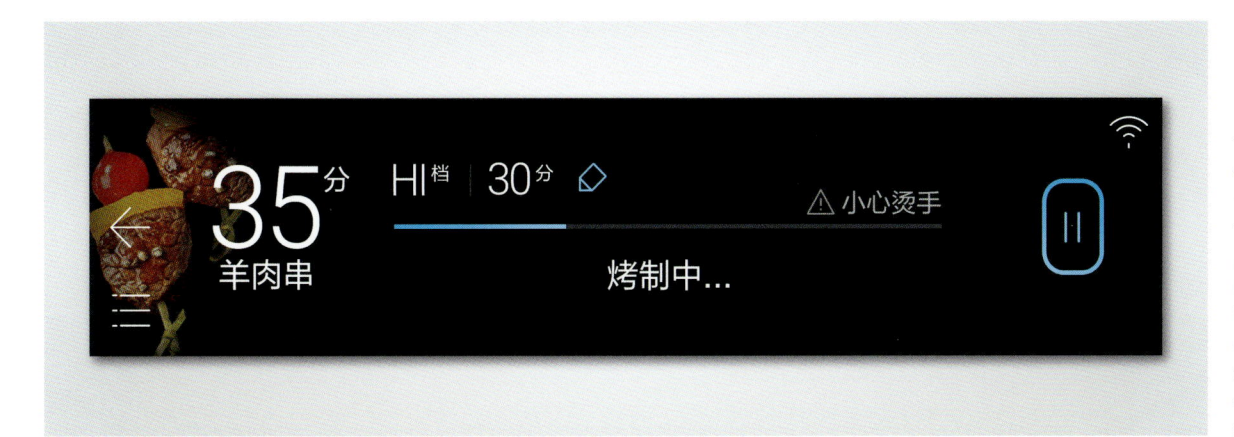

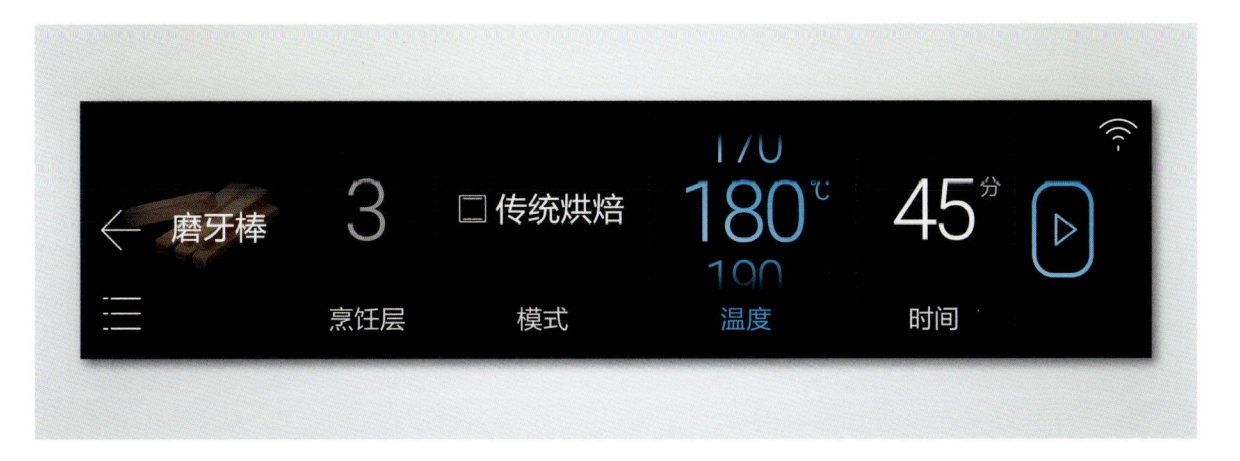

Haier Kitchen Set

[User Interface Design]

The user experience design for the Cascarte kitchen appliances system was redesigned with the objective of a holistic experience in mind. The product appearance follows an easy-to-understand logic in terms of functionality. It also integrates the button design in a natural manner. Through highlighting the operating elements with different levels of contrast, the display design conveys a sense of profoundness and spaciousness. The individual images, the text and the combination of design elements all aim to convey the premium quality of the system.

Client
Haier Group
Qingdao, China

Design
Haier Innovation Design Center
Qingdao, China
Qingdao Hairigaoke Model Co. Ltd.
Qingdao, China

Project Team
Chen Meng
Zhao Siyuan
Sun Yan
Wen Yanbo
Han Cong

Casarte Pulsator Washing Machine

[User Interface Design]

The interface of the Casarte Pulsator washing machine communicates the key message of "wisdom washing". The design, which features a linear element, achieves a dynamic effect. The intelligently configured display indicates the current washing status and provides users with all information in a clear manner. The visualisation of the different washing programs, with its memorable stereo effect, offers an intensive experience, giving users a familiar feeling and facilitating the learning process.

Client
Haier Group
Qingdao, China

Design
Haier Innovation Design Center
Qingdao, China
Qingdao Hairigaoke Model Co. Ltd.
Qingdao, China

Project Team
Sun Luning
Han Cong
Zhang Jiahui
Zhang Wenqi
Zeng Guohao
Wang Qiaoqiao
Wu Xiaolong

Hyperreality Screen

[Screen Design]

This user interface for wall-mounted water dispensers allows users to individually select the water temperature with a patented technology. The design with separately arranged touchscreen buttons on a hyperreality screen offers intuitive operation. The respective water temperature is displayed in numbers and also appealingly associated with the possible preparation method for the respective water temperature. Energy-saving LEDs enable cost-effective use.

Client
Wuhu Midea Kitchen & Bath Appliances Manufacturing
Foshan, China

Design
Wuhu Midea Kitchen & Bath Appliances Manufacturing
Foshan, China

Project Team
Li Jianping
Zhang Jian
Gao Jianjian

MIMOT Robotic Vacuum Cleaner

[User Experience Design, Smart Home Solution]

Client
Guangdong Midea Kitchen Appliances
Manufacturing Co., Ltd.
Foshan, China

Design
Guangdong Midea Kitchen Appliances
Manufacturing Co., Ltd.
Foshan, China

Project Team
Kang Junmuck (Chief Designer)
Kim Woon Hyoung (Designer)
Kim So Young (Designer)
Luo Junyang (Design Strategic Planning)

Apps	Interface & User Experience Design	Spatial Communication	Red Dot: Junior Award	Designer Profiles	Jury Portraits	Index
206	236	336	426	564	642	668

The UX design for the MIMOT robotic vacuum cleaner was developed with the objective of creating an alive-feeling robot product. The concept combines a convenient remote controller, an intuitive mobile app and emotional light effects in order to provide useful functions and a close robot experience in all daily life scenarios. The UI light design is restrained and underlines the functions of the vacuum cleaner, while the AUI design in combination with the light effects emphasises the clear and joyful sound experience.

Publishing & Print Media	Posters	Typography	Illustrations	Sound Design	Film & Animation	Online
4	64	92	116	126	138	172

PRISM Live Studio

[User Interface Design]

Client
NAVER Corp.
Seongnam, South Korea

Design
NAVER Corp.
Seongnam, South Korea

Project Team
Sung Yul Yang (Creative Direction)
Jiyoung Park (UI Design)
Youngok Choi (UI Design)
Yukyung Chun (UI Design)
Sun Lee (UI Design)
Ara Lee (Graphic/Motion Design)
Gyuwon Kim (Graphic/Motion Design)
Juhyeon Jang (Graphic/Motion Design)
Junseok Jang (Graphic/Motion Design)
Minhyung Chun (Graphic/Motion Design)

→ Clip online

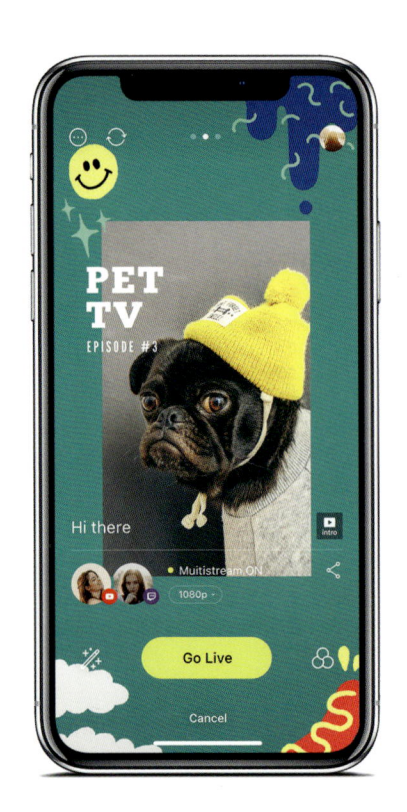

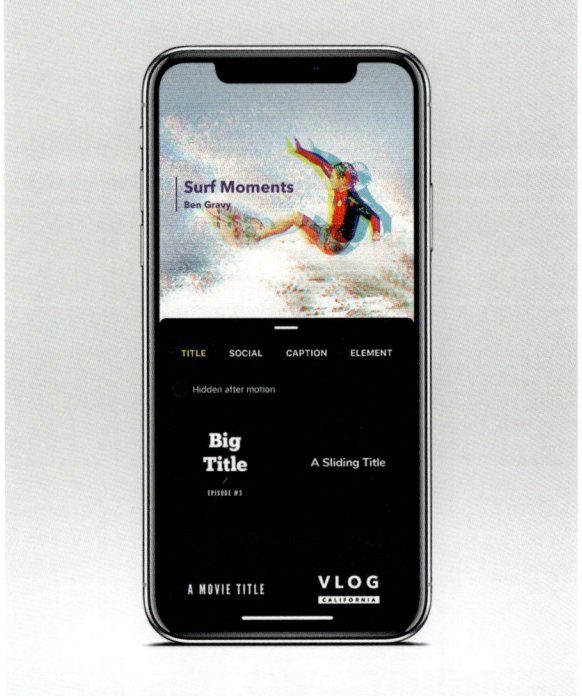

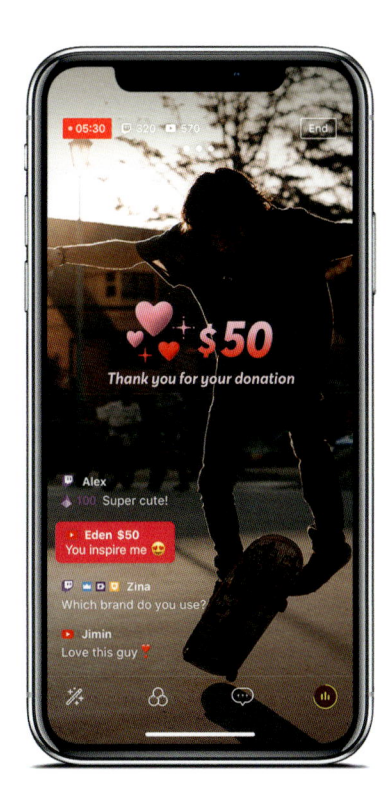

Apps	Interface & User Experience Design	Spatial Communication	Red Dot: Junior Award	Designer Profiles	Jury Portraits	Index
206	236	336	426	564	642	668

PRISM Live Studio is a one-stop live streaming application that enables anyone to create content on a professional level. Its UX design is centred on the concept of offering a high-quality live streaming experience so that broadcasting is made enjoyable and accessible. Creating engaging content is easy thanks to multiple features, such as AR interactive filters. The distinctive "broadcasting interface design" allows content creators to effortlessly manage their live stream feed and interact with their viewers.

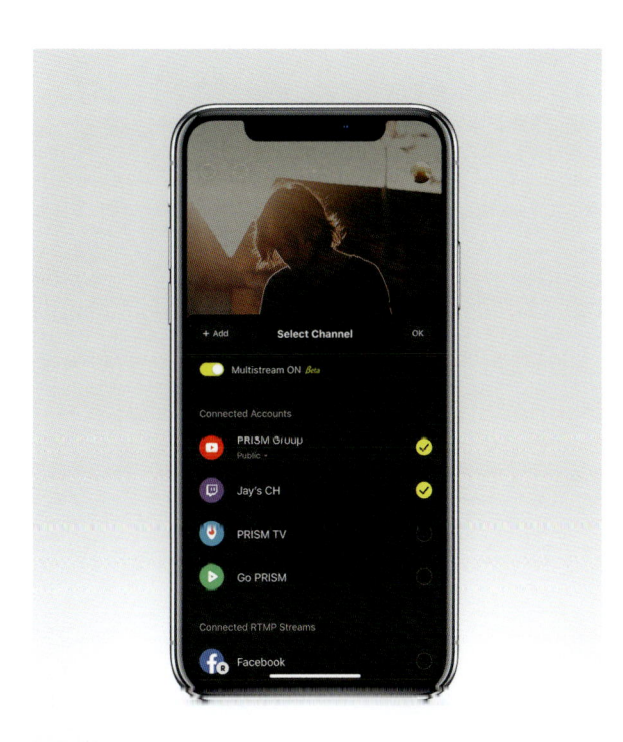

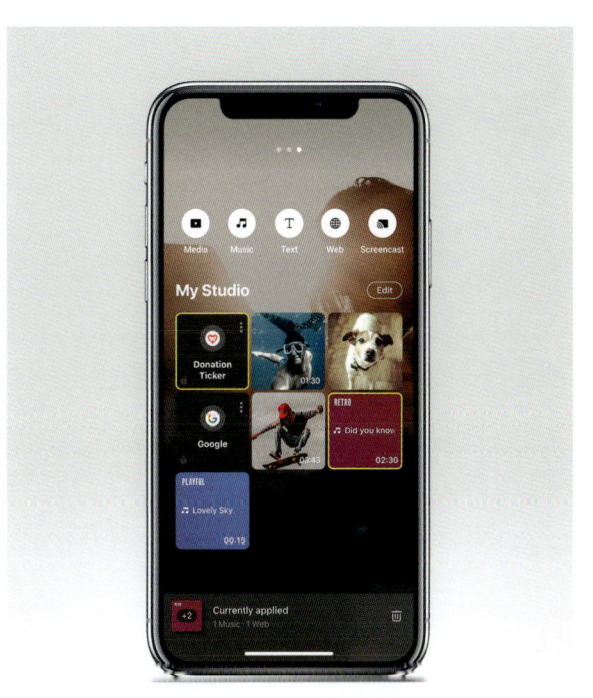

Publishing & Print Media	Posters	Typography	Illustrations	Sound Design	Film & Animation	Online
4	64	92	116	126	138	172

Huawei Vision X65
[User Interface Design]

The Huawei Vision X65 smart TV software system offers an intelligent and seamless television experience. Users do not have to look for the remote control but can use their phone to operate the unit instead. Through a consistent experience across all devices, they are given the feeling of intuitively interacting with the TV, as if they held it in the palm of their hand. The user interface allows for control using air gestures and for mirroring on one's phone, thus enabling users to navigate across the TV. In addition, they can also relive their memories from galleries on a range of other devices.

Client
Huawei Device (Shenzhen) Co., Ltd.
Shenzhen, China

Design
Huawei Device (Shenzhen) Co., Ltd.
Shenzhen, China

Project Team
Ding Yi
Ge Peng
Zhang Ting
Xie Cheng
Wang Zongwei
Hu Yue
Yu Yang
Xie Shu
Zhuang Qing
Tang Chang
Yang Bin

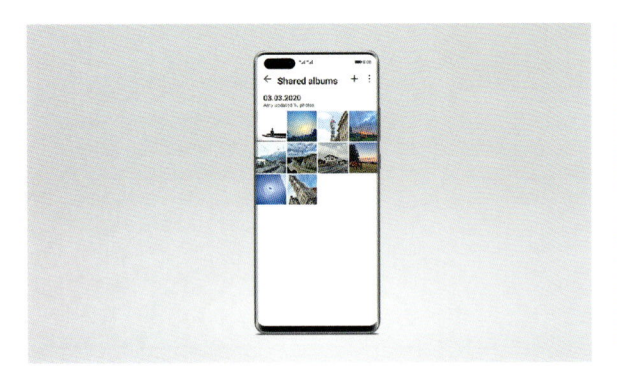

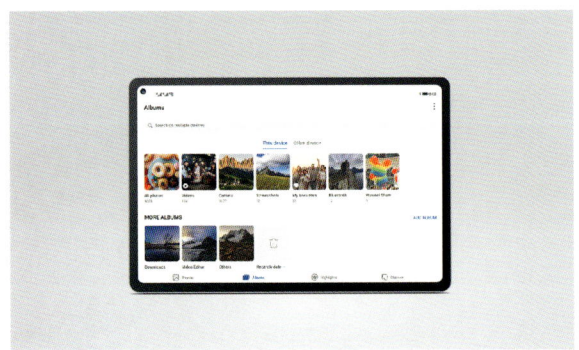

Huawei AI Fitness

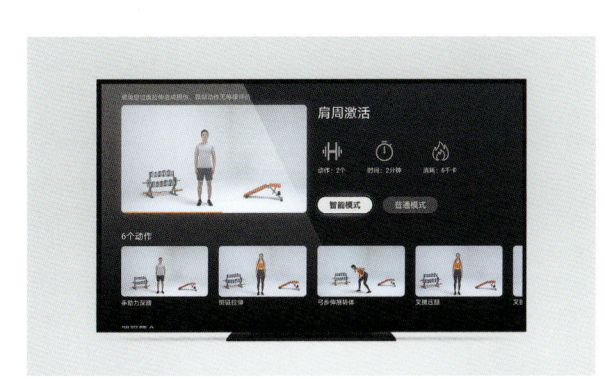

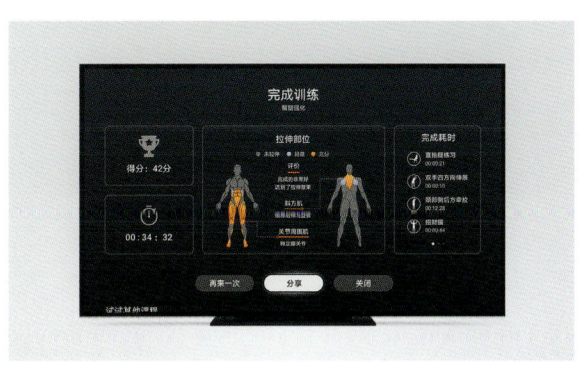

[Fitness Solution]

Huawei AI Fitness is a health solution that combines cameras with large screens to address growing health needs. The user experience design integrates elements such as bone node recognition technology for precise verification of standing or lying down positions, slow speed, different clothing, the lighting environment of a variety of scenes, and real-time contrast between the user's and the coach's actions. When the user's actions are not up to standard, an intelligent voice coach conveys the feeling of "private" instructions, prompting them to improve on the movement.

Client
Huawei Technologies Co., Ltd.
Shenzhen, China

Design
Huawei Technologies Co., Ltd.
Shenzhen, China

Project Team
Jiabing Yan (Strategic Planning)
Xiaohan Chen (Strategic Planning)
Hang Liu (Strategic Planning)
Xindi Yu (Designer)
Lei Li (Marketing Manager)
Yonghang Jiang (Technical Direction)
Huiyue Lin (Technical Direction)
Lei Huang (Technical Direction)
Jie Zhao (Technical Direction)
Chunhui Ma (Technical Direction)
Xiaomeng Liu (Technical Direction)

My JBL Headphones App – Club Series Experience

[Mobile User Interface Design]

The My JBL Headphones app provides users with the experience of their own hearing preference enhanced by JBL headphones using Personi-Fi technology. The interface was developed in collaboration with four well-known DJs by measuring their hearing preference and then transferring the synthesised setting to those users with the app via the CLUB series. This allows users to become immersed in a DJ's personal hearing preferences and to create their own. In addition, they can choose their favourite voice assistant and select a Smart Ambient mode for a specific environment.

Client
Harman International Industries, Inc.
Shenzhen, China

Design
Huemen
Shenzhen, China

Project Team
Dishan Song
Shufen Guo
Alexander Efimov

→ Designer profile on page 596
→ Clip online

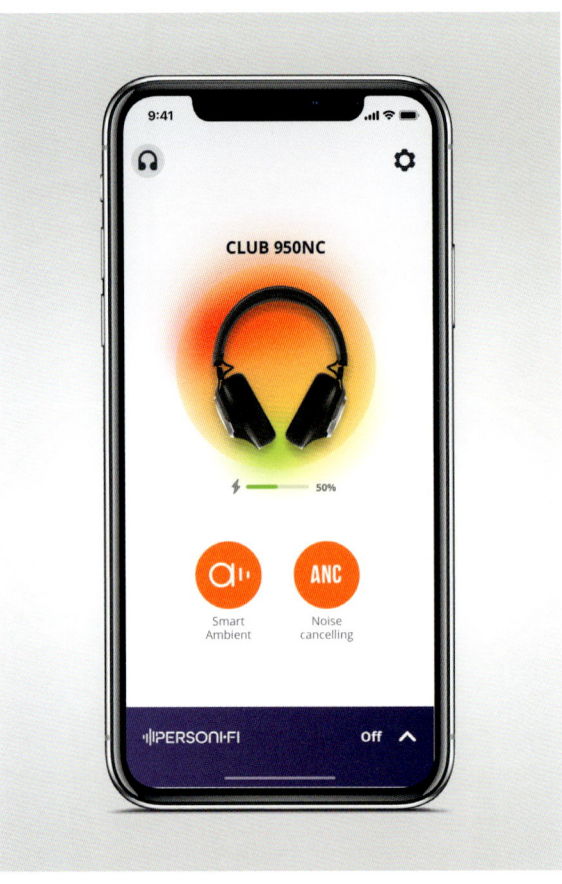

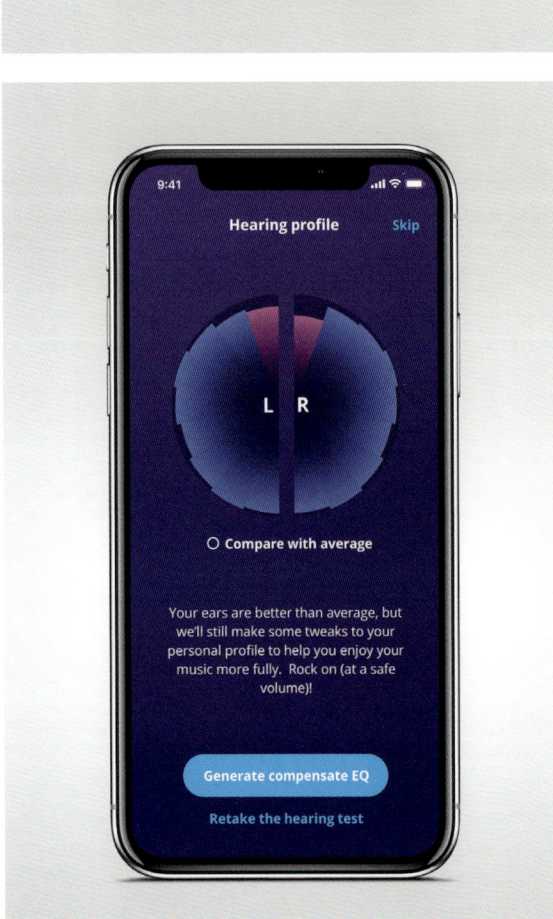

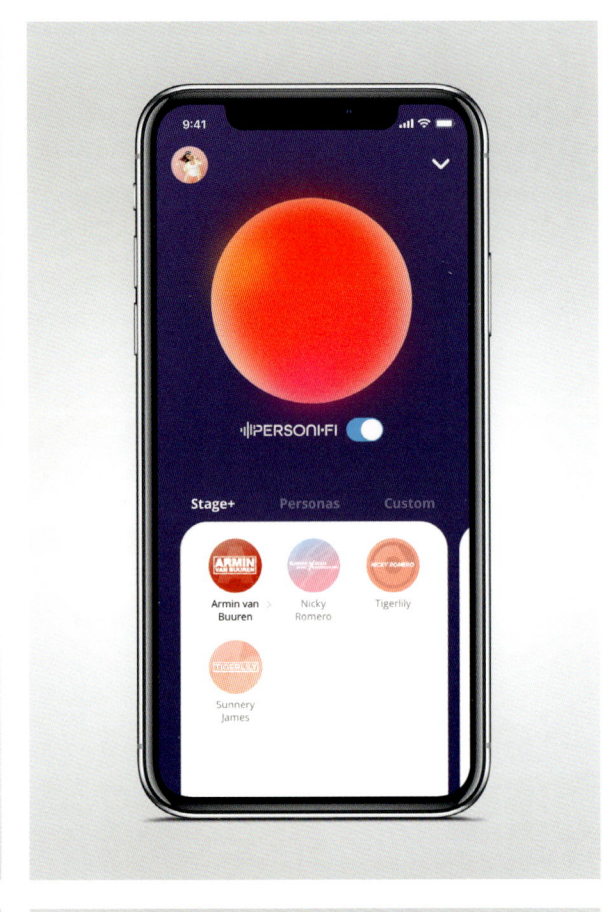

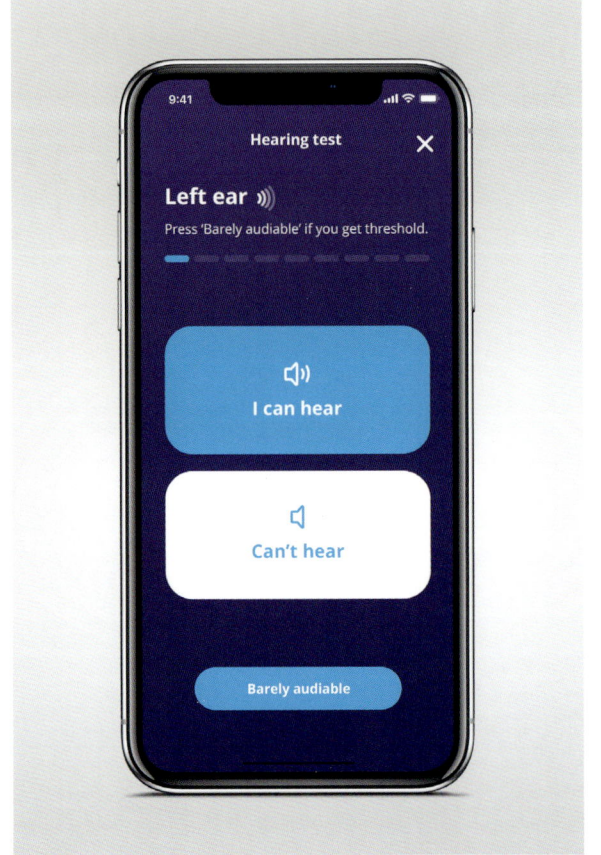

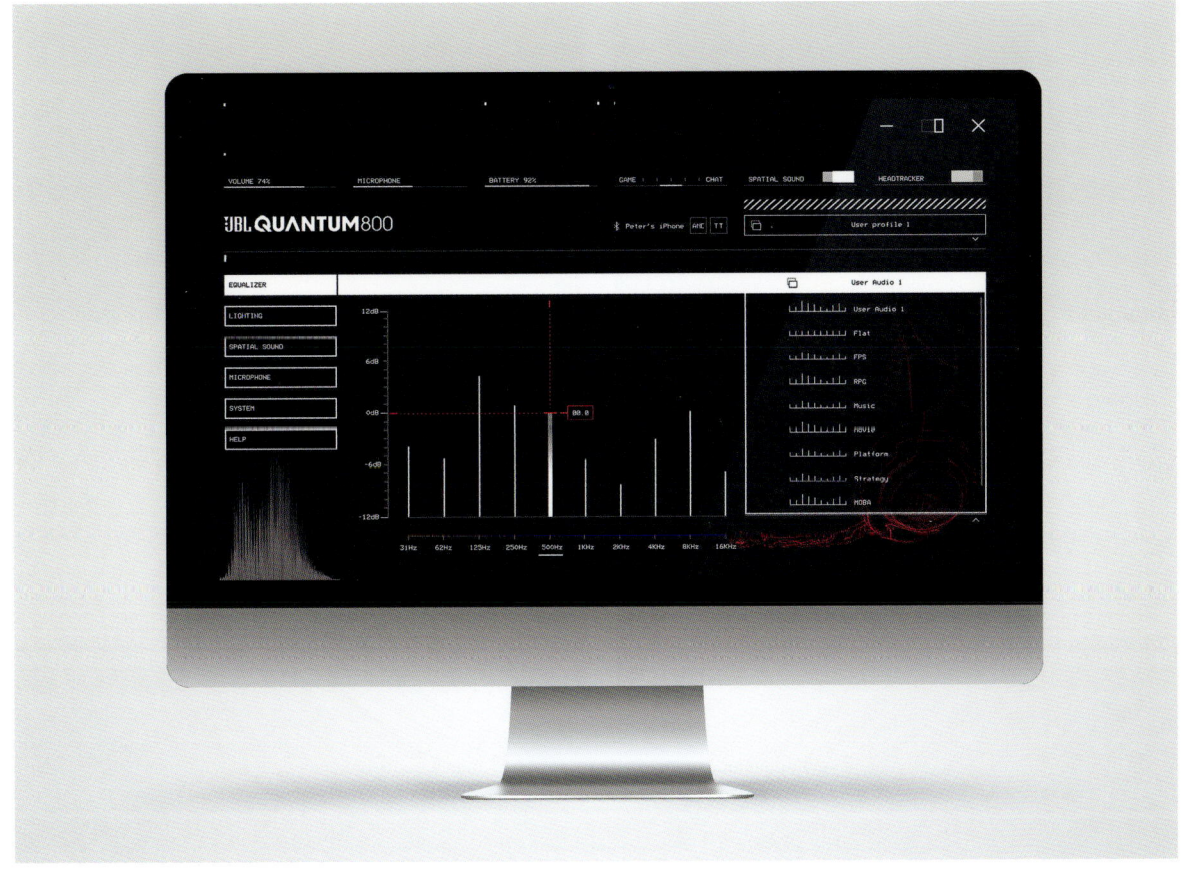

JBL QuantumENGINE

[User Interface Design]

JBL QuantumENGINE is a PC-based app for a new series of JBL Quantum headphones. Designed for gamers, it combines audio controls, multichannel surround sound, multi-zone RGB illumination, 3D audio virtualisation and 3D head-tracking, thus delivering a perfect gaming audio solution. The app also allows users to personalise the JBL Quantum Headphones with 16 million colours, speed, light effects and custom colour shifts. Featuring a "Quantum speculative scenario", the user interface is projecting a dystopian world where advanced technology exists but is available only to a specific set of the population.

Client
Harman International Industries, Inc.
Shenzhen, China

Design
Huemen
Shenzhen, China

Project Team
Cristian Lorca
Dishan Song
Yunji Song
Rongjian Huang

→ Designer profile on page 596
→ Clip online

JBL Partybox 1000

[User Interface Design]

The JBL Partybox 1000 is a powerful party speaker that combines the sound quality of JBL with a dynamic full-panel light show, which is simply activated when users plug in their microphone or guitar. Users can also stream their playlists via Bluetooth or from a USB flash drive. A DJ pad on the top surface allows users to play drums, guitar or piano, as well as to record and to loop on the fly. The product offers an experienced shift from player/listener to a music co-creator, from a mere speaker to a musical instrument.

Client
Harman International Industries, Inc.
Shenzhen, China

Design
Huemen
Shenzhen, China

Project Team
Rongjian Huang
Alexander Efimov

→ Designer profile on page 596
→ Clip online

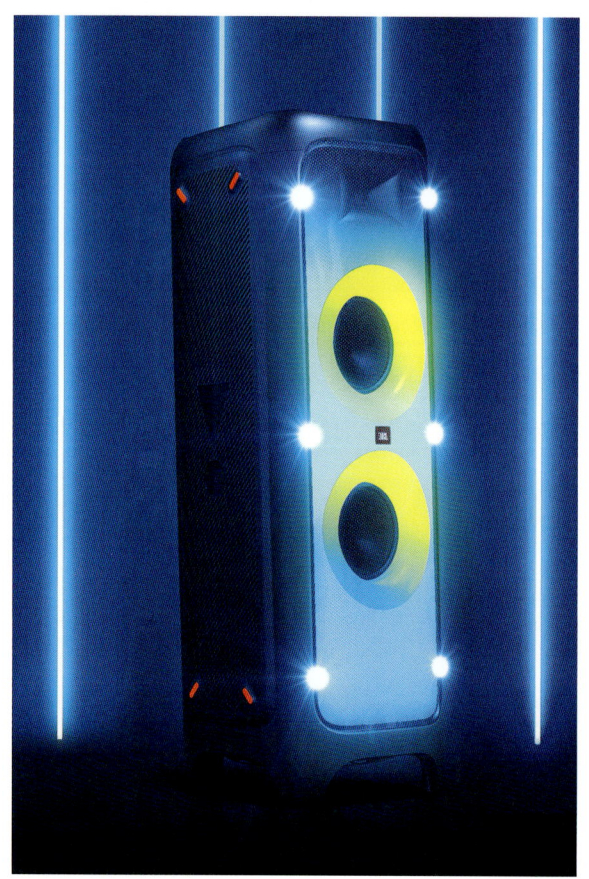

JBL Pulse 4

[User Interface Design]

JBL Pulse 4 is a portable Bluetooth speaker that offers a new experience of one's favourite songs in a unique party ambience. It was designed with the goal of appealing to all of the senses. The speaker features a total of 130 LEDs, which allow for a 360-degree light show. Its wide and complexly designed LED array is meticulously fine-tuned to deliver a stunning light experience. Thanks to the JBL Connect app, individual visualisations can be generated and thematic light shows triggered from anywhere.

Client
Harman International Industries, Inc.
Shenzhen, China

Design
Huemen
Shenzhen, China

Project Team
Rongjian Huang
Dishan Song
Alexander Efimov

→ Designer profile on page 596
→ Clip online

Publishing & Print Media	Posters	Typography	Illustrations	Sound Design	Film & Animation	Online
4	64	92	116	126	138	172

Theater Bonn

[Website Relaunch, Screen Design]

This web application for the Theater Bonn multidisciplinary theatre takes into account the expectations of various target groups. The navigation was reduced to the essentials and bundled to establish a clear structure in order to make finding relevant content quick and intuitive. An overview of the current programme is displayed on the start page, which was implemented using Vue.js and reacts extremely quickly. In addition, the respective detailed views of the events are also located on the start page, along with editorial contributions, including all of the content related to the production.

Client
Theater Bonn
Bonn, Germany

Design
MIR MEDIA – Digital Agentur
Cologne, Germany

Project Team
Matias Ampiainen (Designer)
Sanjay Vohra (Front-End Designer)
Daniel Hihn (Back-End Designer)
Damian Oscik (Back-End Designer)
Thomas C. Böhm (Project Manager)

→ Designer profile on page 608

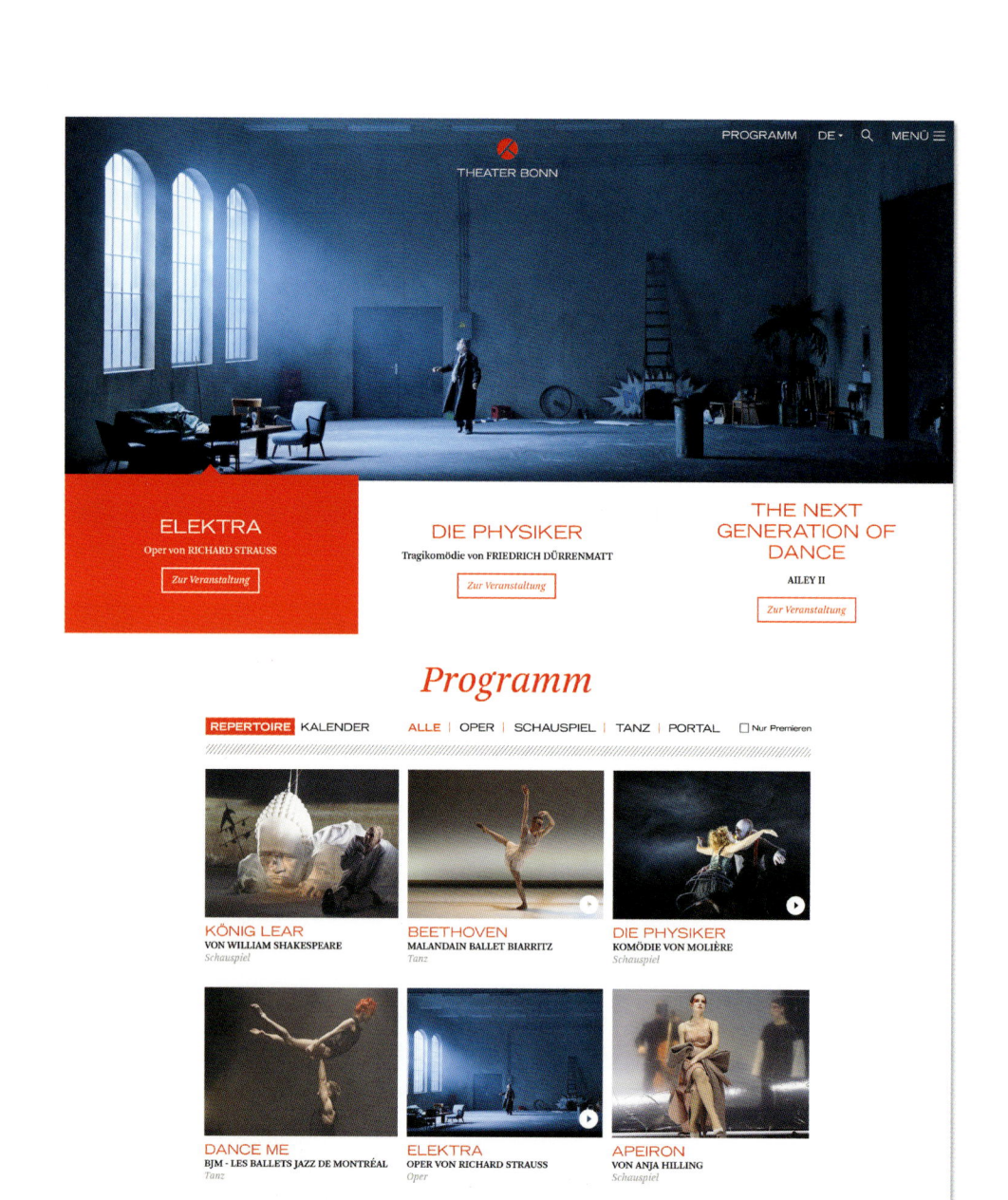

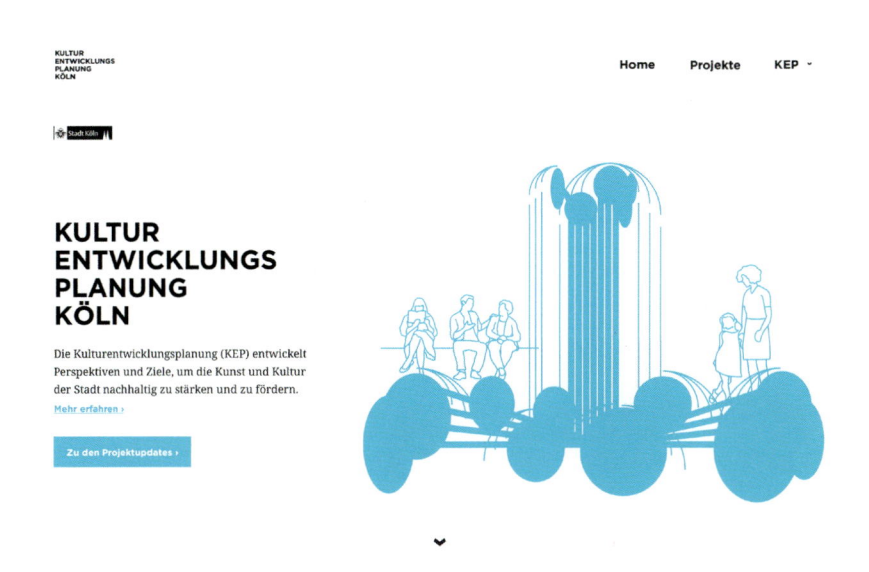

Cultural Development Plan Cologne – kep.koeln

[Website, Screen Design]

The task of the "Cultural Development Plan Cologne – kep.koeln" app is to provide a digital and analogue visualisation of information and data as part of the Cologne Cultural Development Plan (KEP). The preparation of the information was meant to reflect the participatory development of this catalogue of measures, supported by all stakeholders in politics and administration. The implementation by means of consistently user-centred information architecture and a minimalist design implies the highest possible clarity and facilitates the quick and intuitive retrieval of information.

Client
Kulturdezernat der Stadt Köln
Cologne, Germany

Design
MIR MEDIA – Digital Agentur
Cologne, Germany

Project Team
Pawel Jaczewski (Designer)
Matias Ampiainen (Designer)
Steve Schreiner (Designer)
Yannick Schütze (Designer)
Wardy Mango (Front-End Designer)
Mariusz Kosakowski (Back-End Designer)
Thomas C. Böhm (Project Manager)

→ Designer profile on page 608

HBK Essen University of Fine Arts

[Website Relaunch, Screen Design]

Primarily aimed at attracting new students, the redesigned appearance of the University of Fine Arts HBK Essen, Germany, focuses on a low-threshold presentation of content and information. At its centre is the target-group-oriented presentation of moving images, graphics and photographs. An intro film addresses visitors at an emotional level to convey anticipation for the broad curriculum. The different courses are represented with their own visual languages. Information about the degree programmes, the course of study and other details is presented from the perspective of the applicants.

Client
HBK Essen
Essen, Germany

Design
MIR MEDIA – Digital Agentur
Cologne, Germany

Project Team
Katharina Engel (Designer)
Ansgar Hiller (Front-End Designer)
Wardy Mango (Front-End Designer)
Andrzej Sikora (Back-End Designer)
Thomas C. Böhm (Project Manager)

→ Designer profile on page 608

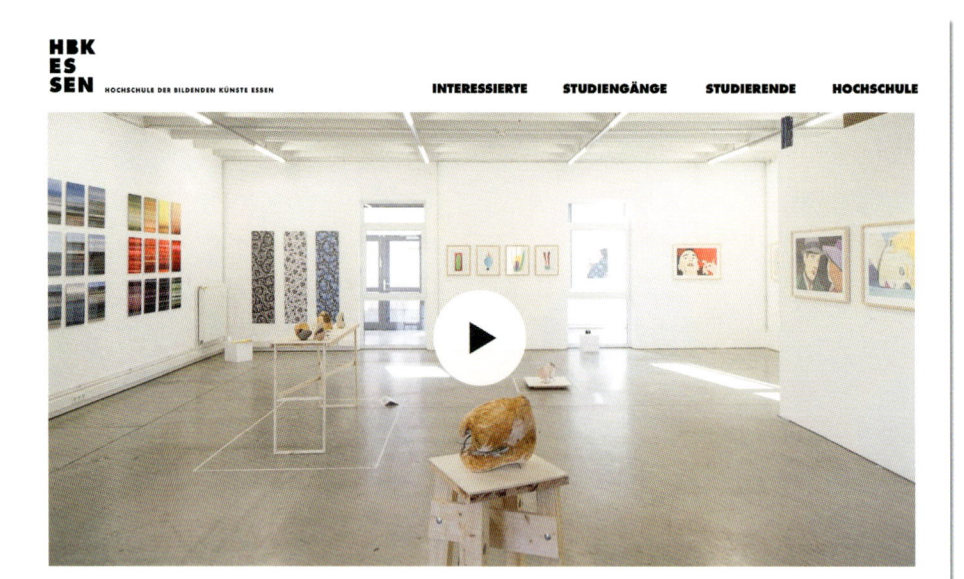

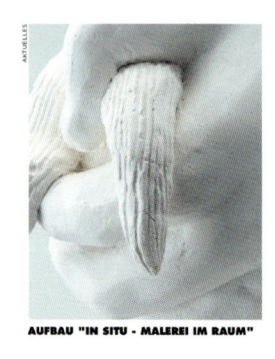

NAVER DATA CENTER GAK

[Brand Website, User Interface Design]

The focus in redesigning the brand website of NAVER DATA CENTER GAK was to communicate the genuine significance and value of the data generated by the data centre. Designed around the key concept "The Visionary Archive", the data is visualised in direct relation to everyday life. The entire concept is based on the principle of constant further development, interaction with the web and the visualisation of changes, for example through the piling up of content when a vast amount of data is accumulated.

Client
NAVER DATA CENTER GAK
Seongnam, South Korea

Design
newtype imageworks
Seoul, South Korea

Project Team
Jinwook Kim (Creative Direction)
Taesoo Im (Art Direction)
Hyungwoo Choi (Web Design)
Jisoo Kim (Web Design)
Yesol Choi (Web Design)
Ahyung Lee (Strategic Planning)

Publishing & Print Media	Posters	Typography	Illustrations	Sound Design	Film & Animation	Online
4	64	92	116	126	138	172

ix3 Design System

[User Interface Design]

Client
ix3, an Aker Solutions Company
Fornebu, Norway

Design
ix3, an Aker Solutions Company
Fornebu, Norway

Project Team
Per Øyvind Olssøn
(Head of Software Foundation)
Viktor Frik (Head of UX Design)
Alina Bezchotnikova (Lead Designer)
Jose Viso Vargas (Designer)
Erik Tallang (Programming)

→ Clip online

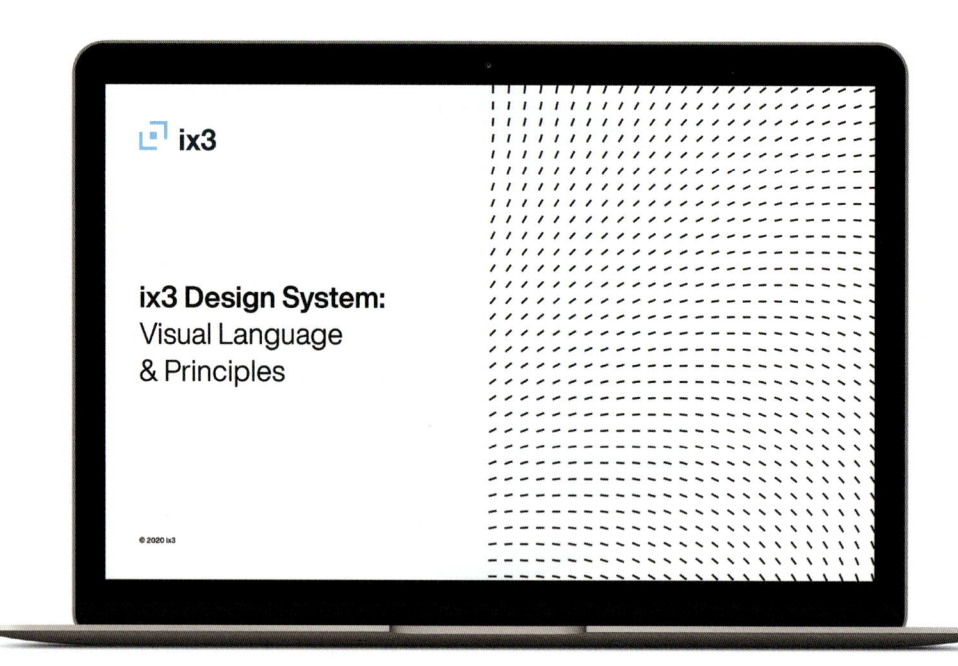

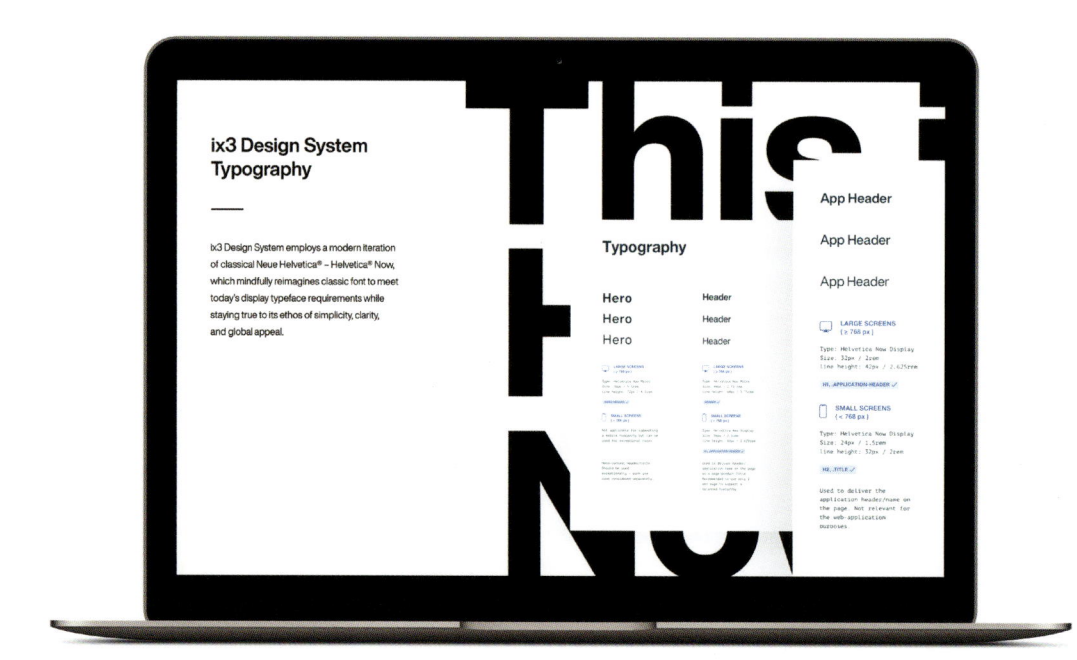

The ix3 Design System is built on the premises of canonical theories and methods. Developed with user-centricity in mind, it establishes an important connection to the brand and its parent organisations. The system makes the design and development of applications more efficient while reducing costs. The well-maintained and continuously expanding ix3 Design System library provides access to common components for all in-house product teams. Its guidelines are written with attention to detail and on the basis of known scenarios and use cases, while its overall design language meets industry standards. The whole system is agile and collaborative in a natural manner and supports over fifteen ix3 products.

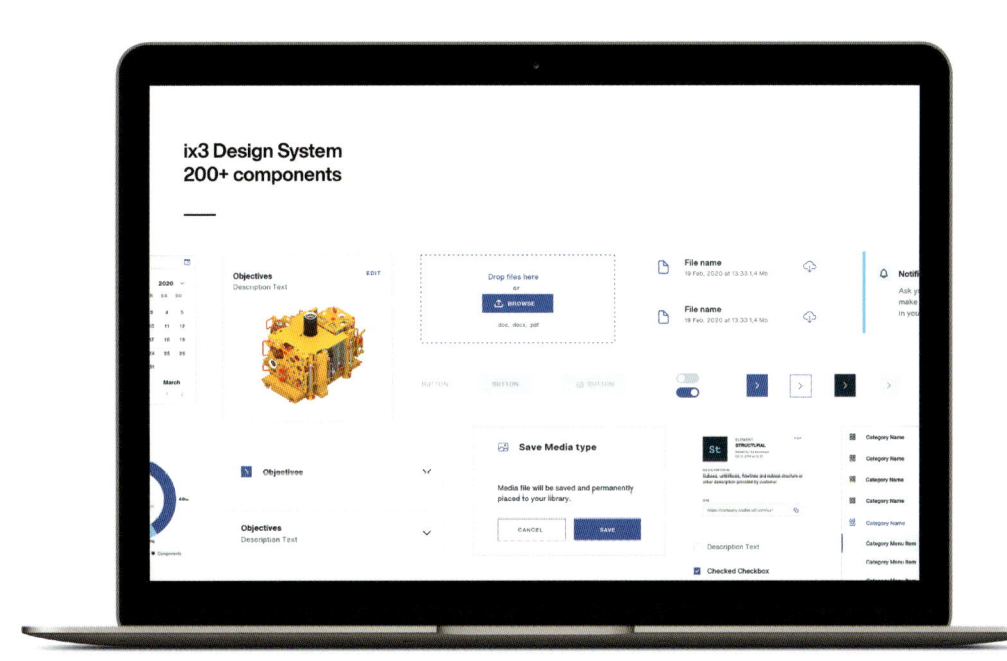

Publishing & Print Media	Posters	Typography	Illustrations	Sound Design	Film & Animation	Online
4	64	92	116	126	138	172

Fontgenic
[Mobile User Experience Design]

Fontgenic is a smartphone app that takes words from objects, such as letters and messages, and combines them with photos to create special memories. It allows users to take writing from pictures or through the camera in real time and use it as an overlay when taking photos. Combining words with associated memories and scenery in a single striking image, it allows more vivid memories to be created. The app was designed with a focus on words as the starting point of the creation process, which begins by extracting the writing before superimposing it onto the image.

Client
FUJIFILM Corporation
Tokyo, Japan

Design
FUJIFILM Corporation Design Center
Tokyo, Japan

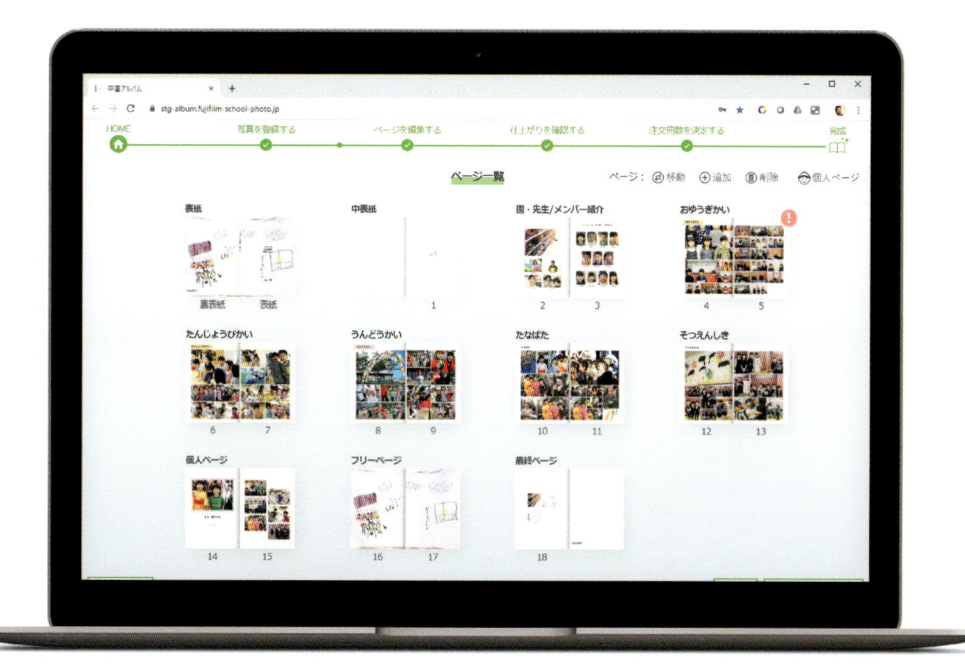

School Photo Graduation Album

[Service Design]

This service was designed for teachers who are responsible for the creation of the photo albums that Japanese nursery schools customarily create to commemorate graduation. As the required pictures have to be selected and then arranged in a layout, considerable time and special care has to be taken to ensure that all of the children are equally represented. The "Participants" function of this app automatically checks for any children who are not present and displays that information on the upper left of the screen to make photo selection both easier and less stressful for teachers.

Client
FUJIFILM Corporation
Tokyo, Japan

Design
FUJIFILM Corporation Design Center
Tokyo, Japan

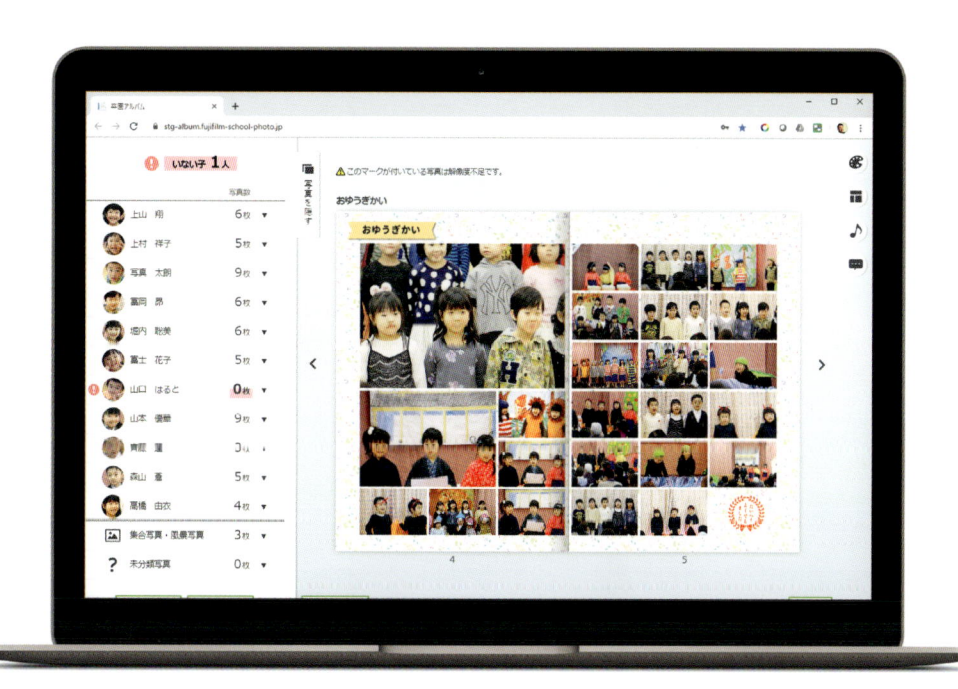

Publishing & Print Media	Posters	Typography	Illustrations	Sound Design	Film & Animation	Online
4	64	92	116	126	138	172

618 Shanghai Street

[Augmented Reality Experience]

618 Shanghai Street is an online interactive AR application that allows users to unveil the history behind a revitalisation project of a series of old buildings in Hong Kong. "Visitors" can thus playfully uncover stories behind the many architectural features remaining on each building. This can be experienced especially in "Bird Street", a landmark in its time that was demolished 30 years ago. It can now be revived by an artistic rendition on users' mobile phones through the use of AR technology. Users are encouraged to share their discoveries among friends on social media.

Client
618 Shanghai Street,
Urban Renewal Authority
Hong Kong

Design
Noiseless Design
Hong Kong

Project Team
Christopher Lee (Creative Director)
Chan Fly (Design)
Morris Lai (Design)
Hung Chung (Design)
Kelvin Ho (3D Modelling)
Isaac Cheung (3D Modelling)
Cherrypicks (Programming)
Vincent Lee (Project Management)
Linus Hui (Project Management)
Wilson Hung (Project Management)
Meiyan Li (Illustration)

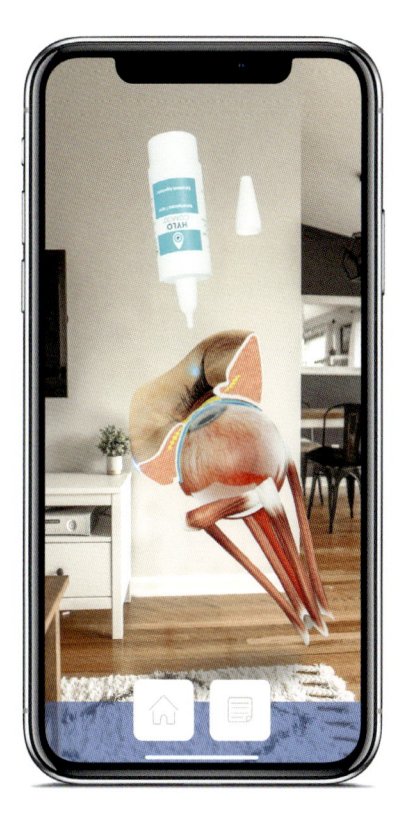

Apps	Interface & User Experience Design	Spatial Communication	Red Dot: Junior Award	Designer Profiles	Jury Portraits	Index
206	236	336	426	564	642	668

The Eye
[Augmented Reality Experience, Health Solution]

Starting this app, an oversized eye appears in the user's space, which can be explored from all angles. In close consultation with the Ursapharm science department, different learning modules were designed for the app. The use of augmented reality opens up new possibilities in exploring complex subjects and making previously unseen processes visible. "The Eye" allows users to dive into the topic of eye health in an intuitive and playful manner.

Client
Ursapharm Arzneimittel GmbH
Saarbrücken, Germany

Design
zeit:raum Gruppe
Saarbrücken, Germany

→ Designer profile on page 640
→ Clip online

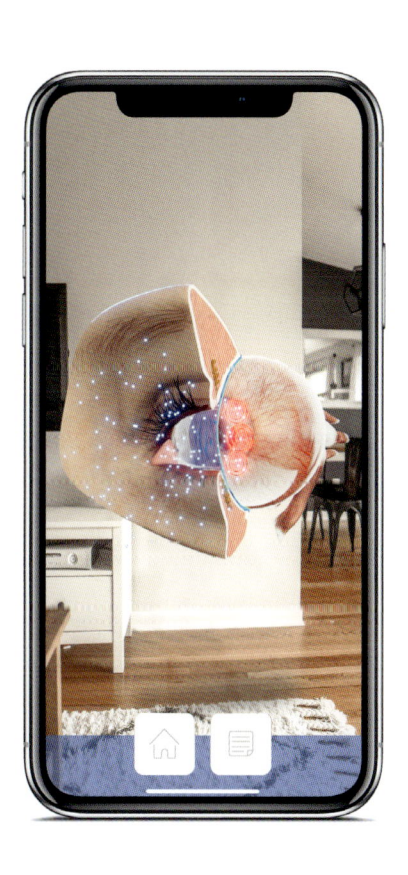

It's your turn, Leonov!

[Website, 3D Computer Graphics]

On 18 March 1965, during the Vostok 2 mission, Alexei Leonov became the first man to exit a spacecraft and walk in space. It was the beginning of a new era of space exploration. Reconstructing the historical moment in a series of 360-degree videos, this website visualises every step that Alexei Leonov took on his way from the spacecraft, through the airlock, to outer space. The video content is complemented by archival recordings, documentary footage and infographics in order to fully recreate the context of the events.

Client
TASS Russian News Agency
Moscow, Russia

Design
TASS Russian News Agency
Moscow, Russia

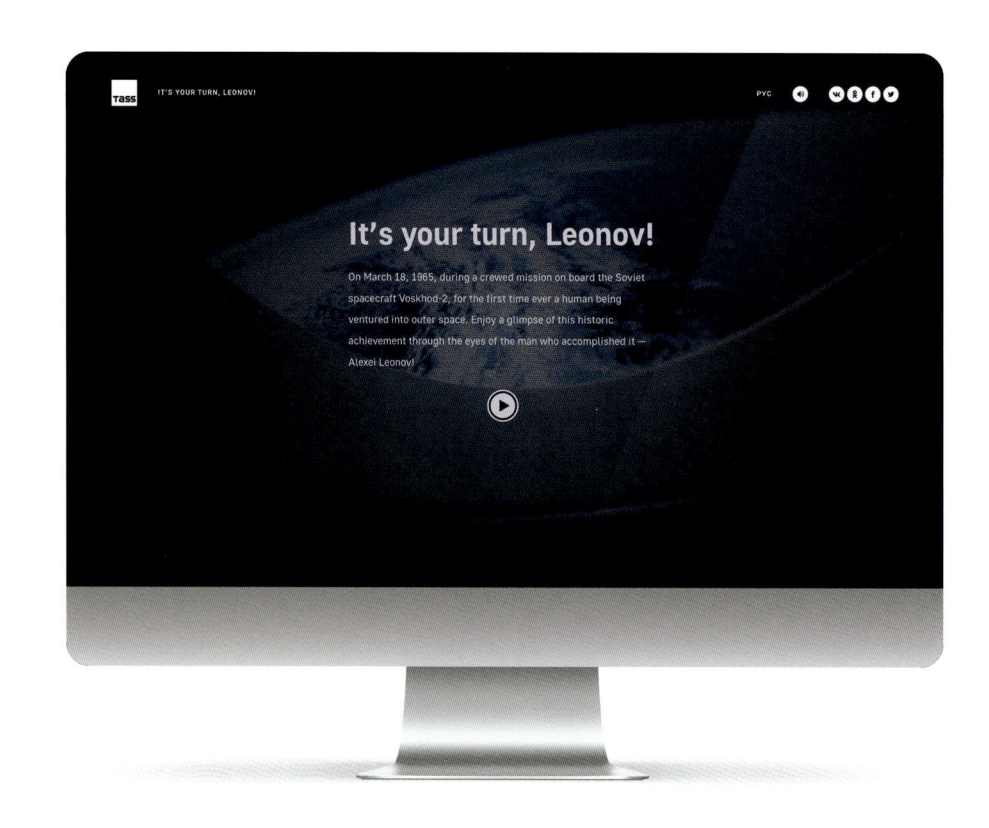

Nemus Futurum

[Interactive Experience Design]

Nemus Futurum is an interactive and comprehensive visitor experience showcasing the Finnish forests. Visitors are guided through sustainable forest management, a sustainable use of forests, forest nature and bioproducts. At the beginning of the tour, visitors are provided with a tablet featuring a bespoke app that helps to contextualise the environment and support the narration of the tour guides. The app uses various methods, such as GPS tracking and augmented reality, to provide a curated digital experience in an awe-inspiring forest setting.

Client
Metsä Group
Espoo, Finland

Design
Great Apes/HiQ Finland
Helsinki, Finland
MKTG Finland
Helsinki, Finland

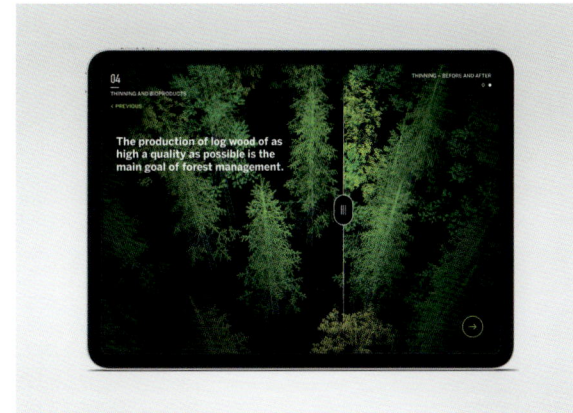

Publishing & Print Media	Posters	Typography	Illustrations	Sound Design	Film & Animation	Online
4	64	92	116	126	138	172

Molecular Futures

[Virtual Reality Experience]

Molecular Futures envisions a virtual future for the specialty chemicals industry. Based on a scenario study by the corporate foresight unit of the company Evonik, the app presents five future scenarios in an everyday setting – a bathroom and a workplace. For each scenario, the interior and products of daily use are designed accordingly. The interactive environments serve as a setting for short stories that portray characters and careers, as well as radio news describing the broader context of the imagined future worlds.

Client
Evonik Industries AG
Creavis
Marl, Germany

Design
Bernhard Hopfengärtner
Berlin, Germany
N O R M A L S
Berlin, Germany

Project Team
Evonik Foresight:
Johannes Mahn (Scenario Content)
Björn Theis (Scenario Content)

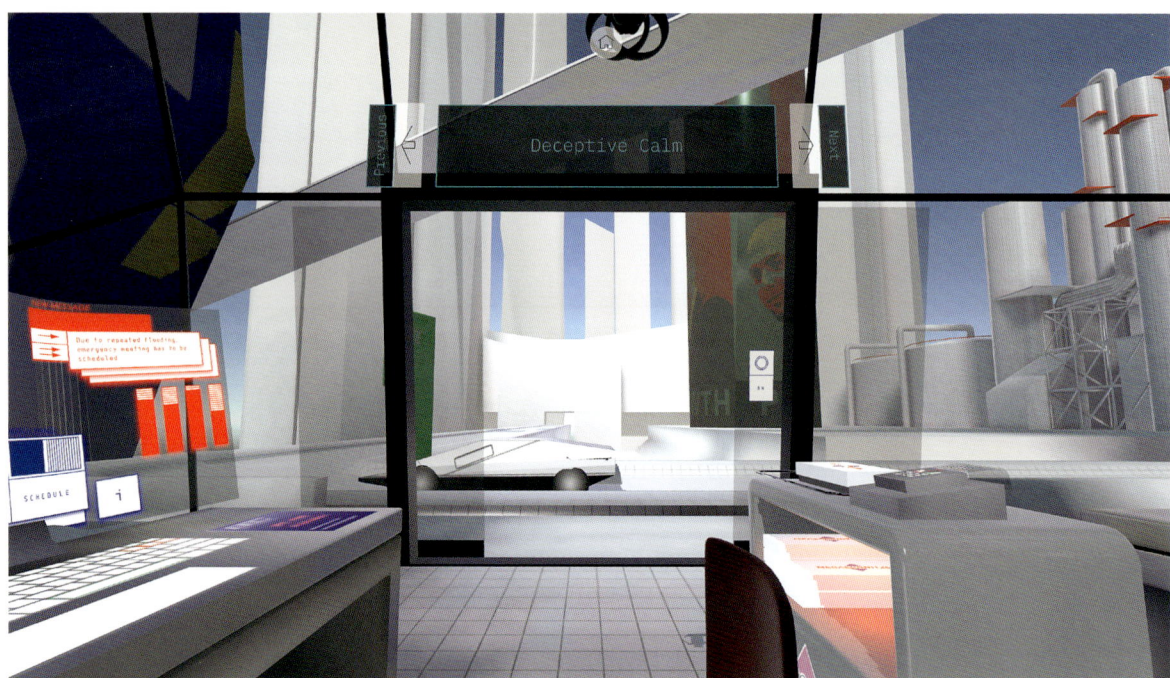

→ Clip online

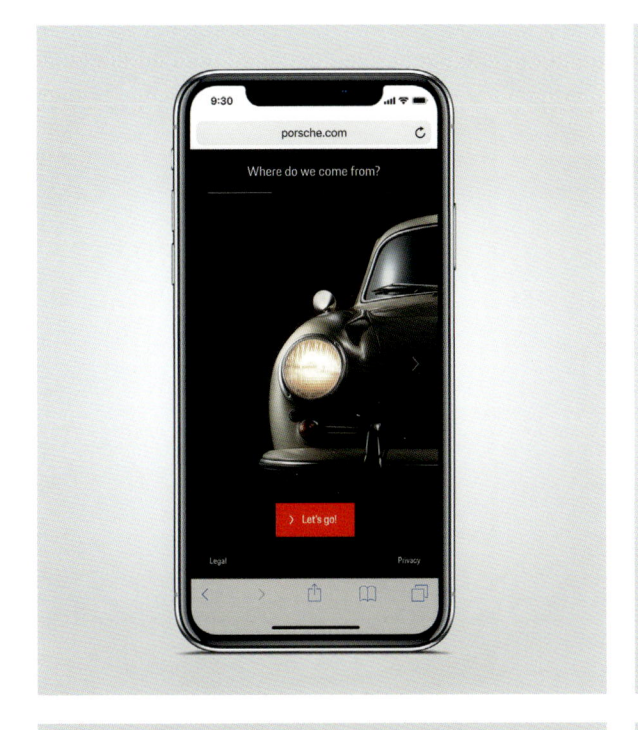

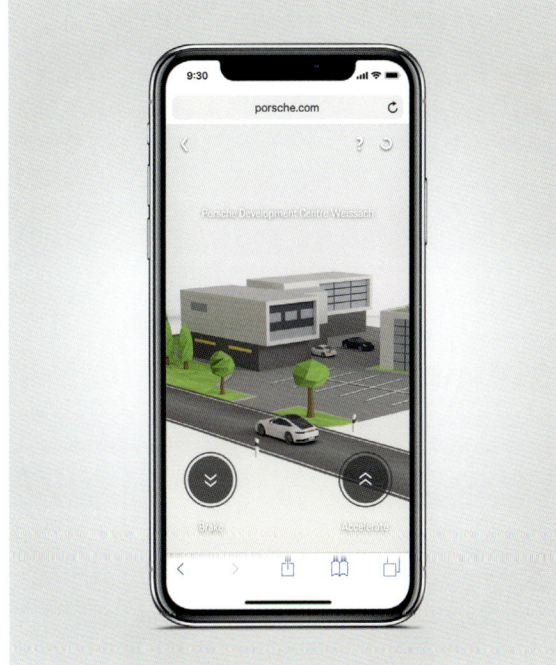

Porsche Digital Brand Academy – The state-of-the-art WebAR Training

[Mobile User Interface Design]

The Porsche Digital Brand Academy is an education app for brand training at Porsche. It consists of three chapters and takes the user on a journey through time starting at the roots of the brand, covering the present and offering an outlook into the future. A Porsche worker guides users through the web-based app as an avatar – providing information, encouraging them to interact with the scenery and rewarding them with emotional content. With the help of the latest WebAR technology from 8th Wall, users can become immersed in an AR scene at the location of choice by using their own smartphone.

Client
Dr. Ing. h.c. F. Porsche AG
Stuttgart, Germany

Design
innovation.rocks consulting gmbh
Vienna, Austria
Keko GmbH
Berlin, Germany

Project Team
innovation.rocks consulting
(Concept, Design, UX/UI):
Deniz Örs (Head of Design)
Sophia Luftensteiner
(User Interface Design)
Alexander Kvasnicka (3D Artist)
Ilker Cirakoglu (Junior Art Director)

Keko (Video & Audio):
Tobias Schwaiger (Creative Director)
Daniel Knisatschek (Senior Copywriter)
Swenja Krosien (Head of Digital Content)

→ Clip online

Connected Car Experience

[Mobility Solution]

This app is built for a new generation of electric and connected vehicles. The solution enables a ubiquitous, connected physical and digital experience. It is based on worldwide studies of Top Notch UX. Throughout the project, the focus was on creating an intuitive interaction that would not in any form obstruct the drivers' experience of driving the car. The app is a central element in the communication between the customer and the connected car.

Client
Tata Motors Ltd.
Mumbai, India

Design
YUJ Designs Pvt. Ltd.
Pune, India

Project Team
Samir Chabukswar (Design)
Neeraj Patel (Development)

→ Designer profile on page 638
→ Clip online

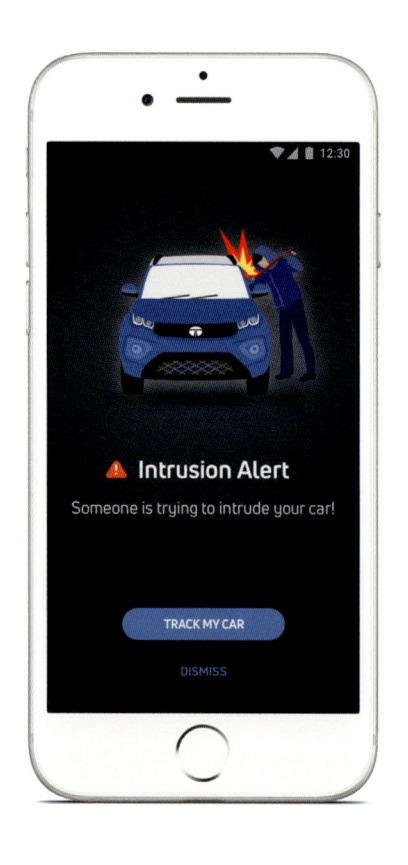

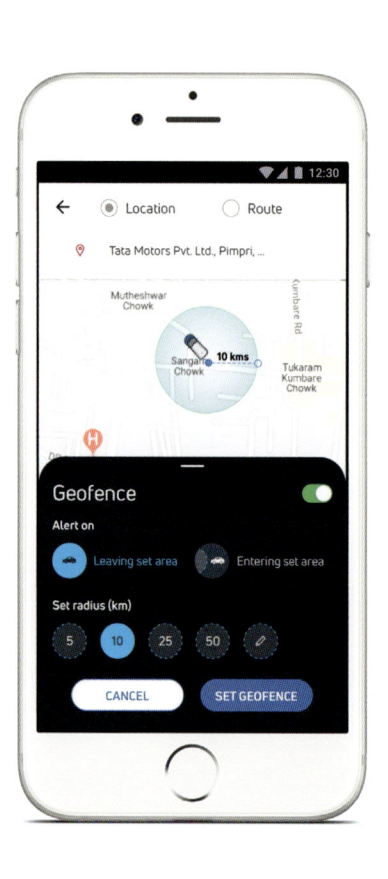

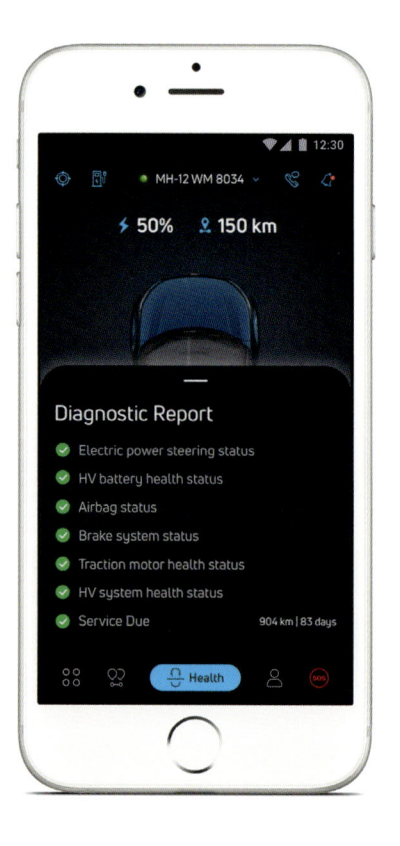

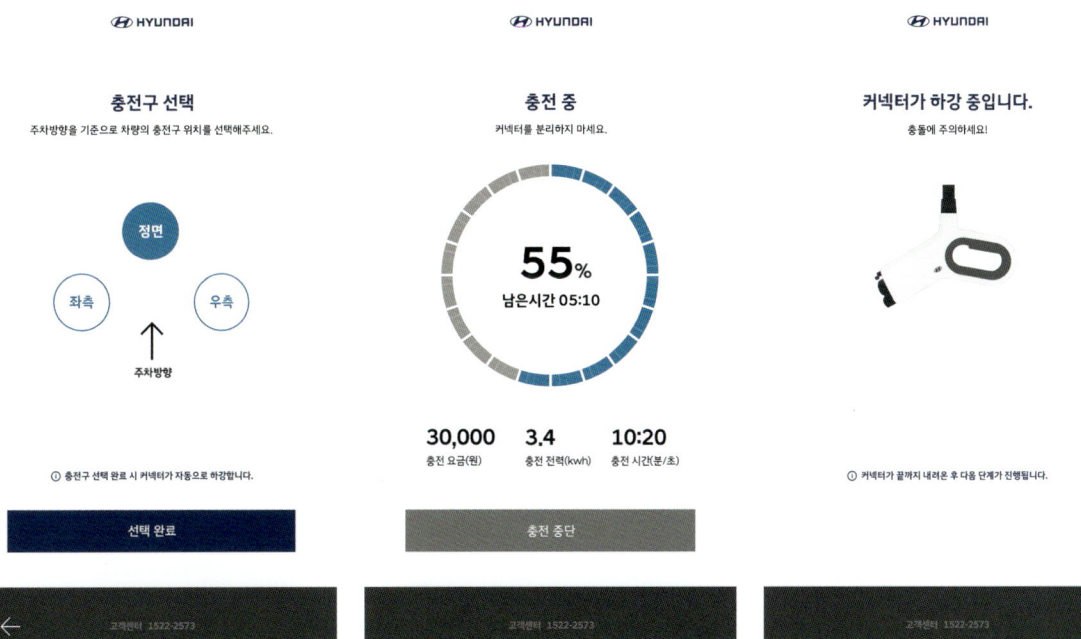

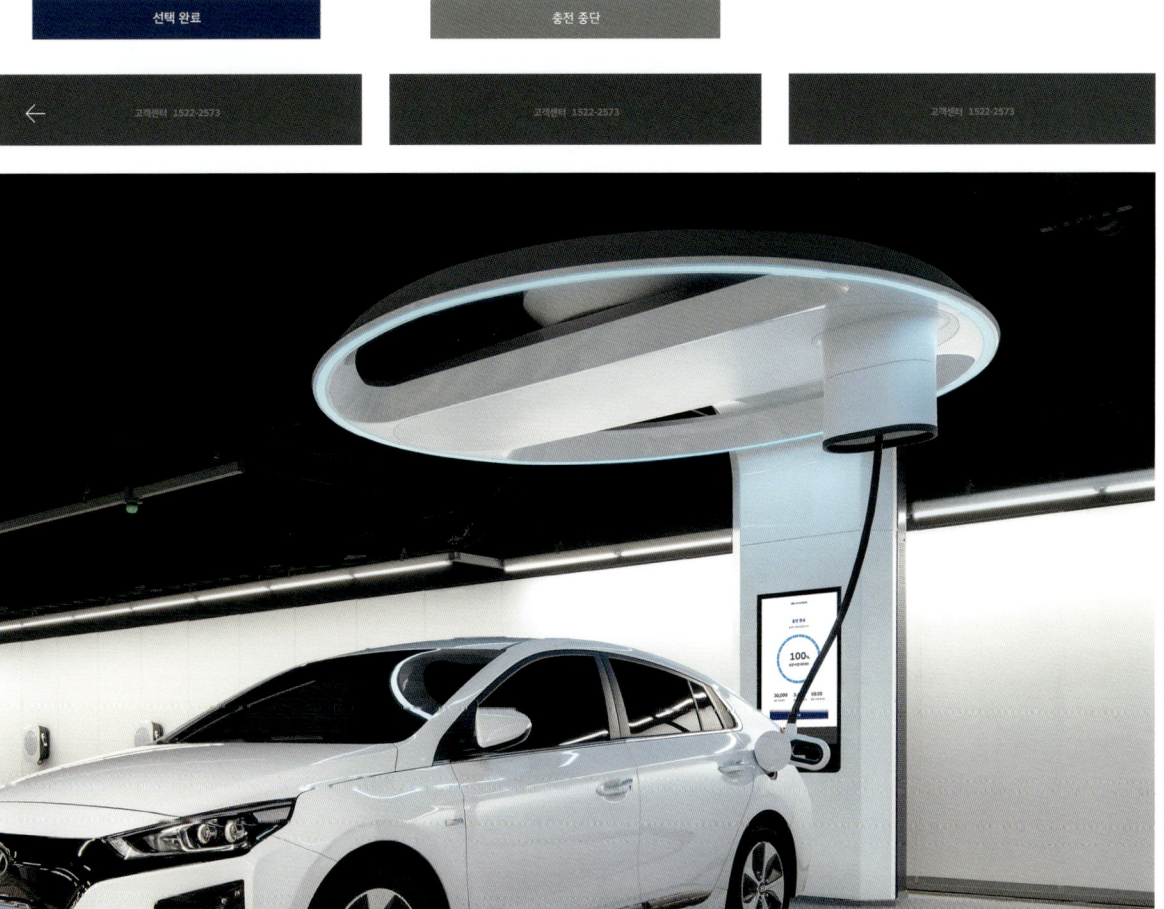

Hyundai Hi-Charger

[User Experience Design]

The Hyundai Hi-Charger offers a new charging experience in the field of electromobility through a "weight-free" system. The design solves the problem that the current high-capacity EV chargers force users to lift a heavy and usually dirty connector to charge their car, as charging ports are in different positions on each vehicle. Based on a "zero-gravity solution", the user can simply choose the location of the vehicle's charging port on a digital screen and a connector then automatically rotates and descends to the selected point for an effortless connection.

Client
Hyundai Motor Company
Seoul, South Korea

Design
Hyundai Motor Company, Creative Works
Seoul, South Korea
McKinsey Design
San Francisco, USA

Project Team
Daeyoung Chaevi (Manufacturer)

Publishing & Print Media	Posters	Typography	Illustrations	Sound Design	Film & Animation	Online
4	64	92	116	126	138	172

carValoo – App for Automatic Damage Notification and Digital Usage History

[User Experience Design]

The carValoo app offers fully automated, digitised car damage detection for fast and precise damage allocation and assessment, complemented by a service that documents the entire life of a car. This eliminates the cost of unassigned damages, reduces expenditures for inspections and increases the operating time. To provide customers with real-time transparency, the minimum viable product was implemented via a web app. The user interface design is based on a collaborative workshop and integrates the ideas of an interdisciplinary team.

Client
thyssenkrupp AG, Automotive Technology
Essen, Germany

Design
Ergosign GmbH
Saarbrücken, Germany

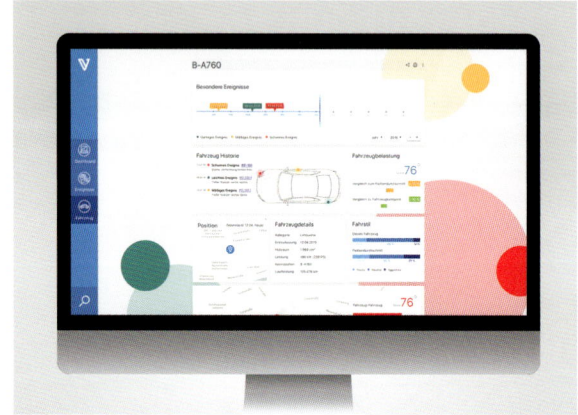

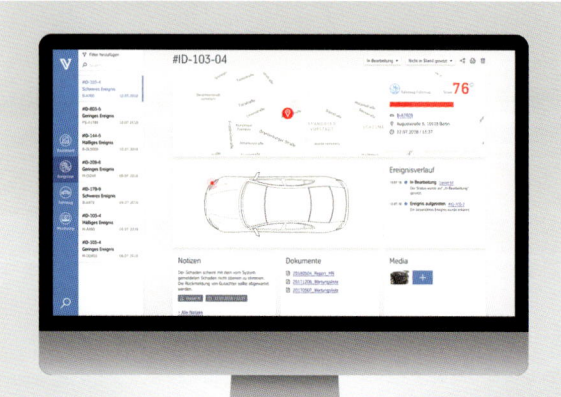

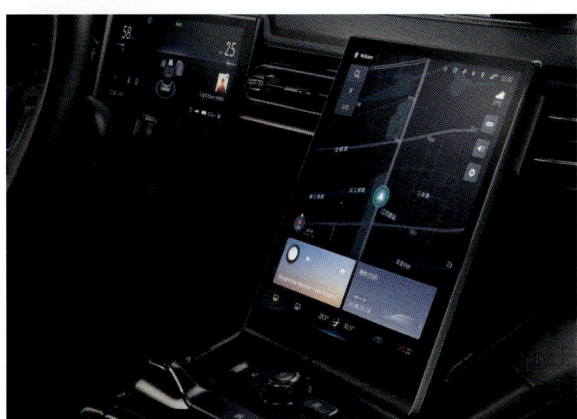

NIO OS

[Human Machine Interface Design]

NIO OS is running on the 11.3" screen of the ES8/ES6. The design allows users to communicate with the car by controlling the abundant functions. The goal has been to create a new driving and car-owning experience. Thanks to the innovative use of Card APP styles and system gestures, the unit is easy to operate when driving or parking. It offers a sophisticated navigation-based home screen, an intelligent recommendation module, a humanised MyCar APP, a customisable Quick Access and an automatic switch for the light and dark mode.

Client
NIO Co., Ltd.
Shanghai, China

Design
NIO Co., Ltd.
Shanghai, China

Project Team
Yuxiang Liu (Creative Direction)
Wenxiao Hu (Creative Direction)
Wei Ding (Creative Direction)
Yiwei Dong (Strategic Planning)
Xin Guan (Digital Concept)
Zhanzhao Liang (Digital Concept)
Caiyun Lian (Digital Concept)

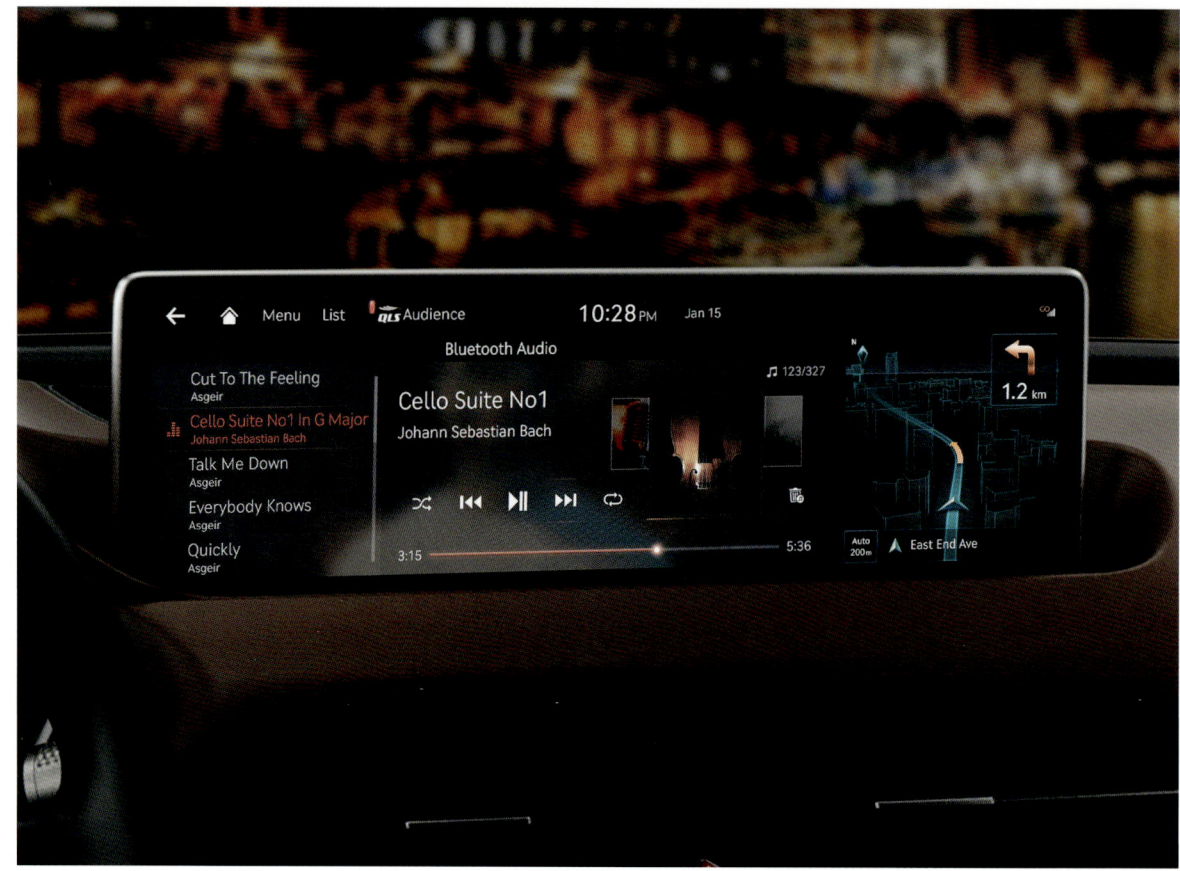

GENESIS Infotainment System – Copper Design

[Automotive Infotainment System, User Interface Design]

A new design was applied to the infotainment system of the Genesis model (GV80/G80) released in 2020. The background was a reinterpretation of the significance of copper-coloured design elements for the brand identity. They play a central role in symbolising the brand's core of athletic elegance. The task was to find a new copper colour system optimised for the digital environment in a running vehicle. This user experience design is the result of a delicate fine-tuning of copper colours and the testing of various metal textures.

Client
Hyundai Motor Company
Seoul, South Korea

Design
Hyundai Motor Company
Seoul, South Korea

MAN Digital Driver Working Place

[User Experience Design, User Interface Design]

This user experience concept for driver working places in the new MAN Truck Generation is determined by the three independently operable systems of "Cluster", "Media System" and "Interior Remote Control". Each system has its own truck-specific controls and is integrated in a holistic interaction concept combined with a contemporary design. The concept meets the special demands for handling a commercial vehicle. Powerful eco and assistance functions allow the driver to operate the vehicle intuitively, thus ensuring efficient and safe driving support in daily routines.

Client
MAN Truck & Bus SE
Munich, Germany

Design
MAN Truck & Bus SE
Munich, Germany

Project Team
Dr. Holger Mohra (Concept Lead)
Thomas Ochs (Graphic Design)
Dr. Martin Zademach (Concept)
David Gerlinger (Concept)
Zie-Na Kim (Concept)
Shiraz Tumasyan (Concept)
Florian Kremser (Concept)

→ Clip online

Spatial Communication

Publishing & Print Media	Posters	Typography	Illustrations	Sound Design	Film & Animation	Online
4	64	92	116	126	138	172

Red Dot: Grand Prix

Fading Stories
[Exhibition Design]

The exhibition "Fading Stories – pass them on" at Fotografiska in Stockholm portrayed 23 survivors of the Holocaust. While the presentation in the physical space was reduced to typographic posters in black and white, photographs and other background information including interviews were accessible via an AR app. Based on quotes from the survivors, the aesthetics of the poster framework were inspired by censured documents with blacked out passages, in order to illustrate how easily stories can be fragmented and corrupted. This demanded the viewers' attention and thus urged the importance of seeing the full story, to see through "alternative facts". Technically, the typographical set-up of the posters worked as a QR code that invited visitors to use their phone camera to unlock each portrait and, once unlocked, to be able to access the full story, the survivor's voice and portrait at any time. The typeface on the posters had a strong visual connection to the Hebrew alphabet and thus created an additional bond between history and present.

Statement by the jury
The way in which the reduced black-and-white design concept of this exhibition plays with the meaning of blacked out content in the quotes from Holocaust survivors is downright outstanding. Just like active remembrance can fade away, so can text quickly become meaningless or corrupted. Featuring blacked out text as QR code effectively turns the hidden words into a key to knowledge – another clever congruence of idea and content, which communicates the topic in a shocking yet extremely successful manner.

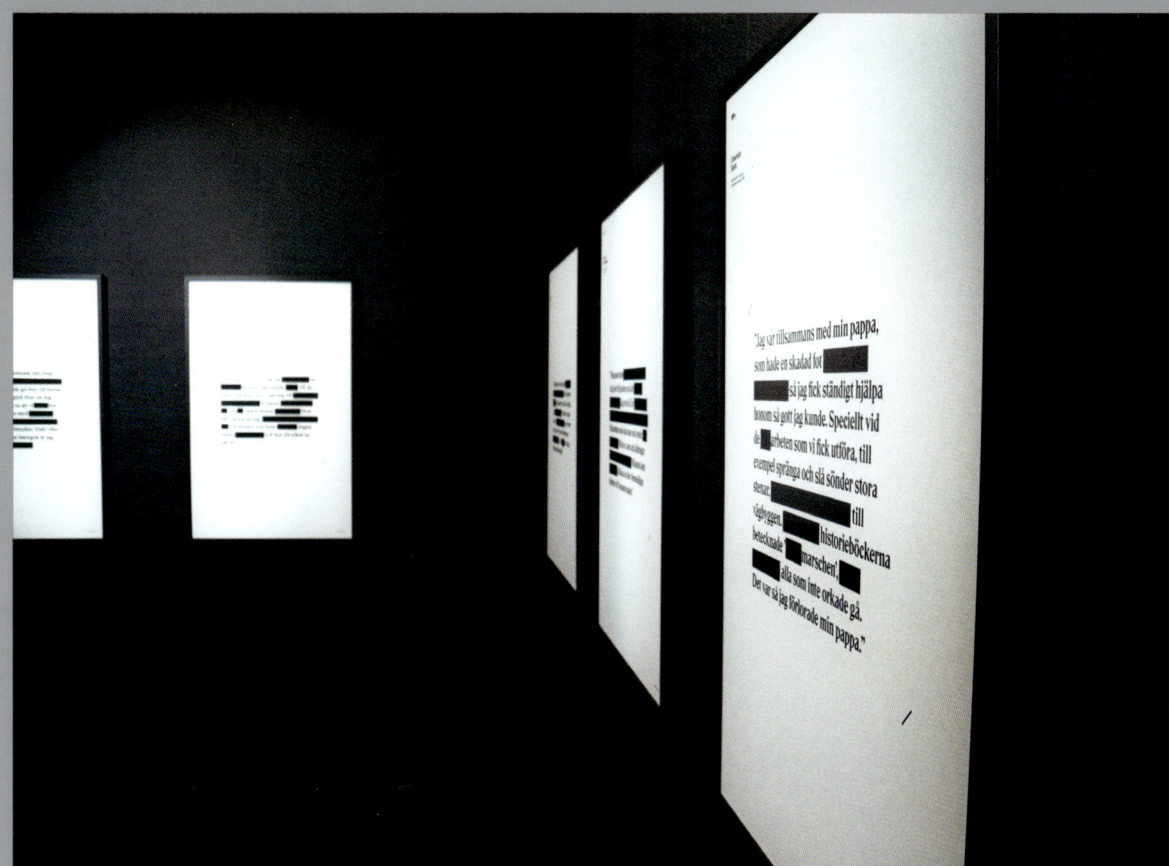

Apps	Interface & User Experience Design	Spatial Communication	Red Dot: Junior Award	Designer Profiles	Jury Portraits	Index
206	236	336	426	564	642	668

reddot winner 2020
grand prix

Client
Raoul Wallenberg Academy
Stockholm, Sweden

Design
Sunny at Sea
Stockholm, Sweden

Project Team
Tobias Ottomar (Creative Direction)
Linnea Hedeborg (Graphic Design)
Johan Wendborg (Strategic Planning)
Farbod Bozorgzad (Project Management)
Vu Phan (Programming)
Oscar Kockum (Programming)

→ Designer profile on page 625

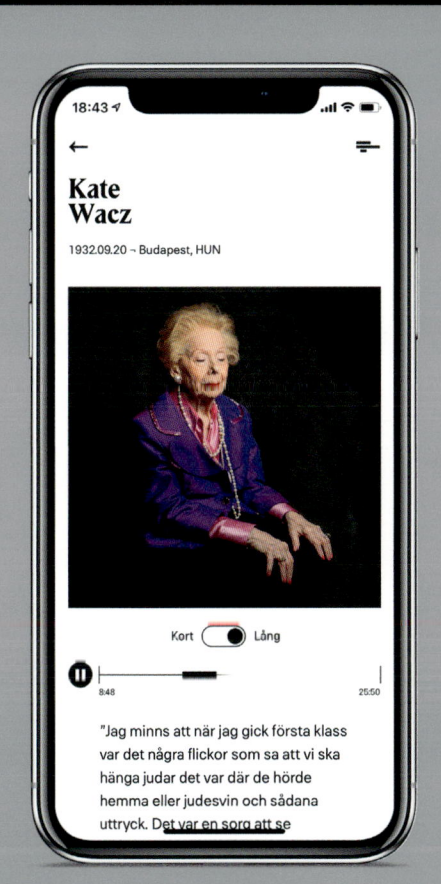

Red Dot: Best of the Best

Festung Xperience
[Exhibition Design]

The reopening of the Dresden Fortress in 2019 was accompanied by "Festung Xperience", an innovative show based on the latest audiovisual technology to immerse visitors in a 360-degree spatial enactment consisting of 25 scenes. The show traces the history of the 16th-century bastion fortification through an audio drama with mixed media including motion, light and sound design. The diverse format enables visitors to submerge themselves into the history of the site and elicits the sensation of being amidst the historic events. The multimedia, multisensorial and largely immaterial scenography even transforms visitors into participants, for example by having them trigger sounds, which appear to come from real sound sources when visitors enter certain areas. The exhibition features no exhibits except for the 1,800 sqm fortress itself, which is preserved in its authenticity and comes to life through a three-dimensional storytelling, an emotional film score as well as space-filling projection mapping.

Statement by the jury
This project is part of a new discipline in exhibition design, where history meets high-tech and gamification provides the link between experience and knowledge transfer. The multimedia "fireworks", with which this project creates a vivid and highly immersive sense of past events in the Dresden Fortress, have been implemented to a very high standard with illustrations, films, animations and sounds that are consistently detailed and engaging.

Client
Staatliche Schlösser, Burgen
und Gärten Sachsen gGmbH
Dresden, Germany

Design
TAMSCHICK MEDIA+SPACE GmbH
Berlin, Germany

Project Team
Charlotte Tamschick (Creative Direction)
Gaël Perrin (Art Direction)
Jan Köpper (Creative Producing)
Hanna Stoff (Project Management)
Tobias Ziegler (Project Management)
Mattis Gutsche (Motion Design)

→ Designer profile on page 627
→ Clip online

Red Dot: Best of the Best

Go! Go! South Pole – Adventurous Horizon

[Exhibition Design]

Can adventures inspire learning and how can a brand present its statements in order to have an influence on society? As their tenth anniversary approached in 2018, the Gamania Cheer Up Foundation initiated the Big Dream project "Go! Go! South Pole" and thus set the record for the first cross-country skiing group at the South Pole. In the extreme environment, the group reached the "end of the earth" by cross-country skiing, forging through wind and snow at 30 degrees Celsius below zero and wind speeds of up to 50 metres per second. In the exhibition, visitors were invited to explore the Antarctic journey through AR, digital internet technology and bodily sensations such as of a harsh storm and extremely cold temperature, enabling visitors to experience various scenes in this rough, inhospitable environment. The adventures at the South Pole were structured into six narrative chapters, in order to not only inspire a sense of adventure among visitors but also to actually create immersive adventures themselves through ice, snow or a protective tent.

Statement by the jury
The exhibition project "Go! Go! South Pole" succeeds in conveying an experience of the ice and snow atmosphere of the Antarctic in a truly captivating manner by activating various sensory levels. By being confronted with icy cold temperatures and extreme winds, visitors could not only immerse in the adventure of this project, but also experience the unapproachable continent authentically and thus gain a better understanding of it.

Apps	Interface & User Experience Design	**Spatial Communication**	Red Dot: Junior Award	Designer Profiles	Jury Portraits	Index
206	236	336	426	564	642	668

Client
Gamania Cheer Up Foundation
Taipei City, Taiwan

Design
InFormat Design Curating
Taipei City, Taiwan

Project Team
Albert Liu (Project Initiator)
Eric Chen (Project Curator)
Gamania Brand Center (Project Planning)
Gamania Chief Technology Office
(Technology Support)
Gamania Corporate Marketing Office
(PR Coordination)
The Chen Studio (Merchandise Planning)
Li-Chou Yang
(Antarctica Expedition Film Director)
Hao-Shen Lin
(Antarctica Expedition Filming)

Yao-Pang Wang (Project Curator)
Doris Hu (PR Coordinator)
Pulp Chen (Copywriting Coordinator)
Jue-Ning Chen (Exhibition Planning)
Li-Ching Liu (Exhibition Planning)
Rae Hsu (Exhibition Planning)
Hao Zhuang (Visual Design)
Tzu-Lin Liu (Visual Design)
Yun-Da Tzou (Visual Design)
Che-Wei Chang (Spatial Design)
Yi-Yang Peng (Spatial Design)
Ingrid Weng (Administration)

→ Designer profile on page 598
→ Clip online

Red Dot: Best of the Best

BLINK – The End is in Sight
[Exhibition Design]

The Sightsavers campaign "BLINK – The End is in Sight" has the aim of eradicating trachoma, an eye infection disease that can lead to blindness, by 2025. Seeking to generate public awareness of the disease, the exhibition was hosted at London's OXO Gallery and featured the work of several award-winning photographers including Nick Knight. The idea was to digitally "hack" the gallery space and drive a visual narrative of the disease. The effects of trachoma were mimicked in an interactive interface with innovative technology to visualise the diminishing ability to blink. The technology gradually eroded each photograph leaving pictures abstractly distorted until the original images were destroyed. The increasingly fractured graphics thus imitated the decreasing eyesight and led visitors around the exhibition space. By thus visualising the slowly progressing character of trachoma within an everyday context, the exhibition successfully raised awareness of the disease and connected visitors to the issue.

Statement by the jury
The Sightsavers campaign manages in a masterful and ingenious manner to stage the devastating progression of trachoma eye infection. Using innovative technology, this process is mimicked in a visually easy-to-understand approach, allowing the loss of vision to be virtually experienced in a sophisticated and emotionally touching way. Public attention for this disease has thus been successfully generated.

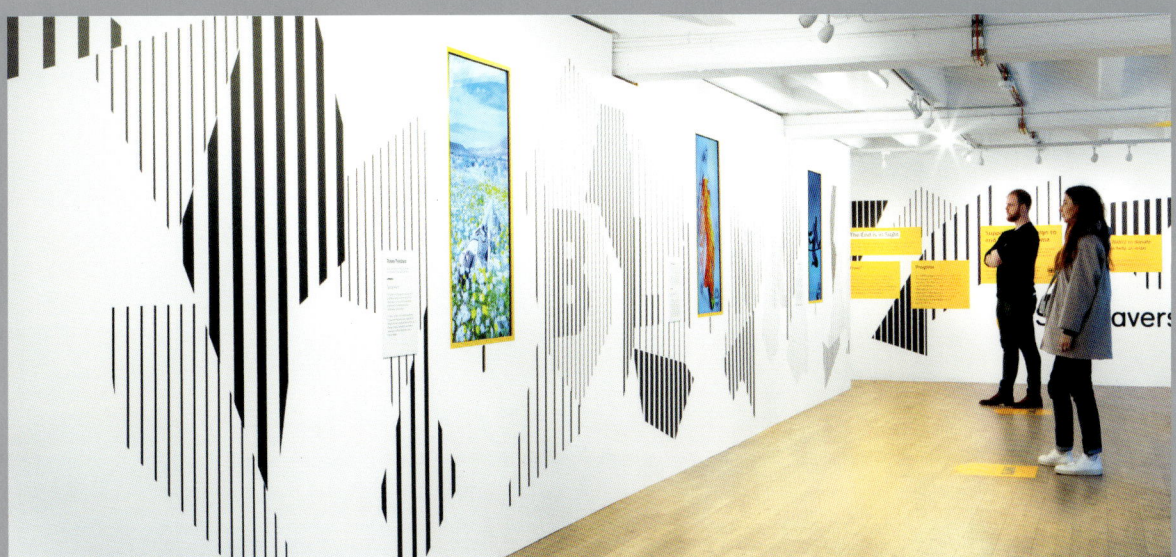

Apps	Interface & User Experience Design	**Spatial Communication**	Red Dot: Junior Award	Designer Profiles	Jury Portraits	Index
206	236	336	426	564	642	668

Client
Sightsavers
Chippenham, United Kingdom

Design
MET Studio
London, United Kingdom
Jason Bruges Studio
London, United Kingdom

Project Team
MET Studio:
Peter Karn (Creative Director)
Darren Lewis (Art Direction)
Jackson Iredale (Designer)
Diana Shayakhmetova (Art Worker)

Jason Bruges Studio:
Jason Bruges
(Creative Director Digital Production)
Adam Wadey
(Senior Designer Digital Production)
Joel Luther-Braun
(Designer Digital Production)

Eric Langham (Content Director),
Barker Langham
Alice Magagnin (Content Researcher),
Barker Langham

→ Designer profile on page 607

345

Red Dot: Best of the Best

Tape Art by TAPE THAT
[Exhibition Design]

Tape art is art made out of adhesive tape. It is a new art form that has grown rapidly over the last ten years. The Berlin-based Tape That Collective designed an exhibition space of 380 sqm inside the Songshan Cultural and Creative Park in Taipei. Within the exhibition, they created eight tape art installations and exhibited over 40 tape paintings created by collectives. Working on-site, all artists included the spatiality of the exhibition space in their themes ranging from camouflage and illusion to a mirror house and a night-view corridor. Moreover, special sounds and light installations turn the event into an immersive art experience. Easy to adhere, tear and change – with sophisticated patterns and skills, the lines and colours of approximately 7,000 cuts of tapes transformed the otherwise plain and little exciting space into a fancy place of great aesthetic value and emotional depth.

Statement by the jury
The remarkable thing about this exhibition is that it is made of simple materials and yet achieves such a rich visual effect. It is with the help of ordinary, ubiquitous adhesive tapes, which skilfully adorn the space with strong graphic patterns and different colours, that it has become possible to present a variety of spatial perceptions and to evoke a multifaceted sense of liveliness.

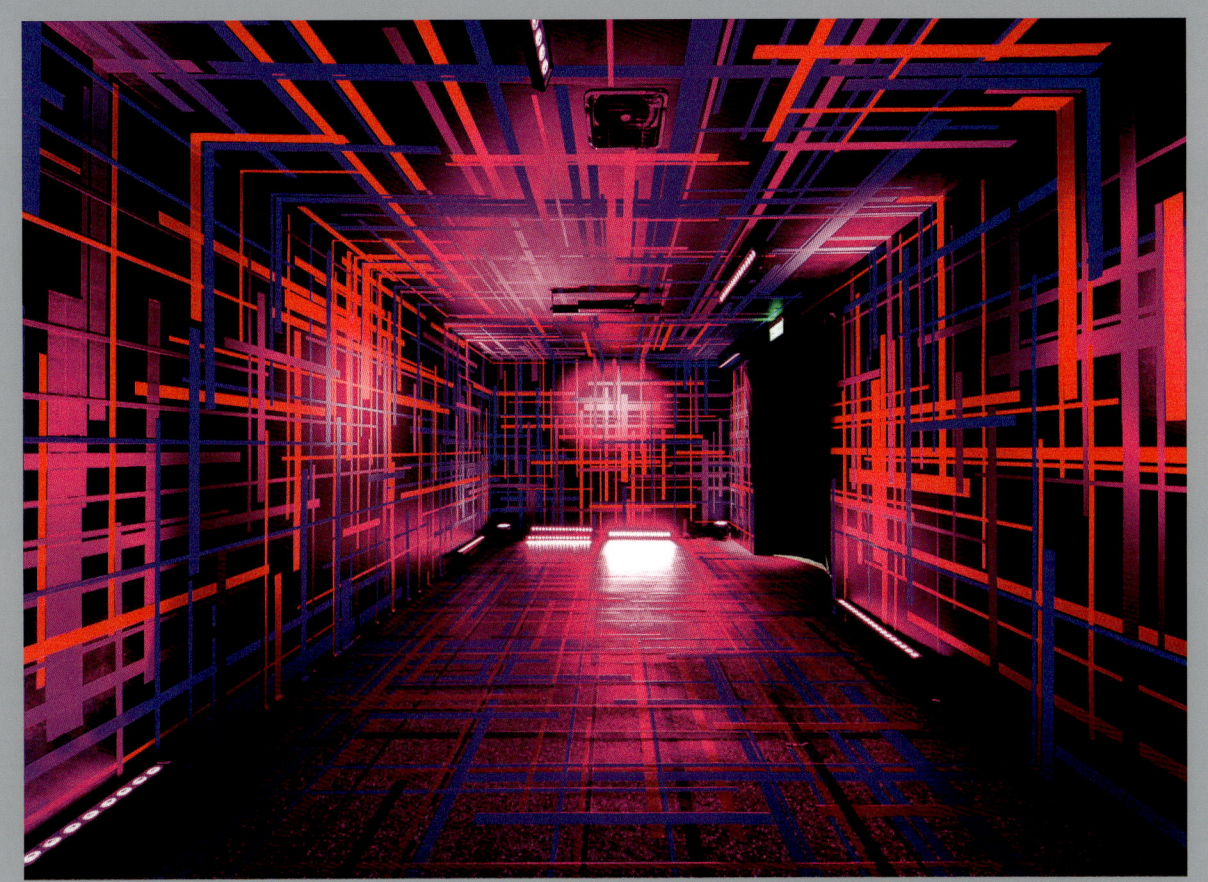

Apps	Interface & User Experience Design	**Spatial Communication**	Red Dot: Junior Award	Designer Profiles	Jury Portraits	Index
206	236	336	426	564	642	668

Client
FunDesign.tv
Taipei City, Taiwan

Design
Tape That Collective
Berlin, Germany

Project Team
Carrie Chang (Curator)
SK Chen (Curator)
Sandrine Cheng (Curator)
Thomas Meissner (Artist)
Nicolas Lawin (Artist)
Cedric Goussanou (Artist)
Stephan Meissner (Artist)
Stefan Busch (Artist)
Adrian Dittert (Artist)
Atau Hamos (Artist)

→ Designer profile on page 588

Red Dot: Best of the Best

TYPO UTOPIA
[Art Installation]

"TYPO UTOPIA" is a large-scale art installation that shows the fascinating effect of typography, movement and sound on human perception. In a pitch-black room, it uses audiovisual means to transport visitors into the world of ideas of the Bauhaus. The interplay of typographic animations and a multidimensional soundtrack creates a unique emotional experience. Congenially visualising the content of ten quotations by famous Bauhaus representatives including Walter Gropius, Wassily Kandinsky and Paul Klee, the typographic designs reflect the thematic diversity of the Bauhaus universe. Fonts and symbols – sometimes hand-drawn, sometimes constructed – play with spatial illusions, as they float, dance, form a carpet of letters, grow or dissolve. Without additional visual material, emotional images are created from black and white, light, shadow and sound alone. Based on enthusiasm for the power, beauty and meaning of letters, the installation thus gives the letterforms a stage and offers a new approach to the Bauhaus.

Statement by the jury
The "TYPO UTOPIA" installation literally draws visitors into its utopian design, which uses and stages typography in a completely new manner. Fully in the tradition of the Bauhaus, it takes little to achieve a lot, when quotes become spaces or words become films. The resulting spatial, visual and emotional experience is sensational and demonstrates the high level of craftsmanship of this installation.

Apps	Interface & User Experience Design	Spatial Communication	Red Dot: Junior Award	Designer Profiles	Jury Portraits	Index
206	236	336	426	564	642	668

Client
Kunststiftung des Landes
Sachsen-Anhalt
Halle/Saale, Germany

Design
Sisters of Design, Anja Krämer und
Claudia Dölling GbR
Halle/Saale, Germany

Project Team
Alexander Nickmann (Sound Artist)
Oscar Loeser (Technical Production), avk4
Clemens Kowalski
(Technical Production), avk4

→ Designer profile on page 621
→ Clip online

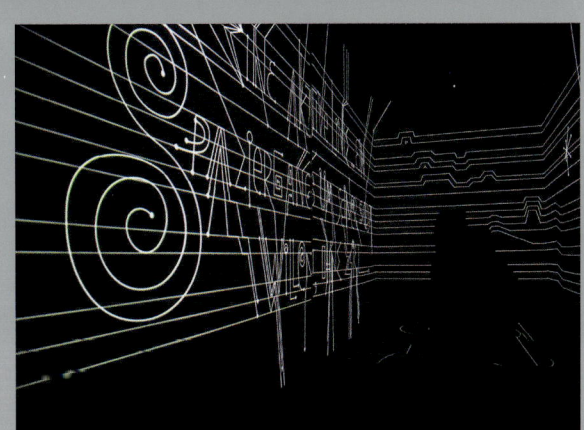

Red Dot: Best of the Best

Light Up 13-Layer Remains
[Light Installation]

An unusual lighting design for the sublime "13-Layer Remains" landmark in Taiwan, this work aims at rejuvenating the old copper smelter plant, which was shut down in the 1970s. Dating back to the Japanese colonial era and also known as the "Potala Palace of Mountain Mines" because of its monumental architecture, the remains of this impressive building were enhanced with 365 sets of luminaires at 15 different angles. Clearly visible from afar, the illumination stages the cultural heritage in an impressive shimmer, whose enveloping amber-coloured light symbolises the fire in copper refining. The various luminance levels, in turn, stand for the individual layers of the rising terrain and, as a whole, transform the building illuminated at night into a great public work of art that resonates warmly with people, while the memory of the mining golden age is rekindled.

Statement by the jury
This monumental light installation convinces with a dramaturgy that is both spectacular and filigree, sustaining a power that transforms the historic monument and landscape in north-eastern Taiwan into a unique artefact. The industrial ruins, which had been contaminated for long, are thus brought back to life after decades of neglect and given a new existence in between nature and culture.

Client
Taiwan Power Company
Taipei City, Taiwan

Design
YI.ng Lighting Design Consultants
New Taipei City, Taiwan

Project Team
Lien Chou (Design)
Wen Ying Chu (Design)
Ping Yi Liu (Design)

→ Designer profile on page 636

TIDES

[Exhibition Design]

The TIDES exhibition at Ventura Centrale during Milan Design Week 2019 took inspiration from the complex "dance of gravity" that leads to the phenomenon of tides. It offered a temporary experience where time, colour and light became fluid like the ocean. The exhibition showcased 100 stools by the designer Kwangho Lee from the series "The Moment of Eclipse". Each eclipse-shaped stool was connected to the next one, forming chains of endless variations. Through an abstract "low tide landscape", the exhibition created an "otherworldly landscape" that invited visitors to take a low tide walk in changing light and colours.

Client
NOROO Group
Seoul, South Korea

Design
NOROO Holdings Co., Ltd.
Seoul, South Korea

Project Team
Kwangho Lee (Creative Direction)
Anny Wang (Art Direction)
Tim Söderström (Art Direction)
Jihye Choi (Spatial Management/Curation)
Nakhoon Choi (Graphic Design)
Andrea Martiradonna (Photography)
Giacomo Costa (Film Direction)

→ Clip online

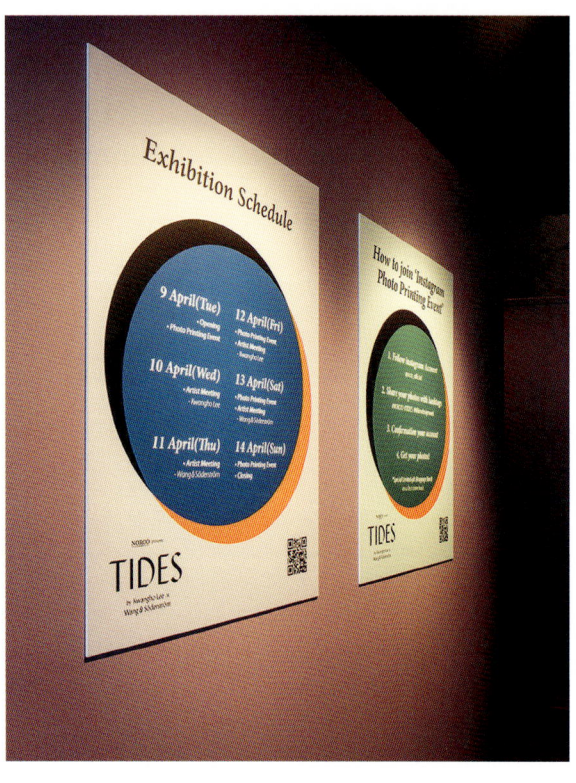

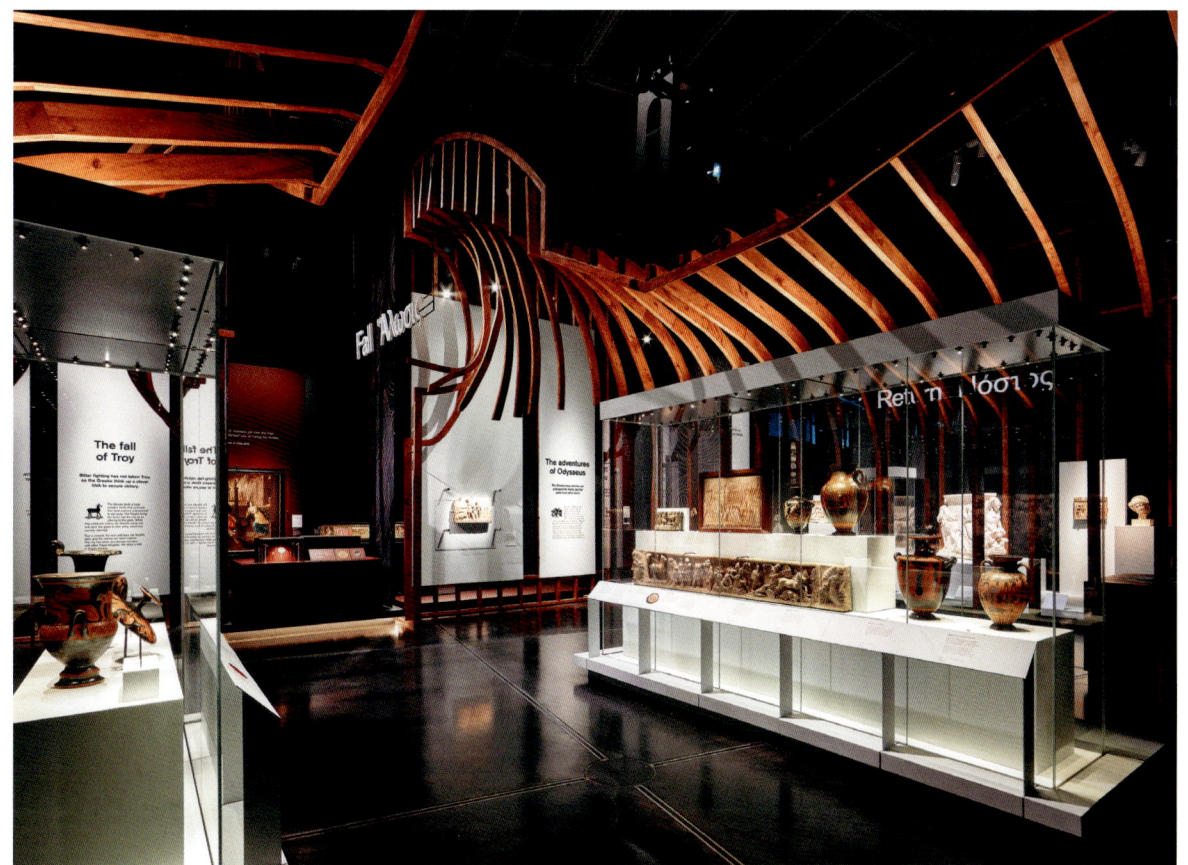

Troy: myth and reality
[Exhibition Design]

The exhibition "Troy: myth and reality" at the British Museum in London, England (November 2019 to March 2020) explored the significance of the subject of Troy and its appeal across time, asking: "Why does this story endure?" A clean, crisp design brought the astonishing objects in the exhibition to life. Dramatic lighting and colour palettes were used to complement the collections, while rich background colours aimed to help multihued paintings glow within the space. The nearly 300 exhibited objects spanned three millennia, from the museum's impressive Greco-Roman artefacts to Heinrich Julius Schliemann's original archaeological findings.

Client
British Museum
London, United Kingdom

Design
Ralph Appelbaum Associates
London, United Kingdom

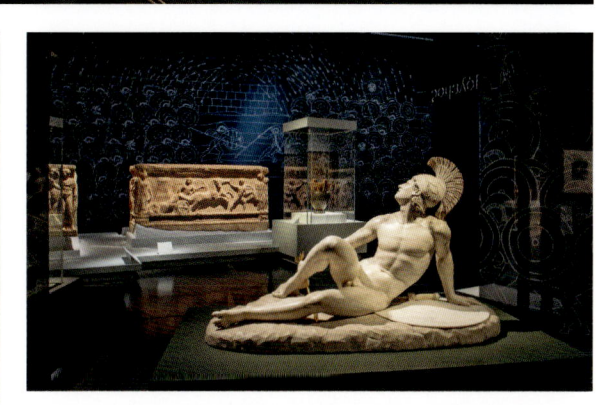

Publishing & Print Media	Posters	Typography	Illustrations	Sound Design	Film & Animation	Online
4	64	92	116	126	138	172

TAIPOWER Cultural Heritage Exhibition – Just Flow 2019

[Exhibition Design]

Client
Taiwan Power Company
Taipei City, Taiwan

Design
Midroom Design Co., Ltd.
Taichung, Taiwan
Plain Design Co., Ltd.
Taichung, Taiwan

Project Team
Taiwan Power Company:
Mei-Ling Yuan (Project Management)
Chih-Hung Chen (Project Management)
Pin-Tzu Su (Project Management)
Pei Chen (Project Management)

Midroom Design:
Chung-Yuan Kuo (Creative Direction)

Plain Design:
Jer-Yu Sheu (Creative Direction)

→ Clip online

This exhibition highlights the potential of hydroelectricity in Taiwan, which has long "hidden among Taiwan's mountains". In exciting images, it chronologically traces the eventful history of Taiwan's hydroelectricity. The story begins over a century ago, when employees from the company TAIPOWER journeyed deep into these mountains. This is complemented by detailed information allowing viewers to understand the local water conditions and topographical features. The key focus, however, is on the challenges and the achievements of those workers who have truly pushed the boundaries and who are impressively presented in a gallery of profile photos as "engineering pioneers".

Archaeological Promenade – James Simon Gallery

[Exhibition Design]

The new James Simon Gallery was conceived as a central entrance and main visitors' centre for the Museum Island in Berlin. The presentation conveying comprehensive content in an innovative manner realises the objective of bringing cultural history to life and making it tangible. It documents the historical development of the Museum Island with its five museums and seven archaeological collections, starting with its modest beginnings as a coin cabinet in the Berlin Palace and ending with the current status as a UNESCO World Heritage Site. The austere and timeless design blends harmoniously into the architecture.

Client
Stiftung Preußischer Kulturbesitz (SPK)
Berlin, Germany

Design
Duncan McCauley
Berlin, Germany

Project Team
Tom Duncan (Creative Direction)
Noel McCauley (Concept)
Gesa Gerstenberger
Di Wu
Tina Raccah

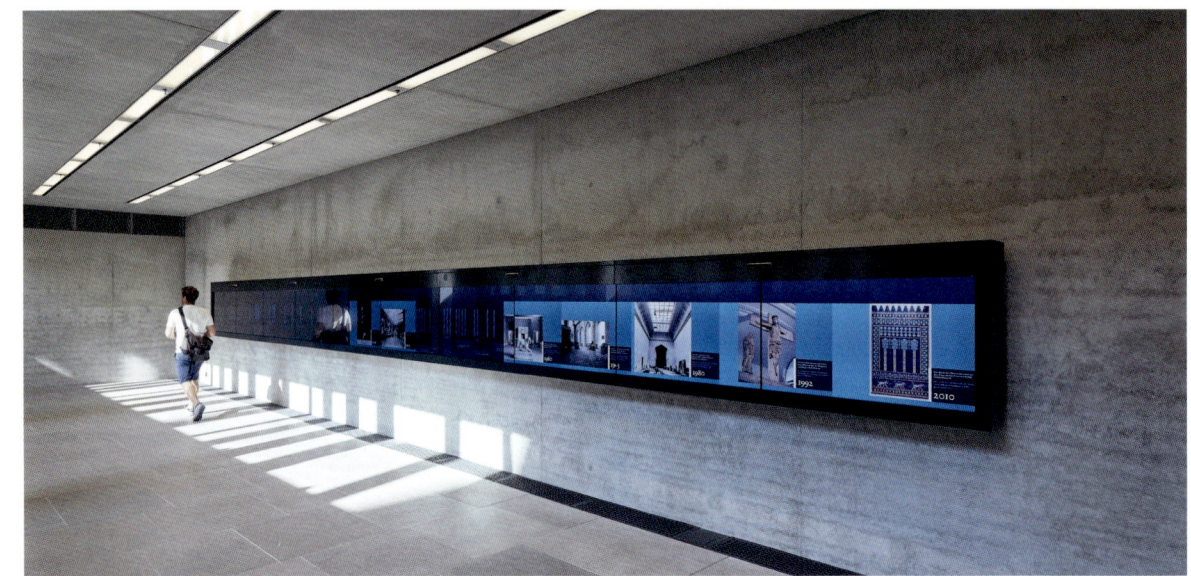

The Select Court Stands from the Palace Museum

[Scenography, Exhibition Design]

This exhibition design creates a dialogue between the existing contemporary spaces and the traditional context of the show's scenography for the Select Court Stands from the Palace Museum, hosted by the Guardian Art Center in Beijing. The scenography of the exhibition took into account the characteristics of the stands and reinterpreted them through a contemporary design concept and with innovative display techniques. It created a dialogue between the past and the present, intending to encourage the visitors to rediscover and rethink the unobtrusive stands.

Client
Guardian Art Center
Beijing, China

Design
Le Chantier Space Design Ltd.
Beijing, China

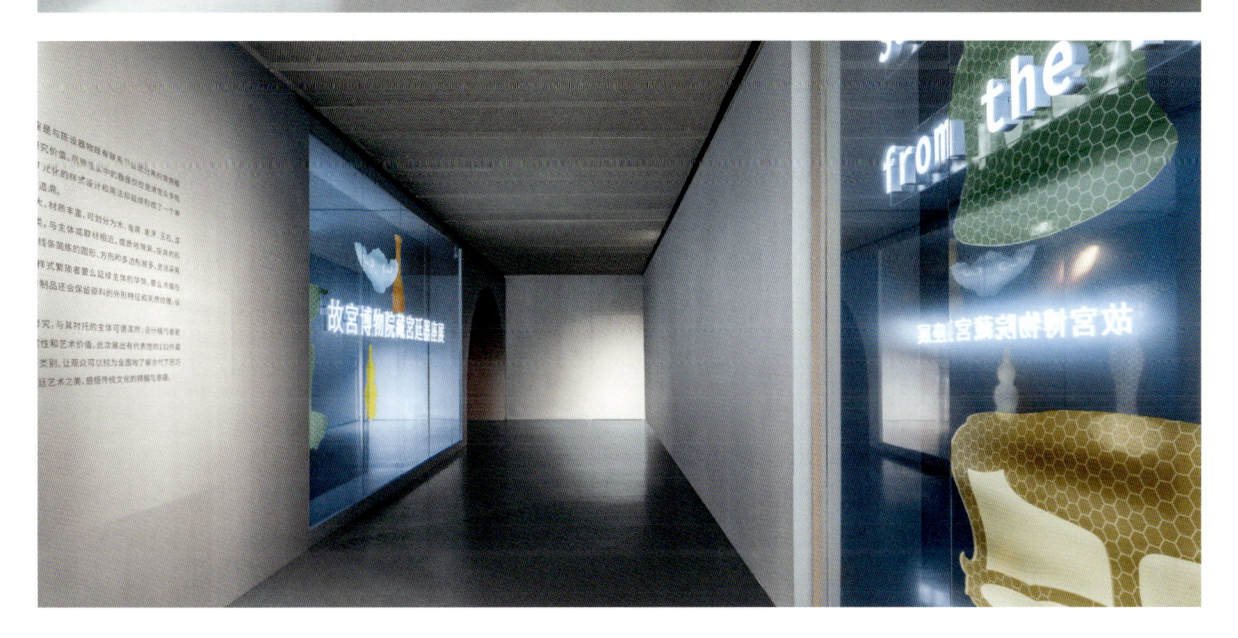

Wilhelm and Alexander von Humboldt

[Exhibition Design]

To illustrate the revolutionary thinking of the brothers Wilhelm and Alexander von Humboldt regarding the social and scientific conditions of their time, the design of this exhibition at the German Historical Museum (DHM) in Berlin, Germany, was inspired by the aesthetics of "Daguerre's Diorama". A historically revolutionary medium at the time, the diorama was characterised by translucent, shifting lighting. Freely interpreted and spatially staged, it "illuminates" the historical framework of the Humboldt brothers, while iconic images from Friedrich J. Bertuch's "Picture Book for Children" reflect the zeitgeist.

Client
Deutsches Historisches Museum
Berlin, Germany

Design
BOK + Gärtner GmbH
Münster, Germany

Project Team
Christian Vogler (Creative Direction)
Rabea Kaup (Creative Direction)
Dominik Kolm (Art Direction)
René Schulze Wienker
(Technical Direction)
Anna Thiemicke (Graphic Design)
Rebecca Sieker (Graphic Design)

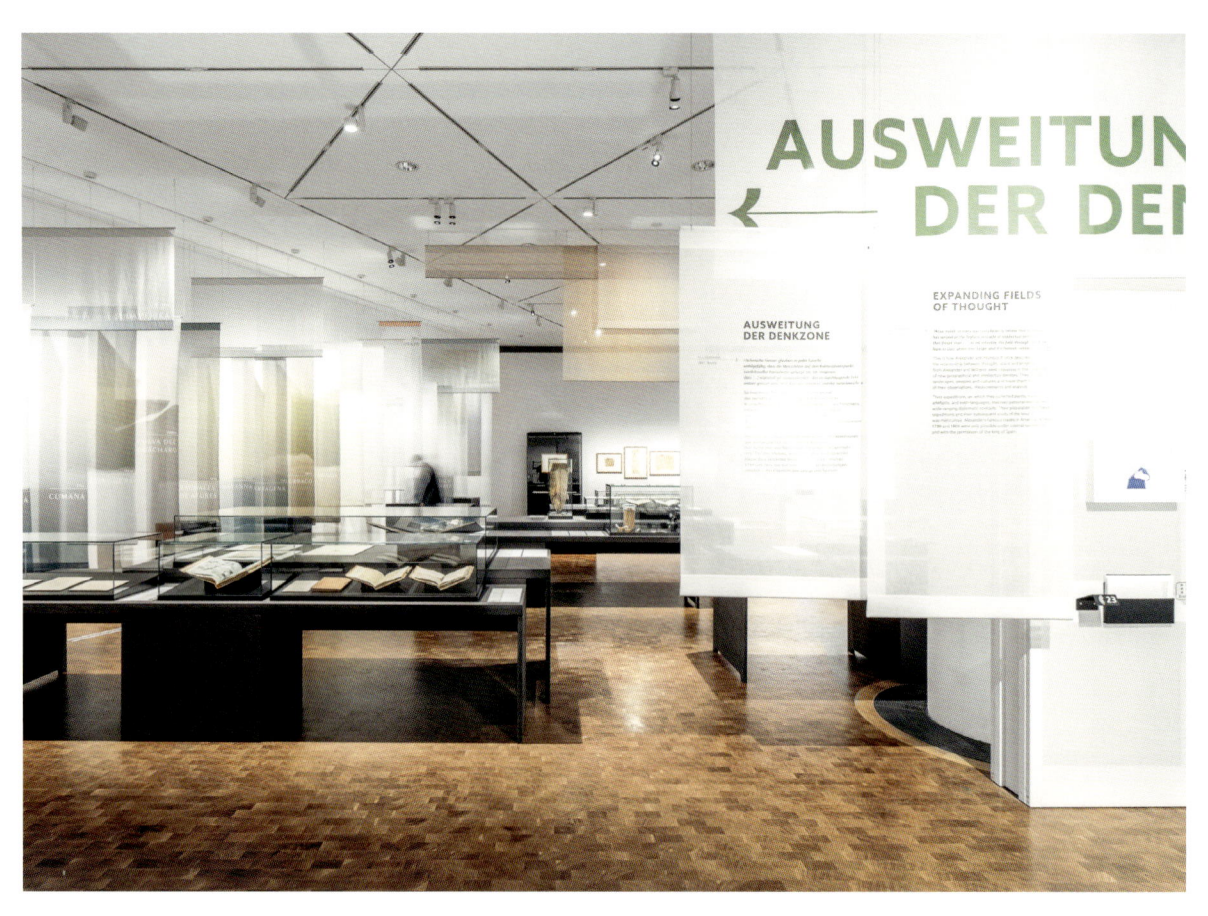

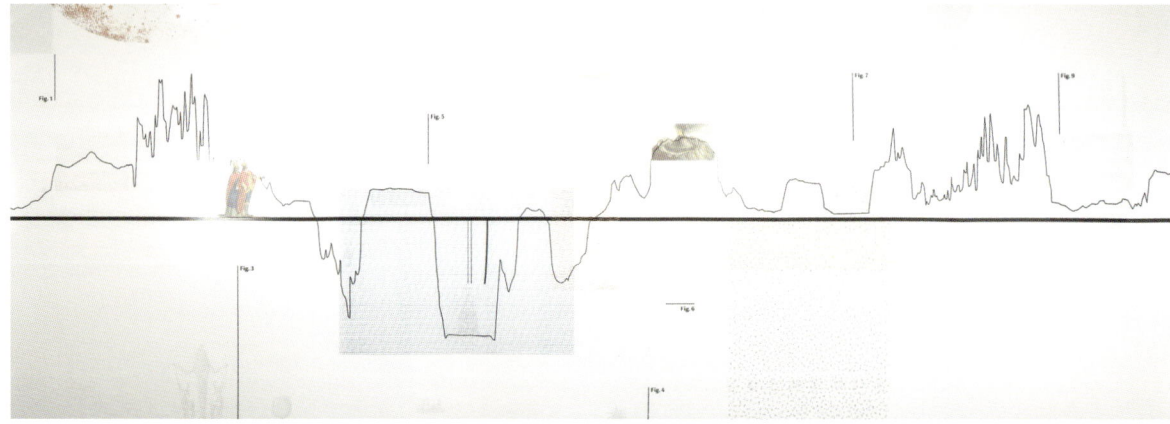

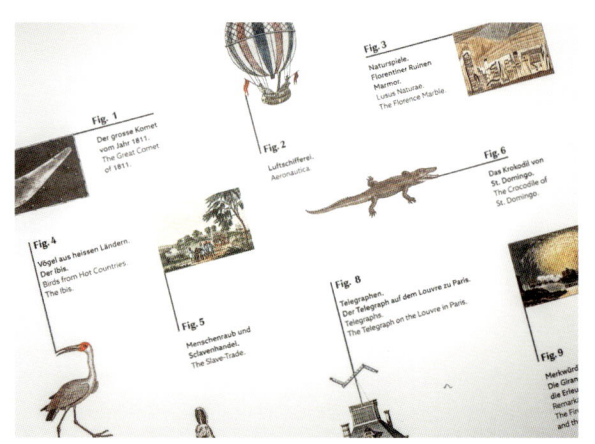

Mycenae – The Legendary World of Agamemnon

[Exhibition Design]

This exhibition follows in the footsteps of the explorers Heinrich Schliemann and Homer, taking visitors on a journey through time from the 19th century to the ancient Greek city of Mycenae. Adopting a circular design, the tour passes through various experience rooms in which architectural reconstruction and abstract interpretation create a contrasting yet harmonious overall picture. The language of form and the colour scheme of the exhibition's graphic and architectural design recalls the look of Mycenaean cities and landscapes. Clay tablets of Linear B – the Mycenaean's own writing system – served as an inspiration for the design of the text hierarchies.

Client
Badisches Landesmuseum
Karlsruhe, Germany

Design
res d Design und Architektur GmbH
Cologne, Germany

Publishing & Print Media	Posters	Typography	Illustrations	Sound Design	Film & Animation	Online
4	64	92	116	126	138	172

ANXIN

[Spatial Design, Exhibition Design]

Conceived as a wooden exhibition hall, this project visualises the diversity and beauty of wood. The shape of veneer shavings served as the main inspiration for the design. The outer layer of a logarithmically curved wall is wrapped around the entire exhibition hall, showcasing a physical structure that creates a mysterious and quiet atmosphere. The design with the large tree logs makes visitors feel as if they were in a forest. The use of discarded wood is intended to show the endless possibilities of wood and the need for regenerative harvesting.

Client
Anxin Weiguang (Shanghai)
imber Company
Shanghai, China

Design
PRID International Design
Shanghai, China
Shanghai Bairen Interior Design &
Engineering Company
Shanghai, China

Project Team
Tu Po Chun (Designer)
Wang Chih Yun (Designer)

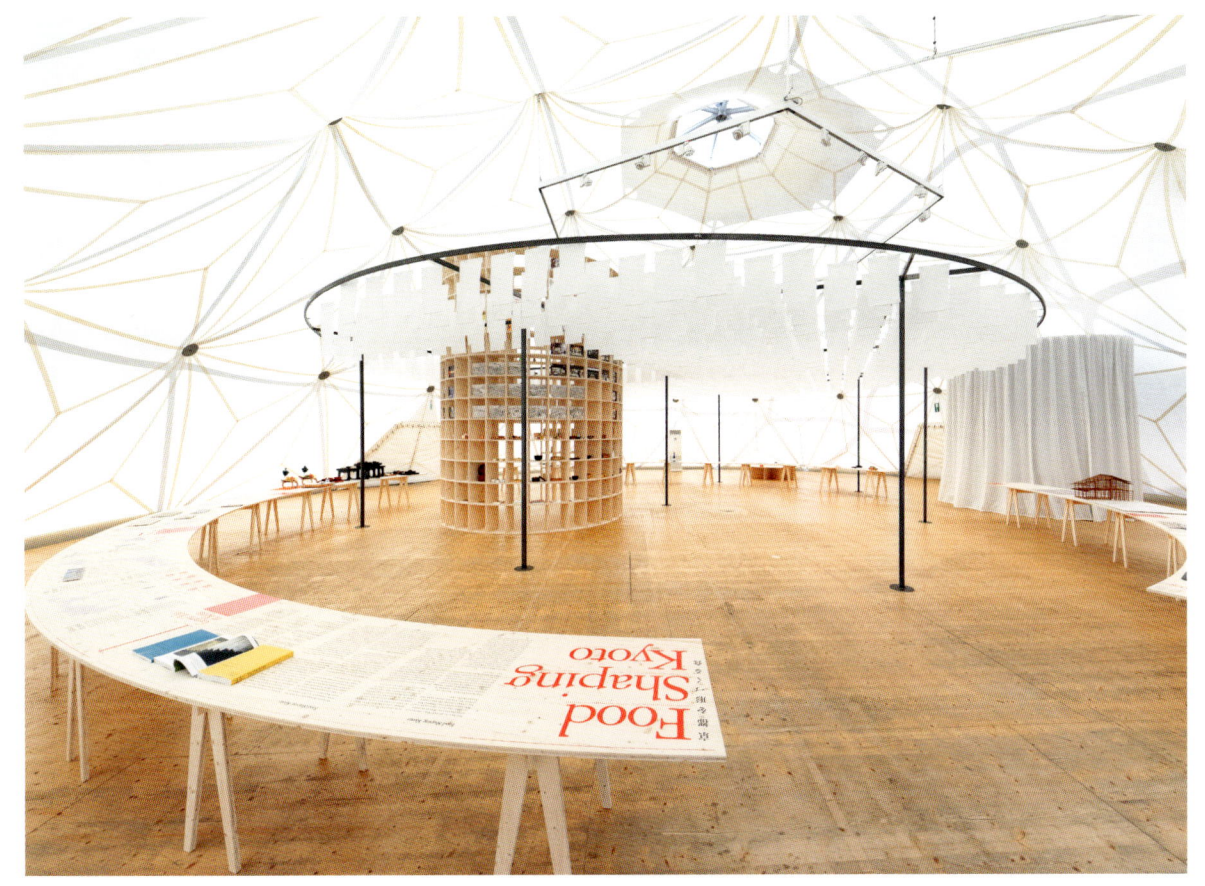

Food Shaping Kyoto

[Exhibition Design]

"Food Shaping Kyoto" documents how the city has been shaped by its culture by visualising it as "food ecosystems". The exhibition showcases the relationship between the city and food through six key words – including water, markets, distribution, urban morphology and the local Gion Festival – that link urban structure and food culture production. This is then depicted by architectural models, food models and tools used at the local Nishiki Market, as well as by drawings, photographs and images. Also designed were tables introducing urban research, a library tower with collected objects and a chamber showing a 360-degree video of the market, which is crucial to Kyoto's food culture.

Client
Vitra Design Museum
Weil am Rhein, Germany

Design
Rahbaran Hürzeler Architects
Basel, Switzerland
Manuel Herz Architects
Basel, Switzerland
KYOTO Design Lab,
Kyoto Institute of Technology
Kyoto, Japan

Project Team
Manuel Herz Architects:
Manuel Herz, Penny Alevizou

Rahbaran Hürzeler Architects:
Shadi Rahbaran, Marcel Wagner

KYOTO Design Lab,
Kyoto Institute of Technology:
Yoshiro Ono, Eizo Okada,
Takayuki Ikegawa, Takuya Miyake

Singapore University of
Technology and Design:
Erwin Viray

Kyoto Institute of Technology:
Kazuhiro Ogata, Kento Yokose,
Heeye Kim, Tomonobu Miyakawa,
Meng Sun, Ryota Manki,
Takashi Hiramoto, Riku Kasai,
Takuya Tsunashima

Harmony between Human and Natural Environment

[Exhibition Design]

The exhibition "Harmony between human and natural environment" addresses the cultural heritage Cordilleras region on the Philippine island of Luzon. By creating a space inspired by the culture of the Ipugao people, who have defined that region, the exhibition provides a place of experience to appreciate their values and diversity. As the Cordilleras rice field terraces have become the emblem of the Ipugao, a symbolic language called "stairs" was created for the exhibition design. The space is structured like the form of the Cordilleras terraces, and the route through the exhibition is subdivided into several thematic sections.

Client
Asia Culture Center/
Asia Culture Institute
Gwangju, South Korea

Design
Asia Culture Institute
Gwangju, South Korea
Joosung Design Lab
Seoul, South Korea

Complete Refurbishment and Redesign of the Deutsches Bergbau-Museum Bochum

[Exhibition Design]

The complete renovation and redesign of the permanent exhibition of the German Mining Museum in Bochum, Germany, presents four thematic tours that connect the general history of mining with that of the Ruhr region. The tours "Hard Coal", "Mining", "Mineral Resources" and "Art and Culture" each have their individual dramaturgy, scenography and specially developed colour coding. The 8,000 sqm of exhibition space combines traditional museum design with a contemporary take on interactive communication.

Client
DMT – Gesellschaft für Lehre und Bildung mbH
Bochum, Germany

Design
krafthaus – Das Atelier von facts and fiction
Cologne, Germany
res d Design und Architektur GmbH
Cologne, Germany

Project Team
Marcus Becker
(Overall Project Management)
Ingo Plato (Project Management Architecture/Concept)
Hendrik Pletz (Concept)
Rebecca Schröder
(Deputy Project Management Design)

Markus Junker (Architecture)
Marléne Gardeweg (Architecture)
Delia Winter (Architecture)
Alexander Hesse (Interior Design)
Katja Petri (Architecture)

Anna Gemmeke (Art Direction)
Katrin Schubert (Art Direction)
Miriam Cremer (Graphic Design)
Philipp Rose (Graphic Design)
Wibke Brode (Graphic Design)
Carina Matzky (Graphic Design)
Agnes Weegen (Graphic Design)
Ribanna Clemens (Graphic Design)

Simin Kianmehr (Photography)

Z Innovation Lab 2019

[Event Design]

Client
Zuni Icosahedron
Hong Kong

Design
Zuni Icosahedron
Hong Kong

Project Team
Zuni Icosahedron:
Mathias Woo (Artistic Director)

Wing Kei Flower Store
(Flower Plaque Production)

→ Clip online

The Z Innovation Lab, held in Hong Kong in 2019, was dedicated to integrating the latest stage technology and innovative ideas in the live arts. Therefore, a giant bamboo "Flower Plaque" installation measuring seventeen by five metres was erected in the Hong Kong Cultural Centre to celebrate its 30th anniversary. The design concept visualises the tradition with an LED display fan showing holograms, light painting and a light web knitted by LED bulbs. The idea was to address, with a touch of technology, the celebratory mood represented by red fabrics, tungsten light bulbs and a traditional peacock positioned on top.

Publishing & Print Media	Posters	Typography	Illustrations	Sound Design	Film & Animation	Online
4	64	92	116	126	138	172

Empire State Building Observatory

[Exhibition Design]

Client
ESRT Observatory TRS, LLC
New York, USA

Design
Thinc Design
New York, USA

Project Team
Thinc Design (Experience Designer)
Beneville Studios, IDEO
(Design Consultants)
JLL (Owner's Representative)
Squint/Opera (Media Designer)
Corgan (Architect)
The Lighting Practice
(Lighting Consultant)
Skanska (Construction Manager)
Intersection (Technology Integrator)
Maltbie (Exhibit Fabricator)
Diversified (Hardware Integrator)
Thorton Tomasetti (Structural Engineer)
Syska Hennessy Group (MEP Engineer)

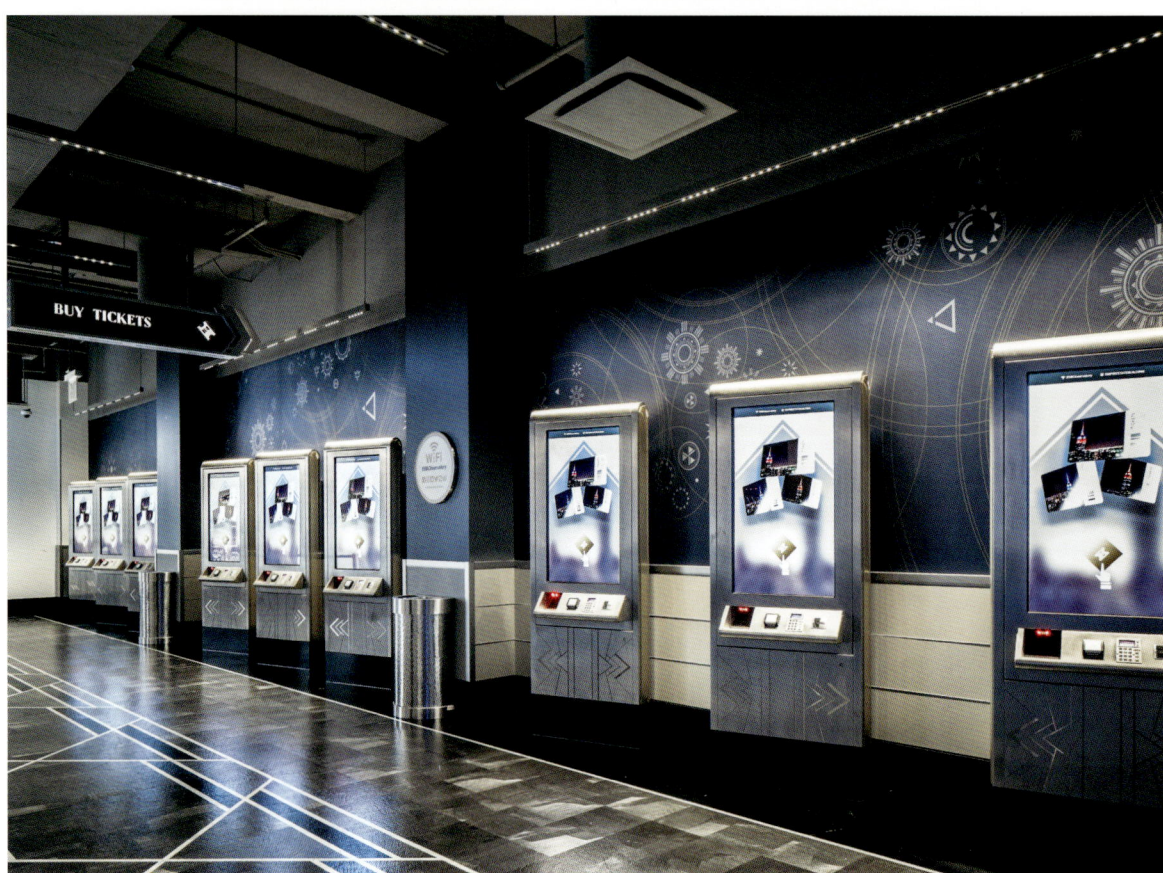

Apps	Interface & User Experience Design	**Spatial Communication**	Red Dot: Junior Award	Designer Profiles	Jury Portraits	Index
206	236	336	426	564	642	668

The redesign and modernisation of the Empire State Building observatories in New York, USA, have added a dedicated visitor entrance with the objective of changing how over four million annual visitors experience the building, while also reducing wait times and adding fascinating impressions. A spectacular, two-story model of the building marks the start of an exciting "journey". Galleries immerse guests in the building's history and mystique through cinematic quality films, immersive environments, interactive screens, models, photographs and authentic artefacts. With a new observatory level on the 80th floor, the viewing area has more than doubled.

Publishing & Print Media	Posters	Typography	Illustrations	Sound Design	Film & Animation	Online
4	64	92	116	126	138	172

Maximilian Schell

[Exhibition Design]

This exhibition presents the actor Maximilian Schell as an artist and Renaissance man. With its panoramic view, the stylised log cabin on the Schell mountain estate in Preitenegg, Austria, forms the pivotal point in the exhibition's central axis. Thanks to a 360-degree photo shown on seven monitors, the hut acts as a juxtaposition to the glamour of Schell's Hollywood career, symbolised by the Oscar he won for "Judgment at Nuremberg". The exhibition is structured using the stylistic device of collage, as it also defines the life and film work of Schell himself.

Client
DFF – Deutsches Filminstitut &
Filmmuseum e.V.
Frankfurt/Main, Germany

Design
mind the gap! design
Karl-Heinz Best
Frankfurt/Main, Germany
Supportarchitekten
Meike Schermelleh
Heusenstamm, Germany

Museum of Literature Ireland

[Exhibition Design]

The new Museum of Literature Ireland (MoLI) in Dublin celebrates the country's storied tradition, providing an overview of Irish language and literature, while exploring how such a small island has produced so many literary giants. As the main challenge was to create an engaging visitor experience out of the written word, the exhibition design displays MoLI's collection dynamically alongside media installations that bring the sights and sounds of Irish literature to life – from windswept hills and oral traditions to Dublin's "dirty" streets and contemporary slang.

Client
National Library of Ireland/
University College Dublin
UCD Naughton Joyce Centre
Dublin, Ireland

Design
Ralph Appelbaum Associates
London, United Kingdom

Sunhyangjeong

[Event Design]

The Sunhyangjeong (Bell Pavilion of Echoing Virtue) was designed to echo a sound of peace and prosperity in Asia at the ASEAN–Republic of Korea Commemorative Summit 2019 in Busan, South Korea. Its overall shape and meaning follow that of traditional Korean bells, although reinterpreted in a modern context applying 5G and AI technology. The pavilion was also designed to empathise with pan-Asian orientalism beyond Korean characteristics. The landscape of oriental painting is linked with the bell and welcomed the target group of Asian leaders with a serene but magnificent echoing sound.

Client
SK Telecom
Seoul, South Korea

Design
GBO
Seoul, South Korea

Project Team
Kwangjin Woo (Designer)
Jaegyun Seo (Designer)
Changhwan Noh (Designer)
H.W. Nam (Designer)

Multiverse

[Public Installation]

Multiverse is an audiovisual installation which explores the evolution of infinite possible universes. Used here are generative graphics and sounds that exploit the theorisation of the existence of the so-called multiverse, that is, a system composed of an infinite number of universes that coexist in parallel outside of our space-time continuum. Through the creation of a succession of digital paintings generated in real time, the installation attempts to represent the eternal birth and death of infinite parallel universes. No single scene repeats in the same form.

Client
BDC – Bonanni Del Rio Catalog
Parma, Italy

Design
fuse*
Campogalliano (Modena), Italy

Project Team
fuse*:
Mattia Carretti (Art Direction)
Luca Camellini (Art Direction)
Samuel Pietri (Programming)
Riccardo Bazzoni (Music/Sound Design)

Daniele Iandolo (Manufacturer), Fiera S.r.l.

→ Clip online

Space Duality

[Virtual Reality Installation]

Space Duality as part of the USM Design Grant was set up as a semester project in the Department of Interior Architecture at HEAD – Genève, Geneva University of Art and Design, in Switzerland. Twelve students developed seven immersive projects that offered a novel and emotional experience related to space. Entering the various VR projects, which were placed inside or on top of specially built pieces of furniture, transfers the viewer into an unseen environment full of surprises. While some of the projects have an "enchanted" charm about them, others challenge one to redefine what "interior spaces" are in general.

Client
Fondation USM
Gümlingen, Switzerland

Design
HEAD – Genève,
Department of Interior Architecture
Geneva, Switzerland

Project Team
Simon Husslein (Studio Tutor)
Lara Grandchamp (Studio Assistant)
Javier Fernandez-Contreras
(Head of Department)
Valentina De Luigi (Scientific Deputy)
Mélissa Ferrara (Student)
Brian Grenier (Student)
Kanya-On Khurewathanakul (Student)
Julia Miclos Moura (Student)
Hyeryeon Nam (Student)
Johanna Picard (Student)
Rébecca Sanmartin (Student)
Caroline Savary (Student)
Sonia Schwerdtel (Student)
Ophélie Surchat (Student)
Lydia Campana (Student)
Aurélie Chêne (Student)

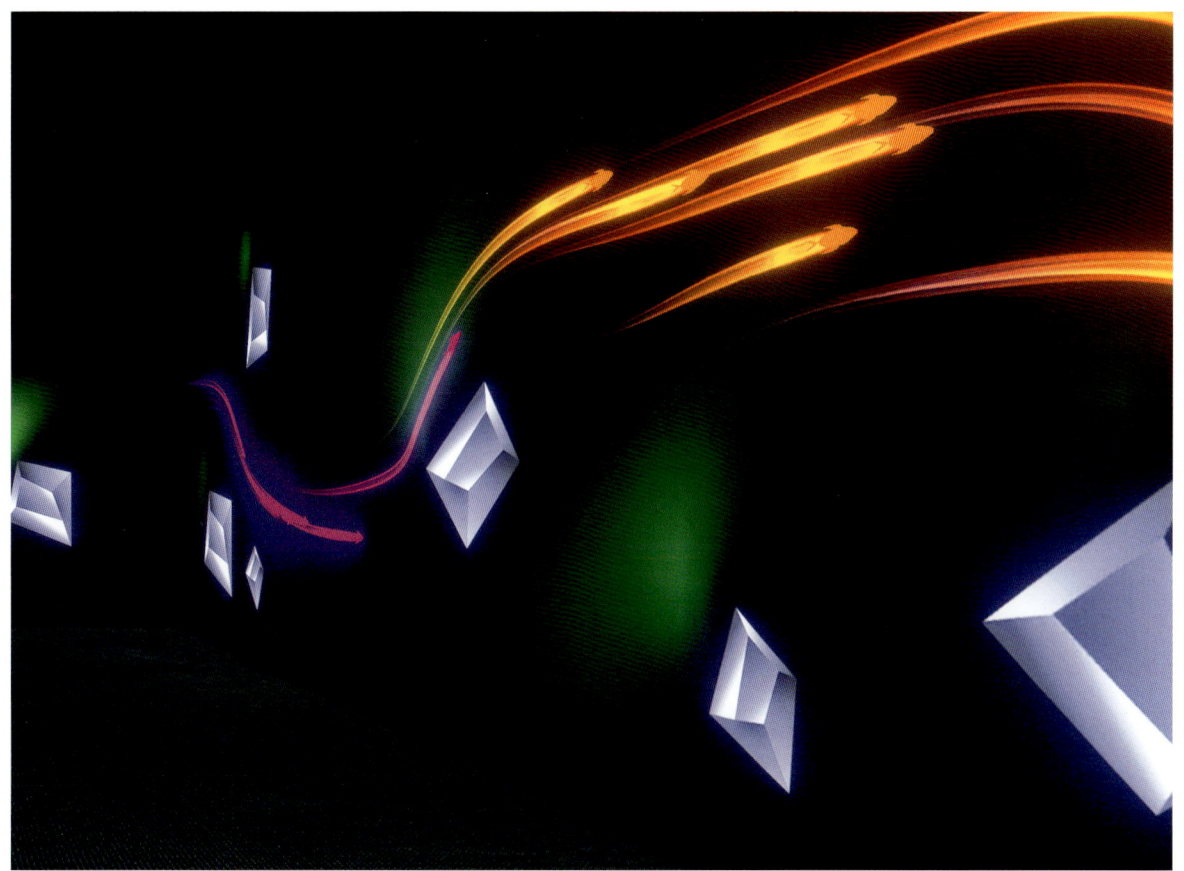

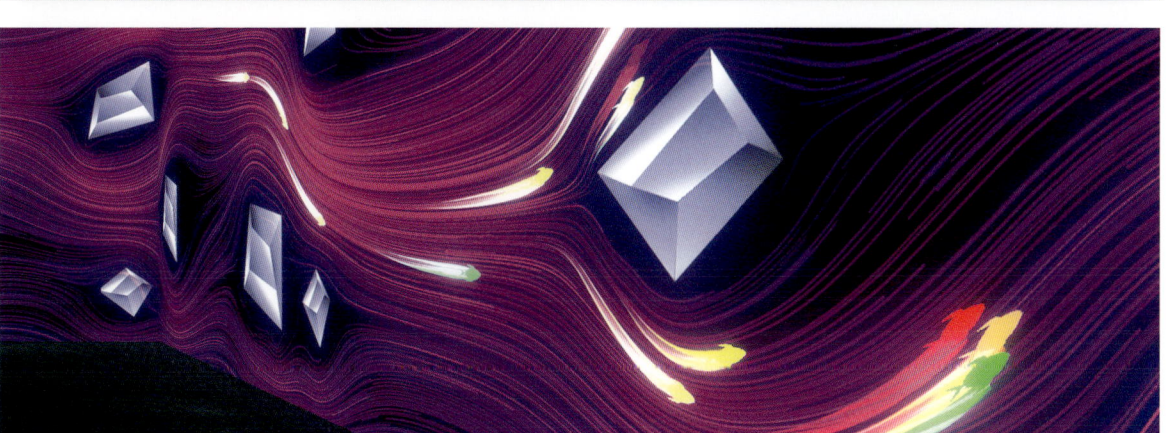

FLUIDS

[Interactive Installation, Exhibition Design]

This interactive installation was exhibited in the Chinese cities of Daqing, Qingdao, Xian and Xingtai in 2019. Its design aimed at piquing curiosity and inviting people to explore and contemplate mankind, life and nature in their interrelationship by offering a poetic and philosophical sensory experience. An immersive feeling of being lost and reborn was evoked, converging into a powerful stream of consciousness. When people interacted with the installation, sensors recognised and judged the position touched and fed it back to the computer for data processing.

Client
Gooest Media Technology Daqing Co., Ltd.
Daqing, China

Design
Gooest Media Technology Daqing Co., Ltd.
Daqing, China

→ Designer profile on page 589
→ Clip online

Publishing & Print Media	Posters	Typography	Illustrations	Sound Design	Film & Animation	Online
4	64	92	116	126	138	172

Sniffing out the Differences

[Installation Design]

Client
Prince Claus Fund
Amsterdam, Netherlands
British Council
London, United Kingdom

Design
Sniffing out the Differences
Hyderabad, India

→ Designer profile on page 622
→ Clip online

"Sniffing out the Differences" is a series of interactive installations. It explores tales and olfactory associations in South Asian cultures from the past, present, and future. The series illustrates how identities and cultures emerge with mobility, and new distinct patterns get formed. The series is a dialogue between our multiple identities in today's globalised world, with the identities articulated in smell and pattern visualisations. Furthermore, it questions the issue of xenophobia and biases, all with the help of smell. The goal is to invite the audience to make sense of culture by experiencing and interacting with it through its distinct smells.

25 Years of Nexon Online Game

[Exhibition Design]

Client
Nexon Computer Museum
Jeju, South Korea

Design
does interactive
Seoul, South Korea

Project Team
Sang Jun Lee (Creative Direction)
Seung Yong Kang (Project Management)
Seul Ki Jang (Strategic Planning)
Seong Hwan Kim (Strategic Planning)
Victor Manselon (Technical Direction)
Valentin Vannay (Programming)

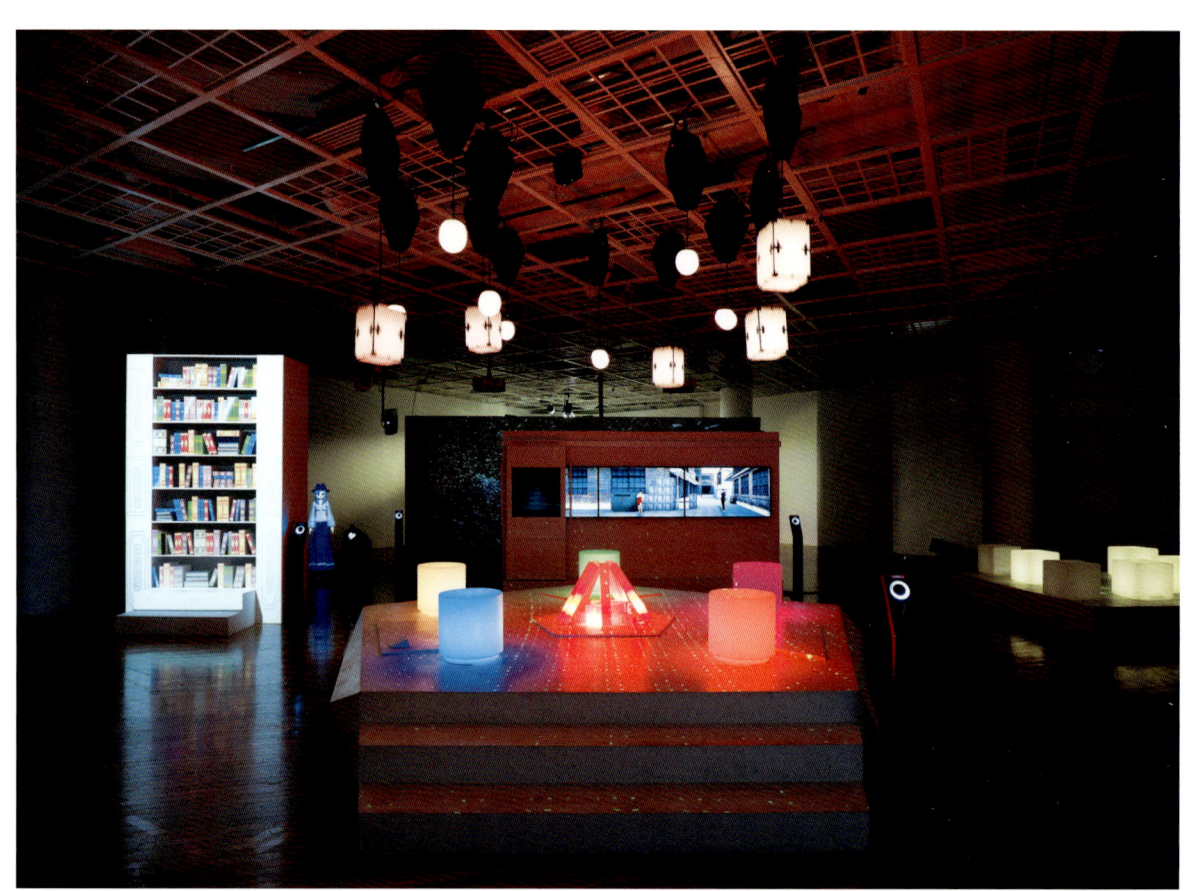

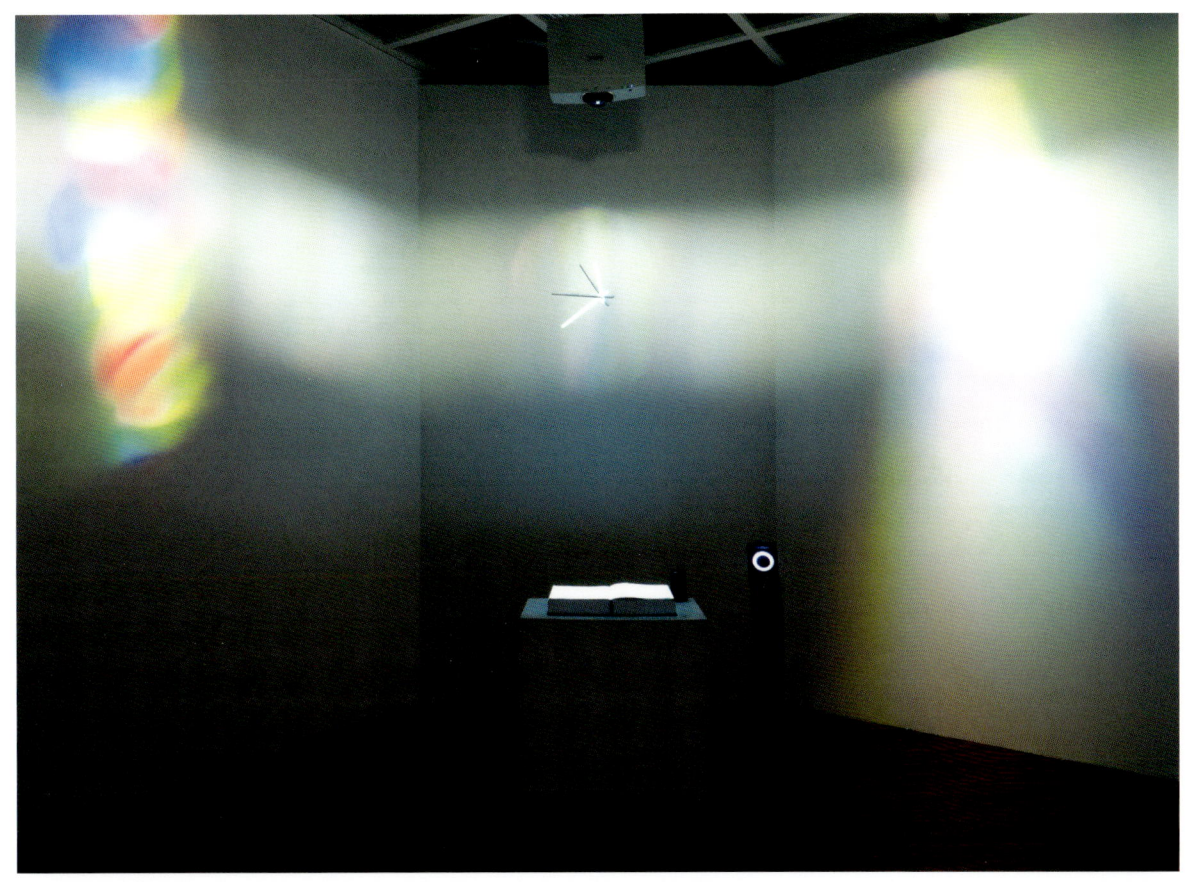

Celebrating the 25th anniversary of Nexon online games in Korea, this fusion exhibition shows the games' past, present and future. It offers a new interpretation of online games by artistically visualising technology. The concept of space is derived from the meaning of the slash (/) symbol, as used in chat window commands, one of the main features of online games. The exhibition is structured around the element of "interaction", characteristic of video games, and thus invites users to experience the show as if actually playing a video game. Inside the exhibition space, visitors can enjoy the content installed on both sides of walls shaped like slashes. A look from the entrance into the exhibition hall reveals eleven exhibits that are virtual reproductions of online games.

Publishing & Print Media	Posters	Typography	Illustrations	Sound Design	Film & Animation	Online
4	64	92	116	126	138	172

RE: ECM

[Exhibition Design]

With "Feel the reverberation of sound" as its motto, this exhibition was conceived as a platform inspired by a table-tennis table. It invited visitors to sit face to face, with a thin cloth between them. Alternating lights illuminated the audience whenever the music changed. The audience had the option of participating as quiet listeners or as actors on stage in the light. They could experience continuous sound, either by listening to music while staying in the space or by creating an imaginary conversation between musicians inside the specific space. Thus, visitors could gain a new artistic experience through the act of creation.

Client
Storage by Hyundai Card
Seoul, South Korea

Design
1990 UAO
Seoul, South Korea
Joosung Design Lab
Seoul, South Korea

Resonance

[Exhibition Design]

The design of the "Resonance by Samsung" exhibition for Milan Design Week 2019 aimed at questioning conventional on-screen technology interactions. The traditional on-screen content experience was replaced with an interplay of lights, forms, shapes and movement that continually changed in response to the visitors. In this part of the experience, breath, sound and touch became the key to unlocking a mesmerising world of possibilities. The surrounding world transformed as people interacted with the installation, evoking a flow of emotions with a bold resonance in their hearts and minds.

Client
Samsung Design Corporate Center
Seoul, South Korea

Design
Cheil Worldwide
Seoul, South Korea
VAVE
Offenbach/Main, Germany

Project Team
Cheil Worldwide:
Jaesan Kim (Head of
Brand Experience Business)
Simon Hong (Executive Creative Director)
Jihoo Kim (Design Director)
Insoo Song (Designer)
Subin Seol (Designer)

VAVE:
Tobias Geisler (Creative Director)
Whan Lee (Senior Designer)
Matthias Sütterlin (Senior Designer)

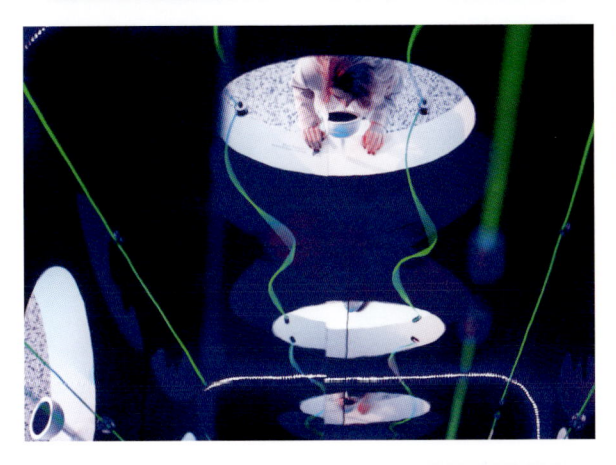

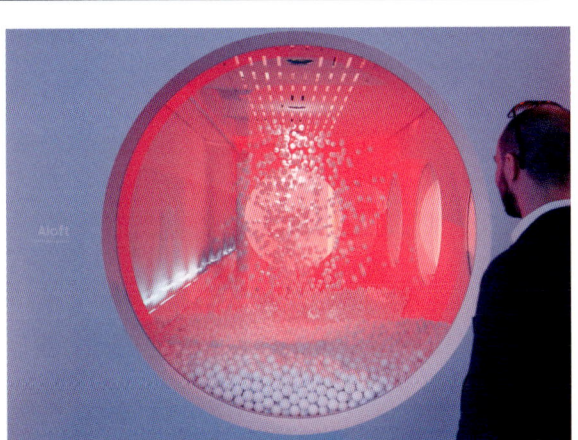

Publishing & Print Media	Posters	Typography	Illustrations	Sound Design	Film & Animation	Online
4	64	92	116	126	138	172

Nemus Futurum
[Interactive Experience Design]

The interactive Nemus Futurum visitor experience showcases Finnish forest management by using cutting-edge technology directly on site. Guided through all significant stages of an 80-year forest cycle, visitors can experience how sustainable forest management has an effect on the climate and forest biodiversity. At the beginning of the tour, visitors are provided with a tablet featuring a bespoke app that helps to contextualise the environment and to support the narration of the tour guides. The app applies various methods, such as GPS tracking and augmented reality.

Client
Metsä Group
Espoo, Finland

Design
Great Apes/HiQ Finland
Helsinki, Finland
MKTG Finland
Helsinki, Finland

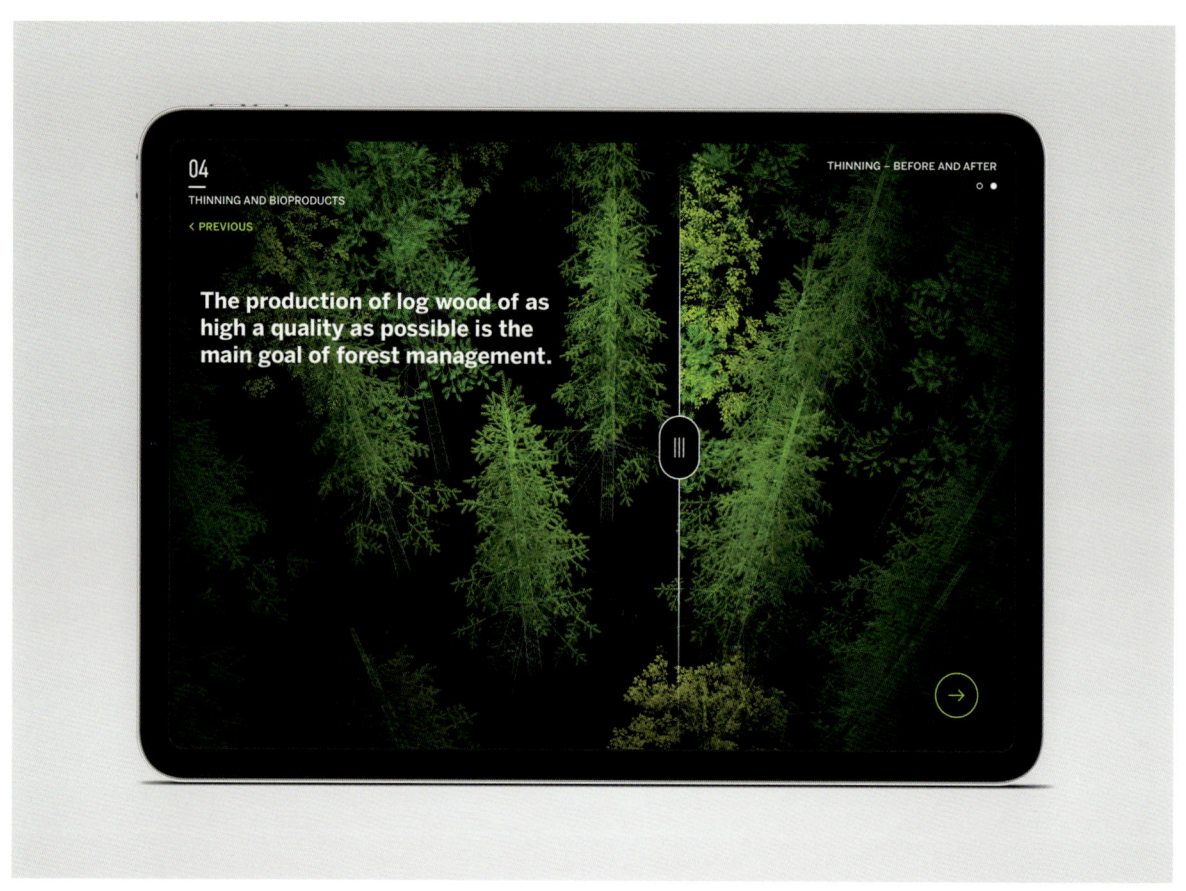

Apps	Interface & User Experience Design	Spatial Communication	Red Dot: Junior Award	Designer Profiles	Jury Portraits	Index
206	236	336	426	564	642	668

Welcome to Samsung Town

[Spatial Communication, Exhibition Design]

During the IFA 2019 in Berlin, "Welcome to Samsung Town" attracted the attention of visitors with its exhibition design featuring various digital interactive experiences. Visitors were invited to cross the bridge in the middle of the exhibition hall and view the entire Samsung Town with the "AR Observatory", which provided the products' location and information through augmented reality. At Samsung Town Square, visitors could also become citizens of the town. A corresponding app allowed them to take selfies and create their own avatars, which were transmitted in real time to Samsung Town for display on a huge interactive media wall.

Client
Samsung Electronics Co., Ltd.
Global Marketing Center
Suwon, South Korea

Design
Cheil Worldwide
Seoul, South Korea

Sony Design Exhibition Milan Design Week 2019 – Affinity in Autonomy

[Exhibition Design]

"Affinity in Autonomy", an interactive exhibition at Milan Design Week 2019, exhibited Sony's vision of a new relationship with robotics. It communicates the belief that the relationship between humans and technology will evolve through the deepening of our understanding of artificial intelligence and its ability to display feelings. Composed of five interactions, visitors could experience step by step the awakening and the growth of the relations between robotics and humans. This relationship is also expressed through the gradual increase in colour as the journey progresses.

Client
Sony Corporation
Tokyo, Japan

Design
Sony Design
Tokyo, Japan

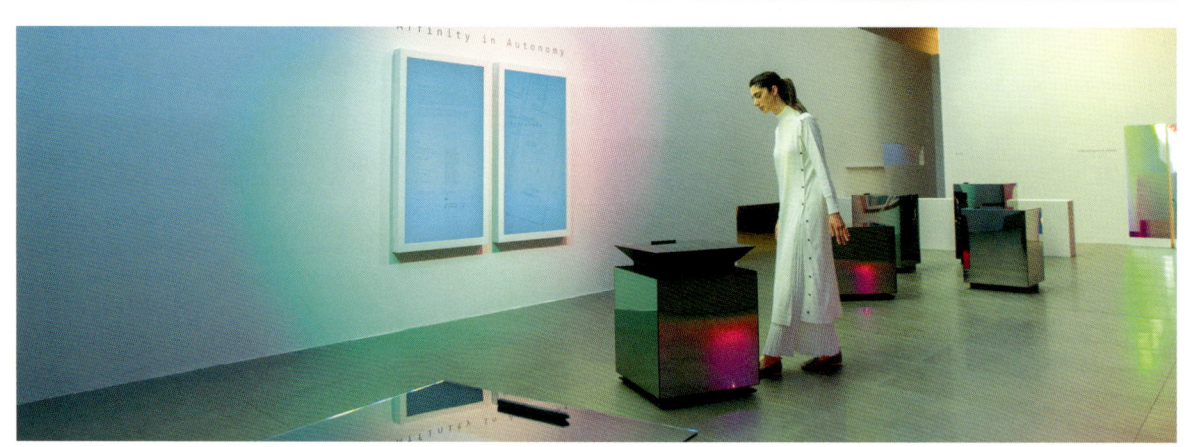

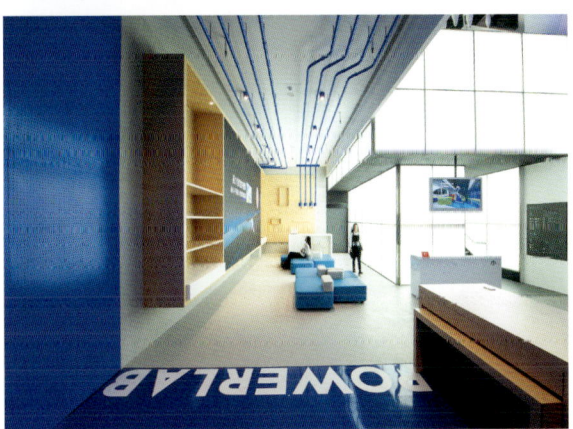

TAIPOWER D/S ONE

[Spatial Design]

The design of the TAIPOWER D/S ONE public facility experience centre visualises the statements of "electricity" as the core, "current" as the operation, and "electrical energy" as the significance of influence. The symbol of lightning is presented in simplified straight lines and fillets that communicate the message of energy savings. This has been interpreted by the "exclamation mark" and "slash" signs as key elements of the visual design. The aim was to turn the concept, knowledge and aesthetics of "intangible power" into a new place easily accessible by the public.

Client
Taiwan Power Company
Taipei City, Taiwan

Design
Cogitoimage International Co., Ltd.
Taipei City, Taiwan

Project Team
David Y.M. Liu (Producer)
Tony C.L. Tsai (Creative Director)
Bungawaty Kosasih (Art Director)

Publishing & Print Media	Posters	Typography	Illustrations	Sound Design	Film & Animation	Online
4	64	92	116	126	138	172

stories/spaces

[Public Installation, Exhibition Design]

Client
1zu33 Architectural Brand Identity
Munich, Germany

Design
1zu33 Architectural Brand Identity
Munich, Germany
OFF OFFICE
Munich, Germany

Project Team
1zu33:
Hendrik Müller (Art Direction)
Georg Thiersch (Art Direction)
Christine Neulinger (Exhibition Design)
Christian Sedlmeier (Exhibition Design)
Elena Schadt (Exhibition Design)
Vianney Lebrun (Exhibition Design)
Stella Funk (Exhibition Design)
Cornelia Laule (Exhibition Design)
Franziska Baldszun (Exhibition Design)
Frederike Mueller (Exhibition Design)
Jana Thiemann (Exhibition Design)

OFF OFFICE:
Markus Lingemann (Art Direction)
Johannes von Gross (Art Direction)
Roman Zimmermanns (Graphic Design)
Oliver Schwamkrug (Music/
Sound Design)
Rupert Maurer (Film Editing)
Melih Bilgil (Film Editing)

Manfred Jarisch (Photography),
Myrzik & Jarisch
Gina Bolle (Photography)

Klaus Schurig (Technical Direction),
Schurig GmbH
Stefan Angenendt (Exhibition
Construction), Winkels Interior
Martin Singer (Media Technology),
Neumann&Müller

The 10th anniversary of the architectural brand agency 1zu33 was celebrated with an experiential exhibition at the AIT-ArchitekturSalon in Munich, Germany. The installation "stories/spaces" unveiled the creative processes behind the agency's work in spatial brand communication. Enveloped by changing light and sound, four double-sided screens were utilised to show the duality between process and result. While sketches and references from the design process were shown on the outer walls, the details of the final project were screened in the inner sanctum. Visitors were invited to leisurely meander between the panels.

OSOL

[Public Installation]

Client
Hwaseong City Government
Hwaseong, South Korea
Gyeonggi Cultural Foundation
Gyeonggi Province, South Korea

Design
SOAP Design Studio
Seoul, South Korea

Project Team
Soonyup Kwon (Architect)
Eungyung Shin (Architect)
Dongsun Chang (Project Management)

Myungho Kang (Photography), PACE
Suman Chun (Film Production), PACE

Youngjune Choi (Construction), ZIUM

OSOL is a permanent art pavilion installed at Gungpyung Pine Habitat (GPH) on the west coast of South Korea. Over 1,000 pine trees have been standing along the tidal beach for 100 years. This beautiful scenery was unveiled to the public after the military wire fences, which had been erected during the Cold War era with North Korea, were torn down. The pavilion aims to lure visitors to the beach by offering shelter from the strong sea wind and the sun. Inspired by the view of the pine forest and light reflections on the sea, the forest-like structure of the pavilion with its anodised aluminium reflects the surrounding colours. The view of the ocean and the pine forest through the pavilion allows visitors to experience the new perspective and harmony of nature.

Snail Garden – Peak-nic
[Outdoor Amusement Facility]

The challenge in designing the Snail Garden outdoor amusement facility located on the top of a hill was that the surroundings of the place were not child-friendly. The project proposes a new form of urban playground that is suitable for the hills and valleys of Busan, South Korea. The subtitle "Peak-nic" (Peak + picnic) denotes a picnic in the mountains. The snail series was inspired by origami and designed with a functional purpose. The six different sculpture-like items are suitable for both children and families, functioning as playground slides, climbing structures, exiting holes or benches.

Client
Daewon Plus Group
Busan, South Korea

Design
EMOTIONplanning
Busan, South Korea
Daewon Plus Group
Busan, South Korea

Project Team
EMOTIONplanning:
Heewon Kim (Creative Direction)
Hyunsu Kim (Graphic Design)
Kyunghyun Kim (Graphic Design)

Daewon Plus Group:
Hyoseob Choi (Creative Direction)
Julia Jung (Text)

Wheels of Life

[Public Installation]

Designed for the opening of Alva Hotel by Royal in Hong Kong, the primary purpose of this art installation has been to promote the importance of upcycling. It is composed of 88 used bicycle wheels collected from the local community. All wheels were set in grid within an oval plan, supported by steel pipes of various heights and rotated at different angles. This resulted in a colourful, leaf-like surface floating with lightness and harmonising with the surrounding greenery. LED tubes installed on the wheels turn the whole installation into an eye-catching sculpture at night.

Client
Alva Hotel by Royal
Hong Kong

Design
O Studio Architects
Hong Kong
Echo Asia Communications
Hong Kong

Project Team
Fai Au (Head of Design)
Samson Tong (Campaign Creative)
Daisy Lee (Concept)

→ Clip online

Publishing & Print Media	Posters	Typography	Illustrations	Sound Design	Film & Animation	Online
4	64	92	116	126	138	172

Liuku
[Urban Installation]

The Fair Centre of Finland, Messukeskus, celebrated its 100th anniversary with a public and interactive art installation. The design met the challenge of "getting people together", which is the unique selling point of the Expo Centre. The installation consists of an adventure space in the shape of a capital M, measuring 7 metres in height and 25 metres in length. Made of sustainable wood and offering dynamic lighting, the interior contains stairs that double as seats and a long slide which pays homage to the slide remembered from the first fair a century ago. The structure is permanent and has been designed to comply with strict child safety regulations.

Client
The Fair Centre of Finland
Helsinki, Finland

Design
Berry Creative
Helsinki, Finland

Project Team
Timo Berry (Creative Direction)
Kaisa Berry (Creative Direction)
Maija Gulin (Design)
Johannes Neumeier (Design)
Riku Sourama (Lighting Design)

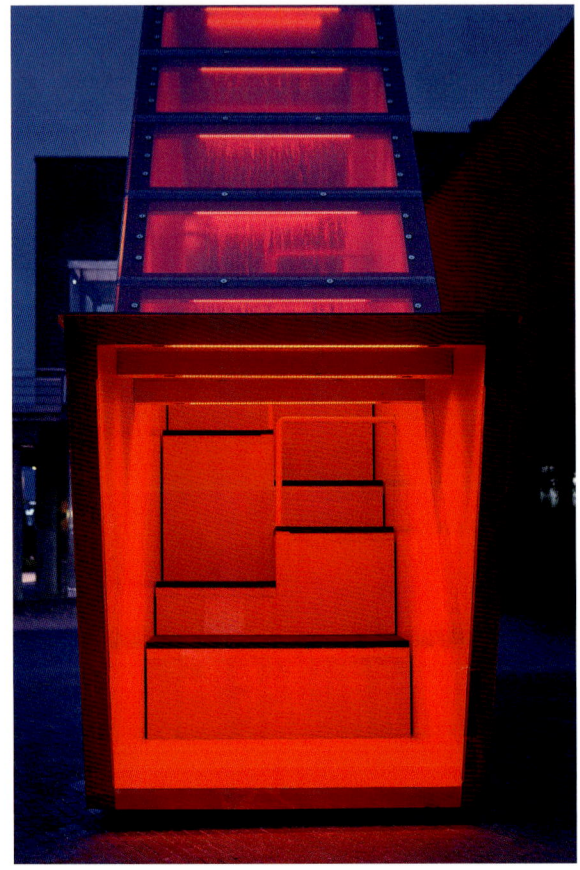

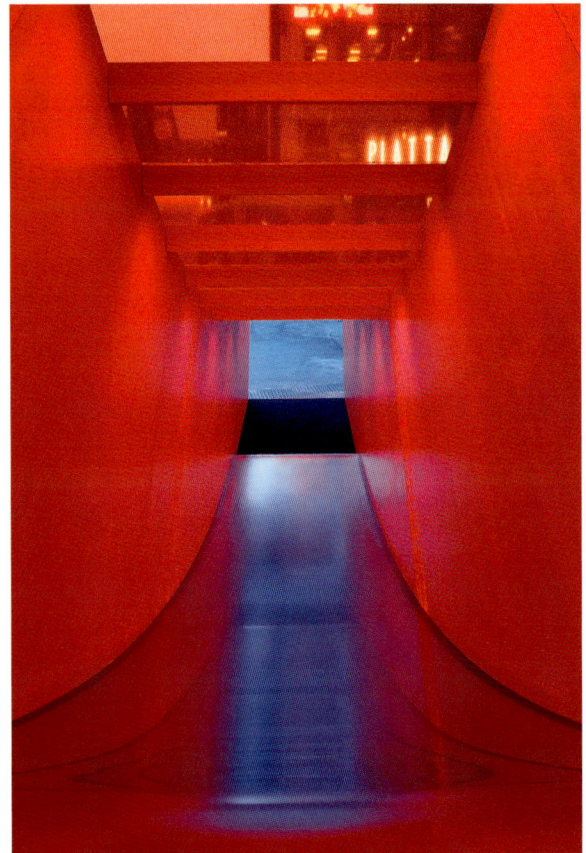

VW Fair Stand IAA 2019 – Enter Vibrant Power
[Event Design]

This trade-fair design for Volkswagen celebrated the company's system change, new products, technologies and genuine world premieres at the IAA 2019 in Frankfurt, Germany. With the core topics of vibrant design and sustainability, the design language was based on clean and modular architecture systematics, as well as a bold use of light and colour. Vibrant walls with energetic gradients and colourful, animated skies created an emotional and inspiring space for experiencing the brand and the products. Framed by a white line above the vibrant space, the new logo "shined" – resembling the concept of light and clarity to convey the all-electric approach of Volkswagen.

Client
Volkswagen AG
Wolfsburg, Germany

Design
MUTABOR Brand Experience GmbH
Hamburg, Germany

Project Team
Ben Erben (Creative Direction)
Gerd Hermes (Creative Direction)
Jan Lenze (Architectural Planning)
Charlotte Valentin-Jessen
(Project Management)

Genesis G90

[Interactive Exhibition Design, Light Installation]

The interactive media project and exhibition "Complete Your Style: G90" celebrated the brand's luxury flagship sedan G90. It took place at the Genesis Studio in Hanam on the outskirts of Seoul, South Korea. Realising a barrier-free environment that allowed visitors to freely experience the design of the G90, the aim was to satisfy the needs of a diverse range of consumers. When a person stepped into the specially built zone in the centre of the studio, the surrounding walls of the zone immediately adopted the colour of that person's outfit, which was automatically recognised by a sensor.

Client
Hyundai Motor Co. (Genesis Motors)
Seoul, South Korea

Design
BLACKSPACE
Munich, Germany
DXS
Seoul, South Korea
Suh Architects
Seoul, South Korea

Genesis Mint

[Event Design]

For the exhibition of Genesis Mint, an electric concept car by the luxury offshoot of the Hyundai brand, a team of designers and architects added an interactive layer to a conventional showroom. Staged at Starfield Hanam on the outskirts of Seoul, South Korea, it invited visitors to take souvenir photographs of themselves next to the vehicle and encouraged them to simultaneously view their images on a display panel located on the back side of the studio. The project, an extension of the earlier Genesis experiment with the G90, was a playful way to bring fashion and art to a vehicle showcase.

Client
Hyundai Motor Co. (Genesis Motors)
Seoul, South Korea

Design
BLACKSPACE
Munich, Germany
PANCOMMUNICATION KOREA
Seoul, South Korea
Suh Architects
Seoul, South Korea

Winter Universiade 2019
[Event Design]

Client
ANO "Directorate Krasnoyarsk 2019"
Krasnoyarsk, Russia

Design
ArtStyle Design Group
Krasnoyarsk, Russia

The event design for the games of the 29th Winter Universiade 2019 in Krasnoyarsk, Russia, combines the principle of harsh Siberian nature with that of the "warmth of human hearts". The graphics symbolise both movement in sports and the dynamic elements of Siberian nature, such as wind, ice and the powerful Yenisey river. The goal was a unique experience encompassing identity, the mascot U-Laika, uniforms, small architectural forms, the Universiade cauldron, torch and awarding ceremonies, all imbued by attributes that had been developed as part of the unified concept "Real Winter". The medals were made of innovative aluminium alloy with precious metals in combination with Swarovski crystals.

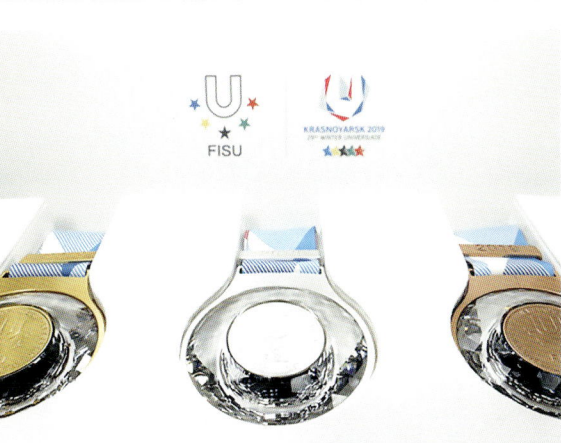

FIFA World Football Museum

[Spatial Design, Event Design]

This spatial communication staged special moments of the FIFA Women's World Cup France 2019. In dedication to female football players and fans all over the world, Hyundai built a temporary museum titled "True Passion Inspires" at the heart of Paris and opened it for free during the tournament to honour women's football and to showcase Hyundai's brand philosophy of innovation and sustainability. The focus was on the maxim of sustainability, as this temporary structure does not do any environmental harm and yet still embraces creativity.

Client
Hyundai Motor Company
Seoul, South Korea

Design
Hyundai Motor Company, Creative Works
Seoul, South Korea

Project Team
Sungwon Jee (Creative Director)
Young Jang (Design Manager)
Sungwhan Kim (Scenographer)
Sukgyu Choi (Graphic Designer)
Seohee Park (Graphic Designer)

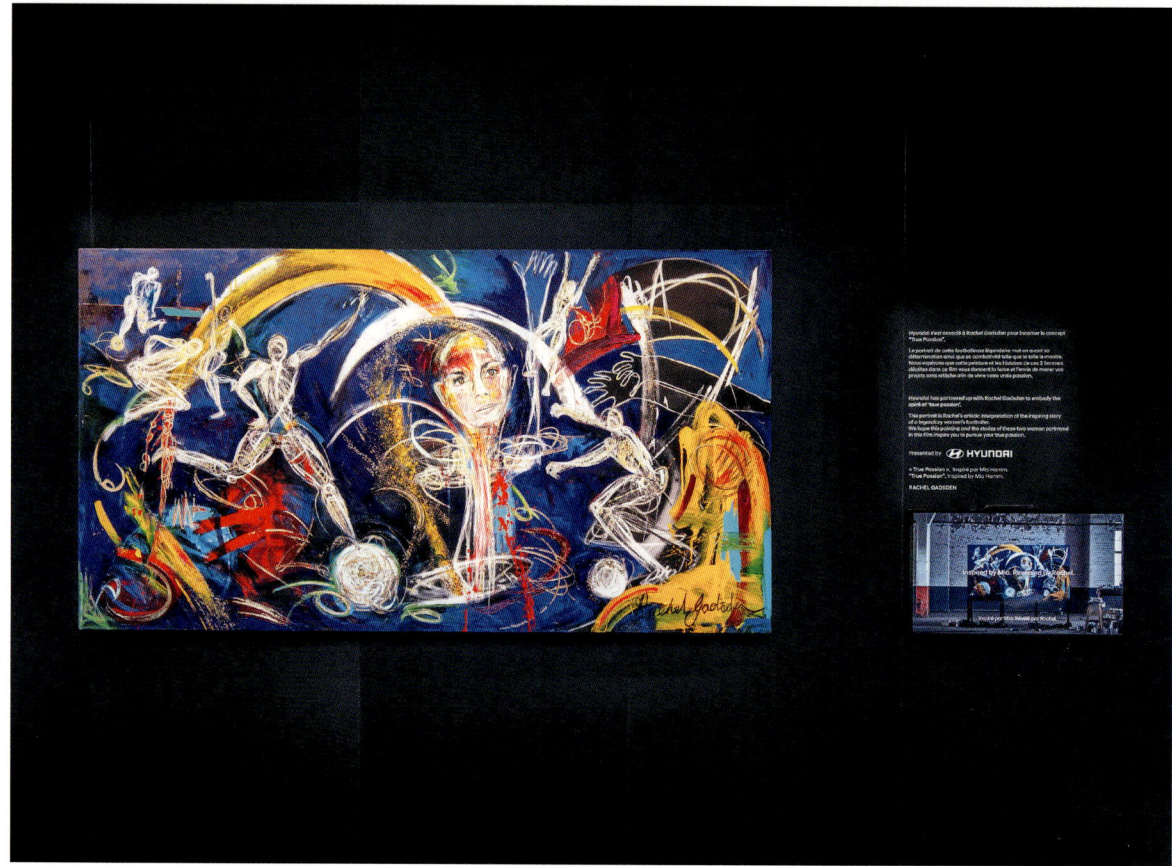

Samsung Galaxy Z Flip & Galaxy S20 Unpacked

[Event Design]

The Samsung Galaxy Z Flip and S20 series were announced in February 2020 during Galaxy Unpacked, held at the Palace of Fine Arts, San Francisco. As the event particularly stood for a new paradigm shift of innovation, it started with the naming of the product. The goal was to deliver a bold and playful visual to emphasise the high-quality smartphone using 11 screens in all. In contrast to previous events in that series, a total of three products and their features were presented during the event.

Client
Samsung Electronics Co., Ltd.
Suwon, South Korea

Design
Cheil Worldwide
Seoul, South Korea
Designfever
Seoul, South Korea

Project Team
Cheil Worldwide:
Jonghee Yoo (Creative Direction)
Sohyun Lee (Creative Direction)
Yeonji Jeon (Account Management)

Designfever:
Jooheon Oh (Art Direction)
Suchun Park (Project Management)
Minsu Lee (Strategic Planning)
Taeyeon Kim (Motion Graphic Design)
Dayun Yun (Design)

Beethoven Tour Bonn and Rhein-Sieg-Kreis

[Orientation System]

For the 250th anniversary of the birth of Ludwig van Beethoven, installations served to invite viewers to discover Beethoven's life stations in the city of Bonn and in the Rhine-Sieg region of Germany. To achieve this, a Beethoven tour was developed comprising digital and analogue information elements. Based on its own word mark, the tour appears as "BTHVN Story" and "BTHVN Region". Information pillars now mark places where Ludwig van Beethoven worked and places that influenced him. The word mark "BTHVN 2020" was used as inspiration for the information system.

Client
Beethoven Jubiläums GmbH
Bonn, Germany

Design
Büro Müller-Rieger GmbH
Munich, Germany
P.medien GmbH
Munich, Germany
Kuhl|Frenzel GmbH & Co. KG
Osnabrück, Germany

Project Team
Büro Müller-Rieger:
Monika Müller-Rieger (Creative Direction)
Hans-Christian Täubrich (Text)

Kuhl|Frenzel:
Jörg Frenzel (Art Direction)
Max-Heinrich Müller (Graphic Design)

P.medien:
Reinhard Körting (Media Design)

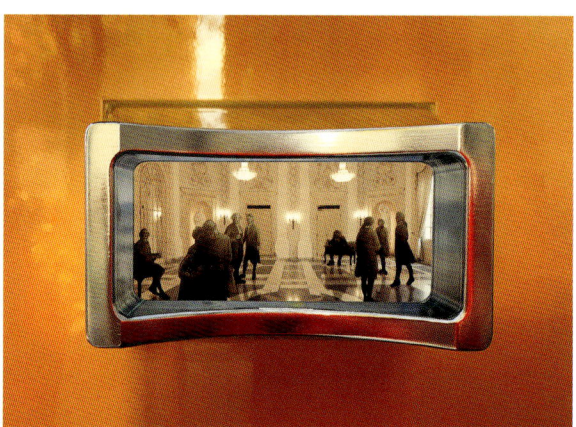

Samsung KX Spec Card

[Information Design]

The spec card was designed for Samsung KX, a retail destination at King's Cross in London, England. The concept was born of reducing the wastage of reprinting price information and having multiple systems of vertically standing versus flat placards and size requirements. The system utilises a common acrylic resin base, so information not only can be printed and adhered to the back of the acrylic; it can also be easily replaced with fresh prints and mounted. The price numbers can also be customised with "roller-deck" style modules and inserted within the routed recess of the spec card.

Client
Samsung Electronics Co., Ltd.
Seoul, South Korea

Design
Cheil Worldwide
Seoul, South Korea

Project Team
Simon Hong (Executive Creative Director)
Hee Young Lee (Product Designer)
Jason Heo (Creative Director)
Soyeon Yoo (Graphic Designer)
Seungtae Kim (Graphic Designer)

Publishing & Print Media	Posters	Typography	Illustrations	Sound Design	Film & Animation	Online
4	64	92	116	126	138	172

Kaohsiung National Stadium

[Orientation System]

Client
Kaohsiung City Government,
Sports Development Bureau
Kaohsiung, Taiwan

Design
Hand Heart Design Firm
Kaohsiung, Taiwan

Project Team
Chih-Yang Hsu
Lien-Chieh Su
I-Hui Lin
I-Chen Lee
Rou-Tzu Pan
Yi-Wen Lu
Pei-Yu Jiang
I-Chieh Chou
Chia-Chen Liu
Yan-Zhu Wang

→ Designer profile on page 592

The design orientation system for the Kaohsiung National Stadium in Taiwan is based on scientific traffic flow arrangements and wayfinding principles. The objective was to make it easily identifiable in terms of colour, image, alphabet and sequential number, from both afar and up close. The concept of a "motionless" logo was inspired and adapted to the streamlined structure of the building, while the inclusive imagery was inspired by Zen philosophy and aims at representing the building's beauty of "movement". To provide visual orientation, the design integrates the colours of the seating in the stadium. The achromatic colour concept used as a background matches the fair-faced concrete.

Puskás Arena Budapest
[Orientation System]

Client
BFK Budapest Development Center
Budapest, Hungary

Design
Graphasel Design Studio
Budapest, Hungary

Project Team
BFK Budapest Development Center:
Balázs Fürjes (Government Commissioner)

Graphasel Design Studio:
László Ördögh (Art Direction)
Dávid Drozsnyik (Art Direction)
Mátyás Beke (Wayfinding Design)
Láng Kristóf (Graphic Design)
Péter Szőke (Graphic Design)
Csaba Dobos (Graphic Design)

Attila Balázs (Photography)

→ Designer profile on page 590
→ Clip online

Puskás Arena opened to the public in November 2019 with the Hungary-Uruguay opening football game. Its visual identity and wayfinding system were developed as part of this large-scale project. A key focus of the design was to give the images and national character of the graphic elements of the navigation system impact. When designing the route, the primary consideration was to get the visitor to their seat as quickly as possible, based on the information on the ticket. To this end, it was necessary to put in place clear, articulate, easily identifiable signage and to plan several reinforcement points between the "stations".

Electric Future

[Spatial Design, Orientation System]

As part of the launch for the new brand Vitesco Technologies, various spatial touchpoints for both indoor and outdoor use were developed for Continental AG. The goal was the worldwide implementation of these touchpoints – for instance as events, trade fairs, signage systems, control systems or vehicles – in order to enhance the visibility and reputation of the brands Vitesco Technologies in the B2B sector. The colour and typography serve not only as the key elements in the guidance system; they also become important components in the industrial architecture of a new business park.

Client
Vitesco Technologies GmbH
Regensburg, Germany

Design
loved GmbH
Hamburg, Germany

Project Team
Vitesco Technologies:
Thomas Hackl (Brand Management)
Birgit Mehlhorn (Brand Management)

loved:
Maik Beimdieck
(Executive Creative Director)
Sebastian Körner (Senior Art Director)
Birte Ludwig (Senior Art Director)
Jonathan Amelung
(Client Service Director)
Carsten Eggers (Account Director)
Frauke Stürmer
(Senior Account Manager)

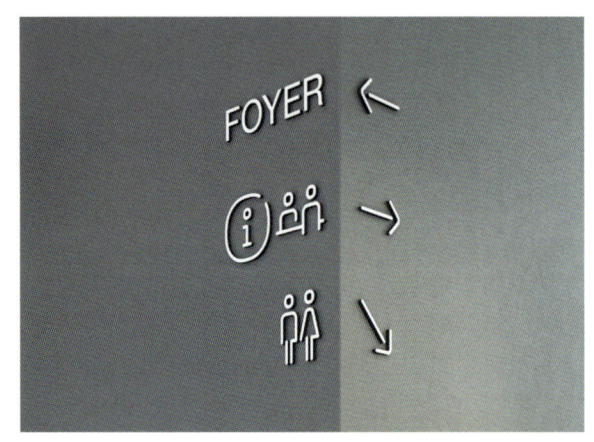

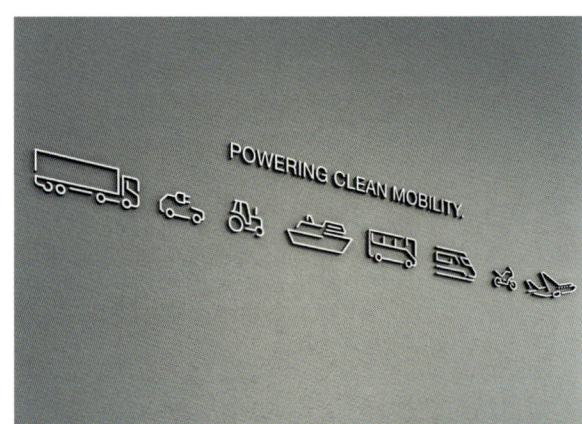

BEOS NOVA
[Orientation System]

This orientation system revitalises the wasteland of an abandoned production site by transforming it into a modern, mixed-use business park for multiple tenants. Establishing a clear reference to the history of the site, which had been used by the manufacturer AVON, the park's name mirrors the letters of AVON to create the anagram NOVA. Based on the corporate shade of orange, a comprehensive colour guidance system identifies all eleven buildings in the complex. In combination with the strong, striking numbers, this enables clear and easy orientation.

Client
BEOS AG
Berlin, Germany

Design
Studio für Gestaltung
Cologne, Germany

Publishing & Print Media	Posters	Typography	Illustrations	Sound Design	Film & Animation	Online
4	64	92	116	126	138	172

ABB's new office in Kraków
[Orientation System]

Client
ABB
Kraków, Poland

Design
Admind Branding & Communications
Kraków, Poland

Project Team
Małgorzata Macuda (Project Manager)
Karolina Pospichil (Creative Director)
Michał Suska (Creative Concept)
Andrzej Firlet (Graphic Design)
Dawid Kułaga (Graphic Design)
Marcin Głąb (Cooperation)
Blank Studio (Cooperation)

→ Designer profile on page 568
→ Clip online

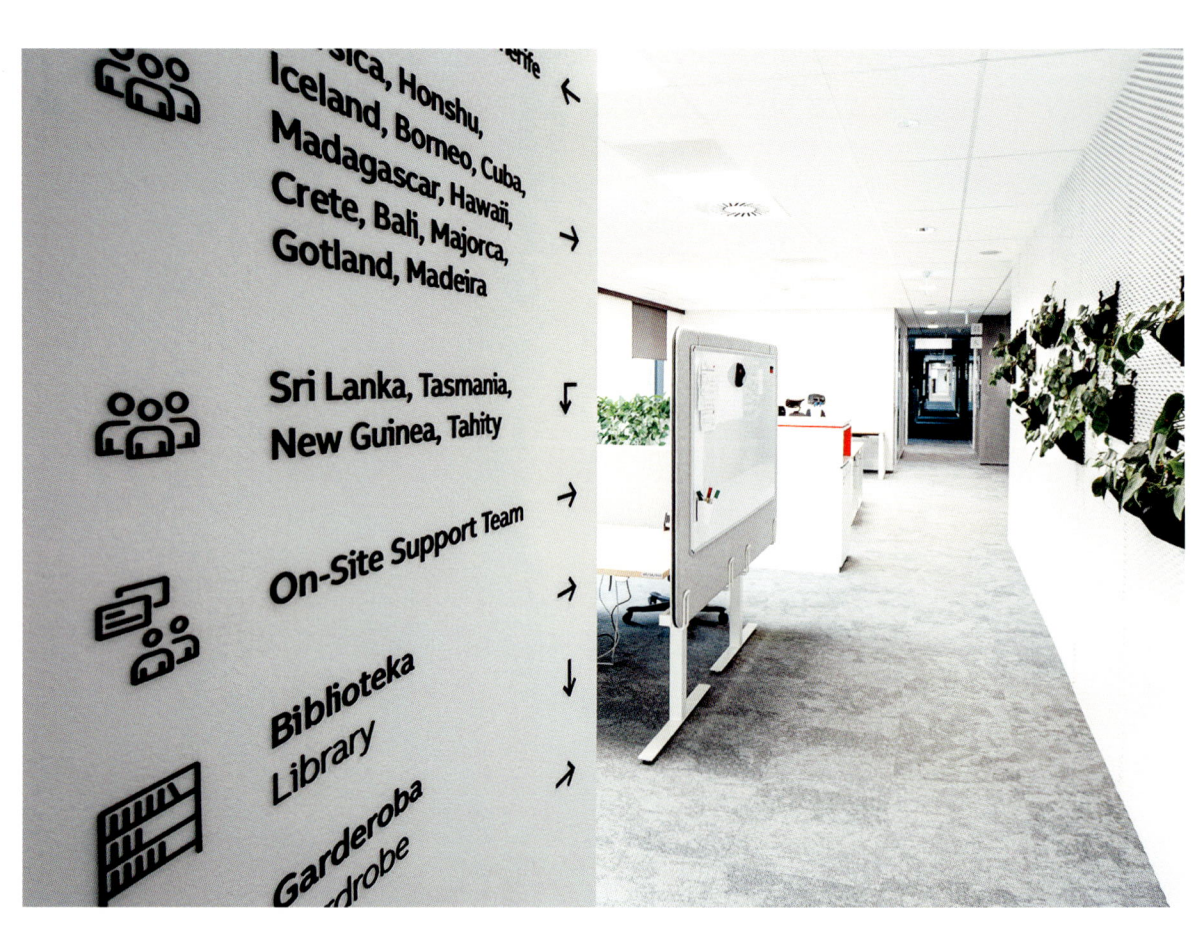

The aim was to create a complete, easy-to-understand wayfinding system coherent with the existing brand guidelines for the new office of the company ABB based in Kraków, Poland. Another challenge was to adjust the design to the interior style and architecture. The solution was to create a system of easy-to-group signs that is both scalable and provides a unified look at a glance. The informational and directional signs have been generously designed to be clearly visible. They showcase a visual lightness so as to not dominate the space. After a test phase and one month of use in the office, and after soliciting the ABB team's opinion, a few final adjustments were made.

Publishing & Print Media	Posters	Typography	Illustrations	Sound Design	Film & Animation	Online
4	64	92	116	126	138	172

Characters – Book House of Tranquillity

[Orientation System]

This orientation system for a hotel has been modelled to present an atmosphere of tranquillity and reverie. Several signs of such an atmosphere, like water, mountains, stones and bamboo, have been matched to the areas of dining, conference, academy and guestrooms. The design absorbs the original cultural elements and extends and restructures them through the strokes of Chinese characters. Other artistically integrated elements are spatial compositions in calligraphy and geometry, as well as lights and shadows for presenting a distinctive visual language from the unique viewing angles of the various spaces.

Client
Water Great Wall Academy Hotel
Beijing, China

Design
Zhengbang Creative Beijing Branding & Technology Co., Ltd.
Beijing, China

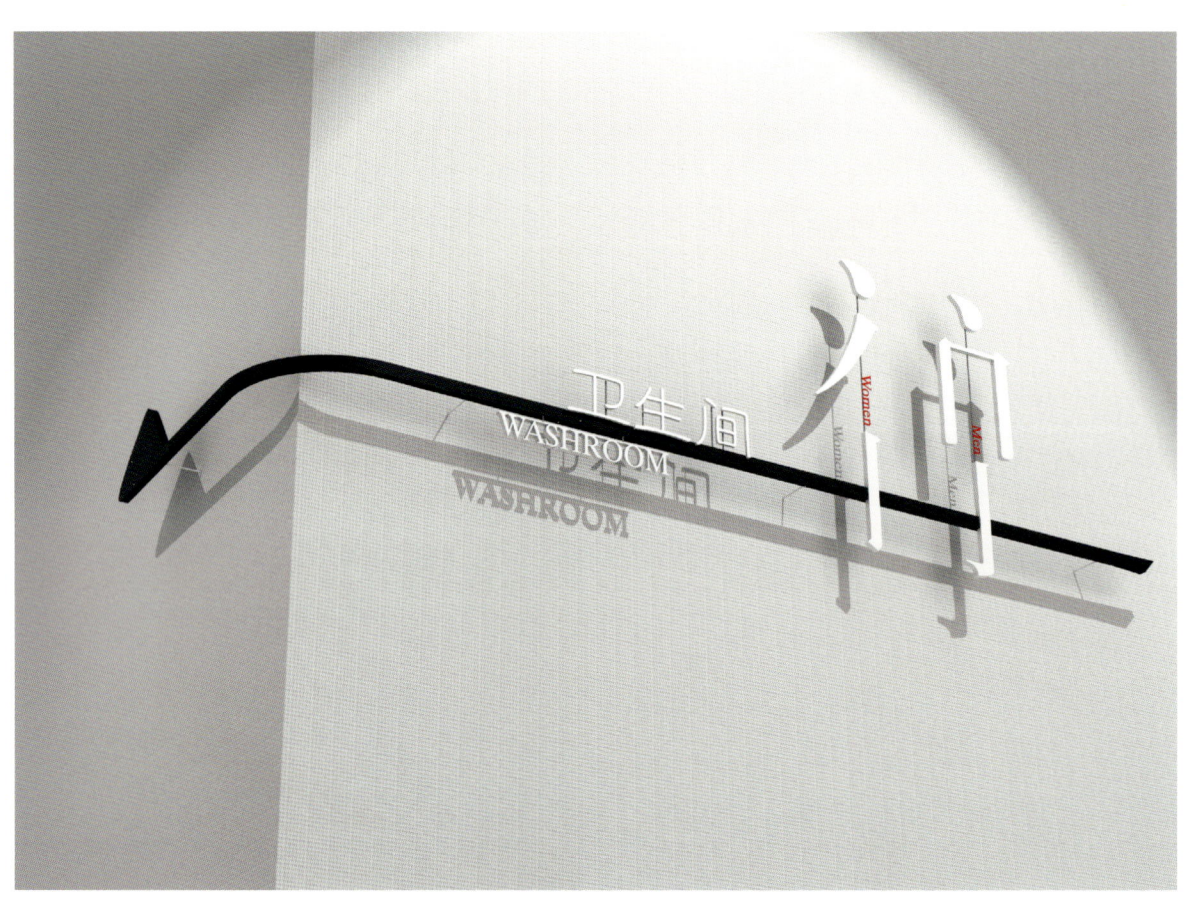

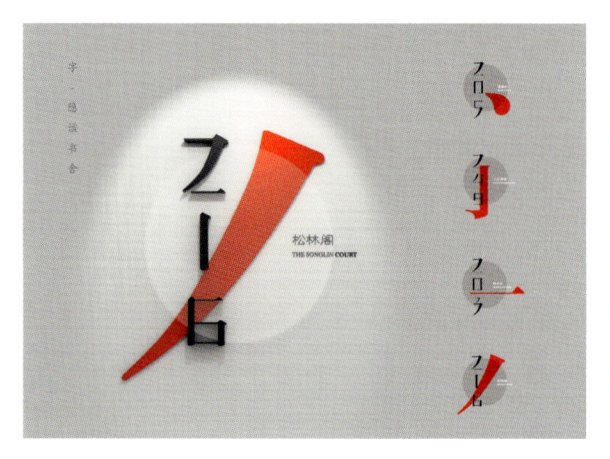

Season's Greetings Festival 2019

[Event Design, Media Show]

Under the theme "The Next 10 Years", the Season's Greetings Festival 2019 in the Gangnam district of Seoul, South Korea, presented a grand-scale multimedia art show. The aim was to express the hopes and wishes of the citizens through DOOH (digital out-of-home) media, a media facade (projection mapping), laser lights and fireworks. Interwoven, all media delivered the message "Don't stop dreaming", thus encouraging the audience to dream of a bright future. Synchronised on six mega-screens in a "free outdoor advertising zone", the art show provided the audience with an immersive media experience.

Client
OOH Freezone Committee
Seoul, South Korea

Design
CJ Powercast
Seoul, South Korea

Publishing & Print Media	Posters	Typography	Illustrations	Sound Design	Film & Animation	Online
4	64	92	116	126	138	172

Taiwan Forward – Presidential Office Building Projection Mapping Show

[Light Installation]

Client
The General Association of Chinese Culture (GACC)
Taipei City, Taiwan

Design
Agi Chen Studio
Taipei City, Taiwan

→ Designer profile on page 580
→ Clip online

Apps	Interface & User Experience Design	**Spatial Communication**	Red Dot: Junior Award	Designer Profiles	Jury Portraits	Index
206	236	336	426	564	642	668

This projection mapping show visualised the collaborative achievement of successive generations of Taiwanese, illustrating how together they have brought peace within both the country and the global community. Designed for the Presidential Office Building on the 108th National Day of the Republic of China (Taiwan), the show highlights and summarises the influences of these generations in the sense of "nourishing a spirit of inclusion and creativity that has fostered understanding and cooperation between Taiwan and the global community". The aim was to turn this building into a "time machine" that looks back on Taiwan's old passion for baseball, the bravery of the country's athletes on the international stage, and the solidarity and visionary spirit of Taiwan's scientists.

2019 Love Kaohsiung Lumière Festival

[Exhibition Design]

Reflecting local culture, the 2019 Love Kaohsiung Lumière was a festival that took the landscape of Kaohsiung, Taiwan, as its starting point for integrating huge lighting installations into the environment. As a multimedia event, the festival incorporated exhibition design, concert technology, installation art, and new media images, as well as contemporary folklore and pop music. The design achieved an interactive experience within an environmentally friendly context. In addition to appreciating the light exhibition from a distance, visitors were also invited to stroll through the dazzling lights and shadows.

Client
Kaohsiung City Government,
Economic Development Bureau
Kaohsiung, Taiwan

Design
B'IN LIVE Co., Ltd.
Taipei City, Taiwan
Chill Co., Ltd.
Taipei City, Taiwan

Project Team
Yi Ying Chen

Mouse Light Fun

[Light Installation]

As part of the Taipei Lantern Festival 2020 in Taiwan, this light installation was created as interactive sculpture. The invitation to build a design piece related to the animal mouse, as it is the Chinese Zodiac of this year, led to experimentation with the opposites of light and shadow. The result, "Mouse Light Fun", goes beyond the principle of a purely decorative sculpture. With its fun and engaging appearance, the installation transformed Taipei into a playground for citizens, inviting them to play with their own "shadow". Adults and children alike enjoyed an experience full of childishness and playfulness.

Client
Taipei City Government,
Department of Information and Tourism
Taipei City, Taiwan

Design
+ing
Taipei City, Taiwan

Project Team
Pei Ken Tsao
Yu Hsuan Chan
Pin Hua Tseng
Fan Hao Tseng
Yun Chiao Lin

→ Clip online

Taiwan Lantern Festival 2020 – Born on the Island

[Light Installation]

Client
Taichung City Government,
Agriculture Bureau
Taichung, Taiwan

Design
Ding Yong Culture Creativity Co., Ltd.
Taipei City, Taiwan
Netizen Productions Co., Ltd.
Taipei City, Taiwan

Project Team
Ming-Hsien Wang (Artwork)
Hide Lin (Artwork)
Ling-Li Tseng (Artwork)
Cheng-Tsung Feng (Artwork)
Nobuyuki Sugihara (Artwork)
Ayaka Nakamura (Artwork)
Kun-Lin Hsieh (Artwork)
Yuan-Ru You (Artwork)
Jiann-Jyn Wu (Artwork)

→ Designer profile on page 585
→ Clip online

The Taiwan Lantern Festival 2020 was held in Taichung, Taiwan, during the outbreak of the Covid-19 pandemic. Focusing on environmental sustainability, the curator team wanted to go beyond conventional practices. Initiated from an architectural perspective and artistic form, the installations used natural materials that were recyclable after the exhibition was over and therefore friendly for the communities and the environment. A cross-functional team, including architects, craftspeople and artists, created a new landscape echoing humanity and nature. It is a reflection and conversation for a post-pandemic lifestyle that is sustainable and holistic, but also focused on peace and harmony.

Infinity Tower Contents
[Spatial Design]

Client
Samsung Electronics Co., Ltd.
Suwon, South Korea

Design
Cheil Worldwide
Seoul, South Korea
Easywith
Seoul, South Korea

Project Team
Samsung:
Eunyoung Lee, Guemjoo Kwon

Cheil:
Matthew Hong (Account Leader)
Jungmin Lee (Account Manager)
Jaehyeon Bae (Account Manager)
Jong-Hee Yoo (Head of Brand Experience Creative Division)
Jungmin Ma (Creative Director)
Heejin Jung (Creative Technologist)
Soyeon Kim (Producer)
Hyun Young Doo (Project Manager)
Minsu Kim (Digital Art Director)
Jihyun Song (Senior Art Director)

Easywith:
Minha Yang (Art Director)
Ji Hun Lee (Project Manager)
Soo Yeon Kim (Project Manager)
Yong Shin Kim (Visual Supervisor)
Jiwon Kang (3D Motion Designer)
Hong Jun Min (Creative Director)
Young Sang Cho (Creative Coder)
Eul Lee (Creative Coder)
Jaehyung Noh (Creative Coder)

→ Clip online

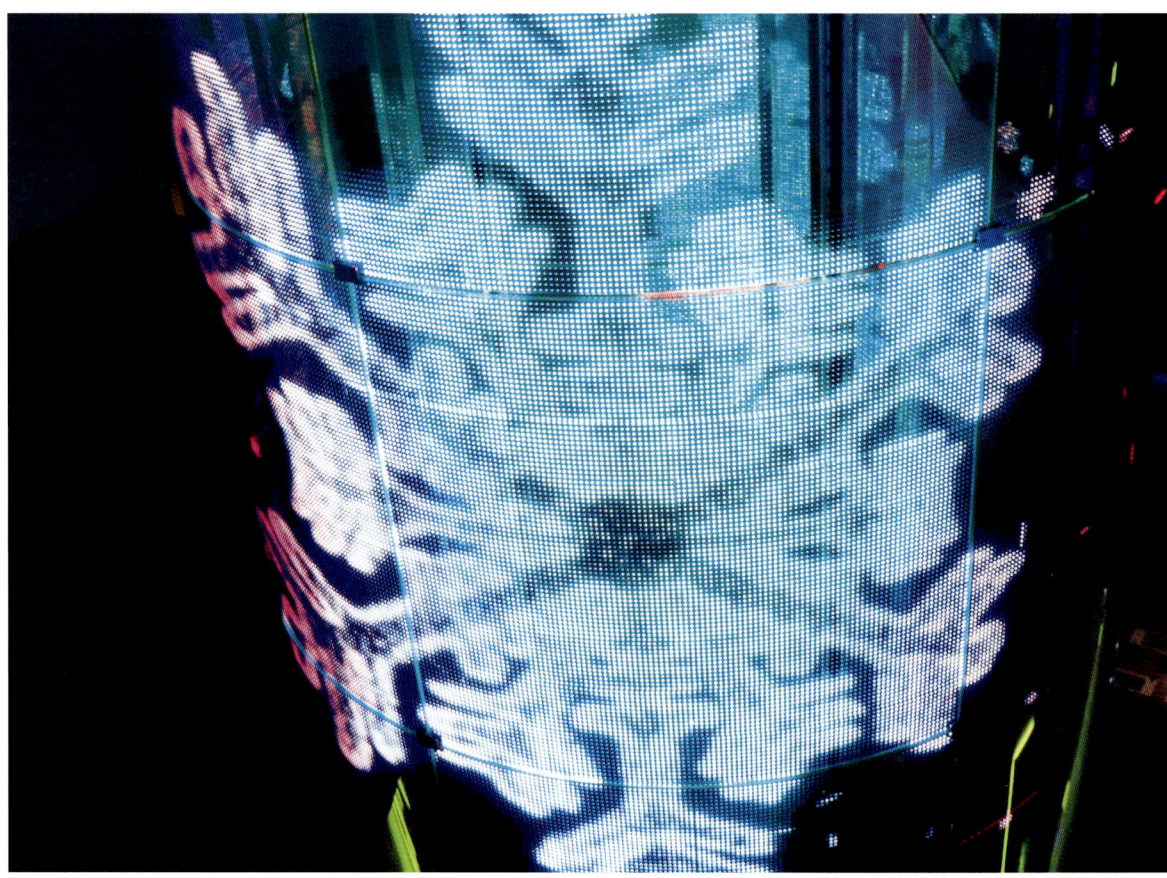

The "Infinity Tower" was installed at the new Samsung Electronics premium brand shop at Gwanggyo Galleria, a landmark department store in South Korea, in 2020. It is a 20-metre-high, transparent LED pillar that stretches across three floors, which offers real-time visualised data of the local weather and time, incorporating rain, wind and cloud real-time flow data from a satellite. The raw data is used to create beautiful, flowing imagery based on an algorithm designed by creative technologists. The tower also displays the time of day, the season of the year and even the changes of the moon. The visualisations are not only of artistic value, but also has a commercial dimension as it can blend data content with lifestyle events such as Christmas or weddings.

adabay – Corporate Office Design

[Interior Design]

Client
adabay GmbH
Munich, Germany

Design
Bespoke
Munich, Germany
adabay GmbH
Munich, Germany

Project Team
Bespoke Interior Design & Production (Concept)

adabay Creative Team (Creative Direction)

Stefan Dünisch (Photography)

→ Designer profile on page 567

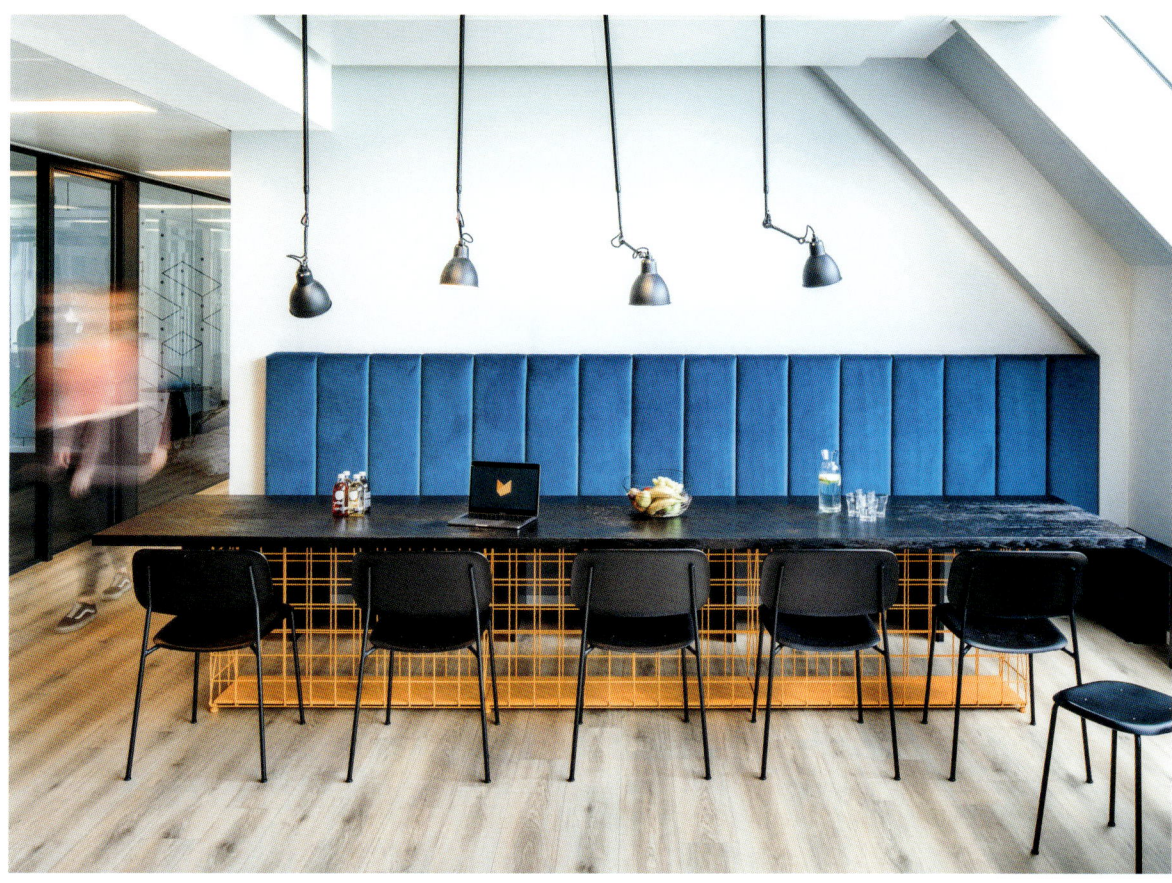

The office design for adabay, a Munich-based digital media agency, welcomes guests with lush, floral patterns into the reception area, giving them a taste of the stylistic fusion awaiting them inside: a monochrome ball pit, a sci-fi room with an interactive flat-screen table, and a jungle room filled with hammocks and wooden stumps. A wall of plants enhances the hall to the large kitchen with pop art accents. The wide range of environments allows the agency to accommodate clients where they feel most comfortable, while keeping their own team inspired in unique co-working spaces. An open-plan office, a conference room full of the latest technology, and the managing director's office with a fun accent wall of old circuit boards give the second floor a more traditional office flair.

The centvingtsept by Pixelis

[Interior Design]

The centvingtsept is a new working environment for the 80 employees of the B-Corp-certified Pixelis branding agency. The design is a reminder of the responsibility that agencies hold in changing the world. Conceived to reflect the co-creation model inherent to the agency, it is defined as a creative, living and organic place that shares the same organisation model, custom-made by and for Pixelis. The ambition of this venue was to make eco-innovation the focal point while designing smart, open spaces to ensure a smooth creative flow.

Client
Pixelis
Paris, France

Design
Pixelis
Paris, France

Project Team
Pixelis:
Edouard Provenzani (President)
Frederic Ly (Designer)

Wildsourcing
Tech Connection
Collectif Quatorze
Akagreen
La Collecterie
Martin Lyonnet
Salem Mostefaoui (Photography)

Studio Ippolito Fleitz Group

[Office Design, Interior Design]

This office design was created against the backdrop of expanding the Ippolito Fleitz Group to a three-storey studio in order to connect the different areas into one organic whole. The design uses the diversity of available interior space to create a communicative and identity-giving environment. This has resulted in various communication zones, while all other parts of the studio have their own stories to tell. The aim here is to express the image of an international, interdisciplinary design studio that works as a dynamic, vibrant and collaged entity.

Client
Ippolito Fleitz Group GmbH
Stuttgart, Germany

Design
Ippolito Fleitz Group GmbH
Stuttgart, Germany

Publishing & Print Media	Posters	Typography	Illustrations	Sound Design	Film & Animation	Online
4	64	92	116	126	138	172

Knowledge Ocean Fire Wolf Creative Book
[Spatial Design]

The design for this bookstore adopts an industrial style, using weatherproof steel throughout the space. The space pillars are also wrapped in this material and function as display frames. Another key design element is the ceiling theme, modelled as a big octopus equipped with multiple antennae that symbolise "the diversity of knowledge". Made of a steel skeleton and solid wood, the bookshelves create an astonishing effect, for they look as if they were breathing. The space between the bookshelves is filled with steel mesh and serves as a display background. Taking into account many merits, this bookstore is also a book bar and an art exhibition hall.

Client
Shenzhen Fire Wolf
International Industrial
Shenzhen, China

Design
Shenzhen Fire Wolf
Graphic Design Co., Ltd.
Shenzhen, China

Project Team
Yang Zhen (Project Management)
Hu Yubin (Graphic Design)
Yang Jialu (Graphic Design)

La Visione – Object Carpet Restaurant

[Interior Design]

The interior design of the Italian restaurant La Visione, located at the centre of the "Object Campus – City of Visions", pursues its basic idea of creating synergy. It aims at positioning the location between different worlds. Thus, it functions as a co-working space, a slash team meeting place and a bar for everyone. However, above all, it was meant to be a point of contact for the company Object Carpet to engage with the world. The objective here was to facilitate a tangible experience of its furnishing expertise in a subtle yet palpable manner. Therefore, textile wall collages of damask and hessian enter into a tantalising dialogue with carpet and cord.

Client
OBJECT CARPET GmbH
Denkendorf, Germany

Design
Ippolito Fleitz Group GmbH
Stuttgart, Germany

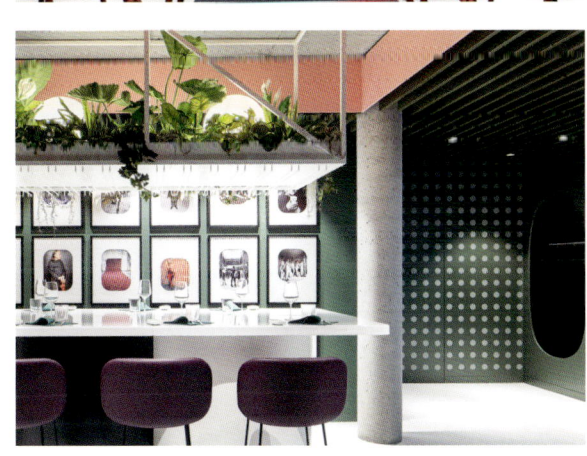

IKEA Pop-up Hotel

[Exhibition Design]

The goal of this project was to push the boundaries of conventional brand collaboration by creating an interactive showcase of innovative lifestyle solutions. The location for the "IKEA Pop-up Hotel" was a historic urban neighbourhood in the city of Taipei, Taiwan. Nine rooms on the third floor were designed to take a creative approach to meeting the specific household needs of families in different phases of life. These spaces were not just static exhibits of products. Rather, they were available as accommodation during the event, allowing guests to enjoy the rooms privately and at their own pace.

Client
IKEA Taiwan
New Taipei City, Taiwan

Design
Smig Creative
Taipei City, Taiwan

Project Team
Tao-Yi Pan (Creative Direction)
Wen Jiun Chiu (Project Management)
Yi-Ping Pan (Visual Design)
Hao Chiang Chen (Visual Design)
Ying-Ching Li
(Customer Advisory Service)
Young-Enn Wang (Interior Design)
Yan-Rong Lu (Decoration Design)
Shih-Ti Kao (Account Management)

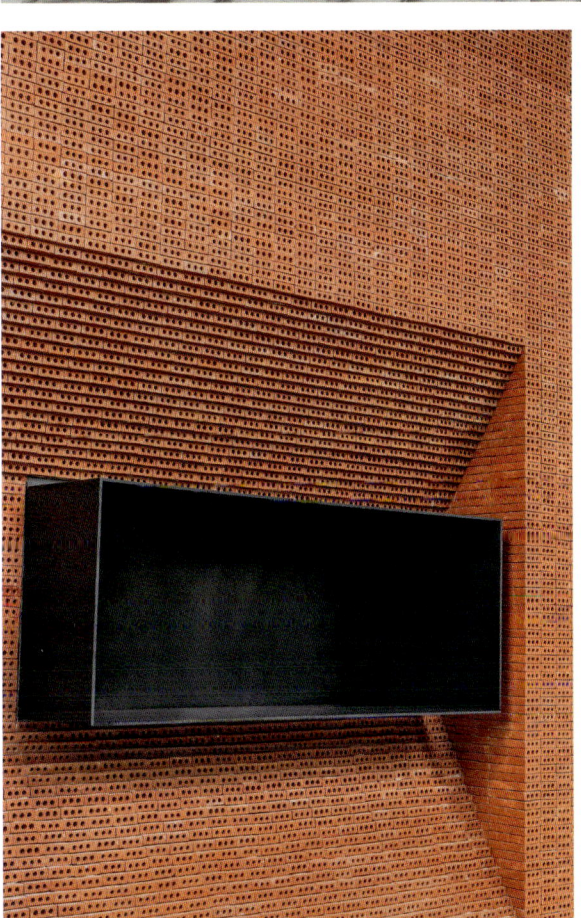

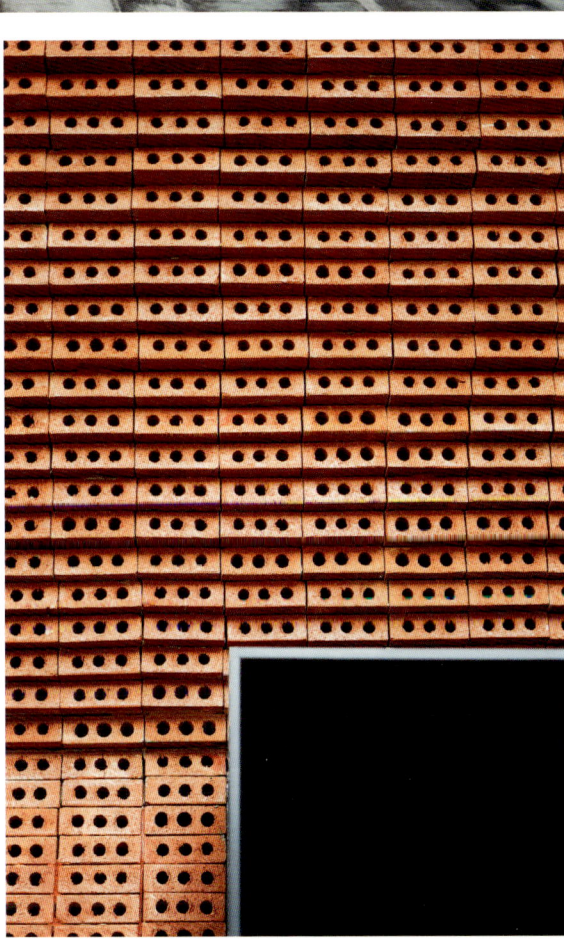

.jpg coffee

[Facade Design, Interior Design]

The interior design for ".jpg coffee" boldly addresses the lively target group of people in Zhujiang New Town, one of the three main business districts in all of China. The shop's simple brick-red facade is all made of jacinth-sintered bricks, which are produced from raw clay. As the colour is simple and harmonious, it forms a strong contrast to the otherwise heavily decorated surroundings in the district. Doing entirely without a logo or any other information related to the two brands on the facade makes the space more pure and architectural.

Client
.jpg coffee
Guangzhou, China

Design
Shenzhen Geomdesign Culture Co., Ltd.
Shenzhen, China

Project Team
Yuzhao Ma (Designer)
Guosu Ye (Designer)

Red Dot: Junior Award

- 428 **Red Dot: Junior Prize nominee**
- 430 **Red Dot: Best of the Best**
- 440 **Publishing & Print Media**
- 490 **Posters**
- 496 **Typography**
- 498 **Illustrations**
- 526 **Film & Animation**
- 542 **Online**
- 543 **Apps**
- 544 **Interface & User Experience Design**
- 560 **Spatial Communication**

Red Dot: Best of the Best [Red Dot: Junior Prize nominee]

Hanzi's Secret
[Educational Game]

Chinese is a highly complex language and one of the world's oldest. There are many regional variants, but they are all linked as they share the same logograms or characters, with one character basically standing for one word. As it can be hard for children to easily understand hundreds of different characters, the Hanzi's Secret project was launched to convey the beautiful characters, their shapes and the stories behind them. The iPad app was designed to help children learn Chinese in a new and entertaining manner. Keeping the basic structure of the Chinese characters, each of the characters is introduced by appearing as a cute cartoon image with a story. After getting to know the building blocks that the characters consist of, children can remember them easily and apply the method of word formation quickly to create more characters independently. The imaginatively designed app contains over 40 animations that have been drawn to excite children and encourage them to spend time learning Chinese characters by making it pleasure and fun.

Statement by the jury
The Hanzi's Secret app inspires with its playful approach conveying that learning the difficult Chinese language could be done with ease and joy. The idea of explaining the characters by introducing their meaning based on their building blocks, which in turn appear in animated picture stories, has been solved and implemented in an enchanting manner. The app thus raises interest in the ancient language and its rich culture to highly stimulating effect.

Client
BiBoBox Studio
Shanghai/Dalian, China

Design
BiBoBox Studio
Shanghai/Dalian, China

Project Team
BiBoBox Studio,
Shanghai Jiao Tong University:
Bo Liu (Art Direction)
Xiaofang Li (Creative Direction)
Zhao Liu (Technical Direction)
Zhuolin Gu (Animation)

BiBoBox Studio, Dalian Minzu University:
Huan Tan (Graphic Design)
Wei Liu (Graphic Design)

→ Designer profile on page 576
→ Clip online

Red Dot: Best of the Best

Colors To Be Heard
[Special Publication]

"Colors To Be Heard" is a work on synaesthesia, the overlapping of two or more senses in perception, such as in seeing sound. Inspired by Chinese folk music, the two volumes present the colour spectrum of eight folk songs created according to the timbre produced by the four folk music instruments of the cucurbit flute, chimes, pipa and erhu. Each volume consists of a colour spectrum and a music score section, which were printed and bound so that one section opens from the left and the other from the right. The colour spectra have been created to match the song melodies and labelled with the professional CMYK data. The right side of each page shows selected colour combinations and visualises them with original illustrations, allowing each folk song to be understood also through the illustration and, in turn, making the colour scheme recognisable in the illustration. The score section presents the eight songs through font design and unique graphic visual effects that aim at expressing the beauty of traditional folk music.

Statement by the jury
This work inspires to listen to Chinese folk music. Following a synaesthetic approach, the opulent colour spectra of the work not only convey the richness of the traditional soundscapes, they also translate the tones and timbres into tactile experiences by featuring embossed printing. The variety of colours is contrasted by a reduced appearance and an excellently implemented notation, making the work extremely exciting to experience.

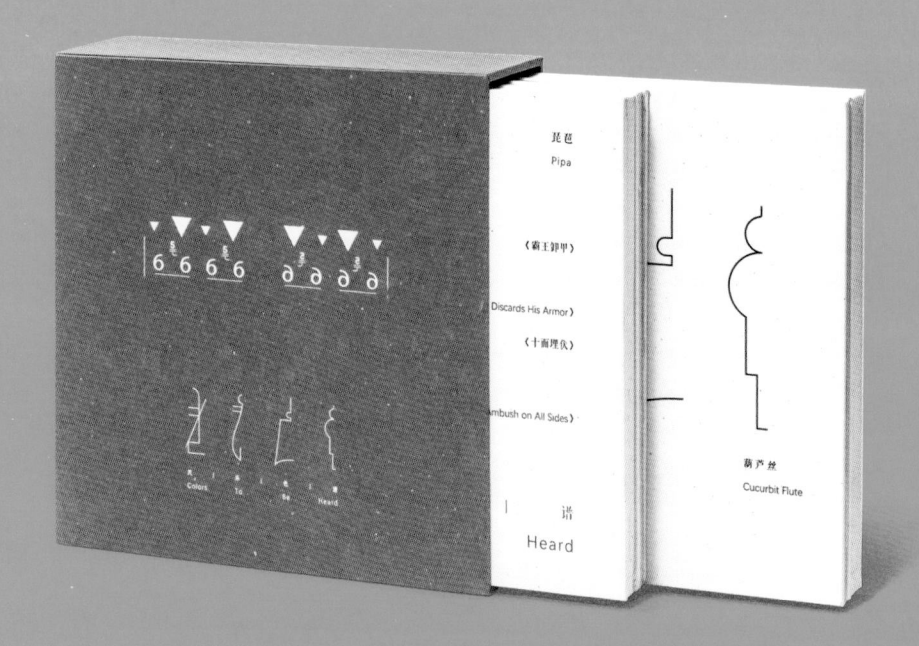

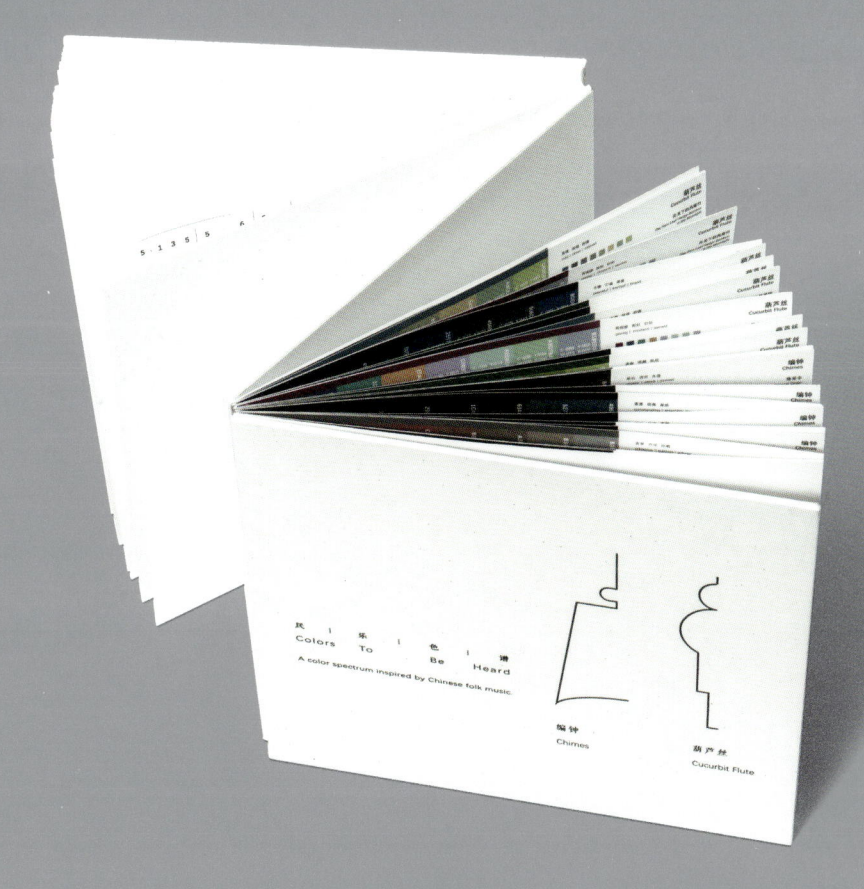

Apps	Interface & User Experience Design	Spatial Communication	Red Dot: Junior Award	Designer Profiles	Jury Portraits	Index
206	236	336	426	564	642	668

University
Shanghai Publishing and Printing College
Shanghai, China

Supervising Professor
Fang Wu

Design
Qing-Ying Zhou, Qi-Wen Li,
Shanghai Publishing and Printing College

→ Designer profile on page 620

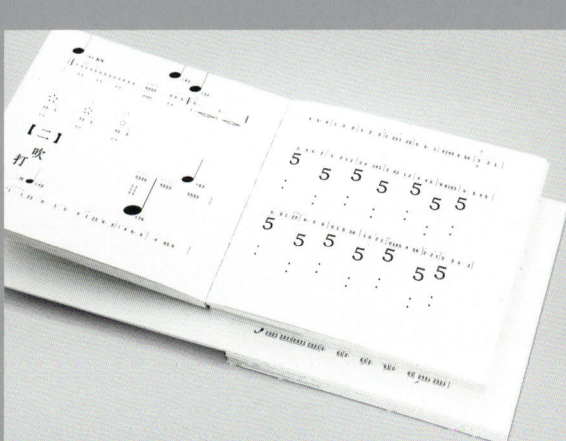

Red Dot: Best of the Best

Long Far Temple
[Book]

The Long Far Temple, a non-official and religion-related long-term shelter for mental patients, existed in Taiwan for nearly a half-century. This book takes an experimental approach in its attempt to present and visualise the atmosphere in the facility such as through the use of various materials. The cover, for example, hand-stitched with white leather, takes the insulation board of isolation rooms in mental hospitals as inspiration, while the linen bookcase wrapping refers to the white clothes which inpatients wear. The elastic band and safety buckle, in turn, are reminiscent of a straitjacket or belts for strapping a patient to a bed. The inner pages feature collages in the form of composite media, as well as black-and-white photographs showing the facility with its walls and fences and which were enhanced by hand-drawn graffiti to depict feelings like fear, despair and helplessness. In a highly engaging and memorable manner, the work thus manages to educate the public about the placement of people with mental disorders in Taiwan and the human rights of these patients.

Statement by the jury
This book on the Long Far Temple in Taiwan has emerged as an outstanding design implementation. The choice of materials featuring both in the unusual binding and as a variety of design elements have added up to creating a highly engaging book. The illustrations, photographs and typographic elements all approach the topic in a sensitive manner inviting viewers to get closer to that reality.

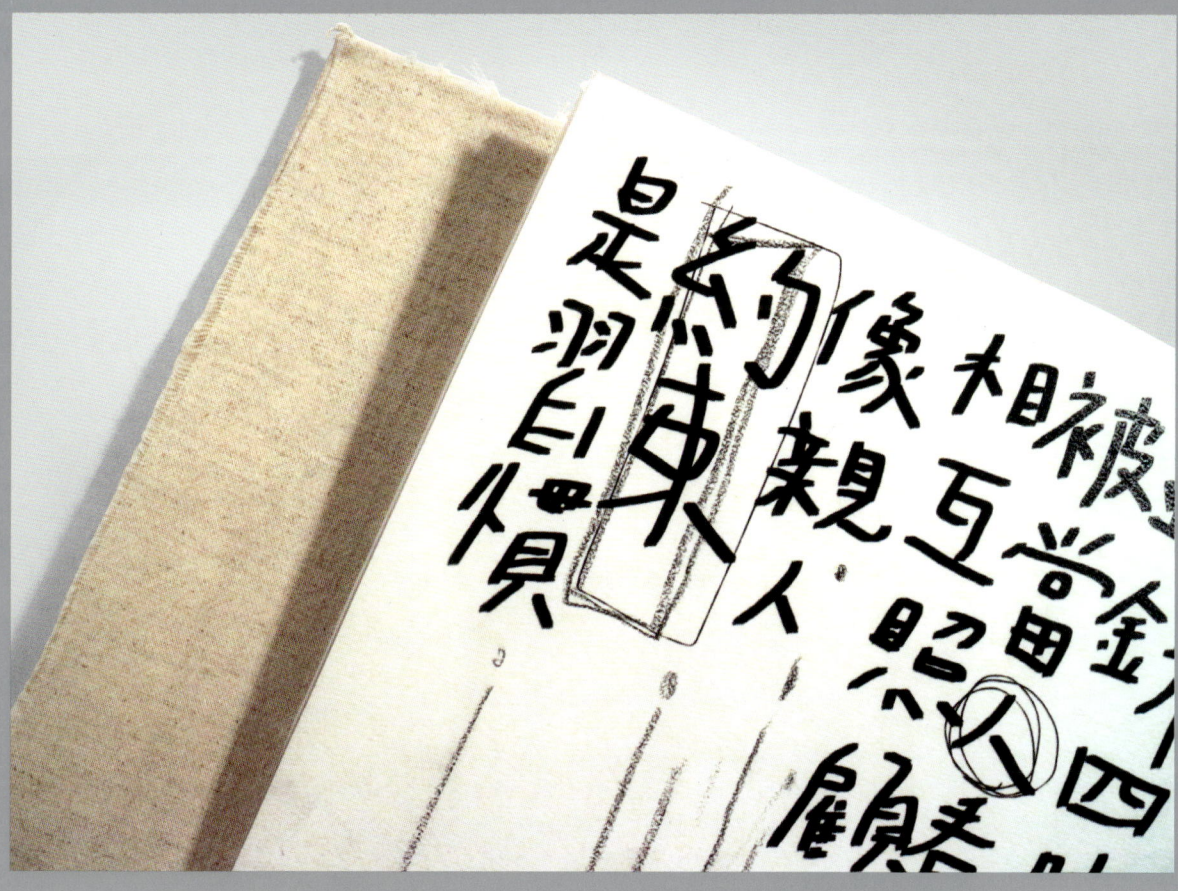

| Apps | Interface & User Experience Design | Spatial Communication | **Red Dot: Junior Award** | Designer Profiles | Jury Portraits | Index |
| 206 | 236 | 336 | 426 | 564 | 642 | 668 |

University
Chaoyang University of Technology
Taichung, Taiwan

Supervising Professor
Yao-Hua Lee

Design
Liang-Ying Huang, Yi-Xuan Sun,
Yu-Jie Jhuang,
Chaoyang University of Technology

→ Designer profile on page 579

Red Dot: Best of the Best

Relentless
[Typographic Artwork]

This three-dimensional typographic artwork was created with the intention of giving a voice to gravity and giving it the opportunity to play a role in delivering the message. Conceptually, the work arose from the mundane action of shuffling a stack of papers in a box and the typically familiar sound it makes when the papers move from left to right and vice versa. The work explores the ways that gravity is usually taken for granted and the impact that it has had on the typographical systems that designers use. Gravity itself thus becomes a designer by changing meaning and generating meaning at the same time. As the papers in the stack are printed on the cut edges and bevelled on one side, among other things, the back and forth movement of the papers causes a shift and distortion of the letters. It is thanks to gravity that the words "Falling into place, flushing neatly by my hand" are finally revealed.

Statement by the jury
This work triggers real joy. It is so simple that even a child can understand how it works. Yet the underlying idea and the achieved effect are all the more enticing when the recipient of this aesthetically designed work realises that and how gravity is at work here in altering words and meanings. The implementation is proof of a high degree of creativity and craftsmanship.

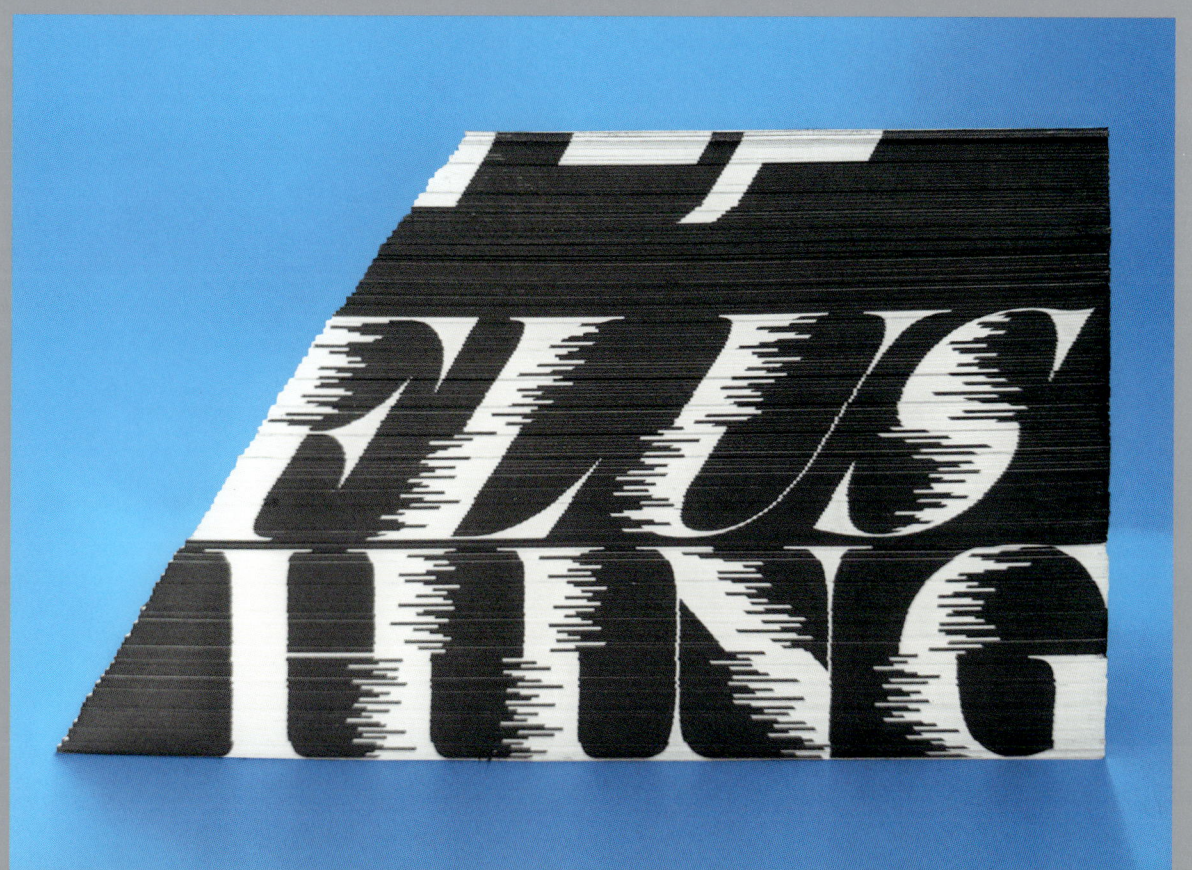

Apps	Interface & User Experience Design	Spatial Communication	**Red Dot: Junior Award**	Designer Profiles	Jury Portraits	Index
206	236	336	426	564	642	668

University
SCAD Savannah College of Art and Design
Savannah, USA

Design
George Stack, SCAD

→ Designer profile on page 619

Red Dot: Best of the Best

WordUpUp
[Educational Game]

WordUpUp is a puzzle-like game designed to help children learn English. Embedded in a colourful world full of fun, the game appeals to children who can already read and invites them in a playful manner to put pictures and words together correctly. There are two themes in the game, the Mysterious Forest and the Lively City, each containing 14 puzzles and 28 English words that need to be found in two levels. The background of the scenes in pastel tones is animated and easy to move simply by scrolling. Cute, interesting and easy-to-like, the illustrations are easy to assign, and the task is to drag an animal in the centre of the forest or – in the city – a bus or utility vehicle onto the figure that appears in the top right corner. If both fit together, just like in a puzzle, the English name appears as a word on the screen and in sound, so that the children can hear the standard pronunciation. When interacting with the game world, the cars can even be made to honk their horns and the animals produce their typical noises.

Statement by the jury
The interactive app WordUpUp was tailored precisely to its target audience of children and as an entering game offers introducing them to a foreign language in a playful manner. The design draws user attention with its coherent concept of simple, cute illustrations and animations, resulting in the app being well-received by both young and old and making them want to start playing the game right away.

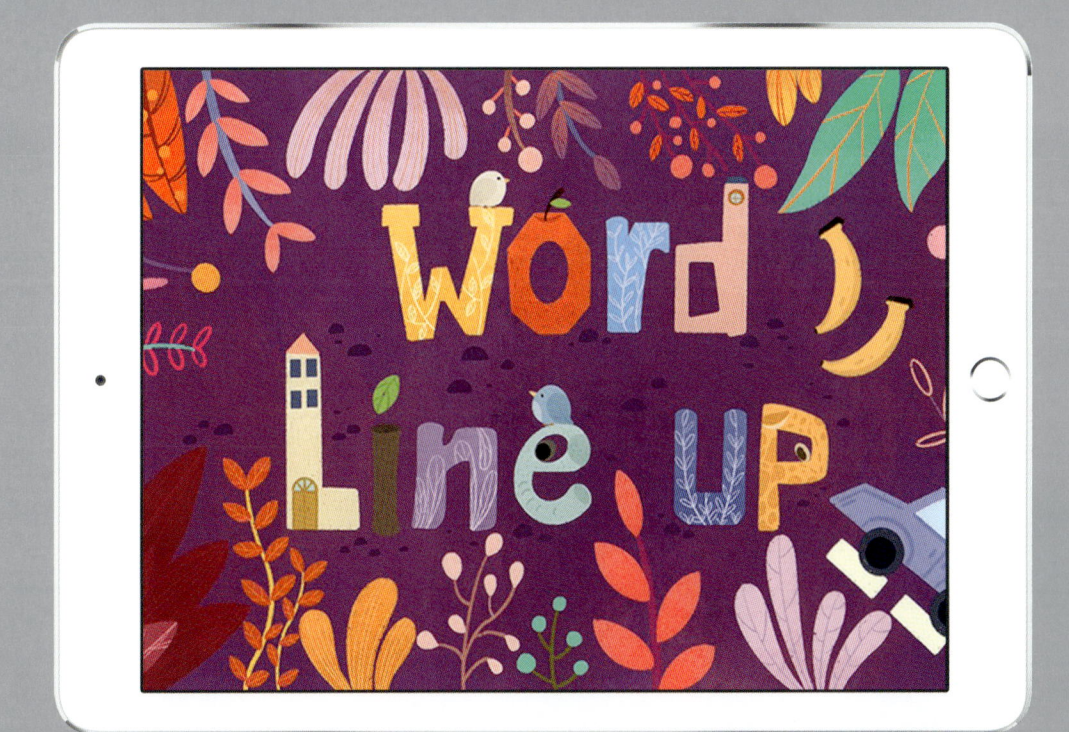

Apps	Interface & User Experience Design	Spatial Communication	Red Dot: Junior Award	Designer Profiles	Jury Portraits	Index
206	236	336	426	564	642	668

Client
BiBoBox Studio
Shanghai/Dalian, China

Design
BiBoBox Studio
Shanghai/Dalian, China

Project Team
BiBoBox Studio,
Shanghai Jiao Tong University:
Xiaofang Li (Creative Direction)
Bo Liu (Art Direction)
Zhuolin Gu (Digital Concept)
Weiwei Ma (Digital Concept)

BiBoBox Studio, Dalian Minzu University:
Lei Bai (Graphic Design)
Jingye Zhang (Graphic Design)

→ Designer profile on page 577
→ Clip online

Red Dot: Best of the Best

AccuPick

[Bin Picking System, User Interface Design]

Solomon's AccuPick is an AI-based system that connects a robot arm and a 3D vision camera. It features an intuitive, concise and easy-to-use interface, the main objective of which is to create intelligent production lines, allowing also users who are less familiar with coding to easily operate the system. Administrators are provided with preconfigured modules that allow users to quickly build projects by a simple drag-and-drop approach – adaptable to the diverse production line requirements across the most different industries. Moreover, with its clean and logical design, AccuPick also provides a variety of functions that can adapt to a wide set of objects that are handled in different production lines. Based on the collected information, the system is able to improve the efficiency of each machine, giving operators a smooth experience and enhancing the organisations' overall performance by creating truly smart production lines.

Statement by the jury

The AccuPick AI-based system scores with an intuitive and intelligent workflow that allows creating all kinds of different production lines. The fact that the modular, icon-based interface can be operated without coding knowledge embodies a particularly low-threshold and therefore easy-to-use solution. In addition, it is outstanding that this simplicity results in greater productivity and enhanced performance.

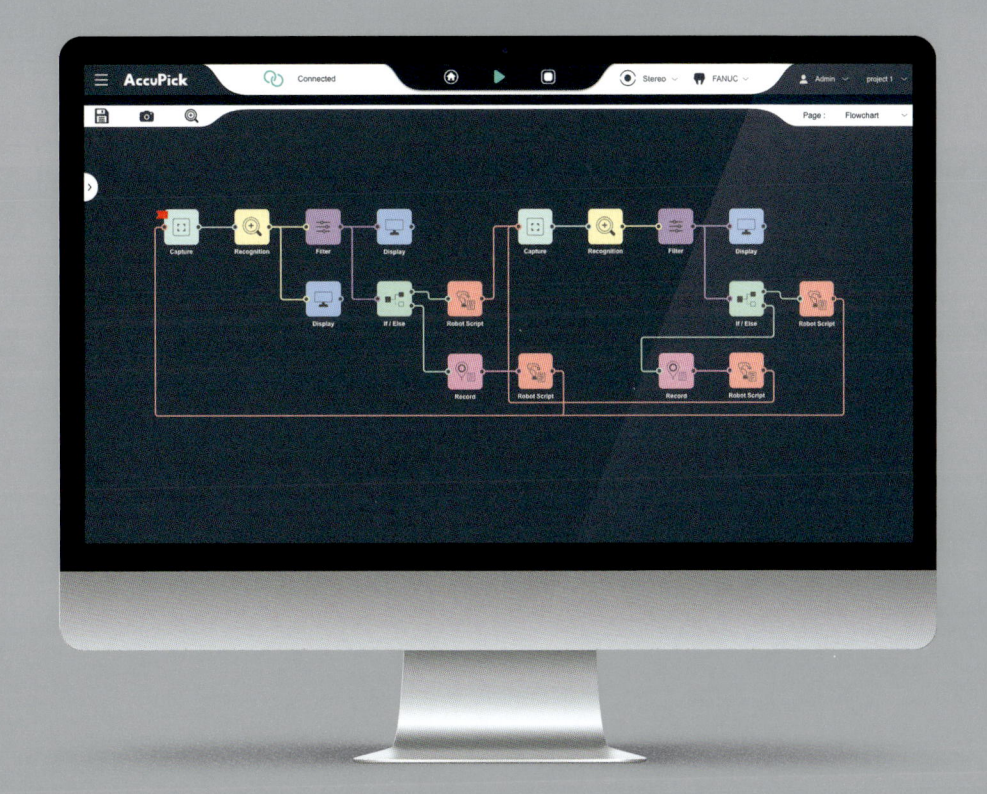

Apps	Interface & User Experience Design	Spatial Communication	Red Dot: Junior Award	Designer Profiles	Jury Portraits	Index
206	236	336	426	564	642	668

Client
Solomon Technology Corporation
Taipei City, Taiwan

Design
Solomon Technology Corporation
Taipei City, Taiwan

Project Team
Chung Hsu Lin (Design)
VBU Group Solomon (Programming)

→ Designer profile on page 623

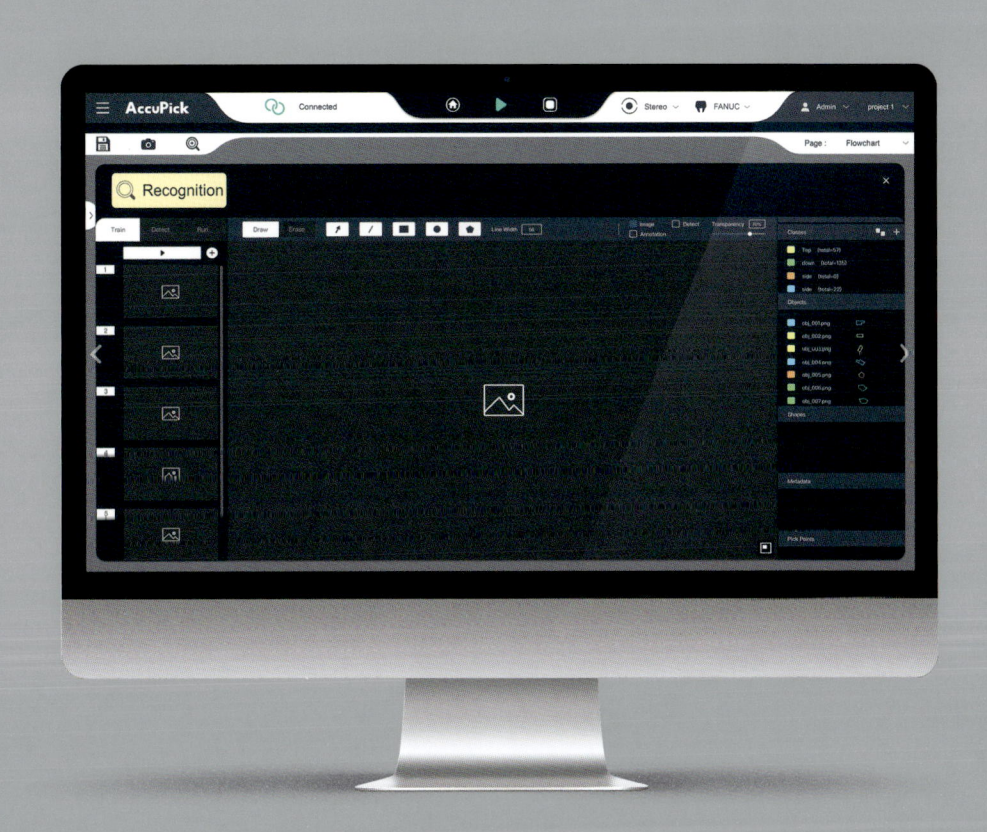

Publishing & Print Media	Posters	Typography	Illustrations	Sound Design	Film & Animation	Online
4	64	92	116	126	138	172

New Wave Movement

[Exhibition Catalogue]

The New Wave Movement of the 1960s to 1980s was chosen as the subject of an exhibition catalogue and accompanying material. A critical analysis describes the phenomenon in typography where punk-influenced designers such as Wolfgang Weingart or Dan Friedman began to break with handed-down conventions, such as the strictly grid-based arrangement of font. With the aim of interpreting this movement from a contemporary perspective, the catalogue examines the design tools of that era and presents them in a fittingly modern layout.

University
SCAD Savannah College of Art and Design
Savannah, USA

Design
Jiatong Li, SCAD

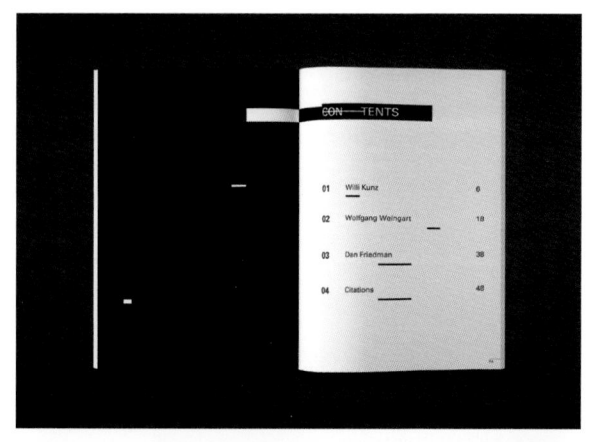

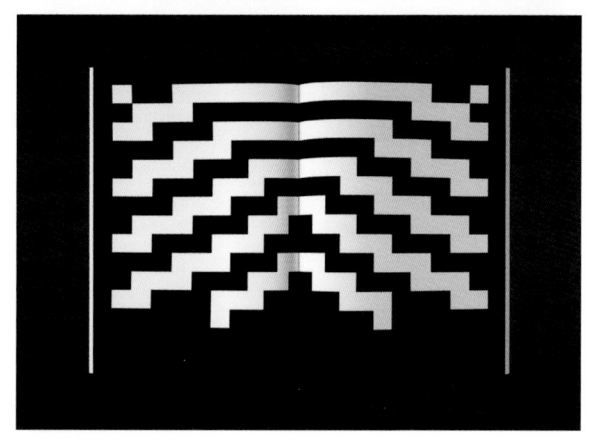

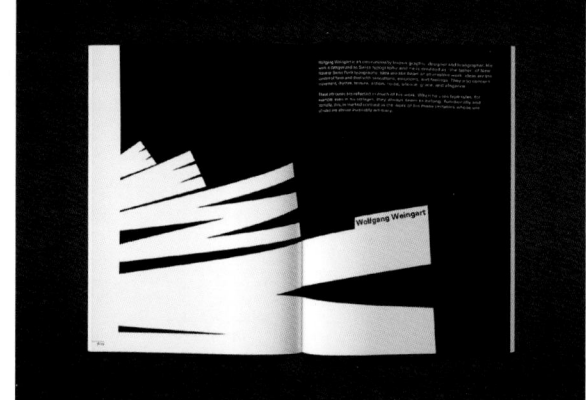

gleich. verschieden. Die Schnittstelle zwischen Social Work & Social Design

[Book]

Design is increasingly seen and used as a political tool. This clear and carefully designed book deals with the question of how design influences our daily lives and whether it is possible to accomplish social and cultural change through design. The rise of globalisation is leading to more exclusion and social injustice. Social design tries to counter this issue, and this piece of work pleads strongly in favour of supporting social organisations through graphic design. The content is tied together with a series of portraits of the Austrian organisation VinziWerke.

University
FH JOANNEUM – University of Applied Sciences
Graz, Austria

Design
Bettina Fink
Graz, Austria

Publishing & Print Media	Posters	Typography	Illustrations	Sound Design	Film & Animation	Online
4	64	92	116	126	138	172

im moment

[Book]

Long before digitalisation, Polaroid allowed photos to be developed immediately for the first time without the need for a dark room or lab. Instant photos helped photography to gain more respect and build a reputation in the art world. This project focuses on Polaroid's functionality, development and significance. The originality of every single image and the surprise of not knowing what outcome to expect led to the creation of these two books – one theoretical, the other practical. Together, they give a clear overview of the power of this medium in an aesthetically pleasing interplay between words and images.

University
FH JOANNEUM – University of Applied Sciences
Graz, Austria

Design
Sophie Ortmeier
Graz, Austria

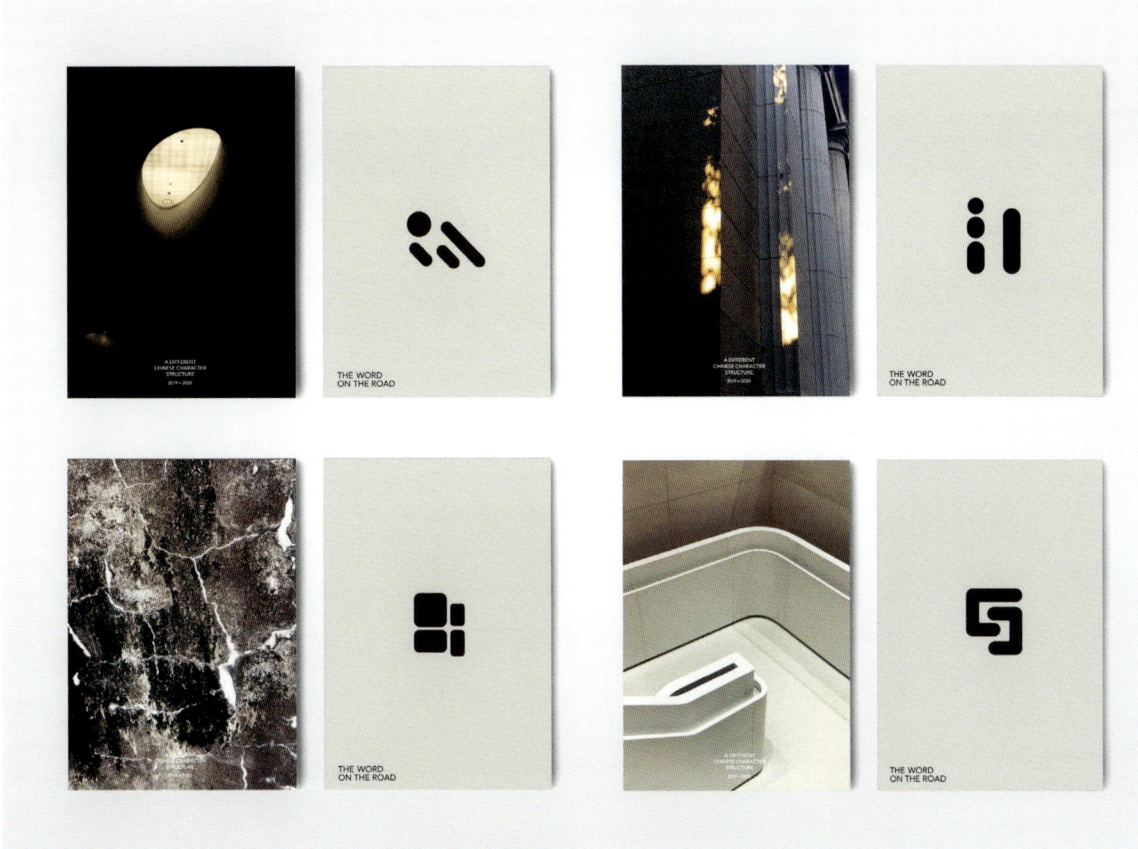

The Word on the Road

[Book]

Our daily life is full of words in different shapes and sizes. The photographs in this carefully executed book with a minimalist design in terms of colour aim to portray the emotions of an image – for example of a chair, house or corner – in such a way as to convey a message. Images, words and messages endeavour to instruct and inspire readers to develop independent thought. The core idea is to remind people to focus on the present and find inner peace as well as to capture the emotion of a moment using photography and transform its message into a new word.

University
Shu-Te University
Kaohsiung, Taiwan

Supervising Professor
Hui-Lin Chiu

Design
Hsuan-Hung Hsu, Chun-Wei Tseng,
Ya-Ching Tseng, Cih-Yan Kang,
Jun-Wei Liu, Chia-Tsan Lin,
Shu-Te University

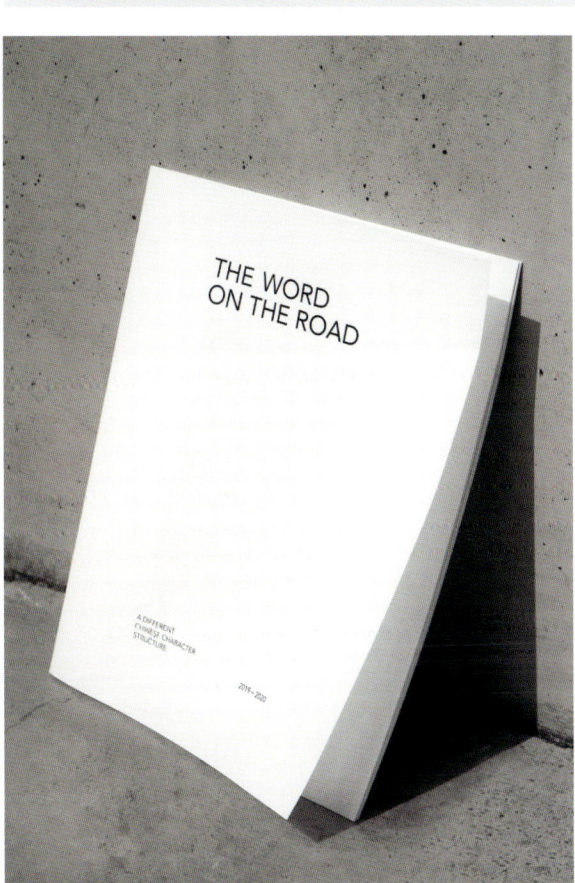

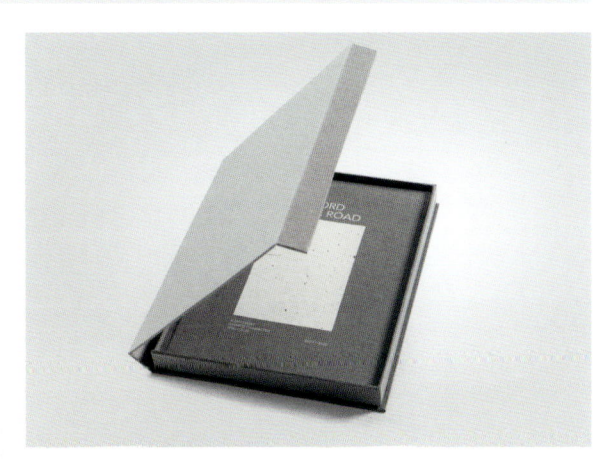

einfach – Leitfaden für barrierefreies Grafikdesign

[Book]

All people have the same right to consume information, but the topic of accessibility has not yet become established in classical information processing designs. How can cognitive barriers in the design of information be broken down in such a way that the end product is equally informative and appealing for people with and without cognitive impairment? The guideline "einfach – Leitfaden für barrierefreies Grafikdesign" (simple – guide to accessible graphic design) focuses on this issue and is intended to help in the development of print products that are both visually appealing and accessible. The guide itself sets a great example by effectively implementing the lessons learnt.

University
FH JOANNEUM – University of Applied Sciences
Graz, Austria

Design
Verena Müller
Munich, Germany

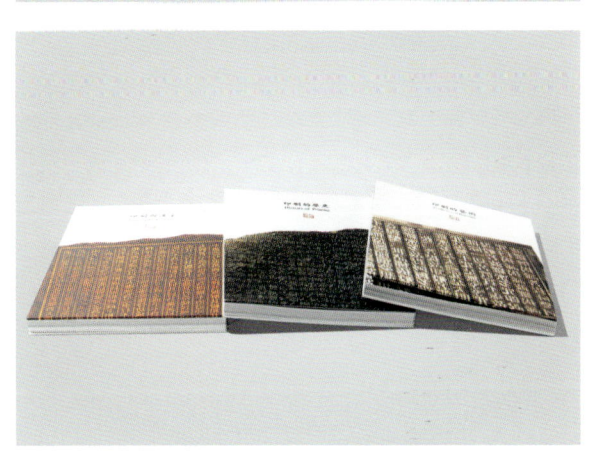

Aesthetics of Chinese Printing

[Book]

Typography has great significance for civilisation and is part of our common cultural heritage. These three books, presented in a lavishly designed wooden boxed set, document the rise and fall of traditional typographical industries as well as the history of artisans who earned their living with hot metal typesetting and lead type. Descriptions of technological terms related to the processes are interspersed with colourful graphics and text-based documents and highlight the dynamic aesthetics of typography as well as the arrangements of the type, resulting in a look that resembles the scrambling and reassembling of a jigsaw puzzle.

University
Chihlee University of Technology
New Taipei City, Taiwan

Supervising Professor
Shih-Lun Chen, Pei-Yuan Chung

Design
Chen-Hao Pang, Kan-Fu Lee,
Hui-Ting Chan, Chia-Yu Lin,
Chihlee University of Technology

Belles from the Tang Dynasty

[Special Publication]

This interactive pop-up book teaches history while keeping its readers entertained. Its design integrates antiquity and modernity and conveys the culture of the Tang Dynasty using famous women as characters and a wealth of details. Five representative female figures of the era were chosen and turned into modern beauties on a fictitious campus, among which are the tough and ambitious Wu Zetian and the romantic, innocent Yu Xuanji. The main aim of the elaborate, lovingly designed book and cards is to use a modern aesthetic to help people learn about each figure's key characteristics in a fun way.

University
Ming Chi University of Technology
New Taipei City, Taiwan

Design
Xuan-Wen Lai, Wan-Yu Chung, Li-Ju Chen, Ming Chi University of Technology

Guan Chuang

[Special Publication]

In the Chinese language, Guan is a homonym that has various meanings, including to detain, to see close up, and to enjoy. This project uses the Chinese characters that mean "to close windows" (pronounced Guan Chuang) to allude to the hidden images in everyday life. The aim is to change images perceived as ugly by combining different lines and patterns on iron-framed windows so that users can enjoy and recognise beautiful views. Six of these windows were related to characteristic Taiwanese sights and complemented by creative products such as booklets or stamps.

University
Shin Min High School
Taichung, Taiwan

Design
Shih Yun Chen, Jia Min Wang,
Li Rong Wang, Ming Xian Wu,
Shin Min High School

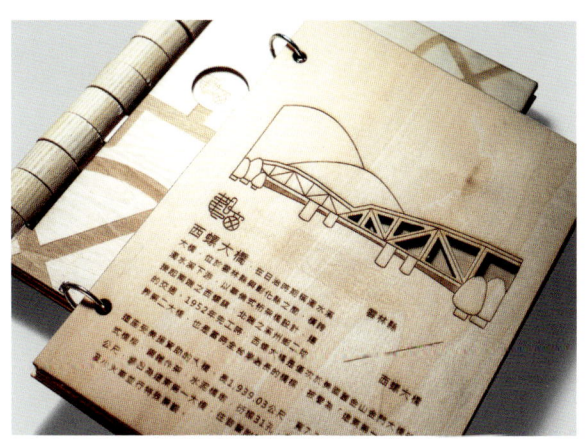

Publishing & Print Media	Posters	Typography	Illustrations	Sound Design	Film & Animation	Online
4	64	92	116	126	138	172

Yan Chen Corner

[Special Publication]

The Taiwanese town of Kaohsiung has preserved some old corner houses in the traditional arcuate shape. This project consists of two parts: the "Old House Creative Book" and the "Old Corner House Picture Book". They combine surrealist illustrations with typical structural characteristics of those corner houses. Each book presents the past, present and future of a corner house. The cover of the first part features hand-drawn illustrations and three-dimensional spatial structures, while the cover of the second part resembles a frame and presents the current facade of the corner buildings inside a plastic cover to symbolise their conservation.

University
Cheng Shiu University
Kaohsiung, Taiwan

Supervising Professor
Sheng-Huang Yu

Design
Chia-Hsuan Chang, Rou-Ya Huang, Yue-Tong Hong, Cheng Shiu University

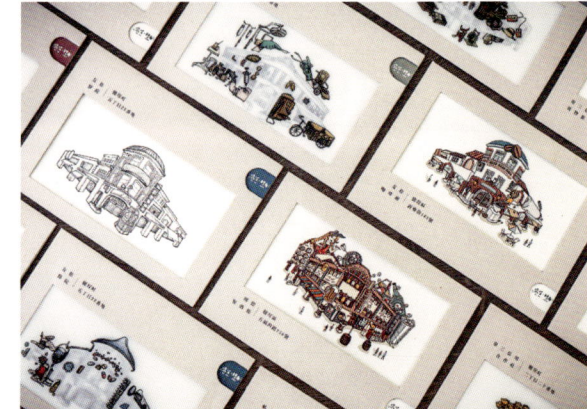

Hall of Eastern Art – Zu-Shi Temple in San Shia

[Special Publication]

The Zu-Shi Temple in San Shia is renowned for its artistic stone and wood carvings and copper sculptures. This publication reflects on the superior traditional craftsmanship, which is today increasingly being lost, as well as the cultural value of Taiwanese temples, focusing on sculptures and blending information and image analyses to create easy-to-understand brochures. By combining the unique colours of the temples and presenting the totem sculptures in powerful images, the publication helps readers understand and appreciate the significance and aesthetic of this art form.

University
China University of Technology
Taipei City, Taiwan

Supervising Professor
Chien-Hsun Chen, Cheng-Ta Lee, En-Ying Lin

Design
Yi-Ting Tung, Hsin-Man Chiang, Pei-Hua Su, Xin-Ya Huang, Shi-Wen Zhang, Department of Visual Communication Design, China University of Technology

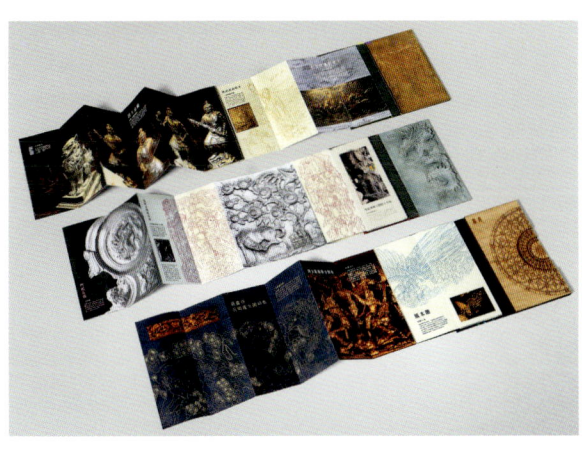

Laozi Said

[Special Publication]

"Laozi Said" structures the classic text of Taoism, the Tao Te Ching, into three chapters. The ancient philosophical concepts are illustrated on foldout pages that can be opened up to create a large poster, similar to how philosophical ideas offer a holistic view of life. The cover of the boxed set is decorated with Chinese calligraphy to represent the abstract concept of Tao and with simplified symbols to denote its morals. The hill is the realm of Laozi, the flowing water symbolises gentleness and the dot is the time allotted to all things on Earth.

University
China University of Technology
Taipei City, Taiwan

Supervising Professor
Chien-Hsun Chen, Sheng-Chuan Chang, Cheng-Ta Lee

Design
Shao-Wei Tang, Guo-Yi Lee, Ming-Huan Chen, Department of Visual Communication Design, China University of Technology

Jujiao Effect

[Special Publication]

Jianjiao is a big religious festival in Taiwan that follows a particular sequence of festivities. Five paintings trace and reinterpreted each stage of the festival in detail using modern media. For instance, fluorescent ink was chosen to reflect the festival's changing appearance from the daytime to nighttime. The project was based on film footage and photos taken during the festival, woven together using contemporary and traditional elements to enable the general public of today to gain a better understanding of the event and greater awareness of this important cultural tradition.

University
Ling Tung University
Taichung, Taiwan

Supervising Professor
Wei-Hsien Lan, Ching-Wei Liu

Design
Wun-Huei Sun, Chiao-Hsuan Yang,
Fang-Yi Lin, Shin-Yu Hsu,
Ling Tung University

Resolution Joss Paper Shop

[Special Publication]

University
Fu Jen Catholic University
New Taipei City, Taiwan

Supervising Professor
Chia-Yin Yu, Fa-Hsiang Hu

Design
Shu-Yi Chiang, Xin-Yi Lee,
Ching-Yu Chao, Fu Jen Catholic
University

Apps	Interface & User Experience Design	Spatial Communication	**Red Dot: Junior Award**	Designer Profiles	Jury Portraits	Index
206	236	336	426	564	642	668

The realisation that many of today's social problems are still yet to be solved or improved prompted the project "Resolution Joss Paper Shop". Using prayers to symbolise the desire to tackle social issues, the project adopts the aesthetic of traditional Chinese paper products known as joss paper, or ghost money. These are sheets of paper traditionally used in Chinese cultures as burnt offerings to gods or to honour deceased family members to ensure their spirit has a good life in the next world. With an attractive, predominantly red and yellow design, the printed work aims to bring greater attention to social problems.

Publishing & Print Media	Posters	Typography	Illustrations	Sound Design	Film & Animation	Online
4	64	92	116	126	138	172

Word Out Our Type

[Special Publication]

This project consists of books, calendars and posters that collate images of the lives of people in Taiwan and its historic cultures and transform them into fonts. Each font is intended to convey the stories of the past and the former way of life. The individual characters and the font's visual characteristics influence and illustrate the quality of the messages delivered. The overall concept revolves around using words to paint pictures to allow memories or even simple traces of life, such as a street scene, to be communicated via typography.

University
Ming Chi University of Technology
New Taipei City, Taiwan

Design
Chi-Chih Chang, Hsin-Pei Chang, Fang-Yu Hsieh, Jou-Yu Huang, Wan-Yi Sheng, Ming Chi University of Technology

Married With A Soul

[Brochure]

"Married With A Soul" describes traditional ghost marriages in Taiwanese culture. They used to be common but have recently become almost taboo, resulting in a decline in numbers. Ghost marriage refers to the wedding between a young woman and her fiancé who has died in an accident. Its true meaning is a family bond that transcends life. The paper structure, which can be folded out into a brochure as well as a star, uses traditional drawings to present this custom and communicate the meaning of one of Taiwan's formerly well-known cultural traditions.

University
Asia University
Taichung, Taiwan

Supervising Professor
Chiung Hui Chen

Design
Siao Jhen Wei, Jia Qi Xie, Yun Chen Hsu, Asia University

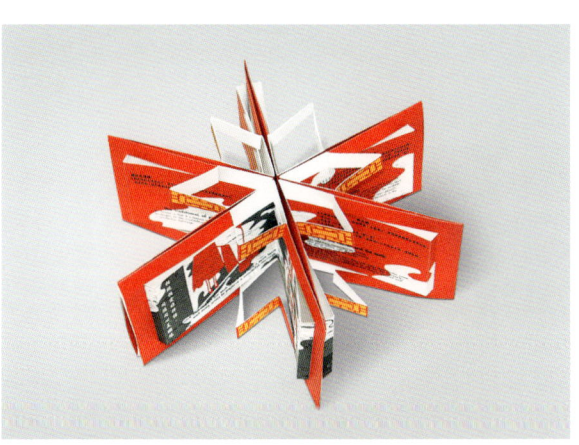

Publishing & Print Media	Posters	Typography	Illustrations	Sound Design	Film & Animation	Online
4	64	92	116	126	138	172

Glyph of Herbal Medicine

[Book]

Chinese characters are made up of various strokes similar to how herbal medicines comprise various ingredients. The three thread-sewn books provide an introduction to 108 ingredients used in herbal medicine and use their properties to create a complete set of Chinese words. The finely drawn illustrations show the structure of the ingredients. The font design is based on the roots of the plants. It incorporates the features, colours and uses of each ingredient to create "Glyph of Herbal Medicine", where you can find the right cure by simply looking at the words.

University
Shu-Te University
Kaohsiung, Taiwan

Supervising Professor
Chih-Che Su

Design
Chia-Lin Wu, Po-Tan Chen, Jia-Hong Lin, Chia-Hui Kuo, Jia-Yi Clou,
Wing-Sze Cheung, Shu-Te University

Twelve Main Meridians

[Special Publication]

A total of twelve meridian systems are at the heart of Chinese medicine. These systems are presented in the three books "The Day", "The Noon", and "The Night". The books are bound with thin strings and copper eyelets, symbolising the fine network formed by these meridians. The whole series provides an introduction to the background and treatment of different acupuncture points with the aim of helping the readers to help themselves. The idea behind the illustrations stems from the decorative patterns on ancient Greek clay pots and murals. These are combined with the characteristics of ancient Chinese characters.

University
Shu-Te University
Kaohsiung, Taiwan

Supervising Professor
Yu-Lung Yang

Design
Wun-Min Yuan, Yu-Zhen Lee,
Jia-Cheng Wu, Xin-Ying Zeng, Ko-Hsin Yu,
Ciang-Yu Cai, Shu-Te University

Publishing & Print Media	Posters	Typography	Illustrations	Sound Design	Film & Animation	Online
4	64	92	116	126	138	172

Odyssey 5125 AD

[Educational Book]

"Odyssey 5125 AD" asks the question of what the Earth would look like in thousands of years following the impact of human civilisation. The publication takes us into the distant future and recounts the adventure of interstellar explorers. Intended for primary school pupils, it contains a storybook and a book depicting the future evolution of animals living on the Earth. The story follows researchers who, upon returning to the Earth, discover animals that live off the waste left by humans, thus confronting them with the dilemma of having to decide whether to clean the Earth or not. Lively comic-style stories are interspersed with detailed information on different animals.

University
China University of Technology
Taipei City, Taiwan

Supervising Professor
Shuo-Ting Wei, Hsiao-Chin Wang,
Chih-Te Kan

Design
Tzu-Han Wang, An-Ching Lin,
Xin-Ping He, Department of Visual
Communication Design,
China University of Technology

Disappearing Castle
[Pop-up Book]

"Disappearing Castle" is a pop-up book that presents detailed models of four historic city gates in Taiwan. Just as the gates were once demolished in real life, the paper models are initially hidden away in the pages only to be revealed when the book is opened. And just as some of them were rebuilt in real life for cultural reasons, the project also wants to preserve the country's long history and communicate it to the younger generations. To do so, the carefully handcrafted cardboard models also replicate the rich ornamentation and unique architecture of these structures.

University
Chihlee University of Technology
New Taipei City, Taiwan

Supervising Professor
Shih-Lun Chen

Design
Yen-Chi Chen, Shu-Ching Chiu,
Wan-Ying Lin, Zih-Syuan Wang,
Man-Ling Zhang,
Chihlee University of Technology

Publishing & Print Media	Posters	Typography	Illustrations	Sound Design	Film & Animation	Online
4	64	92	116	126	138	172

Sun Wu Kong – Somersault and Show Amazing Skills

[Educational 3D Gamebook]

The allegorical meaning of the Chinese classic "Journey to the West" inspired the creation of this educational 3D gamebook for primary school children. The book uses simple imagery to explain the story about the both human and bestial nature of the main character, Wu Kong. A game of dice, DIY finger puppets and question boxes complement the book. What makes it special is that it can be not only read like a normal book but also opened out to let the reader play with the different scenes of the story that artfully pop up.

University
Chaoyang University of Technology
Taichung, Taiwan

Supervising Professor
Jau-Hui Lu

Design
Chia-Li Hsu, Rui-Zhen Wu, Tan Yong Jian, Chaoyang University of Technology

Confusion

[Tabletop Game]

"Confusion" is a life-simulation board game developed for teenagers. The game and its cards are divided into sections that cover school life and everything that follows, with each section having a different set of rules. Players have to take on various tasks, for example, controlling their resource consumption, collecting items, choosing a career, making decisions, carrying out competitions and cooperating with other players. Rich in detail and carefully executed, all of the components can be stored in the specially designed box.

University
China University of Technology
Taipei City, Taiwan

Supervising Professor
Po-Wen Wu, Wei-Feng Kao

Design
Hsiang-En Tung, Qi-Han Zhong,
Yu-Ting Wang, Yen-Lei Ho,
Cheng-Shao Tsai, Department of Visual
Communication Design, China University
of Technology

94513 Zeichen

[Book]

The new, the unknown and the alien are often perceived as threats. Traditions and conventions are barely questioned any more. Thinking that runs counter to the norm and is a source of creativity is the topic of the book "94513 Zeichen" (94513 characters). Made up almost entirely of typography set in a wide range of layouts, it discusses this ability in this time of constant change through various stories and supporting documents. Design, when it is understood as an improvement of the status quo by means of creative compositions, can accompany changes that have great effect and result in the exact opposite of norms.

University
FH JOANNEUM – University of Applied Sciences
Graz, Austria

Design
Paul Pacher
Graz, Austria

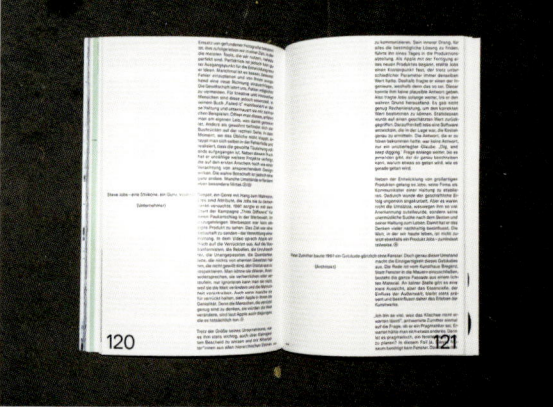

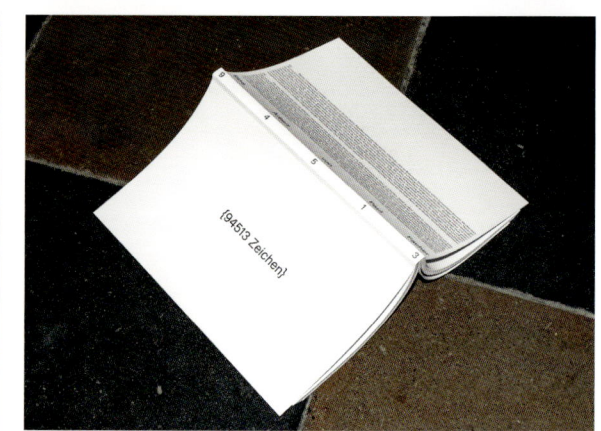

How Long Is Now?
[Book]

How long is now? This question, which has no clear answer even if you limit it to the subjective present, is what this book tackles. Over the course of his research, the author arrives at interesting insights, for instance the observation that "now" is shorter when heard than seen. Featuring a reduced, unobtrusive typeface with orange used sparingly as an additional colour, the design focuses on conveying the book's contents clearly. The results of the book offer a lesson in how to find and optimise designs so that they correspond to our perception.

University
FH JOANNEUM – University of Applied Sciences
Graz, Austria

Design
Benjamin Ressi
Berlin, Germany

→ Designer profile on page 615

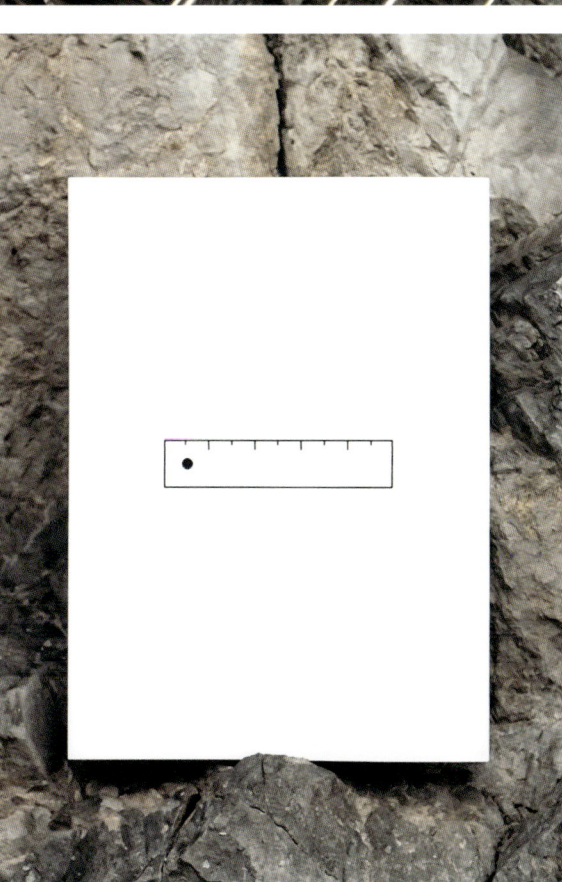

Publishing & Print Media	Posters	Typography	Illustrations	Sound Design	Film & Animation	Online
4	64	92	116	126	138	172

Sandwich Generation

[Special Publication]

For this project, people belonging to the sandwich generation, aged between 25 and 60, were asked about the degree and nature of the stress they had experienced, and the findings were translated into different types of visual diagrams. Five colours were used to represent different causes of stress; overlapping sections indicate stress with multiple causes, while the size of each triangle represents the magnitude of the respective cause. The results of the survey – that almost all stress was caused by work in addition to caring for the family and little free time – are therefore easy to see from the design. The project also offers a self-assessment.

University
Chaoyang University of Technology
Taichung, Taiwan

Supervising Professor
Yao-Hua Lee

Design
Yu Chen, Yi-Chiao Lee, Yu-Xuan Huang, Chaoyang University of Technology

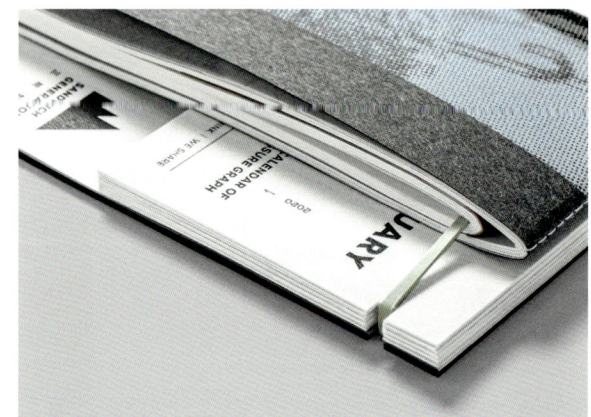

Apps	Interface & User Experience Design	Spatial Communication	**Red Dot: Junior Award**	Designer Profiles	Jury Portraits	Index
206	236	336	426	564	642	668

Symptom of Student

[Book]

Based on the authors' own research, these four books tackle the mentality and behaviour of today's college students, who are presented as lacking discipline and maturity. 52 major symptoms were selected to describe certain types of students: from the cute and naive freshmen to the sophomores who only want to fool around to the zombie-like seniors. The illustrations demonstrate a suitably ironic and dark humour combined with a colour palette that shifts gradually from bright and vibrant to dull and faded as the students age.

University
Shu-Te University
Kaohsiung, Taiwan

Supervising Professor
Hui-Lin Chiu

Design
Hong-Yuan Zhou, Chen-Chen Chang, Yan-Zhen Li, Shu-Te University

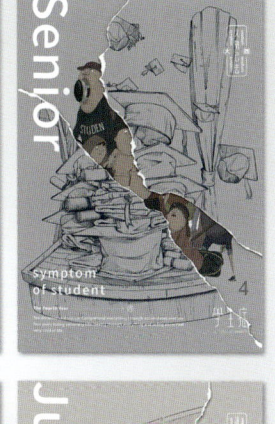

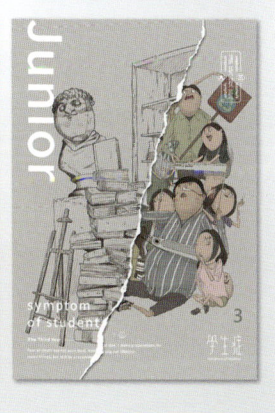

Publishing & Print Media	Posters	Typography	Illustrations	Sound Design	Film & Animation	Online
4	64	92	116	126	138	172

Uncompleted Protest Guidance

[Book]

In democracies, freedom of speech and of assembly are essential for enabling people to express their views. Highly sculptural in its design, this project, consisting of four sets of two books, mainly addresses the topics of demonstrations, work, elections and religion. The social movement is illustrated in a humorous way and presented in the form of two-fold booklets that can be opened out to let opposing viewpoints face each other. There is no right or wrong. What matters is respect for different perspectives and ways of thinking as well as human diversity.

University
China University of Technology
Taipei City, Taiwan

Supervising Professor
Sheng-Chuan Chang, Yao-Yuan Shang, Jung-Shun Huang

Design
Jing-Wen Tzeng, Yi-Jun Chen, Yi-Hsien Sun, Chia-Chi Chen, Jing-Zi Huang, Chu-Wei Chang, Yu-Chen Cheng, Bo-Jia Ciou, Department of Visual Communication Design, China University of Technology

Forward Station
[Special Publication]

"Forward Station" is a book that seeks to embolden people who desire freedom and greater courage by telling the story of Hong Kong citizens who fought the Extradition Law Amendment Bill as well as for democracy. Its message is that it takes real action to solve problems. The book is based on the real experiences of the author. It mixes information from social media and authentic records of those participating in this social movement. The special publication uses different grades of paper and print techniques to symbolise the power of courage.

University
Ling Tung University
Taichung, Taiwan

Supervising Professor
Lu-Hsin Chang

Design
Man-Qi Chiang, Wen-Chien Wu, Tzu-Yun Lai, Yu-Ting Huang, Jia-Yi Lin, Wan-Yu Chang, Ling Tung University

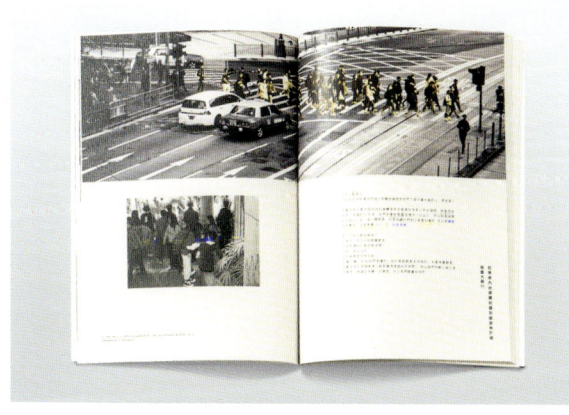

Publishing & Print Media	Posters	Typography	Illustrations	Sound Design	Film & Animation	Online
4	64	92	116	126	138	172

Western-Style Building
[Book]

This book presents eight historical buildings in the southern Chinese village of Shuei-Tou, which are representative of a special type of architecture for which the village is known. The poor soil in the area once prompted many people to look for work abroad. When they returned with money to build their own houses, they mixed the style and experience they had gathered abroad with local elements, combining western culture with Minnan culture. The Asian-style book also features explanations of the buildings' history, interior design and tiled roofs, thus shedding light on the region's unique architectural style and interesting history.

University
Shu-Te University
Kaohsiung, Taiwan

Supervising Professor
Yu-Lung Yang

Design
Jia-Qi Wu, Mei-Ting Huang, Siou-Yuan Lin, Yun-Dian Guo, Tsai-Wei Chen, Ya-Ting Hsu, Shu-Te University

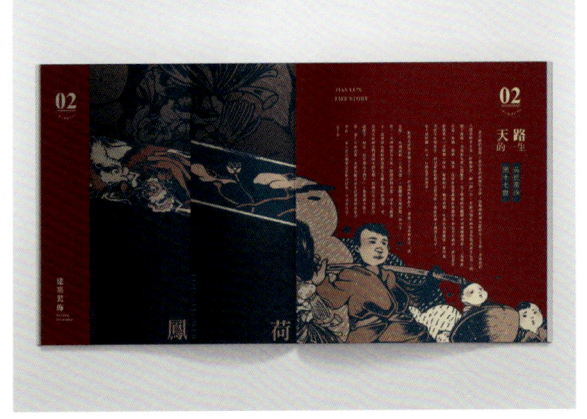

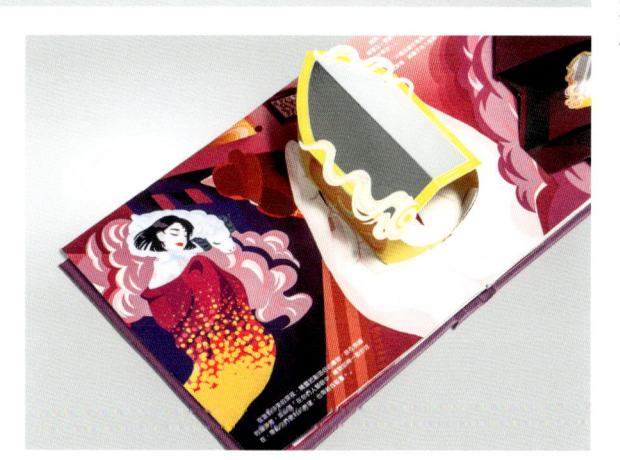

Apps	Interface & User Experience Design	Spatial Communication	**Red Dot: Junior Award**	Designer Profiles	Jury Portraits	Index
206	236	336	426	564	642	668

The Addiction World
[Pop-up Book]

Three great addictions are the subject of this work, which consists of three lavishly produced pop-up books. Despite their often negative physical and environmental consequences, addictions are sometimes difficult to detect in everyday life. In order to draw attention to this phenomenon, the comic-style books use pages that unfold to reveal various deliberately exaggerated 3D scenes. The addictions covered by the books include dependence on the Internet and video games, compulsive shopping and the craving for admiration – all presented in finely crafted details and within the context of the addictions.

University
Asia University
Taichung, Taiwan

Supervising Professor
Hui-Ping Lu

Design
Yen-Ting Huang, Chun-Hao Peng,
Zhi-Mei Wang, Tzu-Wei Kuo,
Asia University

Matchmaking Corner
[Book]

The matchmaking corner is a place in China where middle-class parents can seek out potential partners for their children, using family background, jobs, wealth and appearance as matchmaking criteria. Complex individuals are reduced to superficial personal information on cardboards. The phenomenon represents a magical, microcosm of the Chinese society. This project distilled the main types of singles on display into nine fairly representative characters and created a humorous dictionary. With precise descriptions and attractive illustrations, this piece of work draws attention to the fact that behind each figure lies a social issue in modern-day China.

University
National Yunlin University of Science and Technology
Douliu City, Yunlin County, Taiwan

Design
Fei Li, Handan Zhang, Tianyue Zhao, Hungchang Yu, National Yunlin University of Science and Technology

Women Style

[Stamp Collection Set, Book]

The 20th century marks an important chapter for feminism in Taiwan, with people beginning to understand that women are more than just an adornment for men. This idea has prompted the emergence of a society where gender equality is now becoming a reality. This work separates the years of the economic boom between 1901 and 1960 – seen as the awakening of feminism – from the subsequent period of evolution of feminism that continued into the year 2000. The carefully designed stamp album is rich in detail and has a vintage look. It contains numerous stories and facts to raise the profile of famous women who shaped feminism in Taiwan.

University
Shu-Te University
Kaohsiung, Taiwan

Supervising Professor
Yu-Lung Yang

Design
Yi-Tieh Lin, Yu-Ting Chen, Yu-Chieh Lin, Gao-Ling Hsu, I-Hsuan Tiao,
Shu-Te University

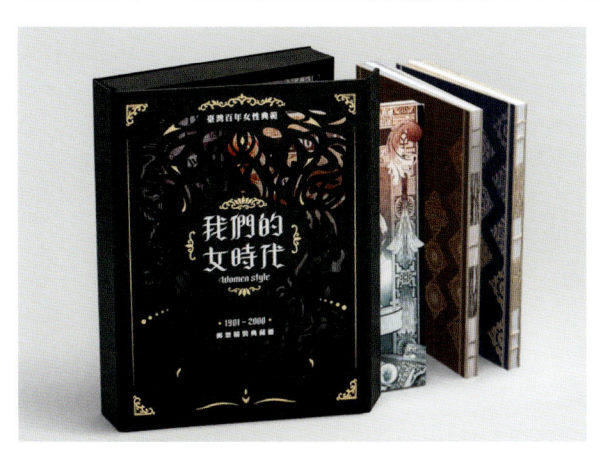

Unfriendly Gift

[Book]

"Unfriendly Gift" is a series of six picture books disguised as six pretty gifts that reveal hidden suffering. They tell the true stories of little girls and young women who were victims of sexual assault by their fathers, teachers, coaches or colleagues – people whom they once trusted. In order to highlight the tension between apparent care and affection on the one hand and unbearable fear on the other, the visual design uses two very different styles. Mild, warm tones applied with soft brush strokes on the book covers stand in contrast with dark, disharmonious tones in rough brush strokes on the inner pages.

University
China University of Technology
Taipei City, Taiwan

Supervising Professor
Shuo-Ting Wei, Hsiao-Chin Wang

Design
Wei-Che Hung, Yu-Jie Wu, Pei-Xuan Li, Jia-Hong Shi, Ching-Yen Shih, Yi-Shan Chen, Department of Visual Communication Design, China University of Technology

Apps	Interface & User Experience Design	Spatial Communication	Red Dot: Junior Award	Designer Profiles	Jury Portraits	Index
206	236	336	426	564	642	668

Unutterable

[Book]

The work "Unutterable", which consists of five books, revolves around people who are embarrassed and ashamed following sexual harassment, and find it difficult to talk about their experience. Expressive imagery, including black-and-white drawings, conveys the distress, intimidation and bewildering emotions as well as the core value of physical autonomy. The story is told by five characters who represent five different perspectives and are each associated with one symbol, such as a mirror, wings or the sun. Different colours and textures are used to create distinction between the books.

University
Chaoyang University of Technology
Taichung, Taiwan

Supervising Professor
Pei-Yu Tseng, Kuo-Min Chuang

Design
Chia-Yu Chen, Ting-Wei Liao, Yi-Ting Jiang, Yi-En Kao, Yu-Zhi Liao, Chaoyang University of Technology

Publishing & Print Media	Posters	Typography	Illustrations	Sound Design	Film & Animation	Online
4	64	92	116	126	138	172

CLICK BAIT

[Special Publication]

The media often uses sensationalism in order to get a higher click-through rate. Exploring this subject matter, this project rewrites a well-known fairy tale in a journalistic style. It visually presents two versions of the story in parallel using two different colours: red represents the explosive nature of news reporting, while blue stands for the actual happenings, thus satirising the confusion created by news stories. The project uses individual pages highlighted with a red frame to draw attention to the fact that we are all affected by this issue and need to be aware of and discuss misleading elements of news.

University
Ling Tung University
Taichung, Taiwan

Supervising Professor
Wei-Hsien Lan

Design
Yong-Yu Lu, Yi-Ting Kao, Ru-Pei Liou, Chun-Teng Wang, Chiao-Fei Han, Yuan-Xuan Ou, Ling Tung University

Bomia-Hohan

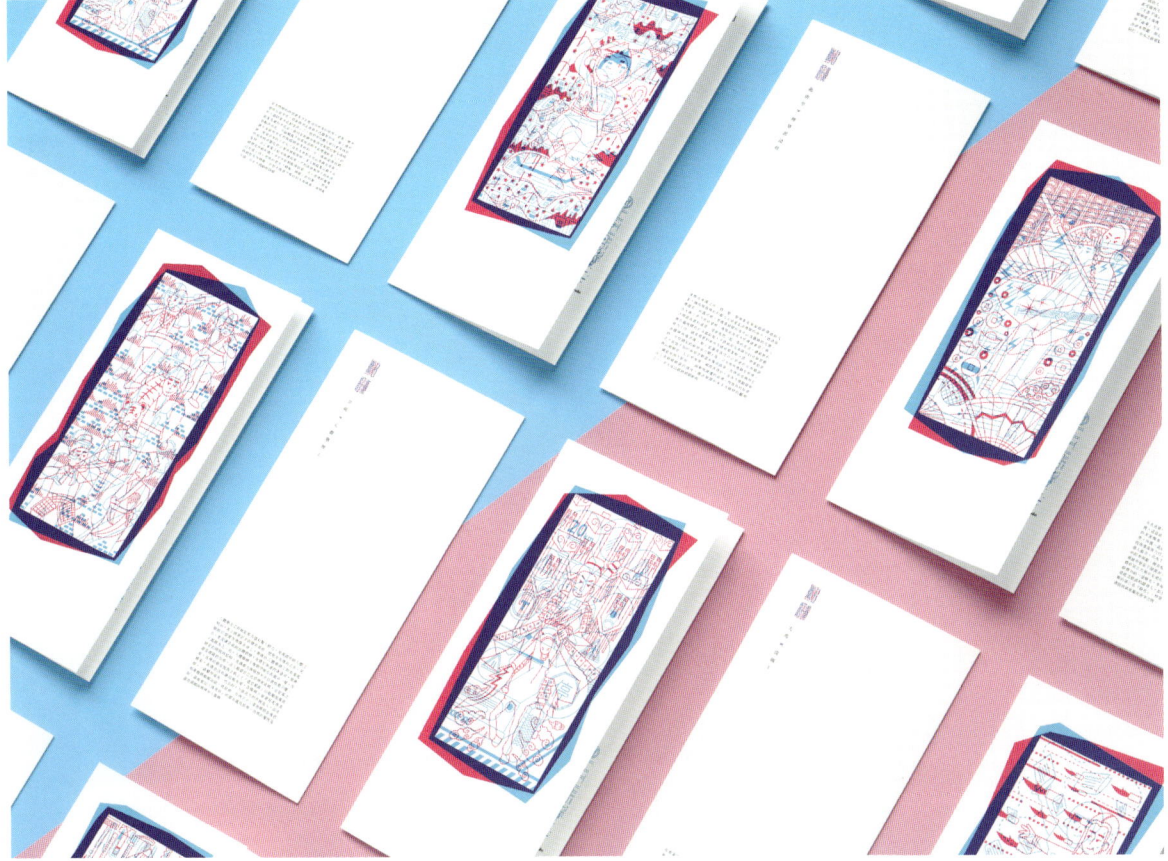

[Special Publication]

This project focuses on changing the stereotypical image people have of contract workers. Alongside traditional Chinese characters, it uses images that, when viewed under either a red or blue filter, reveals the contrast between common public perception of contract workers and the hidden skills and abilities these workers may possess. The various professions are furthermore represented by oriental heroes in order to redefine the image temporary employees have. When the pages are torn out of the flyers, they reveal the underlying courageous attributes of the heroes.

University
National Taipei University of Business
Taoyuan, Taiwan

Supervising Professor
Yu-Ju Lin

Design
Hsiao-Chi Chien, Wei-Hsuan Chen, Department of Commercial Design and Management, National Taipei University of Business

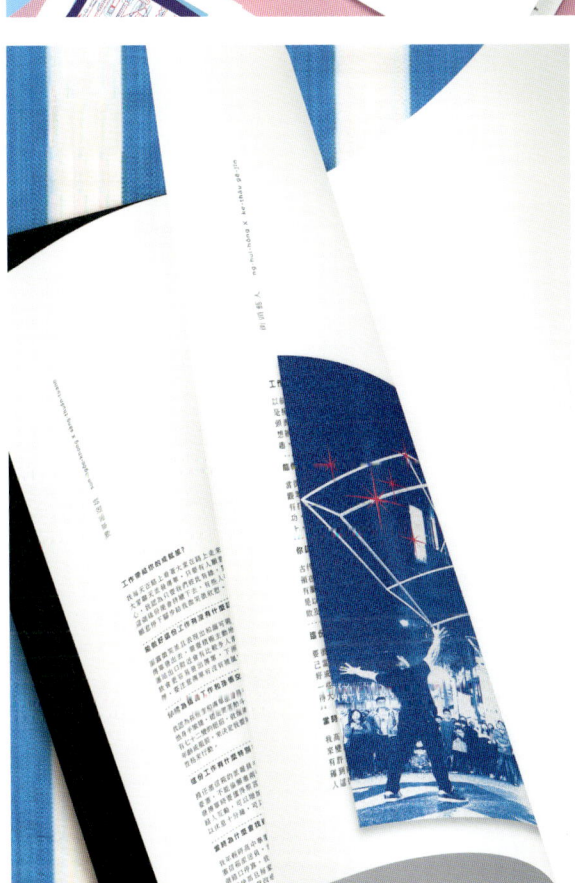

Publishing & Print Media	Posters	Typography	Illustrations	Sound Design	Film & Animation	Online
4	64	92	116	126	138	172

O'SH*T

[Newspaper]

O'SH*T is a biannual newspaper about the race towards fashion and sustainability with a humorous yet dramatic approach. The publication aims to raise awareness about the consequences of consumer habits and production conditions in the fashion industry, educating readers on the impacts of sustainability on our planet and at the same time encouraging them to make more conscious choices. The colours navy and orange are used to highlight the negative and positive sides of sustainability in fashion respectively. Vivid imagery combines linguistic aspects and photography in a creative, easy-to-understand and striking manner.

University
LASALLE College of the Arts
Singapore

Design
Vanessa Koh, LASALLE College of the Arts

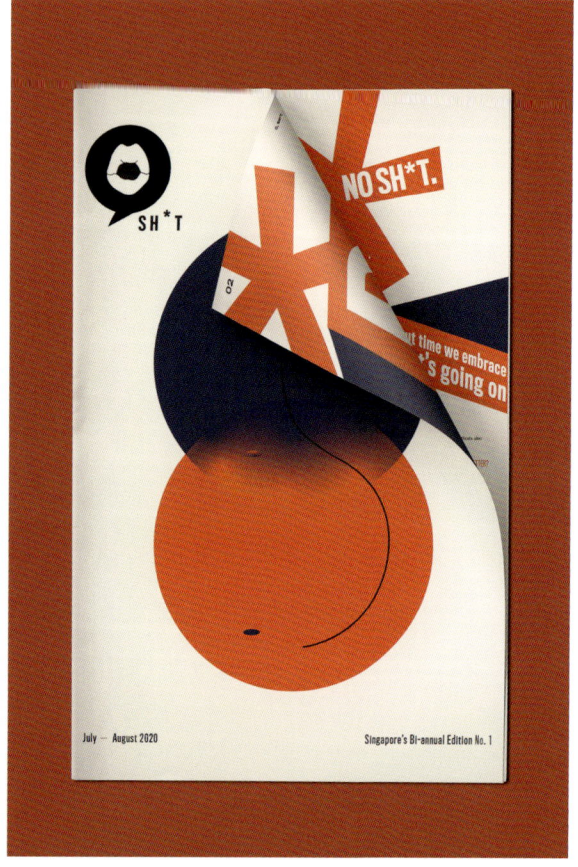

B1 – Land Subsidence of Taiwan

[Special Publication]

The main reason for the growing problem of land subsidence in Taiwan is that excessive amounts of groundwater are being drawn from the ground. This leads to further problems such as soil liquefaction and seawater intrusion. The book provides an introduction to the complex problem of land subsidence and describes the four main reasons that have caused this problem as well as the primary issues arising from it. Using a white font against a black background and just one other colour, red, the book presents countless data in easy-to-understand diagrams and information relating to land subsidence, thus raising public awareness of this issue.

University
Shu-Te University
Kaohsiung, Taiwan

Supervising Professor
Yueh-Ying Chen

Design
Ji-Rong Jiang, Hao-Jiun Yang,
Shang-Yi Huang, Kai-Ping Liao,
Shu-Te University

Publishing & Print Media	Posters	Typography	Illustrations	Sound Design	Film & Animation	Online
4	64	92	116	126	138	172

Paperfly

[Special Publication]

Due to climate change, the number of butterflies in Taiwan, once known as the Butterfly Kingdom for its numerous species, has drastically declined. "Paperfly" aims to raise awareness of environmental protection and ecological conservation among children by encouraging interaction with a set of seven creative and elaborately designed DIY paper products. Information and detailed instructions are provided to allow users to make kinetic butterfly models. The DIY process is designed to raise a person's interest in the state of butterflies in Taiwan and draw attention to their need for protection.

University
Chaoyang University of Technology
Taichung, Taiwan

Supervising Professor
Kuei-To Wang

Design
Yi-Jie Wang, Zhi-Lin Zeng, Fang-Yu Syu, Ya-Lin Hung, Cheng-Ta Hsiao, Chaoyang University of Technology

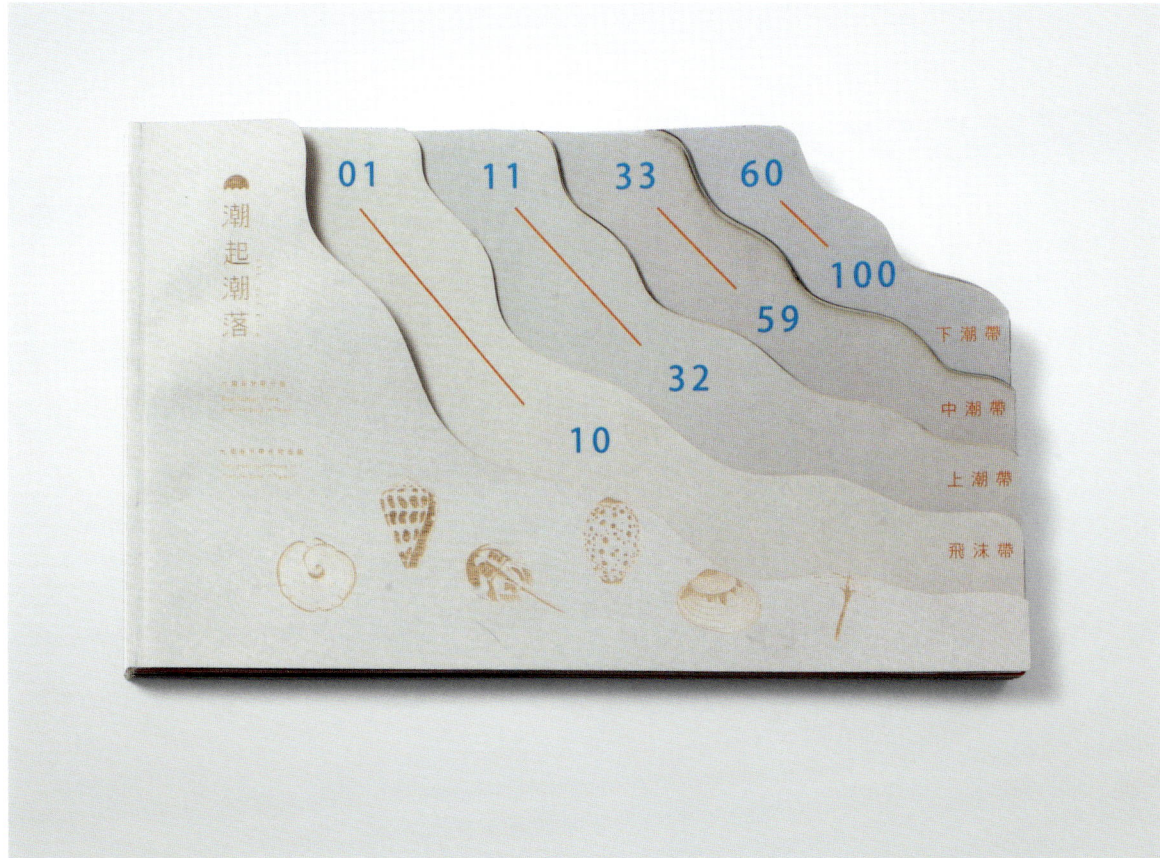

Apps	Interface & User Experience Design	Spatial Communication	Red Dot: Junior Award	Designer Profiles	Jury Portraits	Index
206	236	336	426	564	642	668

Ebb and Flow
[Special Publication]

The intertidal zone in Taiwan is divided into several terrains with different ecologies and vegetation that provide habitats for creatures, all of which change with the sea level. This project focuses on low and high tide, and presents the change of the shoreline, its various layers during the intertidal period and the biological features in an illustrated book, on posters and in a calendar whose design is inspired by the waxing and waning moon. Colours are used to make this natural cycle come alive visually: grey represents the intertidal zone, blue the sea and orange the vitality of the tidal zone.

University
Ling Tung University
Taichung, Taiwan

Supervising Professor
Tyng-Chau Hwang

Design
Hui-Ju Wen, Yi-Fang Tu, Fang-Yu Liu,
Syun Ciou, Wan-Ling Hsieh,
Ling Tung University

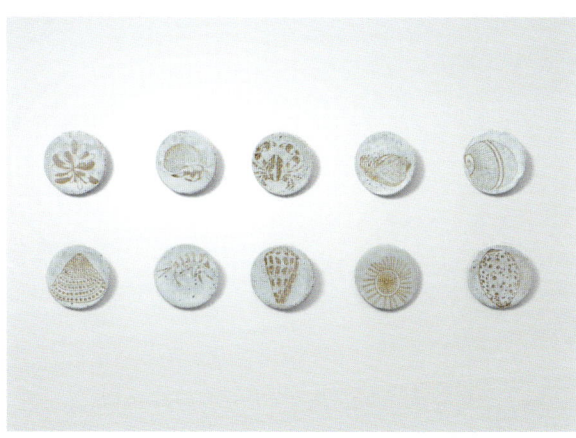

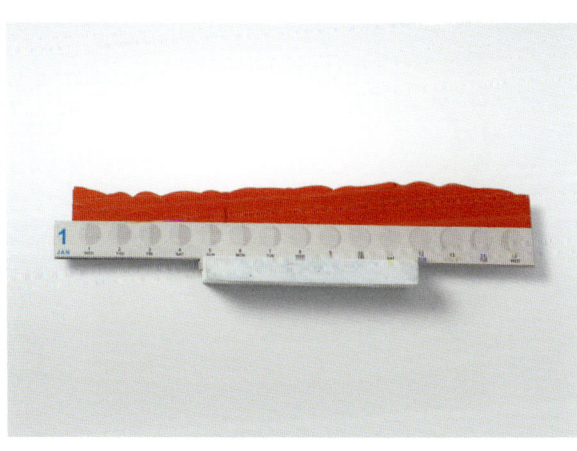

Publishing & Print Media	Posters	Typography	Illustrations	Sound Design	Film & Animation	Online
4	64	92	116	126	138	172

The Fridge

[Book]

Fishery and refrigeration technology have caused unregulated exploitation of maritime habitats to progress at an alarming rate over the years. The use of refrigerators makes it possible to store and preserve more and more food. The ocean may run out of seafood within just a few decades, with refrigerators becoming a deathbed for marine life. The chief element of this book involves detailed representations of fish and other marine species alongside realistic illustrations of refrigerators, thus underscoring the never-ending spiral of ecological disasters.

University
Shu-Te University
Kaohsiung, Taiwan

Supervising Professor
Yu-Lung Yang

Design
You-Ting Yan, Yen-Yun Kung, Jin-Ming Jiang, Chuan-Yi Hung, Cai-Feng Huang, Ya-Shan Xie, Shu-Te University

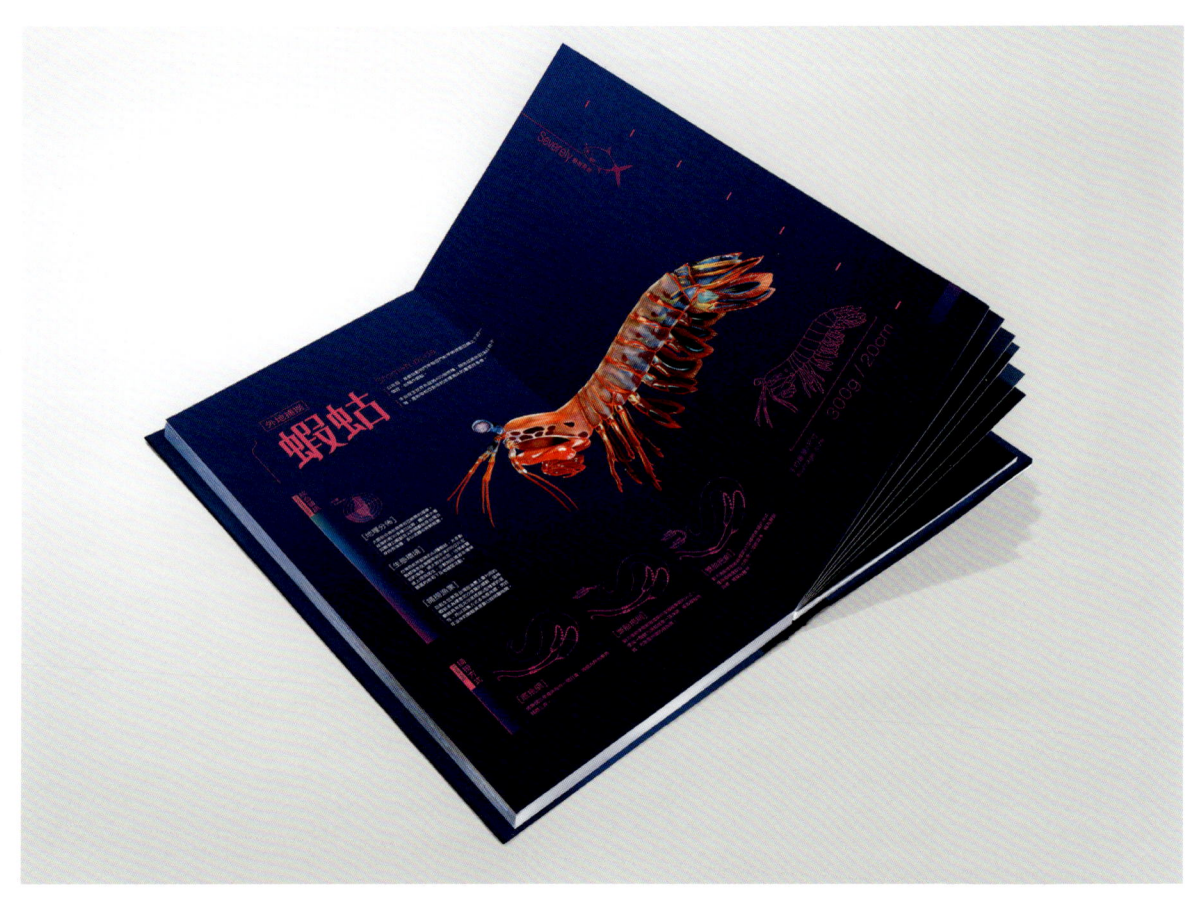

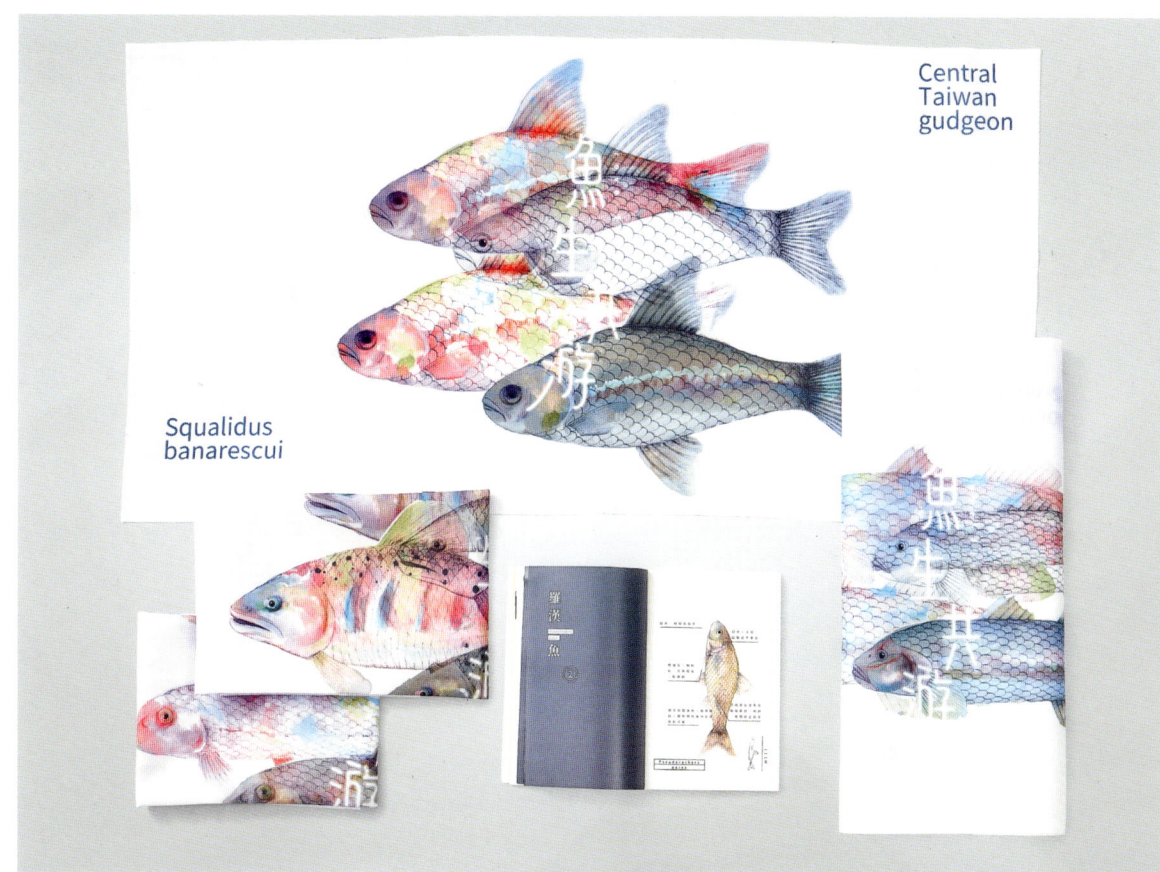

Rove Fish

[Special Publication]

Taiwan not only is rich in culture and nature, but also breeds many native fish species. The "Rove Fish" project presents the breeding of these fish, in particularly the gudgeon, through posters, meticulously thread-sewn booklets and an illustrated guide. Printed in light, friendly colours that replicate water and the shimmering silvery skin of a fish, the various components of the work document the fish's habitat, posture and body in detail and highlight them with flowing illustrations reminiscent of aquatic plants.

University
Ling Tung University
Taichung, Taiwan

Supervising Professor
Ding-Xian Yang, Chung-Yuan Kuo

Design
Li Chign Chang, Yun Chiao Wang, Tz Ying Lin, Xuan Yan Kuo, You Shan Xiao, Pin Wei Lee, Ling Tung University

From Taiwan

[Passport Redesign, Special Publication]

University
Southern Taiwan University of
Science and Technology
Tainan, Taiwan

Supervising Professor
Chia-Chun Lin

Design
Chun-Hao Hsu, Ya-Zhu Hsu, Ya-Hsin Tsai,
Southern Taiwan University of Science
and Technology

Apps	Interface & User Experience Design	Spatial Communication	**Red Dot: Junior Award**	Designer Profiles	Jury Portraits	Index
206	236	336	426	564	642	668

With the development and gradual expansion of the Taiwanese society, its people have more opportunity to interact with foreigners and make friends in different countries. A passport represents a person's identity and country and was chosen as a device to accentuate the scenic and cultural highlights of the country. The characteristic security threads and guilloche – a security feature to prevent the counterfeiting of documents – are key design elements and reproduce the various motifs in classic, light colours. QR codes and interactive AR functions direct users to a website with further information and videos.

Publishing & Print Media	Posters	Typography	Illustrations	Sound Design	Film & Animation	Online
4	64	92	116	126	138	172

Designing mobile systems

[Book]

This bachelor's thesis deals with the ever-increasing digitisation of our everyday lives and shows that the advantages of digital apps can also be applied to sports activities. It focuses on the analysis of economic conditions, the creation of the structural and technical concept as well as the visual design of the mobile app. Questions relating to software requirements and user interface design were determined using research methods and shown in a layout that displays the content and graphics in an easy-to-understand manner.

University
FH JOANNEUM – University of Applied Sciences
Graz, Austria

Design
Julia Krenn
Graz, Austria

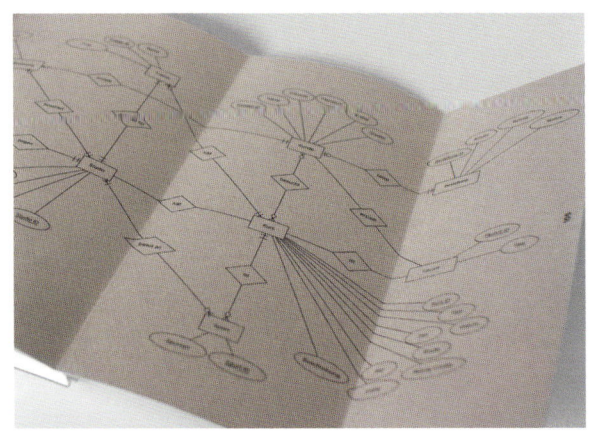

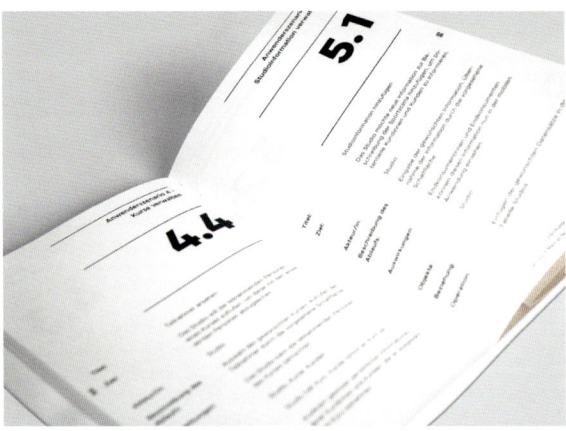

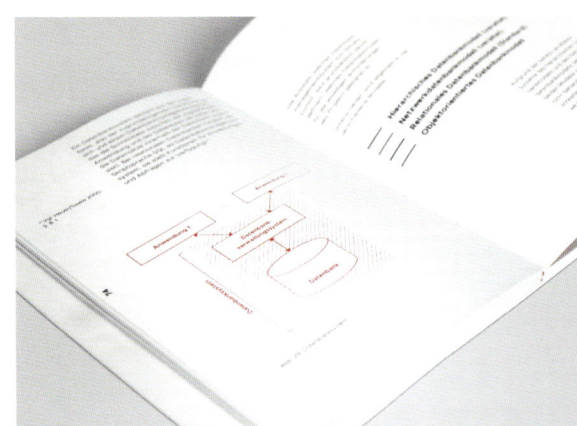

13 Waves

[Guidebook]

Developed for Chinese Taipei Surfing Association, "13 Waves" consists of 13 guide booklets that contain a range of information on ten major surfing spots. They describe the cultural features of the tourist destinations or provide an introduction to modern-day surfing to help the public get to know this sport. Three of the booklets are training guides that also cover topics such as safety and equipment. Supplied as a boxed set, the guides each have a different colour and contain many abstract illustrations that reflect this vigorous water sport.

University
China University of Technology
Taipei City, Taiwan

Supervising Professor
Chien-Hsun Chen, Jung-Shun Huang, Cheng-Ta Lee, Yao-Yuan Shang

Design
Po-Ching Lin, Yu-Wen Kao, Meng-Jie Chen, Wan-Juan Wu, Yu-Xiang Wang, Yu-Chi Li, Department of Visual Communication Design, China University of Technology

Publishing & Print Media	Posters	Typography	Illustrations	Sound Design	Film & Animation	Online
4	64	92	116	126	138	172

Taiwanese Festival
[Special Publication]

This project is based on Taiwan's six best-known lantern festivals. It aims to highlight local folk traditions and promote them in a special, traditional manner. Among these classic festivals is the momentous Bombing Master Han Dan festival in Taitung, where bare-chested men, playing the role of Lord Han Dan, voluntarily have fireworks thrown at them. The vibrant illustrations, printed in lively colours on a black background, are also available on 3D plexiglass light boxes and memorably presents the project's message.

University
Ming Chi University of Technology
New Taipei City, Taiwan

Design
Tzu-Yu Lin, Shun-Wen Hsiao, Jin-An Li, Jing-Wen Huang, Ming Chi University of Technology

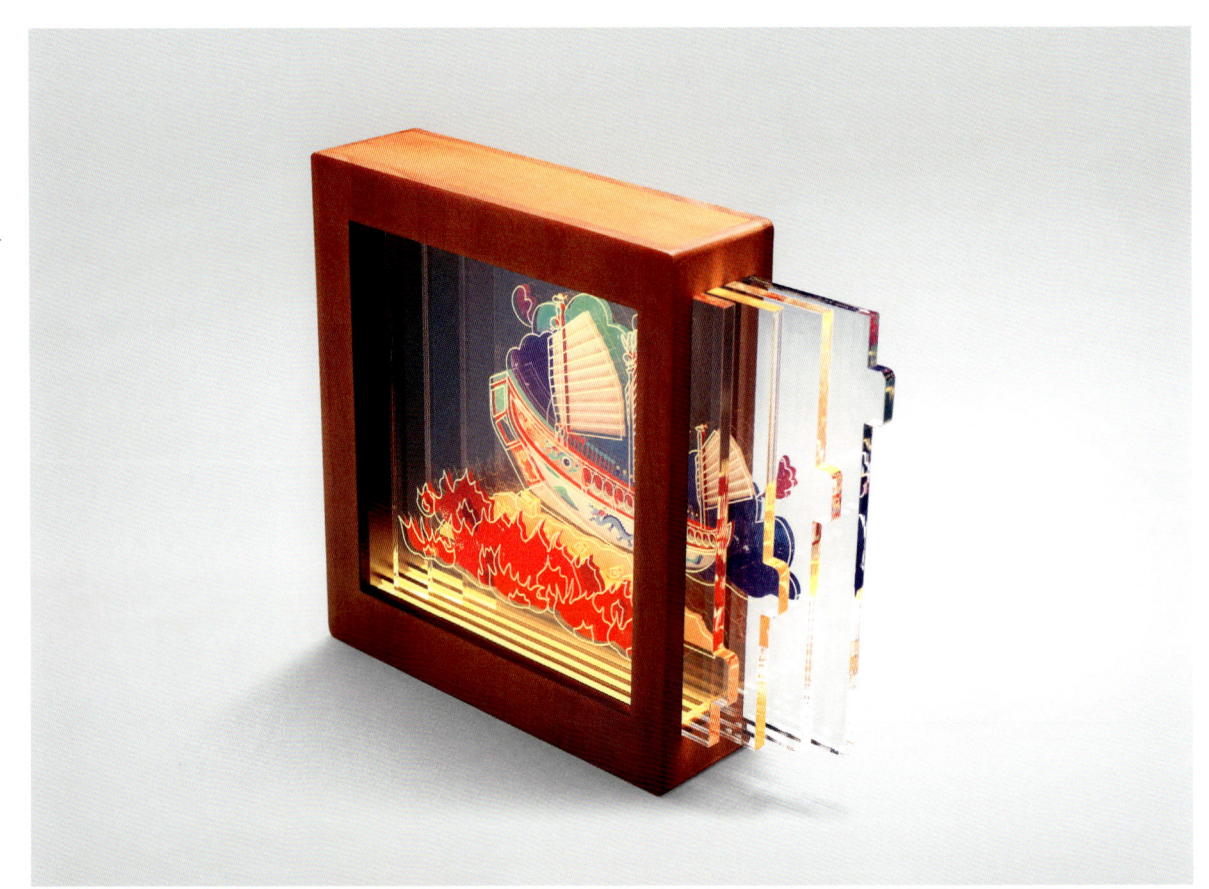

The Sounds of Night Market

[Special Publication]

The night market is the most popular tourist destination in Taiwan and part of its popular culture. This project is based on field research into famous night markets, as well as on audio and video recording. The work presents the lively nature of the goings-on through a mixture of illustrations, sound effects and interactive games. It uses the aesthetic of traditional vinyl records and a wide variety of night market-style packages to convey the unique beauty of this special element of Taiwanese culture and allow users to experience it no matter where they are or what time it might be.

University
China University of Technology
Taipei City, Taiwan

Supervising Professor
Yung-Pin Thao, Hsiao-Chin Wang,
Yuan-Hsun Chuang

Design
Pin-Jung Chen, Ting-Hsuan Hsu,
Chun-Wei Chang, Jia-Hong Xie,
Yu-Jie Hong, Department of Visual
Communication Design,
China University of Technology

Publishing & Print Media	Posters	Typography	Illustrations	Sound Design	Film & Animation	Online
4	64	92	116	126	138	172

Mountain Life

[Stamps, Special Publication]

Taipei City is surrounded by mountains in which ten beautiful countryside trails have been created. This project encompasses the design of stamps and albums depicting these trails, with the aim of encouraging the urban population to rediscover the mountains and nature. The landscape around Taipei is represented in a creative and detailed manner through images that promote nature-based tourism in the country as part of the cultural heritage. The individual stamp albums are each dedicated to a specific section of the trails and its features, and have a unique colour scheme.

University
China University of Technology
Taipei City, Taiwan

Supervising Professor
Chien-Hsun Chen, Cheng-Ta Lee

Design
Chieh-Hsi Liao, Wei-Ling Hou,
Chien Chieh, Hui-Chi Tien,
Department of Visual Communication
Design, China University of Technology

Life in Wenzi

[Special Publication]

"Life in Wenzi" introduces readers to Wenzi, a Taiwanese fishing village that has retained its unique way of life, offers adventure tours and makes sea products. The project consists of an interactive 360-degree, 3D book and also presents the village as a secret realm of the martial arts to allude to the craft of fishing and oyster-shucking. Decorated with oriental-style water colours, the creatively and lavishly produced paper book with interlocking mechanisms features elements that can be folded out, pushed or pulled to let readers experience the diversity of life in Wenzi.

University
Asia University
Taichung, Taiwan

Supervising Professor
Hui-Ping Lu

Design
Chi-Ping Huang, Yu-Jung Chen, Fang-Chun Lin, Yi-Han Huang, Ni-En Tsai, Chia-Yi Lin, Asia University

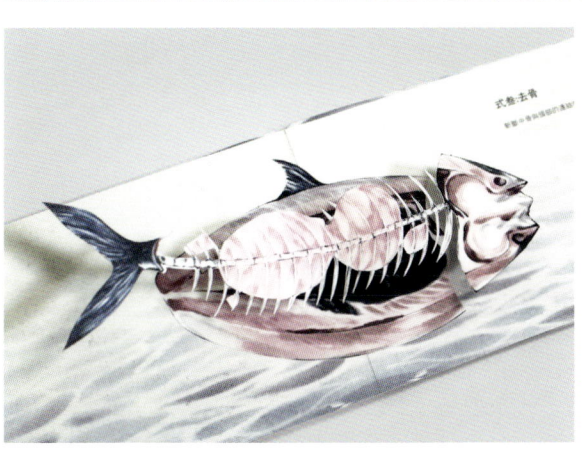

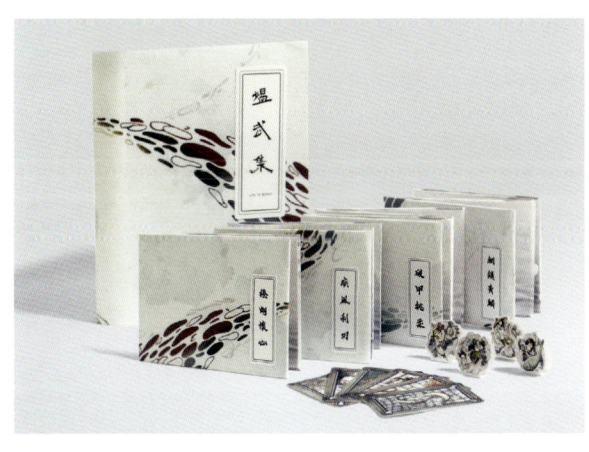

Publishing & Print Media	Posters	Typography	Illustrations	Sound Design	Film & Animation	Online
4	64	92	116	126	138	172

The Word on the Road

[Poster Series]

The emotions in a moment in time are captured by the motifs of the project "The Word on the Road". The photographs show everyday objects and places such as streets, a staircase or a chair, and are an expressive call to focus on the present moment and to pay close attention even in everyday life. Unusual perspectives make the special nature of what initially appears mundane visible and tangible. Each image is created in such a way as to arouse emotions in the beholder, develop its very own imagery and convey messages which in turn can be translated into a new language.

University
Shu-Te University
Kaohsiung, Taiwan

Supervising Professor
Hui-Lin Chiu

Design
Hsuan-Hung Hsu, Chun-Wei Tseng,
Ya-Ching Tseng, Cih-Yan Kang,
Jun-Wei Liu, Chia-Tsan Lin,
Shu-Te University

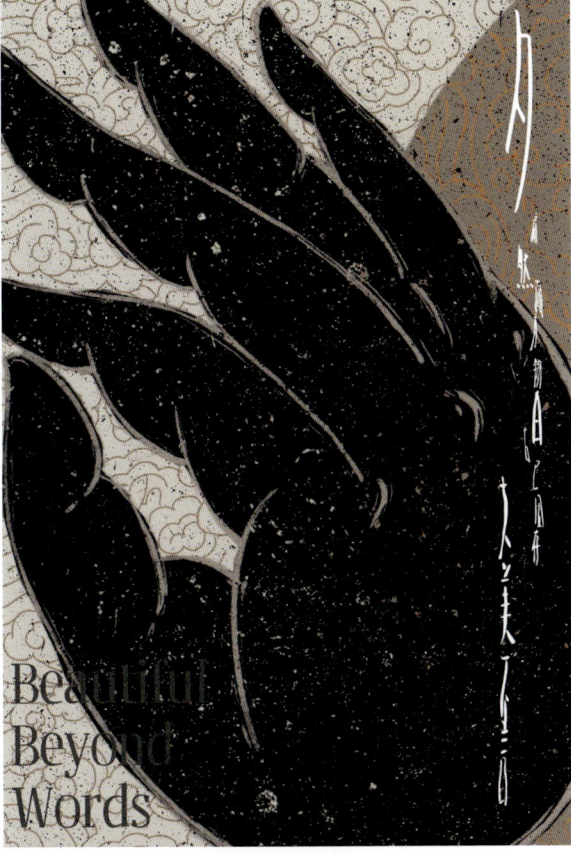

Beautiful Beyond Words
[Art Poster]

The poster series "Beautiful Beyond Words" summarises the thoughts of Chinese philosopher Chuang-tzu on nature in eight motifs and explores the Taoist view of heaven and earth. A stylistic mix of traditional works on paper and modern multimedia methods portrays the changing of the seasons and the movement of time from sunrise to sunset. The abstract design visualises the inseparable link between beauty and nature, which often cannot be explained with words but can be portrayed artistically and understood intuitively.

University
869 school of design
Dalian, China

Supervising Professor
Jiang Xue

Design
Yin He, Zhang Zhibin, Wen Mengxi, Zhang Yanfeng, 869 school of design

→ Clip online

Forbidden

[Art Poster]

"Forbidden" speaks out for freedom of expression and calls on observers to speak, watch and listen. The prohibitions printed in white font against a black background, "Close your eyes", "Shut your mouth" and "Cover your ears", are reinterpreted ad absurdum using simple but all the more effective illustrations. Through the hands covering the eyes, ears and mouth in a bid to curb freedom of opinion and expression, the eyes are still watching, the wide-open mouth is still protesting and the ears are still listening.

Client
JXDesign
Hangzhou, China

University
Zhejiang Gongshang University
Hangzhou, China

Design
Liao Shucheng, Lin Xingmin, Li Shangtan,
Hangzhou College of Commerce,
Zhejiang Gongshang University

THE MOST BEAUTIFUL SCENERY IN TAIWAN IS PEOPLE

HUMAN WARMTH

PLEASURE FROM HELPING OTHERS

HELP EACH OTHER

EPIDEMIC PREVENTION IS LIKE FIGHTING

EPIDEMIC PREVENTION

Taiwan

[Poster Series]

This series of posters communicates Taiwan's characteristics of hospitality and helpfulness as well as its transparent epidemic prevention strategy in a bid to advertise holidays and short stays there. Streamlined motifs and short core messages have a concise and succinct impact. Hands are featured as a repetitive common thread throughout the design. Hands holding each other in a protective and supportive way combine to create an outline map of the country. Each motif and each feature is allocated a clear colour scheme, visually reinforcing the respective message.

University
Chihlee University of Technology
New Taipei City, Taiwan

Supervising Professor
Shih-Lun Chen

Design
Ya-Ci Cai,
Chihlee University of Technology

Publishing & Print Media	Posters	Typography	Illustrations	Sound Design	Film & Animation	Online
4	64	92	116	126	138	172

Creators'
[Event Poster]

What is it that shapes a generation? The poster series "Creators'" makes a bold comparison to find an answer to this question. Like tectonic plates, which move and change the face of the Earth, one motif shows human figures stacked one above the other. They too move and change the world, everyone individually and yet collectively. The printing effects chosen create a special multi-layered impact. A conscious link is created between stone and minerals through the colours used. The change brought about by COVID-19 is also referenced, with one motif depicting figures wearing masks and observing social distancing.

University
Ling Tung University
Taichung, Taiwan

Supervising Professor
Chung-Yuan Kuo, An-Hui Ching

Design
Pei-Cheng Jian, Chia-Hsuan Chang, Wei-Neng Chen, Xin-Hong Guo, Jia-Yi Wu, Jin-Jia Zhang,
Ling Tung University

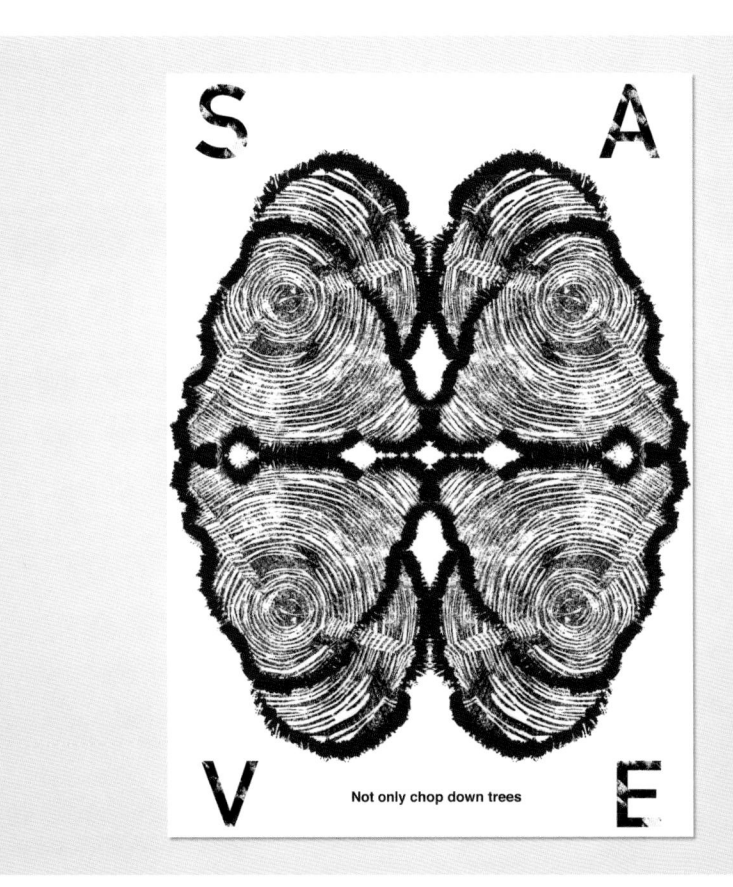

Not Only Chop Down Trees

[Promotional Poster]

This series uses expressive motifs as a plea for reafforestation. Animal species suffering from a loss of forest habitat are at the heart of the posters. Annual rings are used to create black-and-white outlines of species such as turtles and bears. This underscores the symbiotic relationship between species and their habitat, while the dark colours used for the motifs visualise the creeping threat that accompanies deforestation. The slogan "Save me" is positioned prominently and given a bright-red colour.

University
Asia University
Taichung, Taiwan

Supervising Professor
Ming-Lung Yu, Jia-An Lin

Design
Tzu-Hsuan Fan, Asia University

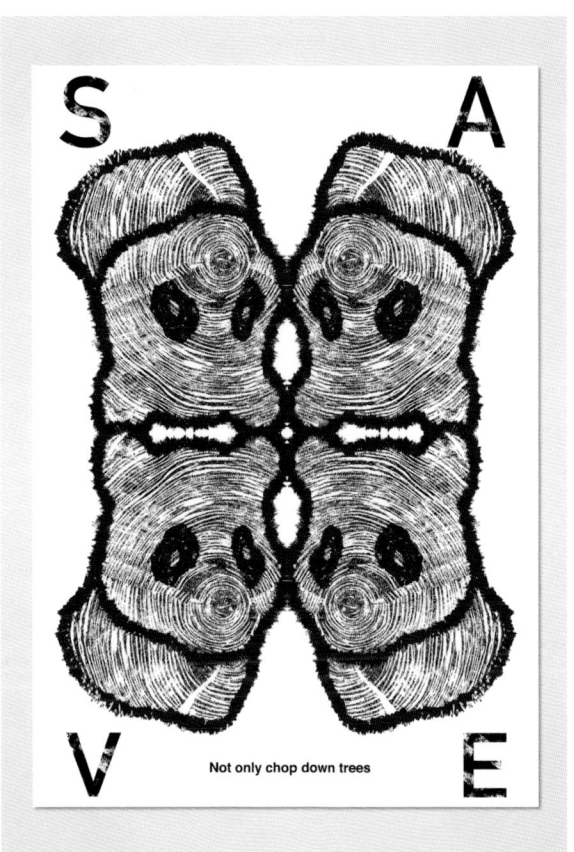

Publishing & Print Media	Posters	Typography	Illustrations	Sound Design	Film & Animation	Online
4	64	92	116	126	138	172

LIBERTYGRAPHY
[Typeface]

The typeface LIBERTYGRAPHY is inspired by the typeface of marching slogans from Taiwan's history. Its dynamic look is reminiscent of the masses in the social movement, who stood up for the democratisation and independence of their country. Thick strokes combined with rounded corners lend the typeface a smooth and rational appeal. The thick strokes on the right aim to symbolise the direction in which people march. The length-to-width ratio of the characters is 10:6 and the centre of gravity is on the left. Depending on the writing direction, the strokes on the right are thick and rounded.

University
Ling Tung University
Taichung, Taiwan

Supervising Professor
Chien-Wen Chen, Wen-Jen Huang

Design
Rui-Ling Qiu, Re-Chi Zhao,
Yi-Hsuan Tsai, Qing-Ru Zhan, Abigail See,
Ling Tung University

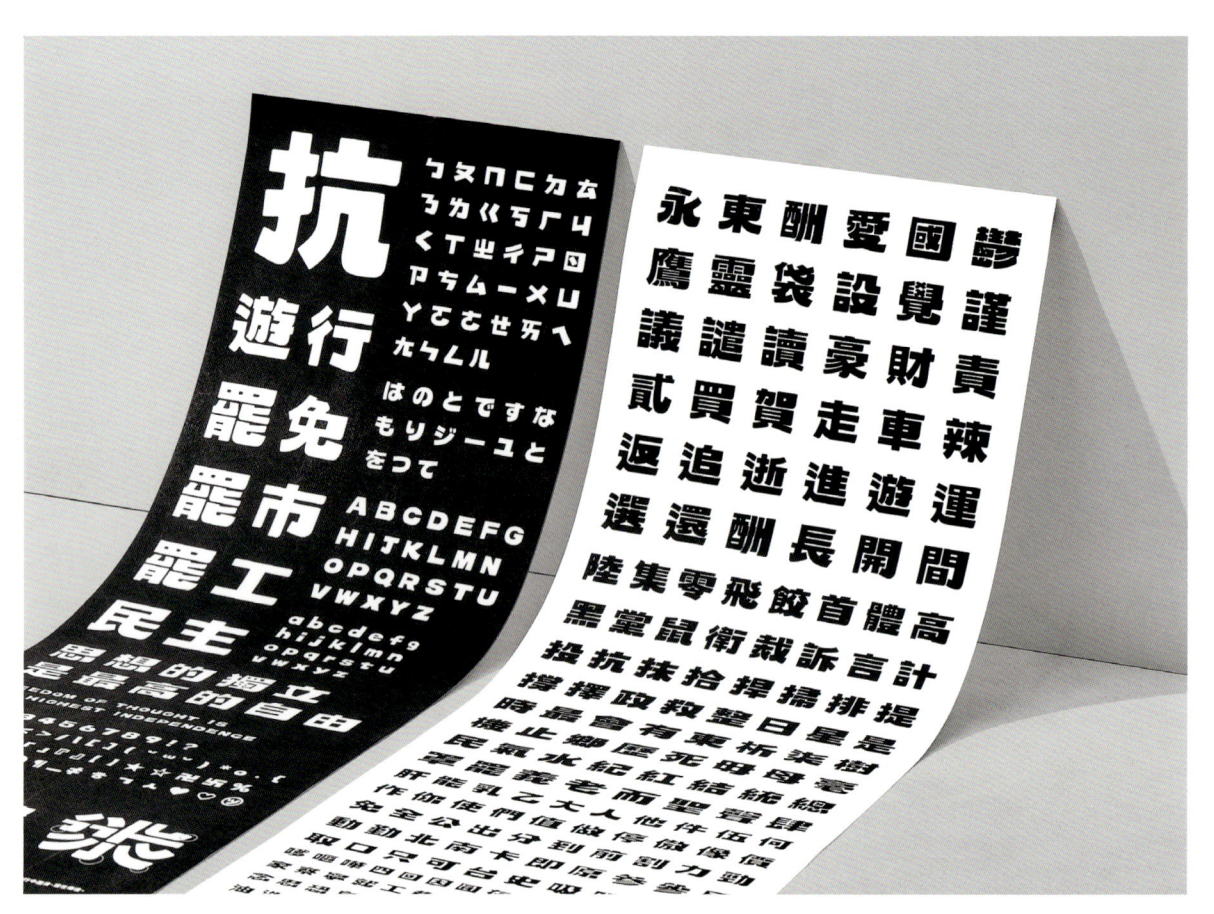

496

Filigran Gothic

[Typeface]

Filigran Gothic is an original typeface inspired by the branches in Fraktur type and the high contrast of fat-face serifs. It is a heavyweight display type intended to be used large on designs such as branding and print media. The typeface's most interesting features include the weight axis variations as well as the mix of translation and expansion strokes. The stroke endings are also remarkably abrupt, which lends the type a three-dimensional appeal and is reminiscent of the brush strokes in calligraphy. The full typeface includes standard ligatures and alternative glyphs that make it versatile for different designs.

University
SCAD Savannah College of Art and Design
Savannah, USA

Design
Allison Davis, SCAD

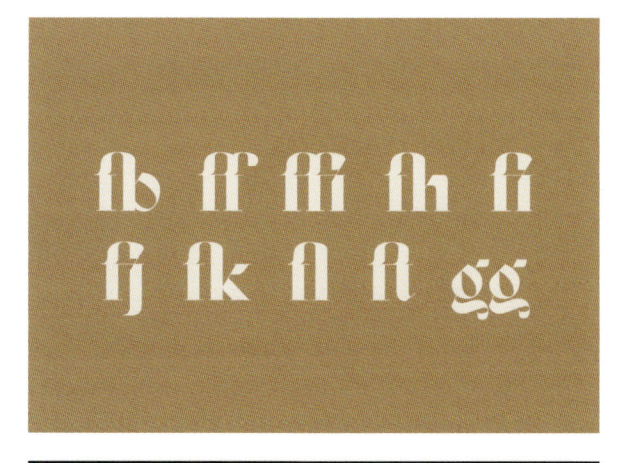

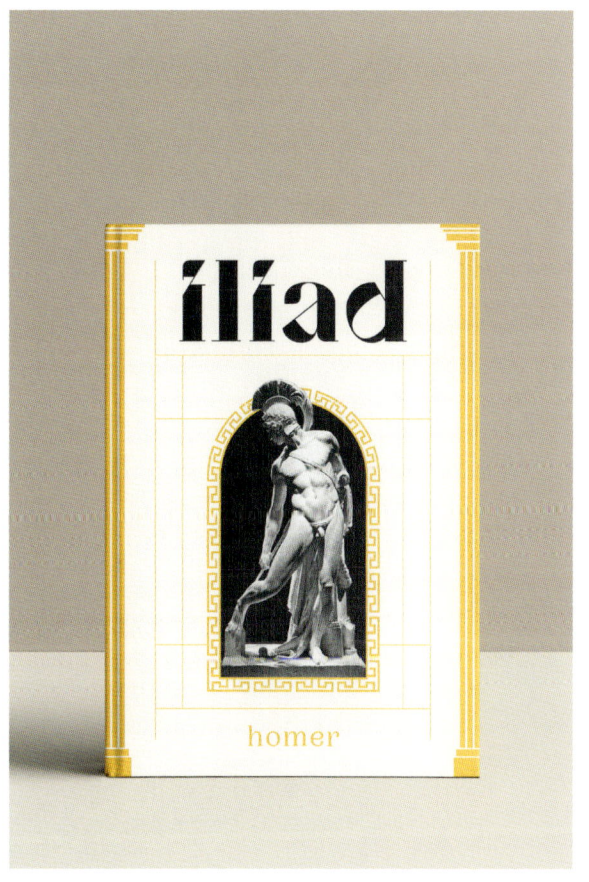

Publishing & Print Media	Posters	Typography	Illustrations	Sound Design	Film & Animation	Online
4	64	92	116	126	138	172

Enter the World of Fish
[Informative Illustrations]

"Enter the World of Fish" summarises information on fish and seafood as well as their origins. The design of posters, fish passports and fish identity cards places great emphasis on visually conveying basic facts in order to change consumers' purchasing behaviour and eating habits, and thereby counteract overfishing. The facts are all accompanied by naturalistic, life-like illustrations of the various fish species. The drawings are surrounded by wave-like patterns and shapes which give the images great dynamism and visual impact.

University
National Yunlin University of Science and Technology
Douliu City, Yunlin County, Taiwan

Supervising Professor
Chia-Wen Lin, Jung Tsao, Nick Chao, Wingly Shih

Design
Yi-Shan Lin, National Yunlin University of Science and Technology

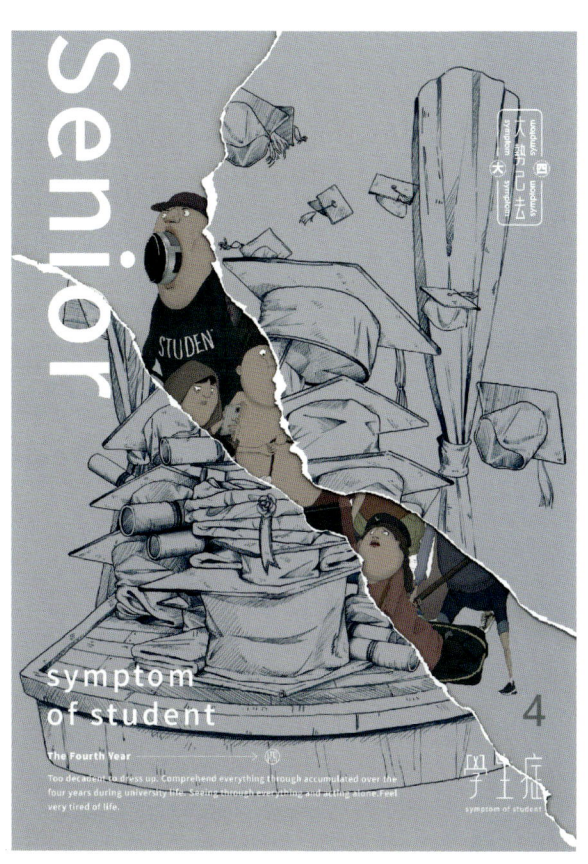

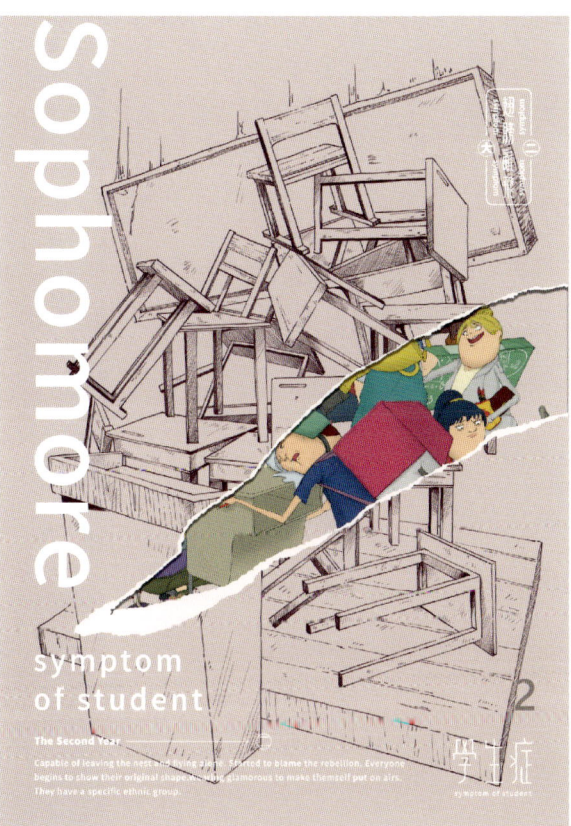

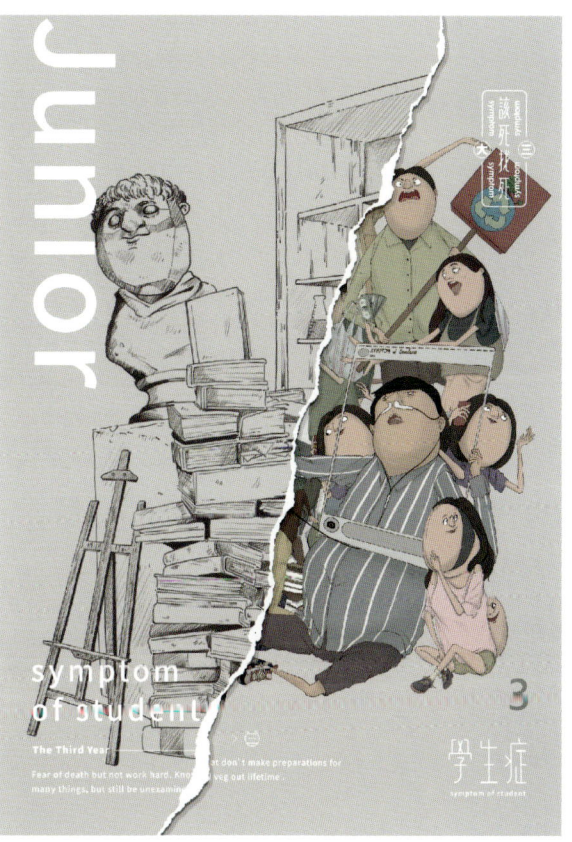

Symptom of Student

[Poster Illustrations]

Student life in Taiwan today is critically but also humorously explored by this series of illustrations. The ironic drawings portray student life from being a college freshman through to being a senior as a sickness-inducing journey full of parties, between stuffed wardrobes and immersed in chaotic disorder. The colouring of the illustrations highlights the students' development. While strong, bright colours predominate in the early period, students in later semesters are characterised by matt, pale tones. The 52 main symptoms covered in the books are intended to make students reflect on their behaviour.

University
Shu-Te University
Kaohsiung, Taiwan

Supervising Professor
Hui-Lin Chiu

Design
Hong-Yuan Zhou, Chen-Chen Chang, Yan-Zhen Li, Shu-Te University

Publishing & Print Media	Posters	Typography	Illustrations	Sound Design	Film & Animation	Online
4	64	92	116	126	138	172

Reunite
[Illustration]

"Reunite" is an experimental work about the current state of the world, reflecting the artist's thoughts. Divided into four separate images, the paintings show the splitting of the world as we know it, as well as the drifting apart of people and other creatures who live on Earth and are experiencing major crises. The faceless figures remain isolated and turn away from each other, all sucked in by and drowning in the maelstrom of events. At the end of this effectively visualised snapshot in time, hope in the Earth itself remains as a constant that brings people together.

University
SCAD Savannah College of Art and Design
Savannah, USA

Design
Jessie Lin, SCAD

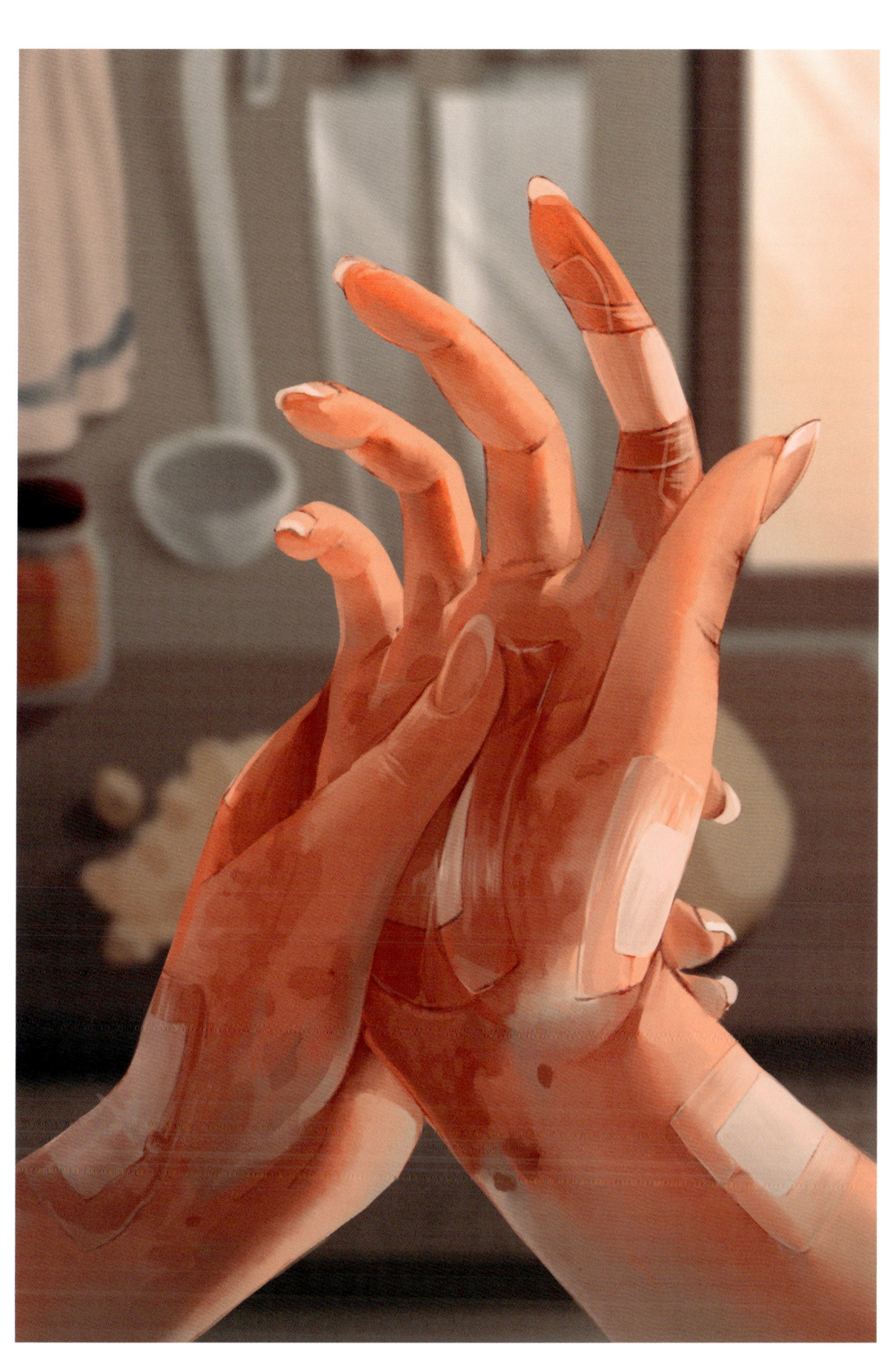

Hands

[Historical Illustration]

"Hands" is based on the invention of adhesive bandages, which were developed by Earle Dickson in 1920. His wife often cut or burnt herself while cooking. He would prepare some gauze which she could apply herself. This thoughtful aspect of the invention is reflected by the bright colours of the illustration. It is dominated by warm, human flesh tones, used not only for the hands themselves but also for the kitchen setting. The close-up of the hands looks intimate and also creates an image of self-care as the bandage allows people to treat themselves instead of needing the help of someone else.

University
SCAD Savannah College of Art and Design
Savannah, USA

Design
Genevieve Bedell, SCAD

Publishing & Print Media	Posters	Typography	Illustrations	Sound Design	Film & Animation	Online
4	64	92	116	126	138	172

Men Smoke
[Editorial Illustration]

The editorial illustration "Men Smoke" represents loneliness and the way in which it is connected to creativity and learning. This painting is based on the feelings the artist experienced over the course of his artistic development. The smoke in the hands of this character expresses not only confusion but also represents a calm and serene feeling. The motif aims to pose questions, to be thought-provoking, and to touch the viewers and make them eager to know the story behind the characters in the painting as well as reflect on ways in which they can release and express their own creative ideas.

University
SCAD Savannah College of Art and Design
Savannah, USA

Design
Ke Gao, SCAD

Yellow Face

[Editorial Illustration]

The editorial illustration "Yellow Face" is an exploratory and experimental piece which shows a narrative from a unique perspective. During the design phase, the aim of the artist was to try out new line work, colours and textures in order to further develop his own style while searching for a future direction for his drawing. The contrasting colouring of the illustration catches the eye immediately. The use of familiar colour combinations is paired with the attempt to break through people's established understanding of object colours.

University
SCAD Savannah College of Art and Design
Savannah, USA

Design
Ke Gao, SCAD

Twelve Main Meridians

[Informative Illustrations]

Meridians are at the core of traditional Chinese medicine. These illustrations introduce the twelve main meridians in three books. Corresponding to the time of day when the various treatments can be used, the book banners differ markedly in their colouring. The illustrations blend Western and Oriental cultural style elements with the aim of communicating knowledge of the meridians as a type of legacy for humankind. The drawings are based on the decorative patterns found on ancient Greek clay pots and murals in combination with ancient Chinese characters.

University
Shu-Te University
Kaohsiung, Taiwan

Supervising Professor
Yu-Lung Yang

Design
Wun-Min Yuan, Yu-Zhen Lee,
Jia-Cheng Wu, Xin-Ying Zeng, Ko-Hsin Yu,
Ciang-Yu Cai, Shu-Te University

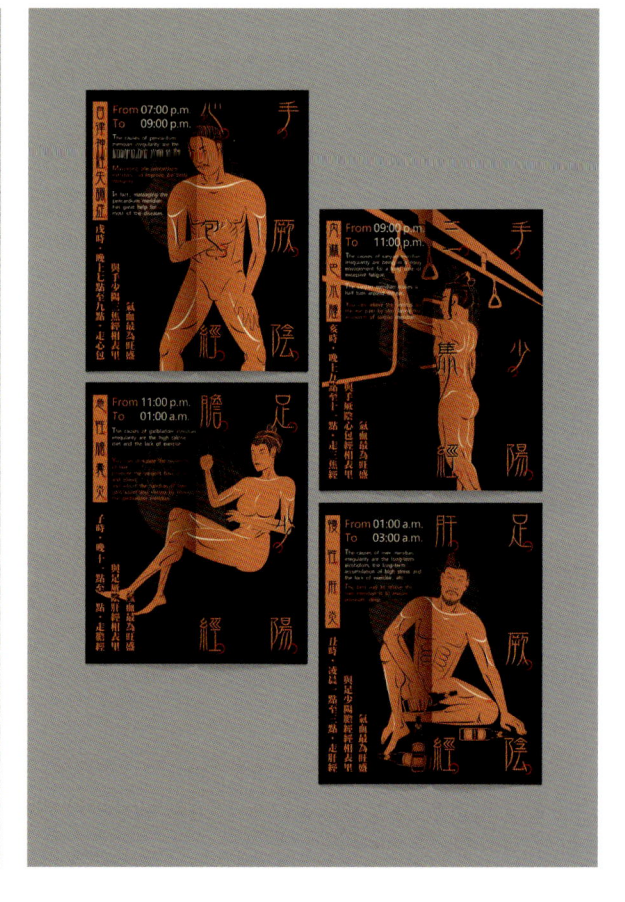

An-Fang

[Illustrations]

The Taiwanese religious ceremony of An-Fang is addressed in these richly detailed illustrations. Fine, bronze-coloured illustrations against a jet-black background capture the Taoist gods and the tradition and rituals behind the celebrations. The colours and execution create a mysterious, mystical atmosphere, which captivates the viewer and draws them into the events depicted. The production process combined modern technology with tradition: ten illustrations, created using technical drawing pens, have been scanned at a high resolution, digitally coloured, printed on rice paper and then mounted in the style of a traditional Taoist scroll.

University
China University of Technology
Taipei City, Taiwan

Supervising Professor
Yuan-Hsun Chuang, Hsiao-Chin Wang, Shuo-Ting Wei, Yung-Ping Tsao

Design
Kai-Xiang Lei, Shyao Hong, Ping-Chih Lai, Cheng-Ping Shih, Ya-Min Cheng, Department of Visual Communication Design, China University of Technology

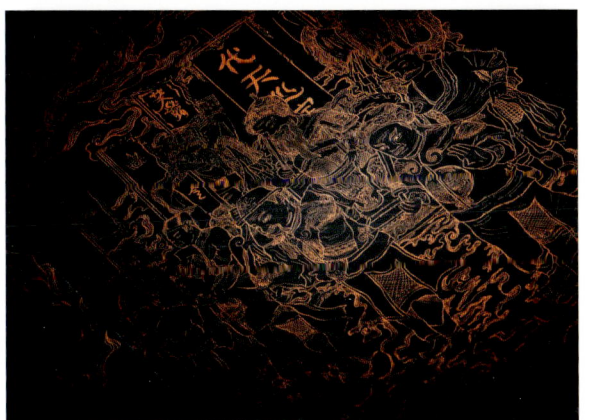

Publishing & Print Media	Posters	Typography	Illustrations	Sound Design	Film & Animation	Online
4	64	92	116	126	138	172

Ruse

[Illustration]

This is an illustration for "The Tale of the Wazir of King Yunan and Rayyan the Doctor". The king's throne and other background content are drawn with complicated lines, showing the extravagant court life. The dying king and the decapitated head of the doctor constitute the foreground. Compared with the complicated depiction of the background, the figures in the foreground are characterised by much plainer styling. That makes them stand out from the secular atmosphere of the background and expresses the absurdity of the fable: the moment when the dead doctor gets his revenge on the evil king is entirely the desire of the storyteller.

University
SCAD Savannah College of Art and Design
Savannah, USA

Design
Jiayun Fan, SCAD

Freyr

[Character Design, Poster Illustration]

The "Freyr" project was inspired by the mythological Norse god of the same name. The illustration represents key features and symbols of the god such as the sword and a piece of fruit, which represents good harvest and fertility. Both help the viewer to recognise and identify Freyr. At the same time, the illustration offers a modern interpretation and design for the character. A printmaking look was chosen in order to evoke a sense of ancient mythology. The overlapping of colours and the wood engraving edges were also designed to produce a vintage feel.

University
SCAD Savannah College of Art and Design
Savannah, USA

Design
Yujia Zhang, SCAD

Publishing & Print Media	Posters	Typography	Illustrations	Sound Design	Film & Animation	Online
4	64	92	116	126	138	172

RAN
[Interactive Illustration]

University
Weißensee Academy of Art Berlin
Berlin, Germany

Supervising Professor
Barbara Junge, Kathi Kaeppel,
Julian Adenauer

Design
Ailun Jiang
Berlin, Germany

→ Designer profile on page 629
→ Clip online

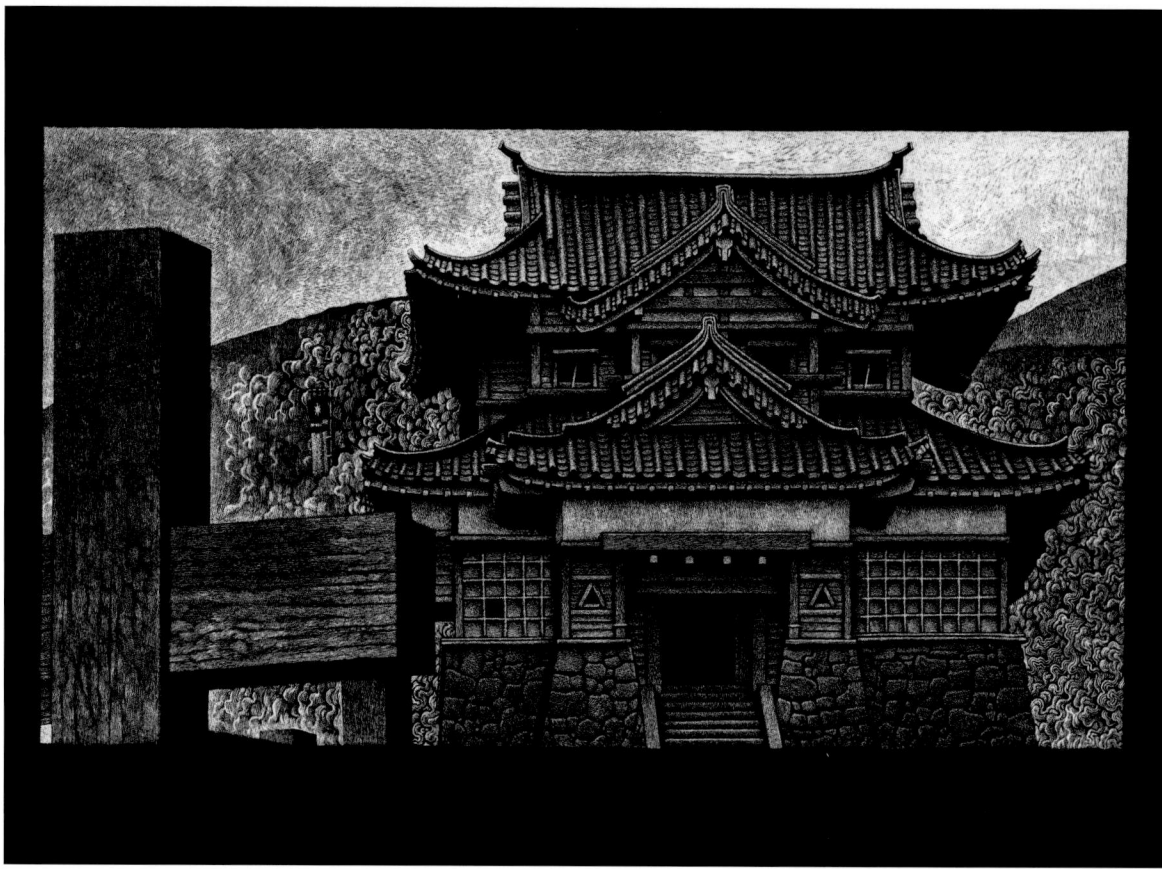

"RAN" is based on the eponymous film by Akira Kurosawa. The interactive scratchboard illustrations reinterpret the dramatic story and the philosophical spirit of the samurai. The characters, clothing, sets and battle scenes are all remarkably realistic in their representation and rich in detail. All drawings are in shades of black, white and grey. The signal colour red is used to accentuate expressive highlights and thus gives the illustrations an additional sense of drama. In combination with haunting sounds, the scenes exert a strong pull which is difficult to resist.

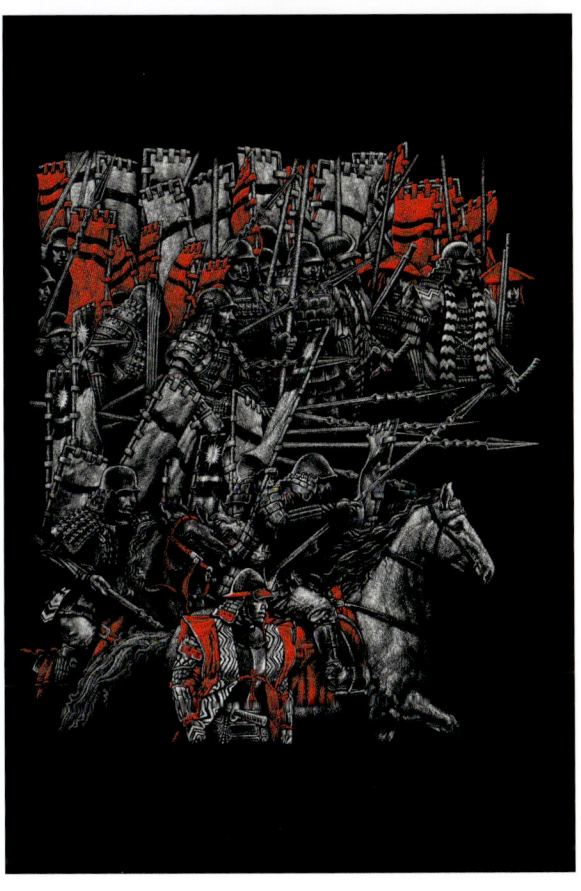

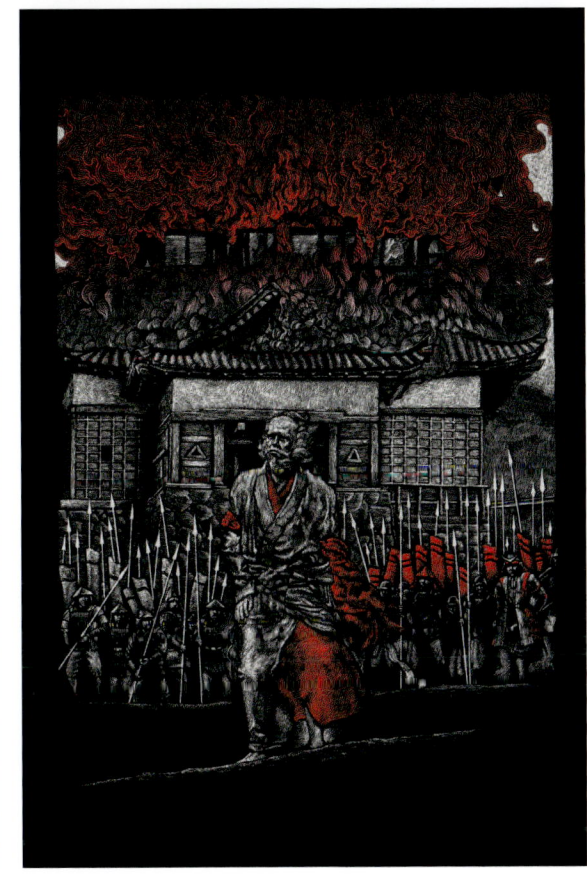

Publishing & Print Media	Posters	Typography	Illustrations	Sound Design	Film & Animation	Online
4	64	92	116	126	138	172

Dracula

[Book Cover Illustration]

This book cover illustration was handcrafted with layers of paper and painted details in gouache. The typography of "Dracula" was specially designed for the project. The novel's themes of power and mystery were the main inspiration for the illustration. The piece's fundamental composition demonstrates Dracula's manipulative power. The vertical composition with red as the predominant colour furthermore references his thirst for blood. The Dracula piece implies the mysteriousness of a character who is unknown throughout most of the story. This mystery is represented by the control this character exerts without showing his face.

University
SCAD Savannah College of Art and Design
Savannah, USA

Design
Dana SanMar, SCAD

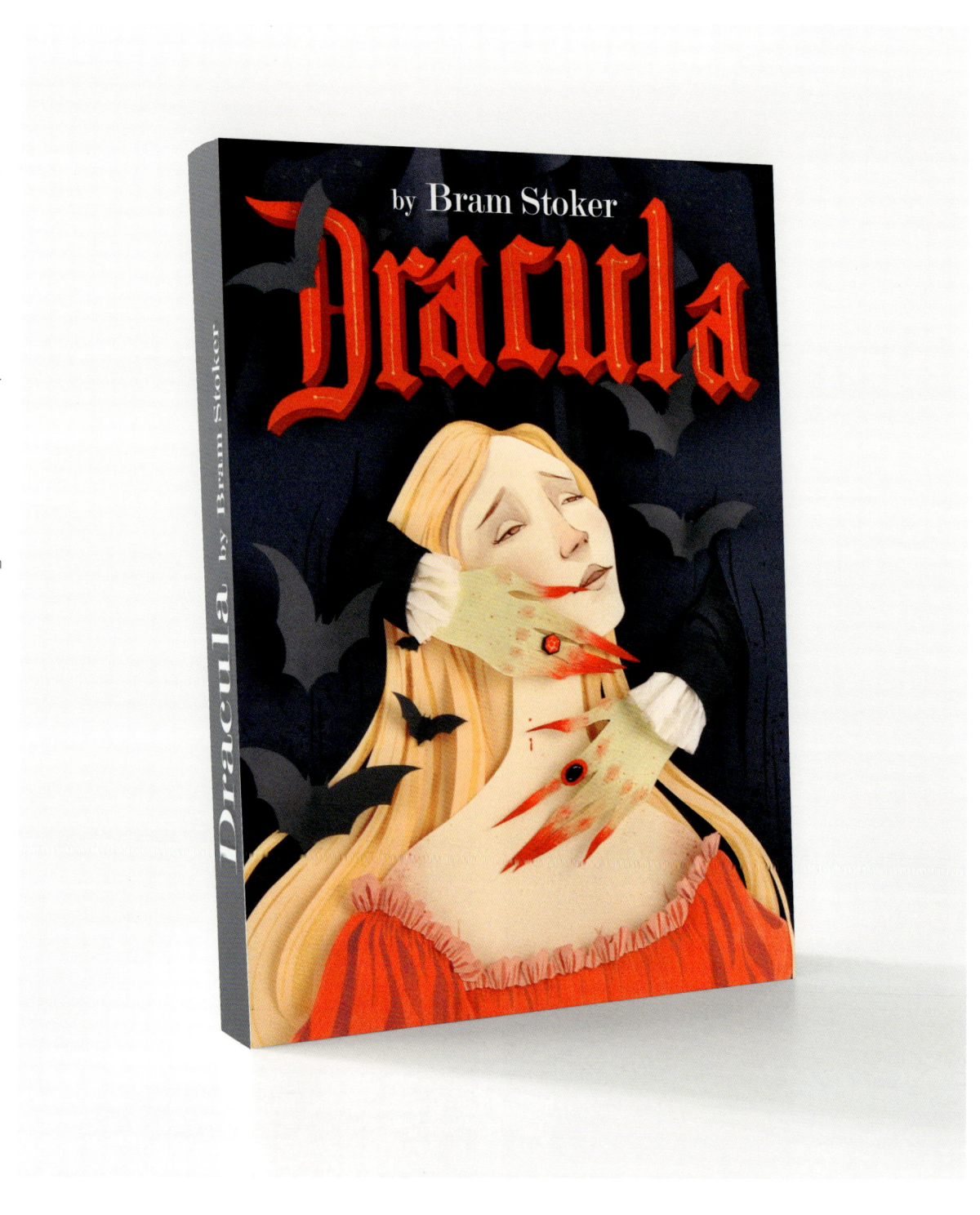

Howl's Moving Castle

[Book Cover Illustration]

This handcrafted book cover illustration for the book "Howl's Moving Castle" expresses the protagonist Sophie's transformation. The story's sense of adventure and magic are visualised by the main character, Sophie, who is floating in the middle of the night. Elements relevant to the story, like the hats and shooting starts, float around her, symbolising her growth. By the end of the story, she has found peace, which is apparent in her resting face. The piece's fundamental composition is one of outward radiation from the flaming heart as a centrepiece.

University
SCAD Savannah College of Art and Design
Savannah, USA

Design
Dana SanMar, SCAD

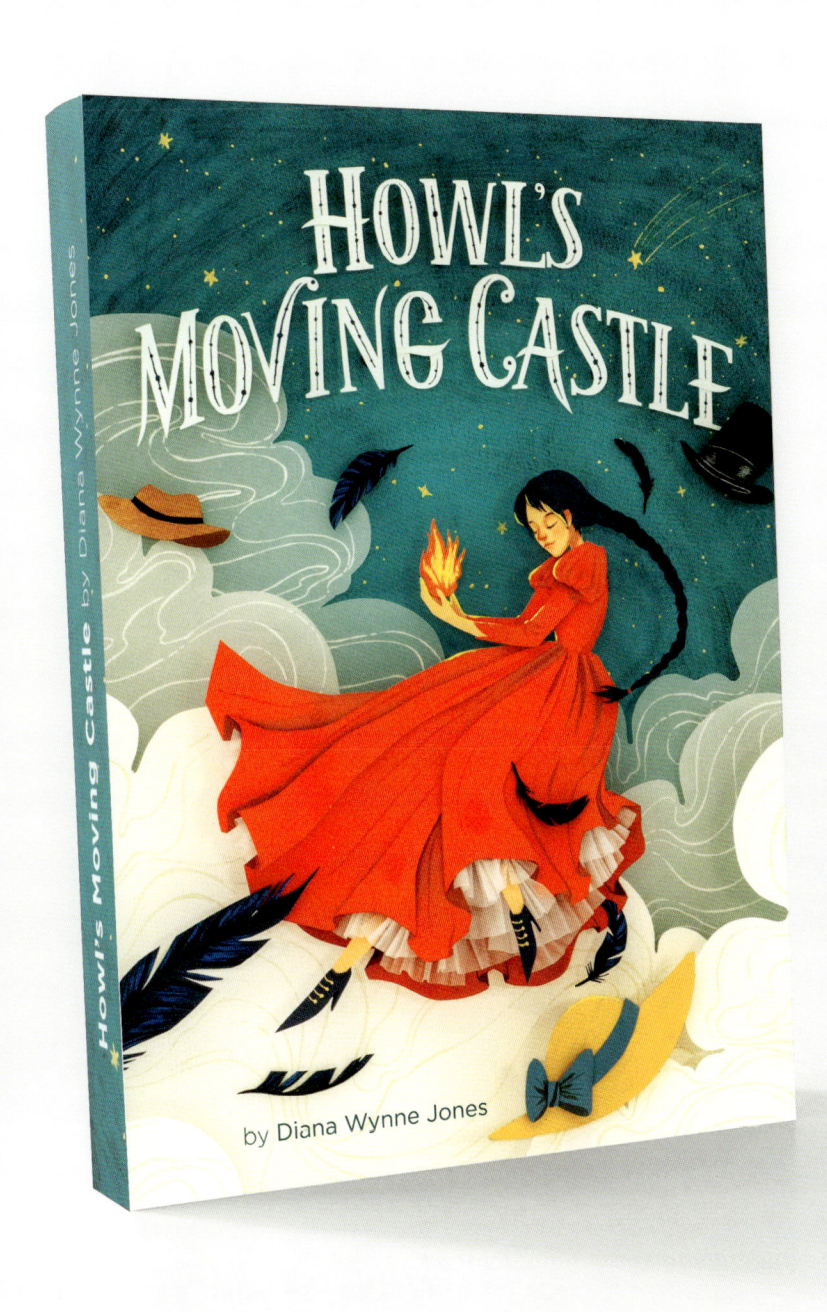

Publishing & Print Media	Posters	Typography	Illustrations	Sound Design	Film & Animation	Online
4	64	92	116	126	138	172

20,000 Leagues Under the Sea

[Book Cover Illustration]

This book cover illustration marries the artistic style of contemporary illustrator Johnny Dombrowski with a classic adventure story. The cover design of Jules Verne's novel "Twenty Thousand Leagues under The Sea" is notable for its graphic novel style, characteristic of Dombrowski's work, and the captivating fine line drawings. The illustration also reproduces the concentrated colour palette used by the illustrator. This reduced colour range creates a powerful atmosphere and a suitable setting for the illustrations of the classic novel.

University
SCAD Savannah College of Art and Design
Savannah, USA

Design
Andrea Siles-Loayza, SCAD

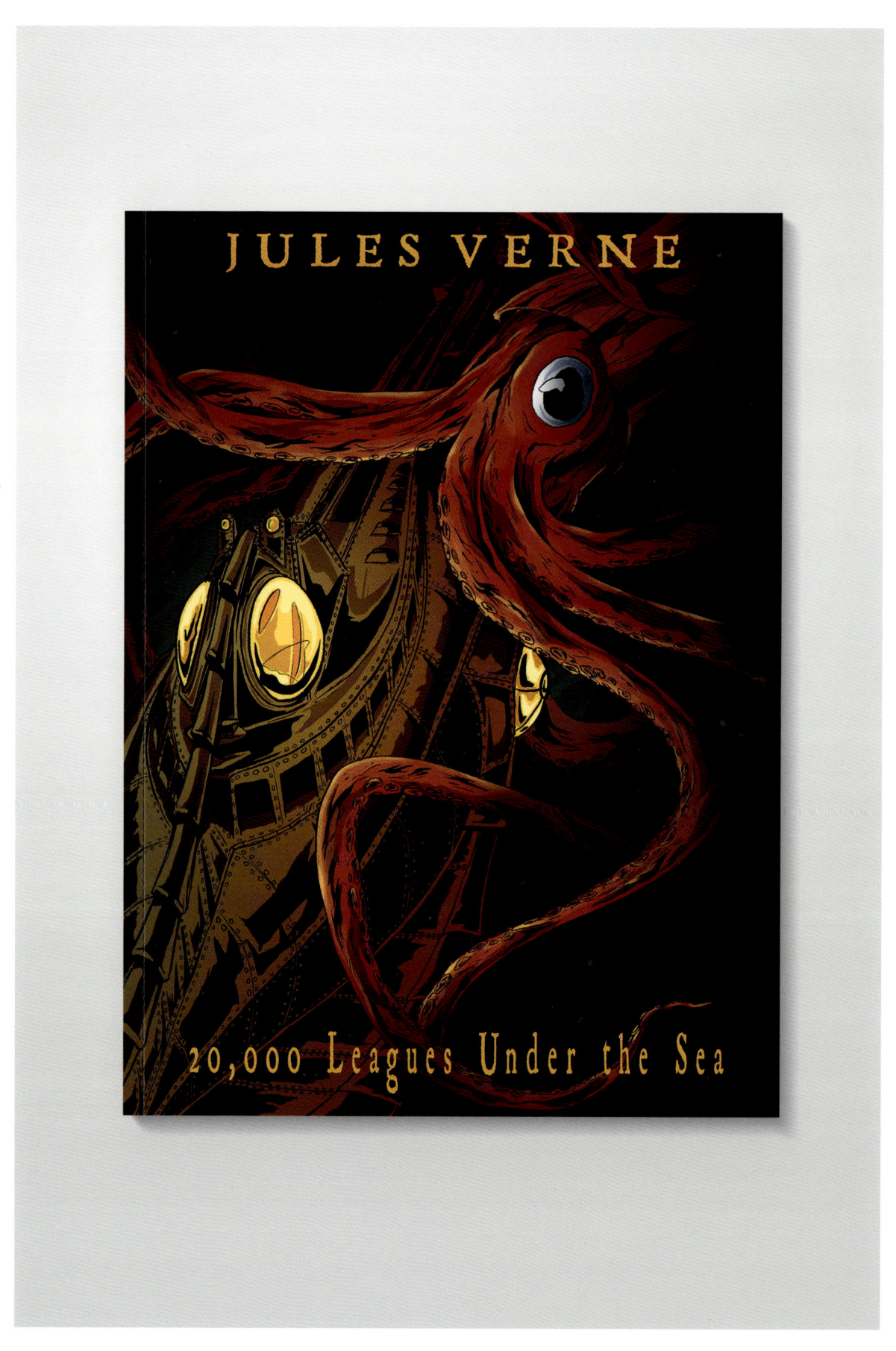

Apps	Interface & User Experience Design	Spatial Communication	Red Dot: Junior Award	Designer Profiles	Jury Portraits	Index
206	236	336	426	564	642	668

Musical Script Book Covers

[Book Cover Illustrations]

The design of this series of musical script book covers is impressive for the unified visual system it creates, which, nonetheless, gives each script a sense of individuality. The initial letter of the respective musical takes up the entire cover, which also references the colours of the show's original branding. The initials and the complete title on the front and back covers are set in Fit typeface, an eye-catching font, which allows for the creation of interesting text shapes as well. The covers have an intentional, slightly worn look as a hint to many pirate copies of scripts on the market.

Client
Elvin Hu
San Francisco, USA

Design
Elvin Hu
San Francisco, USA

→ Designer profile on page 594

Publishing & Print Media	Posters	Typography	Illustrations	Sound Design	Film & Animation	Online
4	64	92	116	126	138	172

Eight Immortals Crossing the Sea

[Illustrations]

The Taiwanese legend of the Eight Immortals can be acted out with the colourful paper figures presented on this cut-out sheet. The intricately and accurately produced illustrations are defined by lovingly rendered details and clearly drawn facial features, visually depicting the abilities of the respective saints while also making it easy to distinguish between the different characters. The choice of material and the ease with which the puppets can be assembled brings Taiwanese puppetry to the mainstream and keeps this tradition alive.

University
Taoyuan Municipal Shou Shan Senior High School
Taoyuan, Taiwan

Supervising Professor
Chao Sheng Yang, Jung Shun Huang

Design
Zi Xuan Wang, Hsi Yu Tseng, Jia Ru Chen, Yen Ying Chen, Taoyuan Municipal Shou Shan Senior High School

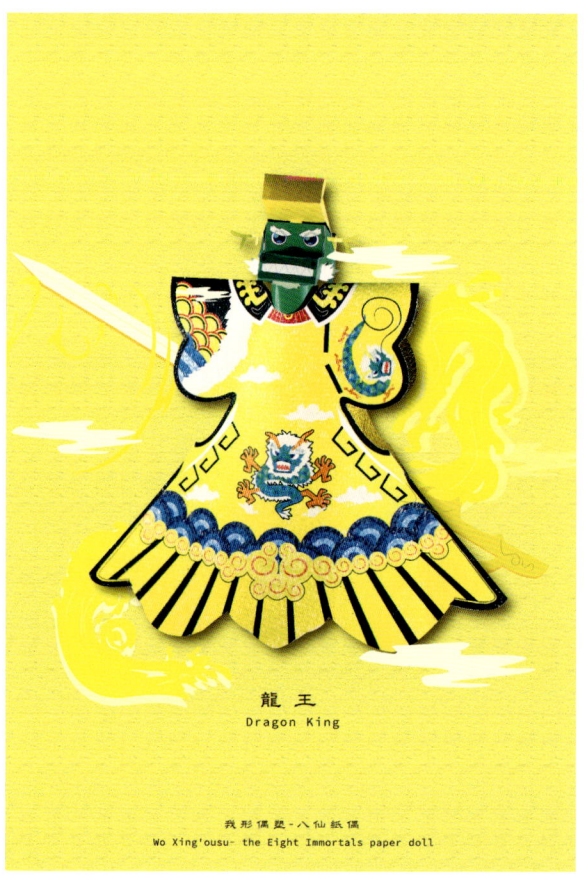

Apps	Interface & User Experience Design	Spatial Communication	Red Dot: Junior Award	Designer Profiles	Jury Portraits	Index
206	236	336	426	564	642	668

Taiwan's Calendar

[Editorial Illustrations]

The Taiwanese postcard calendar provides a colourful illustration for every month of the year. The imagery is deliberately simple and presents a clear overview of the key public holidays, festivities and traditions in each month. Varieties of plant, fruit and vegetable serve as symbols for the various blossom and harvest periods. Adults and children working, celebrating or at play merge with typical Taiwanese landscapes to form riotously colourful and vibrant scenes, giving informative insights into the country and its culture.

University
Asia University
Taichung, Taiwan

Supervising Professor
Hui-Ping Lu

Design
Chi-Man Ieong, Hsiao-Yun Lo,
You-Sin Lien, Asia University

Publishing & Print Media	Posters	Typography	Illustrations	Sound Design	Film & Animation	Online
4	64	92	116	126	138	172

2020 Chungju World Martial Arts Festival

[Promotional Illustrations]

Client
Hanjoo Jho, Planetary Craft
Seoul, South Korea

University
Dongyang Mirae University
Seoul, South Korea

Design
Sewoong Kim, Soonjai Hong,
Jaeseong Choi, Dongyang Mirae
University

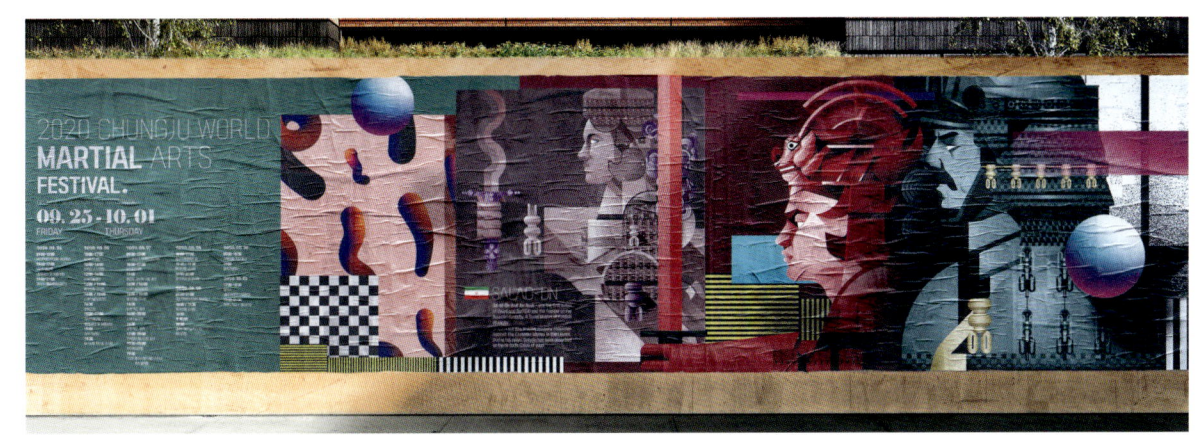

Apps	Interface & User Experience Design	Spatial Communication	Red Dot: Junior Award	Designer Profiles	Jury Portraits	Index
206	236	336	426	564	642	668

Famous generals and kings of the participating countries adorn the flyers, posters, banners, invitations and other marketing material of the Chungju World Martial Arts Festival in Korea. For the event, two different types of illustrations were created. They produce a coherent overall image and combine martial arts, traditions and a variety of cultures. Some of the motifs use predominantly geometric shapes, graphic patterns and bright colours on a black background. The colours and traditional shapes of the participating countries determine the style of the other illustrations.

Homeland

[Illustrations]

The intimate connection between humankind and earth, as well as its importance to the Taiwanese people, is explored in the "Homeland" publication. Its three sections respectively focus on the character of the land, its natural resources and its flora. Like the land itself, the colourful illustrations are very diverse. Each one presents a different and special facet of the relationship between people and nature. The colour scheme of earthy, grey and green tones results in compositions which are unique and yet still form a visually harmonious whole.

University
China University of Technology
Taipei City, Taiwan

Supervising Professor
Chien-Hsun Chen, Sheng-Chuan Chang, Cheng-Ta Lee

Design
Yu-Fang Wu, Yu-Rou Chen, Pin-Wen Chen, Chieh-Chia Lai, Xuan-Yu Lai, Hsiao-Chien Lee, Department of Visual Communication Design, China University of Technology

Western-Style Building

[Informative Illustrations]

The illustrations in this book tell the stories of eight historical houses in a Taiwanese village which were erected by people who worked abroad, earned their living there and built a prestigious home on the return to their native village. Western and oriental architectural styles and traditions converged. These drawings capture this mixture in detail. Supplemented by explanatory chapters on interiors, culture and history, the finely drawn illustrations pay, in a picturesque manner, tribute to a unique building style.

University
Shu-Te University
Kaohsiung, Taiwan

Supervising Professor
Yu-Lung Yang

Design
Jia-Qi Wu, Mei-Ting Huang,
Siou-Yuan Lin, Yun-Dian Guo,
Tsai-Wei Chen, Ya-Ting Hsu,
Shu-Te University

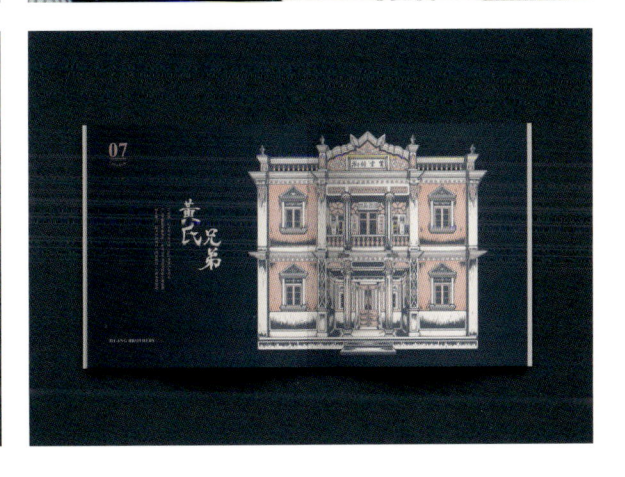

Publishing & Print Media	Posters	Typography	Illustrations	Sound Design	Film & Animation	Online
4	64	92	116	126	138	172

Balance of Nature

[Illustrations]

University
869 school of design
Dalian, China

Supervising Professor
Jiang Xue

Design
Li Hu, Ma Youyuan, Sun Yuting, Ma Xueting, Wei Zixuan,
869 school of design

→ Clip online

Apps	Interface & User Experience Design	Spatial Communication	**Red Dot: Junior Award**	Designer Profiles	Jury Portraits	Index
206	236	336	426	564	642	668

This series of posters and marketing materials illustrates the balance in nature achieved by the harmonious coexistence of all living beings. Landscapes created by geometrically overlapping and complementary shapes are just as much part of the "Balance of Nature" project as the representation of twelve kinds of animal. These stand alone as single abstract motifs but are also part of the mythology of the Chinese dragon, a creature said to be in charge of the balance of nature. With its magical combination of animal features from horns, to a snake body and talons, it is considered to be the leader of all creatures.

Publishing & Print Media	Posters	Typography	Illustrations	Sound Design	Film & Animation	Online
4	64	92	116	126	138	172

Taiwanese Festival

[Promotional Illustrations]

Six typical rites and traditions are the focus of these illustrations, intended to convey Taiwan's rich culture. The images skilfully combine traditional styles with modern elements. The variety and intensity of the colours used give them great expressive quality, which makes them into highly decorative posters or calendars. A light box, specially made for the illustrations, allows the motifs to come to life and reveal their 3D nature.

University
Ming Chi University of Technology
New Taipei City, Taiwan

Design
Tzu-Yu Lin, Shun-Wen Hsiao, Jin-An Li, Jing-Wen Huang, Ming Chi University of Technology

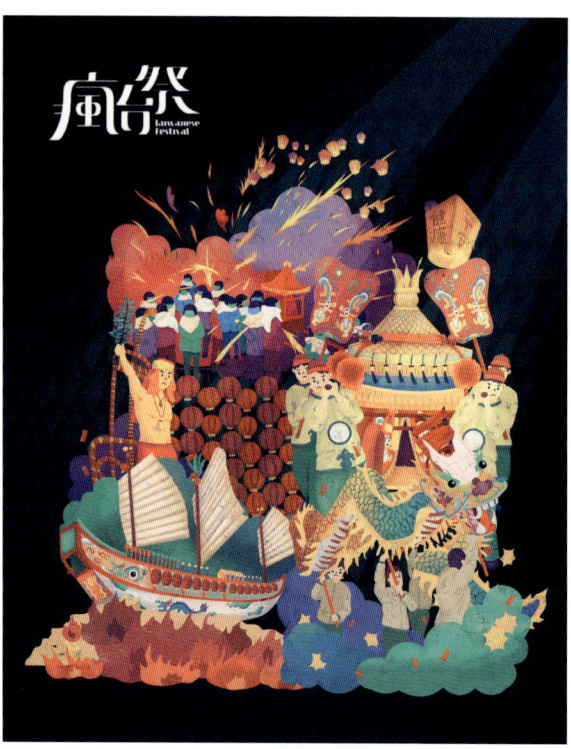

Guei Village – The product of plum in Liouguei

[Packaging Illustrations]

Liouguei in Taiwan is famous for its plum products and for being a habitat to some rare species, such as the peregrine falcon. The plum blossom and different animals have therefore been used as key visual elements of a design range aimed at promoting the town and stimulating tourism. The hand-drawn illustrations are the focal point of the packaging for a range of plum-related products. Depending on the product, the images vary in their colours and arrangement, but they all seamlessly adapt to the different packaging items, all with a geometric tortoiseshell shape.

University
Cheng Shiu University
Kaohsiung, Taiwan

Supervising Professor
Yueh-Hsing Lai, Yu-Jui Yu, Yu-Jin Lin, Shou-Che Wu

Design
Hsing-Ying Hsieh, Cheng Shiu University

Publishing & Print Media	Posters	Typography	Illustrations	Sound Design	Film & Animation	Online
4	64	92	116	126	138	172

PAKAMLIR – Puyuma Xiaomi Bartender

[Packaging Illustrations]

In the language of the Puyuma, one of Taiwan's indigenous peoples, the word "pakamlir" means "special". The millet wine of the same name is served only on certain occasions. The visual design of the bottles is therefore striking and symbolic as well. The illustrations on the labels reference Taiwanese legends. The traditional characters are drawn with great vibrancy and surrounded with dynamic and powerful patterns. The colours of the illustrations reflect those of the respective wine, making it easy to distinguish visually between the different flavours.

University
China University of Technology
Taipei City, Taiwan

Supervising Professor
Jung Shun Huang, Yao Yuan Shang

Design
Chia Chin Yang, Chiao Yu Tsai, Yu Ling Ye, Yu Chieh Li, Po Hsun Chen, Yu Fu Zeng, Shao Chi Ruan, Department of Visual Communication Design, China University of Technology

Bayberry in Yangmei

[Packaging Illustrations]

Adorning the labels of bayberry-vinegar bottles and jam jars, these illustrations depict a grandchild and grandfather and their shared memories of bayberries and the products derived from it. Shades of red dominate the colour scheme of these hand-drawn illustrations and create a direct link to the glossy red fruit at the heart of each image. The deliberately naive, richly imaginative illustration style gives rise to creative image-worlds which convey joie de vivre and are imbued with warmth.

University
China University of Technology
Taipei City, Taiwan

Supervising Professor
Jung Shun Huang, Yao Yuan Shang

Design
Wang Yang Chieh, Fang I Wen,
Yu Lun Cheng, Chen Syuan Jian,
Department of Visual Communication
Design, China University of Technology

Den Tyste

[Narrative Short Film]

Leo is a deaf child who experiences life in the year 1968 in Piteå, Sweden, by careful observation. Through this unique perception, he realises his parents' relationship is deteriorating. "Den Tyste" follows Leo and his mother as they deal with their family's pitfalls. The film explores these two perspectives in experimental ways using intriguing techniques of sound design and cinematography to distinguish between their different perspectives. Shot on 16 mm colour as well as black-and-white film, without any dialogues, "Den Tyste" truly embodies the primary emphasis of purely visual storytelling.

University
SCAD Savannah College of Art and Design
Savannah, USA

Design
Kai Dickson, SCAD

→ Clip online

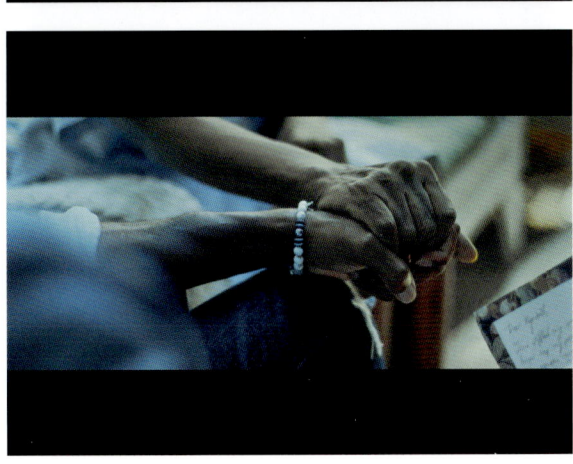

Apps	Interface & User Experience Design	Spatial Communication	**Red Dot: Junior Award**	Designer Profiles	Jury Portraits	Index
206	236	336	426	564	642	668

Willie's Letter

[Short Film]

Set against a southern landscape, "Willie's Letter" tells a parallel story of sacrifice and resurrection across two generations. A depressed father contemplates life while attempting to hold on to his son. A PTSD-diagnosed son embarks on a journey to revisit the place of his father's demise and makes an unexpected discovery. The film is inspired, in part, by the propaganda piece "The Willie Lynch Letter, 1712." The letter discusses the generational trauma of slave descendants and the separation of black families – dynamics which are embedded in this film's father-son relationship.

University
SCAD Savannah College of Art and Design
Savannah, USA

Design
Kiana Woodson, SCAD

→ Clip online

527

Kim's

[Short Film]

"Kim's" is a short film about an immigrant father and his son who finally get to understand each other better, after they learn how to stand up and fight against stereotypes. The purpose of this film was to portray the isolation of an individual through the eyes of a minority in the United States of America during an unexpected state of emergency. The use of 50 mm prime lenses to establish the shallow depth of field in key scenes, like the conference scene, visually highlights the desolation and discomfort the main character is experiencing.

University
SCAD Savannah College of Art and Design
Savannah, USA

Design
Hahn Han, SCAD

→ Clip online

Twine

[Stop-Motion Animation]

A puppet on strings embodies the suffering of women in society in the stop-motion animation film "Twine". The setting is based on Chinese puppet theatre, the epitome of a traditional representation of roles. After the main character has been completely buried by black strings, she plucks up the courage to change the negative labels which have literally been stuck onto her in the form of small, grey pieces of paper into something light and positive. The film relies heavily on the use of perspective, as well as on light and darkness to portray patriarchal suppression.

University
Southern Taiwan University of Science and Technology
Tainan, Taiwan

Supervising Professor
Chian-Fan Liou, Rain Chen

Design
Ya-Zhu Zhang, Ying-Syuan Huang, Fan-Chen Su, Hui-Tong Wu, Pei-Syuan Li, Pei-Ting Tsai, Southern Taiwan University of Science and Technology

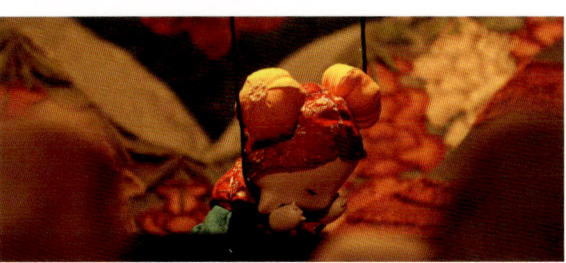

→ Clip online

Publishing & Print Media	Posters	Typography	Illustrations	Sound Design	Film & Animation	Online
4	64	92	116	126	138	172

Ceremony

[Stop-Motion Animation]

The stop-motion film "Ceremony" presents the belief that the dead can find eternal peace only with the blessings of the living. The plot is set in a no-man's land between life and death, where an old man is wandering, lost. The backdrop is one of mountains made of artfully folded joss paper, the golden shimmer of which creates a mysterious atmosphere, while red spider lilies grow from the ground. Both the paper and the lilies are traditionally associated with death. The moment the old man hears his grandchild's loving words of farewell, the flowers turn a pure white and the dead man can rest in peace.

University
Chaoyang University of Technology
Taichung, Taiwan

Supervising Professor
Wei-Jung Feng

Design
Yu-Ting Chang, Tsai-Chuan Huang, Chi-Hsuan Tsen, Chu-Fong Nie, Yi-Yu Chen, Chaoyang University of Technology

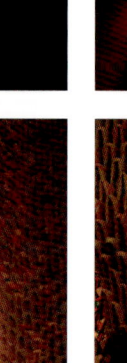

→ Clip online

The Orbit of Memory
[Experimental Animation]

"The orbit of memory" is an experimental animation showing a man who enters a train, setting out on the journey of his life. He meets many people and feels joy and sorrow, with his memories and experiences leaving traces on the train, which finally represents his unique personal history. To help the viewer identify with the protagonist, he is the only character to not have distinctive external features. What makes the design of the animation stand out is the great variety of hand-crafted elements, which create a powerful interplay of different styles and materials such as modelling media, cardboard and paint.

University
Southern Taiwan University of Science and Technology
Tainan, Taiwan

Supervising Professor
Chian-Fan Liou, Rain Chen

Design
Wen-Hsin Lu, Pei-Yu Chou, Yi-June Zhuo, Wei-Chi Ding, Mung-Lin Li, Chih-En Li, Southern Taiwan University of Science and Technology

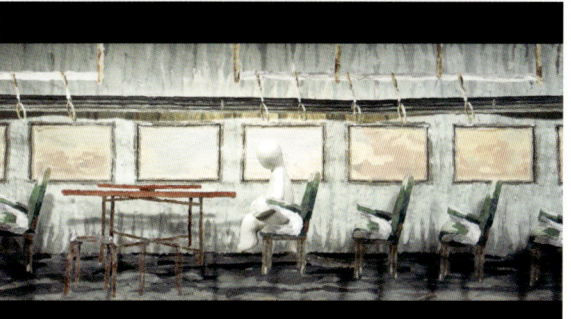

→ Clip online

Publishing & Print Media	Posters	Typography	Illustrations	Sound Design	Film & Animation	Online
4	64	92	116	126	138	172

Mine
[3D Animation]

The 3D animation film "Mine" portrays the possessive behaviour of an obsessive lover. The female protagonist marks various locations in nature with a flag to register her ownership of these territories. The different landscapes serve as allegories for different parts of her lover's body that are gradually occupied by her and defended against rivals. At the end, the lover is completely under her control. The use of bright colours and the charming stop motion style help to soften the sombre content of the story.

University
National Yunlin University of Science and Technology
Douliu City, Yunlin County, Taiwan

Supervising Professor
Ching-Cheng Liu

Design
Hwa-Chin Hsu, Jing-Fen Chiou, National Yunlin University of Science and Technology

→ Clip online

Function

[3D Animated Film]

"Function" is a 3D animated film produced by approximately twenty animation, visual effects and sound design students. The film follows the story of Blu, a recently activated robot, who goes on an adventure to discover his purpose of existence. Through trial and error and through a valuable discovery, Blu comes to realise that he too was designed for a specific reason and has a meaningful role to play. The film was produced utilising multiple software programs for animation design, such as Maya, Zbrush, Substance Painter, Nuke and After Effects.

University
SCAD Savannah College of Art and Design
Savannah, USA

Design
Abby Spencer, SCAD

→ Clip online

ELPIS

[Computer Animation]

People follow a variety of dreams. The animated short film "ELPIS" takes viewers to a fantasy world in which a girl is following a dream. There is no rigid plot line. Instead, emotions predominate. For this reason, the laws of physics do not seem to apply and the narrative threads of certain sequences use the stream of consciousness technique. The imagery is highly symbolic: the motif of the dream is translated into a number of different metaphors, including a meteorite and a white stag. Ultimately, it is up to the viewers to decide what innermost desire they see reflected in the images.

University
Asia University
Taichung, Taiwan

Supervising Professor
Lin Jia-An, Yu Ming-Lung

Design
Chang Chih-Ling, Chiu Te-Cheng, Ding Hao-Yi, Asia University

→ Clip online

BUTCH

[Animated Short Film]

In this mixed-media animated short film, a small-town butcher experiences a meteoric rise to fame after building large sculptures made of meat and faces the grim consequences of desperation. Tragic events, which occurred in the lonely shop, are revealed to show how the town became infamous for the urban legend, known as Butch. The film reflects on the pressure that comes with demands artists are exposed to, the results of turning passion into a source of income, and the way artists fall in and out of love with their art, while slowly being consumed by it.

University
SCAD Savannah College of Art and Design
Savannah, USA

Design
Max Johnson, SCAD

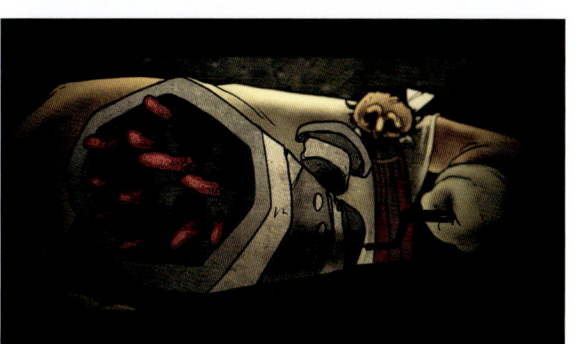

→ Clip online

Publishing & Print Media	Posters	Typography	Illustrations	Sound Design	Film & Animation	Online
4	64	92	116	126	138	172

The Millennials

[Hand-Drawn Animation]

University
Chaoyang University of Technology
Taichung, Taiwan

Supervising Professor
Wei-Jung Feng

Design
Shao Yu Lu, Ya Shen Lee, Kuan Lin Chiu,
Chaoyang University of Technology

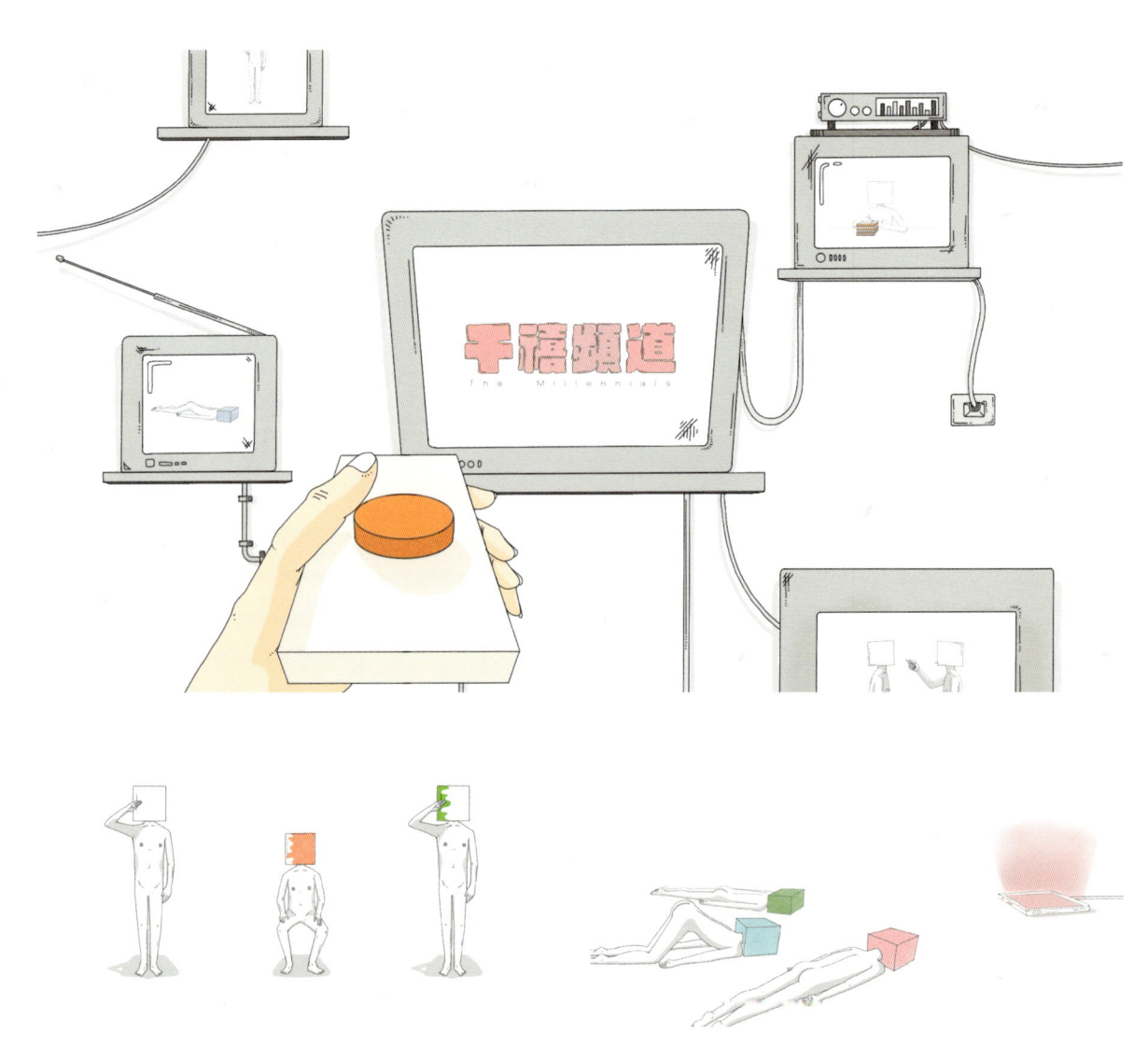

→ Clip online

This film takes a critical look at the media habits of millennials. In short chapters with titles such as "herd behaviour" and "phishing", various phenomena of the internet and the culture of mobile communication are taken to absurd extremes. Reminiscent of classic newspaper caricatures, the style of the hand-drawn animations is minimalist, as is the sound design. The intention behind this is to leave the film open to interpretation by viewers. The sparse visuals also underscore the characters' alienation from their environment.

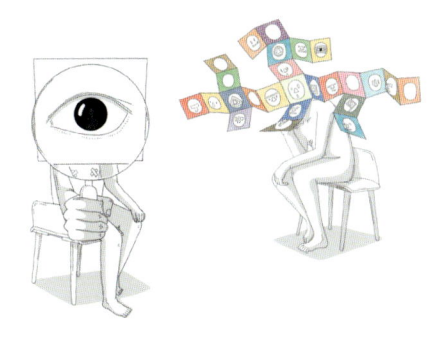

Publishing & Print Media	Posters	Typography	Illustrations	Sound Design	Film & Animation	Online
4	64	92	116	126	138	172

Our House Is On Fire

[Illustrated Kinetic Typography Animation]

"Our House Is On Fire" is an animated, illustrated kinetic typography video which visualises a speech by 16-year old climate activist Greta Thunberg at the World Economic Forum in 2019. It highlights the importance and urgency of the rising global temperatures and serves as a call to action to our lawmakers and citizens to act before it is too late. The project features a blend of illustrations and handwritten type, and uses the music "Ether Oar" by The Whole Other as an accompaniment to Greta Thunberg's speech.

University
SCAD Savannah College of Art and Design
Savannah, USA

Design
Katsy Garcia, SCAD

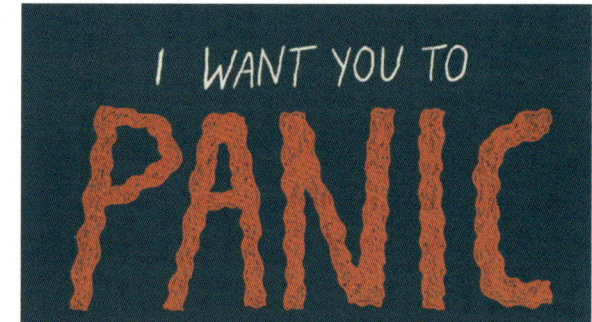

→ Clip online

To My Younger Self
[Computer Animation]

"To My Younger Self" describes the designer's feelings about her own life experiences in an abstract yet emotional way. Ever since she can remember, she has been forced to travel from place to place due to the situation of her family. In the film, a paper plane represents her as a person. Other geometric objects and origami figures symbolise the different situations she has experienced. The intention of the film is not just to send a message to the designer's younger self, but also to others who are going through similar circumstances.

Client
Kim Lin
Los Angeles, USA

Design
Kim Lin
Los Angeles, USA
Kexin Yang
Chengdu, China
James Findlater
London, United Kingdom

→ Designer profile on page 604
→ Clip online

Publishing & Print Media	Posters	Typography	Illustrations	Sound Design	Film & Animation	Online
4	64	92	116	126	138	172

Annecy Animation Film Festival 2019 Opening Title

[Computer Animation]

The theme of the Annecy Animation Film Festival 2019 is Japanese animation. This opening title was created to combine Japanese culture and elements of nature in Annecy. Inspired by the poster on the festival's website, the storyline depicts a Japanese girl looking through a telescope to see the festival. The telescope also acts as a connection between these two different cultures. The zoetrope, a traditional animation device, was employed to symbolise this festival's long history.

University
SCAD Savannah College of Art and Design
Savannah, USA

Design
Yifan Sun, SCAD

→ Clip online

Civilizations: PBS Title Sequence

[Opening Title, After Effects]

This project sought to redesign the opening title for "Civilizations", an art history documentary series. The goal was to create a piece which more clearly distinguishes the show from other similar programmes. Thus, the conceptual basis for the project was to visually demonstrate how art movements evolve into one another over time. This was accomplished by iteratively rearranging abstract geometric forms to represent various historical artworks. This use of abstraction also solved the challenge of creating a visually unified piece while depicting the highly varied aesthetics throughout art history.

University
SCAD Savannah College of Art and Design
Savannah, USA

Design
Luke Gibson, SCAD

→ Clip online

Publishing & Print Media	Posters	Typography	Illustrations	Sound Design	Film & Animation	Online
4	64	92	116	126	138	172

Renew

[Social Service App, Online Platform]

Renew is a social service platform that helps refugees to get work, residency and insurance. It makes job recommendations, assists in providing continued education to facilitate connection with the market and gives refugees the required insurance to increase their chances of being hired. Apart from offering accommodation options and supportive information regarding development opportunities for children, it connects local schools, social services, cooperative education and homestay. Children of refugees are thus able to grow up in a stable environment, and the potential social problems that refugees may face are reduced.

University
Ming Chi University of Technology
New Taipei City, Taiwan

Supervising Professor
Kai-Chu Li

Design
Chang-Yu Lung, Chieh-An Chung,
Zi-Shan Zhang,
Ming Chi University of Technology

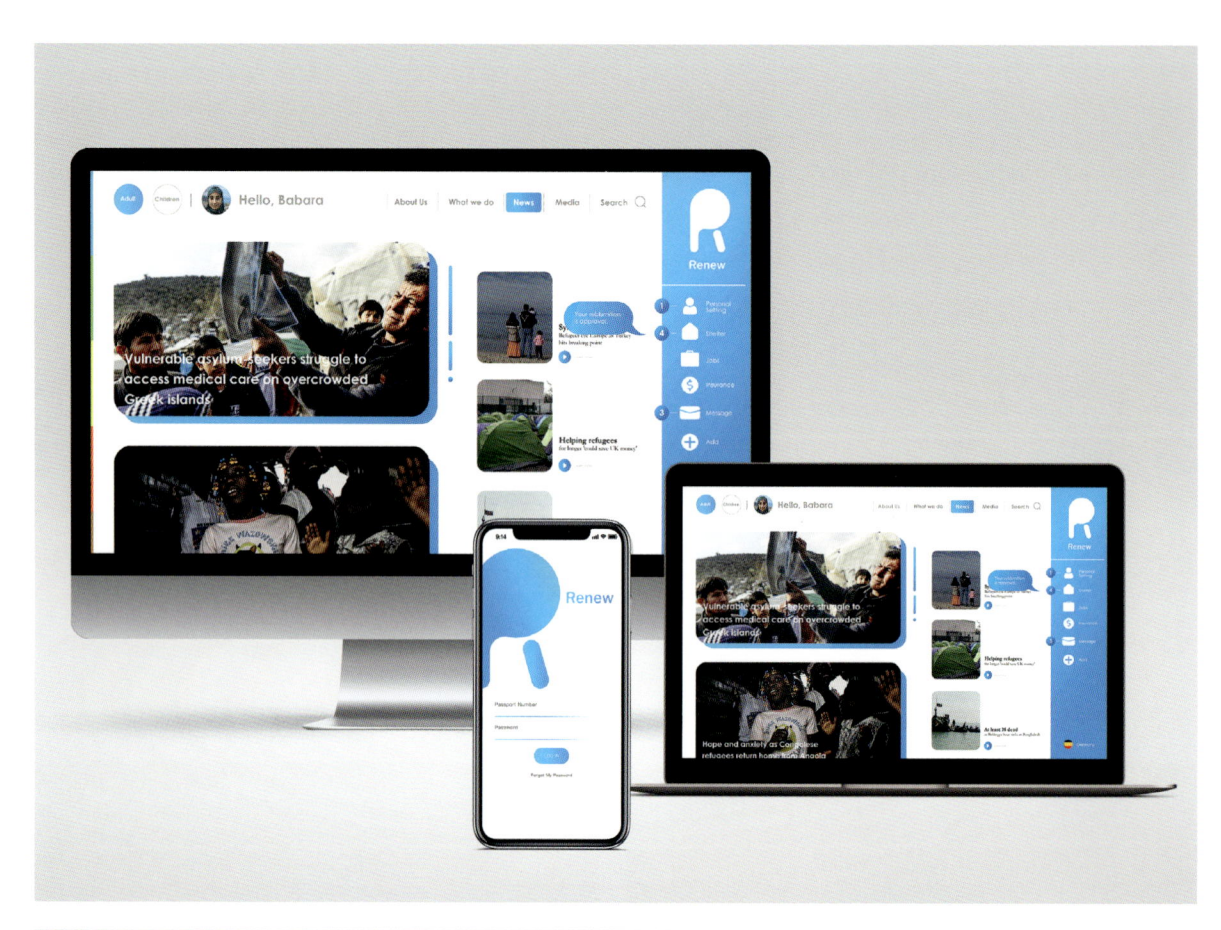

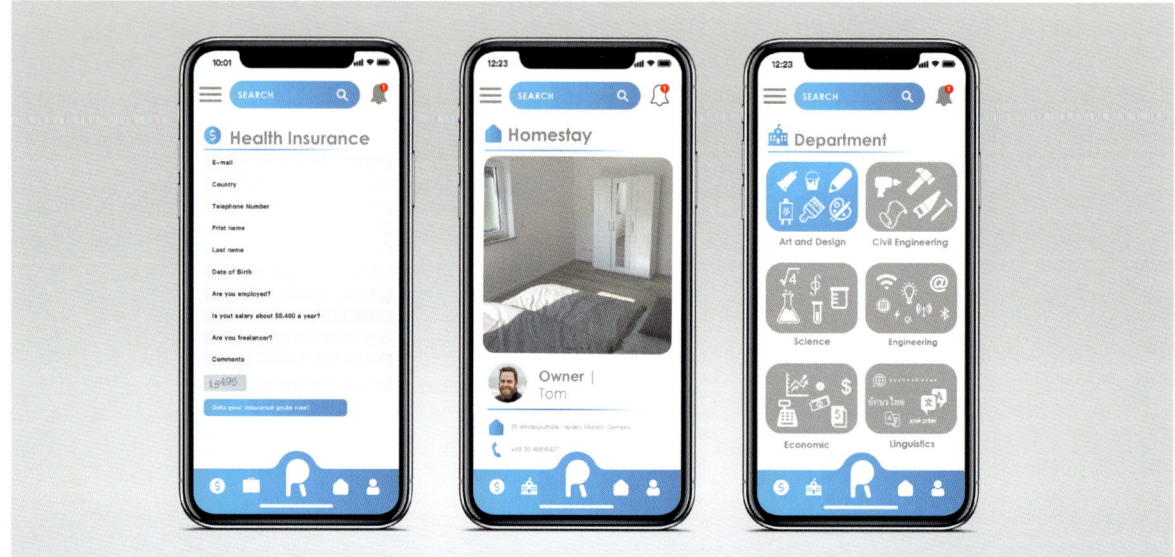

Apps	Interface & User Experience Design	Spatial Communication	Red Dot: Junior Award	Designer Profiles	Jury Portraits	Index
206	236	336	426	564	642	668

Basis

[Family Communication App]

Basis is an app focused on bringing long-distance families together. It is designed for adult family members who live in different locations, such as parents and their children who are at college, siblings who have moved apart but want to stay in contact, or multigenerational families who live spread across the country. The app is used to organise and maintain an open line of communication through features designed for creating events, playing games and sharing content. Thanks to an integrated gesture-tracking camera, together with a TV, parties can be hosted, group video calls made, and party games played.

University
SCAD Savannah College of Art and Design
Savannah, USA

Design
Emma Fowler, Mara Healy,
Hadyn Hawkins, Lydia Goshen,
Darren Wells, SCAD

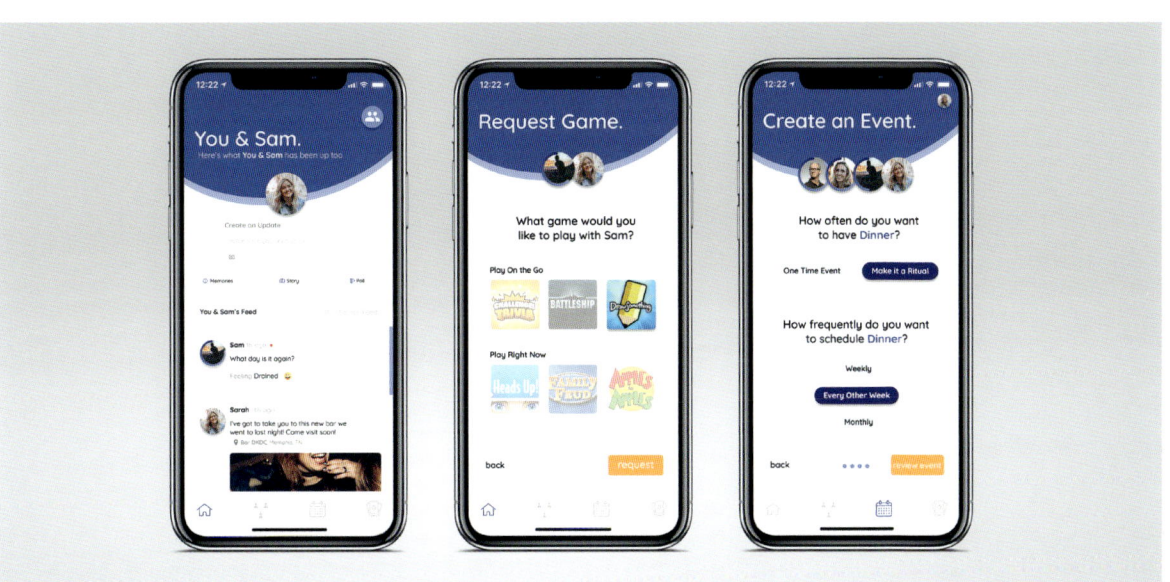

Summer Hero Clip – For prevention of heatstroke
[Wearable Health Solution]

The Summer Hero Clip is a user-friendly wearable device for the prevention of heatstroke that can be clipped onto hats or sleeves. It predicts the heat index, calculated by measuring the atmospheric temperature and humidity every minute. Once the device detects that the temperature has reached an "extreme caution level", it alerts the wearer with an alarm sound. If the risk level remains unchanged or stays at a higher level after an hour since the first alarm, a second warning sound will launch. The warnings are aimed at helping users avoid the risk of heatstroke.

Client
LG Electronics Inc.
Seoul, South Korea

University
Dongseo University
Busan, South Korea

Supervising Professor
Dosang Ryu, Mikyeong Moon

Design
Chanyang Lee, Dahyeon Kang,
Jeonghoon Park, Doheon Kim,
Dongseo University

Voice Sticker for Blind

[Health Solution]

The design of Voice Sticker for Blind tackles the issue that visually impaired people face many inconveniences in their daily lives. It focuses on situations where it is difficult for them to distinguish certain items from similar products. The concept applies the technology of the Arduino board, combined with a voice recorder, speaker module and a relay module, to activate a recording sticker. The use of recorded voice messages improves the quality of life of the visually impaired and gives them more security.

Client
3M
Seoul, South Korea

University
Dongseo University
Busan, South Korea

Supervising Professor
Dosang Ryu, Mikyeong Moon

Design
Hyeonji Kim, Soojung Ha,
Ryungyeong Kim, Sooyeon Lee,
Dongseo University

Press Recording & Tap Speaking

[Power Strip for Blind People]

Press Recording & Tap Speaking is a voice-recording power strip for visually impaired people. It addresses the fact that, with the high number of electronic devices in use today, visually impaired individuals have difficulty distinguishing between the different power outlets of congested power strips. The design concept is based on communicating with the power strip. A voice recording button next to each electrical outlet allows users to distinguish between the plugs. The recording and playback of the sound is intuitive thanks to press-and-tap operation.

Client
Belkin
Los Angeles, USA

University
Dongseo University
Busan, South Korea

Supervising Professor
Dosang Ryu, Mikyeong Moon

Design
Nahyun Kim, Nayeong Kim,
Wooseong Kim, Seongheon Song,
Dongseo University

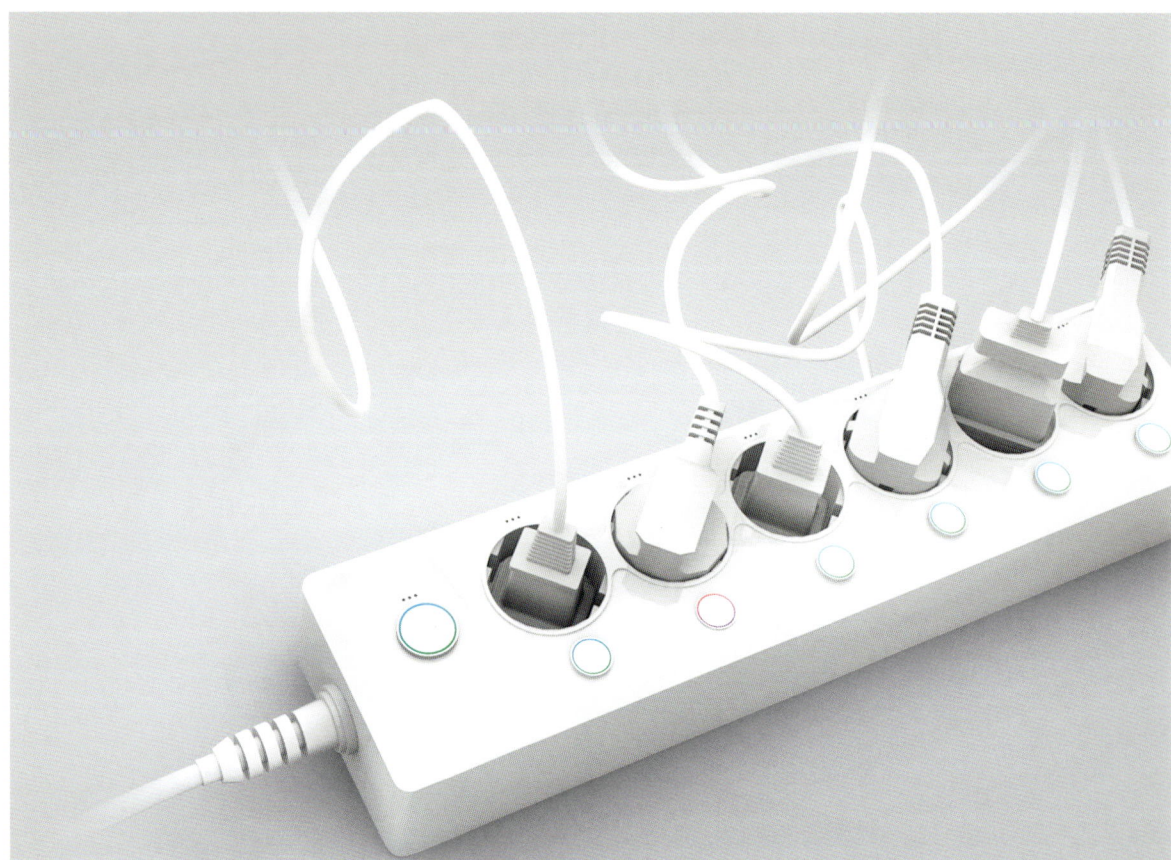

Apps	Interface & User Experience Design	Spatial Communication	Red Dot: Junior Award	Designer Profiles	Jury Portraits	Index
206	236	336	426	564	642	668

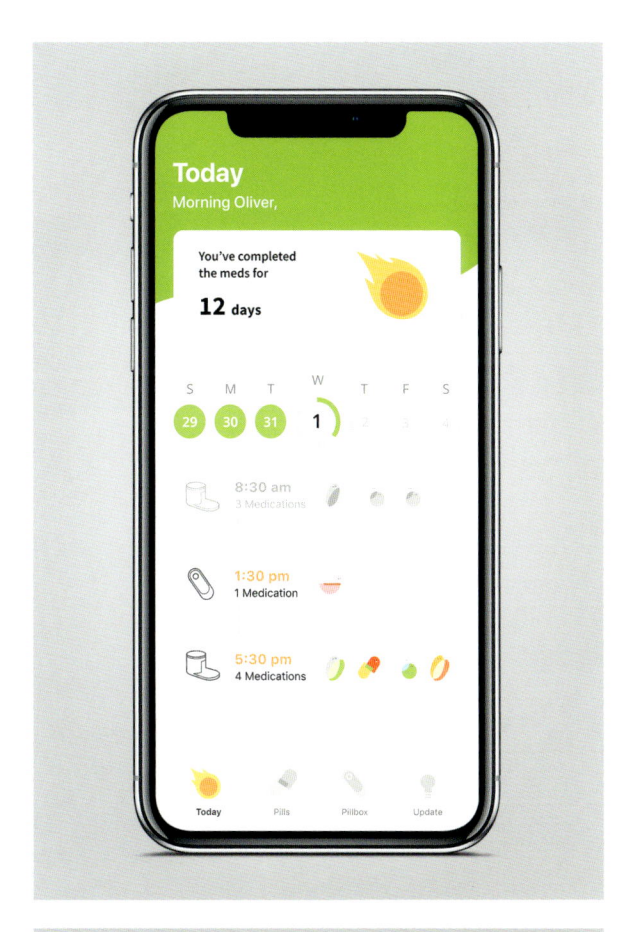

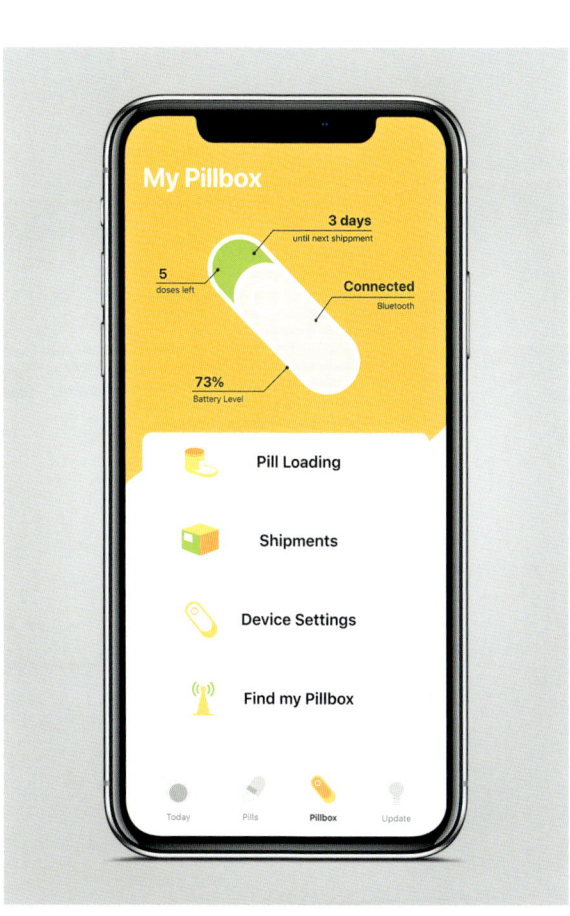

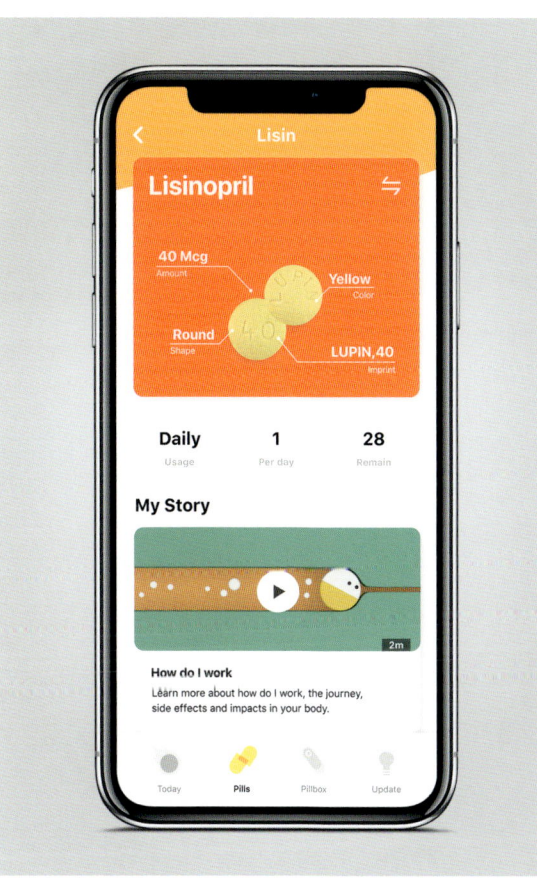

Seamless Health

[User Experience Design,
User Interface Design]

Seamless Health dedicates itself to the problem of non-adherence to medication in the USA. It consists of an app, a smart pillbox, a station and refill packs, and it offers connectivity to doctors and pharmacies. The app provides easy-to-follow medical information directly targeted at users and their conditions in the form of animated videos and easily understandable text. The "Smart pillbox" reminds and encourages them to take their medication on time, tracking their adherence. The product houses all of the medications, and it acts as a refill station and a wireless charging pad for the portable pillbox.

University
SCAD Savannah College of Art and Design
Savannah, USA

Design
Eika Johanna Weber, Matt Moore,
Emily Ip, SCAD

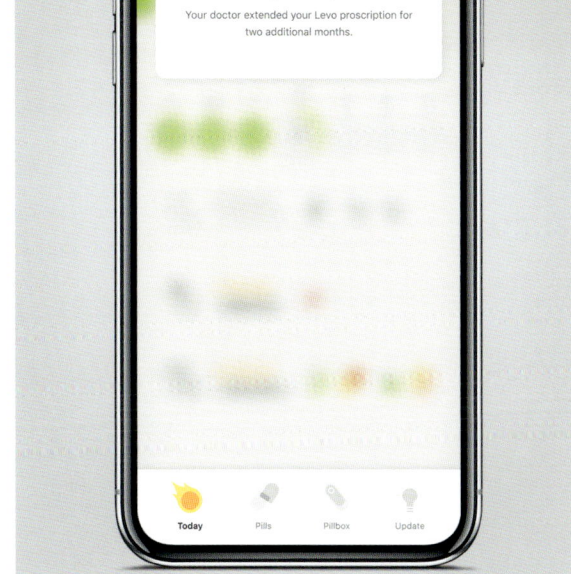

Lighthouse

[User Experience Design,
User Interface Design]

This device aims to encourage active listening and empathy within a conversation among group members. Individual voice data is visualised and represented with changes of colour and opacity in real time. For example, if a person speaks in an aggressive manner, their light on the device will turn red or if a person is not contributing much to the conversation their light will fade away. The Lighthouse app visualises the data of the users' conversation performance, thus leading to better communication skills.

University
SCAD Savannah College of Art and Design
Savannah, USA

Supervising Professor
Sung Park

Design
Yun Kim, Jonathan Sanchez,
Savannah Wilkinson, Yeji Han,
Dahyun Lee, SCAD

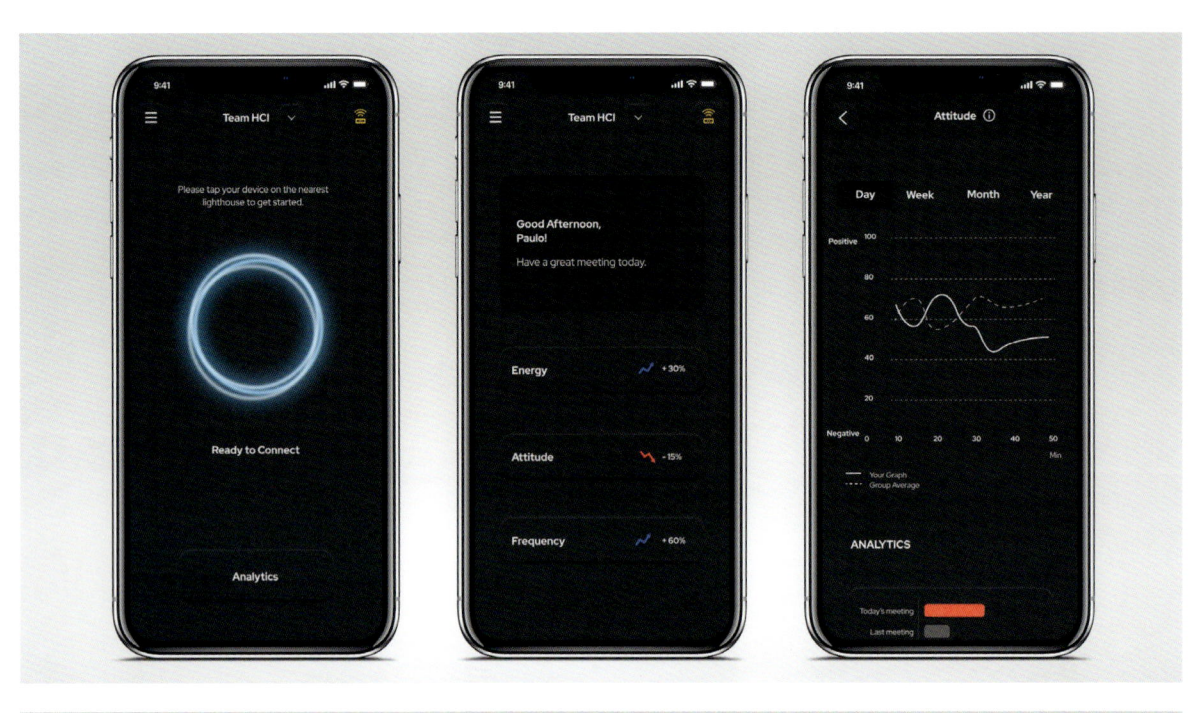

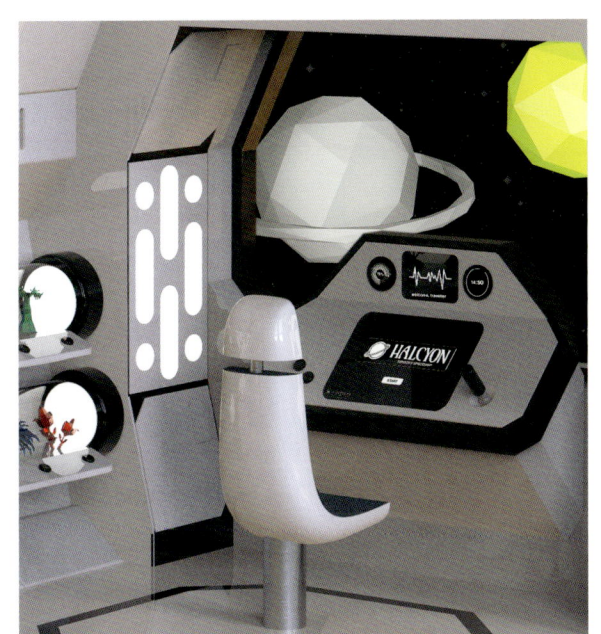

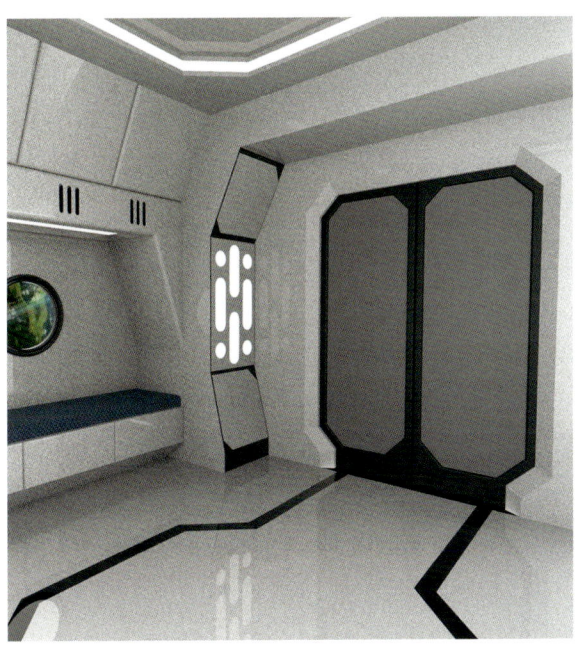

Halcyon Sensory Spaceship

[User Experience Design, User Interface Design]

Halcyon Sensory Spaceship is designed for people with sensory issues, as seen for example in people with autism. The device can be utilised in public areas, such as amusement parks or shopping malls, where disturbing signals can be high. The UX design puts users in the "captain's seat", while the environment adapts entirely to their sensory needs as they travel through a galaxy. They enter a calm and dim environment and go through various steps designed to mitigate a panic attack or other anxiety symptoms.

University
SCAD Savannah College of Art and Design
Savannah, USA

Design
Calyssa Nowviskie, Jena Martin,
Andrew Bretnall, SCAD

Token

[User Interface Design]

Token is a tactile toolkit that focuses on mutual understanding between authority figures and students during disciplinary conversations in school. It aims to foster a positive change in student behaviour and to encourage empathy within the institutional discipline system through three steps: identifying the situation and people involved, facilitating perspective-taking by using emojis and setting goals with a follow-up application. The toolkit builds a system with circles to represent places, actor tokens to represent people and emojis to represent emotion.

University
SCAD Savannah College of Art and Design
Savannah, USA

Design
Maria Ruiz, Eli Clein, Seungpil Lee, Connelly Morris, Esther Holliday, SCAD

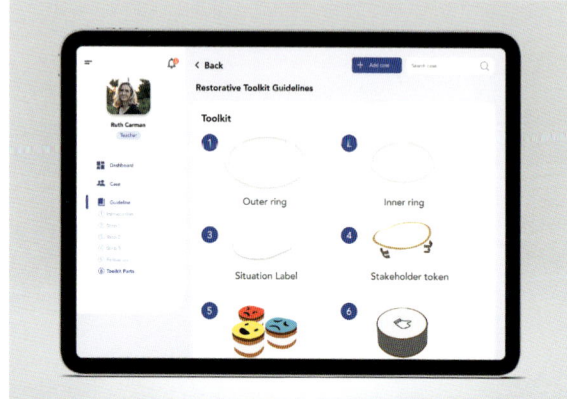

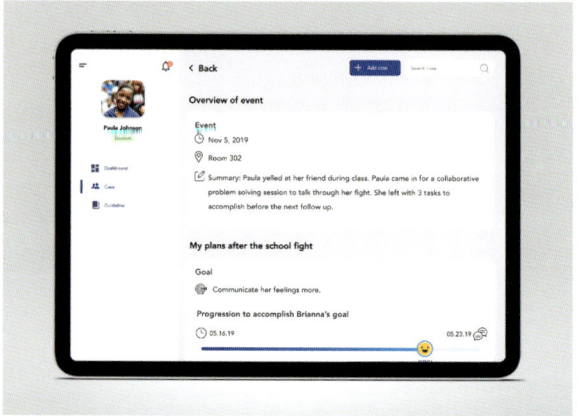

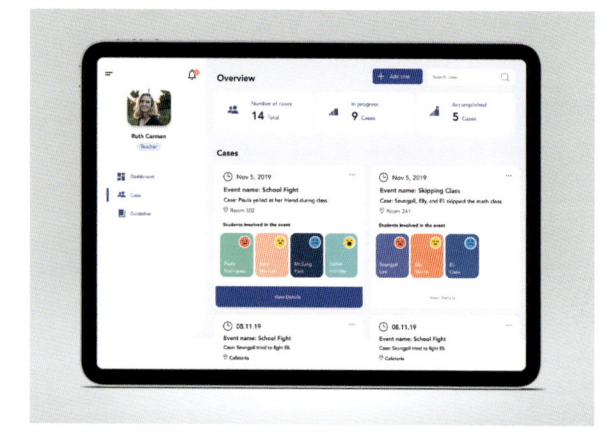

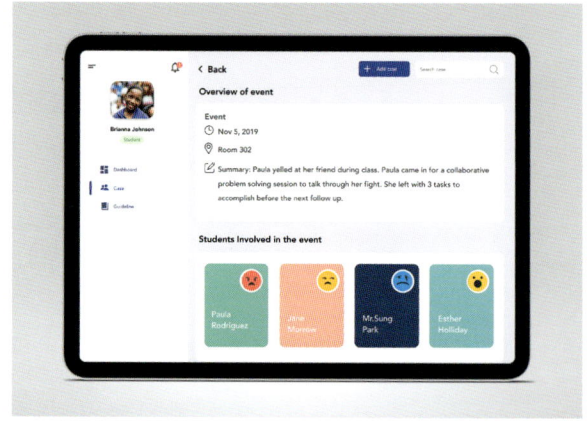

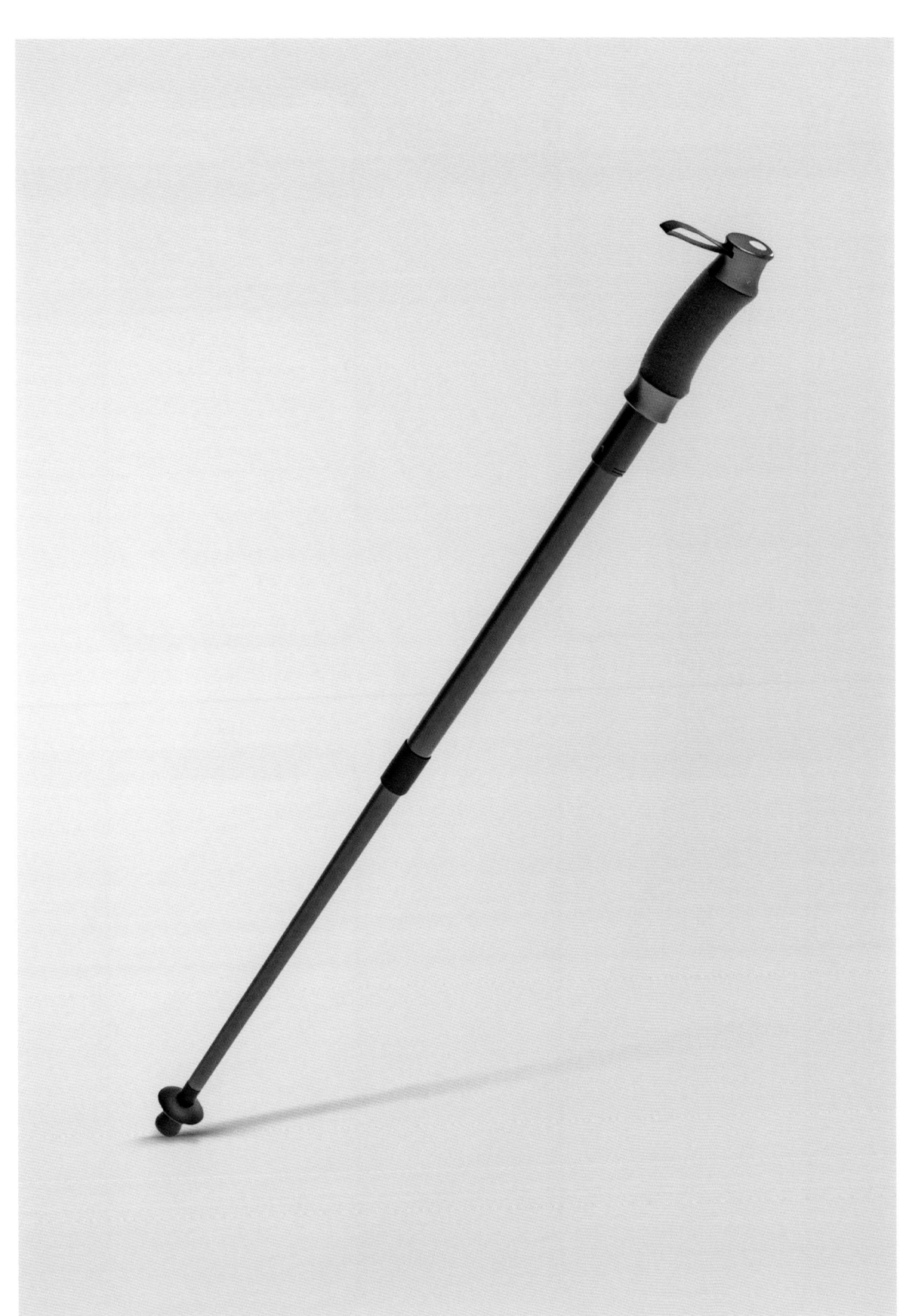

Frequency-Shield Trekking Pole

[Mountaineering Safety Equipment]

The Frequency-Shield Trekking Pole was developed for encounters with wild animals in the outdoors, which are occasionally dangerous. The aim was to develop a product which protects both humans and animals against injury and which also functions as a basic trekking pole. The design takes advantage of the differences in the range of hearing between animals and humans. The trekking pole emits frequencies that humans cannot hear, but which cause animals to run away.

Client
BlackYak
Seoul, South Korea

University
Dongseo University
Busan, South Korea

Supervising Professor
Dosang Ryu, Mikyeong Moon

Design
Hoyeon Shin, Hyeyeon Kim,
Haeyeong Song, Hyuntae Ryu,
Dongseo University

Publishing & Print Media	Posters	Typography	Illustrations	Sound Design	Film & Animation	Online
4	64	92	116	126	138	172

CAIR

[User Experience Design,
User Interface Design]

CAIR was designed against the backdrop that contemporary communication behaviour is dangerous in traffic. People are used to do things like pushing news alerts, text messages and social media, which puts them in distracting situations that can ultimately cause the death of the driver or of others. CAIR is a next-generation driving assistant that provides a safe yet seamless driving experience and prevents distracted driving. As an AI device designed to be user-friendly, it allows drivers to stay focused on the road without being distracted by anything that happens inside the car.

University
SCAD Savannah College of Art and Design
Savannah, USA

Design
Seungpil Lee, Esther Holliday,
Wonil Choi, SCAD

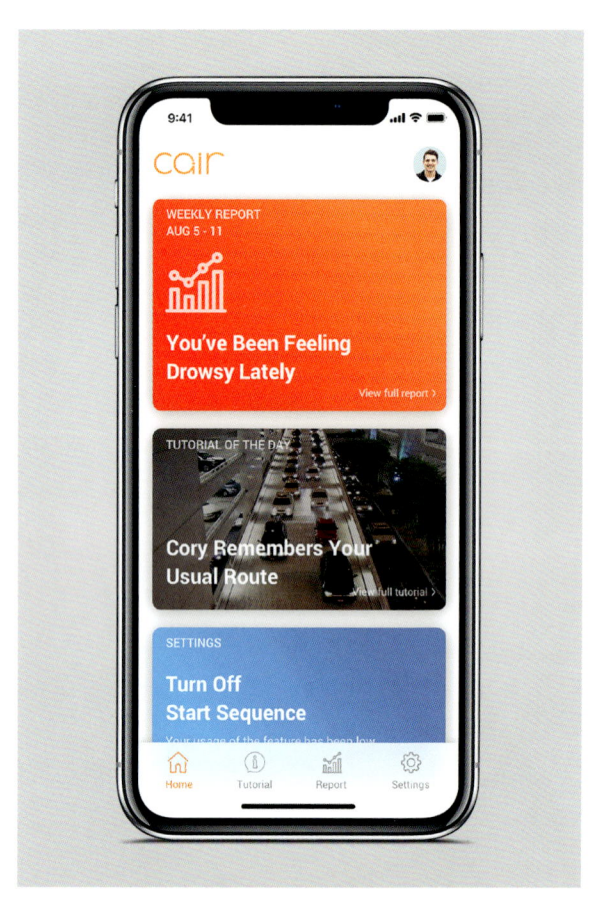

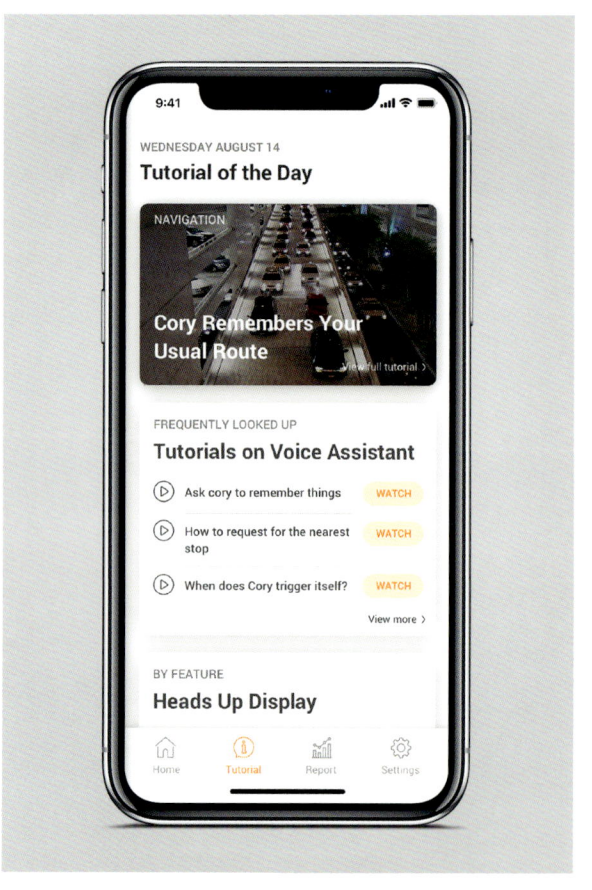

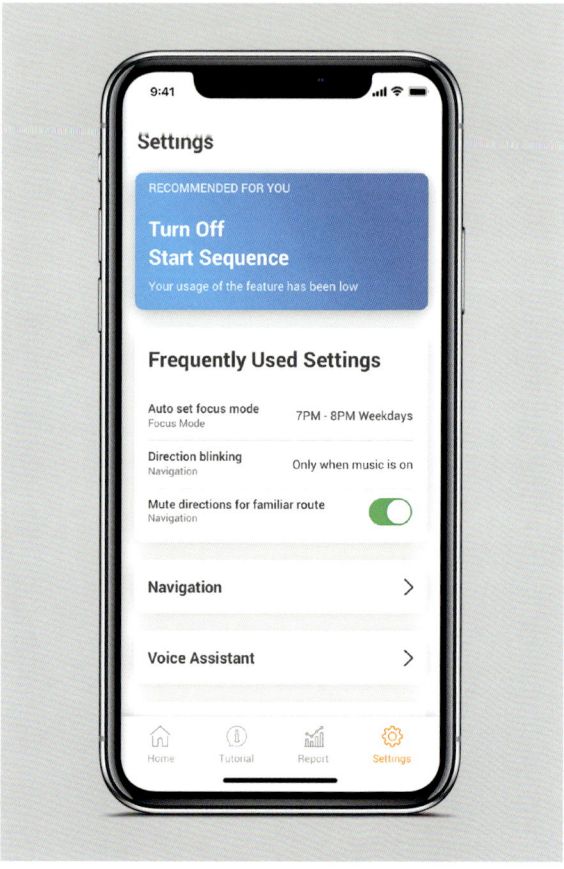

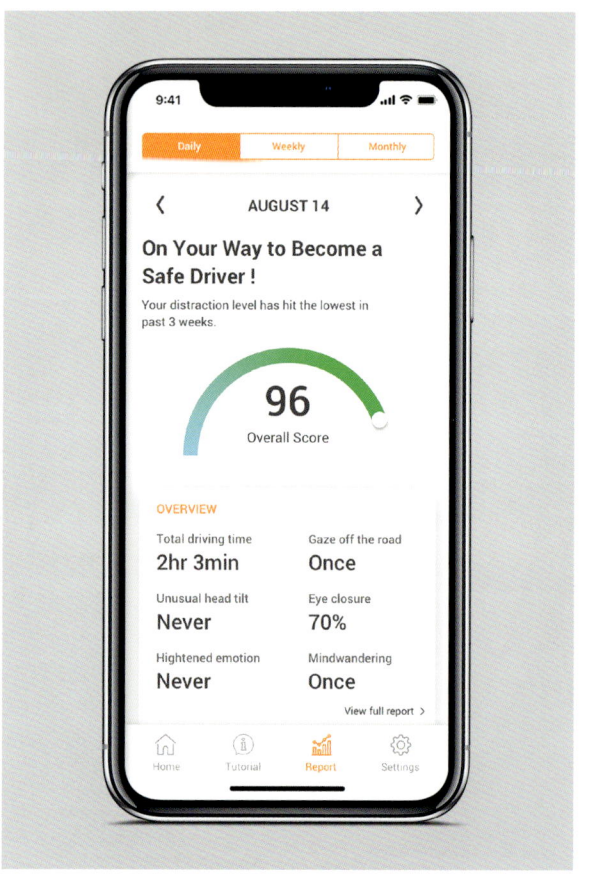

Safety Tail

[Traffic Accident Prevention System]

Safety Tail was developed to address the high number of accidents in tunnels. These accidents are often caused by too little distance between cars. Drivers lack a sense of speed and distance, because a large part of the accessible visual information is missing in tunnels. This traffic accident prevention system is based on sensors attached to the wall of the tunnel. They detect the speed and distance between cars and trigger red lights that indicate the proper safety distance, thus making it clear to drivers whether they are keeping a safe distance or not.

Client
Korea Expressway Corporation
North Gyeongsang Province, South Korea

University
Dongseo University
Busan, South Korea

Supervising Professor
Dosang Ryu, Mikyeong Moon

Design
Sujung Choi, Yulim Lee, Hyeontae Kim, Jaeheon Lee, Dongseo University

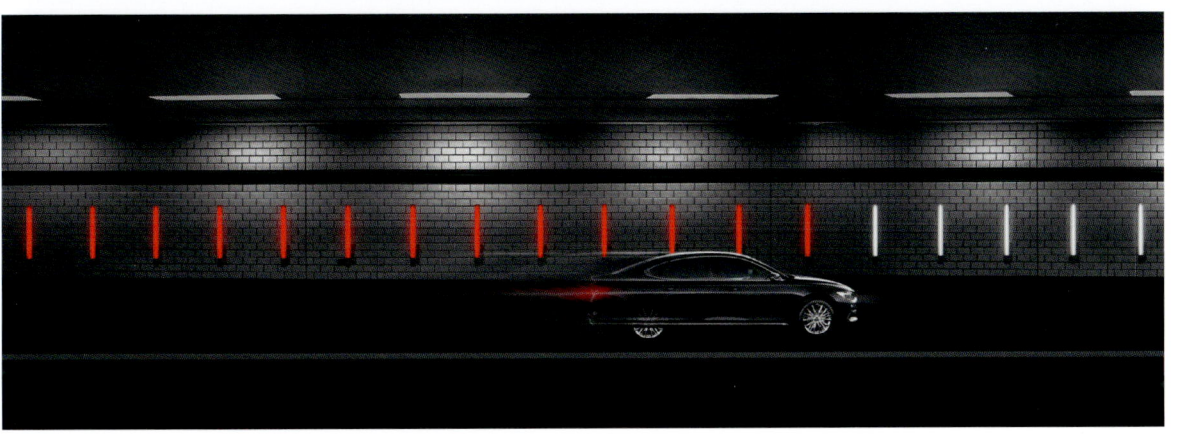

Safe Space for Street Cleaner

[Wearable Technology Solution]

To protect street cleaners working in traffic in Korea, this wearable concept combines three technologies. First, an Optical Try Display installed on the helmet integrates holographic technology to lock light into a specific space and project images onto the body of the street cleaner with the intention of protecting him through better visibility. Second, the Gyro Sensor technology keeps the hologram and the road horizontal at all times. And third, the switch on the helmet incorporates the so-called Lens Shift, which allows street cleaners to resize the hologram to suit their situation.

Client
3M
Seoul, South Korea

University
Dongseo University
Busan, South Korea

Supervising Professor
Dosang Ryu, Mikyeong Moon

Design
Harin Noh, Daekyum Kang, Minsoo Kim, Hyeongmun Choi, Dongseo University

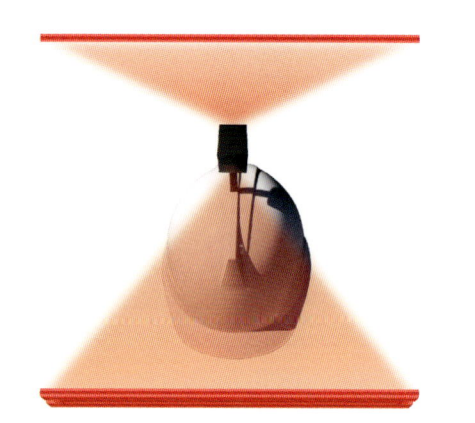

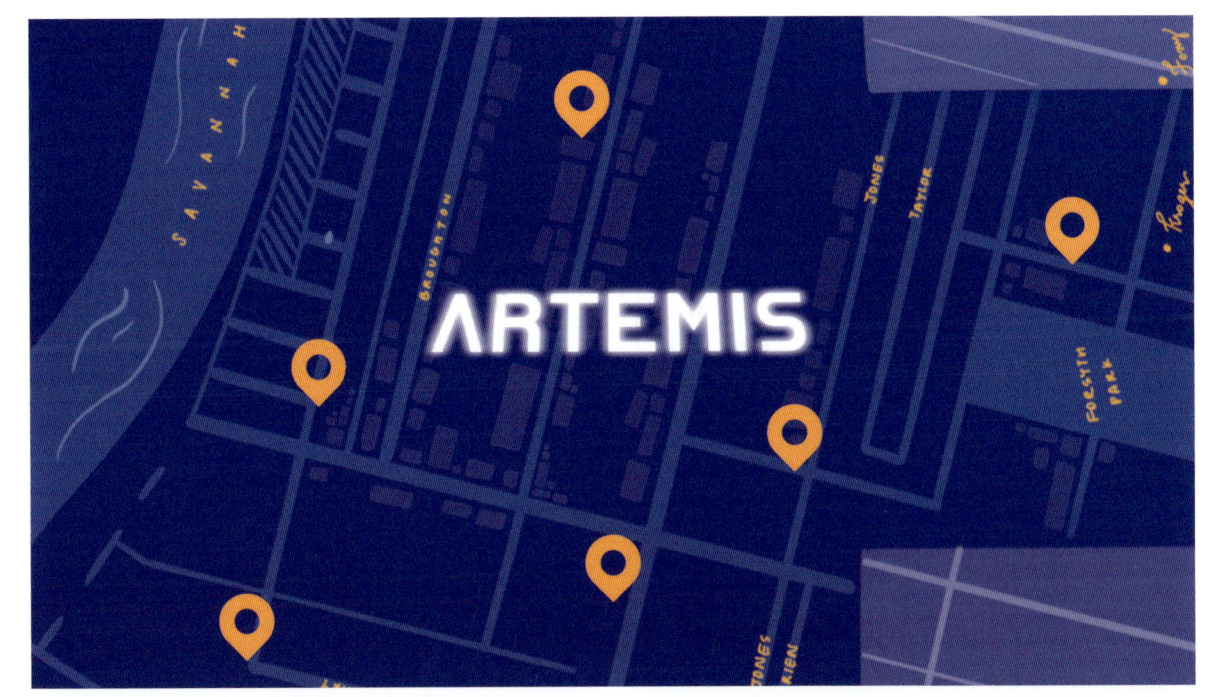

Artemis

[Virtual Reality Simulator]

Artemis focuses on the intention to turn self-defence training into an immersive experience by replicating realistic assault scenarios and conditions. Designed as a virtual reality game, it emulates realistic scenarios and educates users on preventative personal safety methods. Through comprehensive interactive storytelling, users are better prepared for the training situations. With every in-game decision, the story evolves differently, aiming to provide a unique experience and individual feedback applicable to the real world.

University
SCAD Savannah College of Art and Design
Savannah, USA

Design
Erin Imhof, Isabella Gardner, Fama Ndiaye, Lekha Veeramachaneni, Josh Willey, Griffin Bliss, SCAD

Publishing & Print Media	Posters	Typography	Illustrations	Sound Design	Film & Animation	Online
4	64	92	116	126	138	172

Humwire

[Mobile User Interface Design]

Humwire is a communication medium for musicians. As a native application, it allows users to discover, jam and collaborate with serious and professional musicians nearby. It thus validates the legitimacy of artists and their content by requiring users to sign in to upload tracks and send friend requests. The design also puts an emphasis on displaying relevant content in a way that is as streamlined and accessible as possible. Sharing and saving tracks and artists is an added feature that allows musicians to keep track of potential future opportunities.

University
SCAD Savannah College of Art and Design
Savannah, USA

Design
Michael MacWilliams, SCAD

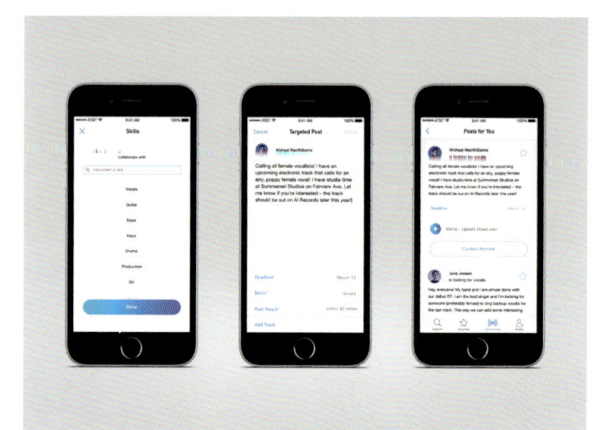

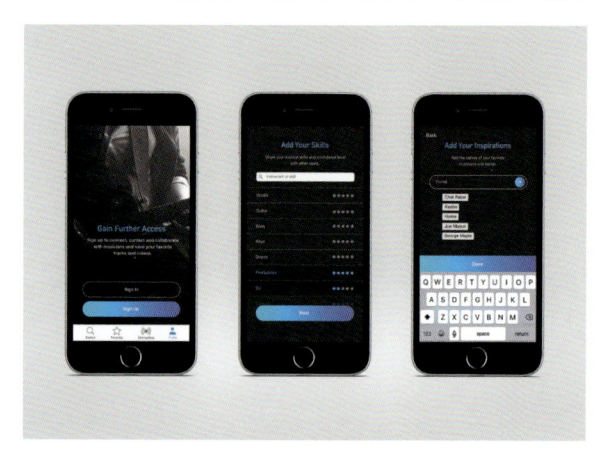

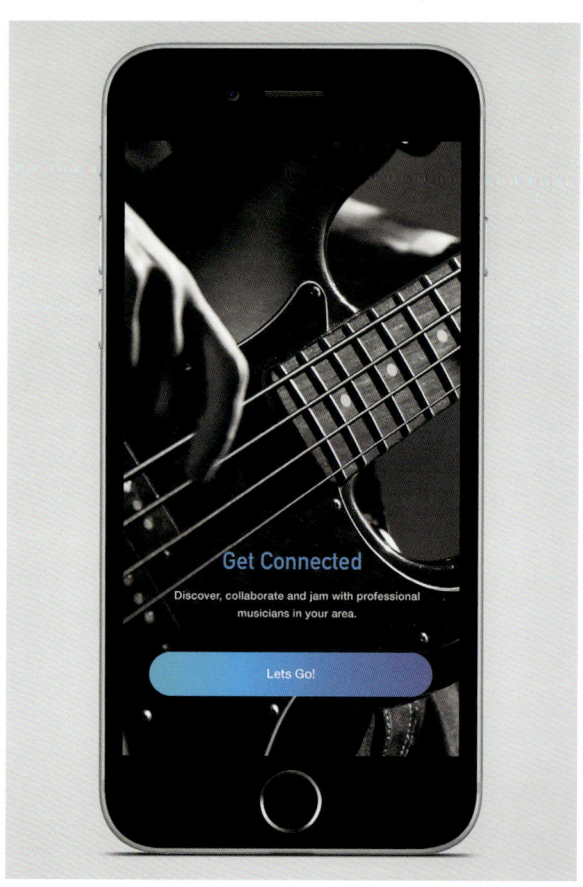

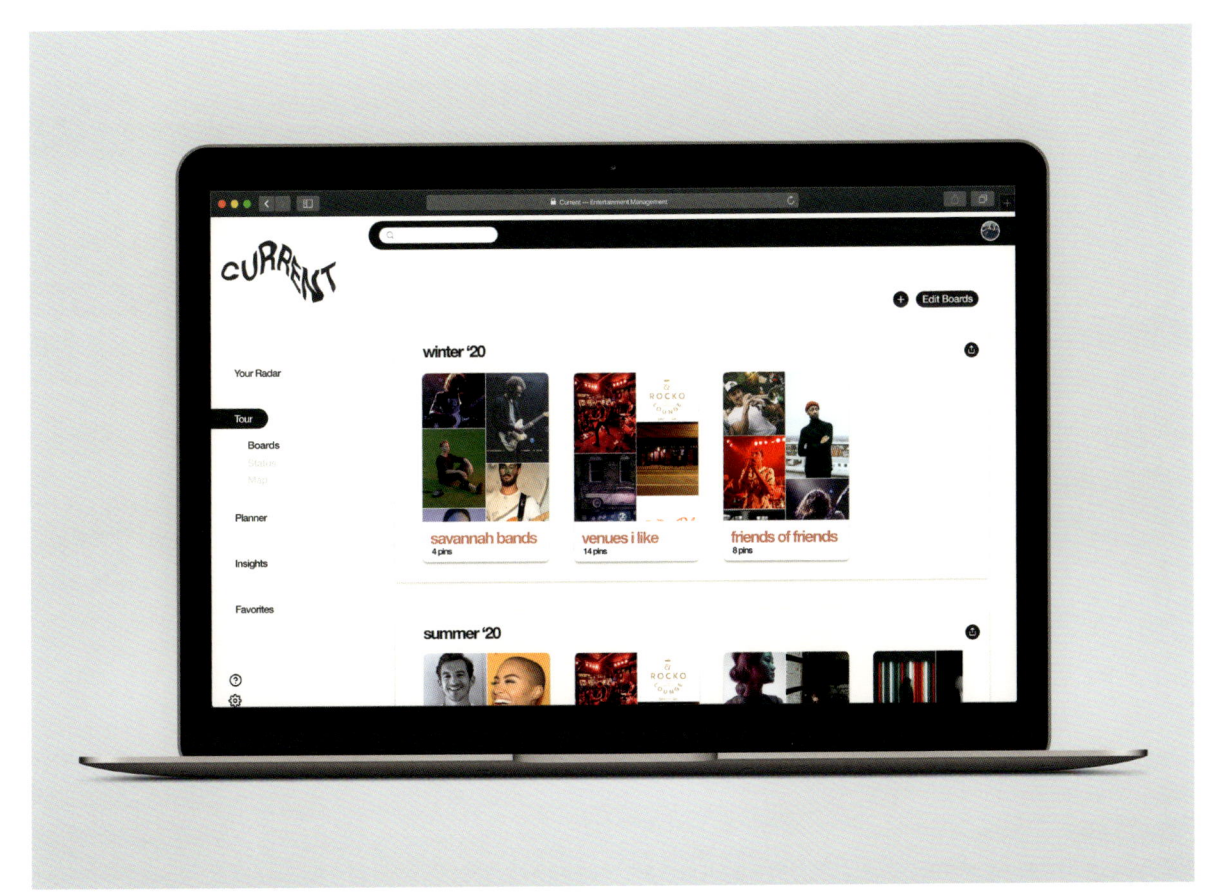

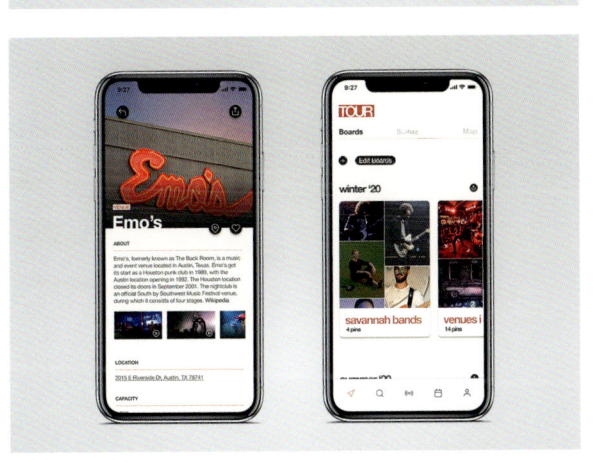

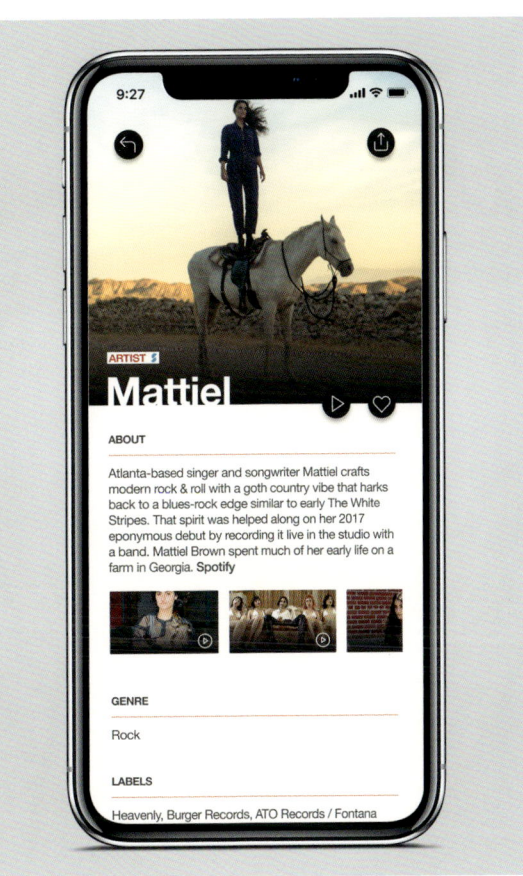

Current: AI Driven Entertainment Management Powered by Independent Musicians

[User Experience Design, User Interface Design]

Since touring is the most important source of income for many musicians, this user experience design is perfectly tailored to their needs. "Current" aims to maintain the essence of the DIY musician scene by supporting tours, while providing a resource enabling independent musicians to understand their network across the country. As a mobile and desktop app, it offers ways to communicate, build tours easily and review venues. Designed in the style of popular rock zines, it allows the musicians to connect with one another on tour and find venues in new cities according to their preferences, all powered by machine learning.

University
SCAD Savannah College of Art and Design
Savannah, USA

Design
Vanessa Jaber, Drew Murray, Mara Healy, Samantha Wall, SCAD

Pineapple, Banana or Lemon?

[Augmented Reality Hybrid Board Game]

"Pineapple, banana or lemon?" is a cooperative game for four players. For its development, the existing literature on games and play was examined, and hybrid games on the market were tested, compared and observed in respect to their digital and analogue components. Finally, rapid prototypes were used to gain insight into various areas of hybrid games. The information was then used to build an iteratively designed game prototype and expand it with an augmented reality smartphone application, making it emerge as an exciting type of hybrid game.

University
FH JOANNEUM – University of Applied Sciences
Graz, Austria

Supervising Professor
Maja Pivec

Design
Simon Wünscher
Weiz, Austria

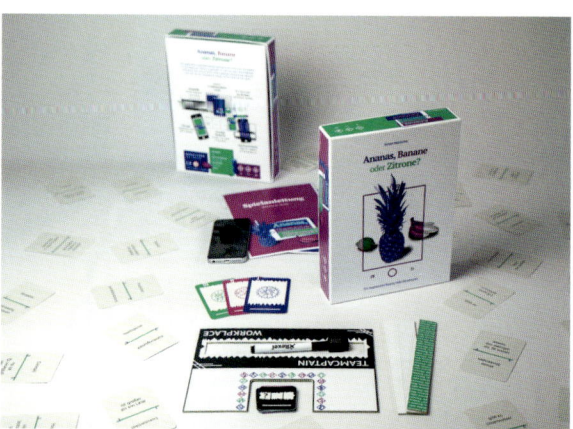

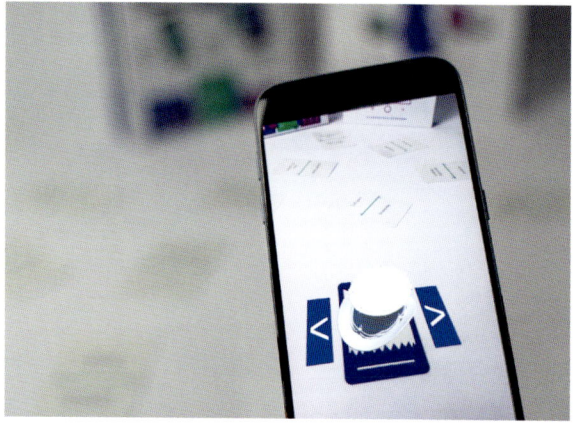

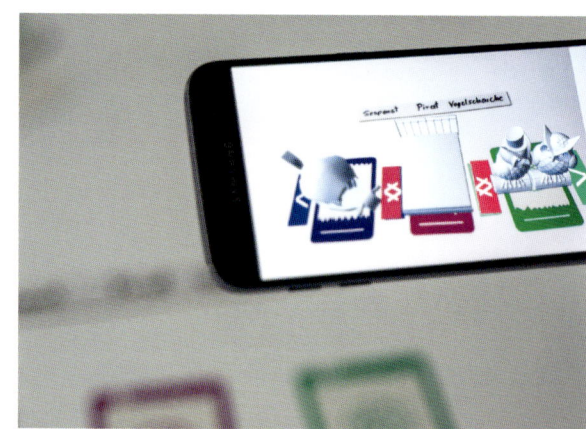

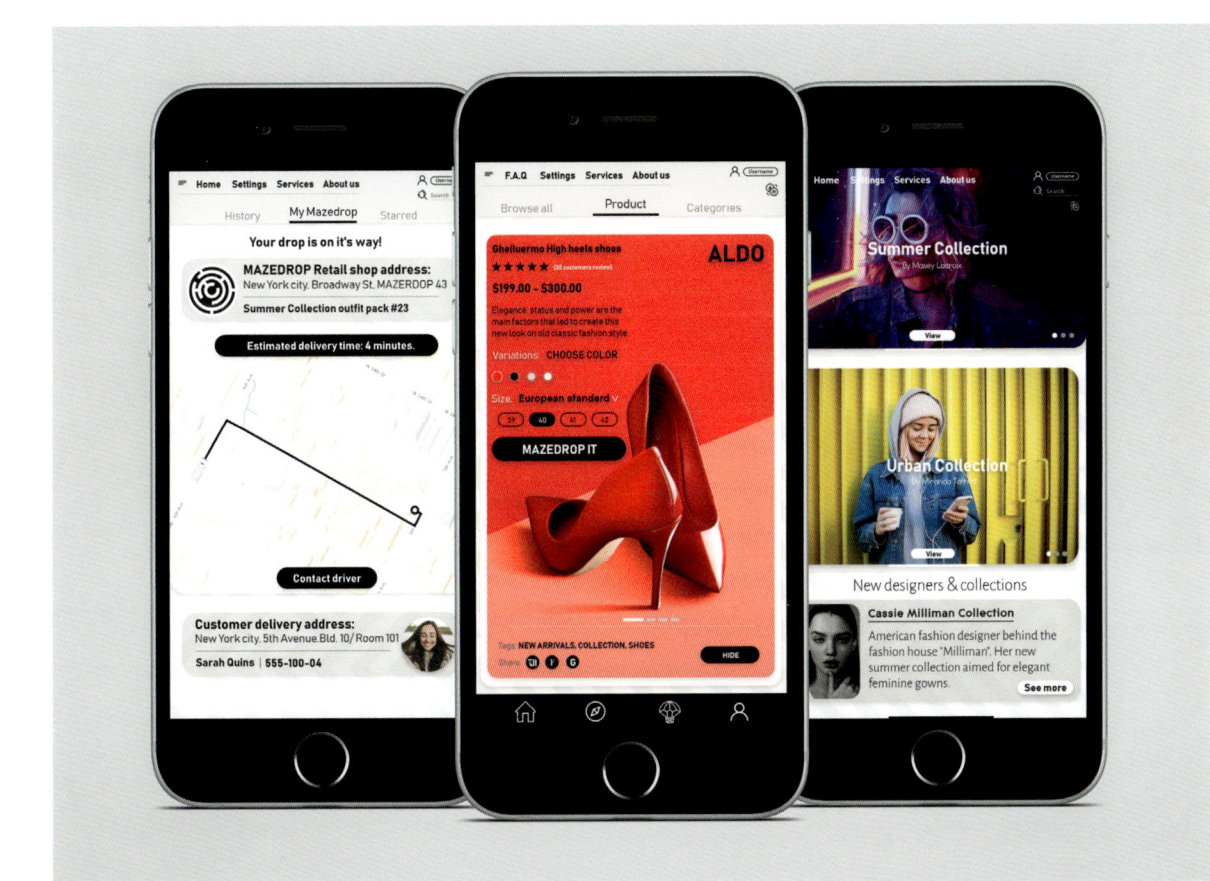

MAZEDROP

[User Experience Design,
User Interface Design]

The main goal of the current user experience and user interface design for MAZEDROP, an e-commerce platform and cloth retailer, was to simplify internet shopping by increasing its usability, thus making it more intuitive, straightforward and visually enjoyable. In addition to the shopping experience, the app includes features such as a discover section that offers news as well as information on trends and events to keep users up to date at all times. Built on a minimalistic style, the design relies on a clear layout to focus the user's attention on the content.

University
Shanghai Jiao Tong University
Shanghai, China

Supervising Professor
Tao Xi

Design
Denis Tsoy, Shanghai Jiao Tong University

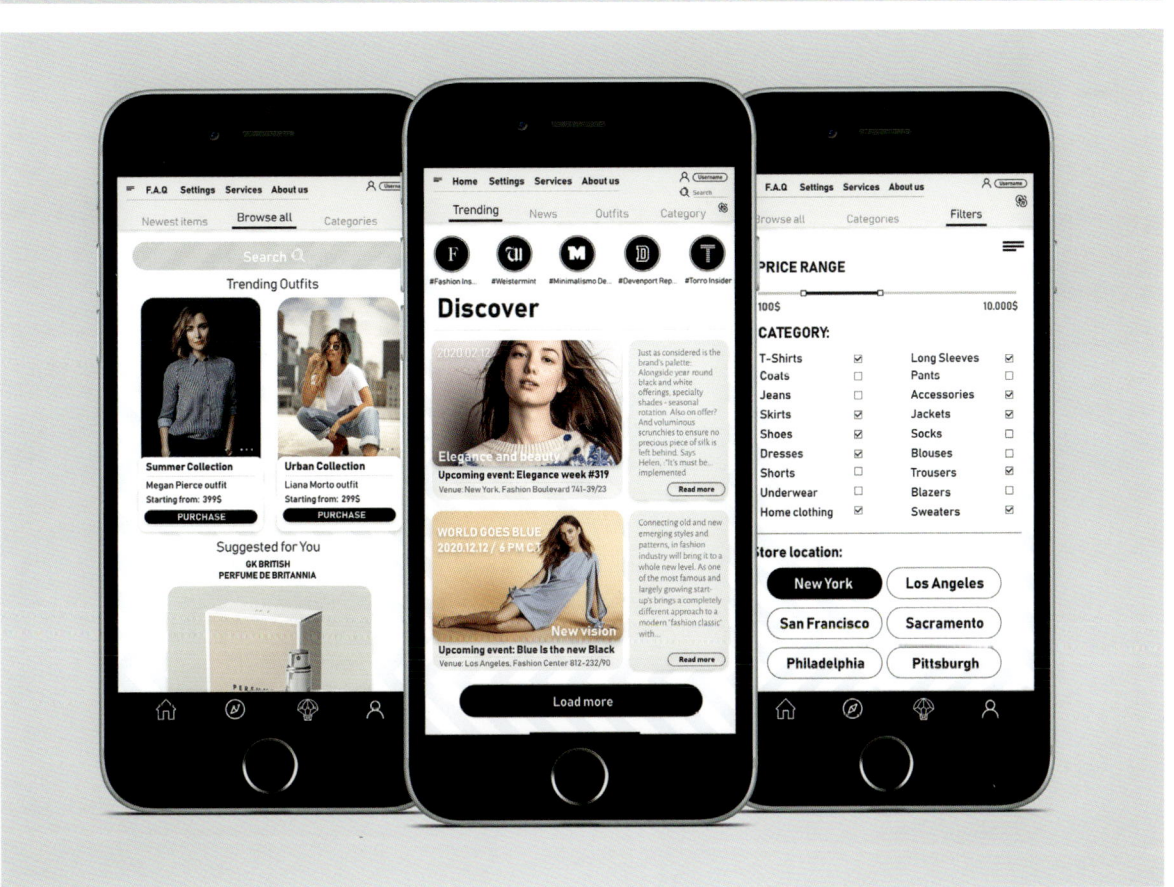

Loom

[Exhibition Design]

Designed and built as a student project for the "Tuchmacher-Museum", a historic cloth-making institution in Bramsche, Germany, the "Loom" exhibition allows visitors to experience for themselves the art of spinning yarn. Using an original, historic loom as a guide, an interactive station mimics the process of spinning yarn in a less complex representation. Visitors are digitally immersed in the process of creating yarn, guided by a chatbot that reacts to their real-time input. An AR overlay visualises the movement of the original loom, connecting visitors to the past.

University
University of Applied Sciences Osnabrück
Osnabrück, Germany

Design
Aljoscha Theil, Jonas Mai,
Julian Ruthemeyer, Maximilian Berndt,
Perihan Isik, Sebastian Winter,
Tom Janssens, University of Applied
Sciences Osnabrück

Reminiscence of Flowers

[Interaction Design]

With the concept of bringing different sensory experiences to an audience, the design of this device aims to document "Taiwan's flowers, fragrance and memory". Three kinds of flowers were selected by the Taiwanese people themselves as being the most representative of Taiwan. In addition, people's memories and stories about the flowers were also collected. The overall device is a 245 × 180 cm darkroom, three walls of which feature interactive paper sculpture devices on the theme of plum blossoms, magnolias and Phalaenopsis, allowing users to freely experience three kinds of interactions.

University
Tatung University
Taipei City, Taiwan

Supervising Professor
Shu-Yuan Lin

Design
Hsiao-Jung Chen, Tsai-Shiuan Yu, Qu-Ya Chen, An-Ro Chen, Tatung University

Publishing & Print Media	Posters	Typography	Illustrations	Sound Design	Film & Animation	Online
4	64	92	116	126	138	172

The Cover Story

[Urban Communication]

University
Southern Taiwan University of
Science and Technology
Tainan, Taiwan

Supervising Professor
Rain Chen, Chian-Fan Liou

Design
Hsin-Hua Lee, Wei-Ling Kuo,
Tzu-Ting Chang, Yu-Wei Chen,
Jia-Ying Chi, Southern Taiwan University
of Science and Technology

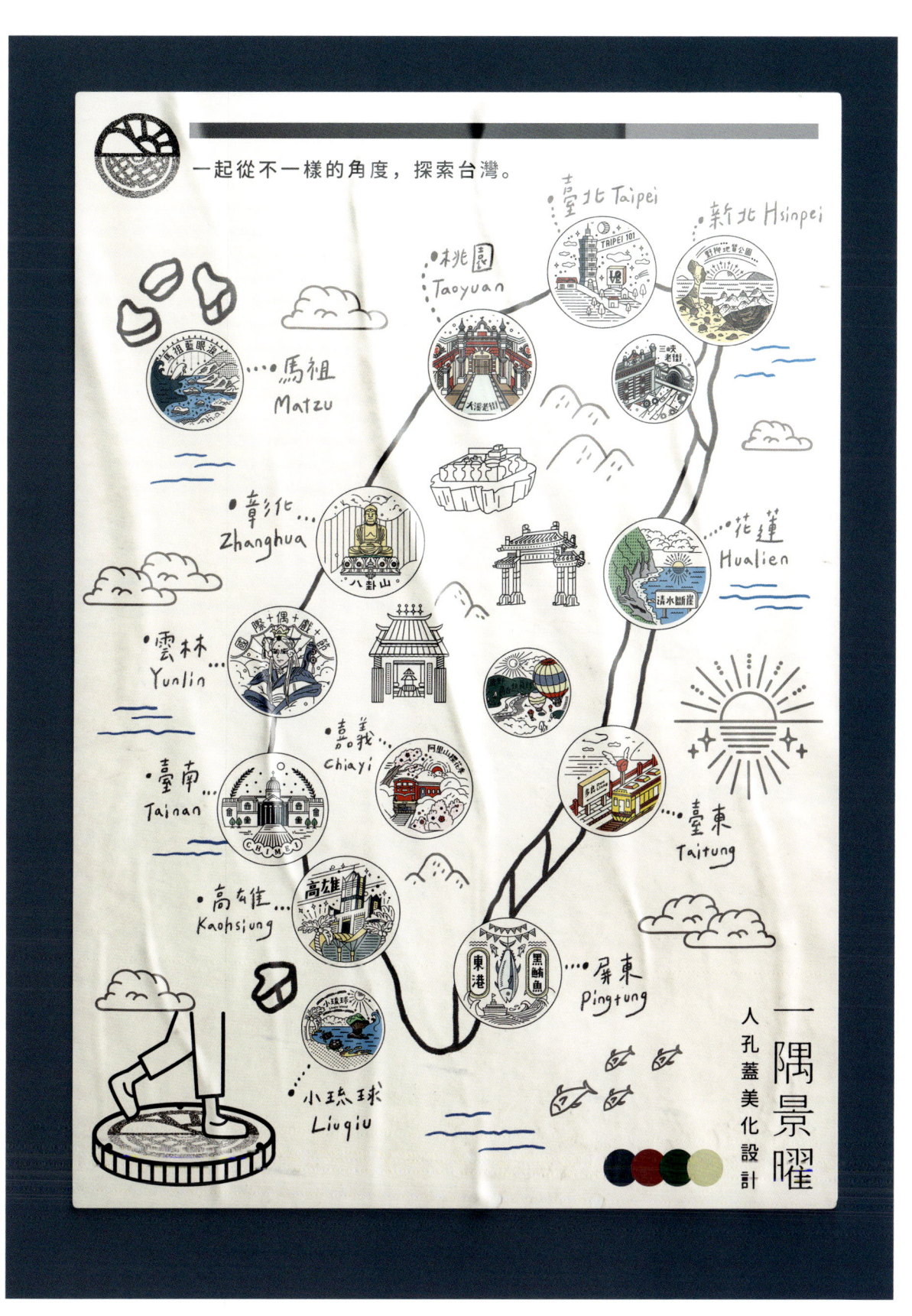

This project aims to promote and connect the island of Taiwan's many cities by decorating manhole covers with images of iconic sights. Turning them into a medium, the idea was also to change the image of manholes. The designs are subdivided into the four categories of architecture, old streets, landscapes and festivals. Each category is given a fitting colour palette and text, making it easy for viewers to learn about the place or event depicted while appreciating the design. To introduce the manhole covers, the brochure's content pages offer brief introductions and descriptions of individual manhole covers and show the colour palette used.

Designer Profiles

1508
Christoffer Kildahl, Per Jackson, Tore Rosbo
— Ask why.

Red Dot: Best of the Best
→ Online: page 178–179

The 1508 studio consists of 35 inquisitive designers trying to ask bold questions and challenge conventional strategies and structures – balancing empathy and value. With 20 years of experience in design and the transformation of services, brands and organisations, they have collected a few awards and achieved some meaningful impact, especially with their approach and solutions. Among a very long list of clients are Carlsberg, Novo, SMK (the National Gallery of Denmark), the Royal Danish Theatre, the National Olympic Committee and Sports Confederation of Denmark and HAY.

What does design mean to you?
We don't know what is going to happen next. Creating future solutions calls for a new mindset. A mindset based on hypotheses, purpose and experiments that connects solutions with users, transforms organisations and develops great experiences for strong relationships. We try to ask what really matters, to create from what we have learnt and come up with sustainable solutions that have the ability to evolve. Connecting people and technology through design.

What was your solution to making all works of art in the SMK accessible?
The key for creating the experience of SMK Open was to provide an overview of options and possibilities, while encouraging engagement and play in an exciting set-up. Aligning the solution to the digital and analogue profile of SMK was very important. Layout and typography are therefore precisely calibrated to fit both the feeling of being in the museum physically and the rest of the digital profile.

adabay
— We're creating a new digital world.

Red Dot
→ Spatial Communication: page 418–419

adabay is a young team of coders, designers and online marketing specialists providing the full range of digital services from concept to product design, technical implementation and marketing campaigns. The agency consists of a team of twenty-somethings working for clients such as Mammut, HypoVereinsbank, Munich Re, Johanniter, THW, UniCredit and BayWa.

What does design mean to you?
Design isn't something that just falls into place. Design is deliberate. Design creates change and communicates without needing any words. Design is the fine balance of pleasing visuals, interesting compositions and strong, persuasive messaging.

Where do you see future challenges in communication design?
In the fact that our world continues to evolve rapidly. New platforms, technologies and devices are created every single day. Cultures continue to intersect, creating new social trends and values that must be considered when designing new products.

What was your intention in designing your awarded work?
Our main goal was to design an office space that acts as an extension of adabay's new digital world, promotes collaboration and enables the creation of great products. The bottom floor houses multiple co-working spaces that inspire the team and visitors with adabay's signature touch of playful craziness. The second floor features a more typical office flair and gives the team more than enough space to move and collaborate freely.

Admind Branding & Communications
Karolina Pospischil
— Find ways to build connections –
between people, ideas, emotions.

Red Dot
→ Spatial Communication: page 406–407

Karolina Pospischil graduated from the Jagiellonian University in Krakow, Poland, and was a student at the School of Brand Strategy SAR. She is co-founder of the Grube Poster Studio and runs the creative teams at Admind, guiding their strategic development and supervising creative concepts. At the Annecy International Animation Film Festival, she was recognised for her short film "The Guardian" that later won awards at the Arizona Film Festival, CIFF, River Film Festival, SPARK Animation, Animac Lleida and Mecal Barcelona. She has worked for brands such as OFFF Barcelona, the Jewish Culture Festival, the Children's Film Festival Galicja, Krakow Festival Office, Alter Publishing House and Jagiellonian University.

Where do you see future challenges in communication design?
I hope communication design will not start biting its own tail, focusing too much on trends (both in terms of aesthetics and current topics) instead of taking social and environmental responsibility. Empathy is not the end of communication.

To what extent do you think new technologies are changing design?
The change brought about by new technologies is more a slow evolution than a rapid revolution. As designers, we are looking for new ways to use technology – existing and new – to create convenience and ease of use for all users.

What drives you to create something new?
The value it brings during the whole process – if it's fun, surprising, comes with a new point of view and creates a community.

Alty
— Great design is always about making complex things clear and easy to use.

Red Dot
→ Apps: page 212
→ Apps: page 229

Alty was founded in 2009 as a design and development service company and, today, is made up of dozens of great creators who are united by one idea: to create successful digital products that serve people all over the world, solve their problems on a daily basis and, as a result, create truly happy lives.

To what extent do you think new technologies are changing design?
We think that this is a mutual process. Designers are inspired by new technologies. And technologies evolve because designers bring a lot of innovations that are big challenges from a technical point. There are no limits!

Why did you become a designer?
Design is what actually changes people's lives for the better. We are happy to see how our work makes people's lives easier and happier.

What drives you to create something new?
Just one small thing – the desire to change the world! We really love the time we live in. Even the craziest ideas can be brought to life. Ten or twenty years ago, we could not even dream about that.

What makes your work unique?
We have accumulated huge experience because of a strong focus on narrow niches. And through design we don't just solve the target audience's problems, but help businesses to succeed, achieve business goals and market themselves.

AMI DESIGN
Amy M. F. Tsai
— Give all that you have to what you are doing; if not, then don't even bother.

Red Dot
→ Posters: page 87

Amy M. F. Tsai completed her doctoral degree in design at Swinburne University of Technology and currently teaches creative product design to university students in Taiwan. She has recently become president of KAPAarts, an association of artists who share her passion for the arts. Her expertise spans the planning and curation of exhibitions to various visual designs as well as installation artworks, with several of her works having won international design awards. Her design studio AMI DESIGN specialises in visual communication and brand design.

What does design mean to you?
Design is my way to stay away from being one of the "walking dead".

To what extent do you think new technologies are changing design?
All technologies have become a part of the lifestyle that we are familiar with; it is just presented in a new format. I am not a believer in the notion that anything can change design. On the contrary, it is design that has been changing what is around us and the narrative about us.

What are the biggest challenges in a creative's everyday life?
You ponder the value and the meaning of the existence of each creature/subject. It can drive one wild with incredulity when one sees how easy it is for others to dismiss or overlook the wonders of the world that are before them.

Amorepacific
Kanghwan Jeon
— A good design requires extreme communication.

Red Dot: Best of the Best
→ Online: page 182–183

Red Dot
→ Online: page 196

After graduating from Hongik University in 2012, Kanghwan Jeon started working in the digital design field at a design agency. Three years later, he became an in-house designer at Ticket Monster, a social commerce company, on a full-fledged service. After a short venture experience in 2017, he has been working as a designer at Amorepacific.

Where do you see future challenges in communication design?
I think that the era of not seeing each other in person has come faster because of COVID-19. This phenomenon will create more intense competition in the digital market. We must survive this competition. I am convinced that communicating clearly while conveying the values of the client will be most important in this area.

What was your intention in designing your awarded work?
We thought it was a problem that men's skincare brands communicate in the same way as women's brands do. So we thought about creating a persona called "Bro" who shares useful "Tips" in a familiar way. The project is designed to capture the value of the brand through familiar illustrations, interesting texts and layouts that resemble cartoons.

How has humour been translated visually in the adverts for the Bro&Tips skincare range?
In order to communicate with elements that key customers will like, we tried to express humour in frames using strong lines just like in cartoons. We also sought to communicate with customers through witty illustrations, humorous copywriting and bold typography.

Publishing & Print Media	Posters	Typography	Illustrations	Sound Design	Film & Animation	Online
4	64	92	116	126	138	172

APOLLO Content Company
Soyoung Kim
— Be faithful to the basics.
Every design needs a reason.

Red Dot
→ Film & Animation: page 154–155

Soyoung Kim is currently executive director of ANSSil's brand design integrator. Before, she worked as the art director of the opening and closing ceremonies of the 2018 Winter Olympics in Pyeongchang, South Korea, and as an art director, producer and creative director for TV CF and in the film, music video, media arts industries and others. She has already won several design awards

To what extent do you think new technologies are changing design?
New technologies and design can create a new level of enjoyment for all different lifestyles and also can elicit communication. So, designers should be open-minded and try to find new designs and new values that can harmonise with new technologies.

Why did you become a designer?
In my childhood, I loved drawing and people praised my work. This is the driving force of my creativity. Now I feel happy when I create, and creating is when I can be myself. I want to pass this happiness on to others through my designs.

What was your intention in designing your awarded work?
It is a line animation concept trailer for ANSSil's brand launch. The purpose of the concept trailer is to attract attention and make customers curious about the brand. Motivated by the "string" core of the mattress, we composed the trailer with minimalistic lines to describe ANSSil's brand identity.

Appedu Design Institute
Wei-Ching Lin
— Success comes naturally to those who follow their passions.

Red Dot
→ Illustrations: page 125

Wei-Ching Lin currently works as a user interface designer and as a front-end web developer at a tech company designing user interfaces, writing front-end web programs and creating web animations. He has a lot of experience in website design and also studies the usage patterns of digital software and the overall user experience.

What does design mean to you?
Design is all around us – in the things we use and wear. For me, design is a way of life.

To what extent do you think new technologies are changing design?
Artificial Intelligence (AI) has taken over some aspects of website design, such as analysing users' browsing patterns to create banner advertisements that speak to different groups of users. The trend towards the use of AI in design is especially noticeable in digital media advertising. However, I believe that human creativity and imagination cannot be replaced by AI.

What makes your work unique?
Creating artwork that one does not see in everyday life. Most of the artwork I design portrays imaginary landscapes or dream fantasies.

What was your intention in designing your awarded work?
To evoke love in people's hearts – to love the ecosystem and to love Mother Earth.

Aught
Tomaz Goh
— Design with clarity, simplicity and thoughtfulness

Red Dot
→ Film & Animation: page 165

Before founding Aught in 2013, Tomaz Goh worked for globally renowned creative branding and advertising agencies such as Bartle Bogle Hegarty (BBH), Interbrand and The Partners. He has judged for the Crowbar Awards in Singapore and was both a guest speaker and guest examiner at First Media Design School and Raffles Design Institute respectively. He was also a featured artist for Tiger Beer's "Tiger Translate" initiative and the Uniqlo UT x Cannes Lions collection. Among his clients are Lenzing AG, NTT i-Cast Japan, Tourism Authority of Thailand, Singtel and Nespresso.

What does design mean to you?
It is a process and a means to an end. Personally, it boils down to two things: action (putting your thoughts into something tangible) and progression (making things better).

To what extent do you think new technologies are changing design?
New technologies are constantly changing. Only time will tell if they will significantly affect the future or if they are just a temporal, fleeting thing. As much as these things do, at times, aid us, design is fundamentally very human, something we can never deviate from. We need to ask what we can do with what we have and, more importantly, why we should do so. There is a need to strike a good balance between technology and design.

What drives you to create something new?
The belief that nothing is permanent drives me to create new things. All that is new now will not be so tomorrow.

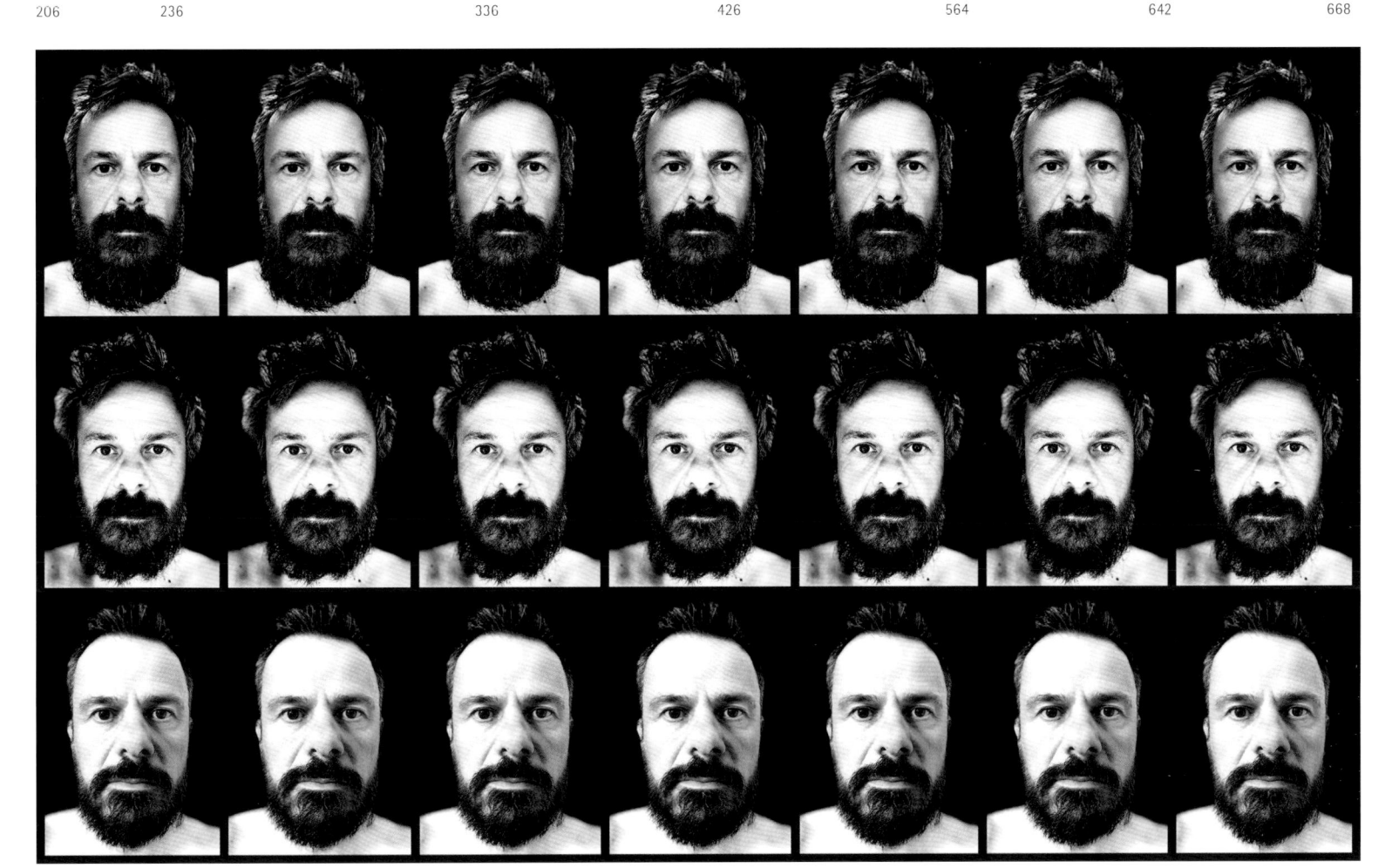

B&tW Studio
Lee Bradley
— We are all born with genius.
(Milton Glaser)

Red Dot: Best of the Best
→ Publishing & Print Media: page 10–11

B&tW Studio is a design and communications practice based in Leeds, United Kingdom. Founded in 2005 by creative director Lee Bradley, it has become well known for its ability to combine big ideas with meticulous attention to detail. By staying deliberately small, the studio can give each project the attention it deserves. The "&t" in its name stands for the belief in partnership, collaboration and making connections – between people and ideas, brands and audiences, design and business.

How can designers be ahead of their time?
Embrace change and discover new technologies. Use your natural ideas (talent) and mix with the forever changing world we live in.

What do you need in order to be creative?
Discover the great outdoors and visit inspirational places and architecture. Share ideas and build on the strength of others. It's about big ideas but working as a team to develop that winning formula and let those skills unite. Let the world and what's around you inspire you. It's all there to engage with.

To which aspect did you pay special attention when designing your award-winning work?
We wanted to produce a book that wasn't just the normal photographer's showcase of work. We gave it a purpose and relevance based around the journey John Angerson took to photograph his work. This created a narrative and told a compelling story. It was about making a collector's piece and defining a legacy for John's concept and the hard work he put into it.

BiBoBox Studio
Zhao Liu, Wei Liu, Huan Tan, Zhuolin Gu, Xiaofang Li, Bo Liu
— A good story makes studying inspiring.

Red Dot: Junior Award
Best of the Best
→ Apps: page 428–429

BiBoBox Studio focuses on mobile application design, experience innovation design, digital entertainment design and creative game design for children. The team always adheres to the design service philosophy of quality, taste and stability. The BiBoBox team consists of product and user strategy experts, interactive experience designers, animation designers, illustrators, programmers and engineers from different disciplines.

What does design mean to you?
Design is the way we think and the way we express ourselves.

Where do you see future challenges in communication design?
The way people communicate is changing quickly. We can see an endless stream of interaction methods and dazzling visual styles. The resources we can use are growing exponentially, thus making decisions difficult.

To what extent do you think new technologies are changing design?
Design is all about solving problems in an unexpected but correct way. New technologies may broaden our imagination.

What was your intention in designing your awarded work?
Our product combines a good story with an attractive, interactive design to inspire and guide children to achieve educational goals. The aim is to allow children to learn and play at the same time.

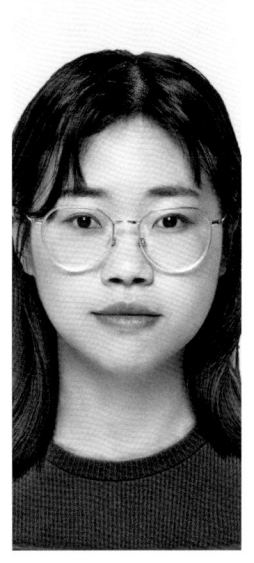

BiBoBox Studio
Jingye Zhang, Lei Bai,
Weiwei Ma, Zhuolin Gu,
Xiaofang Li, Bo Liu
— A good story makes studying inspiring.

Red Dot: Junior Award
Best of the Best
→ Apps: page 436–437

BiBoBox Studio focuses on mobile application design, experience innovation design, digital entertainment design and creative game design for children. The team always adheres to the design service philosophy of quality, taste and stability. The BiBoBox team consists of product and user strategy experts, interactive experience designers, animation designers, illustrators, programmers and engineers from different disciplines.

Why did you become a designer?
Because we believe we have the power and passion to create a better life.

What drives you to create something new?
Self-discipline and imagination.

What and how do children who cannot read learn with your WordUpUp game?
Making learning fun and relaxing can reduce the fear of learning a foreign language. The colourful illustrations provide an enjoyable aesthetic experience and teach children about cute animals and everyday things in life. They can interact with the magical objects and learn the meaning and pronunciation of words. For example, in the Mysterious Forest theme, children drag a mole onto a mound of dirt. The mole then comes out of the ground to say hello and is followed by the word and pronunciation of "mole". In this way, the children can connect the image and behaviour of the mole with the word that describes it.

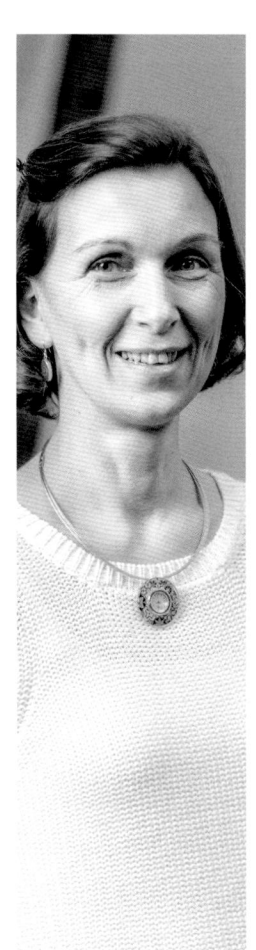

CaderaDesign
Amelie Reich, Tom Cadera,
Eva Wolz, René Fleischer,
Anna Radlbeck,
Henning Muschko
— Understanding technology.
Designing for people.

Red Dot: Best of the Best
→ Interface & User Experience Design: page 244–245

CaderaDesign was founded by its managing director Tom Cadera in 1992. Based in Würzburg, Germany, it is one of the leading agencies for user experience design in the field of machinery and industry, developing both hardware and software solutions. The team of CaderaDesign consists of designers and IT specialists who work on user experience design and industrial design projects in an inter disciplinary way. After completing his studies in industrial design at the Braunschweig University of Art, Tom Cadera specialised in designing the interface between man and highly complex technology. Between 1997 and 2008, he was also a lecturer at the Furtwangen University.

Where do you see future challenges in communication design?
Interaction with products is something that is in a constant state of flux. New technologies have led to user interfaces that are getting ever smaller and less tangible. People need something they can "grasp". It is an extremely exciting challenge to get the balance right when seeking to produce safe and emotionally satisfying interaction.

What was your intention in designing your awarded work?
Our prime motive was to conceive graphics that make highly complex processes understandable and therefore manageable in a quick and intuitive way. This enables the user to ensure the quality and efficiency of the production process. A carefully considered concept with attractive and self-explanatory illustrations was therefore a must. The design of an innovative basic layout with a sidebar was the enabler for achieving this.

Chaoyang University of Technology
Yi-Xuan Sun, Liang-Ying Huang, Yu-Jie Jhuang
— Try to do anything to inspire more possibilities.

Red Dot: Junior Award
Best of the Best
→ Publishing & Print Media: page 432–433

Yi-Xuan Sun, Liang-Ying Huang and Yu-Jie Jhuang are students from the Department of Visual Communication Design at Chaoyang University of Technology, Taiwan. Liang-Ying Huang, the leader of the awarded project, was responsible for illustration design and graphic editing. Yi-Xuan Sun was in charge of manual binding and copywriting, and Yu-Jie Jhuang was responsible for the layout design and planning programme.

How can communication design arouse emotions?
By acting as a social observer.

What inspires you?
The conversations within our team inspire us.

How would you describe your style of design?
Adventurous and unrestricted.

What was your intention in designing your awarded work?
By taking this true story about mental health in Taiwan as the entry point and transforming it into a magazine of visual imagery from an objective perspective, we hoped to stimulate the public and make people think about the issue. When collecting the project data, we felt different emotions about the background story and the dialogue with patients, family members and the outside world. We then used the stacking and patchwork methods to express what we felt.

How do you think this award will impact your life?
This award gives us great encouragement and recognition.

Agi Chen Studio
Agi Chen
— Seeking a creative way to collect memory and transform it into a new perception.

Red Dot
→ Spatial Communication: page 410–411

Agi Chen is an experienced creative who works across multiple fields and the media languages of contemporary culture to penetrate public spaces through cross-border thinking and multimedia creation. She established her studio to integrate creatives from different fields and began to put together large-scale architectural projection mapping productions. She served as visual coordinator of the 2017 Summer Universiade opening ceremony, as the art director of the Presidential Office Building projection mapping show and the 2018 Taipei 101 New Year's Eve Celebration, transforming projection mapping into transcendent media that reshapes the collective memory.

What does design mean to you?
The ability to create communications with new sensations.

Where do you see future challenges in communication design?
One challenge is how to transform collective memory into an intelligent interface.

Why did you become a designer?
To give free thoughts and feelings more space.

What drives you to create something new?
My curiosity about everything in existence.

What was your intention in designing your awarded work?
To refashion the collective memory of Taiwan by transforming the 100-year-old Presidential Office Building into a projection mapping theatre with a focus on the environment.

COBE

Red Dot: Grand Prix
→ Apps: page 208–209

COBE specialises in CX design, UI/UX design and software development. The agency combines a user-centred design approach with a proprietary UX identity method (UXi). Using findings from neuroscience and behavioural economics, this method integrates brand values into the design of digital products and creates an emotional connection between the user, the product and the brand behind it. Founded in 2012 by Felix van de Sand, Anatol Korel and Daniel Wagner, the team currently has 50 members based in Munich and Osijek. Among its clients are Vodafone, Porsche and ProSiebenSat.1.

Why did you become a designer?
Eight years ago, we realised that UX design would play an important role in future. We knew that we wanted to be involved in making digital history.

At whom is FYEO targeted and why should one download it?
FYEO is designed to appeal to everyone who enjoys listening to podcasts and generally likes audio content. FYEO is intended to show users that the app and the experience will make audio content even more enjoyable and inspiring. Of course, the FYEO Originals are the icing on the cake and are staged and presented accordingly. FYEO is simply the digital stage for this type of audio content.

Custom Interactions
Dr. Michaela Kauer-Franz,
Sascha Hiller, Marta Piqué,
Philipp Kohl, Dr. Benjamin Franz
— Everybody's time is valuable –
an inspiring interface with 3DUX.

Red Dot
→ Interface & User Experience Design: page 276–277

Custom Interactions is a data-driven UX design company founded in 2013. The team of 15 people helps clients to build products with outstanding user experience based on a data-driven UX design approach (3DUX). Custom Interactions focuses on the design of critical interfaces, where good design plays a major role in ensuring the safety of people and work efficiency such as in the mobility and medical sectors.

What does design mean to you?
Invisible support and guidance that enable ease of use, confident decision-making and clear navigation, paired with good visual design that enhances the experience even further.

What drives you to create something new?
Besides the trust that clients place in us to support their needs and help with their projects, it is also always inspiring to see and work in an industry that constantly changes and adapts. It never gets boring.

What makes your work unique?
Supporting and reassuring the user in critical situations about making the right decision, whether it is in security, transportation and aviation or in medical environments.

What was your intention in designing your awarded work?
Ease of use, simplicity and quick decision-making were intentions that always were on top of our list of things to accomplish with our UI for this project.

Dentsu
Kazuhiro Shimura
— One's interests are the source of ideas to solve social issues.

Red Dot
→ Apps: page 235

Kazuhiro Shimura has a background in biotechnology and began his career at Dentsu in 2007. He subsequently joined the Toyota Future Mobility Development Division and was involved in the development of "i-ROAD", the three-wheeled electric vehicle and its mobility-related services. He has designed numerous successful innovative solutions for clients' businesses using technology and data, in addition to creating effective ads. As a creative director, he has received multiple international awards in renowned competitions such as the Cannes Lions, One Show, Clio Awards, D&AD Awards, London International Awards, Spikes Asia and Adfest.

What does design mean to you?
Design is about coming up with ideas to solve the various challenges that exist in our world.

What was your intention in designing your awarded work?
I often buy tuna as sashimi at the grocery store, but sometimes it doesn't taste as good as I expect it to. I had been wondering whether something could be done to improve this hit-or-miss experience, which happens despite the tuna looking the same. Then, I saw a professional broker examining tuna on the news. That gave me the idea to learn about the inspection skills of professional tuna merchants and spread technology offering that grading expertise across the globe. As of 2020, tuna qualified by TUNA SCOPE has not only been used domestically and in some countries abroad; it has also begun to be employed on a global scale as part of a project subsidised by the Japan Fisheries Agency. In this way, my desire to continue eating delicious tuna has inspired the development of TUNA SCOPE.

Design In Situ
Selin Oezcelik Mörth, Nagehan Kurali Alan
We create untold digital stories.
We believe in participation.

Red Dot
→ Online: page 197

Design In Situ was founded by Selin Oezcelik Mörth and Nagehan Kurali Alan in 2010 as an interdisciplinary design studio to create digital experiences as a service. The interdisciplinary background of the team allows the studio to shape users' emotions using creative technologies in different spaces. With that aim, Design In Situ creates interactive installations, digital environments or visual identities by combining different design disciplines for online platforms, retail environments, museums, events and public spaces for global brands such as Nike, Samsung, Coca-Cola and Vitra.

Where do you see future challenges in communication design?
The future of communication design will be challenged by the amount of adaptation to technological change. While staying in line with design fundamentals, we will have to be brave and flexible enough to try different approaches in design practice. Interdisciplinarity has always been and will continue to be a fundamental requirement to overcoming the future challenges of design experiences.

To what extent do you think new technologies are changing design?
New technologies have enabled us to discover new realms of design. The integration of technology into physical spaces has led to new creative methods of communication.

Why did you become a designer?
We were always intrigued by the opportunities of tackling and solving problems methodologically while at the same time cultivating aesthetic skills and assets.

Ding Yong Culture Creativity
— Design and art for a sustainable perspective of the future.

Red Dot
→ Spatial Communication: page 414–415

The cross-functional team of Ding Yong Culture Creativity includes architects, craftsmen and artists. They create new landscapes that echo humanity and nature. The aim is to incite reflection and conversation for a post-pandemic, sustainable and holistic lifestyle of peace and harmony. In the past, the team has realised projects for the World Expo 2015 in Milan, the London Design Biennale 2016 and the Taiwan Lantern Festival, and also carried out other large-scale planning.

What does design mean to you?
Design is about the future environment of mankind.

Where do you see future challenges in communication design?
In the quality of aesthetics and social communication.

To what extent do you think new technologies are changing design?
New technologies are changing thinking in the production process and leading to different imaginative solutions.

Why did you become a designer?
It was fate.

What drives you to create something new?
Imagining the future.

Publishing & Print Media	Posters	Typography	Illustrations	Sound Design	Film & Animation	Online
4	64	92	116	126	138	172

Anna Farkas
– Less is more thought.

Red Dot: Grand Prix
→ Publishing & Print Media: page 6–7

Anna Farkas graduated in graphic design from the Hungarian University of Fine Arts. In 1999, she founded her own studio, Anagraphic. She mainly designs logos, identities and publications. Her work has been recognised by numerous awards. In particular, her unique lunar cycle calendar, the Anaptár, on which she also wrote her doctoral thesis, has been singled out for awards and has, to date, won nine international prizes.

What does design mean to you?
Design for me means solving problems.

Why did you become a designer?
My grandmother, Anna F. Györffy, was one of Hungary's most versatile children's book illustrators of the last 60 years, with many of her books being published abroad. Seeing her love for her work and how she used her time as she thought best, I already decided as a child that I too wanted to do something like that when I grew up.

How do the scientific and the artistic merge in your awarded work?
"Anaptár" is a unique, informative poster calendar that is not only a work of beauty but also a source of fascinating new discoveries. It is much more than a traditional ephemeris. The publication provides lots of information besides enumerating days. Visualising data on the sun and the moon in a new way, the calendar shows the movement of these heavenly bodies in the sky, and, because of the radial arrangement, this huge amount of astronomical data is incorporated in a new, spectacular, complex and yet easily comprehensible system.

Freshheads
Carola Jansen
— Design is not about you, it's about your audience. Design on behalf of their needs.

Red Dot: Grand Prix
→ Online: page 174–175

Carola Jansen completed her bachelor's degree in 2009 and afterwards started working as an all-round design freelancer for many different clients in smaller and bigger companies. After several years of working freelance, she joined Freshheads, a Dutch agency that provides multidisciplinary teams for digital innovation, in 2017. At Freshheads she has the opportunity to collaborate with great developers on challenging projects for international clients.

What does design mean to you?
Design is a powerful tool to tell a story and create meaningful products. It speaks to people's subconscious and communicates feelings through experience. I believe that the best designs are the ones where aesthetics, technology and functionality are brought together.

What are the biggest challenges in a creative's everyday life?
The biggest challenge is not to let yourself be held back by restrictions imposed by others, yourself, technologies or your clients. It is important to be aware of blocking factors and to try to eliminate them. Give the creative process space and let it flow.

What was your intention in designing your awarded work?
Because of my passion for both art and design, I became very enthusiastic about the opportunity to contribute to this art project that impacts people's lives on so many levels. The biggest challenge in designing the website was to make the tattoos be more than just a letter. They had to show the global impact, but also the individual stories, so people would be able to understand the importance of this art project.

Publishing & Print Media	Posters	Typography	Illustrations	Sound Design	Film & Animation	Online
4	64	92	116	126	138	172

FunDesign.tv/Tape That Collective
— First-ever exhibition in Asia dedicated to tape art!

Red Dot: Best of the Best
→ Spatial Communication: page 346–347

Taipei-based FunDesign.tv is a content provider with business activities in numerous countries in Asia, including mainland China, as well as in Europe. As a media platform, one of the company's focal points is its dedication to design and art exhibition curating, artistic creativity development and cross-cultural exchange. Thus in 2019 Taipei was ignited by a visual party of lines, patches of colour and fluorescence that was part of the award-winning tape art exhibition, curated by Carrie Chang, SK Chen and Sandrine Cheng. Founded in 2011, Tape That Collective is a team of artists with roots in the urban art movement, consisting of Cedric Goussanou, Atau Hamos, Stephan Meissner, Thomas Meissner, Adrian Dittert, Stefan Busch and Nicolas Lawin. Their tape artworks can be found, amongst others, in underground nightclubs, abandoned buildings, showrooms and galleries. While focused on Berlin, the collective is active in many other cities with recent and ongoing projects.

What makes your work unique?
When working with tape, one of the most important techniques is to work in layers. Playing with depth, shapes and the room itself, tape art builds a perfect scene in which to get lost in time and space. The emancipation of tape art as a self-sufficient medium is most likely due to and also intertwined with the beginning of the urban art movement. Its removable and temporary nature makes tape a rewarding medium to use on any surface it sticks to, thus making it easy to integrate into urban environments.

Gooest Media Technology Daqing
Kevin Guang Sun
— To make art more interesting.
To make art digital
and give it a new form.

Red Dot
→ Spatial Communication: page 373

Kevin Guang Sun is a new media technology practitioner, designer and software development engineer. In 2010, he co-founded Gooest Media Technology Daqing Co., Ltd., where he is deputy general manager and technical director. His work includes the digital representation of public art in specific venues, interactive multimedia programmes and the implementation of immersive installations, exploring the convergence between digital technologies and physical entities. He has won several awards in renowned competitions such as the VEGA Digital Awards and the MUSE Creative Awards.

To what extent do you think new technologies are changing design?
Developments in design have always gone hand in hand with new technological advances. Every technological innovation will bring revolutionary change for design. From Impressionist paintings to the invention of the camera, many artists and design masters have been influenced by the direction modern art has taken. Therefore, new technologies will lead to strong developments in art and design.

What drives you to create something new?
I like to abstract concrete objects and use various new technologies to realise some of my ideas and express them in graphic code. I hope that these ideas will have a certain commercial value and meet the sensory needs of most people.

What are the biggest challenges in a creative's everyday life?
The biggest challenge for future design must be how to meet the psychological needs of users, and how to make design close to life.

Publishing & Print Media	Posters	Typography	Illustrations	Sound Design	Film & Animation	Online
4	64	92	116	126	138	172

Graphasel Design Studio
Csaba Dobos, Kristóf Láng, Mátyás Beke, László Ördögh, Dávid Drozsnyik, Péter Szöke
— We love creating unique visual communication.

Red Dot
→ Spatial Communication: page 402–403

Graphasel Design Studio was established within the Hungarian University of Fine Arts by a small team of friends in Budapest in 2003. The name "Graphasel" was created by linking the two words "graphic" and "asasel" (Azasel). The team is led by the two founders, László Ördögh and Dávid Drozsnyik, who graduated from the university as graphics majors in 2005. The studio primarily specialises in image design and artistic visual identities. In addition to creative work, the design studio puts great emphasis on the positioning and communication of the brands it is entrusted with.

What does design mean to you?
We believe that beyond functionality, design is a game for the senses. For us, this means that design is a complex adventure; the combination of the experiences seen, felt and perceived. If a person, experiencing something for the first time, remembers it later, the design becomes a communicable story in their mind. If that story is similar to what we formulated at the beginning of the design process, then we are spot on.

What are the biggest challenges in a creative's everyday life?
Maintaining teamwork and team dynamics requires constant attention. Integrating individual creative processes into a well-designed system and controlling the processes is the biggest challenge in everyday life. We believe in teamwork and have experienced that the most successful projects are those we have created when we are in tune with each other, like a symphony orchestra.

Guangzhou City Construction College
Fojun Li
— Do my best and let it be.

Red Dot
→ Typography: page 112–113

Fojun Li is vice president and associate professor of the School of Art and Design at Guangzhou City Construction College. He is the founder of Iseead Design (Shenzhen) Co., Ltd., an agency providing brand and corporate image design and design services for famous enterprises such as C'estbon, Pepsi, Founder, etc. He is a member of the Association Typographique Internationale (ATypI), the International Council of Graphic Design Associations, a national member of the design committee of the China Packaging Federation, director of the Commercial Art Designer Association of Guangdong and vice president of the Shenzhen Intellectual Creative Design Property Association.

What does design mean to you?
If I can, I will make design a lifelong pursuit. It is not only a hobby, but a job. And it is the impulse that makes me indefatigable, regardless of the weather or time of day.

What drives you to create something new?
New design ideas and creative forms emerge because customers are constantly putting forward design projects that meet the needs of the market.

What makes your work unique?
I have devoted myself to design sustainability, our heritage, its reconstruction and activation. I advocate the dissemination of modern oriental aesthetics. Relying on modern design techniques, I explore rare traditional woodcut books all year round, and regenerate them in a computer font library, so that endangered rare fonts are preserved.

Publishing & Print Media	Posters	Typography	Illustrations	Sound Design	Film & Animation	Online
4	64	92	116	126	138	172

Hand Heart Design Firm
— Visualize the invisible value.

Red Dot
→ Spatial Communication: page 400–401

Founded in 2013, Hand Heart Design has been focusing on the design of brand identities. The company regularly designs the corporate social responsibility report for several large-scale enterprises such as Taiwan China Airlines, Delta Electronics, AU Optronics, Shin Kong Financial Holding and the brand and environmental identity system for Tainan Public Library, Kaohsiung Medical University and the Kaohsiung National Stadium.

What does design mean to you?
Design is the solution to an issue; the design creates value and a way of thinking.

Why did you become a designer?
Our homeland, Taiwan, is a pretty island. The Portuguese discovered it 400 years ago and gave Formosa a beautiful name. The city of Kaohsiung, where we grew up, modernised and introduced industrialisation, but it is gradually losing its original appearance with all kinds of advertisements disfiguring the neat streets. We hope to contribute our capabilities to make the city more beautiful and allow the world to become a better place.

What are the biggest challenges in a creative's everyday life?
To explore, observe, discover, collect and see all the different kinds of details hidden in daily living; to enable the extraordinary through the ordinary; and to make simplicity not that simple through determination, judgment and the process of elimination.

Ming-Chi Hsieh Art Studio
Ming-Chi Ken Hsieh
— To create marvellous, contemporary work through design and creativity by lining up emotions.

Red Dot
→ Posters: page 79
→ Posters: page 86

Ming-Chi Hsieh graduated from art university and holds a PhD in design. He gained more than 25 years of experience working with famous design companies, before founding his own agency, Ming-Chi Hsieh Art Studio. He has won numerous domestic and international awards.

What does design mean to you?
A way to keep talking with the world.

Where do you see future challenges in communication design?
The change of consumer behaviour has an impact on the future design so design is not just about communication and storytelling, it is also about image.

Why did you become a designer?
I always seek to achieve the most elegant balance between design and creation. My aim is to record the beauty of life and to create the most marvellous contemporary work through constant effort.

What drives you to create something new?
I am curious about the unknown world. Images are part of everyone's life. As soon as the day dawns, we are flooded with millions of images. There are pictures and videos. People communicate them to gain approval or to feel part of society. Humans are like a puzzle, a collection of images. When everyone shows the world we live in through pictures, what will that look like? I am curious.

Mingpu Elvin Hu
— Design is not just what it looks like and how it works. Design is how it feels.

Red Dot: Junior Award
→ Illustrations: page 513

Elvin Hu is an award-winning designer, currently based in San Francisco. Before starting his current position as an interaction designer at Google, he spent a few years studying design and photography at Cooper Union in New York City. In the past, during his time at MetaDesign, he has worked on branding projects for companies like Volkswagen. His personal projects have received worldwide attention from media outlets such as The Verge, GQ, Wired, etc., and won him prestigious awards, e.g. from the Type Directors Club.

How can communication design arouse emotions?
Everything people experience and see in daily life has been designed – explicitly or not, and these designs become part of their memories. Designs we produce gently remind the viewers of the existence of such experiences and encourage them to relive the feelings they had and synthesise them with the new information we present them with.

What goals have you set for your future career?
I want to work on projects that empower people to create things they desire to produce and bring high-quality design and technology to places they have not traditionally reached.

What inspires you?
Nature, trivial things we tend to ignore and many aspects of Asian culture.

How would you describe your style of design?
Simple, authentic and straightforward.

Huawei Technologies, UCD Center

Zhenzhen Li, Binghua Xu, Yilin Wang, Nan Qiao, Xin Meng, Chi Xu, Ye Zhao, Haidong Yang, Shaolei Wang, Xue Yang
— Building a fully connected, intelligent world with better design.

Red Dot: Best of the Best
→ Interface & User Experience Design: page 242–243

With in-depth research into user experience, human-computer interaction and user interface technologies, the UCD Center of Huawei Technologies Co., Ltd. was founded in 2005 and is dedicated to improving the usability and overall experience of key products such as the network O&M, the Cloud and AI, as well as consumer devices. Binghua Xu, Zhenzhen Li and Yilin Wang are user experience designers at the UCD Center. They regularly win awards with their projects in international design competitions.

What does design mean to you?
Creating beautiful things and making life better.

What was your intention in designing your awarded work?
We would like to benefit more people in need.

How do you think this award will impact your life?
It is recognition and encouragement of our design work. It will also motivate us to continue exploring and designing to improve user experiences.

Huemen
Dishan Song, Alexander Efimov, Yunji Song, Mo Wang, Rongjian Huang, Shufen Guo, Sankun Liu
— Power global brands through a collaborative and personalised approach.

Red Dot
→ Interface & User Experience Design: page 312
→ Interface & User Experience Design: page 313
→ Interface & User Experience Design: page 314
→ Interface & User Experience Design: page 315

Huemen is a design agency with a global team of great problem solvers, strategists, thinkers, researchers and designers who work together to foster innovation at scale. They design and deliver meaningful experiences that give brands a competitive advantage and long-lasting relevance.

What does design mean to you?
Changing the world in a beautiful way.

Where do you see future challenges in communication design?
Today's connected world is seeing a convergence of ecosystems – from the car to the home, the office and everything in between. Intelligent, immersive, intuitive and individualised user experiences will win out over products and technologies.

To what extent do you think new technologies are changing design?
Technologies open new doors of possibilities to solve customers' needs.

What are the biggest challenges in a creative's everyday life?
The balance between a better user experience and technical/project constraints.

Hufax Arts/FJCU
Fa-Hsiang Hu
— We create, design and imagine.

Red Dot
→ Typography: page 110

Fa-Hsiang Hu is an assistant professor at the Department of Applied Arts at Fu Jen Catholic University (FJCU), director of the Taiwan Graphic Design Association, director of the Taiwan Poster Design Association and executive creative director of Hufax Arts. His works have been recognised by the Taiwan Visual Design Award and numerous awards from leading design organisations worldwide, including the D&AD Awards, London International Awards, Red Dot Award, New York Type Directors Club, Communication Arts Award of Excellence, Graphis Awards, the Golden Pin Design Award, Hong Kong Designers Association Global Design Awards and International Design Awards.

To what extent do you think new technologies are changing design?
In an era of ever-changing new technologies, every moment brings with it the possibility of change. Design will also be inspired by new technologies.

What drives you to create something new?
I am driven by my disagreement with certain old things and wrong concepts. I hope to improve them with innovative design and creativity.

What makes your work unique?
In addition to the design form, perhaps my upbringing and Asian background and culture, coupled with imagination and curiosity, have become important factors in my work.

Publishing & Print Media	Posters	Typography	Illustrations	Sound Design	Film & Animation	Online
4	64	92	116	126	138	172

InFormat Design Curating
— Curating is the way that we make design happen.

Red Dot: Best of the Best
→ Spatial Communication: page 342–343

InFormat Design Curating is dedicated to renovating the process of design. Its core value is the spirit of curating and striving for the perfect solution for each project. After researching and analysing content and developing working strategies, the multiple award-winning studio integrates visual and interior design teams in planning and thus combines novel ideas with professional ability. The studio's services include exhibition curating, interior and visual design, project planning and multimedia installation production for international clients such as Samsung, Elle, GQ, Danchu, Taiwan Design Center, Real Tokyo Office or Kris Yao Artech.

To what extent do you think new technologies are changing design?
Our senses can now travel through the axes of time and space thanks to the rapid advances of technologies such as AR and VR, which include the reconstruction of scents. New technologies have increased the flexibility of experience design, as well as the flexibility of design itself.

What drives you to create something new?
Discovering new perspectives amid the hidden narrative trends of society and extracting their inner meaning in a world that continues to change is a challenge that offers immense satisfaction.

What are the biggest challenges in a creative's everyday life?
What's necessary is a persistent appetite for exploration. Don't stop at curiosity; take a step further and try to analyse and embrace it.

Jäger & Jäger
Nico Nolle, Daniela Eisele, Olaf Jäger, Regina Jäger, Reinhard Thomas, Michael Haberbosch, Tanja Weich
— The best is yet to come.

Red Dot: Best of the Best
→ Publishing & Print Media: page 12–13

Jäger & Jäger is an owner-operated brand identity and corporate communication agency. With more than 350 national and international design awards, it is among the German agencies who have won the most awards and was named European Design Agency of the Year in 2013.

What does design mean to you?
Life itself. Work. Attitude. Content. Form. Structure. Expression... Something that is impossible to elude wherever one may be.

Where do you see future challenges in communication design?
In today's here today, gone tomorrow attitude.

To what extent do you think new technologies are changing design?
Design's field of activity is becoming more comprehensive. It has, for instance, become an active co-creator of change processes.

What are the biggest challenges in a creative's everyday life?
Time (and sometimes also the client, but only sometimes).

What makes your work unique?
Hopefully, mainly the idea (but definitely also the details).

Publishing & Print Media	Posters	Typography	Illustrations	Sound Design	Film & Animation	Online
4	64	92	116	126	138	172

Killing Mario
Jin Young Ju, Min Jee Park,
Yu Ji Son, Bang Wool Seo,
Seong Yun Choi,
Se Hyung Chang
— We take a unique approach to our projects to deliver differentiated results.

Red Dot
→ Publishing & Print Media: page 28–29
→ Publishing & Print Media: page 30–31

Killing Mario is a brand communication company founded in 2008. The team members that worked on the LOTTE Duty Free's heritage book include creative directors, copywriters and designers who teamed up previously to work on major projects for prominent companies such as Samsung Electronics, LOTTE and Paradise Group.

What does design mean to you?
Design is the most lucid and beautiful means of expressing the myriad emotions felt over the course of a lifetime.

To what extent do you think new technologies are changing design?
New technologies provide the means for the public to experience design in more diverse ways. The essence of design does not change. Creators and viewers alike may find greater inspiration through these novel applications.

What are the biggest challenges in a creative's everyday life?
Unlike fine art, design presupposes persuasion and empathy. In this sense, the first gateway and the most demanding step for a designer is client communication.

What makes your work unique?
The ability to see things from a new perspective even though we are all looking at the same objects and phenomena. Sometimes a silly, ludicrous and maybe even trivial idea can bring about great innovation.

Klim Type Foundry
Kris Sowersby
— Typefaces reflect a culture's priorities and aspirations.

Red Dot: Best of the Best
→ Typography: page 94–95

Klim Type Foundry, based in Te Whanganui-a-Tara/Wellington, Aotearoa/New Zealand, was founded by Kris Sowersby. He has received numerous accolades such as: being named an ADC Young Gun in 2010; being accepted as a member of the prestigious Alliance Graphique Internationale in 2013; and receiving the John Britten Black Pin in 2015, the highest award given by the Designers Institute of New Zealand. In 2019, he was named an Art Laureate by the Arts Foundation of New Zealand. Having designed custom fonts for clients such as the Financial Times, PayPal, National Geographic, the Bank of New Zealand, Trade Me and the Hokotehi Moriori Trust, his fonts are included in Apple's operating system, MacOS Catalina 10.15.4.

What does design mean to you?
Design is the means to an end.

Why did you become a designer?
Becoming an artist wasn't a viable career choice.

What makes your work unique?
I don't think my work is particularly unique. But it is well crafted, which is possibly more important in typeface design.

What was your intention in designing your awarded work?
I wanted to capture the analogue materiality of Akzidenz-Grotesk, especially the medium weight used in Unimark's legendary wayfinding system for the New York City Subway.

KW43 BRANDDESIGN
– Harnessing creativity effectively.

Red Dot: Best of the Best
→ Interface & User Experience Design: page 240–241

KW43 BRANDDESIGN was founded in 1998. The agency specialises in corporate identity and design. In 2005, it also became an accredited agency for strategic brand design in the interdisciplinary and holistic service portfolio of Grey Germany, led by Jan-Philipp Jahn (chief executive officer) and Francisca Maass (chief creative officer). Grey Germany's KW43 in Düsseldorf is under the creative management of executive creative director Jürgen Adolph. The agency is part of the international, New York-based Grey Group and thus belongs to WPP, one of the world's largest groups of companies in the communications services sector. With numerous awards to its name, the agency works for clients such as Barmer, Deichmann, Grohe, Intersnack, Württembergische, Wüstenrot and Zwiesel Glas.

What does design mean to you?
Design is a translation of strategy – and in equal measure also strategy in itself.

To what extent do you think new technologies are changing design?
To a considerable extent. Design is the interface between humans and technology. As technology interfaces advance or new ones are created, design also has to advance and reinvent itself. That doesn't mean that design principles will all change at the same pace.

What are the biggest challenges in a creative's everyday life?
Not to take oneself and what one does too seriously. And thus to reconcile oneself to the fact that a great idea does not guarantee it will be put into practice.

LG Uplus
Ju Hyun Park, Seo Woo Lee,
Min Hyung Cho
— Design is good. Life is good.

Red Dot
→ Apps: page 220–221

LG Uplus is a South Korean cellular carrier owned by LG Corporation. It was established in 1996 and has been transforming the lives of customers ever since. Continuing into the era of 5G and IoT, LG Uplus continues to create higher standards of service and make its customers happy. Ju Hyun Park, Seo Woo Lee and Min Hyung Cho have been working together in the UX centre of LG Uplus for around three years in different roles.

What does design mean to you?
Design improves user satisfaction and loyalty through the utility, ease of use and pleasure provided by the interaction with a product or service. Design is also an act of creating trust in a brand.

Where do you see future challenges in communication design?
Technological and social changes. As we are a telecom company, we have to keep up with new technology flows like 5G or AI. Social changes are also extremely important nowadays, and we have to consider the need for a zero-contact environment.

What makes your work unique?
Our ideas have been shaped through our camaraderie. We have played games together and chatted a lot. We were full of inspirational ideas which led to our project.

What was your intention in designing your awarded work?
The design was meant to create a sense of unity within the game environment so that the design elements of the service do not feel alien to the elements of the game.

Publishing & Print Media	Posters	Typography	Illustrations	Sound Design	Film & Animation	Online
4	64	92	116	126	138	172

Kim Lin
— Every single thing in your life can provide inspiration for brilliant design.

Red Dot: Junior Award
→ Film & Animation: page 539

Kim Lin was majoring in 3D character animation when she first got into art school in the USA. She gained experience in the world of building animation for three years, both at school and in studios, and then realised her heart was still more attached to the initial design process. Shifting her focus to making storyboards and style frames, she got in touch with motion graphics in her junior year at college. After four years of studying art and design, she is now starting her career as a motion designer and illustrator in the USA.

What goals have you set for your future career?
To continue exploring the field of design and animation. There are always new trends and thoughts coming up in this field, which inspire me with passion.

What inspires you?
Everything that happens in my life. It could be people, or it could just be a book that I read about. Once you want to design, anything can be the right inspiration.

How would you describe your style of design?
Most of my works are illustrative and have saturated pastel colours. Overall, I think they have a gentle, positive feeling.

How do you think this award will impact your life?
This award definitely provides me with approval of my design skills and gives me more confidence. I believe this award will lead me to create more and more brilliant designs.

Littlevoice
Dmytro Izotov, Vladimir Khokhlov
— Deeply explore the problem. Relentlessly iterate. Don't stop until it resonates.

Red Dot
→ Interface & User Experience Design: page 293

Dmytro Izotov and Vladimir Khokhlov have honed their craftsmanship at companies like Microsoft, Nokia, Philips, Skype and Sony. They first worked together on various high-profile user interface design transformations at Skype and Microsoft before founding their own design agency, Littlevoice, in 2018. The agency helps businesses differentiate their connected products, retain and attract customers or unlock growth. With offices in London and Kyiv, its clients include Konica Minolta, Leica Camera and Michelin.

Where do you see future challenges in communication design?
In the ability to understand and form opinions on how today's culture, socio-economic drivers and technological and business trends will impact human behaviour and vice versa, and therefore how to predict what the world will look like in the future.

Why did you become a designer?
Dieter Rams once said: "You cannot understand good design if you do not understand people." Sometimes the importance of understanding people gets overlooked but here at Littlevoice we all share a passion for the holy trinity: good honest design, how technology works and what makes people tick. It's why we became designers in the first place.

What are the biggest challenges in a creative's everyday life?
The ability to suspend if not eliminate your fear of failure. Fear stifles creativity.

Merry Go Round
— Keep filming fun.

Red Dot
→ Film & Animation: page 152

Merry Go Round is a group of partners who are passionate about visual storytelling. They began collaborating in Taipei in 2007 and provide integrated marketing, strategy planning, video production, equipment rental, sales and technical consulting, space rental, film courses and other multifaceted services. Their documentary "Go Grandriders" set new documentary box office records in Taiwan and Hong Kong. Their commercial work includes Gong Yoo's ZenFone 4 Asia-Pacific TV commercial, and they have filmed in collaboration with Jay Chou and G.E.M. The "Tik Tok" music video has racked up over ten million views on YouTube.

Where do you see future challenges in communication design?
In the era of an explosion of information, the speed of information dissemination has been expanding and the carrier of communication has many forms. Fragmentation of content is a prominent feature of this era. With the accelerated pace of work and life, "fragmented" reading has emerged and gradually become mainstream. It may eventually lead people to lose patience with deep reading. Finding the most effective way to communicate and convey a deeper, more complex, emotional message, may be the big challenge of communication design.

What makes your work unique?
We always try to deliver the essence of what should be told in the video in various creative ways. From our perspective, if we cannot only fully express what the client wants, but also put in some of our own life experience or something we care for, that is really great.

Apps	Interface & User Experience Design	Spatial Communication	Red Dot: Junior Award	**Designer Profiles**	Jury Portraits	Index
206	236	336	426	564	642	668

MET Studio/
Jason Bruges Studio/
Barker Langham
— Be accountable for the incredible.

Red Dot: Best of the Best
→ Spatial Communication: page 344–345

With nearly 40 years of experience in planning, designing and delivering cultural hubs, museums, brand experiences, expos, visitor centres, exhibitions and attractions, MET Studio combines strategic vision and insight with cutting-edge creativity to bring to life environments and experiences that truly connect with audiences. For the award-winning project "BLINK", MET Studio collaborated with internationally acclaimed installation designer Jason Bruges Studio and leading interpretation consultants Barker Langham.

What does design mean to you?
For us design is very much about bringing the artistic and the technical together. Design shapes the world around us and has to be inspiring. However, to have true value it also must be functional and serve a practical purpose. Good design is the perfect balance between these things.

What was your intention in designing your awarded work?
For "BLINK" we really wanted to put the subject and condition in an everyday context that visitors could emotionally connect with. We wanted to avoid the clichéd charity approach of showing victims. The fact that, simply through the act of blinking, visitors are permanently destroying beautiful artworks really seemed to encapsulate the reality of trachoma perfectly. Thus, we developed an interactive interface and innovative blink-tracking technology that mimicked the effects of trachoma by eroding the artworks blink by blink, pixel by pixel. As visitors viewed the pieces, they involuntarily and permanently distorted them – much like the condition of trachoma that gradually and painfully erodes sight with every blink.

MIR MEDIA – Digital Agentur
Oliver Priester,
Eva-Maria Schreiner
— Find a balance between following the rules and ignoring them.

Red Dot
→ Interface & User Experience Design: page 316
→ Interface & User Experience Design: page 317
→ Interface & User Experience Design: page 318

Eva-Maria Schreiner and Oliver Priester studied design at the KISD Köln International School of Design. After one year studying abroad in Nagoya, Japan, they graduated in hypermedia in 1997. The same year, the joint agency MIR MEDIA was founded. Based in Cologne, Germany, it is a full-service digital agency and has been accompanying brands, companies and institutions through the digital transformation ever since. The main focus is on cultural institutions and cultural event organisers. In 2017, the 20-strong team was listed in the BVDW ranking of the 30 most creative digital agencies in Germany.

Where do you see future challenges in communication design?
Media is changing rapidly. We want to influence these changes at the forefront.

To what extent do you think new technologies are changing design?
Design always was and is fluid. It will constantly change. But its core principles – form, function, quality, clarity, the intention to communicate – will always define good design.

What are the biggest challenges in a creative's everyday life?
Fighting for free time to work on the creative process.

What makes your work unique?
Focusing on real people with real needs.

Monotype
Malou Verlomme
— Think less, look more.

Red Dot: Best of the Best
→ Typography: page 98–99

Malou Verlomme is senior type designer for Monotype and has been with the company since 2016. His Camille typeface has the honour of being part of the collection at France's Centre National des Arts Plastiques (CNAP). His typefaces include Madera, Placard Next, as well as Ecam and Totem, published with the type foundry LongType, which he co-founded in 2012. In 2016, he designed the Johnston100 typeface for TfL for extensive use throughout the London Underground. He has a graphic design degree from the École Duperré in Paris and an MA degree in typeface design from the University of Reading.

What does design mean to you?
Design is beauty within constraint. When functionality dictates form, there is a moment of bliss when everything unfolds in its own natural way. This is the beauty of design.

To what extent do you think new technologies are changing design?
In the world of type, technologies have always played a predominant role. In fact, type is a technology. Since the invention of printing, type design has gone through four different technologies (hand punchcutting, mechanical punchcutting, phototypesetting and digital). Typefaces are always the fruit of the technologies that saw them emerge and there is no such thing as a simple transfer of a design from one to the other. There can only be adaptations which can be more or less successful. I think it's important to understand that in our field, technology is intrinsic, not contextual.

monsun media
Michael Hantke
— Stay hungry.

Red Dot
→ Publishing & Print Media: page 59
→ Publishing & Print Media: page 63

The brand agency monsun media has been creating identity-based brand communication for national and international B2B companies under the direction of Michael Hantke since 2002. The company's original digital focus quickly changed to a holistic brand approach and to the conception and support of integrative communication projects. Part of this development is the expansion of competencies in the areas of CGI and 3D used in brand staging for clients from the automotive, plant engineering, mechanical engineering and construction industries, complemented by expertise in VR.

What does design mean to you?
Design is an art form that intentionally triggers emotions and actions in a very original way.

To what extent do you think new technologies are changing design?
Technologies do not change the content of a communication project. They only expand the framework of what we can create.

Why did you become a designer?
Because we have a special ability to observe. The joy is to give our observations a perfectly fitting form of expression.

What was your intention in designing your awarded work?
The quality of our work should directly represent the brand personality. In addition, our work is intended to trigger curiosity, natural inspiration and knowledge in viewers – and therefore to lead them to reflect on themselves.

Moscow High School 548 Tsaritsyno

Nikita Semionov, Sasha Volkov, Misha Borisov, Dima Kaderkaev, Zhenya Timoshenkova, Vlad Sarychev, Nata Makashvili, Dima Sobaev, Lera Agescheva
— What happened in Auschwitz should never happen again!

Red Dot: Best of the Best
→ Online: page 176–177
→ Interface & User Experience Design: page 238–239

Red Dot
→ Illustrations: page 122
→ Film & Animation: page 166

The nine students at the Moscow High School 548 Tsaritsyno created the award-winning work "Lessons of Auschwitz" after visiting the Memorial in Poland. They are all between 14 and 16 years old and expressed their feelings and reactions in VR animations under the creative guidance of Russia's leading XR artist Denis Semionov. The film was a collaboration between RT Creative Lab, headed by award-winning producer Kirill Karnovich-Valua, Denis Semionov and Phygitalism Studio, which specialises in mixed reality productions.

What was your intention in designing your awarded work?
The aim was to show how history can deeply resonate with our generation and that we are capable of transmitting our emotions through art and digital design, retelling history with current technology. Learning how to draw in virtual reality, we managed, for example, to come up with individual sketch ideas that through the animation of names and real quotes from Holocaust survivors emphasise how critical it is that we never again allow such inhumanity. The innovation lies in merging our virtual avatars with our VR illustrations in one project. We used the Unity program to combine volumetric video with animation. The videos were then processed with special shader effects.

What makes your work unique?
The challenge we faced with our project was to find the balance between innovative visual design and the very sensitive topic we were addressing. The recognition from such an esteemed panel of judges as the Red Dot Jury tells us that our film hit the right note and tone, of which we are really proud.

Publishing & Print Media	Posters	Typography	Illustrations	Sound Design	Film & Animation	Online
4	64	92	116	126	138	172

ORVIBO
Shaobin Wu, Weina Li, Junbin Huang, Xijiao Li, Qingquan Fu, Lan Xiao
— Good design always starts with people.

Red Dot
→ Interface & User Experience Design: page 298

ORVIBO uses innovative technology, products and design to create smart home systems that make human-computer interaction, high-quality living experiences and space management more convenient and efficient for users. Shaobin Wu is vice president of design, responsible for strategic planning, Xijiao Li is responsible for interaction design and user interface design, Weina Li is product manager, Qingquan Fu is art director, Lan Xiao is interface designer and Junbin Huang is kinetic designer. In addition to interface design, they also create user experience design for the IoT ecosystem and home AI centre.

What does design mean to you?
Design reshapes the interaction between people and the environment to make life better and more efficient.

Why did you become a designer?
We can infuse our emotions into our designs and allow our values to permeate the world.

What are the biggest challenges in a creative's everyday life?
The balance between design and business value has always been our biggest challenge.

What makes your work unique?
Living space is the most important component of life. It is about security, comfort, pleasure or warmth. It is about love, about dignity. Technology is changing the way people connect with their environment.

peetz & le peetz design
Sebastian Peetz
— Think the extraordinary and something incredible will develop of its own accord.

Red Dot
→ Publishing & Print Media: page 16–17

Sebastian Peetz studied at the American Art Center College of Design in Switzerland, graduating with a scholarship to study in Los Angeles. Following a period in London, he worked for French typographer Philippe Apeloig in Paris, later also as his partner. In 1996, Sebastian Peetz opened a studio in Hannover, Germany, serving clients such as the Wilhelm Busch Museum, the Fête de la Musique, the City of Hannover and the society of friends of the Sprengel Museum. He has also exhibited some of his artistic work in Germany and abroad. At peetz & le peetz design, Sebastian Peetz creates corporate designs, signage, posters, catalogues, books, annual reports and marketing concepts. The in-house publishing company lepeetzpress produces art books and calendars.

What does design mean to you?
To involve all competencies in solving a task: skill, mood, economics, experience and uniqueness.

Where do you see future challenges in communication design?
Communication design is part of every future-oriented model. Whether it is for a carpenter or a newly invented economic concept, a material from synthetic biology or the packaging of a neural storage unit – the key is always to convey information clearly through print, colour, graphics.

What are the biggest challenges in a creative's everyday life?
The successful combination of one's private life and creativity, of self-determination and that which is determined by external factors.

Publishing & Print Media	Posters	Typography	Illustrations	Sound Design	Film & Animation	Online
4	64	92	116	126	138	172

Pinion Digital
Saltanat Tashibayeva
— Move to your goal as fast as you can; if you can't, lie down in that direction.

Red Dot
→ Online: page 204
→ Apps: page 213

Saltanat Tashibayeva is a senior product designer at fromAtoB by Pinion Digital, a Berlin-based mobility travel agency dedicated to changing the way people travel. Originally from Kazakhstan, she has worked in the USA, Belarus and Germany, and currently lives in San Francisco. Prior to joining fromAtoB, she worked at Wargaming, an award-winning developer and publisher of many game brands, and as a graphic designer for companies such as Montblanc and Saks Fifth Avenue. She also acts as a writer and blogger, serves as a jury member at Awwwards.com and the Webby Awards, and organised the 2019 UX/UI Design Conference.

What are the biggest challenges in a creative's everyday life?
Starting from scratch. It's always hard to begin and see things through. This is something you have to overcome every single day.

What was your intention in designing your awarded work?
Our company creates products that help the traveller to get from point A to point B in one click, without having to turn to other applications and services. Today, there are a million travel and ticketing services out there, but not one that offers all the needed functionality and information as a one-stop shop. My intention in designing the fromAtoB product was to achieve a combination of ease of use, information accessibility and, of course, aesthetic pleasure for our users.

Benjamin Ressi
— Create what you'd like to see more often in the world.

Red Dot: Junior Award
→ Publishing & Print Media: page 463

Benjamin Ressi initially studied philosophy before switching to design and completing his bachelor's degree in information design at the Department of Media and Design at FH JOANNEUM in Graz, Austria. Following a six-month internship at nulleins™ brand creation, he has been working in Berlin as a freelance interdisciplinary designer and develops designs for a whole range of projects.

How can communication design arouse emotions?
I believe design is stimulating when it seeks to establish an electrifying connection between viewer and object, and develops this connection using creative tools. Sensitive design renders thoughts and the intention behind them visible and thereby enables the viewer to see themselves reflected within it. Design thereby creates an invisible space within which emotions can develop their full impact. To put it another way: if one invests lots of emotions in the design, it is also able to elicit these same emotions from the viewer.

Do you prefer to play it safe when designing a new project or are you keen to experiment?
I think it's especially rewarding to experiment when starting a new project. Your head is still free of preconceptions and it's easy to develop new ideas. It is also often easier to rein things in than it is to push boundaries if your rational mind is filled with fixed notions.

How would you describe your style of design?
Surreptitiously eye-catching.

RT/Phygitalism Studio
Kirill Karnovich-Valua,
Denis Semionov, Ivan Yunitskiy
— We should trust younger generations more to express themselves in art and design.

Red Dot: Best of the Best
→ Online: page 176–177
→ Interface & User Experience Design: page 238–239

Red Dot
→ Illustrations: page 122
→ Film & Animation: page 166

For the award-winning project and social experiment "Lessons of Auschwitz", RT Moscow brought nine students from a Moscow high school to the Memorial in Poland to personally experience this historic site. After the trip, the 14- to 16-year-old kids expressed their feelings and reactions in VR animation with the aim of showing how history can be retold and reimagined by younger generations through digital art. The film was created in collaboration between RT Creative Lab, headed by award-winning producer Kirill Karnovich-Valua, Russia's leading XR artist Denis Semionov and Phygitalism Studio, which specialises in mixed reality productions.

What was your intention in designing your awarded work?
Today, in a mostly digital world, it is important to bridge the gap and keep younger generations interested in learning history. The victims' stories of the Holocaust and horrors of Auschwitz are always with us but must be retold by and for new generations. So, our challenge was to find a new digital approach to visual storytelling and create an innovative yet moving and touching artistic tribute.

To what extent do you think new technologies are changing design?
Up until now, many saw the VR headset as an entertainment tool or just a gadget for gamers that had no place in art. Now this opinion has changed. We are witnessing a dramatic increase in creative works involving XR technology. Mixed reality is definitely emerging as a new trend for brands: it opens endless possibilities for them to stand out and create an immersive innovative storytelling project.

Samsung SDS, CX Innovation Team
Dooyeon Kim, Jungwon Kim, Jaehwa Lee
— Change your design routine.

Red Dot
→ Interface & User Experience Design: page 263

Based in South Korea, Samsung SDS is a global company that provides enterprise IT services and solutions. Through design thinking, design systems and agile validation, the CX Innovation Team of Samsung SDS analyses diverse customer behaviours from multiple perspectives based on customer experience (CX) expertise, develops business strategies to improve service/system usability and creates new and better customer experience.

What does design mean to you?
For us, as enterprise UX designers, design is a clear visual language that helps customers use valuable products without wasting time. Design is also about creating a unique, personal and visually inspiring world.

To what extent do you think new technologies are changing design?
New technology expands the realm of design and inspires designers. New designs are being created using technologies that have never been before, and technologies that have not been before require designers' insights for better usage.

What was your intention in designing your awarded work?
Communicating with data or machines is no different from talking with friends. But the conversations with data or machines were sometimes rather rough and disconnected. Through our design, we have just helped them have a smoother, easier conversation.

SAP SE – The Tools Team

Astrid Kadel,
Jonathan Edward Lee,
Angie Salama, Roman Kostka,
Sarina Claudia Walter,
Nikola Freudensprung
— We take UX seriously and work seriously, but we don't take ourselves too seriously.

Red Dot
→ Interface & User Experience Design: page 290–291

The Tools Team is an autonomous multidisciplinary team inside SAP, located in the USA, India and the SAP headquarters in Germany. They are designers, product managers, developers and technologists. Some of their products and services are internal and some external. Everything they create is need-based, designed to support individual contributors and teams in a tangible way.

Where do you see future challenges in communication design?
Design has to adapt to new upcoming technologies very quickly and it will become accessible to more and more people. Design therefore also has to become more accessible and open. In addition, the rapid change and the constant phenomenon of individualism will lead us to think even more about how we can tailor designs to single-user needs. The core of design, however – digging into a process, listening to people, gaining a deep understanding for their needs and having the necessary creativity to adapt solutions to people's lives – will remain unchanged.

Why did you become a designer?
It's simply great to work on things that help people and at the same time feel and look beautiful. At the end of the day, we like imagining their delight in using our products because of the intuitive experience and beautifully crafted interfaces. That's pure joy for us.

What are the biggest challenges in a creative's everyday life?
Working with assumptions vs. insights. Challenging the status quo. Convincing the decision makers that there's a simpler way to do things.

SCAD Savannah College of Art and Design
George Maxwell Stack
— All great things can (and must) be made better.

Red Dot: Junior Award
Best of the Best
→ Typography: page 434–435

George Maxwell Stack holds a BFA degree with an emphasis in graphic design and studies at the Savannah College of Art and Design in Atlanta, Georgia. He currently works as a communication designer at the telecommunication provider Hargray and was previously a brand designer at Border States Electric.

What goals have you set for your future career?
I entered the graduate programme at Savannah College of Art and Design with the intention of transitioning into teaching. An MFA will allow me to find a new role, inspiring the next generation of creative thinkers.

Do you prefer to play it safe when designing a new project or are you keen to experiment?
Experimentation and play are an invaluable part of any creative process. In my experience, the best solutions always come as the result of allowing ample room for and, at times, encouraging failure.

What relationship is there between typography and gravity in your award-winning design?
This three-dimensional typography piece was created with the intention of giving a voice to gravity and allowing it to play a role in delivering the message. Referencing the mundane act of flushing a stack of papers, this work explores the ways that we take gravity for granted and the impact that it has had on the typographical systems that we use as designers. Gravity becomes the designer by flushing the papers and revealing the words: "Falling into place, flushing neatly by my hand."

Shanghai Publishing and Printing College
Fang Wu, Qi-Wen Li, Qing-Ying Zhou
— A problem well stated is a problem half solved.

Red Dot: Junior Award
Best of the Best
→ Publishing & Print Media: page 430–431

Qing-Ying Zhou and Qi-Wen Li are studying visual communication design at Shanghai Publishing and Printing College. Fang Wu is their professional teacher in the bookbinding and design course. They share a passion for the cultural creativity of modern books and look forward to proving their expertise in fair and impartial professional competitions around the world.

How can communication design arouse emotions?
Through the change of colours and graphics that make people engage with the design project.

What goals have you set for your future career?
To expand the professional field and become independent designers.

What inspires you?
Dreams and responsibilities.

How would you describe your style of design?
As a concise, modern, free and readable design style.

What was your intention in designing your awarded work?
To allow people to understand the charm of Chinese ethnic musical instruments and to use them for colour and synaesthesia designing the work.

How do you think this award will impact your life?
It means recognition and will allow us to be able to insist.

Sisters of Design
Claudia Dölling, Anja Krämer
— In SOD we trust.

Red Dot: Best of the Best
→ Spatial Communication: page 348–349

Claudia Dölling and Anja Krämer are graphic designers, font lovers and founders of the studio Sisters of Design in Halle/Saale, Germany, established in 2004. Only recently, they have begun to dive deeper into digital worlds such as animation, video installation and VR. Fascinated by these new possibilities for visualising content and the power of movement, their work mainly focuses on typography as a material. For the project "TYPO UTOPIA", the two designers also received the European Design Award 2020.

Where do you see future challenges in communication design?
The increasing need to design immaterial things requires new design approaches and the courage to break new ground.

What are the biggest challenges in a creative's everyday life?
Not to let ourselves be absorbed by the daily work routine but to develop our own approach.

What was your intention in designing your awarded work?
To present the ideas of Bauhaus artists in an immersive way and to explore the effect of typography, movement and sound on human perception. Based on our great enthusiasm for the power, beauty and meaning of letters, we wanted to give letter forms a stage and offer a surprisingly new approach to the Bauhaus universe. Our typographical designs reflect the respective content and are based on the visual language of Bauhaus. Font and symbols play with spatial illusions, soar, dance, form a carpet of letters, expand or dissolve.

Sniffing out the Differences Team
Kadambari Sahu
— Be Bold. Experiment. Create.

Red Dot
→ Spatial Communication: page 374–375

Kadambari Sahu is senior vice president of design at ValueLabs and leads the team of UX designers. She studied at the National Institute of Design, India, and went on to a post-graduate degree in new media design. She subsequently became the co-founder of the studio Akalpya Imaginations, before working as manager and new media designer at Tata Consultancy Services and as lead interaction designer at Pramati Technologies. Her work has won several accolades and was exhibited, among others, in New York and Las Vegas.

What does design mean to you?
Design for me is creation with intent. It is the process of arriving at innovative solutions to serious user problems through empathy and a strong understanding of the user's needs and desires.

To what extent do you think new technologies are changing design?
With ever-increasing amounts of behavioural data collection and processing capabilities, we are rapidly moving towards a future where we are proactively influencing user behaviour instead of reacting to it. This puts great power into the hands of designers, who need to understand the implications of these changes and how they affect our society and planet. Empathy, caution and an inclination towards doing what is good for the user are key.

What makes your work unique?
I try to experiment a lot with both the medium of interaction and narration. I use the medium to create unique experiences that affect people viscerally.

Solomon Technology Corporation
— Vision with intelligence.

Red Dot: Junior Award
Best of the Best
→ Interface & User Experience Design: page 438–439

Solomon Technology Corporation was founded in 1973. Its contributions to the development of vision systems and automation have been widely recognised, allowing it to position itself as one of the top 200 technology companies in Taiwan.

How can communication design arouse emotions?
At Solomon, we strive to make creativity a way of life. Our design team not only puts a lot of effort into creating products that are visually appealing, but it also strives to connect with our customers by listening to their needs, helping them to ease their constraints.

Do you prefer to play it safe when designing a new project or are you keen to experiment?
Innovation is the force that drives us forward. Only through constant experimentation and failures can we gain experience to come up with innovative and practical solutions.

What was your intention in designing your awarded work?
Solomon's aim was to provide our customers with a simplified and intuitive user interface that helped to make their production process smoother and more efficient.

What is your personal vision for the future?
In the future, our goal is to continue providing customers with innovate solutions and to become the leader of 3D vision systems and industrial artificial intelligence, by making robots smarter and easier to use.

Springload
Dan Newman, Zak Brown
— Making the things that matter, better.

Red Dot: Best of the Best
→ Typography: page 96–97
→ Online: page 184–185

Dan Newman and Zak Brown work at Springload, Te Pipitanga in Aotearoa/New Zealand. The digital agency cleverly uses technology in a human-centred approach. Dan Newman has a master's degree in computer graphic design from the Whanganui School of Design and the University of Waikato. He has also studied at the University of Applied Sciences Upper Austria and the University of Nottingham on a scholarship as a visiting researcher. Zak Brown attended the College of Creative Arts at Massey University, where he received a Bachelor of Design with first class honours.

What does design mean to you?
It's a set of rules and systems that visually organise information and experiences. A way of problem solving and communicating.

To what extent do you think new technologies are changing design?
Significantly. The experiences people have with and that are enabled by new technologies/media are constantly in flux.

What are the biggest challenges in a creative's everyday life?
Continuing to find new sources of inspiration and meaning in the work we do with such uncertain times for society and our planet.

What was your intention in designing your awarded work?
The experience needed to be effortless, informative and interesting, and we wanted people to encounter a straightforward licensing process. Aesthetically, Klim wanted the redesign of the site to complement Söhne, which is their new brand font.

Sunny at Sea
Tobias Ottomar, Linnea Hedeborg
— Don't think – feel. Great design is intuitive and speaks to your heart.

Red Dot: Grand Prix
→ Spatial Communication: page 338–339

As creative director, Tobias Ottomar leads all conceptual and creative work at Sunny at Sea, a user-centred design and development agency in Stockholm, Sweden. He has a degree in graphic design from Berghs School of Communication and over 15 years of experience as art and creative director. Working for clients such as TUI, Google, Absolut or Telenor, he has won awards at D&AD, the ADC Awards, Rebrand 100, Guldägget, the European Design Awards and the German Design Award. Linnea Hedeborg is a multidisciplinary senior designer and has worked in Sweden as well as internationally for agencies and in-house teams on brands such as Google, Lonely Planet, eBay and Carlton & United Breweries. She has a bachelor's degree in graphic design from the University of Canberra and a bachelor's degree in packaging design from the Mid Sweden University. Her work has won awards at D&AD, the ADC Awards and Guldägget.

What was your intention in designing your awarded work?
Our intention was to carry personal witness statements from one generation to another in order to keep these stories alive. We live in a time where news is harder to verify and truth is no longer regarded as the most important thing. It is more about quick reporting and winning arguments. The generation that lived through World War II is slowly dying. To transmit their truths and ensure that they can continue to exist is such an important task in trying to prevent this from happening again. We also wanted to ensure that these stories were received by the younger generation with as little noise as possible. We therefore applied innovative and interesting technology to the experience in order to adapt it to their lives.

Supercharge
Sara T. Kocsis, Bence Lukacs, Erika Somogyi, Adam Sandor, Balazs Fonagy
— We build futures, not just tech.

Red Dot
→ Interface & User Experience Design: page 255

Supercharge is an innovation partner for companies helping them to be trailblazers in the digital era. With roots in product development and offices in Budapest, London and Amsterdam, the decade-old agency unites over 130 digital experts – strategists, designers and engineers. They approach projects with a balance of practicality, scientific thinking and empathy towards people and find the right way between visionary thinking and feasible solutions with a relentless focus on value creation.

Where do you see future challenges in communication design?
The challenge lies in the astonishing complexity that arrives with breakneck digitalisation of the world. With everything in continuous flux, designers need to be multifaceted, to some extent understanding all domains that influence their work: people, business and tech as well.

What drives you to create something new?
New solutions emerge from new challenges. The world is changing faster than ever – and that statement isn't just a platitude, but a fact supported by a magnitude of data – and survival in such environment depends on constantly coming up with new, better answers. Innovation is not a choice anymore, it is a necessity – a necessity that pleases our team a lot due to our curious nature.

What makes your work unique?
Our unique understanding of people, business and technology enables us to create products that are truly fit for the future.

TAMSCHICK MEDIA+SPACE
Marc Tamschick,
Charlotte Tamschick,
Ashraf El Sharkawy
– Our passion is the fusion
of media + space.

Red Dot: Best of the Best
→ Spatial Communication: page 340–341

TAMSCHICK MEDIA+SPACE is an interdisciplinary studio for media-enhanced scenography, staging architectural spaces and their contents narratively with the help of media. As one of Europe's leading specialists for spatial media, such as for facade and architecture projections, the studio addresses companies and institutions ranging from museums and exhibition venues to fairs and showrooms, expos and events. With 20 years of specialist experience in the conception, design, production and implementation of spatial media productions, it focuses on the immersive, tangible, haptic dimension of digital media in spaces and engages visitors in emotional and audiovisual walk-in environments.

What drives you to create something new?
The desire to establish new formats in scenography, to inspire people and move them emotionally, but also the desire to convey contents that are difficult to understand in an entertaining way.

What are the biggest challenges in a creative's everyday life?
The many, constantly new ideas that need to be generated and conveyed with precision and clarity in convincing concepts, but also the demands of leading and motivating a large, young creative team with different individual needs and experiences.

What makes your work unique?
Seeking experiments that have not been seen before. All projects tell a story on which the design is based.

We Are Social
Jason Breen,
Vladimir Crvenkovic,
Tom Johnson
— Colourless green ideas
sleep furiously.

Acer
— Breaking barriers between
people and technology.

Red Dot
→ Online: page 201

Jason Breen, a creative director from Toronto, Canada, has worked over 15 years in China in creative development as well as on integrated interactive and digital immersive solutions. At BBDO, he worked on the Silver Effie award-winning campaign for Visa during the 2018 Summer Olympics in Beijing. Vladimir Crvenkovic, the head of design from Serbia, has ten years of experience in designing identities and visual systems for brands and various cultural organisations. Tom Johnson, the copywriter, originally from Britain, has previously worked as a writer for a UNESCO NGO. At We Are Social, all three work together on projects for Acer products, such as ConceptD or Acer Predator, and have been recognised in international competitions.

What does design mean to you?
Doing less for more; stripping back to deliver the idea in its purest form. The campaign with Acer's ConceptD was a great example of this. "Let Creators Be Creators" is not only the brand slogan but the campaign's guiding principle; we simply give creatives the platform and tools to create rather than pushing them too heavily in a "branded" direction.

What makes your work unique?
Authenticity is the goal of our work rather than uniqueness. What we produce, or what anyone produces for that matter, is by necessity an interweaving of different influences, direct and indirect. It is far better to create something authentic which beautifully serves its purpose than to obsess over being unique.

Weißensee Academy of Art Berlin
Ailun Jiang
— Every project is determined both by the designer and the viewers.

Red Dot: Junior Award
→ Illustrations: page 508–509

Ailun Jiang began studying visual communication at Zhejiang University in Hangzhou, China, in 2008. After completing his Bachelor of Arts, he focused on illustration and moving images, and began studying at Weißensee Academy of Art Berlin in 2014. For his thesis "RAN", he spent a year working on interactive illustrations and was awarded at the Indigo Design Award, the 3×3 International Illustration Show No.17, the Joseph Binder Award and the JIA Illustration Award, among others.

What goals have you set for your future career?
I would initially like to find a job in the areas of graphic and motion design in order to gain additional professional experience. My dream is one day to set up my own studio.

What inspires you?
One can find inspiration everywhere in everyday life. Sometimes, small, inconspicuous objects conceal a wonderful world. They are so unremarkable that we often ignore them. They allow me to express my abstract thoughts or big issues more specifically and metaphorically. I am furthermore convinced that music allows good ideas to surface in my mind.

How would you describe your style of design?
As fluid as water. I find it difficult to define my style precisely myself as I believe that style cannot be viewed in isolation, but only in relation to materials, techniques, concepts and the many other elements that form the basis of a project.

White City Project Foundation
Ivan Aleksandrov
— Study the old but create the new.

Red Dot: Best of the Best
→ Publishing & Print Media: page 8–9

Ivan Aleksandrov graduated in 2004 from Moscow State University of Printing Arts. He is a member of the Moscow Union of Artists, the illustrators group Volshebnaya Pila and the International Board on Books for Young People (IBBY). From 2004 to 2013, he worked as a tutor on book design at his university. Since 2018, he has been teaching graphic design at the Institute of Modern Art in Moscow. His books have won several international awards in competitions such as the BIB Awards (Slovakia, 2007), the CJ Picture Book Festival (South Korea, 2009) and the European Design Awards in 2020. Since 2013, he has worked as an art director at the White City Project Foundation.

What drives you to create something new?
The passion for creating systems inspires me most of all. It is a really indescribable feeling when the "rules of the game" you've set at the beginning seem to be defined by the design.

What was your intention in designing your awarded work?
The main intention was to organise a very complicated structure of text and visual content in a straightforward and clear way. The idea of the design came from the subject itself and the general message of the project. I realised that for me it was a book not only about place but about time as well. We made the decision to produce a small but extremely thick volume to reflect the high concentration of historical events and cultural uniqueness in one place, where the buildings of different times mix to create an unrepeatable architectural ensemble.

why do birds
— Treat every project like it's something that you've never done before.

Red Dot: Grand Prix
→ Sound Design: page 128–129

Red Dot
→ Sound Design: page 134–135

why do birds is one of the leading audio branding agencies, operating across the globe for international companies like Hyundai, Siemens, SEAT, DiDi Chuxing, Telefónica, N26 or GORE-TEX. Having won the most renowned awards in the industry, it brings together the disciplines of audio and visual design with extensive expertise in branding. Founded in 2010, the agency is active in teaching and research at a number of universities. It employs 20 people in its Berlin office, working on audio, graphic and motion design, software development and service design projects.

Where do you see future challenges in communication design?
The audio sector is becoming increasingly important in communication design. There will be a strong shift towards voice-based services. Brands need to figure out how they can position themselves in an invisible environment via audio.

What drives you to create something new?
The desire to stand out from the crowd, to create something better – something that touches the unexpected.

What is the idea underlying the new sound logo?
From healthcare to Med-Tech: we had the chance to translate the brand's strategic shift into sound and to create an audio experience of premium character. The project included health-oriented sounds and innovative software for sound implementation.

wir sind artisten
Miri Ringerthaler, Alex Stieg, Anne Hochkönig
— We can't spit fire.

Red Dot
→ Publishing & Print Media: page 26–27

wir sind artisten (we are artists) is a studio for design, specialising in branding, editorial and book design, corporate publishing, web design, exhibition design, packaging design and more. With precision and a customer-specific approach, it finds solutions that delight the eye and exercise the mind. Founded by Alex Stieg, the team consists of passionate designers who are located in the heart of Salzburg, Austria.

What does design mean to you?
For us, design means boiling down complex issues to a simplified mode of expression; and yes, the details make the design.

To what extent do you think new technologies are changing design?
In some areas, we will arrive at a certain level of interchangeability or homogenisation of design. New technologies, however, also foster new developments that relate to craftsmanship.

What drives you to create something new?
How a blank sheet of paper turns into a finished design; to see "your" own product in public and to see that the design "works".

What was your intention in designing your awarded work?
Restaurant Ikarus in Salzburg, Austria, offers visitors one of the most exciting restaurant concepts. We wanted to focus on the tool each guest chef has – their hands – and on handwritten menus in order to emphasise the unique personality of each guest chef.

Xiaomi Intelligent Hardware Division, User Experience Design Center
Wei Yu, Nandier, Beiyi Zhang, Xiaoxiao Shi, Lipeng Ge, Liang Tan

Red Dot
→ Interface & User Experience Design: page 297

The User Experience Design Center of the Xiaomi Intelligent Hardware Division focuses on design practice and theoretical research at the cutting edge of science and technology. Its numerous achievements in the field of artificial intelligence, multimodal interaction and virtual reality interaction in recent years have received awards in competitions such as the Red Dot Award and the International Design Excellence Awards multiple times over.

To what extent do you think new technologies are changing design?
New technological advances can enrich and even change the content of design and the design process, especially in the field of user experience design. With the advance of AI technology, IoT and 5G technology, human-computer interaction has evolved from interface interaction in the era of the mobile internet to multimodal interaction. Users can naturally and conveniently use voice, vision and interface interaction to operate devices and experience content. We believe that experience design content in the future will lead to more segmentation and new professional directions.

What was your intention in designing your awarded work?
AIS'UI is an interactive system with VUI and GUI designed for all family members so they can access internet content or information and control their smart devices with ease. Our product strategy is therefore based on improving multimodal interaction capability and the intelligent home control experience, as well as the efficiency of long-distance interaction by enriching content and services, and developments in the field of emotional design.

Beijing Xiaomi Mobile Software Co., Ltd.
Shao Chen, Jiawei Liu, Zhuoqun Sun, Jiayan Li, Tianyu Zhou, Anqi Wen
— Wonderful design is often attributed to various perspectives.

Red Dot
→ Apps: page 214–215

The MIUI Design Team at Beijing Xiaomi Mobile Software Co., Ltd. is responsible for the overall design work of the Xiaomi Smartphone System and focuses on exploring different options of user experience design. Within ten years, it has grown into a professional team of over 50 design specialists, whose work covers all aspects of mobile phone experiences from the operating system to essential applications.

What does design mean to you?
Design makes us appreciate the beauty of life and has become part of our lives.

Where do you see future challenges in communication design?
The emergence of an endless stream of new media and platforms. In view of this ever-changing situation, the challenge lies in getting design to convey information more accurately with high fidelity so that users can obtain the information they want at a lower cost while making the experience convenient and natural.

Why did you become a designer?
It all starts from our enthusiasm for design. We believe the design profession and our creative work can improve people's lives.

What makes your work unique?
It is enthusiasm and solidarity that makes our work unique. Without enthusiasm, we would lose the driving force to create extraordinary work. Without solidarity, we wouldn't be able to evaluate the quality of the work. Both of them are therefore indispensable.

Beijing Xiaomi Mobile Software Co., Ltd.
Xuewei Cui
— Less, but better.

Red Dot
→ Apps: page 217

Xuewei Cui is a user experience designer of Xiaomi's IoT, responsible for the UI/UX design of Xiaomi wearable products and Mijia smart devices, such as Xiaomi watches, the Mijia printer series, Mijia transportation series or Xiaomi fan series. Her work ranges from defining product function to the logic of interaction, visual displays and the animation connection to other aspects that improve product quality and make the equipment more intelligent. She has already won awards in competitions such as the iF Design Award and the Red Dot Award.

Where do you see future challenges in communication design?
Designers need to understand forward-looking knowledge in different fields. They need to explore and master the prevailing design methodology in the industry and continuously improve their design skills.

Why did you become a designer?
I am an idealist, a designer who loves art and hopes to use design to reach people's hearts. I think the most important skill of a designer is to develop his or her own imagination, to keep their love of design and always to continue learning.

What makes your work unique?
My design provides users with a variety of printing solutions and solves users' printing needs in the fastest and most convenient way. It turns out to be simple and practical, with certain innovations in function and design.

YI.ng Lighting Design Consultants
Lien Chou, Wen Ying Chu, Ping Yi Liu
— Lighting design allows us to see more beauty.

Red Dot: Best of the Best
→ Spatial Communication: page 350–351

YI.ng Lighting Design Consultants is an international architectural lighting consultancy founded by Wen Ying Chu and Ping Yi Liu in Taipei City, Taiwan, in 2009. Its portfolio encompasses a wide variety of architectural lighting types with the goal of designing and creating outstanding lighting environments that enrich architectural and lighting culture. With lighting as a tool, the designers can heighten the impact of architectural features, transform spaces, reveal the aesthetic qualities of a space and intensify the experience of an environment.

What does design mean to you?
In addition to properly solving problems, design also needs to create beauty and convey certain messages.

Where do you see future challenges in communication design?
In conveying information to the public accurately and elegantly via design.

What drives you to create something new?
As we are not good at words, we want to use lighting to say something.

What was your intention in designing your awarded work?
What we want to convey is not just lighting. Lighting whispers about our relationship with nature and our relationship with the land. Taiwan is actually beautiful, but we forget how beautiful it is. Please forget the lighting for a while and feel the land under your feet. The lighting is dedicated to all those who live in this country together.

Shenzhen Yimu Technology
Tianyi Chen
— Integrate design into products and become the hallmark of the brand.

Red Dot
→ Interface & User Experience Design: page 280

Tianyi Chen graduated from Carnegie Mellon University in Pittsburgh, USA, in 2011. He was subsequently responsible for the design and development of numerous apps, websites and information systems that demonstrate his experience in information system architecture and implementation. As the co-founder of a start-up in 2015, he was in charge of the product design and development of IoT products and a big data platform, designed to solve environmental problems. He has received several awards in competitions such as the Red Dot Award and the iF Design Award.

What does design mean to you?
The most important way for me to communicate feelings to my audience is through visual sensations and unique experiences.

To what extent do you think new technologies are changing design?
Design innovation depends on the application of new technologies, new materials and new processes, and on grasping and meeting the real needs of consumers.

Why did you become a designer?
To turn what is in one's mind into a necessity that improves life.

What was your intention in designing your awarded work?
While ensuring water safety, my aim was to make water quality public and transparent, so that ordinary users can find out what the water quality is in real time and can minimise damage due to sudden water pollution incidents.

Publishing & Print Media	Posters	Typography	Illustrations	Sound Design	Film & Animation	Online
4	64	92	116	126	138	172

YUJ Designs
Prasadd Bartakke,
Samir Chabukswar
— To deliver valuable human experiences that impact businesses globally.

Red Dot
→ Interface & User Experience Design: page 330

YUJ Designs is a leading UX design studio with offices in India (Pune and Bangalore) and the USA. Its vision is to help businesses create value through user experience design. Founded in 2009 by Samir Chabukswar, chief executive officer, and Prasadd Bartakke, chief experience officer, it has gained substantial experience from working on more than 2,500 successful design and research projects for Fortune 100 and 500 companies.

What does design mean to you?
Design shapes experiences. At YUJ Designs, we believe good design drives human behaviour and creates unique and memorable experiences. At a product or service design level, design must make sense to humans and businesses providing the products/services, in achieving the goals of each. Design, in that sense, is a return-on-investment generating tool, a means to identify unspoken desires, satisfy verbalised and unmet requirements, and a means to engage humans in productive activity.

Why did you become a designer?
YUJ Designs was formed with the vision of helping businesses create value through user experience design and with the aim of putting India on the world design map. We wanted to bring that aspect to the fore, that great design can come from India.

What drives you to create something new?
Empathy towards humans and the potential that design has to make an impact are the primary drivers for us to create new businesses, services, processes and designs.

Zeichen & Wunder
Marcus von Hausen, Irmgard Hesse

Red Dot: Best of the Best
→ Online: page 180–181

Irmgard Hesse studied communication design in Munich and founded her own design studio while she was still a student. After an extended stay in Salvador da Bahia, Brazil, she took part in various exhibitions with her own works in Germany. To this day, the intense engagement with contents forms the basis for her design concepts. Zeichen & Wunder stands for real substance in brand management and design. Marcus von Hausen began working as an independent designer for a number of agencies during his studies in philosophy and communication design in Munich, Germany. In 1991, he founded his first design studio working on corporate design, book design, illustration and photography commissions. After a period in Toronto, Canada, he and Irmgard Hesse together set up the Zeichen & Wunder agency in 1995.

What does design mean to you?
The ability to constantly keep creating an impetus that opens up new perspectives or sets things in motion.

To what extent do you think new technologies are changing design?
Deep down not at all. One always has to get to the core of the matter regardless of technological possibilities. People will always be people, after all.

What was your intention in designing your awarded work?
Producing some momentum in an established, somewhat inflexible design system and so win over the very young for the wonderful German newspaper Süddeutsche Zeitung.

zeit:raum Gruppe
Stefan Pfeifer, Markus Frei, Valery Reck
— Design has to become more expressionistic and risky to stay relevant.

Red Dot
→ Interface & User Experience Design: page 325

Markus Frei, art director at zeit:raum XR, grew up in southern Germany. He graduated from art college after a short earlier stint in regional television and went on to join zeit:raum in 2016. Stefan Pfeifer, technical director at zeit:raum XR, developed a particular affection for 3D real-time and game development during his bachelor's degree in applied computer science. Valery Reck, visual designer at zeit:raum, started his career as a self-taught designer and later graduated with a bachelor's degree in intermedia design.

Where do you see future challenges in communication design?
We believe design will be more and more influenced by big data. Big data is the engine that powers the algorithms of the current generation of artificial intelligence. We are talking about design, not art, here – and design is purpose-driven. It has a goal and this goal can be reached faster by combining algorithms and big data. We believe, design has to become more expressionistic, risky and have a direct dialogue with art in order to stay relevant.

To what extent do you think new technologies are changing design?
It is our belief that future challenges in communication design are inevitably linked to the rise of new technologies, which will influence how we think about and design our products. One change already taking place is that technology will become increasingly more wearable. From smart watches to smart clothes, wearable augmented reality devices and beyond, new challenges and design philosophies will arise.

Zhejiang Gongshang University, Institute of Brand Development
Ping Yang, Kaihao Zhu, Kan Zhao, Wenjun Xu, Linkun Li

Red Dot
→ Typography: page 102

The Institute of Brand Development of Zhejiang Gongshang University is located in Hangzhou, China, and was established in 2015. The institute is a comprehensive platform for external design services within the Art and Design College of Zhejiang Gongshang University, jointly established by the Market Supervision Administration of Zhejiang Province and Zhejiang Gongshang University. It provides brand design support focusing on the economic, social and cultural development characteristics of Zhejiang Province to government and to institutions, and helps business sectors grow through innovation-driven brand development strategies. Amongst others, it has worked for the World Internet Conference (Wuzhen Summit), Alibaba Group and Ant Financial Group.

What does design mean to you?
Design means a process of constantly challenging, accepting questions, trying to fail, continuing to create and finally realising an idea. All the challenges and failures in this process are valuable rewards.

Why did you become a designer?
The love of new and beautiful things and the love of expression is probably the biggest reason for becoming a designer. Becoming a designer is a natural progression when you have a good grounding in drawing and aesthetics.

What are the biggest challenges in a creative's everyday life?
It's a challenge to remain curious and creative over time, not to become dependent on familiar creative methods and to keep trying new creative paths.

Jury Portraits

Publishing & Print Media	Posters	Typography	Illustrations	Sound Design	Film & Animation	Online
4	64	92	116	126	138	172

01 | 02

Renne Angelvuo
Finland

01 | 02 NOODELIST
NOODELIST is an innovative plant-based instant noodle brand founded by Thuong Tan with her start-up company in California in 2018. Primarily targeted at Californian millennial techies, the packaging design of this extremely nutritious dish is clear and bold, differing from the ordinary bulky products.

Renne Angelvuo studied advertising, marketing and design at the Institute of Marketing in Helsinki and followed this up with an arts degree from the Free Art School Helsinki. Since 1980, he has been working as an art director in advertising and design. In 1994, he launched the company PRIORITY Advertising & Design, and in 2004 set up Win Win Branding, which is today called Win Win Design. Renne Angelvuo has years of expertise in packaging design, industrial design, branding and packaging innovations. His clients include many big Finnish and international brands such as Nokia, MySQL, Nestlé, Metsä Tissue, UPM-Kymmene and Saarioinen. He was president of the European Packaging Design Association from 2015 to 2018 and is still a member of the board.

What innovations are there in regard to minimalism in packaging design?
There are ingenious structural solutions and the use of fibre-based packaging materials with great visuals and a minimalist approach.

What characterises good packaging design?
Some things don't change, which means that packaging design must be eye-catching and visible to get people's attention and to communicate in almost no time the product benefits to achieve memorable branding.

Who or what inspires you in your daily work as a designer?
The real inspiration for me are challenging consumers, rapidly changing consumer trends and the need to please these smart millennial consumers.

Apps	Interface & User Experience Design	Spatial Communication	Red Dot: Junior Award	Designer Profiles	Jury Portraits	Index
206	236	336	426	564	642	668

01

Prof. Masayo Ave
Germany/Japan

01 DESIGN GYMNASTICS A.B.C.
Typeface collection discovered in nature
by Masayo Ave in 2009–2018, presented at
Venice Design 2019.

Professor Masayo Ave is the founder of the design studio MasayoAve creation and SED.Lab, Sensory Experience Design Laboratory, in Berlin. Merging culture and disciplines, she brings to bear her expertise in her sensory-based innovative design works and also in the field of design education. A graduate in architecture from Hosei University in Japan, her design career began in Milan in the early 1990s. Taking a sensorial and imaginative approach to basic design principles, her focus on material exploration and experimental design development brought her critical fame and many international design awards. In the early 2000s, Masayo Ave also became involved in the field of design education and was appointed a professor at Berlin University of the Arts, the Estonian Academy of Arts and recently at Berlin International University of Applied Sciences. As a prominent design teacher, she has also been dedicating her career to developing a new design education programme for children and young people that encompasses sensory-based design experiences.

What appeals to you about working as a professor and teacher in addition to being a designer?
It is a process of sharing my latest learnings and experiments in the professional field, and of encouraging the younger generation to expand their future activities beyond the narrow limit of one discipline. I also consider it a mission to transfer the almost forgotten wisdom of my grandparents' generation to my grandchildren's generation.

How did you develop your passion for design?
By keeping alive my inborn sense of wonder and by renewing my own delight in the mysteries of the Earth and living.

Publishing & Print Media	Posters	Typography	Illustrations	Sound Design	Film & Animation	Online
4	64	92	116	126	138	172

01 | 02

Špela Čadež
Slovenia

01 | 02 Steakhouse
Short animated film about the invisibility of psychic violence in a couple's long-standing relationship. 9 minutes; produced by Finta, Contemporary Art Institute, Ljubljana, Slovenia.

Špela Čadež was born in 1977 and graduated in graphic design in Ljubljana, Slovenia, in 2002. She continued her studies at the Academy of Media Arts Cologne, Germany, and has been working as an independent animation director and producer since 2008. Her films have been screened worldwide. "Boles" (2013) has received 50 awards, distinctions and nominations including a Grand Prix at the DOK Leipzig and Best Debut Award at the Hiroshima International Animation Festival. Špela Čadež' latest film "Nighthawk" (2016) has to date received 23 awards and distinctions including the Grand Prix at the Holland Animation Film Festival (HAFF) and at the Animafest Zagreb. It has been screened at international festivals such as the Sundance Film Festival, the Clermont-Ferrand International Short Film Festival and the Annecy International Animation Film Festival.

Do you live by a certain philosophy?
I believe the best thing in life is to find work that you love doing. Then you don't really go to work. I'm lucky to have a job like that.

What do you consider to be the main challenges but also the appeal of working as an animation director?
The biggest challenge is to have patience, to motivate the whole team and believe in the film through the long process of production.

How did you experience this year's jury session for the Red Dot Award: Brands & Communication Design?
Meeting with the other judges and having discussions in person cannot be replaced with online work. But we did our job as best as we could, so let's all hope that our old reality comes back soon.

Eric Chang
Taiwan

01 | 02 Audi A1
During the COVID-19 pandemic, most people were quarantined at home. Online gaming became more popular than ever among young people. Audi A1 scored a coup with a popular game, Animal Crossing, and a design that created an online car showroom to display the new A1 model and introduced car features throughout the game. The game attracted countless players to visit the virtual showroom and made appreciation of the car more fun and interesting.

01 | 02

Eric Chang holds a master's degree from the University of Wisconsin in Madison, USA, and currently teaches at National Chengchi University, Taiwan. Specialising in marketing, direct marketing, customer relationship management (CRM) and digital marketing, he has in-depth knowledge of the theory and application of integrated and digital marketing. He has advised clients in a wide array of industries. Eric Chang joined McCann Worldgroup, Taiwan as CEO in 2018, providing clients with such services as digital marketing strategies and digital media planning, CRM strategy consulting and communications planning. He previously worked for Ogilvy more than 20 years and served as vice president of business development for OgilvyOne in the Asia-Pacific region.

What do you enjoy most about your job in the areas of marketing communication and digital marketing?
Communication is not only a skill or tool to use to talk to your consumers or target audience but a science, and it is alive. It evolves as technology develops, and cultures, societies and the environment change. As designers or marketers, we need to evolve as well, to follow the trend, learn from the past and change our mindset to adapt to the new normal. Throughout my career, I have therefore also learned, grown and evolved, which makes my life more enjoyable.

What developments can we expect to see in digital advertising over the next few years?
Digital is everywhere, in everything. Digital advertising is all advertising, digital marketing represents all marketing. There is no online or offline, we are all in-the-line.

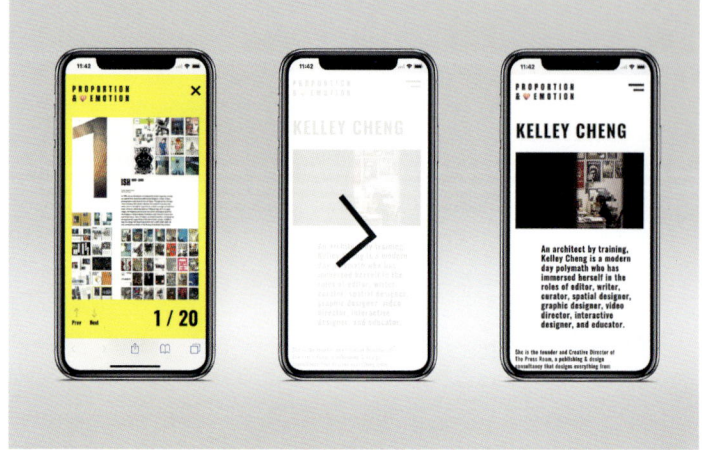

01 | 02

Kelley Cheng
Singapore

**01 | 02 Proportion & Emotion:
20 Years in Design with Kelley Cheng**
The exhibition showcased the multidisciplinary design works of Kelley Cheng as she exercised her sensibilities in the different genres of design in putting together this exhibition. Online exhibition design, key visual and app.

A leading designer in Singapore, Kelley Cheng is an architectural graduate turned polymath whose activities range from magazine editor, public speaker and art gallery owner to designer. She runs her own publishing and design consultancy, The Press Room, a multidisciplinary studio designing everything from books, brands, graphics and documentaries to spaces, stages and film sets. Her projects include the Youth Olympic Games, i Light Marina Bay Light Art Festival, Singapore Pavilion at the World Expo 2012 Yeosu Korea, President's Design Award 2013 and 2016. In collaboration with Studio Milou Architects, The Press Room won the President's Design Award 2015 for the National Gallery Singapore wayfinding design. Kelley Cheng serves as adjunct lecturer in the Industrial Design department at the National University of Singapore, and as a visiting professor at the China Academy of Art, Hangzhou. In 2009, she was celebrated as one of the "Great Women of Our Time" and in 2010 as one of the "50 Most Inspirational Women" in Singapore.

What has most influenced your many years of working as a designer?
I have been deeply influenced by architecture and many architects, especially the Modernists like Mies van der Rohe and Le Corbusier. A lot of my work is driven by content and context, both of which are the fundamentals of developing an architecture.

How would you define design?
A good design is often about solving problems and serving a practical need, be it something as simple as a poster or something as big as a piece of architecture.

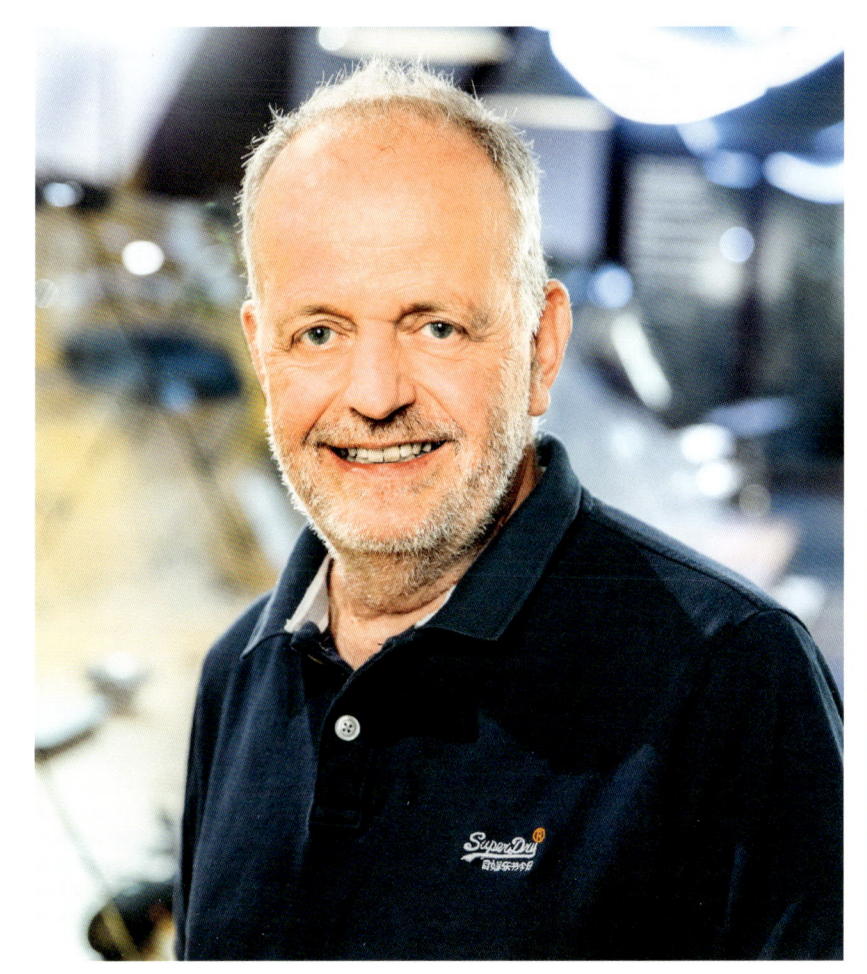

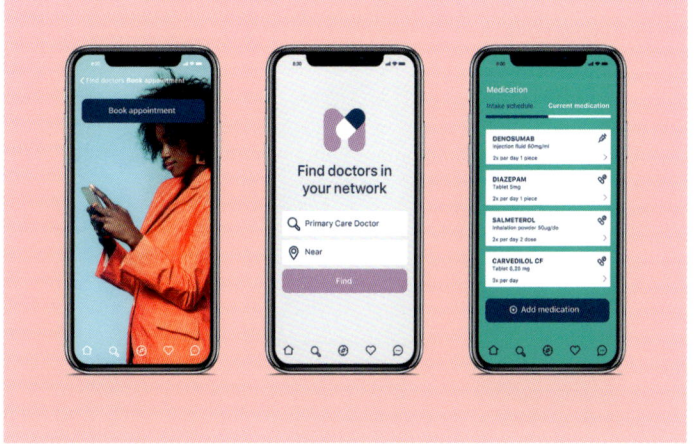

Prof. Michel de Boer
Netherlands

01 | 02 Medxpert
The Medxpert brand has been created around an innovative personal health record app. It unlocks all of one's medical data in an innovative way and may be shared with healthcare providers, doctors and specialists. The personal health record can be used anywhere in the world and is based on international medical and software standards. All data is stored in a private database on the phone and is always up to date. The brand's app has been designed to be accurate, open, simple, friendly, objective and knowledgeable.

01 | 02

Professor Michel de Boer became creative managing partner at Studio Dumbar in 1989. In 2011, he set up his own design office, MdB Associates, with associated offices in Germany, Korea and Hong Kong. He has worked for clients such as Apple, Allianz, Shell, Nike, Jaguar and Mercedes-Benz, and has won numerous awards, amongst them prestigious D&AD gold awards. A special D&AD achievement award was given to him in 2012 when he ranked in the top ten as one of the most awarded designers of all times. Michel de Boer has also won multiple Red Dot awards. In 2014, he opened his Chinese office: De Boer Wang Studio in Shanghai. In 2018, he was appointed Professor of Practice in Innovation Branding Design that is part of the Master's Design Programme at Tongji University College of D&I. Michel de Boer is a member of Alliance Graphique International (AGI).

Why is it so important for brands to think holistically?
It is a key for brands to match a well-defined strategy. This needs to be translated into a clear vision, embedded with strong brand personality characteristics, which enables the company to position the brand in an appropriate manner. This holistic approach should be mirrored by a design which aligns the brand perfectly with the market

The Red Dot Award was last year expanded to include "Brands". What is your opinion of this development?
The time when branding was equated to a logo or a visual identity, or to advertising or marketing is way behind us. Branding is about values, needs, lifestyles, personalities, expressions and confidence. It is the bedrock of the quality of life. I am happy that the Red Dot Award recognises the importance of branding. So it is a very good initiative!

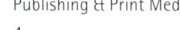

01

Andrea Finke-Anlauff
Germany

01 CCI A3 Joystick
CCI A3 is an AUX-N multifunction joystick for all ISOBUS devices which is extremely innovative with its simple touch display controls and vibration feedback. Depending on the grid selected, it recognises the right sequence of keys, allows for blind operation via vibration feedback and can also easily be controlled by hand thanks to the ergonomic hand rest.

Andrea Finke-Anlauff studied product and graphic design in Braunschweig (Germany), Barcelona and Helsinki, and graduated from the Braunschweig University of Arts with a diploma. During her studies, she already worked for Nokia in Great Britain, Japan and Finland, and signed a consultancy agreement with Nokia in 1992. In 1994, she founded the company mangodesign, which specialises in product design and interaction design, and which has been able to secure numerous awards and patents ever since. As the executive creative director, Andrea Finke-Anlauff works on innovative projects, services and future visions for her long-term clients from the automotive, consumer electronics and agricultural technology industries. In 2003, she co-founded the design manufacturer mangoobjects, which specialises in small-scale series and individual product presentations. In 2019, both companies became part of Gofore Germany GmbH. Andrea Finke-Anlauff has taught at various art schools and universities and has acted as a jury member for several international design awards.

What was your first design project?
My first design project, which was subsequently also mass-produced, was the Nokia 8110, the "banana phone", also used in the film "The Matrix". After 25 years, it was redesigned in 2018 and brought back as a classic.

What makes your work as a jury member special?
The ability to evaluate and enjoy design solutions, as well as judge them purely based on the quality of their merits together with colleagues from different cultures who share the same values.

Gustavo Greco
Brazil

01 | 02 Teatro Feluma
Signage system for the Teatro Feluma in Belo Horizonte, Brazil, which plays with light and form.

01 | 02

Gustavo Greco is the founder and creative director of Greco Design. He is professor of the brand management postgraduate course at PUC Minas and also director of ABEDESIGN, the Brazilian Association of Design Companies. Moreover, he acts as a juror in the D&AD Awards, Cannes Lions, Prémios Lusos, FIAP, 10th Brazilian Graphic Design Biennial, El Ojo de Iberoamérica and iF concept design award. Gustavo Greco received awards from e.g. the Cannes Lions, D&AD Awards, Red Dot Award, iF Design Award, El Ojo de Iberoamérica, London International Awards, Bienal Iberoamericana de Diseño and HOW International Design Awards.

You act as a jury member for several design competitions. What makes them relevant in your opinion?
Design competitions set creative standards, educate, inspire and promote good design. They increase people's awareness of the importance of design. An award-winning project is a relevant project.

To what extent is design changed by new technologies?
Technologies and design are inseparable, influencing each other mutually. But I see technologies as a means to an end and not the end in themselves; as a means of putting into practice the way designers think, always focused on human beings.

How did you experience this year's jury process?
We converted the familial environment during the jury session into a digital process. Even so, the search for highly qualified international talent and the commitment to achieving special results made it a very distinguished moment.

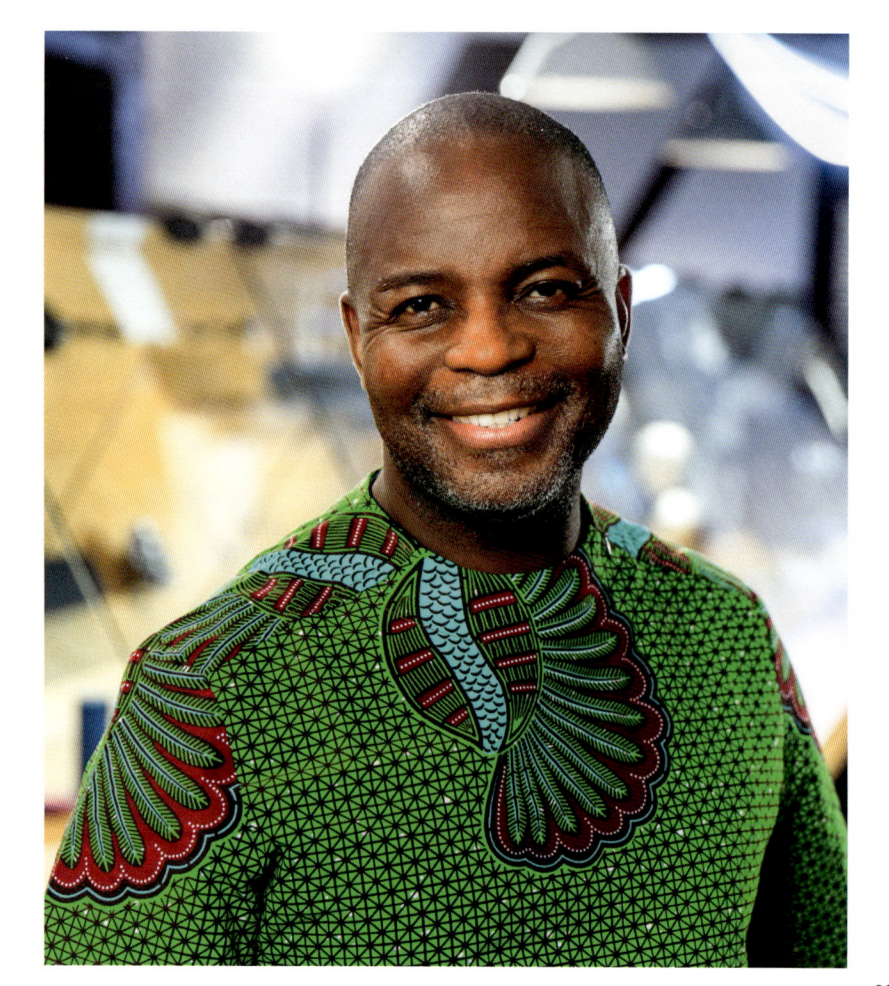

Publishing & Print Media	Posters	Typography	Illustrations	Sound Design	Film & Animation	Online
4	64	92	116	126	138	172

01 | 02

Thebe Ikalafeng
South Africa

01 Grosso Foods Group
Brand activation for a new Africa-focused agri-business enterprise.

02 Africa Brand Leadership Academy
A new global/African visual identity and applications for the re-branding of the Brand Leadership Academy as the Africa Brand Leadership Academy.

Thebe Ikalafeng is a leading global African brand and reputation architect, advisor and author. He has worked on over 100 local and global brands across Africa and has been recognised by New African Magazine as one of the 100 Most Influential Africans. He is the founder of the Brand Africa and Brand Leadership Group, a non-executive director of Cartrack Holdings, World Wide Fund for Nature and South African Tourism. Thebe Ikalateng holds BSc and MBA degrees from the Marquette University (USA), and followed the executive education programmes at Wits Business School and Harvard Business School. He has been to every country in Africa and every continent in the world.

What key qualities must brands have for consumers to trust them?
While in the past it was enough just to fulfil the functional standard, today consumers expect brands to contribute to their well-being and quality of life, to be ethical, just and respectful. This year of 2020 has been the definitive year in which these standards have been tested – where brands have been challenged to take a stand.

How does a brand stay memorable?
A brand stays memorable when it is relevant, irreverent and unexpectedly delivers on its promise.

How must a brand present itself in the competition in order to merit an award from you?
With simplicity, craftsmanship, elegance and differentiation.

Hjalti Karlsson
USA

01 Reykjavík Art Museum
Branding and identity. The Reykjavík Art Museum is the pre-eminent art museum in Iceland, with three locations across the capital, each focusing on different decades and artists. The new branding and design identity for the museum needed to speak to both local and international audiences.

Hjalti Karlsson founded the award-winning design studio karlssonwilker inc. with partner Jan Wilker in 2000. He has launched a number of notable creative projects over the course of his career, including work for MINI/BMW, Bloomberg Businessweek, Nintendo, Swatch, Museum of the Moving Image, Vitra and Reykjavík Art Museum. He is a recipient of the Torsten and Wanja Söderberg Prize and has been featured in numerous publications. Hjalti Karlsson has served on design juries internationally, also in the position of chairman of the design jury at the Clio Awards and for Red Dot Design Award. He lectures regularly around the globe and is a member of the Alliance Graphique Internationale (AGI). Hjalti Karlsson was born and raised in Reykjavík, Iceland, and is an alumnus of Parsons School of Design.

What role does teamwork play in your day-to-day work?
Teamwork is very important. We are a team of six designers, and we collaborate on pretty much everything in the studio. It's very important that our designers do not have too much of an ego to work here. And the same goes for clients.

Why is holistic brand communication so important for success?
Holistic brand communication – a cohesive look and feel through all applications – is very important for brands. If companies do not have it, then the brand communication will fall flat and not work at all.

What made you become a graphic designer?
My father was a bank manager and my mother a nurse, but she loved to paint. My interest in design came from her.

01 | 02

Akira Kobayashi
Germany

01 **Akko & Akko Rounded**
Type Design

02 **Neue Frutiger**
Type Design (with Adrian Frutiger)

Akira Kobayashi, born in 1960, started his career as a type designer at Sha-Ken Co., Ltd. in 1983. In 1989, he studied calligraphy and typography in London. On his return to Japan in 1990, he joined Jiyu-Kobo. From 1993 to 1997, he worked for TypeBank, where he designed a Latin alphabet to match the digital Japanese fonts of the foundry. Afterwards, he became a freelance type designer and won numerous international awards. In 2001, he moved to Germany to assume his current position as type director at Monotype GmbH. Akira Kobayashi has also collaborated with the two pre-eminent designers Adrian Frutiger and Hermann Zapf to modernise their earlier type designs. He is a frequent speaker at international type conferences and a juror in prestigious international design competitions.

What mistakes do you frequently notice in typography design?
The meaning of the content of the written language should take precedence while typography should remain in the background. Typography only makes sense if it allows the text to express itself.

What new challenges do you believe lie ahead in the field of typography?
Type design and typography will increasingly be responsible for designing texts in different languages.

What advice would you give young designers for a successful career start?
In typography, it is always important to think of the white space around the letters or punctuation marks. Train yourself not just to focus on the black letters, but also on the white background.

01 | 02

Prof. Shu-Chang Kung
Taiwan

01 | 02 Bethlehem Foundation
Early treatment and education centre for children with developmental impairments in Tainan, Taiwan.

Professor Shu-Chang Kung studied architecture and design at the Harvard Graduate School of Design and in 1997 established AURA Architects & Associates in Taipei. He is currently professor at the Graduate Institute of Architecture at National Chiao Tung University, Taiwan, and vice chairman of the Taiwan Design Alliance. His work has received many international awards. Shu-Chang Kung has served as Taiwan's representative at the Hong Kong & Shenzhen Bi-City Biennale of Urbanism/Architecture and at the Next-Gene 20 of the 11th International Architecture Biennale in Venice, both in 2008. He was also the chief curator of the Taipei Pavilion at the Hong Kong and Shenzhen Bi-City Biennale of Urbanism/Architecture in 2011–2012, and of the Harvest Blessings Pavilion at the 2018 Taichung World Flora Exposition.

What characterises good spatial communication?
Good spatial communication comes from good storytelling. It has to profoundly touch people and change our future for the better.

How has this design field changed in recent years?
Recently, I was deeply moved by a series of diverse and outstanding works that integrated interdisciplinary thinking from creative technologies with human sensibilities to respond to the critical challenges the environment and our society face.

Where do you expect to see the greatest changes in future design degree courses?
The most important future challenge for design is to maintain the essence of human sensibility and interactions.

Herwig Kusatz
Austria

01 Wiener Linien
Sound architecture for the Wiener Linien, the public transport services of the city of Vienna, Austria.

Herwig Kusatz studied biomedical engineering at the Graz University of Technology and updated his professional training with a full-time MBA at the NIMBAS Graduate School of Management in Utrecht, the Netherlands. He developed an interest in a strategic approach to the use of acoustics and founded the company Sound Strategy in 2005. His first customer was the sporting goods designer and manufacturer adidas, who commissioned him to produce the music for its in-store videos in all performance stores worldwide. The first sound strategies were delivered to Generali and Almdudler, followed by Wien Energie, Doctors Without Borders, Wien Tourismus, Slow Food, Vöslauer, ARD. ZDF medienakademie, ORTOVOX and Wiener Linien. Herwig Kusatz has won numerous international awards and, following an increasing number of requests, began sharing his knowledge of the design of audio processes in the university sector.

What skills should a good sound designer have?
An understanding of the interaction between the different human senses and their psychological effect. A thorough knowledge of acoustic parameters such as timbre, rhythm, melody, harmony and volume. And comprehensive skills in embedding the sound concept in applications.

How would you describe a sound designer's creative process?
Understanding the wishes and problems of the customer. Analysing existing concepts and applications for the topic in question. Presenting solution concepts. Mapping out, expanding and adapting the selected solutions with professional expertise.

Prof. Laurent Lacour
Germany

01 User Centric Customer
Ad for Commerz Real, Commerzbank Group.

01

Professor Laurent Lacour studied visual communication and art at the University of Art and Design in Offenbach, Germany. He is managing partner of the design studio "hauser lacour" that carries out extensive and award-winning works, e.g. branding and corporate design projects, among others for Siemens, Swiss Re, Munich Re, De Gruyter Wissenschaftsverlag, Fraport AG and Deutsche Börse Group. Its portfolio also includes projects for clients from the cultural sector, such as Kölner Philharmonie, Museum für Moderne Kunst in Frankfurt or Max-Planck-Institut Florenz. Laurent Lacour has taught at the universities of Zurich, Basel, Karlsruhe and Darmstadt. In 2011, he started a full professorship at the design department of the University of Applied Sciences in Düsseldorf.

How did you experience this year's jury session?
Of course, it was really different from past years. We worked independently in the digital space. Coordination with the other judges was a little bit more efficient. I very much liked that you could concentrate so well on the work and that you gained time through the digital approach to judging.

What role does storytelling play in branding today?
Modern brands are flexible, highly adaptive and organised in terms of processes. This has to do with the digital touchpoints. On this basis, storytelling is the focus of every modern brand development. That will continue to evolve. In the future, designers will have to think like filmmakers: in storyboards, strong narrative imagery and moving images.

Publishing & Print Media	Posters	Typography	Illustrations	Sound Design	Film & Animation	Online
4	64	92	116	126	138	172

01

Uwe Melichar
Germany

01 PaperHelp
As a design response to the challenging COVID-19 pandemic, sustainable cardboard masks were developed – functional packaging for the face in communicative paper packs of ten.

Uwe Melichar, born in 1968, studied communication design at the Muthesius University in Kiel and worked at the brand agency FACTOR for 25 years. He was the agency's managing partner and built up the packaging division. In 2020, he left the FACTOR and started his new business, MELICHAR Bros. Under the slogan "Increase Value, Decrease Waste" the company focusses on sustainable packaging solutions. In his work-life, Uwe Melichar has realised projects for adidas, Bosch, C&A, Gardena, Omron and Miele. Together with his team, he develops packaging and communication design for clients in Japan, Russia, China, the USA and various European countries. He is also a lecturer at several universities, such as the University of Augsburg, is a member of the Type Directors Club New York and president of the European Brand & Packaging Design Association (epda).

Which materials will prevail in packaging design in future?
The future lies in rapidly renewable raw materials. Paper pulp, paper foam are technologies that make it possible to produce cellulose-based packaging elements that can be freely shaped.

How would you describe the development of packaging solutions in recent years?
After many years in which aesthetics predominated, genuine solutions are increasingly playing an important role: packaging that explains the product, that makes portioning and removal of the contents easier and that is resealable. In recent years, companies have been taking on more responsibility and creating easier, lighter and smarter packaging. Products are being given a stage, with packaging in combination with intelligent storytelling offering a brilliant mise en scène.

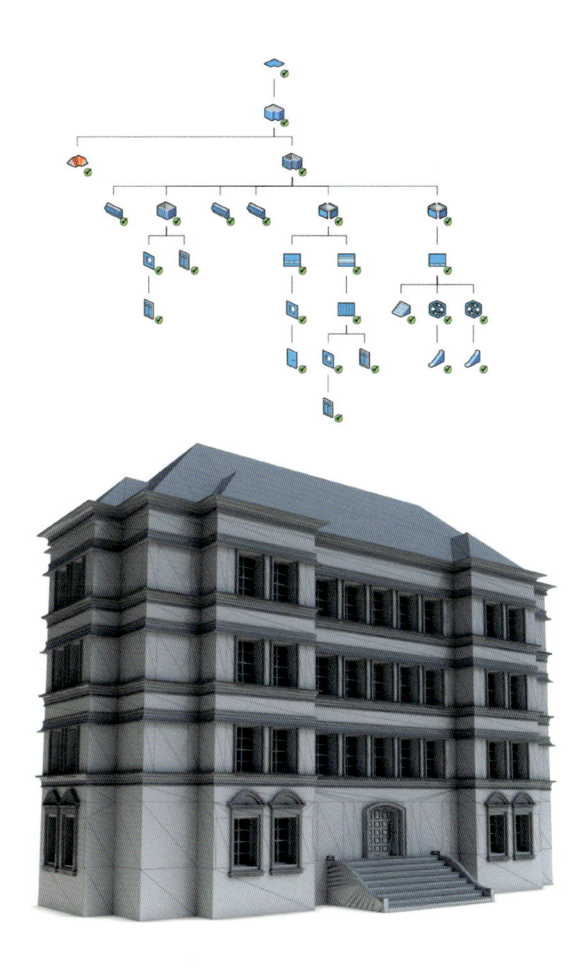

Prof. Dr. Christof Rezk-Salama
Germany

01 Procedural Architecture
Procedural generation of buildings for an ongoing research project on smart cities.

Professor Dr. Christof Rezk-Salama studied information technology at the Friedrich-Alexander University in Erlangen/Nuremberg, Germany, and subsequently obtained his PhD with honours. After working as a design engineer at Siemens Medical, he completed his postdoctoral qualification at the University of Siegen in 2009. He then taught and conducted research as a professor in the Department of Game Design at the Media Design University of Applied Sciences in Düsseldorf, Germany. In 2012, he accepted a professorship for game development in the Department of Computer Science at the University of Applied Sciences in Trier, Germany.

How will games and their designers evolve on mobile devices?
A difficult question. The truly innovative ideas in gaming tend to come from small, independent developers. The gaming market for mobile platforms is by now so saturated that it is not the most innovative game concepts that make it, in my opinion, but rather those that can achieve greater visibility due to enormous marketing budgets.

What is the likely future job description of a game designer?
Good game design is characterised by intuitive ease of use, barrier-free access, intrinsic motivation and, above all, fairness for widely different ways of playing, which is achieved through dynamic balancing. Analysing all of this and applying it to technological devices are the core competencies required for digitalisation, in my view. I therefore expect that game designers will be represented more in all areas of digital transformation.

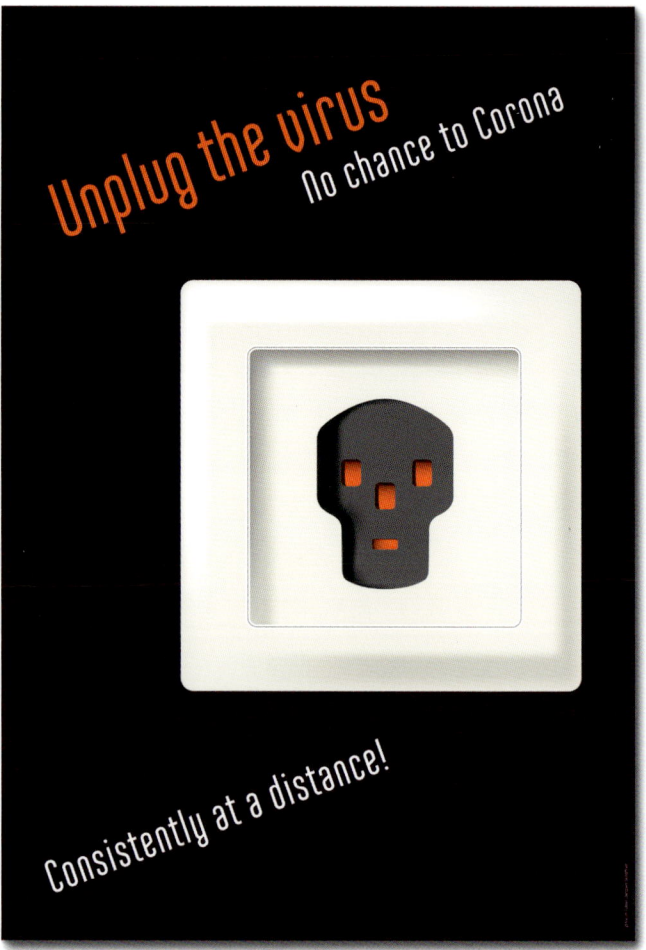

Jean Jacques Schaffner
Switzerland

01 COVID-19 Pandemic
The worldwide COVID-19 pandemic has shown how vulnerable complex societies are. How can politics adequately communicate with people? Today, merely communicating numbers and facts is no longer enough. As part of a big campaign, proposals were submitted to highlight the potential of professional communication.

Jean Jacques Schaffner, born in Basel, Switzerland, in 1954, studied graphic design at Basel Art School. This was followed by further training as a photographer and as a TV music director as well as study stays in Paris, London, San Francisco and at the University of Utah. In 1976, he founded Schaffner & Conzelmann Designersfactory in Basel, a full-service communication and design agency and one of the most renowned agencies in Switzerland. From 2000 to 2003, Jean Jacques Schaffner was president of the European Packaging Design Association. Since 2019, he has been working as an independent consultant, photographer, film producer, design juror and spokesperson under the name jjsscc.

What options are available for turning brands into three-dimensional experiences?
The time when interior design was limited to the mere decoration of physical spaces is long gone. Today, the objective is rather to design sensory experiences. The task that has to be solved is the bringing together of sound, colour, light projections and, of course, also spatial elements in one context. Never before has it been so important to be able to think in an interdisciplinary way.

What drives you to keep reinventing design?
A look at the design developments across the world, challenges me anew every day to improve. I consider it a privilege to have so much good design available and to be able to measure myself against it. That is why I still continue to take part in design tenders. Competition keeps you fit.

Niels Schrader
Netherlands

01 | 02 Acid Clouds
Acid Clouds is a photographic research project in collaboration with Roel Backaert that traces the physical impact of virtual data in the Netherlands as data storage is currently reaching the point where digital concerns hit physical constraints. The increasing number of heavily secured data centres in the Netherlands is documented using night-time photography. The unique features of these energy-draining structures made it possible to identify the motives and actions concealed in today's global cloud infrastructure.

Niels Schrader is a concept-driven information designer with a fascination for numbers and data. He is the founder of the Amsterdam-based design studio Mind Design, member of the Alliance Graphique Internationale (AGI) and, together with Ramon Amaro and Sheena Calvert, co-founder of the Queer Computing Consortium (QCC). He graduated with a degree in communication design from the University of Applied Sciences in Düsseldorf and completed his academic studies with the master's programme in design at the Sandberg Institute in Amsterdam. In addition to his design practice, Niels Schrader has lectured at various academies and universities in and outside of Europe. Together with Roosje Klap, he is head of the graphic design department and Non-Linear Narrative master's programme at the Royal Academy of Art in The Hague.

What big app developments are you expecting to see in the next few years?
One of the most significant developments will probably be the introduction of the 5G standard. It will expand mobile data transfer capacities and so provide the basis for new types of smartphone apps. In addition, the embedding of artificial intelligence and machine learning is likely to increase.

What makes your work as a jury member special?
One of the most appealing aspects of jury work is, of course, to witness what inspires a new generation of designers; to see how young people deal with important social issues and integrate that into their design work. In that sense, the Red Dot: Junior Prize is, to my mind, the most important award of the competition.

Publishing & Print Media	Posters	Typography	Illustrations	Sound Design	Film & Animation	Online
4	64	92	116	126	138	172

Bettina Schulz
Germany

01 BS Bettina Schulz – Logo and word mark

02 Collage of work samples

01 | 02

Bettina Schulz, born in Munich in 1974, was editor-in-chief of the international trade magazine "novum – World of Graphic Design" from 2001 until 2019. She had been a member of the editorial team since 1994 and had also worked as a freelance journalist and copywriter for various international trade magazines and customers in industry. She is a member of a number of juries for international design competitions, e.g. the European Design Awards, Designpreis der Landeshauptstadt München, Best of Content Marketing, Global Illustration Award, DesignEuropa Awards, IIID Award. She is furthermore a founding member of the Creative Paper Conference and set up her own copywriting and editorial agency in Munich in July 2019.

How has the quality of entries for the print category changed in the last few years?
I have the impression that the growing digitalisation of life means high-quality print products are appreciated more, which also shines the spotlight onto sustainability. A beautiful brochure is kept longer than a cheap flyer. Print media transport much more nowadays than just information – in a subtle way, they also convey brand values.

What appeals to you about copywriting and journalism?
The intense immersion in brand environments, in companies and their values, and the development of a unique customer language are what make copywriting such an interesting profession. As a journalist, on the other hand, the discovery of new issues and trends, the networking and the opportunity to be part of the opinion-forming process make it both a great job and a great responsibility.

Sylvia Vitale Rotta
France

01 La vache qui rit
Global worldwide redesign of the identity of the famous French brand "La vache qui rit" (The Laughing Cow). Launched in 130 countries.

01

Sylvia Vitale Rotta, born in Tanzania, studied at the London School of Arts. Together with Nick Craig she founded Team Créatif in 1986. Today, it is a group of four agencies, which include branding and packaging, retail, market services, as well as a production and digital platform. Team Créatif has become a reference for branding and packaging identity on the international market, working in 52 countries worldwide with 250 employees. In 2008, Sylvia Vitale Rotta was appointed president of the first design jury at Eurobest and, in 2009, acted as president of the design category at Cannes Lions. In 2013, she was part of the jury at Dubai Lynx. She has given classes at Parisian schools such as Istec and Estacom, École intuit.lab and has also participated in the TEDxParis conference. In 2017, she was awarded the Chevalier de la Légion d'Honneur, granted by the French Ministry of Foreign Affairs and International Development which is bestowed in recognition of an exceptional design career spanning more than 30 years.

What are the most important trends in packaging design?
Firstly, naturalness. All brands are chasing after the natural look; they use fewer colours, more white and simpler packaging. Sometimes, the product deserves a more natural design, sometimes it is a bit played up. However, the consumers' quest for an accessible, non-industrial design is key to successful sales. What is great is when the packaging itself is sustainable.

What advice would you pass on to young designers?
Design is a fantastic profession. Believe you can make a difference to people, brands and products. Never forget to work really hard and it will pay off.

Publishing & Print Media	Posters	Typography	Illustrations	Sound Design	Film & Animation	Online
4	64	92	116	126	138	172

01

Thilo von Debschitz
Germany

01 The Fascination with Building
Calendar for SOKA-BAU, the German building industry's social security fund, Wiesbaden, Germany.

Thilo von Debschitz studied communication design at the RheinMain University of Applied Sciences in Germany. After positions as an art director in various companies, he founded the Q design agency in Wiesbaden in 1997 together with Laurenz Nielbock. The agency has since won numerous international awards. In addition to his agency work, Thilo von Debschitz writes books with a focus on the visual arts. He attracted great attention with his rediscovery of the info graphics pioneer Fritz Kahn and the publication of the monograph dedicated to him. Thilo von Debschitz has taught at the RheinMain University of Applied Sciences and at the IMK, the Institute of Marketing and Communication in Wiesbaden. Today, he is also a regular guest speaker at conferences on the topic of design.

What makes print media persuasive in your opinion?
Our communications are dominated by digital media that are generally designed for speed. We all benefit from that, of course. Print media as a rule steer clear of this transience. Those who make the most of this medium's strengths – through a successful mix of content, design and materiality – will generate long-lasting awareness.

In view of the current situation, what is your assessment of this year's online jury process?
It was brilliant to see how quickly the Red Dot Team set up a digital solution for this year's competition. However, in our category, touching and feeling the entries is especially important. Paper, finishes, binding all cry out for haptic perception. That made the qualitative evaluation based on photos challenging. My exchange with other jury members was therefore particularly intense.

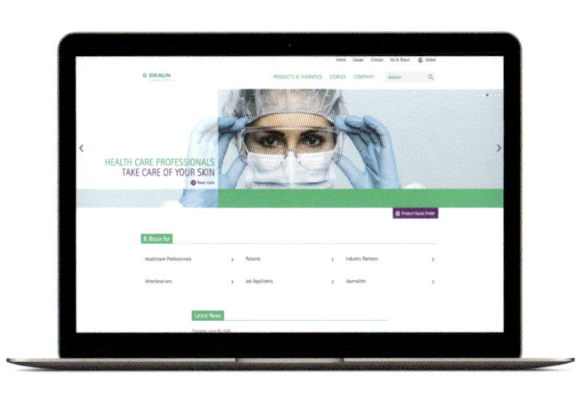

Apps	Interface & User Experience Design	Spatial Communication	Red Dot: Junior Award	Designer Profiles	Jury Portraits	Index
206	236	336	426	564	642	668

01 | 02

Peter Philippe Weiss
Switzerland

01 Mobi24
Storytelling project for the phone applications of the Swiss insurance company Mobiliar..

02 B. Braun
Integral corporate sounds for B. Braun, a supplier of the healthcare sector, Melsungen, Germany. Thanks to an innovative layer/stem structure, the sound elements of the corporate sound library can repeatedly be reassembled in a new way and edited. The B. Braun corporate sound is used worldwide.

Peter Philippe Weiss is an international sound consultant, composer, sound artist, sound designer, producer, author and referee. He also lectures at various universities. In 1994, he founded Corporate Sound AG, the first communication agency specialising in acoustic brand staging that works for international clients in the fields of exhibitions, architecture, museums, events, electronic media and product design. Peter Philippe Weiss is also involved in artistic sound projects and, among others, in 2005 realised a sound installation in Basel, Switzerland, which created new rooms with highly realistic soundscapes in the already existing sound surrounding. In 2009, his "unterwelten" (underworlds) could be heard from the drains in the city of Basel, and, in 2015, he published the book "Wenn Design die Materie verlässt" (When design leaves matter).

What do you find fascinating about the work of a sound designer?
Design and design thinking are constantly evolving. As a designer one has to keep up with the times without ever losing one's inner compass.

Where do you find inspiration for new sound ideas?
In films, in nature or in town when an electric transformer cabinet suddenly produces the hum of a wonderful chord.

What skills should a good sound designer have?
Good sound designers should be open and have a good feel for the context of the sound application. They should also not only work with prefabricated sounds but should experiment with sounds.

Publishing & Print Media	Posters	Typography	Illustrations	Sound Design	Film & Animation	Online
4	64	92	116	126	138	172

01

Holger Windfuhr
Germany

01 Digitec
Cover of Frankfurter Allgemeine Digitec, a special section on all things digital.

Born in the United States, Holger Windfuhr studied psychology at the University of Michigan and graphic design at the U5 Academy in Munich. In 2010, he completed the Kellogg-WHU Executive MBA Program. He began his career as a member of the development team at "Focus" magazine and then moved to the German edition of "Forbes". After co-founding the digital consulting agency "The Media Machine" in New York, he joined "Money" magazine at Time Inc. and then "House & Garden" at Condé Nast. Returning to Germany, he redesigned "impulse" at Gruner+Jahr. From 2000 to 2016, he was the creative head of the German business magazine "WirtschaftsWoche" and guided the visual aesthetics of the brand. Holger Windfuhr is art director of the German daily newspaper "Frankfurter Allgemeine Zeitung", the Sunday newspaper "Frankfurter Allgemeine Sonntagszeitung" and the "Frankfurter Allgemeine Magazin". He is a member of the Art Directors Club and has won numerous design awards.

How has the role of design in print media evolved in recent years?
Haptic qualities have not lost their significance – although an increasing number of readers are, of course, consuming digital content. But it's a question of objectives. Complex concepts and ideas are still more easily digested on paper than in digital form. What matters is offering readers an intelligent mix of analogue and digital content and making the most of the strengths of each medium.

What makes your work as a jury member special?
Red Dot is a truly international competition. Time and again, it is fascinating and enriching to see projects from all over the world.

Apps	Interface & User Experience Design	Spatial Communication	Red Dot: Junior Award	Designer Profiles	Jury Portraits	Index
206	236	336	426	564	642	668

01 | 02

Prof. Dr. Seung Hun Yoo
South Korea

01 Re:Scent
Re:Scent is an interaction design for a digital scent candle that provides bedside lighting with a soothing scent for those suffering from sleep disorder. Design: Seung Hun Yoo, Mina Lee, Sumin Park.

02 Faro
Faro is a UX design concept for local community intelligence in Seoul, Korea. The combination of IoT lighting, sensors, vision systems and mobile apps transforms the old residential neighbourhood into a highly connected smart town. Design: Seung Hun Yoo, Yuni Kim, Doi Kim, Jongeun Lee.

Professor Dr. Seung Hun Yoo is the founder of the CO:UX Design Lab at the School of Art & Design, Korea University. He holds a master's degree in design and a PhD in industrial engineering. He has worked at Samsung Mobile among others and designed many of the company's flagship mobile handsets. After seven years of working as UX Director at Samsung's Korea headquarters and at design offices in the USA, he began working at Korea University in cognitive UX design research studies and education in 2012. His CO:UX Design Lab performs UX design based on users' cognitive behaviour research. Seung Hun Yoo and his team are currently conducting cross-disciplinary UX design projects such as transparent UX display design, medical UX design and next-generation wearable devices.

What are the next big AI innovations you expect to see over the coming years?
The development of AI has focused on finding the areas that need AI help. Now we are entering the stage of finding opportunities for the coexistence of humans and AI. The next big challenge for us will be to utilise AI to reshape human thinking and emotions.

Will UX design and AI increasingly influence our everyday life?
There are already many UX designs today that suggest information to users tailored to their needs based on AI support. Many of our daily information devices are getting smarter thanks to AI. There is no doubt that the final interaction of daily living environments and users is inspired by AI. And the human thinking, feelings and idea generation will be influenced by AI.

Apps	Interface & User Experience Design	Spatial Communication	Red Dot: Junior Award	Designer Profiles	Jury Portraits	**Index**
206	236	336	426	564	642	668

Index Designers

0–9

+ing
www.facebook.com/plusing
Vol. 2: 413

1508
www.1508.dk
Vol. 2: 178–179, 566
Vol. 1: 251

1990 UAO
Vol. 2: 378

1zu33 Architectural Brand Identity
www.1zu33.com
Vol. 2: 24, 384–385

203 X Infographics Lab
www.203x.co.kr
Vol. 2: 74

52 graden noorderbreedte
www.52graden.com
Vol. 2: 34

A

Acer Inc.
www.acer.com
Vol. 2: 201
Vol. 1: 459, 619

adabay GmbH
www.adabay.rocks
Vol. 2: 418–419, 567

Admind Branding & Communications
www.admindagency.com
Vol. 2: 406–407, 568
Vol. 1: 306–307, 620

Akbank T.A.S.
www.akbank.com
Vol. 2: 228

Slavojka Akrapovič
Vol. 2: 132

Akrapovič Kreativa d.o.o.
www.akrapovic.com
Vol. 2: 132, 158

Alty
www.alty.co
Vol. 2: 212, 229, 569

AMI DESIGN
www.amytsai.myportfolio.com
Vol. 2: 87, 570

Amoeba
www.amoeba.co.kr
Vol. 2: 220–221

Amorepacific
www.apgroup.com
Vol. 2: 182–183, 196, 571
Vol. 1: 119

ampersand.studio
www.ampersand.studio
Vol. 2: 44, 45

Analogy
www.analogydesign.co
Vol. 2: 299

APOLLO Content Company
www.anssil.com
Vol. 2: 154–155, 572

Appedu Design Institute
www.appedu.com.tw
Vol. 2: 106, 107, 125, 573

Ralph Appelbaum Associates
www.raai.com
Vol. 2: 353, 369

ArtStyle Design Group
www.artstyle.su
Vol. 2: 394–395

Asia Culture Institute
www.aci-k.kr
Vol. 2: 362

ASUS
www.asus.com
Vol. 2: 148, 149, 150

Aught Pte. Ltd.
www.aug.ht
Vol. 2: 165, 574

B

B'IN LIVE Co., Ltd.
www.bin-live.com
Vol. 2: 412

B&W Studio
www.bandwstudio.co.uk
Vol. 2: 10–11, 575

Baidu Online Network Technology (Beijing) Co., Ltd.
www.baidu.com
Vol. 2: 281

Shanghai Bairen Interior Design & Engineering Company
Vol. 2: 360

Peter Bankov
www.bankovposters.com
Vol. 2: 82, 108

Barker Langham
www.barkerlangham.co.uk
Vol. 2: 344–345, 607

BASIC® x Google
https://store.google.com
Vol. 2: 202–203

Bay Designagentur Bastian Nemitz
www.bay-designagentur.de
Vol. 2: 54–55

Genevieve Bedell SCAD Savannah College of Art and Design
www.scad.edu
Vol. 2: 501

beierarbeit GmbH
www.beierarbeit.de
Vol. 2: 72, 73, 78, 104

Berry Creative
www.berrycreative.fi
Vol. 2: 390
Vol. 1: 241, 625

Bespoke
www.bespoke.eu
Vol. 2: 418–419

BiBoBox Studio
www.bibobox.com
Vol. 2: 428–429, 436–437, 576, 577

BLACKSPACE
www.black.space
Vol. 2: 392, 393

Jörg Block
www.joergblock.de
Vol. 2: 118–119

BOK + Gärtner GmbH
www.bokundgaertner.de
Vol. 2: 358

brandung GmbH & Co. KG
www.brandung.de
Vol. 2: 205

Bronce Estudio
www.broncestudio.com
Vol. 2: 58
Vol. 1: 138–139

Jason Bruges Studio
www.jasonbruges.com
Vol. 2: 344–345, 607

Busch-Jaeger Elektro GmbH Mitglied der ABB-Gruppe
www.busch-jaeger.de
Vol. 2: 300

C

CaderaDesign GmbH
www.caderadesign.de
Vol. 2: 244–245, 578

CADS GmbH
www.cads.at
Vol. 2: 248

Ya-Ci Cai Chihlee University of Technology
www.chihlee.edu.tw
Vol. 2: 493

Chi-Chih Chang, Hsin-Pei Chang, Fang-Yu Hsieh, Jou-Yu Huang, Wan-Yi Sheng Ming Chi University of Technology
www.mcut.edu.tw
Vol. 2: 454

Chia-Hsuan Chang, Rou-Ya Huang, Yue-Tong Hong Cheng Shiu University
www.csu.edu.tw
Vol. 2: 448

Chang Chih-Ling, Chiu Te-Cheng, Ding Hao-Yi Asia University
www.asia.edu.tw
Vol. 2: 534

Li Ching Chang, Yun Chiao Wang, Tz Ying Lin, Xuan Yan Kuo, You Shan Xiao, Pin Wei Lee Ling Tung University
www.ltu.edu.tw
Vol. 2: 481

Yu-Ting Chang, Tsai-Chuan Huang, Chi-Hsuan Tsen, Chu-Fong Nie, Yi-Yu Chen Chaoyang University of Technology
www.cyut.edu.tw
Vol. 2: 530

Chapeau Studios
www.chapeaustudios.com
Vol. 2: 146

Cheil Worldwide
www.cheil.com
Vol. 2: 32, 379, 381, 397, 399, 416–417
Vol. 1: 174, 304, 540–541

Chia-Yu Chen, Ting-Wei Liao, Yi-Ting Jiang, Yi-En Kao, Yu-Zhi Liao Chaoyang University of Technology
www.cyut.edu.tw
Vol. 2: 473

Publishing & Print Media	Posters	Typography	Illustrations	Sound Design	Film & Animation	Online
4	64	92	116	126	138	172

Index Designers

Hsiao-Jung Chen, Tsai-Shiuan Yu, Qu-Ya Chen, An-Ro Chen
Tatung University
www.ttu.edu.tw
Vol. 2: 561

Pin-Jung Chen, Ting-Hsuan Hsu, Chun-Wei Chang, Jia-Hong Xie, Yu-Jie Hong
Department of Visual Communication Design,
China University of Technology
www.cute.edu.tw
Vol. 2: 487

Shih Yun Chen, Jia Min Wang, Li Rong Wang, Ming Xian Wu
Shin Min High School
www.shinmin.tc.edu.tw
Vol. 2: 447

Yen-Chi Chen, Shu-Ching Chiu, Wan-Ying Lin, Zih-Syuan Wang, Man-Ling Zhang
Chihlee University of Technology
www.chihlee.edu.tw
Vol. 2: 459

Yu Chen, Yi-Chiao Lee, Yu-Xuan Huang
Chaoyang University of Technology
www.cyut.edu.tw
Vol. 2: 464

Aqi Chen Studio
www.agichen.com
Vol. 2: 410-411, 580

Man-Qi Chiang, Wen-Chien Wu, Tzu-Yun Lai, Yu-Ting Huang, Jia-Yi Lin, Wan-Yu Chang
Ling Tung University
www.ltu.edu.tw
Vol. 2: 467

Shu-Yi Chiang, Xin-Yi Lee, Ching-Yu Chao
Fu Jen Catholic University
www.aart.fju.edu.tw
Vol. 2: 452-453

Hsiao-Chi Chien, Wei-Hsuan Chen
Department of Commercial Design and Management, National Taipei University of Business
www.ntub.edu.tw
Vol. 2: 475

Chill Co., Ltd.
www.facebook.com/chillchillcoltd
Vol. 2: 412

chilli mind Design Team
www.chilli-mind.com
Vol. 2: 189, 191, 233

Sujung Choi, Yulim Lee, Hyeontae Kim, Jaeheon Lee
Dongseo University
www.dongseo.ac.kr
Vol. 2: 553

Yu Te Chou (ODd)
www.oddchou.wordpress.com
Vol. 2: 137

CJ Powercast
www.cjpowercast.com
Vol. 2: 409

CLEVER°FRANKE
www.cleverfranke.com
Vol. 2: 188, 234, 274
Vol. 1: 94-95, 162, 629

Clim Studio
www.studioclim.com
Vol. 2: 168

COBE GmbH
www.cobeisfresh.com
Vol. 2: 208-209, 581

Cogitoimage International Co., Ltd.
www.cogitoimage.com
Vol. 2: 383

Cognite AS
www.cognite.com
Vol. 2: 262

Colijn IT
www.colijn-it.nl
Vol. 2: 194

Contrast Foundry
www.contrastfoundry.com
Vol. 2: 109

CREVV
www.crevv.com
Vol. 2: 75
Vol. 1: 113, 142, 172-173, 467

Custom Interactions GmbH
www.custom-interactions.com
Vol. 2: 276-277, 582

D
Daehong Communications
www.daehong.com
Vol. 2: 30-31

Daewon Plus Group
www.daewonplus.co.kr
Vol. 2: 388
Vol. 1: 514

Daishin Securities
Daishin Financial Group
www.daishin.com
Vol. 2: 232

Allison Davis
SCAD Savannah College of Art and Design
www.scad.edu
Vol. 2: 407

denkwerk
www.denkwerk.com
Vol. 2: 285

Dental Wings GmbH
www.codiagnostix.com
Vol. 2: 249

Dentsu Inc.
www.dentsu.com
Vol. 2: 235, 583
Vol. 1: 294-295, 302, 324-325, 630, 631

Design In Situ
www.design-insitu.com
Vol. 2: 197, 584

Designfever
www.designfever.com
Vol. 2: 397

Kai Dickson
SCAD Savannah College of Art and Design
www.scad.edu
Vol. 2: 526

Ding Yong
Culture Creativity Co., Ltd.
Vol. 2: 414-415, 585

does interactive
www.does.kr
Vol. 2: 376-377

Shanghai Dongxiang
Culture Communication Co., Ltd.
www.bangqian.net
Vol. 2: 81

Duncan McCauley
www.duncanmccauley.com
Vol. 2: 356

DXS
Vol. 2: 392

E
E.ON Solutions GmbH
www.eon.com
Vol. 2: 283

Easywith
www.easywith.com
Vol. 2: 416-417

Echo Asia Communications
www.echoasiacomm.com
Vol. 2: 389

EF Hello
www.efhello.com
Vol. 2: 210

Eidetic Korea
www.eideticmarketing.com
Vol. 2: 67

Elastique. GmbH
www.elastique.de
Vol. 2: 160, 161

EMOTIONplanning
www.emotionplanning.com
Vol. 2: 388
Vol. 1: 514

Enhancers S.p.A.
www.enhancers.it
Vol. 2: 222-223

Ergosign GmbH
www.ergosign.de
Vol. 2: 261, 332

F
F209 GmbH
www.f209.de
Vol. 2: 268-269

Jiayun Fan
SCAD Savannah College of Art and Design
www.scad.edu
Vol. 2: 506

Tzu-Hsuan Fan
Asia University
www.asia.edu.tw
Vol. 2: 495

Anna Farkas
Anagraphic
www.anagraphic.hu
Vol. 2: 6-7, 586

Index Designers

Feedmee
www.feedmee.de
Vol. 2: 144

James Findlater
Vol. 2: 539

Bettina Fink
www.bettinafink.com
Vol. 2: 441

Shenzhen Fire Wolf
Graphic Design Co., Ltd.
www.fw119.com
Vol. 2: 422
Vol. 1: 409

florianmatthias
www.florianmatthias.com
Vol. 2: 211

Emma Fowler, Mara Healy,
Hadyn Hawkins, Lydia Goshen,
Darren Wells
SCAD Savannah College of
Art and Design
www.scad.edu
Vol. 2: 543

Freshhcads
www.freshheads.com
Vol. 2: 174–175, 587

Fu Jen Catholic University
www.aart.fju.edu.tw
Vol. 2: 110, 597

FUJIFILM Corporation
Design Center
http://design.fujifilm.com
Vol. 2: 216, 322, 323
Vol. 1: 469

FunDesign.tv
www.fundesign.tv
Vol. 2: 346–347, 588

fuse*
www.fuseworks.it
Vol. 2: 371

Fuum Studio
www.fuumstudio.com
Vol. 2: 165

G

Ke Gao
SCAD Savannah College of
Art and Design
www.scad.edu
Vol. 2: 502, 503

Ying Gao
Zhejiang Gongshang University
www.zjgsu.edu.cn
Vol. 2: 105

Katsy Garcia
SCAD Savannah College of
Art and Design
www.scad.edu
Vol. 2: 538

GBO
www.gbo.kr
Vol. 2: 370

GE Healthcare
www.gehealthcare.com
www.edisondesignsystem.com
Vol. 2: 246

Genese Werbeagentur GmbH
www.genese-md.de
Vol. 2: 19
Vol. 1: 310, 312

Shenzhen Geomdesign
Culture Co., Ltd.
www.geomdesign.com
Vol. 2: 425

Ger Ger
www.gerger.com
Vol. 2: 42

Luke Gibson
SCAD Savannah College of
Art and Design
www.scad.edu
Vol. 2: 541

Gooest Media
Technology Daqing Co., Ltd.
www.gooest.net
Vol. 2: 373, 589

grafikatelier Engelke & Neubauer
www.grafikatelier.de
Vol. 2: 14

Grand Quest
www.grandquest.de
Vol. 2: 43

Graphasel Design Studio
www.graphasel.com
Vol. 2: 402–403, 590

Grass Jelly Studio
www.grassjelly.tv
Vol. 2: 170, 171

Great Apes / HiQ Finland
www.greatapes.fi
Vol. 2: 327, 380

Grey Germany / KW43
BRANDDESIGN
www.grey.com
Vol. 2: 240–241, 602

Groothuis
Gesellschaft der Ideen und
Passionen mbH
www.groothuis.de
Vol. 2: 41

Guangzhou City
Construction College
www.gzccc.edu.cn
Vol. 2: 112–113, 591

H

Haier Innovation Design Center
www.haier.com
Vol. 2: 156, 157, 163, 302, 303, 304

Qingdao Hairigaoke Model Co. Ltd.
Vol. 2: 156, 157, 163, 302, 303, 304

Hahn Han
SCAD Savannah College of
Art and Design
www.scad.edu
Vol. 2: 528

Hand Heart Design Firm
www.handheart.com.tw
Vol. 2: 400–401, 592

HAWK University of
Applied Sciences and Art
Faculty of Design
www.hawk.de
Vol. 2: 20

Yin He, Zhang Zhibin,
Wen Mengxi, Zhang Yanfeng
869 school of design
Vol. 2: 491

HEAD – Genève
Department of Interior
Architecture
www.hesge.ch/head
Vol. 2: 372

Herburg Weiland
www.herburg-weiland.de
Vol. 2: 35

Manuel Herz Architects
www.manuelherz.com
Vol. 2: 361

HMI Project GmbH
www.hmi-project.com
Vol. 2: 258, 259

Hong Da Design Studio
www.hddw-design.com
Vol. 2: 25

Bernhard Hopfengärtner
www.berndhopfengaertner.net
Vol. 2: 328

Hsing-Ying Hsieh
Cheng Shiu University
www.csu.edu.tw
Vol. 2: 523

Ming-Chi Ken Hsieh
Ming-Chi Hsieh Art Studio
www.isart8.blogspot.com
Vol. 2: 79, 86, 593

Chia-Li Hsu, Rui-Zhen Wu,
Tan Yong Jian
Chaoyang University of
Technology
www.cyut.edu.tw
Vol. 2: 460

Chun-Hao Hsu, Ya-Zhu Hsu,
Ya-Hsin Tsai
Southern Taiwan University of
Science and Technology
https://vc.stust.edu.tw
Vol. 2: 482–483

Hsuan-Hung Hsu, Chun-Wei Tseng,
Ya-Ching Tseng, Cih-Yan Kang,
Jun-Wei Liu, Chia-Tsan Lin
Shu-Te University
www.vcd.stu.edu.tw
Vol. 2: 443, 490

Hwa-Chin Hsu, Jing-Fen Chiou
National Yunlin University of
Science and Technology
www.yuntech.edu.tw
Vol. 2: 532

Elvin Hu
www.elvin-hu.com
Vol. 2: 513, 594

Xianming Hu
Vol. 2: 56

Publishing & Print Media	Posters	Typography	Illustrations	Sound Design	Film & Animation	Online
4	64	92	116	126	138	172

Index Designers

Chi-Ping Huang, Yu-Jung Chen, Fang-Chun Lin, Yi-Han Huang, Ni-En Tsai, Chia-Yi Lin
Asia University
www.asia.edu.tw
Vol. 2: 489

Liang-Ying Huang, Yi-Xuan Sun, Yu-Jie Jhuang
Chaoyang University of Technology
www.cyut.edu.tw
Vol. 2: 432–433, 579

Yen-Ting Huang, Chun-Hao Peng, Zhi-Mei Wang, Tzu-Wei Kuo
Asia University
www.asia.edu.tw
Vol. 2: 469

Huawei Device (Shenzhen) Co., Ltd.
www.huawei.com
https://consumer.huawei.com
Vol. 2: 296, 310

Huawei Technologies Co., Ltd.
www.huawei.com
www.huaweicloud.com
Vol. 2: 242–243, 252, 260, 266, 267, 272, 275, 279, 289, 294, 295, 311, 595

Huemen
www.huemendesign.com
Vol. 2: 312, 313, 314, 315, 596

Hufax Arts
www.hufax.com.tw
Vol. 2: 110, 597

Human
Burza d.o.o.
www.humaninteraction.com
Vol. 2: 200

Human After All
www.humanafterall.studio
Vol. 2: 48

Wei-Che Hung, Yu-Jie Wu, Pei-Xuan Li, Jia-Hong Shi, Ching-Yen Shih, Yi-Shan Chen
Department of Visual Communication Design,
China University of Technology
www.cute.edu.tw
Vol. 2: 472

Hyundai Motor Company Creative Works
www.creativeworks.kr
Vol. 2: 331, 334, 396
Vol. 1: 308–309, 511

I

IBM
www.ibm.com/cloud
Vol. 2: 264, 265

Chi-Man Ieong, Hsiao-Yun Lo, You-Sin Lien
Asia University
www.asia.edu.tw
Vol. 2: 515

Erin Imhof, Isabella Gardner, Fama Ndiaye, Lekha Veeramachaneni, Josh Willey, Griffin Bliss
SCAD Savannah College of Art and Design
www.scad.edu
Vol. 2: 555

InFormat Design Curating
www.informat-design.com.tw
Vol. 2: 342–343, 598

Innocean Worldwide
www.innocean.com
Vol. 2: 145
Vol. 1: 292–293, 645

innovation.rocks consulting gmbh
www.innovation.rocks
Vol. 2: 329
Vol. 1: 135

intive GmbH
www.intive.com
Vol. 2: 219

Ippolito Fleitz Group GmbH
www.ifgroup.org
Vol. 2: 421, 423

ix3
an Aker Solutions Company
www.ix3.com
Vol. 2: 320–321

J

Vanessa Jaber, Drew Murray, Mara Healy, Samantha Wall
SCAD Savannah College of Art and Design
www.scad.edu
Vol. 2: 557

Jäger & Jäger
www.jaegerundjaeger.com
Vol. 2: 12–13, 599

Japan Mountaineering & Sport Climbing Association
www.jma-climbing.org
Vol. 2: 90–91
Vol. 1: 163

Pei-Cheng Jian, Chia-Hsuan Chang, Wei-Neng Chen, Xin-Hong Guo, Jia-Yi Wu, Jin-Jia Zhang
Ling Tung University
www.ltu.edu.tw
Vol. 2: 494

Ailun Jiang
www.jiangailun.com
Vol. 2: 508–509, 629

Ji-Rong Jiang, Hao-Jiun Yang, Shang-Yi Huang, Kai-Ping Liao
Shu-Te University
www.vcd.stu.edu.tw
Vol. 2: 477

Max Johnson
SCAD Savannah College of Art and Design
www.scad.edu
Vol. 2: 535

Joosung Design Lab
www.joosungdl.co.kr
Vol. 2: 362, 378

K

Keko GmbH
www.keko.de
Vol. 2: 329
Vol. 1: 135

kest werbeagentur gmbh
www.kest.net
Vol. 2: 51

Killing Mario
www.killingmario.com
Vol. 2: 28–29, 30–31, 600

Hyeonji Kim, Soojung Ha, Ryungyeong Kim, Sooyeon Lee
Dongseo University
www.dongseo.ac.kr
Vol. 2: 545

Nahyun Kim, Nayeong Kim, Wooseong Kim, Seongheon Song
Dongseo University
www.dongseo.ac.kr
Vol. 2: 546

Sewoong Kim, Soonjai Hong, Jaeseong Choi
Dongyang Mirae University
www.dongyang.ac.kr
Vol. 2: 516–517

Yun Kim, Jonathan Sanchez, Savannah Wilkinson, Yeji Han, Dahyun Lee
SCAD Savannah College of Art and Design
www.scad.edu
Vol. 2: 548

Klangerfinder
www.klangerfinder.de
Vol. 2: 130–131

Klim Type Foundry
www.klim.co.nz
Vol. 2: 94–95, 96–97, 184–185, 601

Knock-Knock Animation
www.artstation.com/kka
Vol. 2: 169

Vanessa Koh
LASALLE College of the Arts
www.lasalle.edu.sg
Vol. 2: 476

Xiangguo Kong
Vol. 2: 114–115

Kopfkunst
Agentur für Kommunikation GmbH
www.kopfkunst.net
Vol. 2: 164
Vol. 1: 303

krafthaus
das Atelier von facts and fiction
www.factsfiction.de
Vol. 2: 363

Julia Krenn
www.juliakrenn.com
Vol. 2: 484

Kuhl|Frenzel GmbH & Co. KG
www.kuhlfrenzel.de
Vol. 2: 398

Kuudes
www.kuudes.com
Vol. 2: 21, 23

KW43 BRANDDESIGN
www.kw43.de
Vol. 2: 240–241, 602

KYOTO Design Lab
Kyoto Institute of Technology
www.d-lab.kit.ac.jp
Vol. 2: 361

L

La Loupe GmbH
Benjamin & Julia Skardarasy
www.laloupe.com
Vol. 2: 15

Chih-Chun Lai
The Graduate Institute of Design Science, Tatung University
www.ttu.edu.tw
Vol. 2: 79, 86

Index Designers

Xuan-Wen Lai, Wan-Yu Chung,
Li-Ju Chen
Ming Chi University of Technology
www.mcut.edu.tw
www.instagram.com/belles_td
Vol. 2: 446

Le Chantier Space Design Ltd.
Vol. 2: 357

Chanyang Lee, Dahyeon Kang,
Jeonghoon Park, Doheon Kim
Dongseo University
www.dongseo.ac.kr
Vol. 2: 544

Hsin-Hua Lee, Wei-Ling Kuo,
Tzu-Ting Chang, Yu-Wei Chen,
Jia-Ying Chi
Southern Taiwan University of
Science and Technology
https://vc.stust.edu.tw
Vol. 2: 562–563

Seungpil Lee, Esther Holliday,
Wonil Choi
SCAD Savannah College of
Art and Design
www.scad.edu
Vol. 2: 552

Ya-Wen Paulina Lee
Ming-Chi Hsieh Art Studio
www.isart8.blogspot.com
Vol. 2: 86

Kai-Xiang Lei, Shyao Hong,
Ping-Chih Lai, Cheng-Ping Shih,
Ya-Min Cheng
Department of Visual
Communication Design,
China University of Technology
www.cute.edu.tw
Vol. 2: 505

LG Electronics Inc.
www.lg.com
Vol. 2: 103

LG Uplus
www.uplus.co.kr
Vol. 2: 220–221, 603

Chaosheng Li
Zhejiang Gongshang University
www.zjgsu.edu.cn
Vol. 2: 105

Fei Li, Handan Zhang,
Tianyue Zhao, Hungchang Yu
National Yunlin University of
Science and Technology
www.yuntech.edu.tw
Vol. 2: 470

Fojun Li
Guangzhou City
Construction College
www.gzccc.edu.cn
Vol. 2: 112–113, 591

Li Hu, Ma Youyuan, Sun Yuting,
Ma Xueting, Wei Zixuan
869 school of design
Vol. 2: 520–521

Jiatong Li
SCAD Savannah College of
Art and Design
www.scad.edu
Vol. 2: 440

Qi-Wen Li, Qing-Ying Zhou
Shanghai Publishing and
Printing College
www.sppc.edu.cn
Vol. 2: 430–431, 620

Chieh-Hsi Liao, Wei-Ling Hou,
Chien Chieh, Hui-Chi Tien
Department of Visual
Communication Design,
China University of Technology
www.cute.edu.tw
Vol. 2: 488

Liao Shucheng, Lin Xingmin,
Li Shangtan
Hangzhou College of Commerce,
Zhejiang Gongshang University
www.zjgsu.edu.cn
Vol. 2: 492

Jessie Lin
SCAD Savannah College of
Art and Design
www.scad.edu
Vol. 2: 500

Kim Lin
www.chiaochinglin.com
Vol. 2: 539, 604

Po-Ching Lin, Yu-Wen Kao,
Meng-Jie Chen, Wan-Juan Wu,
Yu-Xiang Wang, Yu-Chi Li
Department of Visual
Communication Design,
China University of Technology
www.cute.edu.tw
Vol. 2: 485

Tzu-Yu Lin, Shun-Wen Hsiao,
Jin-An Li, Jing-Wen Huang
Ming Chi University of Technology
www.mcut.edu.tw
www.facebook.com/
TaiwaneseFestival
Vol. 2: 486, 522

Wei-Ching Lin
Vol. 2: 125, 573

Yi-Shan Lin
National Yunlin University of
Science and Technology
www.yuntech.edu.tw
Vol. 2: 498

Yi-Tieh Lin, Yu-Ting Chen,
Yu-Chieh Lin, Gao-Ling Hsu,
I-Hsuan Tiao
Shu-Te University
www.vcd.stu.edu.tw
Vol. 2: 471

Littlevoice
www.littlevoice.io
Vol. 2: 293, 605

Logitech
www.logitech.com
Vol. 2: 146, 147

Logitech Creative Team America
www.logitech.com
Vol. 2: 153

Logitech Creative Team Europe
www.logitech.com
Vol. 2: 168

Loocreative
www.loocreative.com
Vol. 2: 154–155

loved GmbH
www.loved.de
Vol. 2: 40, 49, 76, 121, 133, 159,
404
Vol. 1: 137, 300, 301, 313, 314, 315

Shao Yu Lu, Ya Shen Lee,
Kuan Lin Chiu
Chaoyang University of
Technology
www.cyut.edu.tw
Vol. 2: 536–537

Wen-Hsin Lu, Pei-Yu Chou,
Yi-June Zhuo, Wei-Chi Ding,
Mung-Lin Li, Chih-En Li
Southern Taiwan University of
Science and Technology
https://vc.stust.edu.tw
Vol. 2: 531

Yong-Yu Lu, Yi-Ting Kao,
Ru-Pei Liou, Chun-Teng Wang,
Chiao-Fei Han, Yuan-Xuan Ou
Ling Tung University
www.ltu.edu.tw
Vol. 2: 474

Chang-Yu Lung, Chieh-An Chung,
Zi-Shan Zhang
Ming Chi University of Technology
www.mcut.edu.tw
Vol. 2: 542
Vol. 1: 607, 611, 613

Lunit Inc.
www.lunit.io
Vol. 2: 253

Luxlotusliner
www.luxlotusliner.de
Vol. 2: 140–141

M

Michael MacWilliams
SCAD Savannah College of
Art and Design
www.scad.edu
Vol. 2: 556

MAN Truck & Bus SE
www.man.eu
Vol. 2: 335

ManvsMachine
www.mvsm.com
Vol. 2: 147

mattweis
www.mattweis.de
Vol. 2: 143
Vol. 1: 270–271

McKinsey Design
www.lunar.com
www.mckinseydesign.com
Vol. 2: 48, 331

Mengdom Design Lab
www.mengchih.com
Vol. 2: 77
Vol. 1: 212

mensemedia
Gesellschaft für Neue Medien mbH
www.mensemedia.net
Vol. 2: 192, 193

Publishing & Print Media	Posters	Typography	Illustrations	Sound Design	Film & Animation	Online
4	64	92	116	126	138	172

Index Designers

Merry Go Round Inc.
www.mgrstudio.net
Vol. 2: 152, 606

MET Studio
www.metstudiodesign.com
Vol. 2: 344-345, 607

Wuhu Midea
Kitchen & Bath Appliances
Manufacturing
www.midea.com
Vol. 2: 305

Guangdong Midea
Kitchen Appliances
Manufacturing Co., Ltd.
www.midea.com
Vol. 2: 306-307

Midroom Design Co., Ltd.
www.midroomlab.com
Vol. 2: 354-355

mind the gap! design
Karl-Heinz Best
www.mindthegap-design.com
Vol. 2: 22, 368

MIR MEDIA
Digital Agentur
www.mir.de
Vol. 2: 316, 317, 318, 608

MIUI Design Team
Beijing Xiaomi
Mobile Software Co., Ltd.
www.miui.com
Vol. 2: 214-215, 634

MKTG Finland
www.mktg.fi
Vol. 2: 327, 380

Monotype
www.monotype.com
Vol. 2: 98-99, 609

monsun media GmbH
www.monsun-media.com
Vol. 2: 59, 63, 610

Moscow High School 548
Tsaritsyno
www.mhs548.ru
Vol. 2: 122, 166, 176-177, 238-239, 611

Sarah Müller
www.muellersarah.de
Vol. 2: 46

Verena Müller
www.behance.net/Verenamue2de3
Vol. 2: 444

Büro Müller-Rieger GmbH
www.buero-mueller-rieger.de
Vol. 2: 398

MUTABOR Brand Experience GmbH
www.mutabor.de
Vol. 2: 391
Vol. 1: 510

N

NAVER Corp.
www.navercorp.com
Vol. 2: 218, 308-309

Netizen Productions Co., Ltd.
www.facebook.com/netizen.productions
Vol. 2: 414-415

Netrix Digital
www.netrixdigital.com
Vol. 2: 199

Netural GmbH
www.netural.com
Vol. 2: 224

newtype imageworks
https://newtype.design
Vol. 2: 319

NiEW Design
www.niew.it
Vol. 2: 271

NIO Co., Ltd.
www.nio.com
Vol. 2: 333

Harin Noh, Daekyum Kang,
Minsoo Kim, Hyeongmun Choi
Dongseo University
www.dongseo.as.kr
Vol. 2: 554

Noiseless Design
www.noiseless-design.com
Vol. 2: 324
Vol. 1: 536, 653

N O R M A L S
www.normalfutu.re
Vol. 2: 328

NOROO Holdings Co., Ltd.
www.norooholdings.com
Vol. 2: 352

Calyssa Nowviskie, Jena Martin,
Andrew Bretnall
SCAD Savannah College of
Art and Design
www.scad.edu
Vol. 2: 549

O

O Studio Architects
www.ostudioarchitects.com
Vol. 2: 389

OFF OFFICE
www.offoffice.eu
Vol. 2: 24, 384-385

István Orosz
www.utisz.blogspot.com
Vol. 2: 80

Sophie Ortmeier
www.sophieortmeier.com
Vol. 2: 442

Shenzhen ORVIBO
Technology Co., Ltd.
www.orvibo.com
Vol. 2: 298, 612

P

P.medien GmbH
www.pmedien.com
Vol. 2: 398

P7S1 Experience Design
www.prosiebensat1.com
Vol. 2: 208-209

Paul Pacher
www.paulpacher.com
Vol. 2: 462

Gabor Palotai Design AB
www.gaborpalotai.com
Vol. 2: 88

PANCOMMUNICATION KOREA
www.pancomgroup.com
Vol. 2: 393

Chen-Hao Pang, Kan-Fu Lee,
Hui-Ting Chan, Chia-Yu Lin
Chihlee University of Technology
www.chihlee.edu.tw
Vol. 2: 445

PARADISE GROUP
Brand & Design Dept.
www.paradise.co.kr
Vol. 2: 28-29

Paratype Ltd.
www.paratype.ru
Vol. 2: 100, 101

peetz & le peetz design
Sebastian Peetz
www.peetz.de
Vol. 2: 16-17, 613

PEN.Inc.
www.pen-design.jp
Vol. 2: 90-91
Vol. 1: 163

Pergamen s.r.o.
www.pergamen.sk
Vol. 2: 38

Philips Experience Design team
www.philips.com
Vol. 2: 247, 250, 251, 256-257
Vol. 1: 473, 507

Phygitalism Studio
www.phygitalism.com
Vol. 2: 122, 166, 176-177, 238-239, 616

Pinion Digital GmbH
www.fromatob.com
Vol. 2: 204, 213, 614

Pixelis
www.pixelis.com
Vol. 2: 420
Vol. 1: 230

Pixonal
www.pixonal.com
Vol. 2: 188, 234, 274

Plain Design Co., Ltd.
www.plaindesign.com.tw
Vol. 2: 354-355

PlusX
www.plus-ex.com
Vol. 2: 198
Vol. 1: 133, 143

Polestar
www.polestar.com
Vol. 2: 33
Vol. 1: 206-207, 661

PRID International Design
www.prid-design.cn
Vol. 2: 360

Index Designers

Q

Rui-Ling Qiu, Re-Chi Zhao,
Yi-Hsuan Tsai, Qing-Ru Zhan,
Abigail See
Ling Tung University
www.ltu.edu.tw
Vol. 2: 496

R

Rahbaran Hürzeler Architects
www.rharchitekten.ch
Vol. 2: 361

Ibán Ramón
Design Studio
www.ibanramon.com
Vol. 2: 66
Vol. 1: 195

Rath & Winkler
www.rath-winkler.at
Vol. 2: 211

res d
Design und Architektur GmbH
www.resd.de
Vol. 2: 359, 363

Benjamin Ressi
www.benjaminressi.com
Vol. 2: 463, 615

RT
www.rt.com
https://romanovs100.com
Vol. 2: 122, 166, 176–177, 238–239, 616

Maria Ruiz, Eli Clein, Seungpil Lee,
Connelly Morris, Esther Holliday
SCAD Savannah College of
Art and Design
www.scad.edu
Vol. 2: 550

S

S.F. Express (Hong Kong) Limited
www.sf-express.com
Vol. 2: 284, 286, 287

S12
www.s12.de
Vol. 2: 130–131

Samsung Research America
www.sra.samsung.com
Vol. 2: 186–187

Samsung SDS
www.samsungsds.com
Vol. 2: 263, 617

Shenzhen Sandulixian Design Ltd.
Vol. 2: 70, 83, 89

Dana SanMar
SCAD Savannah College of
Art and Design
www.scad.edu
Vol. 2: 510, 511

SAP SE – The Tools Team
www.sap.com
Vol. 2: 290–291, 618

Sberbank
www.sberbank.ru
Vol. 2: 226–227

SenseTeam
www.senseteam.org
Vol. 2: 18
Vol. 1: 194

Serviceplan Group
www.serviceplan.com
Vol. 2: 47

Shenzhen Institute of Beidou
Applied Technology Co., Ltd.
www.sibat.cn
Vol. 2: 273

Hoyeon Shin, Hyeyeon Kim,
Haeyeong Song, Hyuntae Ryu
Dongseo University
www.dongseo.ac.kr
Vol. 2: 551

Siemens AG / Siemens Ltd.
Digital Enterprise Lab (DE-L),
Process Automation,
Digital Industry
www.siemens.com.cn
Vol. 2: 190

Signify Design team
www.signify.com
Vol. 2: 225

Andrea Siles-Loayza
SCAD Savannah College of
Art and Design
www.scad.edu
Vol. 2: 512

Simon Electric (China) Co., Ltd.
www.simon.com.cn
Vol. 2: 301

Sisters of Design
Anja Krämer und
Claudia Dölling GbR
www.sistersofdesign.de
Vol. 2: 348–349, 621

Sixtyseven Pictures GmbH
www.sixtyseven-pictures.com
Vol. 2: 158

Smig Creative
www.smigcreative.com
Vol. 2: 424

Sniffing out the Differences
www.sniffingoutthedifferences.com
Vol. 2: 374–375, 622

SOAP Design Studio
www.s-oap.com
Vol. 2: 386–387

Suzhou SoFeng
Culture Media Co., Ltd.
www.sofengdesign.com
Vol. 2: 71

Solomon Technology Corporation
www.solomon-3d.com
Vol. 2: 438–439, 623

Sony Design
www.sony.net/design
Vol. 2: 382

Abby Spencer
SCAD Savannah College of
Art and Design
www.scad.edu
Vol. 2: 533

Spiilka Design Büro
www.spiilka.com
Vol. 2: 288

SPIN
www.spin.co.uk
Vol. 2: 32

Springload
www.springload.co.nz
Vol. 2: 96–97, 184–185, 624

George Stack
SCAD Savannah College of
Art and Design
www.scad.edu
Vol. 2: 434–435, 619

Stockholm Design Lab
www.sdl.se
Vol. 2: 33
Vol. 1: 206–207, 661

Strömlin
www.stromlin.dk
Vol. 2: 178–179

Studio für Gestaltung
www.studio.cologne
Vol. 2: 405

Studio Sonda
www.sonda.hr
Vol. 2: 39
Vol. 1: 395

Suh Architects
www.suharchitects.com
Vol. 2: 392, 393
Vol. 1: 535, 669

Wun-Huei Sun, Chiao-Hsuan Yang,
Fang-Yi Lin, Shin-Yu Hsu
Ling Tung University
www.ltu.edu.tw
Vol. 2: 451

Yi-Xuan Sun, Liang-Ying Huang,
Yu-Jie Jhuang
Chaoyang University of
Technology
www.cyut.edu.tw
Vol. 2: 432–433, 579

Yifan Sun
SCAD Savannah College of
Art and Design
www.scad.edu
Vol. 2: 540

Sunny at Sea
www.sunnyatsea.se
Vol. 2: 338–339, 625

Supercharge
www.supercharge.io
Vol. 2: 255, 626

Superunion
www.superunion.com
Vol. 2: 134–135

Supportarchitekten
Meike Schermelleh
www.supportarchitekten.de
Vol. 2: 368

Publishing & Print Media	Posters	Typography	Illustrations	Sound Design	Film & Animation	Online
4	64	92	116	126	138	172

Index Designers

T

T9 Brand
www.t9brand.com
Vol. 2: 69

TAMSCHICK MEDIA+SPACE GmbH
www.tamschick.com
Vol. 2: 340–341, 627

Shao-Wei Tang, Guo-Yi Lee,
Ming-Huan Chen
Department of Visual
Communication Design,
China University of Technology
www.cute.edu.tw
Vol. 2: 450

Tape That Collective
www.tapethatcollective.com
Vol. 2: 346–347, 588

TASS Russian News Agency
www.tass.ru
Vol. 2: 123, 326

The Techno Creatives
www.technocreatives.com
Vol. 2: 162, 254, 278

Aljoscha Theil, Jonas Mai,
Julian Ruthemeyer,
Maximilian Berndt, Perihan Isik,
Sebastian Winter, Tom Janssens
University of Applied Sciences
Osnabrück
www.hs-osnabrueck.de
Vol. 2: 560

Thinc Design
www.thincdesign.com
Vol. 2: 366–367

Timothy Motion
www.timothymotion.com
Vol. 2: 151

TOFU Studio
www.tofu.pl
Vol. 2: 60

ToThree Design
www.tothree.cn
Vol. 2: 61

Transform Design
www.transform.tw
Vol. 2: 57

Denis Tsoy
Shanghai Jiao Tong University
www.sjtu.edu.cn
Vol. 2: 559

TTMM Sp. z o.o.
www.ttmm.is
Vol. 2: 231

Hsiang-En Tung, Qi-Han Zhong,
Yu-Ting Wang, Yen-Lei Ho,
Cheng-Shao Tsai
Department of Visual
Communication Design,
China University of Technology
www.cute.edu.tw
Vol. 2: 461

Yi-Ting Tung, Hsin-Man Chiang,
Pei-Hua Su, Xin-Ya Huang,
Shi-Wen Zhang
Department of Visual
Communication Design,
China University of Technology
www.cute.edu.tw
Vol. 2: 449

Jing-Wen Tzeng, Yi-Jun Chen,
Yi-Hsien Sun, Chia-Chi Chen,
Jing-Zi Huang, Chu-Wei Chang,
Yu-Chen Cheng, Bo-Jia Ciou
Department of Visual
Communication Design,
China University of Technology
www.cute.edu.tw
Vol. 2: 466

U

UNFOLD Design & Motion Studio
www.unfold-design.de
Vol. 2: 142

UNITE Design
www.ud47.com.tw
Vol. 2: 84–85

University of Applied Sciences
Osnabrück
www.hs-osnabrueck.de
Vol. 2: 282

Up Strategy Lab
www.upstrategylab.com
Vol. 2: 292

User Interface Design GmbH
www.uid.com
Vol. 2: 270

V

Panos Vassiliou
www.parachutefonts.com
Vol. 2: 111

VAVE
www.vavestudio.com
Vol. 2: 379

W

Prof. Dirk Wachowiak
www.dirkwachowiak.de
Vol. 2: 52–53

waf.berlin GmbH
www.waf.berlin
Vol. 2: 50
Vol. 1: 276

Tzu-Han Wang, An-Ching Lin,
Xin-Ping He
Department of Visual
Communication Design,
China University of Technology
www.cute.edu.tw
Vol. 2: 458

Wang Yang Chieh, Fang I Wen,
Yu Lun Cheng, Chen Syuan Jian
Department of Visual
Communication Design,
China University of Technology
www.cute.edu.tw
Vol. 2: 525

Yi-Jie Wang, Zhi-Lin Zeng,
Fang-Yu Syu, Ya-Lin Hung,
Cheng-Ta Hsiao
Chaoyang University of
Technology
www.cyut.edu.tw
Vol. 2: 478

Zi Xuan Wang, Hsi Yu Tseng,
Jia Ru Chen, Yen Ying Chen
Taoyuan Municipal Shou Shan
Senior High School
www.sssh.tyc.edu.tw
Vol. 2: 514

We Are Social
www.wearesocial.cn
Vol. 2: 201, 628

Eika Johanna Weber, Matt Moore,
Emily Ip
SCAD Savannah College of
Art and Design
www.scad.edu
Vol. 2: 547

Siao Jhen Wei, Jia Qi Xie,
Yun Chen Hsu
Asia University
www.asia.edu.tw
Vol. 2: 455

Hui-Ju Wen, Yi-Fang Tu,
Fang-Yu Liu, Syun Ciou,
Wan-Ling Hsieh
Ling Tung University
www.ltu.edu.tw
Vol. 2: 479

WESOUND GmbH
www.wesound.de
Vol. 2: 136

where studio
www.facebook.com/wherrrrrrre
Vol. 2: 62

White City Project Foundation
www.facebook.com/
WhiteCityProject
Vol. 2: 8–9, 630

why do birds
www.whydobirds.de
Vol. 2: 128–129, 134–135, 631

wir sind artisten
www.wirsindartisten.com
Vol. 2: 26–27, 632

Kiana Woodson
SCAD Savannah College of
Art and Design
www.scad.edu
Vol. 2: 527

Chia-Lin Wu, Po-Tan Chen,
Jia-Hong Lin, Chia-Hui Kuo,
Jia-Yi Clou, Wing-Sze Cheung
Shu-Te University
www.vcd.stu.edu.tw
Vol. 2: 456

Jia-Qi Wu, Mei-Ting Huang,
Siou-Yuan Lin, Yun-Dian Guo,
Tsai-Wei Chen, Ya-Ting Hsu
Shu-Te University
www.vcd.stu.edu.tw
Vol. 2: 468, 519

Yu-Fang Wu, Yu-Rou Chen,
Pin-Wen Chen, Chieh-Chia Lai,
Xuan-Yu Lai, Hsiao-Chien Lee
Department of Visual
Communication Design,
China University of Technology
www.cute.edu.tw
Vol. 2: 518

Simon Wünscher
www.simonwuenscher.at
Vol. 2: 558

Index Designers

X

Xiaomi Inc.
www.mi.com
Vol. 2: 297, 633
Vol. 1: 458, 460, 461, 462, 463, 486

Beijing Xiaomi
Mobile Software Co., Ltd.
www.mi.com
Vol. 2: 214–215, 217, 634, 635

Y

Y1 Digital AG
www.y1.de
Vol. 2: 195

You-Ting Yan, Yen-Yun Kung,
Jin-Ming Jiang, Chuan-Yi Hung,
Cai-Feng Huang, Ya-Shan Xie
Shu-Te University
www.vcd.stu.edu.tw
Vol. 2: 480

Chia Chin Yang, Chiao Yu Tsai,
Yu Ling Ye, Yu Chieh Li,
Po Hsun Chen, Yu Fu Zeng,
Shao Chi Ruan
Department of Visual
Communication Design,
China University of Technology
www.cute.edu.tw
Vol. 2: 524

Kexin Yang
Vol. 2: 539

Yellow Octopus Pte. Ltd.
www.yellowoctopus.com.sg
Vol. 2: 36–37

YI.ng Lighting Design Consultants
www.yinglighting.wixsite.com/yldc
Vol. 2: 350–351, 636

Shenzhen Yimu
Technology Co., Ltd.
www.yimu.info
Vol. 2: 280, 637

Hangzhou Yizhijia
Network Technology Co., Ltd.
www.enjoybuy.vip
Vol. 2: 167

Wun-Min Yuan, Yu-Zhen Lee,
Jia-Cheng Wu, Xin-Ying Zeng,
Ko-Hsin Yu, Ciang-Yu Cai
Shu-Te University
www.vcd.stu.edu.tw
Vol. 2: 457, 504

YUJ Designs Pvt. Ltd.
www.yujdesigns.com
Vol. 2: 330, 638

Z

Zeichen & Wunder
www.zeichenundwunder.de
Vol. 2: 180–181, 639

zeit:raum Gruppe
www.zeitraum.com
Vol. 2: 325, 640

Gregor Zemljič
www.gregor-zemljic.com
Vol. 2: 132

Ya-Zhu Zhang, Ying-Syuan Huang,
Fan-Chen Su, Hui-Tong Wu,
Pei-Syuan Li, Pei-Ting Tsai
Southern Taiwan University of
Science and Technology
https://vc.stust.edu.tw
Vol. 2: 529

Yujia Zhang
SCAD Savannah College of
Art and Design
www.scad.edu
Vol. 2: 507

Zhejiang Gongshang University
www.zjgsu.edu.cn
Vol. 2: 102, 641
Vol. 1: 167, 211, 412

Bangqian Zheng
www.bangqian.net
Vol. 2: 68

Zhengbang Creative Beijing
Branding & Technology Co., Ltd.
www.zhengbang.com.cn
Vol. 2: 120, 408

Hong-Yuan Zhou, Chen-Chen
Chang, Yan-Zhen Li
Shu-Te University
www.vcd.stu.edu.tw
Vol. 2: 465, 499

Qing-Ying Zhou, Qi-Wen Li
Shanghai Publishing and
Printing College
www.sppc.edu.cn
Vol. 2: 430–431, 620

Biwei Zhu
Wilbur Design Studio
https://zhubiwei.zcool.com.cn
Vol. 2: 124

Nicole Zimmermann
www.nicolezimmermann.com
Vol. 2: 230

Zuni Icosahedron
www.zuni.org.hk
Vol. 2: 364–365

Publishing & Print Media	Posters	Typography	Illustrations	Sound Design	Film & Animation	Online
4	64	92	116	126	138	172

Index Clients/Universities

0–9

1zu33 Architectural Brand Identity
www.1zu33.com
Vol. 2: 24, 384–385

3M
www.3m.com
Vol. 2: 545, 554

618 Shanghai Street
Urban Renewal Authority
https://618.ura-vb.org.hk
Vol. 2: 324

869 school of design
Vol. 2: 491, 520–521

A

A1 Telekom Austria
www.bob.at
Vol. 2: 230

ABB
www.abb.com
Vol. 2: 406–407

Acer Inc.
www.acer.com
Vol. 2: 201
Vol. 1: 459

adabay GmbH
www.adabay.rocks
Vol. 2: 418–419

adidas AG
www.adidas.de
Vol. 2: 219

Akbank T.A.S.
www.akbank.com
Vol. 2: 228

Akrapovič d.d.
www.akrapovic.com
Vol. 2: 132, 158

alamak!project
www.alamakproject.com
Vol. 2: 137

ALIBABA GROUP
www.alibabagroup.com
Vol. 2: 102

Alva Hotel by Royal
www.alva.com.hk
Vol. 2: 389

Amorepacific
www.apgroup.com
Vol. 2: 182–183, 196
Vol. 1: 119

ampersand.studio
www.ampersand.studio
Vol. 2: 45

John Angerson
www.johnangerson.com
Vol. 2: 10–11

ANO "Directorate Krasnoyarsk 2019"
www.krsk2019.com
Vol. 2: 394–395

ANSSil
www.anssil.com
Vol. 2: 154–155

Anxin Weiguang (Shanghai)
Timber Company
www.anxinfloors.com
Vol. 2: 360

Appedu Design Institute
www.appedu.com.tw
Vol. 2: 106, 107, 125

ARD Design und Präsentation
www.ard-design.de
Vol. 2: 140–141

Arphic Technology Co., Ltd.
www.arphic.com.tw
Vol. 2: 25

Artsway Media (Shanghai) Co., Ltd.
www.artsway.com.cn
Vol. 2: 68

Asia Culture Center
Asia Culture Institute
www.aci-k.kr
Vol. 2: 362

Asia University
www.asia.edu.tw
Vol. 2: 455, 469, 489, 495, 515, 534
Vol. 1: 571, 585, 586, 589, 597, 600, 606

Associació València Capital del Disseny
www.designvalencia.eu
Vol. 2: 66
Vol. 1: 195

ASUS
www.asus.com
Vol. 2: 148, 149, 150, 151

AUDI AG
www.audi.com
Vol. 2: 49
Vol. 1: 300

AURORA School for Artists / INKA Research Group
HTW Berlin –
University of Applied Sciences
https://inka.htw-berlin.de
Vol. 2: 46

Axel Springer SE
www.axelspringer.com
Vol. 2: 134–135

B

Badisches Landesmuseum
www.landesmuseum.de
Vol. 2: 359

Baidu Online Network
Technology (Beijing) Co., Ltd.
www.baidu.com
Vol. 2: 281
Vol. 1: 38–39

Bavaria Film GmbH
www.bavaria-film.de
Vol. 2: 143

Bayerischer Rundfunk
BR Fernsehen
www.br.de
Vol. 2: 144

BDC – Bonanni Del Rio Catalog
www.bonannidelriocatalog.com
Vol. 2: 371

Bechtle AG
www.bechtle.com
Vol. 2: 50
Vol. 1: 276

Beethoven Jubiläums GmbH
www.bthvn2020.de
Vol. 2: 398

Beijing Forestry University
www.bjfu.edu.cn
Vol. 2: 56

Belkin
www.belkin.com
Vol. 2: 546

Benevento Publishing
www.beneventopublishing.com
Vol. 2: 26–27

BEOS AG
www.beos.net
Vol. 2: 405
Vol. 1: 242–243

BFK
Budapest Development Center
www.puskasarena.com
Vol. 2: 402–403

BiBoBox Studio
www.bibobox.com
Vol. 2: 428–429, 436–437

Bielefelder Philharmoniker
Bühnen und Orchester
der Stadt Bielefeld
www.bielefelder-philharmoniker.de
Vol. 2: 72, 73

Bitartean
www.bitartean.org
Vol. 2: 58

BlackYak
www.blackyak.com
Vol. 2: 551
Vol. 1: 143

BMW Group
www.bmw.de
Vol. 2: 160, 161
Vol. 1: 290–291

British Council
www.britishcouncil.org
Vol. 2: 374–375

British Museum
www.britishmuseum.org
Vol. 2: 353

Brückner Maschinenbau
GmbH & Co. KG
www.brueckner-maschinenbau.com
Vol. 2: 259

Busch-Jaeger Elektro GmbH
Mitglied der ABB-Gruppe
www.busch-jaeger.de
Vol. 2: 300
Vol. 1: 48–49

Index Clients / Universities

C

Chaoyang University of Technology
www.cyut.edu.tw
Vol. 2: 432–433, 460, 464, 473, 478, 530, 536–537
Vol. 1: 558, 566, 570, 572, 578, 593

Cheng Shiu University
www.csu.edu.tw
Vol. 2: 448, 523
Vol. 1: 573, 575, 596

Chihlee University of Technology
www.chihlee.edu.tw
Vol. 2: 445, 459, 493
Vol. 1: 594, 599

China International Travel Service
www.cits.net
Vol. 2: 120

China University of Technology
www.cute.edu.tw
Vol. 2: 449, 450, 458, 461, 466, 472, 485, 487, 488, 505, 518, 524, 525
Vol. 1: 565, 598, 601

Cognite AS
www.cognite.com
Vol. 2: 262

Colijn IT
www.colijn-it.nl
Vol. 2: 194

D

Daewon Plus Group
www.daewonplus.co.kr
Vol. 2: 388
Vol. 1: 514

Daimler Truck AG
www.daimler-truck.com
Vol. 2: 193

Daishin Securities
Daishin Financial Group
www.daishin.com
Vol. 2: 232

denkwerk
www.denkwerk.com
Vol. 2: 285

Dental Wings GmbH
www.codiagnostix.com
Vol. 2: 249

Dentsu Inc.
www.dentsu.com
Vol. 2: 235

Department of Municipalities and Transport
www.dmt.gov.ae
Vol. 2: 188, 234, 274

Deutsche Telekom AG
www.telekom.com
Vol. 2: 130–131

Deutsches Historisches Museum
www.dhm.de
Vol. 2: 358

DFF – Deutsches Filminstitut & Filmmuseum e.V.
www.dff.film
Vol. 2: 22, 368

Ding Ding Co., Ltd.
www.facebook.com/DingDingYYXL
Vol. 2: 110

discovering hands Service GmbH
www.discovering-hands.de
Vol. 2: 240–241

DMT – Gesellschaft für Lehre und Bildung mbH
www.dmt-lb.de
Vol. 2: 363

Dongseo University
www.dongseo.ac.kr
Vol. 2: 544, 545, 546, 551, 553, 554

Dongyang Mirae University
www.dongyang.ac.kr
Vol. 2: 516–517

E

E.ON Solutions GmbH
www.eon.com
Vol. 2: 283

EasyCard Corporation
www.easycard.com.tw
Vol. 2: 152

EF Education First
www.efhello.com
Vol. 2: 210

FRITZ EGGER GmbH & Co. OG
www.egger.com
Vol. 2: 224

EMMA
Espoo Museum of Modern Art
www.emmamuseum.fi
Vol. 2: 23

Epple Druckfarben AG
www.epple-druckfarben.com
Vol. 2: 59

ESRT Observatory TRS, LLC
www.esbnyc.com
Vol. 2: 366–367

Euroboden GmbH
www.euroboden.de
Vol. 2: 35

EvoBus GmbH
www.evobus.com
Vol. 2: 192

Evonik Industries AG
Creavis
www.evonik.com
Vol. 2: 328

F

The Fair Centre of Finland
www.messukeskus.fi
Vol. 2: 390

Shenzhen Fengchao Technology Co., Ltd.
www.fcbox.com
Vol. 2: 286

FH JOANNEUM
University of Applied Sciences
www.fh-joanneum.at
Vol. 2: 441, 442, 444, 462, 463, 484, 558

FICEP S.p.A.
www.ficepgroup.com
Vol. 2: 271

Fintech Band
www.monobank.ua
Vol. 2: 229

Shenzhen Fire Wolf International Industrial
www.fwqqq.com
Vol. 2: 422

Floating Homes GmbH
www.floatinghomes.de
Vol. 2: 63

FounderType
Beijing Founder Electronics Co., Ltd.
www.foundertype.com
Vol. 2: 112–113, 114–115

Fu Jen Catholic University
www.fju.edu.tw
Vol. 2: 452–453
Vol. 1: 562–563, 568, 602

FUJIFILM Corporation
www.fujifilm.com
Vol. 2: 216, 322, 323
Vol. 1: 469

FunDesign.tv
www.fundesign.tv
Vol. 2: 346–347

G

Gamania Cheer Up Foundation
www.gamaniacheerup.org
Vol. 2: 342–343

Gapwaves AB
www.gapwaves.com
Vol. 2: 162

GE Healthcare
www.gehealthcare.com
Vol. 2: 246

Gebrüder Weiss Gesellschaft m.b.H
www.gw-world.com
Vol. 2: 41

The General Association of Chinese Culture
GACC
www.gacc.org.tw
Vol. 2: 410–411

Gooest Media Technology Daqing Co., Ltd.
www.gooest.net
Vol. 2: 373

Google
https://store.google.com
Vol. 2: 202–203

Publishing & Print Media	Posters	Typography	Illustrations	Sound Design	Film & Animation	Online
4	64	92	116	126	138	172

Index Clients / Universities

GSD Holding
www.gsdholding.com
Vol. 2: 197

Guardian Art Center
www.cguardianart.com
Vol. 2: 357

Gwangju Design Biennale
www.gdb.or.kr
Vol. 2: 105

Gyeonggi Cultural Foundation
www.ggcf.kr
Vol. 2: 386–387

H
Haier Europe
www.haier-europe.com
Vol. 2: 222–223

Haier Group
www.haier.com
Vol. 2: 156, 157, 163, 302, 303, 304

Halyk Bank
www.halykbank.kz
Vol. 2: 212

HandInScan Zrt.
www.handinscan.com
Vol. 2: 255

Landeshauptstadt Hannover
Bewerbungsteam ECoC 2025
www.klh25.de
Vol. 2: 16–17

Harman International
Industries, Inc.
www.harman.com
Vol. 2: 312, 313, 314, 315

HBK Essen
www.hbk-essen.de
Vol. 2: 318

Heidolph Instruments
GmbH & Co. KG
www.heidolph-instruments.com
Vol. 2: 270

Stadt Hildesheim
www.hildesheim.de
Vol. 2: 20

Hochschule Macromedia
Faculty of Creative Arts
https://creative.macromedia-fachhochschule.de
Vol. 2: 52–53

Elvin Hu
www.elvin-hu.com
Vol. 2: 513

Huagang Building Decoration
Materials Co., Ltd.
Hanbrand Company
www.hanbang.com.cn
Vol. 2: 124

Huawei Device (Shenzhen) Co., Ltd.
www.huawei.com
Vol. 2: 296, 310

Huawei Technologies Co., Ltd.
www.huawei.com
Vol. 2: 242–243, 252, 260, 266, 267, 272, 275, 279, 289, 294, 295, 311

Human
Burza d.o.o.
www.humaninteraction.com
Vol. 2: 200

Human Rights Tattoo
www.humanrightstattoo.org
Vol. 2: 174–175

Hungarian University of Fine Arts
Doctoral School
www.doktori.mke.hu
Vol. 2: 6–7

Hwaseong City Government
www.hscity.go.kr
Vol. 2: 386–387

Hyundai Motor Co.
(Genesis Motors)
www.genesis.com
Vol. 2: 392, 393
Vol. 1: 535

Hyundai Motor Company
www.hyundai.com
Vol. 2: 145, 331, 334, 396
Vol. 1: 292–293, 308–309, 511

I
IBM
www.ibm.com/cloud
Vol. 2: 264, 265

IKEA Taiwan
www.ikea.com.tw
Vol. 2: 424

Institut finlandais
www.institut-finlandais.fr
Vol. 2: 21

International Federation of
Sport Climbing
www.ifsc-climbing.org
Vol. 2: 90–91
Vol. 1: 163

IP SYSCON GmbH
www.ipsyscon.de
Vol. 2: 282

Ippolito Fleitz Group GmbH
www.ifgroup.org
Vol. 2: 421

Island-image Art Club de Taipei
www.isart8.blogspot.com
Vol. 2: 79, 86

ITG.digital
www.itg.digital
Vol. 2: 199

ix3
an Aker Solutions Company
www.ix3.com
Vol. 2: 320–321

J
Hanjoo Jho
Planetary Craft
Vol. 2: 516–517

JKU
Johannes Kepler Universität Linz
www.jku.at
Vol. 2: 51

.jpg coffee
Vol. 2: 425

JXDesign
Vol. 2: 492

K
Kaohsiung City Art Promotion
Association
Vol. 2: 87

Kaohsiung City Government
Economic Development Bureau
https://edbkcg.kcg.gov.tw
Vol. 2: 412

Kaohsiung City Government
Sports Development Bureau
https://sports.kcg.gov.tw
Vol. 2: 400–401

KIEFEL GmbH
www.kiefel.com
Vol. 2: 244–245

Klim Type Foundry
www.klim.co.nz
Vol. 2: 94–95, 96–97, 184–185

KLS Martin Group
www.klsmartin.com
Vol. 2: 248

Knock-Knock Animation
www.artstation.com/kka
Vol. 2: 169

Korea Expressway Corporation
www.ex.co.kr
Vol. 2: 553

Krass Optik
www.krass-optik.com
Vol. 2: 195

Kulturdezernat der Stadt Köln
www.stadt-koeln.de
Vol. 2: 317

Kunststiftung des Landes
Sachsen-Anhalt
www.kunststiftung-sachsen-anhalt.de
Vol. 2: 348–349

KWS SAAT SE & Co. KGaA
www.kws.com
Vol. 2: 189

Kyiv Academy of Media Arts
www.k-a-m-a.com
Vol. 2: 75

L
La Loupe GmbH
Benjamin & Julia Skardarasy
www.laloupe.com
Vol. 2: 15

LASALLE College of the Arts
www.lasalle.edu.sg
Vol. 2: 476
Vol. 1: 560

LG Electronics Inc.
www.lg.com
Vol. 2: 103, 544
Vol. 1: 506

LG Uplus
www.uplus.co.kr
Vol. 2: 220–221

Index Clients / Universities

Kim Lin
www.chiaochinglin.com
Vol. 2: 539

Ling Tung University
www.ltu.edu.tw
Vol. 2: 451, 467, 474, 479, 481, 494, 496
Vol. 1: 569, 577, 583, 591, 605

Logitech
www.logitech.com
Vol. 2: 146, 147, 153, 168

LOTTE Duty Free
www.lottedfs.co.kr
Vol. 2: 30–31
Vol. 1: 106–107

Lunit Inc.
www.lunit.io
Vol. 2: 253

Luxembourg For Tourism
www.visitluxembourg.com
Vol. 2: 44

Shenzhen Luyao
Culture Media Ltd.
Vol. 2: 70

M
MAN Truck & Bus SE
www.man.eu
Vol. 2: 335

Masternaut
www.masternaut.com
Vol. 2: 293

May Art Foundation
www.mayartfoundation.com
Vol. 2: 69

McKinsey Design
www.mckinseydesign.com
Vol. 2: 48

Metsä Group
www.metsagroup.com
Vol. 2: 327, 380

Wuhu Midea
Kitchen & Bath Appliances
Manufacturing
www.midea.com
Vol. 2: 305

Guangdong Midea
Kitchen Appliances
Manufacturing Co., Ltd.
www.midea.com
Vol. 2: 306–307

Ming Chi University of Technology
www.mcut.edu.tw
Vol. 2: 446, 454, 486, 522, 542
Vol. 1: 581, 587, 607, 611, 613

Ministry of Digital Transformation of Ukraine
www.thedigital.gov.ua
Vol. 2: 288

Mitteldeutscher Rundfunk
www.mdr.de
Vol. 2: 142

Monotype
www.monotype.com
Vol. 2: 98–99

Morgenpost Verlag GmbH
www.mopo.de
Vol. 2: 136

N
National Library of Ireland /
University College Dublin
UCD Naughton Joyce Centre
www.moli.ie
Vol. 2: 369

National Taipei University of Business
www.ntub.edu.tw
Vol. 2: 475

National Yunlin University of Science and Technology
www.yuntech.edu.tw
Vol. 2: 470, 498, 532
Vol. 1: 559, 580

Gobierno de Navarra
www.navarra.es
Vol. 2: 58

NAVER Corp.
www.navercorp.com
Vol. 2: 218, 308–309

NAVER DATA CENTER GAK
www.navercorp.com
Vol. 2: 319

Nexon Computer Museum
www.nexoncomputermuseum.org
Vol. 2: 376–377

Nextview Netherlands B.V.
www.nextviewconsulting.com
Vol. 2: 34

NIO Co., Ltd.
www.nio.com
Vol. 2: 333

NOROO Group
www.norooholdings.com
Vol. 2: 352

O
OBJECT CARPET GmbH
www.object-carpet.com
Vol. 2: 423

OOH Freezone Committee
Vol. 2: 409

István Orosz
www.utisz.blogspot.com
Vol. 2: 80

Shenzhen ORVIBO
Technology Co., Ltd.
www.orvibo.com
Vol. 2: 298

Andreas Oster Weinkellerei
www.ao-weine.de
Vol. 2: 12–13

P
Panasonic India
www.panasonic.com/in
Vol. 2: 299

Parachute Typefoundry
www.parachutefonts.com
Vol. 2: 111

PARADISE GROUP
www.paradise.co.kr
Vol. 2: 28–29

Paratype Ltd.
www.paratype.ru
Vol. 2: 100, 101

Philips
www.philips.com
Vol. 2: 247, 250, 251, 256–257
Vol. 1: 473, 507

Pingtung County Government
www.cultural.pthg.gov.tw
Vol. 2: 77
Vol. 1: 212

Pinion Digital GmbH
www.fromatob.com
Vol. 2: 204, 213

Pixelis
www.pixelis.com
Vol. 2: 420

Plus10 GmbH
www.plus10.de
Vol. 2: 268–269

PlusX
www.plus-ex.com
Vol. 2: 198

Polestar
www.polestar.com
Vol. 2: 33
Vol. 1: 20–23, 206–207

Dr. Ing. h.c. F. Porsche AG
www.porsche.com
Vol. 2: 329
Vol. 1: 135, 264–265

Prince Claus Fund
www.princeclausfund.org
Vol. 2: 374–375

ProSiebenSat.1 Digital GmbH
www.prosiebensat1.com
Vol. 2: 208–209

R
Raoul Wallenberg Academy
www.rwa.se
Vol. 2: 338–339

Rijeka 2020 d.o.o.
www.rijeka2020.eu
Vol. 2: 39

Röben Tonbaustoffe GmbH
www.roeben.com
Vol. 2: 164
Vol. 1: 303

RSG Group GmbH
www.rsggroup.com
Vol. 2: 205

RT
www.rt.com
Vol. 2: 82, 108, 109, 122, 166, 176–177, 238–239

S
S.F. Express (Hong Kong) Limited
www.sf-express.com
Vol. 2: 284, 287

Samsung Design Corporate Center
www.design.samsung.com
Vol. 2: 379

Samsung Electronics Co., Ltd.
www.samsung.com
Vol. 2: 32, 381, 397, 399, 416–417
Vol. 1: 174, 304, 540–541

Samsung Research America
www.sra.samsung.com
Vol. 2: 186–187

Publishing & Print Media	Posters	Typography	Illustrations	Sound Design	Film & Animation	Online
4	64	92	116	126	138	172

Index Clients / Universities

Samsung SDS
www.samsungsds.com
Vol. 2: 263

SAP SE
www.sap.com
Vol. 2: 290-291

Sberbank
www.sberbank.ru
Vol. 2: 226-227

SCAD Savannah College of
Art and Design
www.scad.edu
Vol. 2: 434-435, 440, 497, 500,
501, 502, 503, 506, 507, 510, 511,
512, 526, 527, 528, 533, 535, 538,
540, 541, 543, 547, 548, 549, 550,
552, 555, 556, 557
Vol. 1: 552-553, 574, 576, 579, 584

Schneider Electric
Automation GmbH
www.se.com
Vol. 2: 258

Alfred H. Schütte GmbH & Co. KG
www.schuette.de
Vol. 2: 261

Serviceplan Group
www.serviceplan.com
Vol. 2: 47

Shanghai Jiao Tong University
www.sjtu.edu.cn
Vol. 2: 559
Vol. 1: 556

Shanghai Publishing and
Printing College
www.sppc.edu.cn
Vol. 2: 430-431

Shenzhen Transportation
Operation Command Center
http://jtys.sz.gov.cn
Vol. 2: 273

Shin Min High School
www.shinmin.tc.edu.tw
Vol. 2: 447

Shu-Te University
www.stu.edu.tw
Vol. 2: 443, 456, 457, 465, 468,
471, 477, 480, 490, 499, 504, 519

SieMatic Möbelwerke
GmbH & Co. KG
www.siematic.com
Vol. 2: 54-55

Siemens
www.siemens.com.cn
Vol. 2: 190

Siemens AG
https://support.industry.siemens.com
Vol. 2: 233

Siemens Healthineers
Siemens Healthcare GmbH
www.siemens-healthineers.com
Vol. 2: 128-129

Sightsavers
www.sightsavers.org
Vol. 2: 344-345

Signify
www.signify.com
Vol. 2: 225

Simon Electric (China) Co., Ltd.
www.simon.com.cn
Vol. 2: 301

SK Telecom
www.sktelecom.com
Vol. 2: 370
Vol. 1: 130, 254

SMA Solar Technology AG
www.sma.de
Vol. 2: 191

Smiths Detection Inc.
www.smithsdetection.com
Vol. 2: 276-277

SMK
Statens Museum for Kunst
www.smk.dk
Vol. 2: 178-179

Suzhou SoFeng
Culture Media Co., Ltd.
www.sofengdesign.com
Vol. 2: 71

Solomon Technology Corporation
www.solomon-3d.com
Vol. 2: 438-439

Sony Corporation
www.sony.net
Vol. 2: 382

Southern Taiwan University of
Science and Technology
www.stust.edu.tw
Vol. 2: 482-483, 529, 531,
562-563

Spolok svätého Vojtecha
www.ssv.sk
Vol. 2: 38

Springer Fachmedien
Wiesbaden GmbH
www.springer.com
Vol. 2: 118-119

Staatliche Schlösser, Burgen und
Gärten Sachsen gGmbH
www.schloesserland-sachsen.de
Vol. 2: 340-341

Staatskanzlei und Ministerium für
Kultur des Landes Sachsen-Anhalt
www.stk.sachsen-anhalt.de
Vol. 2: 19

STARLUX Airlines
www.starlux-airlines.com
Vol. 2: 57

Stiftung Preußischer Kulturbesitz
(SPK)
www.preussischer-kulturbesitz.de
Vol. 2: 356

Storage by Hyundai Card
www.hyundaicard.com
Vol. 2: 378

Street H
Culture Magazine for
Hongdae Area
Vol. 2: 74

Süddeutsche Zeitung
Digitale Medien GmbH
www.sz.de
Vol. 2: 180-181

T
Taichung City Government
Agriculture Bureau
www.agriculture.taichung.gov.tw
Vol. 2: 414-415

Taipei City Government
Department of Cultural Affairs
www.culture.gov.taipei
Vol. 2: 170

Taipei City Government
Department of
Information and Tourism
www.tpedoit.gov.taipei
Vol. 2: 413

Taipei Music Center
https://musiccenter.taipei
Vol. 2: 170

Taiwan Power Company
www.taipower.com.tw
Vol. 2: 350-351, 354-355, 383

Taoyuan Municipal Shou Shan
Senior High School
www.ssssh.tyc.edu.tw
Vol. 2: 514

TASS Russian News Agency
www.tass.ru
Vol. 2: 123, 326

Tata Motors Ltd.
www.tatamotors.com
Vol. 2: 330

Tatung University
www.ttu.edu.tw
Vol. 2: 561

terraplan
Grundstücksentwicklungs-
gesellschaft mbH
www.terraplan.de
Vol. 2: 14

The Harlequin's Carnival Ltd.
Universal Music Ltd., Taiwan
www.umusic.com.tw
Vol. 2: 171

The Unseasonal
www.theunseasonal.com
Vol. 2: 42

Theater Bielefeld
Bühnen und Orchester
der Stadt Bielefeld
www.theater-bielefeld.de
Vol. 2: 78, 104

Theater Bonn
www.theater-bonn.de
Vol. 2: 316

thyssenkrupp AG
Automotive Technology
www.thyssenkrupp.com
Vol. 2: 332

Land Tirol
www.tirol.gv.at
Vol. 2: 211

Tonhalle Düsseldorf
www.tonhalle.de
Vol. 2: 43

ToThree Design
www.tothree.cn
Vol. 2: 61

Index Clients / Universities

Tourism Authority of Thailand
Singapore Office,
Royal Thai Embassy
www.tourismthailand.sg
Vol. 2: 165

TTMM Sp. z o.o.
www.ttmm.is
Vol. 2: 231

U
UNICEF Poland
www.unicef.pl
Vol. 2: 60

UNITE DESIGN
www.ud47.com.tw
Vol. 2: 84-85

University of Applied Sciences
Osnabrück
www.hs-osnabrueck.de
Vol. 2: 560

Up Strategy Lab
www.upstrategylab.com
Vol. 2: 292

Urban Planning
Land & Resources Commission of
Shenzhen
Vol. 2: 18

Ursapharm Arzneimittel GmbH
www.ursapharm.de
Vol. 2: 325

Fondation USM
www.fondationusm.org
Vol. 2: 372

V
Veoneer
www.veoneer.com
Vol. 2: 278

Erik Videgård
Stureplansgruppen
https://videgard.se
Vol. 2: 88

Vitesco Technologies GmbH
www.vitesco-technologies.com
Vol. 2: 404
Vol. 1: 137

Vitra Design Museum
www.design-museum.de
Vol. 2: 361

Vitrolife AB
www.vitrolife.com
Vol. 2: 254

Volkswagen AG
www.volkswagen.de
Vol. 2: 133, 159, 391
Vol. 1: 32-33, 301, 510

W
Water Great Wall Academy Hotel
Vol. 2: 408

WCG
Smilegate
www.wcg.com
Vol. 2: 67

Weißensee Academy of Art Berlin
www.kh-berlin.de
Vol. 2: 508-509

where studio
www.facebook.com/wherrrrrrre
Vol. 2: 62

White City Project Foundation
www.facebook.com/
WhiteCityProject
Vol. 2: 8-9

X
Xiaomi Inc.
www.mi.com
Vol. 2: 297
Vol. 1: 458, 460, 461, 462, 463, 486

Beijing Xiaomi
Mobile Software Co., Ltd.
www.mi.com
Vol. 2: 214-215, 217

Y
YCH Group Pte. Ltd.
www.ych.com
Vol. 2: 36-37

Shenzhen Yimu
Technology Co., Ltd.
www.yimu.info
Vol. 2: 280

Shenzhen Yiqi
Culture Development Ltd.
Vol. 2: 83, 89

Hangzhou Yizhijia
Network Technology Co., Ltd.
www.enjoybuy.vip
Vol. 2: 167

Youth against AIDS
www.youth-against-aids.org
Vol. 2: 40, 76, 121
Vol. 1: 313, 314, 315

Z
Zhejiang Gongshang University
www.zjgsu.edu.cn
Vol. 2: 492

Zhejiang Literature & Art
Publishing House
www.zjwycbs.cn
Vol. 2: 81

Zuni Icosahedron
www.zuni.org.hk
Vol. 2: 364-365

reddot edition

Editor
Peter Zec

Project supervision
Vito Oražem

Project and editorial management
Sophie Angerer

Editorial work
Kirsten Müller (supervision), Essen
Mareike Ahlborn, Essen
Bettina Derksen, Simmern
Karin Kirch, Essen
Karoline Laarmann, Dortmund
Bettina Laustroer, Wuppertal
Astrid Ruta, Essen
Regina Schier, Essen
Corinna Ten-Cate, Wetter

"Red Dot: Agency of the Year"
Dr. Stefanie Roenneke, Bochum

Statement "Red Dot: Junior Prize"
Kelley Cheng, Singapore

Translation
Heike Bors-Eberlein, Tokyo
Stanislaw Eberlein, Tokyo
Bill Kings, Wuppertal
Tara Russell, Dublin
Regina Schier, Essen
Philippa Watts, Exeter

Proofreading
Klaus Dimmler (supervision), Essen
Mareike Ahlborn, Essen
Jörg Arnke, Essen
Dawn Michelle d'Atri, Kirchhundem
Bill Kings, Wuppertal
Karin Kirch, Essen
Regina Schier, Essen
SPRACHENWERFT GmbH, Hamburg
Philippa Watts, Exeter

Client service
Claudia Auerswald, Kevin Boix, Anastasija Delidova,
Yier Huang, René Klügling, Anja Lakomski, Yongchen Li,
Yen-Ming Lin, Judith Lindner, Louisa Mücher,
Lena Poteralla, Lena Wohlfarth, Yiming Zeng

Layout
Lockstoff Design GmbH, Meerbusch
Saskia Rühmkorf (supervision)
Christina Jörres
Katja Kleefeld
Alexandra Korschefsky
Stephanie Marniok
Lena Möllmann

Photographs
Albrecht Fuchs, Vol. 1, page 648
Veera Konsti, Vol. 1, page 625
Attila Balázs, Vol. 2, page 590
Demodern – Creative Technologies, Vol. 2, page 136
Ekaterina Kazantseva, Vol. 2, page 630
Krstan Petrucz, Vol. 2, page 586
Tomomi Takano, Vol. 2, page 361
Marc Theis, Vol. 2, page 613
Simon Vogel, Vol. 2, page 359
Johannes Zinner, Vol. 2, page 656
World Map designed by freepik.com, Vol. 1, page 8

Jury photographs
eventfotograf.in (Schuchrat Kurbanov,
Alex Muchnik), Essen

Company photographs

Production
gelb+, Bernd Reinkens, Düsseldorf

Lithography
gelb+, Bernd Reinkens (supervision),
Düsseldorf
Wurzel Medien GmbH, Jonas Mühlenweg,
Düsseldorf

Printing
Dr. Cantz'sche Druckerei Medien GmbH,
Esslingen

Bookbinding
Buchbinderei Schaumann GmbH,
Darmstadt

International Yearbook Brands & Communication Design 2020/2021
ISBN: 978-3-89939-228-9

Publisher
Red Dot GmbH & Co. KG
Kollwitzstraße 32
10405 Berlin

Red Dot Edition
Design Publisher
Sabine Wöll
edition@red-dot.de

© 2020/2021 Red Dot GmbH & Co. KG

All rights reserved, especially those of translation.
No liability is accepted for the completeness of the information.

The competition "Red Dot Award: Brands & Communication Design" is the continuation of the "Red Dot Award: Communication Design" and "German Prize for Communication Design". The "International Yearbook Brands & Communication Design" is the continuation of the "International Yearbook Communication Design" and "red dot communication design yearbook".

The Deutsche Nationalbibliothek lists this publication in the Deutsche Nationalbibliografie; detailed bibliographic data are available in the Internet at http://dnb.ddb.de